GLOBALIZATION

GLOBALIZATION

Encyclopedia of
Trade, Labor, and Politics

Volume 1

Ashish K. Vaidya, Editor

A B C CLIO

Santa Barbara, California   •   Denver, Colorado   •   Oxford, England

Library of Congress Cataloging-in-Publication Data is available from the Library of Congress.

ISBN: 1-57607-826-4
E-ISBN: 1-57607-827-2

09 08 07 06   10 9 8 7 6 5 4 3 2 1

This book is also available on the World Wide Web as an e-
book. Visit http://www.abc-clio.com for details.

ABC-CLIO, Inc.
130 Cremona Drive, P.O. Box 1911
Santa Barbara, California 93116-1911

This book is printed on acid-free paper.
Manufactured in the United States of America

Contents

Acknowledgments, ix
Introduction, xi

GLOBALIZATION
Encyclopedia of Trade, Labor, and Politics

Volume 1

Volume 2

Acknowledgments

This project has brought together more than 80 experts from around the world to write about various issues of globalization. It has been an arduous task but immensely rewarding. I wish to acknowledge the contributors for all their hard work and dedication. I appreciate the staff and support at ABC-CLIO for their patience and guidance, especially Jim Ciment, Wendy Roseth, and Christine Marra. I also wish to thank my student assistants, Ioulia Tsoi and Merissa Stith, who very ably performed the difficult task of keeping the project on track.

I wish to thank my family, Nivedita, Jaanhvi, and Avaneesh, for their support, love, and encouragement.

I wish to acknowledge and thank my mother, Padma, for her unflinching belief in my abilities, my late father, Kamalakar, for inculcating a global perspective in me, and my sister, Shobhana, who is a source of inspiration always.

Ashish K. Vaidya

Introduction

Globalization: Encyclopedia of Trade, Labor, and Politics is a comprehensive reference work on post–World War II issues of globalization. It examines the phenomenon of globalization from an economic, international business, political, legal, and environmental perspective. Written by scholars, the articles are easily accessible to students, business and industry leaders, lawyers, policy makers, academicians, and general readers.

The encyclopedia is intended as a reference book for undergraduate and graduate students, as well as academicians, in the areas of economics, international business, finance, political science, sociology, law, and environmental studies. The two volumes and its associated web site will serve as a valuable resource guide for practitioners in these fields as well. The encyclopedia is divided into four parts: Trade and Investment Issues; Major Business and Economic Sectors; International Blocs and Organizations; and Other Issues.

Part One: Trade and Investment Issues

Part One is dedicated to the discussion of major trade and investment-related issues within a global context. Each essay deals with a history of the subject, current events and issues, and potential developments. The entries in this section deal with issues such as balance of payments and capital flows, currency crisis and contagion, exchange rate movements, international monetary relations, and government policy. With rapid technological developments in communications and transportation, globalization has changed the shape of international production. This section also focuses on the issue of economic integration, foreign direct investment and joint ventures, economic

growth, technology and technical change. It also addresses the effects of globalization on developing nations and emerging markets. Each entry includes appropriate statistical information in the form of tables and graphs to illustrate the growth and progress of the subject.

Part Two: Major Business and Economic Sectors

Part Two is devoted to entries on major business and economic sectors of the international economy. Like Part One, this section includes discussions of the history, current issues, and future developments for each sector, specifically as they pertain to globalization, but each entry focuses more on trends and changes. Agriculture, chemicals, textiles and apparel, computers, energy, financial services, food and beverages, media, pharmaceuticals, and transport, both manufacturing and service, are examined.

Part Three: International Blocs and Organizations

Part Three is a description of the major world trade organizations and blocs. Each entry in this section deals with a specific trade organization or bloc, including the EU (European Union), APEC (Asia Pacific Economic Cooperation), NAFTA (North American Free Trade Agreement), and the WTO (World Trade Organization). It also contains entries on international financial institutions that deal with trade issues such as the World Bank, the IMF (International Monetary Fund), WHO (World Health Organization), and specific agencies within the United Nations. Each entry contains a brief description of the organization/bloc, a list of member countries, the organizational structure purpose and profile, and economic and socioeconomic data on statistical indicators.

Part Four: Other Issues

Part Four focuses on major environmental, legal, political, and cultural issues within the context of globalization. The effects of globalization have been felt in the areas of global security, the environment, food safety, public health, and social policy. Entries in this section deal with natural resources, energy use, climate change, pollution, and conservation. Given the impact of globalization on cities, urban development, and population growth, this section also addresses those concerns from a historical perspective as well as with consideration to future developments. Entries also discuss the legal, political, and cultural aspects of global-

ization, including concerns of international labor rights and standards, human rights, conflict and cooperation, intellectual property rights, corruption, gender, foreign aid, and trade laws.

The phenomena of globalization has been perhaps the most significant development in the post–World War II era. Globalization has transformed the world economy with an impact has been widely felt in all venues. Its force has led to greater interaction amongst peoples and nation states and has challenged the very foundations of our economic, political, and social systems. This encyclopedia provides the information vital to shedding light on the vital subject of globalization.

PART ONE

Trade and Investment Issues

Antidumping and Countervailing Duties

Antidumping action and countervailing duties are trade measures that have been subject to General Agreement on Tariffs and Trade (GATT) regulation from the inception of the GATT organization in 1947. Both of these trade measures are covered by Article VI of the agreement. This article differs from other articles in GATT in that it is concerned with "unfair trade," whereas the others are concerned with reducing trade restrictions that distort production and consumption in the world economy. Dumping and subsidization were perceived as being "unfair" to domestic competitors and therefore practices tending to undermine respect for the rules of the international trading system and the willingness of countries to liberalize international trade. The GATT law that laid down the unfair trading rules of the world trading system carried over to the World Trade Organization (WTO) when it came into being in 1995.

From the time the GATT rules were introduced, there have been numerous complaints from the exporting countries subject to antidumping actions and, to a lesser extent, those subject to countervailing duties. Both antidumping actions and countervailing duties harm the exporting countries, and there is therefore a clash of interests between exporting and importing countries. Exporting countries have claimed that dumping duties are often applied when they should not be under the letter of the GATT law, and that antidumping actions, and sometimes countervailing duties, are used to discourage cheap imports rather than unfair trading. These rules are still hotly debated.

Dumping Actions

Scope of GATT Rules

Article VI of GATT (1947) defined dumping as a situation in which "the price of the product exported from one country to another is less than the comparable price, in the ordinary course of trade, for the like product when destined for consumption in the exporting country." The difference between the "normal value" and the "export price" is called the "margin of dumping." The duty cannot exceed 100 percent of the dumping margin.

A second form of antidumping action is permitted. This is a "price undertaking," defined as "satisfactory voluntary undertakings from any exporter to revise its prices or to cease exports to the area at dumped prices so that authorities are satisfied that the injurious effect of the dumping is eliminated." The exporter can raise prices no more than the margin of dumping. This measure resulted from British and Canadian complaints during the Kennedy Round (1964–1967) that the U.S. Treasury (which at that time was responsible for dumping investigations) had been slow in its dumping investigations and had encouraged producers to give a price undertaking even though the Tariff Commission inquiry might not have resulted in a finding of injury and the imposition of a duty. It was incorporated into the Antidumping Code drawn up in the Kennedy and Tokyo rounds of GATT negotiations.

Under GATT/WTO rules, antidumping actions apply solely to trade in goods. No provision for antidumping in services was introduced into the General Agreement on Trade in Services (GATS) in the Uruguay Round that was concluded in 1993. It is generally believed that antidumping action makes little sense in the context of services trade because of the different nature of this trade; services often have to be delivered in the country in which the consumers buy the services, and the intangibility and the bundling of services make it difficult to establish unit prices.

Article VI allows members to take antidumping action on imports of a good when dumping occurs, but there is no obligation on them to do so. The government of the importing country has discretion. Before an antidumping duty is imposed or a price undertaking given, two requirements or tests must be met: It must be established that the good is dumped, and that the dumping causes or threatens material injury to an established domestic industry or materially retards the establishment of a domestic industry. This form of action has the consequence that the GATT/WTO law deals not with the regulation of dumping itself but with the regulation of antidumping measures.

Problems of Dumping Investigation

Dumping investigations are initiated in response to a complaint from the industry in the importing country to its government. In some countries, the determination of dumping is carried out by one agency, and the determination of injury by a second agency. For example, in the United States, the Department of Commerce determines whether dumping has taken place, and the International Trade Commission determines whether this has caused injury to the domestic industry. In other countries, one agency may make both determinations. These procedures make antidumping actions a form of tariff with very high costs of administration to the government and to the private parties involved.

In most countries taking antidumping action, the legislation requires that the action be taken when there is a complaint from the do-

mestic industry followed by a positive finding of dumping and a positive finding of injury to the domestic industry. Hence, the dual tests required by the WTO rules as a necessary condition of action have become in practice a sufficient condition. This process ignores the interests of domestic buyers. In many cases, buyers are other firms purchasing intermediate goods rather than final consumers. A few countries—and the European Union—have a national-interest provision in their legislation. Importing countries do not consider the interests of the exporters in other countries.

The process of price-to-price comparisons of like products required for the determination of goods dumping is not straightforward. If there is no like product sold on the domestic market, or if the product is sold on terms that do not reflect its costs or in such small quantities that fair comparison is not possible, alternative comparisons may be made. As one alternative, the export price of the good that is allegedly dumped may be compared with the price at which the product is sold when exported to another country. A second alternative is a constructed price based on the cost of production and a reasonable calculation of administrative costs, sales, and other costs and profit. Additional problems arise in the case of goods exported from nonmarket economies such as China. These have led to additional rules.

Similarly, the determination of injury is not straightforward. The definition of a domestic industry, a determination of whether the industry is being injured or threatened by injury, and findings about whether the dumped imports are responsible for this injury, have all been subject to contention in many dumping cases.

The conflict of interests, administrative costs, and uncertainties in the rules have prompted a succession of reforms in attempts to improve the discipline in the rules. The Antidumping Code drawn up in the Kennedy and Tokyo rounds gave greater precision to the definitions of Article VI relating to like products, dumping, injury, and domestic industry. It laid down for the first time procedures and rules of administration, covering time limits for the period of investigation and for the retroactivity of antidumping duties, the rights of interested parties to be heard, rules of evidence, and other administrative matters.

The introduction of the code also saw the extension of dumping to situations in which the goods were sold below (average) cost. The code allowed a determination of dumping if the export price is less than the cost of production of the good exported, but only if there are no sales of the like product in the exporting country or if a proper comparison cannot be made between the export and the domestic price. Moreover, the code introduced two new measures. First, it allowed a price undertaking. Second, it introduced a provision for preliminary duties. Both became widely used.

The Uruguay Round Agreement on the Implementation of Article VI made a strong attempt to tighten the regulation of governments' antidumping actions. The agreement set out yet more detailed rules concerning the determination of dumping, including dumping at below average cost, as well as concerning the determination of injury and the establishment of a causal link between dumping and injury. It also set out more detailed procedures to be followed in initiating and conducting dumping investigations and clarified the role of settlement panels in disputes concerning antidumping actions taken by members. It introduced a "sunset clause" requiring an antidumping duty to terminate within five years unless a fresh review determines that the expiration of the duty would be likely to lead to continuation or recurrence of dumping and injury. Under the Single Undertaking, which obliged all WTO members to accept all of the rules in the Uruguay Round Agreement, this agreement and the earlier code relating to dumping became binding on all members.

The agreement allowed, for the purpose of determining injury, consideration of the combined effect of dumped imports from more than one supplying country. This combined ef-

fect was called "cumulation," and its inclusion in determination of injury codified a relatively new principle in international trade law. With the experience of six years of application of the Uruguay Round amendments, this new feature can now be seen as a substantial change. Before the Uruguay Round Agreement, the practice was used on a limited scale, but it could be argued that it did not conform to GATT law. The Uruguay Round Agreement made the practice WTO-legal. This has increased the coverage of complaints and their likelihood of meeting the injury test in countries that use this provision. Since the formal introduction of the cumulation, studies have shown that a clear majority of antidumping cases in the United States and the European Union have involved the principle.

On balance, it is not clear whether the changes to the GATT/WTO rules since their inception have strengthened or weakened the discipline on countries taking antidumping actions. These rule changes have maintained the basic features of antidumping measures for more than fifty years.

Despite the changes, the discipline applied by the WTO rules to country action against dumped imports is still weak. In some countries, the procedures allow protection virtually on demand. Over the ten years 1987–1997, the proportion of all completed antidumping investigations that resulted in the imposition of definitive measures was 51 percent for all countries reporting to the GATT/WTO. It was 64 percent for the United States and 62 percent for the European Union (Miranda, Torres, and Ruiz 1998, Table 24). In most countries, a higher proportion of applications fail because of a negative finding on the injury test than because of a negative finding on the dumping test. In the United States, over the past decade the Department of Commerce has rarely issued negative determinations of dumping.

The Pattern of Antidumping Actions
Antidumping actions have risen rapidly since the conclusion of the Uruguay Round negotiations. The WTO Committee on Antidumping

produces semiannual reports that give data on the number of antidumping investigations and measures adopted by members of the organization. Until the mid-1980s, only the United States, Australia, New Zealand, and countries that are now members of the European Community took antidumping action regularly. In 1990, only nine members were reported as taking antidumping action during the year. In recent years, the WTO reported that several members had taken antidumping actions. The main new users have been Mexico, Brazil, South Africa, India, and Korea.

More countries are introducing legislation providing for antidumping duties, though there is no obligation for them to do so under WTO rules. These include developing and transition economies such as China. As of December 31, 2000, sixty-three countries (counting the European Union as a single member) had notified the WTO that they had legislation providing for antidumping action. Thus, antidumping action is becoming a standard tool of international trade policy.

As important as the frequency of action is the magnitude of the levels of protection resulting from the actions. There are no systematic data on this aspect. Empirical studies done for some years show that, in the United States and the European Union, dumping margins are on average two to three times higher than the rates of tariffs on ordinary imports, and in Australia they were five times the average tariffs on the same goods.

Moreover, the imports that are subject to antidumping actions are predominantly sourced from developing and transition economies. WTO statistics show that, after the EU countries, the most frequent targets are China, Korea, Chinese Taipei, and a number of other East Asian exporters. Hence, antidumping action has become another of the issues that divide the developed and the developing countries in the WTO. It has led to an increasing number of formal complaints from exporting countries under the dispute settlement procedures of the WTO in recent years.

Pressure for More Reforms in the WTO
Continued dissatisfaction among the members of the WTO with the antidumping rules was recognized in the Ministerial Declaration issued at Doha in November 2001, in which the parties agreed to engage in negotiations aimed at clarifying and improving disciplines included in the antidumping rules. However, the declaration also stated the ministers' intention of "preserving the basic concepts, principles and effectiveness of these Agreements." There is a basic conflict between the view of the major countries taking antidumping actions and the countries whose exports are subject to these actions. There are likely to be strong demands from exporting countries, especially developing and transition countries, for major changes to the rules, but there is unlikely to be much support among the developed countries for changing antidumping provisions in a substantial way. This clash of views is one of the major challenges of the current round.

In the longer term, more far-reaching reforms are possible. International trade economists, unlike officials from national governments, have been widely opposed to antidumping action. From the time of the publication of the classic study of dumping by Jacob Viner (1926), international trade economists have regarded dumping as a form of price discrimination. There is a conflict of interest within the importing country: Buyers gain from dumping, and domestic sellers of substitute goods lose. Apart from infrequent cases of predatory and strategic dumping, dumping is beneficial rather than harmful to the national welfare of the country in which the goods are dumped. Consequently, national welfare is reduced if an antidumping duty is imposed unless the terms-of-trade effect of the duty is large. This is the standard analysis of a tariff, based on equal weighting of the welfare losses to buyers and the gains to sellers from an antidumping action. This conclusion holds a fortiori for a price undertaking as the higher price is received by the foreign supplier rather than the home government or, alternatively, demand is diverted to higher cost alternative import sources. Both cases result in a higher cost of imports. Empirical studies of the welfare effects of antidumping actions confirm that the importing countries taking the actions are net losers (see Blonigen and Prusa 2003).

In practice, according to trade economists, most antidumping action is a form of protection against imports from the cheapest sources rather than action against "unfair trade." As voluntary export restraints and other nontariff barriers have been curtailed by the GATT and WTO, antidumping action is being used as a substitute form of nontariff barrier that is still permissible under the WTO rules. The marked cyclical pattern of new antidumping actions and the heavy concentration in certain industries (see Miranda, Torres, and Ruiz 1998), especially steel and chemical products, support this view.

To reestablish a link to harmful unfair trading, a number of economists have recommended that a third competition test be added to the dual tests of dumping and injury currently required under existing WTO law. The basis for this view is that pricing behavior is appropriately examined under the standards-of-competition analysis and law. This approach has in fact been adopted in a number of regional trading agreements. The European Union; the European Economic Area (EEA) Agreement, a treaty between the European Union and the European Free Trade Area; and the Closer Economic Relations (CER) Agreement between Australia and New Zealand have all banned the use of antidumping measures on intra-area trade, preferring instead to rely on the application of area-wide competition law to deal with instances of anticompetitive pricing. The Canada-Chile Free Trade Agreement simply bans antidumping actions on bilateral trade without any backstop provision for the application of competition law.

The experience of the GATT over almost fifty years indicates that reform of the antidumping law will be a difficult and slow process. Antidumping action is likely to remain one of the major concerns in the WTO with regard to the rules relating to goods trade.

Countervailing Duties

In several respects, the WTO rules relating to countervailing (antisubsidy) duties follow closely the rules relating to antidumping actions, but there are important differences. Subsidies are government measures, whereas dumping is a private action. The subsidies of a nation may inhibit imports as well as encourage its exports. GATT's Article VI, which contains the original rules regulating the use of countervailing duties, is supplemented by Article XVI, which contains rules that regulate the use of subsidies themselves.

Scope of GATT Rules
Article VI states, "The term 'countervailing duty' shall be understood to mean a special duty levied for the purpose of offsetting any bounty or subsidy bestowed, directly or indirectly, upon the manufacture, production or export of any merchandise." As with antidumping duties, a countervailing duty may be levied only if there is proof of subsidization and of injury or threatened injury to the domestic industry, and the amount of the duty cannot exceed the estimated value of the subsidy.

Article XVI ("Subsidies") is concerned with the trade-distorting effects of subsidies. It has two sections. Section A relates to subsidies in general. Subsidies are defined broadly as financial contributions by a national or subnational government. This section requires that each government notify GATT of all subsidies that have the effect of increasing exports or reducing imports. The only limitation on the use of subsidies in general is a weak provision for consultation between governments. Section B concerns export subsidies. These are defined quite broadly to include tax incentives and other concessions related to export performance. The section prohibits export subsidies on all goods other than primary products, and governments are exhorted to avoid the use of export subsidies on primary products.

The Tokyo Round produced a Subsidies Code that refined the rules. Paralleling the new rules in the Tokyo Round Antidumping Code, there were new provisions in the Subsidies Code for provisional countervailing measures, retroactivity, and procedures and rules of administration. There was also provision for undertakings, either by the government of the exporting country agreeing to eliminate or limit the subsidy, or by the exporter agreeing to revise its price, so that the injurious effect of the subsidy would be eliminated. However, unlike price undertakings for dumped goods, these undertakings have been used rarely. Consequently, for practical purposes, countervailing measures are limited to countervailing duties. There are supplementary provisions relating to developing countries.

Article XVI and the Subsidies Code imposed effective discipline on non-primary-product export subsidies only. As subsidies not based on exports and export subsidies on primary products are not prohibited, many governments have increased their use of these measures in a world trading environment where greater discipline has been imposed on other border measures. This has created a web of conflicting interests. Countries that export goods that compete in world markets with goods from other countries that benefit from subsidies, as well as countries that export goods subject to countervailing duties, have sought more discipline on subsidies and countervailing actions. Countries that assist domestic import-competing or export industries by means of subsidies, or those that use countervailing duties, generally oppose greater discipline.

The Uruguay Round Agreement

The Uruguay Round resulted in an Agreement on Subsidies and Countervailing Measures. This represents a radical change of approach from Article XVI and the Subsidies Code, and one that diverged from the approach of the Uruguay Round Agreement on antidumping

measures. The new agreement imposed for the first time some binding discipline on subsidies based on production and nontrade factors by putting restrictions on their use. There are additional rules for developing countries that allow them a longer time to conform to the new rules and in some circumstances to maintain export subsidies indefinitely.

The agreement adopts what is called a "traffic light" approach. There are three categories of subsidies: prohibited ("red"), actionable ("amber"), and nonactionable ("green"). The prohibited category comprises "import-substitution subsidies" (defined narrowly as those contingent on the use of domestic over imported goods), as well as the export subsidies previously prohibited, and other subsidies likely to have adverse effects on other member countries. The nonactionable category comprises subsidies that are not specific to individual enterprises or industries and other subsidies designated "green," including assistance for basic research or to disadvantaged regions and environmental requirements. Only subsidies in the amber category may be subject to countervailing duties.

All categories of subsidies may be challenged by one member or members bringing a complaint against another member or members under the dispute settlement procedures of the WTO. For the actionable category of subsidies, a complaint may be based on one of three types of adverse effects: injury to the domestic industry of an importing country; the nullification or impairment of benefits accruing to another member from tariff concessions or improved market access into the subsidizing members; or serious prejudice (the loss of exports of another member, either into the market of the subsidizing member or in a third country). The last two effects allow exporting countries affected adversely by the production-based subsidies of another country to make a complaint that might result in the reduction or elimination of a subsidy.

Several complaints have been made under these provisions. Indeed, alleged breaches of the Agreement on Subsidies and Countervailing Measures have been a common subject of the complaints surfacing in the WTO dispute settlement procedures. Most of these have concerned subsidies rather than countervailing duties, as there is less scope for the miscalculation of subsidy levels than for the margin of dumping. As a result of decisions of WTO panels and the Appellate Body, several areas of government budgetary assistance previously regarded as outside GATT discipline have been judged to be prohibited subsidies within the terms of the Uruguay Round Agreement. This applies, for example, to the Foreign Sales Corporation regime of the U.S. Internal Revenue Code and to Brazilian and Canadian interest equalization payments on export sales of regional aircraft.

The rules and procedures relating to action through the imposition of countervailing subsidies are essentially the same as those relating to antidumping action under the Antidumping Agreement. For example, in the assessment of injury to domestic industry, imports from multiple countries may be cumulated, and there is a five-year limit and provision for retroactivity.

The Uruguay Round Agreement on Agriculture has rules relating to subsidies on agricultural products that supplement those in the Agreement on Subsidies and Countervailing Measures. Article 13 has a temporary and partial derogation from the rules of the Agreement on Subsidies and Countervailing Measures for subsidies on agricultural products. In broad terms, this Agreement on Agriculture followed the tariff-lights categories of the Agreement on Subsidies and Countervailing Measures. Domestic agricultural support measures for subsidies in the "Amber Box," that is, actionable subsidies that distort trade, were the subject of negotiations. The end result was a 20 percent reduction in the aggregate levels of government agricultural support measures. This was the first time in the history of the GATT that reductions in subsidies on agriculture were achieved through negotiation. There is no parallel in the negotiations on industrial goods, where the negotiations in all GATT rounds were confined to tariffs and nontariff measures not including subsidies. This difference in treatment of subsidies in the agricultural and industrial sectors derives principally from the fact that the proportion of assistance that comes from subsidies rather than from tariffs and other border restrictions is higher for domestic producers of agricultural products than for the industrial sector. This is true of the European Union and the United States.

Countervailing actions apply solely to goods. In relation to services, GATS Article XV has its own provisions on subsidies. These are, however, confined to a relatively weak provision allowing for consultations among members, a provision for future negotiations on subsidies affecting services, and a commitment to examining the need for countervailing measures.

The Pattern of Countervailing Duties

The number of members with legislation providing for countervailing duties and the number of countervailing duty applications have risen since the end of the Uruguay Round. As of December 31, 2000, fifty-two countries had notified the WTO that they had legislation providing for countervailing measures. As with antidumping actions, the principal countries taking action have been developed countries, chiefly the United States and the countries of the European Union. The principal countries whose subsidies are subject to action are developing countries plus, in this case, EU countries.

The industries targeted are broadly the same industries as those subject to frequent antidumping actions, notably metal products and chemicals, as well as some agricultural products. Typically, imports subject to countervailing duties have also been subject to antidumping actions: This is the pattern in the United States, the European Union, and Australia, which have been the most frequent users of countervailing duties. This provides a direct link, in practice, between the use of antidumping actions and countervailing duties, and it suggests a common protective motive for these actions.

However, countervailing duty actions are taken much less frequently than antidumping actions. In 1999–2000, the WTO Committee on Subsidies and Countervailing Measures reported that only five countries took countervailing duty actions during the year. The number of countervailing duties in force on June 30, 2000, was less than one-tenth the number of antidumping measures.

Pressure for More Reform in the WTO

Since the Uruguay Round, there has been some continuing concern over the discipline exercised over subsidies and actions to countervail subsidies and the procedures under Article VI and the Agreement on Subsidies and Countervailing Measures. Developing countries have some dissatisfaction with the agreement, but this centers on the transition period for them to conform to the rules and on special and differential treatment issues.

The Ministerial Declaration at Doha in November 2001, again under the section relating to WTO rules, agreed that there would be negotiations aimed at clarifying and improving the discipline applied to countervailing duties. Action to countervail subsidies may also be considered under the services negotiations.

Countervailing duties lower the national welfare in importing countries that impose the duties, as well as in the exporting countries, because they distort production and consumption, like an ordinary tariff. Empirical studies have confirmed the losses. In the case of subsidized trade, however, there is no doubt that the subsidies themselves distort world production and world trade. Unlike dumping, therefore, there is a case for action against subsidized trade by reducing the levels of the subsidies themselves.

There is no provision, however, in the Doha Ministerial Declaration for negotiating the levels of industrial subsidies. This continues the practice throughout the history of the GATT of excluding industrial production-based subsi-

dies from the set of trade-distorting measures that are covered by these negotiations. However, some regional trading agreements have disciplined the use of subsidies that distort intra-area trade. The 1957 Treaty of Rome—which established the European Community—prohibits all "state aids" (subsidies) that distort intra-area trade, though these controls have proven to be ineffective in practice, and it prohibits the use of countervailing duties on imports from member countries, as they are a form of customs duty. The CER Agreement between Australia and New Zealand has gone further in removing all subsidies that affect bilateral trade.

The absence of any provision for negotiating down subsidy levels for industrial subsidies is an anomaly, as the declaration provides for negotiations to phase out all forms of export subsidies and to reduce substantially trade-distorting domestic support in the agricultural sector, in fisheries, and in services. Unless the levels of industrial subsidies are reduced, countervailing duties on actionable subsidies, and, in some cases, formal complaints under the dispute settlement procedures, are the only forms of action possible against subsidies. Imposing greater discipline on levels of subsidies that assist export- and import-competing producers is unfinished business.

P. J. Lloyd

See Also National government policies; Non-tariff barriers; Protectionism; Subsidies; Tariffs; Technical barriers to trade; GATT; World Trade Organization (WTO); US Trade laws

References

Blonigen, B. A., and T. J. Prusa. "Antidumping." In *Handbook of International Trade*, Vol. I. Edited by E. K. Choi and James Harrigan, Oxford: Blackwell Publishing, 2003.

Boltuck, R., and R. E. Litan, eds. 1991. *Down in the Dumps: Administration of the Unfair Trade Laws*. Washington, DC: Brookings Institution.

Finger, J. M. 1993. *Antidumping: How It Works and Who Gets Hurt*. Ann Arbor: University of Michigan Press.

Marvel, H. P., and E. J. Ray. 1995. "Countervailing Duties." *Economic Journal* 105 (November): 1576–1593.

Messerlin, P. A., and G. Reed. 1995. "The US and EC Antidumping Policies." *Economic Journal* 105 (November): 1565–1575.

Miranda, J. R., A. Torres, and M. Ruiz. 1998. "The International Use of Anti-Dumping." *Journal of World Trade Law* 32, no. 5: 5–71.

Tavares, J., C. Macario, and K. Steinfatt. 2001. "Antidumping in the Americas." *Journal of World Trade* 35, no. 4: 555–574.

Vautier, K. M., and P. J. Lloyd. 1997. "A Case Study of Anti-Dumping and Countervailing Duties in Australia." Pp. 129–142 in K. M. Vautier and P. J. Lloyd, eds., *International Trade and Competition Policy: CER, APEC and the WTO.* Wellington: Institute of Public Policy.

Vermulst, E., and F. Graafsma. 2001. "WTO Dispute Settlement with Respect to Trade Contingency Measures." *Journal of World Trade* 35, no. 2: 209–228.

Viner, J. 1926. *Dumping: A Problem in International Trade.* Geneva: League of Nations.

World Trade Organization. *Annual Report.* Geneva: WTO, various years.

Balance of Payments and Capital Inflows

The balance of payments is a summary statement that, in principle, records all the transactions of the residents of a nation with the residents of all other nations during a particular period of time, usually a calendar year. The United States and some other nations also keep such a record on a quarterly basis. The primary purpose is to obtain reliable and up-to-date information on transactions between domestic residents and foreign residents. As trade and investment flows expand and globalization of international business becomes a reality, domestic monetary and regulatory policy no longer focuses on domestic markets alone but increasingly has to take into account foreign developments as well. The information collected is used to help support trade negotiations, formulate policy, and analyze the impact of that policy and the policies of foreign countries on international transactions.

Interest in maintaining records of international transactions predates data collection within other economic accounts. During much of the seventeenth and eighteenth centuries, the dominant economic policy was mercantilism. Mercantilism describes the theory that a nation's economic prosperity can be reflected by the stock of precious metals accumulated in the public treasury. As a way of accumulating gold and silver, mercantilism suggests that a nation should sell more output to foreigners than it bought from them. To achieve this, nations restricted imports through such devices as tariffs and quotas. But the restrictions reduced international trade and thereby reduced the gains that arose from the division of labor, specialization, and exchange. Tensions between advocates and opponents of free trade were a recurrent theme during the time when mercantilism was popular. Since then, economists, policymakers, and others have had an intense theoretical and empirical interest in the measurement of international transactions.

Concurrent with the changes in the world economy were efforts to modernize economic accounting standards and provide more detailed guidance in areas of emerging interest. Since the Bretton Woods Agreement in 1945, the International Monetary Fund (IMF) has had primary responsibility for setting international standards for the compilation of balance of payments accounts. In 1993, the IMF released the fifth edition of its *Balance of Payments Manual* (BPM), which replaced a 1977 edition. The United States took a leadership role in the coordinated international effort that culminated in the release of the new BPM. The manual was modeled upon existing U.S. accounts, especially in areas such as foreign direct investment, where the United States is clearly the world's leader. In other areas, the new BPM amended rules governing the United States and other major industrial nations.

In the United States, official balance of payments accounts are maintained by the Bureau of Economic Analysis (BEA), a division of the U.S. Department of Commerce. U.S. international transactions accounts are published every January, April, July, and October in the *Survey of Current Business,* a monthly publication of the BEA.

Balance of payments accounting standards have not remained static. Over time, they have evolved in response to changes in concerns and changes in the structure and organization of the world economy. For instance, when the Eurodollar market gained significance in the 1950s, during the Cold War, the Soviet Union shifted dollar deposits out of the United States and placed them in London banks. Further, dollars were becoming considerably more abundant in Britain and Europe because of the existence of legal ceilings, through Regulation Q of the Federal Reserve, on the interest rates that could be paid by U.S. banks on their time and savings deposits. Many U.S. depositors chose to place their dollars in Europe, where higher interest rates were available, and the Euro banks were quite willing to receive them.

Beginning in the 1960s and continuing throughout the 1970s and 1980s, world financial markets changed dramatically. Financial innovation produced new instruments that widened the scope for transactions, fostering the development of new markets in financial futures, junk bonds, and swaps. Also in the 1980s, Regulation Q was phased out. Financial liberalization occurred worldwide. Scandinavia, Latin America, Asia, and the United States were especially affected. Before the shift toward liberalization, banks in many Latin American countries were owned by the government and subject to interest rate restrictions, as in Scandinavia. Moreover, lending was restricted to government and other low-risk borrowers. With the deregulation trend, many countries liberalized their credit markets. International lending exploded, and financial capital became more internationally mobile. Countries with large imbalances between domestic saving and investment, such as Japan, became lenders on international financial markets.

Since the 1980s, there has been mounting evidence of the growing interdependence of national economies and the strong interconnections among them. Clearly, there has been a remarkable proliferation in the volume of international transactions for which records must be maintained as well as in the types of international transactions that occur, necessitating revisions in the manner in which records are collected and maintained. The shift in the nature of cross-border financial flows has heightened interest in the quality of the balance of payments accounts maintained by the United States and other countries to measure international securities flows and holdings. To a large extent, the data improvement efforts are driven by changing needs and changing economic conditions.

Definitions of International Transactions

Since a nation's balance of payments account is the statistical record of all economic transactions taking place between its residents and the rest of the world, the notion of a "resident" is fundamental to balance of payments principles. In international transactions statistics, a resident may be an individual, branch, partnership, associated group, association, estate, trust, corporation, or other organization or government entity. An economist speaking about the transactions of U.S. residents, for example, would have in mind not only the transactions of individual Americans but also transactions of U.S. firms and of the U.S. government at all levels.

For individuals, it can be difficult to determine who is a "resident" and who is not, but certain standards have been adopted in international transactions statistics. For example, a U.S. resident means any person resident in the United States or subject to the jurisdiction of the United States. A foreign resident would be any person resident outside of the United States or subject to the jurisdiction of a country other than the United States. As a general rule, tourists, diplomats, military personnel, and temporary migrant workers are all regarded as residents of the countries from which they come. For example, the expenditures of Japanese tourists purchasing U.S. goods are regarded as a U.S. export because the transaction involves U.S. sales to foreign residents, the Japanese tourists. The expenditures of U.S. tourists in foreign countries are treated as imports in the U.S. balance of payments because they involve the purchase of foreign goods by U.S. residents. The income received by Mexican temporary migrants working on U.S. farms would also be classified as an import. The transaction represents a purchase of foreign services by U.S. residents and is therefore an international transaction included in the category "services transactions." Furthermore, the U.S. system defines foreign residents as individuals or institutions residing outside the United States on a permanent or long-term basis, regardless of whether they are U.S. citizens. U.S. residents are defined in a like manner. For instance, a U.S. citizen who retires to Spain is a foreigner for purposes of the data.

In most cases, a transaction clearly is or is not an international transaction. However, in some cases in which the seller provides the good or service in the country of the purchaser, questions may arise as to whether the transaction should be regarded as an international transaction or a local sale by a foreign affiliate. Foreign affiliates of U.S. firms can be broken down into foreign subsidiaries and branches according to their legal status. The "foreign subsidiary" is legally incorporated into the country in which it operates, whereas the "branch" is considered an extension of the parent company and is not incorporated abroad. Affiliates of multinational companies are regarded as residents of the countries in which they are located rather than as residents of the countries of their owners. As a result, transactions between the parent company in the United States and a foreign affiliate are recorded as transactions between a U.S. firm and a foreign resident. Therefore, if a U.S. resident's foreign activity or operation is incorporated abroad, it is a foreign affiliate and regarded as a foreign resident. Honda USA, for example, is considered a U.S. firm, and General Motors Canada is considered foreign.

If a U.S. person's foreign activity or operation is *not* incorporated abroad, its status is based on the weight of the evidence with regard to specific factors. In general, an unincorporated foreign operation of a U.S. company is considered to be a foreign affiliate if the operation (1) pays foreign income taxes; (2) has a substantial physical presence abroad (for example, plant and equipment or employees); (3) maintains financial records so that it can prepare its own financial statements; (4) takes title to the goods it sells and receives the revenues from its sales; or (5) receives funds for its own account from customers for the services it performs. An unincorporated foreign operation of a U.S. company is generally *not* considered to be a foreign affiliate if the operation (1) pays no foreign income taxes; (2) has limited physical assets or employees permanently located abroad; (3) has no financial statements; (4) conducts business abroad only for the U.S. company's account and not for its own account; and (5) receives funds to cover its expenses only from the U.S. entities. Operations meeting the second set of criteria are considered operations of the U.S. company, and their sales within the foreign country are recorded in U.S. international transactions accounts as exports to that country. In contrast, sales abroad by foreign affiliates of U.S. companies are regarded as transactions between foreign residents and are not included as a U.S. balance of payments transaction.

Criteria for determining which U.S. activities do or do not constitute a U.S. affiliate of a foreign entity are parallel to those listed above. For example, sales within the United States by U.S. affiliates of foreign companies are considered transactions between two U.S. residents and would not be included in the U.S. international balance of payments accounts.

Breakdown of the Accounts

A nation's balance of payments account is broken up into three primary accounts: (1) the current account (CA); (2) the capital account (KA); and (3) the official reserve transactions account. The current account records a nation's trade in goods, services, interest income, and gifts with the rest of the world. The capital account measures a nation's nonofficial trade in short-term assets, long-term assets, and foreign direct investment. The official reserve transaction account records transactions by monetary authorities. Specifically, the official reserve transaction account for the United States records changes in U.S. official reserve assets carried out by the Federal Reserve Bank and any changes in foreign official assets in the United States carried out by foreign central banks. Each of these three accounts is in turn divided into subaccounts, as described below.

Current Account

The current account is composed of four subaccounts: (1) merchandise trade; (2) services; (3) investment income; and (4) unilateral transfers. Merchandise trade consists of trade in all raw materials and manufactured goods. Together with the Census Bureau and the U.S. Customs Service, the BEA continues to make improvements in the measurement of the statistical account of exports and imports. Until mid-1993, the merchandise balance was reported in the media. Since then, the merchandise trade account has been combined with a second subaccount, services, to determine the balance of goods and services.

The second subaccount within the current account, trade in services, refers to economic activities whose outputs are other than tangible goods. This category includes, but is not limited to, banking, other financial services, insurance, transportation, communications, data processing, advertising, accounting, construction, design, engineering, management consulting, real estate, professional services, entertainment, education, and health care. Royalties and license fees paid for the use of a work or invention, when the copyright or patent is held by a resident citizen of another country, are also counted as payments for a service.

The third subaccount within the current account, investment income, includes interest payments and dividends because they are considered payments for the services of capital that is working abroad. The profits earned by a factory owned by a foreign resident, for example, are payments for the services of the capital embodied in that factory. It is important to distinguish yearly payments for the services of capital, which appear in the current account, from the original investment itself, which appears in the capital account. The net balance on the merchandise, services, and investment income subaccounts yields the current balance of goods, services, and income.

Unilateral transfers, or gift transactions, the fourth subaccount of the current account, consist of government transfers to foreign residents, foreign aid, personal gifts to friends and relatives abroad, personal and institutional charitable donations, and the like. Money sent abroad by a U.S. resident to friends or relatives would be included in U.S. unilateral transfers. Net unilateral transfers equal the unilateral transfers received from abroad by U.S. residents minus unilateral transfers sent to foreign residents by U.S. residents. U.S. net unilateral transfers have been negative each year since World War II, except for 1991, when the U.S. government received sizable transfers from foreign governments to help pay their share of the Persian Gulf War.

Economists add the net unilateral transfers to the balance of goods, services, and income to derive the balance on the current account. The balance on the current account is reported quarterly in the United States.

Capital Account

When economists talk about capital, they usually mean the physical goods employed to produce goods and services. Sometimes, capital is just another word for money. The capital account records a country's nonofficial, international transactions involving purchases or sales of financial assets and real assets. Within the capital account, the key distinction is between foreign direct investment and portfolio capital. Portfolio investment, in turn, is divided into long-term and short-term assets.

The first subaccount within the capital account is direct investment. Direct investment means the ownership or control, directly by one person, of 10 percent or more of the voting stock of an incorporated business enterprise or an equivalent interest in an unincorporated business enterprise. Direct investment would also describe the construction of a new factory or enterprise as well as the purchase of real estate. Direct investment is measured by the Department of Commerce's BEA.

Securities and banking flows are classified as cross-border portfolio investments. Portfolio investment is the ownership or control, by a single investor or an affiliated group, of less than 10 percent of the voting equity of an incorporated business enterprise or an equivalent interest in an unincorporated enterprise. The earliest measurement effort was an 1853 Department of Treasury survey of foreign holdings of U.S. public and private securities conducted in response to congressional concern about the increasing level of U.S. debt held by foreigners. In 1934, in connection with the banking emergency, the United States began to collect monthly data on transactions in long-term securities and monthly and quarterly data on other financial flows, such as bank and nonbank lending and borrowing and holdings of short-term financial flows. Currently, the U.S. Treasury collects data on cross-border portfolio investment through the Treasury International Capital (TIC) reporting system. In addition to the TIC system, surveys of foreign holdings of U.S. securities continue intermittently by the Department of Commerce.

Long-term portfolio investment involves international transactions in financial assets with an original term to maturity greater than one year. Such investments consist of purchases of capital market securities, such as stocks and long term-bonds and bank loans with terms to maturity of greater than one year. Cross-border transactions in equities and long-term debt securities are measured at mar-

ket value through monthly reports filed by transactors, which are mainly brokers and dealers. Data are collected at the aggregate level by country.

Short-term capital flows involve assets with original terms to maturity of less than one year. Examples include transactions in money-market instruments such as treasury bills, commercial paper, certificates of deposit, and repurchase agreements. Also included as short-term capital flows are any international shifts in the ownership of liquid funds such as checking deposits or cash. Foreign holdings of U.S. short-term securities are measured in the aggregate, at face value, through monthly reports filed by banks and brokers and quarterly reports filed by corporate borrowers. U.S. holdings of foreign short-term securities are measured in the aggregate, at face value, through monthly reports filed by banks and brokers and quarterly reports filed by custodians and investors. All such holdings are commingled with other types of assets, such as time and demand deposits.

U.S. securities are defined as securities issued by institutions resident in the United States. Neither the currency in which a security is denominated nor the exchange on which a security trades determines whether a security is domestic or foreign. Therefore, a security issued in Germany by a U.S. resident firm that is denominated in euros is a U.S. security. Likewise, a security issued by a Canadian firm that trades in the United States and is denominated in U.S. dollars is a foreign security. American Depositary Receipts (ADRs) are considered foreign securities because, although they are issued by U.S. institutions, their purpose is to serve as proxies to facilitate the trading of the foreign securities the ADR represents.

When the BEA publishes the official balance of payments data, it augments the TIC transactions data with data on stock swaps. Stock swaps occur through cross-border mergers and acquisitions and involve the exchange of stock in the target company for stock in the new firm, in the case of a merger, or in the acquiring firm, in the case of an acquisition. For example, when British Petroleum, a UK firm, acquired Amoco, a U.S. firm, in an equity financed deal worth a reported $48 billion, holders of stock in the now defunct Amoco were given stock in newly formed BP Amoco, a UK firm. From a balance of payments perspective, the net transaction records the U.S. residents' acquisition of $48 billion in UK equities less the value of Amoco stock held by foreigners. The value of foreign stocks acquired by U.S. residents in stock swap arrangements has increased sharply in recent years.

All transactions in the current and capital accounts are called autonomous transactions because they take place for business or profit motives and independently of balance of payments considerations. Autonomous items are sometimes referred to as "the items above the line." The sum of the various subaccounts of the current account and the private capital account constitute the overall balance of payments. In general, the balance of payments can be a negative value, a positive value, or a sum totaling zero. The economic interpretation of a balance of payment disequilibrium will be addressed in Section VIII.

Official Reserve Transactions Account

The official reserve transaction account records official reserve transactions carried out by domestic and foreign central banks. For the United States, for example, the net balance consists of the difference between the change in the U.S. central bank's holdings of official reserves and the changes in foreign central banks' holdings of official assets in the United States. The international reserve assets include four items: gold holdings, foreign exchange reserves, credits issued by the IMF, and Special Drawing Rights (SDRs). SDRs, an asset created by the IMF, are described as "paper gold," and their value is defined in terms of a fixed-proportion, weighted mix of four currencies—U.S. dollars, Japanese yen, British pounds, and euros. Transactions in official reserve assets are called "accommodating transactions" or "items below the line" because they result from and are needed to balance international transactions.

The official reserve transactions balance can be used to measure the intervention of monetary authorities in foreign exchange markets.

Double-Entry Bookkeeping

Balance of payments accounts are maintained according to the principles of double-entry bookkeeping. In this method, each international transaction is recorded twice—as a credit on one side of the ledger and as a debit of equal amount on the other side. Double-entry bookkeeping thus acknowledges the fact that in general every transaction has two sides: When we sell something, we receive a payment for it, and when we buy something, we have to pay for it.

Say, for example, that a U.S. resident visiting France spends $2,000 on hotels, meals, and entertainment. In other words, he purchases travel services from foreigners and makes a payment to them in return. The United States would debit $2,000 under the services subaccount of the current account and simultaneously credit $2,000 to short-term capital flows because, in receiving the U.S. payment, the French are augmenting their holdings of U.S. short-term financial assets.

In another example, suppose the U.S. government gives a gift of $500 to an African government. Again, the transaction would be recorded twice. The payment itself is a unilateral transfer. Therefore, the United States would debit the subaccount of the current account in the amount of $500. However, the payment is received by the African government, and this side of the transaction represents an increase in foreign claims on the United States. Therefore, the United States would credit $500 to the U.S. short-term capital flow subaccount of the capital account.

Tables 1–3 itemize the types of credit and debit transactions recorded in a nation's balance of payments. Since the balance of payments consists of several individual accounts, a deficit in one account must be offset by a surplus in another account.

Table 1: Current Account Credit and Debit Entry Items Only

Current Account: Credit Items	Current Account: Debit Items
Exports of goods	Imports of goods
Exports of services	Imports of services
Interest income earned from investments in a foreign country	Interest income paid to other country's residents from their investments in the home country
Unilateral transfers or gifts received from abroad	Unilateral transfers or gifts made to foreigners

Table 2: Capital Account Credit and Debt Entry Items Only

Capital Account: Credit Items	Capital Account: Debit Items
An increase in foreign-country ownership/holdings of home country's assets in the form of direct investment, long-term capital, or short-term capital	A reduction or sale of financial assets held in the home country by foreign residents
A reduction in home-country ownership/holdings of foreign country's financial assets in the form of direct investments, long-term capital, or short-term capital	An increase in home-country resident's holdings of foreign financial assets and foreign direct investment

Table 3: Official Reserve Transactions Credit and Debit Entry Items Only

Official Reserve Transactions: Credits	Official Reserve Transactions: Debits
Foreign central banks acquire official reserves (currency or bank accounts) in the home country	Foreign central banks decrease or sell their assets (currency or bank accounts) in the home country
The home country's central bank reduces or sells some of its international reserve assets or its assets of foreign currency	The home country's central bank increases its international reserve assets or its holdings of foreign currency

Statistical Errors in Balance of Payments Accounts

In principle, the balance of payments should record all international economic transactions between the residents of one nation and the rest of the world. In practice, many international economic transactions are hard to cap-ture through any systematic procedures of data collection. The literally millions of transactions of the residents of a nation with the rest of the world cannot appear individually in the balance of payments accounts. As a summary statement, the balance of payments aggregates all transactions into a few major categories. Errors are bound to occur for several reasons.

First of all, some transactions may be valued incorrectly, resulting in data gaps in the accounts. In the United States, much of the data are generated by survey responses. For most of the surveys, the reporting period used is the fiscal year of the reporter, and in most cases, the reporter's fiscal year coincides with the calendar year, so that the published statistical aggregates track calendar year activity fairly closely. But based on comparisons with partner country data, port audits, and other sources of information, the Census Bureau estimates that goods exports are underestimated by as much as 3 to 7 percent of the published value. Second, some transactions may be omitted entirely from the accounts. This is because transactors may undervalue transactions so that they fall below the threshold reporting level, may fail to file the required documentation, may file documents with incomplete information, or may intentionally undervalue shipments to avoid quotas and tariffs. Finally, some gaps are believed to exist in the coverage of the e-commerce services. With the increased use of the Internet, some transactors may not be aware of the nationality of their foreign counterparties. In some cases, transactors may not even be aware they are transacting business with foreign residents. Internet-generated transactions are not currently covered by existing BEA surveys. Therefore, balance of payments accounts list the "statistical discrepancy," that is, the best available estimates of the measurement errors.

Economic Meaning of Imbalances

The joint sum of the current account, the capital account, and the statistical discrepancy determines the overall balance of payments status of a country. Although the totals of payments and receipts are equal in theory, there will be inequalities—that is, deficits or surpluses—in particular kinds of transactions. For example, if a country is observed to run a deficit in the current account, then in all likelihood the country will have an equal surplus in the capital account and vice versa.

Contrary to the general perception, the existence of a current account deficit is not in itself a sign of a bad economic policy. If a country has a current account deficit, it simply means the country is importing capital. Importing capital is no more unnatural than importing shoes or automobiles. The deficit is a response to conditions within the country. A country is more likely to have a deficit in its current account if it has higher exchange rates or price levels vis-à-vis its trading partners or if it is observed to have lower barriers to trade.

If a country is running a current account surplus, and its private residents are not acquiring foreign assets, then it must be the central bank that is acquiring foreign assets. Because every debit has an offsetting credit somewhere, the sum of a country's current account, capital account, statistical discrepancy, and official reserve transactions must sum to zero. This must be true because it is an accounting identity.

Data

Historical data for the U.S. balance of payments accounts are included in Tables 4 through 7 and Figures 1 through 5.

R. M. Payan

See Also Currency Crisis and Contagion; Dollarization; Exchange Rate Movements; Foreign Direct Investment and Cross-Border Transactions; International Financial Markets; International Monetary Fund (IMF)

References

Caves, Richard E., Jeffrey A. Frankel, and Ronald Winthrop Jones. 1999. *World Trade and Payments: An Introduction.* 8th ed. Reading, MA: Addison-Wesley.
Griever, William, Gary Lee, and Francis Warnock. 2001. "The U.S. System for Measuring Cross-Border Investment in Securities: A Primer with a Discussion of Recent Developments." *Federal Reserve Bulletin,* October 2001.

Table 4: Summary Calculation of Balance of Payments Subaccounts in the United States, 2003 (in billions of U.S. dollars)

	1985		1990		1995		2000		2003	
Current account balance (CAB)	$-118.1		$-80.0		$-109.5		$-413.4		$-530.7	
Trade balance	-122.2		-111.0		-174.2		-452.4		-547.6	
Capital account balance		123.6		55.7		10.2		370.0		283.1
Reported capital account	107.1		30.5		-13.9		432.8		295.1	
Statistical discrepancy	16.5		25.2		24.1		-62.8		-12.0	
Official reserve settlements (ORS) balance	5.5		-24.3		-99.3		-43.4		-247.6	
U.S. official reserve assets, net	-3.9		-2.2		-9.7		-0.3		1.5	
Foreign official assets in the U.S., net	-1.6		26.5		109.0		43.7		246.1	
Overall balance of payments		0.0		0.0		0.0		0.0		0.0

Notes: The precise figure for the reported capital account is obtained by adding (1) U.S. government assets other than official reserve assets, net; (2) U.S. private assets, net; (3) other U.S. government liabilities; and (4) other foreign assets in the United States, net. In the calculation of the ORS balance some foreign official assets in the United States that are not regarded as international reserves by foreign monetary authorities are excluded.

Source: U.S. Department of Commerce.

Table 5: The U.S. Capital Account Balance, 1985–2003 (in billions of dollars)

	1985	1990	1995	2000	2003
Capital account balance	$123.6	$55.7	$10.2	$370.0	$280.6
I. U.S. assets abroad, net	-40.9	-79.1	-342.5	-569.5	-284.96
U.S. government assets other than official reserve assets, net	-2.8	2.3	-1.0	-0.9	0.54
U.S. private assets, net	-38.1	-81.4	-341.5	-568.6	-285.5
II. Foreign assets in the U.S., net	1484	109.6	328.58	1,002.3	580.04
Other U.S. government liabilities	0.84	1.9	-0.12	-1.8	-0.56
Other foreign assets in the U.S., net	147.2	107.7	328.7	1,004.1	580.6

Note: The Capital Account Balance is obtained by summing rows I. and II.
Source: U.S. Department of Commerce, Bureau of Economic Analysis.

International Monetary Fund. 1993. *Balance of Payments Manual.* 5th ed. Washington, DC: IMF.

Kozlow, Ralph. 2000. "International Accounts Data Needs: Plans, Progress, and Priorities." Bureau of Economic Analysis (BEA). Presentation to the BEA Advisory Committee. Washington, DC: November 2000.

McEachern, William. 2003. *Macroeconomics.* 6th ed. Mason, OH: Thomson South Western Publishing.

Mishkin, Frederic. 2004. *The Economics of Money, Banks, and Financial Markets.* Boston, MA: Pearson Addison-Wesley.

Rivera-Batiz, Francisco, and Luis Rivera-Batiz. 1994. *International Finance and Open Economy Macroeconomics.* 2d ed. Hertfordshire, UK: Prentice Hall.

Salvatore, Dominick. 2001. *International Economics.* 7th ed. New York: John Wiley and Sons.

Stein, Herbert. 2002. "Balance of Payments." *The Concise Encyclopedia of Economics,* http://www.econlib.org.

U.S. Department of Commerce, Bureau of Economic Analysis. Survey of Current Business. Washington DC: Government Printing Office, http://www.bea. doc.gov.

———. "Form BE-82 Instruction Booklet: Annual Survey of Financial Services Transactions between U.S. Financial Services Providers and Unaffiliated Foreign Persons." Washington, DC: U.S. Government Printing Office.

———. 1997. "U.S. International Transactions: Revised Estimates for 1974–96." Survey of Current Business. Washington, DC: U.S. Government Printing Office.

U.S. Government Printing Office. 1990. *The Balance of Payments of the United States: Concepts, Data Sources, and Estimating Procedures.* Washington, DC.

Yarbrough, Beth, and Robert Yarbrough. 2000. *The World Economy: Trade and Finance.* 5th ed. Orlando, FL: Harcourt College Publishers.

Table 6: Summary Calculation of Balance of Payments Subaccounts in the United States, 2003 (in billions of U.S. dollars)

Current account balance (CAB)		$-530.7
Trade balance	-547.6	
Capital account balance		283.1
Reported capital account	295.1	
Statistical discrepancy	-12.0	
Official reserve settlements (ORS) balance		-247.6
U.S. official reserve assets, net		1.5
Foreign official assets in the U.S., net		246.1
Overall balance of payments		0.0

Notes: The precise figure for the reported capital account is obtained by adding (1) U.S. government assets other than official reserve assets, net; (2) U.S. private assets, net; (3) other U.S. government liabilities; and (4) other foreign assets in the United States, net. In the calculation of the ORS balance some foreign official assets in the United States that are not regarded as international reserves by foreign monetary authorities are excluded.

Source: U.S. Department of Commerce.

Table 7: Summary of U.S. International Transactions, 2003 (in millions of dollars)

Transaction	*2003*
Exports of goods, services, and investment income	$1,314,888
Merchandise goods, excluding military	713,122
Services and military goods	307,381
Income receipts on investments	294,385
Imports of goods, services, and investment income	-1,778,117
Merchandise goods, excluding military	-1,517,011
Services and military goods	-256,337
Income payments on investments	-261,106
Unilateral transfers, net	-67,439
U.S. assets abroad, net [increase/capital outflow (-)]	-283,414
U.S. official reserve assets, net	1,523
U.S. government assets, other than official reserve assets, net	537
U.S. private assets, net	-285,474
Foreign assets in the United States, net [increase/capital inflow (+)]	829,173
Foreign official assets, net	248,573
Other foreign assets, net	580,600
Allocations of Special Drawing Rights	601
Statistical discrepancy	-12,012

Source: U.S. Department of Commerce, Bureau of Economic Analysis.

Figure 1: The U.S. Current Account Balance (deficit)

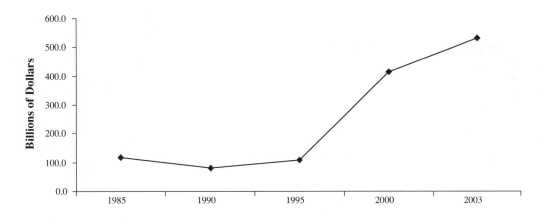

Figure 2: The U.S. Capital Account Balance (surplus)

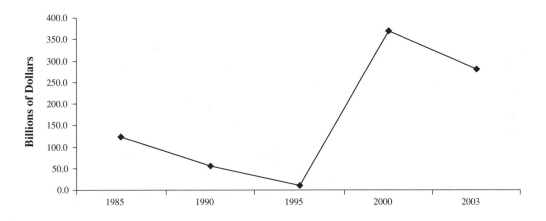

Figure 3: The U.S. Official Reserve Settlements Balance

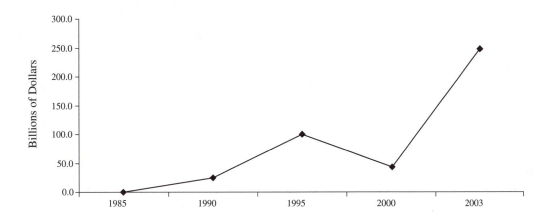

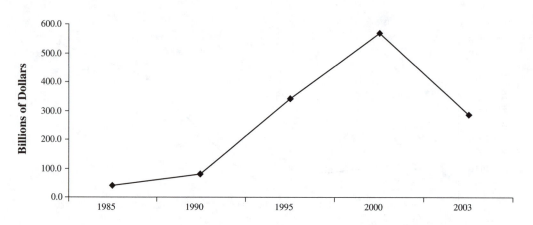

Figure 4: Increase in U.S. Assets Abroad

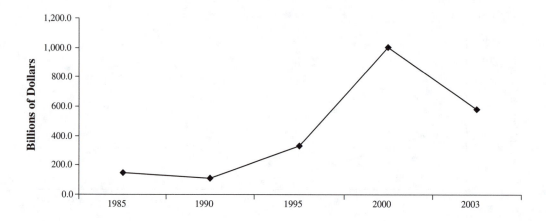

Figure 5: Increase in Foreign Assets in the United States

Currency Crisis and Contagion

There is from time to time much talk in the press, and indeed in all forms of media, of currency crises. These are sometimes said to spread as a result of "contagion"—rather like an illness. But what are "currency crises"? What is meant by "contagion" in this context? The starting point for answering such questions lies in the study of financial crises in general.

Financial Crises

Numerous definitions of financial crises exist. In a 2003 speech, Andrew Crockett, chairman of the Bank for International Settlements, approached the problem by first defining financial stability—the situation that a financial crisis disrupts. "I will take financial stability to be a situation in which the capacity of financial institutions and markets to efficiently mobilise savings, provide liquidity, and allocate investment is maintained unimpaired" (Crockett 2003). He went on: "Note that in my definition, financial stability can be consistent with the periodic failure of *individual* financial institutions, and with fluctuations of prices in markets for financial assets. The failure of individual institutions is of concern only if it leads (as it sometimes can) to an impairment of the basic intermediation role of the financial system at large. And asset price volatility is of concern only if it leads to a severe misallocation of capital" (ibid., 4).

Then, after discussing the reasons that such crises would be costly, he gave examples of crises:

The past decade or so has provided ample evidence of the costs of financial instability. At the international level, think of the Mexican crises of 1994–95; think of the East Asian crises of 1997–98; think of the Argentine crisis that began in 2001 and is still far from reaching its end.

At the national level, there are also examples of financial instability in advanced industrial countries. These include: banking crises of Spain and the Nordic countries in the 1980s; the S and L crisis in the United States; and the financial bubble in Japan, whose costs are still being felt today. Closer to home [the speech was given in London, England], if one defines instability broadly, is the ERM (Exchange Rate Mechanism) crisis of 1992.[1] (ibid., 7)

What can be summarized, distilled, from these examples? What, on the basis of these examples, is a "financial crisis"? A broad definition, illustrated by this range of examples, might posit that the term encompasses big changes in exchange rates, big fluctuations in stock markets, collapses in banking systems, and also what might be called "partial collapses" in banking systems, episodes when banks survive but with their balance sheets in such poor condition that they can do little new lending—they cannot fulfill one of their core purposes, the transmitting of funds from lenders to borrowers. Such a broad definition would once have been regarded as extraordinary, for although the study of dramatic episodes in financial markets is not new, in the early days of its study a definition rather narrower than that suggested by Andrew Crockett's examples would certainly have been taken as given.

Crashes and Crises

Until this century, only problems within the banking system itself were seen as financial crises. Crashes of financial or other asset markets were the consequence of prior "manias," a result of human gullibility and folly, a proper subject of study by the disinterested observer but not requiring any policy action. This attitude is vividly summarized in the title of Charles Mckay's (1845) classic, *Extraordinary Popular Delusions and the Madness of Crowds.*

Crises in the banking system, however, were regarded as serious, even dangerous, occurrences. Anna Schwartz, in a recent statement of this view, described such events as "real" crises. "Such a crisis is fuelled by fear, that means of payment will be unavailable at any price, and in a fractional reserve banking system leads to a scramble for high-powered money" (Schwartz 1986, 11). In contrast to these "real" crises are "pseudo" crises. These involve "a decline in asset prices, of equity stock, real estate, commodities, depreciation of the exchange value of the national currency; financial distress of a large non-financial firm, a large municipality, a financial industry, or sovereign debtors" (ibid., 24). Such loss of wealth causes distress, but it is not in itself a financial crisis. A "pseudo" crisis is simply an unusually large case of mistaken investment, and mistaken investments are inevitable in an uncertain world. A "real" financial crisis occurs when the stability of the whole banking system is threatened.

Such "real" crises have been quite rare. Certainly, on this definition episodes frequently described as crises—such as Latin America in the early 1980s and Russia in 1998—were not crises outside these countries, and they may not have been crises in the sense in which Schwartz uses the term inside these countries.[2] According to Schwartz, no such crisis has oc-

curred in Britain since 1866,[3] or in the United States since 1933.

Schwartz's definition says nothing of the cause of the crisis. In that regard, as in the definition itself, it follows in the tradition of Henry Thornton (1802) and Walter Bagehot (1873). Their approach aimed at clarifying a problem and then going on to propose a solution. A "real" crisis in the Schwartz sense is dangerous because it can lead to an unanticipated and undesired collapse in the stock of money, and such an unanticipated squeeze will cause a recession, perhaps a depression. The monetary squeeze is produced both by a fall in the money multiplier (as cash shifts from the banking system to the public) and in bank deposits. To prevent this squeeze, Thornton, Bagehot, Schwartz, and other writers in this tradition have all suggested a similar course of action, recommending that the central bank of whichever country experiences such a shock should lend freely on collateral. It should not restrict lending to the classes of security (usually quite narrow) that it would accept for discount at normal times. Advances should be made without limit, on demand, but at a rate of interest above the precrisis rate. These loans should be made to the market—that is, to anyone who brings in acceptable security. In addition (and argued in particular by Bagehot), it should be made clear that the central bank will act in that way should there ever be a crisis: This reduces the likelihood of runs because knowledge that the central bank will supply liquidity makes it seem less urgent to scramble for it.

What can trigger such a "real" crisis? Robert Harry Inglis Palgrave (1889), under the heading "Crises, Commercial and Financial," provided first a definition of crises and then a description of the development of several nineteenth-century crises. "Times of difficulty in commercial matters are, when pressure becomes acute, financial crises." His description of the events of 1825 is a good example:

The next serious crisis occurred in 1825, one of the most severe through which the commercial *and banking* [emphasis added] systems of the country had ever passed. At this date speculation ran very high, for the most part in loans and mining adventures, and other investments abroad. The foreign exchanges were so much depressed as to be the cause of a nearly continuous drain on the bullion of the Bank. Many and heavy banking failures, and a state of commercial discredit, preceded and formed the earlier stage of the panic. The tendency to speculation, and the undue extension of credit, was preceded, probably caused, and certainly favoured and promoted, by the low rate of interest which had existed for some time previously; and this low rate of interest was apparently prolonged by the operations of the Bank of England. (Palgrave 1889, 457)

Palgrave supplied several examples of such chains of events and referred to Thomas Tooke (1838) and Leone Levi (1888) as providing many more details.

To summarize so far, the view developed in the nineteenth century and restated in the twentieth, by Schwartz and others, is that crashes in financial markets are not in themselves crises. They can lead to runs on the banking system and thus produce "real" crises. One can lead to the other by starting a scramble for liquidity.[4] But to quote Palgrave, "Commercial crises may take place without any reference to the circulating medium as has been exemplified in Hamburg and elsewhere."

There is plainly a rather fundamental difference of view between, on the one hand, Andrew Crockett, and on the other all those writers who define a financial crisis narrowly, thinking of it as essentially any event that produces a sharp and undesired fall in the quantity of money. To qualify as a crisis on that definition, a big fluctuation in an exchange rate would have to produce a sharp, substantial, and unexpected monetary contraction. The issue of whether a fluctuation in the exchange rate, without first causing a monetary contraction, can produce recession is discussed below.

Stable Exchange Rates and Economic Stability?

The International Monetary Fund (IMF) was established with the preservation of exchange rate stability as its main objective. Why, in the years that it was first designed and then set up (roughly speaking, from 1941 to 1948), was exchange rate stability seen as so important? To understand this emphasis, it is necessary to look back to the period between World War I (which ended in 1918) and World War II (which broke out in 1939).

The story has several strands that need to be identified. After World War I, the nationalism that played its part in bringing the war about continued and even intensified. This was manifest in various ways, finding its economic expression in increased barriers to trade, wrangling over war debts, and reparation payments. It generally soured international relations. It was this climate, together with the failure of the faulty restored gold standard, compounded by the ineptitude of the Federal Reserve in the years 1928–1932, that initiated and exacerbated the Great Depression in the United States, which in turn had worldwide ramifications. The resulting mixture of dirty/managed exchange rates in the 1930s provoked a series of competitive devaluations—something future designers of the international monetary system would want to avoid.

What has to be remembered is that the principal participants in the planning of that system were the United States and the United Kingdom—the two major economies in the free world (and the key currency countries, though there was to be an attempt to destroy this concept). This is important because the final outcome—the establishment of the IMF and other associated institutions—had perhaps more to do with British and American monetary and trade matters than with a wider concern with, and analysis of, the world economy, though some of that was obviously involved.

Another important element in the story was capital movements. World War I, and its unsatisfactory outcome for the resolution of many issues, had created a great deal of political uncertainty in Europe and stimulated a corresponding amount of capital flight. Some flight was prompted by fear that the capital would not be able to be moved. From World War I through the 1920s, there was flight from all parts of Europe. There was, too, a "normal" change in the direction of capital flows when, for example, American investment in Germany began to be returned in the late 1920s as the New York Stock Exchange boomed. But the really large movements of capital were provoked by increasing uncertainty generated at the turn of the decade by the spreading world depression and other political developments. When the Nazis emerged as the second-largest party in the Riechstag in 1930, things got worse. In the summer of 1931, the Bruning government introduced exchange controls, and a standstill on short-term debt owed abroad was negotiated. Not surprisingly, capital flight increased. There were fears that Britain would do something similar, and in September 1931 it did. Many other countries followed suit soon after, and it was at that point that exchange controls proliferated.

Although Britain did not suffer greatly in the Great Depression (output fell less than 6 percent against the U.S. fall of around 35 percent), it nevertheless behaved as if it were affected. For example, it reversed its free trade policies of almost a century and introduced a general tariff. At the same time, Britain saw in its empire a possible solution to trade and output concerns, for it contemplated turning the empire into a customs union. At the Ottawa conference of 1932, it did something less than that but nevertheless signed a large number of trade agreements with empire partners, and more significantly, extended preferential treatment to empire countries—imperial preference. This is of significance because of the extent to which it upset Britain's biggest trading partner, the United States. Tension between the United States and the United Kingdom had also blown up earlier over Britain's share of reparation payments from Germany after World War I.

Ever-spreading trading barriers, in part arising out of the depression and in part in retaliation against the United States for the introduction of the Smoot-Hawley tariff in 1930, provoked further impediments to international discourse. All manner of obstacles appeared: quotas, bilateral settlements, clearing arrangements, exchange controls, and invisible barriers to trade. Some would go so far as to say that all this led inexorably to World War II. Whether or not that is too strong a conclusion, it is clear that great damage was done to the international economy: International trade collapsed between 1930 and 1935 and had barely made any recovery by 1939. International economic relations had deteriorated, to a disastrous or potentially disastrous extent, depending on one's view of the origins of World War II.

It is here that the direct link with the 1930s comes into view. Given what was widely accepted would be Britain's balance of payments position after the war (little to export with still strong demand for imports), it was felt that some safeguards would be needed if Britain were to abandon the imperial preferential apparatus. In order to develop a plan that would allow Britain to do this, in 1941 John Maynard Keynes drafted his proposal for an International Clearing Union—the basis of the "Keynes Plan" for the new international monetary system. Keynes himself described it as utopian. It seemed to cover all international finance, from postwar reconstruction through development finance, an investment board, and so on. And of course the British were keen to restore the position of sterling after the war, in part to demonstrate Britain's ability to maintain its status as a leading power. It was not at all clear that the United States was supporting of Britain's stance. The scheme would attend primarily to short-run balance of payments adjustments. The institution would issue a new international currency (the "bancor"), which would be held and used by central banks for settling the external account. The union would be there to provide liquidity, with a view to keeping exchange rates stable. The plan was put forward in the midst of continuing Anglo-

American talks on monetary and trade matters that ran through the war. Through Harry Dexter White, the United States proposed a more limited stabilization fund. It is important to remember at this stage that the United States had established its own exchange stabilization fund in 1934 to operate under the control of the secretary of the treasury. The White plan was more conservative than Keynes's in that it saw the new institution's reserves being made up of national currencies and gold rather than envisioning an institution with the power to create new money.

By the spring of 1944, the two proposals had been combined to form "The Joint Statement of Experts on the Establishment of an International Monetary Fund." The concentration was on developed industrial countries, and although the stabilization fund was initially to be a policeman with discretionary powers, it was to rely on the member countries behaving responsibly. Later that year, the plan developed into the Bretton Woods Agreements to establish the IMF and the World Bank. The White plan reflected the interests of a creditor nation, the Keynes plan those of a debtor.

The aims for the new international financial architecture reflected concerns of the times and the upheavals of the interwar years. The plan called for stable and "realistic" exchange rates; countries in difficulty were to have access to adequate international reserves to smooth short-term problems. Good behavior would be expected; some codes of behavior were put into place. This ambition in a sense aimed to incorporate the good aspects of the past (the international pre-1914 gold standard) while removing the problems of the 1930s (restrictions and emphasis on domestic survival).

An Inherent Problem

The reasons for the existence of the IMF, and of the system of pegged exchange rates that it was designed to preserve, show that only pegged exchange rates were thought to be desirable. But note, too—and this is of the greatest im-

portance—that countries were intended to remain free to change their exchange rate. Keeping the exchange rate fixed was a commitment that could be overridden, if the consequences of keeping it fixed would be severe domestic disruption. The system was of "fixed but adjustable" rates.

Now, there is a fundamental design problem with this system. The problem was set out very clearly in 1953, well before examples of the fundamental flaw first appeared, by Milton Friedman. (Other writers on the subject at around the same time were F. A. Lutz [1954], E. Sohmen [1957], and L. B. Yeager [1959]). Friedman summarized his argument as follows:

> Because the exchange rate is changed infrequently and only to meet substantial difficulties, a change tends to come well after the onset of the difficulty, to be postponed as long as possible, and to be made only after substantial pressure on the exchange rate has accumulated. In consequence, there is seldom any doubt about the direction in which an exchange rate will be changed, if it is changed. In the interim between the suspicion of a possible change in the rate and the actual change, there is every incentive to sell the country's currency if a devaluation is expected—or to buy it if an appreciation is expected. (Friedman 1953, 164)

His point was that an arrangement of "fixed but adjustable" rates is an illusion. Rates must be either truly fixed—in effect one currency—or free to float. Subsequent work has developed this idea and set out a variety of models in which Friedman's original insight is confirmed time and time again. Examples of this literature include P. R. Krugman (1979), R. P. Flood and P. M. Garber (1984), P. M. Garber and L. E. O. Svensonn (1995). A particularly straightforward exposition was provided by Obstfeld and Rogoff (1995).

Obstfeld and Rogoff made a crucial point:

> If central banks always have the reserves to crush speculation, why do they suffer period-

ic humiliation in foreign exchange markets? The problem, of course, is that very few central banks will cling to an exchange rate target without regard to what is happening in the rest of the economy. Domestic political realities will not allow it, even when agreements with foreign governments are at stake. (Obstfeld and Rogoff 1995, 79)

Another point worth bringing out is that there can be attacks on a currency, substantial foreign exchange reserve loss, and depreciation, with rational expectations, even when no shock is currently present. In the Flood and Garber analysis noted above, an attack occurs because some policy that is being pursued domestically—monetary expansion, say—is inconsistent with the goal of keeping the exchange rate pegged. Subsequent work constructs models in which there can be an attack that shifts the exchange rate even without such an inconsistency. Such attacks in reality are rare and unlikely. What the models actually do is underline the unsustainability of the "fixed but adjustable" exchange rate regime so long as domestic objections take priority over external agreements.

Overview So Far

It may be useful at this point to pause and take stock and then look ahead. First it was shown how modern and comparatively unusual it is for an exchange rate movement *in itself* to be seen as a crisis. Then it was shown how an attachment to a system of "fixed but adjustable" exchange rates developed. It has also been shown that, despite that system's attractions, it is fundamentally incompatible with capital mobility.

The next step must be to consider why capital mobility is regarded as so important that having it is more important than having a regime of fixed but adjustable exchange rates. That done, it is necessary to consider some examples of "currency crises." Examples, that is to

say, of countries that have experienced sharp depreciations of their currency and domestic economic turmoil. Did the currency depreciation cause the domestic crisis? Also examined are examples of countries that experienced depreciations without having "domestic crises." What are the key differences between the two groups of countries? Differences between developing and developed countries are relevant here. That leads on to contagion. What *exactly* is contagion? How often has it occurred? Why is it often mentioned as an aspect of a currency crisis?

The Importance of Capital Mobility

Economists have over many years demonstrated and measured the gains from freedom of trade in goods. That in itself has an important implication for capital mobility. This follows from balance of payments accounting. Remember that a balance of payment is a set of accounts; it has to balance. If the current account is in surplus, then the capital one must be in deficit (see Chrystal and Wood 1988).

This, in turn, means that a restriction on the capital account can imply a restriction on the current account, and hence loss of some of the gains from trade.

Further, although examples of calculations of the benefits of capital mobility cannot be provided, illustrations abound. One notable example occurred between 1869 and 1878, when the United States ran, on average, a current account deficit of around 1 percent of gross domestic product (GDP) every year. The deficit then continued, at a lower average level, for another ten years. This permitted domestic investment to exceed domestic saving by a very substantial amount for some twenty years. That investment, among other things, allowed the development of the railroads and the opening up of the West. The United States developed more rapidly than it otherwise would have. Without the investment, the nation would have lost a substantial amount of income. Furthermore, any measure of that income loss would underestimate the loss to the world as a whole. The development of the United States raised real wages throughout a good part of Europe by lowering the price of grain, then a major component of workers' expenditure. That benefit, too, would have been lost without capital mobility.

Currency Crises

The East Asian Crises

The East Asian crises were certainly not all identical, but they did have common features. There were asset price booms, followed by crashes, followed by problems in banking systems and flight from currencies. As the preceding narrative shows, that is not a new story. Commentators who expressed surprise at crises arising in the absence of public-sector problems had formed their expectations on a narrow slice of history.[5] Why the asset price crash led so rapidly to large-scale banking problems and then to problems with currencies has been neatly summarized by Ronald McKinnon, who said that "banks and other financial institutions were poorly regulated but their depositors were nevertheless insured—explicitly or implicitly—against bankruptcy by their national governments. The resulting moral hazard was responsible for the excessive build up of short-term foreign-currency indebtedness" (McKinnon 2000, 3).[6]

This buildup of foreign-currency indebtedness was encouraged by the pegged exchange rate regime. Because of the guarantees, there was undiversified lending as well as undiversified borrowing by banks. In addition, and again because of the guarantees, the problem was large in scale, and the banks had little collateral to offer in exchange for liquidity from the central bank. These problems, themselves substantial, were exacerbated by many of the banks involved having to make loans on the direction of government rather than according to commercial criteria.

In short, the system could not have been worse designed either to provide stability or to facilitate lender of last resort (LoLR) action; and even had LoLR action been feasible, the fall in value of the East Asian currencies undermined the capital position of the banks via their net foreign-currency indebtedness. Crash turned into crisis. Would crash without crisis have led to serious economic difficulties? The evidence from the past is that it would not.

"Problem-Free" Crises

Currency crises are not new, nor are they confined to developing countries. One of the most famous of currency crises, and one of major symbolic importance, occurred in 1931. That was when Britain finally left the gold standard. Britain had been on that standard, linking its currency firmly to gold, for around 200 years. The standard had delivered long-run stability of prices. Occasionally, in times of war, Britain had left the standard, but these had been "suspensions"—temporary leavings of the standard, with the declared intention of returning. Britain always had returned, and it did so in 1925, after the suspension occasioned by World War I. But there was still a far from smoothly working world economy, and in 1931, after a struggle, including raised interest rates, Britain finally abandoned gold, and with no intention to return. (For an accessible account of the events leading up to Britain's leaving gold, see Capie, Mills, and Wood 1985.) Was the abandoning of gold a crisis for Britain? The answer to this question is a clear no: The economy grew strongly, and there was a period of steady, essentially noninflationary growth until almost the outbreak of war in 1939.

The great Austrian economist Joseph Schumpeter wrote of it as follows: "In England there was neither panic nor—precisely owing to the way the thing had been done or, if the reader prefer, had come about—loss of 'confidence' but rather a sigh of relief" (Schumpeter 1939, 956). Remarkably, exactly the same could have been written about what happened when Britain left the ERM in 1992. Britain had struggled to maintain the exchange rate. Just as Milton Friedman had described in 1953, ERM had made clear which way the currency was going to move. It was a one-way bet. And in another echo of the past (that is, of 1931), Britain's leaving the ERM was followed by a period—about ten years—of strong low-inflation growth. So currency crises need not be crises, although they plainly can be.

But what turns currency crises into crises for the economy? Before answering that question, it is useful to review the concept of contagion. For in the course of clarifying what that is, the crucial factors turning currency crises to economic crises will be exposed.

Currency and Contagion

Suppose a country experiences some sort of financial panic or crisis in its banking system. Lenders in other countries are then, quite reasonably, unwilling to lend to it. One argument for this causing international problems is that third countries, untarnished by these domestic difficulties, nevertheless lose their creditworthiness. This is sometimes called the "tequila effect," after what supposedly happened in the aftermath of Mexico's 1994 difficulties. It is argued on the same basis that a bailout of the original country is required, lest contagion produce a wave of crises across the world, with quite likely disastrous effects.

What evidence is there for this "contagion" actually occurring? Models can undoubtedly be constructed to show it is likely. But has it happened in recent years? Two cases are often cited—Argentina in 1995 as a result of Mexico in 1994, and the problems in the rest of Asia after the collapse of Thailand's currency (the baht) in July 1997. We consider these in turn.

Argentina had adopted an arrangement in all essential features comprising a currency board in March 1994. The peso was convertible one-to-one with the U.S. dollar. Inflation fell, and fiscal discipline was restored. Private capital started to flow in. Unfortunately, although

monetary and fiscal arrangements had been reformed, no such changes had affected the banking system. It was undercapitalized, and although the central bank had regulatory powers, no improvement in the banking system was effected. Nor, in the event that problems hit this frail system, was the central bank in a position to act as lender of last resort: A currency board arrangement prevents this.

The Argentinian banking system was thus not only fragile: It had no possibility of central bank liquidity support. A cliché is sometimes apt, and that is the case here: The Argentinian banking system was an accident waiting to happen. Thus the conventional view of Argentina's problems, in which Argentina is an innocent victim of Mexico's circumstances, misses an important part of the story. The timing is correct: After Mexico's problems, depositors at Argentinian banks did withdraw their pesos and convert them into U.S. dollars, producing, as was inevitable in the absence of a lender of last resort, a sharp monetary contraction. Gross domestic product fell by over 5 percent in 1995, and unemployment rose from 10 percent to 17 percent. This led, in turn, to a sharp move into deficit by the public sector. No fewer than 205 banks failed in 1995.

It may be the case that observing Mexico led Argentinians to a careful evaluation of their own country's economic situation, and thus to the Argentinian crisis. But was that contagion? Rather, it was the reverse: It was rational action prompted by a warning from elsewhere, not irrational panic in response to an irrelevant signal.

And what of Southeast Asia? There can be no claim that Thailand was an innocent victim of bad luck. The baht collapsed not for that reason but because of surging short-term foreign borrowing, a banking system whose main activity was speculative property lending, and a corrupt government. What about the other countries that suffered in the fallout? Indonesia, Malaysia, and the Philippines all had to give up their exchange rate pegs. Was this "contagion"? The case for that is not persuasive. Every one of these countries had adopted an exchange rate peg as a way of reducing inflation. That policy worked: Low inflation and manifest investment opportunities led to large capital inflows. These inflows were allowed to affect the domestic money supply. In consequence, prices rose, first of nontradables and then, via the pressure of these on costs generally, of tradables. The real exchange rates started to appreciate despite the nominal rates being pegged. This led to a rapidly widening current account deficit—far from always bad, but invariably a signal that the cause should be investigated.

It started to be noticed that the banking systems of these countries were not lending prudently what they had borrowed. Nonperforming loans were high and rising, especially in the state-owned banks. Local lenders were quite well informed, and there was, in consequence, a risk premium on domestic securities. This led banks (and firms) to borrow in foreign currency while lending substantially in domestic currency. Again, like Argentina, the situation was an accident waiting to happen. Thailand may have been the catalyst, but these countries were not innocent bystanders affected by the resulting explosion. Thailand, after all, was followed only by those countries that were themselves in dangerous situations. Whether these countries might have got by had Thailand not triggered their collapse is an interesting question, but only superficially so, for it is unanswerable. It is plain, though, that they could not go on as they were.

In summary, it is hard to make the case that contagion was the source of problems in these often-cited episodes. The "tequila effect" on the basis of these episodes—including the one that gave it its name—is an effect without consequences.

Overview and Conclusions

What general points can be made about currency crises and contagion? The first is that currency crises—sudden collapses or upward shifts (although these are much less common) in an exchange rate—are a product of a particular exchange rate system. This is a pegged exchange rate, one that is fixed subject to the proviso that if domestic difficulties become too great it will be changed. Milton Friedman in 1953 pointed out the inherent instability of such a system. Since then, numerous authors, some listed above, have formalized and developed that insight. It is understandable that the world was attracted to such a system; the fact remains that such a system is fundamentally flawed.

But currency crises need not become economic crises. Indeed, as the experience of Britain in both 1931 and 1992 shows, a currency crisis may end in preventing, if not an economic crisis, certainly severe economic hardship. What turns a currency crisis into an economic crisis is when the exchange rate collapse interacts with the country's financial system—in particular, its banking system—and severely damages it.

Contagion, the transmission of crises from one problem-free country to another, though perhaps conceivable in principle, is hard to find in practice. What is noticeable is that one currency crisis, of the sort that leads to an economic crisis, frequently triggers another by prompting observers to look around for countries with similar symptoms. But that is not contagion.

Geoffrey Wood

See Also Balance of Payments and Capital Flows; Dollarization; Exchange Rate Movements; International Financial Markets; International Indebtedness; International Monetary Fund (IMF)

Endnotes

1. The last item refers to the practical breakup of the system of pegged exchange rates that had prevailed between most of the countries of the European Union. The pound sterling floated and caused countries to develop their exchange rates against the DM (Deutsch Mark).

2. This is not to say they were not severe problems for the countries concerned.

3. In this Schwartz followed Palgrave: "One of the most remarkable and instructive facts is negative, viz., that there has been really no panic in England since 1866" (Palgrave 1894, 462).

4. This theory of the origin of banking panics is clearly related to what Calomiris and Gorton (1991) called the "asymmetric information approach."

5. Goodhart and Delargy (1998) also remarked on this.

6. This indebtedness explains why breaking the link with the dollar, for these countries the counterpart of the Bank of England's suspension of the Bank Charter Act in 1866, was of little help.

References

Bagehot, W. 1962 [1873]. *Lombard Street: A Description of the Money Market.* Homewood, IL: Irwin.

Calomiris, C. W., and G. Gorton. 1991. "The Origin of Banking Panics: Models, Facts, and Bank Regulations." In R. G. Hubbard, ed., *Financial Markets and Financial Crises.* Chicago: University of Chicago Press.

Capie, F.H., T.C. Mills and G.E. Wood, "Debt Management and Interest Rates: The British Stock Conversion of 1932", *Applied Economics,* 18, 1111–1126.

Chrystal, K. Alec, and Geoffrey E. Wood, "Are Trade Deficits a Problem?" Federal Reserve Bank of St. Louis, Review 70 (January/February 1988), pp. 3–11.

Crockett, Andrew. 2003. "International standard setting in financial supervision." Lecture by Andrew Crockett, General Manager of the BIS and Chairman of the Financial Stability Forum, at the Cass Business School, City University, London, 5 February. http://www.bis.org/speeches/sp030205.htm

Flood, R. P., and P. M. Garber. 1984. "Collapsing Exchange-Rate Regimes: Some Linear Examples." *Journal of International Economics* 17. August 1984, v. 17, iss. 1–2, pp. 1–13

Friedman, M. 1953. "The Case for Flexible Exchange Rates." In M. Friedman, *Essays in Positive Economics.* Chicago: University of Chicago Press.

Garber, P. M., and L. E. O. Svensson. 1995. "The Operation and Collapse of Fixed Exchange Rate Regimes." In G. Grossman and K. Rogoff, eds., *Handbook of International Economics,* vol. 3. North Holland, Amsterdam: Elsevier.

Goodhart, C., and P. J. R. Delargy. 1998. "Financial Crises: Plus ça Change, plus c'est la Même Chose." *International Finance* 1, no. 2.

Handbook of International Economics Vol. 3. http://books.elsevier.com/elsevier/?isbn=0444815473. Edited by G. M. Grossman, Princeton University, Princeton, NJ. K. Rogoff, Harvard University, Cambridge, MA.

Krugman, P. R. 1979. "A Model of Balance of Payments Crises." *Journal of Money, Credit, and Banking* 11.Vol. 11, No. 3 (Aug. 1979), pp. 311–325

Levi, L. 1872. *History of British Commerce and of the Economic Progress of the British Nation, 1763–1870.*

Lutz, F. A. 1954. "The Case for Flexible Exchange Rates." *Banca Nazionale del Lavaro Review* 7.

Mckay, C. 1932 [1841]. *Extraordinary Popular Delusions and the Madness of Crowds.* New York: Farrar, Straus and Giroux.

McKinnon, Ronald I., *The International Dollar Standard and the Sustainability of the U.S. Current Account Deficit.* Brookings Papers on Economic Activity. Vol. 2001, No. 1 (2001), pp. 227–239.

Obstfeld, Maurice, and Kenneth S. Rogoff. 1995. "The Mirage of Fixed Exchange Rates," *Journal of Economic Perspectives* 9, Fall 1995, No. 4, pp. 73–90.

Palgrave, R. H. I. 1889, 1894. *Dictionary of Political Economy.* London: Macmillan.

Schumpeter, J. 1939. *Business Cycles.* New York: McGraw Hill.

Schwartz, A. J. 1986. "Real and Pseudo Financial Crises." In F. H. Capie and G. E. Wood, eds., *Financial Crises and the World Banking System.* London: Macmillan.

Sohmen, E. 1957. "Demand Elasticities and Foreign 'Exchange Market.'" *Journal of Political Economy* 65. Vol. 65, No. 5 (Oct. 1957), pp. 431–436.

Thornton, H. 1978 [1802]. *An Enquiry into the Effects of the Paper Credit of Great Britain.* With an introduction by F. A. Hayek. Fairfield, NJ: Augustus Kelly.

Tooke, T. 1838. *History of Prices.* London: Longman, Brown, Green and Longman (becomes Tooke and Newmarch, published 1858).

Yeager, L. B. 1959. "The Misconceived Problem of International Liquidity." *Journal of Finance* 14.

Dollarization

Currency substitution occurs when residents of a country extensively use foreign currency alongside or instead of the domestic currency.[1] When the foreign currency used is the U.S. dollar, the phenomenon is called "dollarization." Commonly, the term serves as shorthand for the use of any foreign currency by another country. The issues that dollarization raise, used in this broad sense, are identical for countries in the region around South Africa using the South African rand, for example, as for a country of, say, Eastern Europe considering adopting the euro. Thus, in common usage, dollarization is synonymous with currency substitution in general, that is, a country adopting a foreign currency as its own. Definitions for related terms are the same whether the currency being substituted is the dollar, the euro, the yen, or some other currency. Dollarization has three main varieties: unofficial dollarization, semiofficial dollarization, and official dollarization. These three types are described below. This discussion of dollarization in its broad sense is followed by a brief examination of dollarization in Latin America. In the Latin American context, "dollarization" is normally employed to refer specifically to the use of U.S. currency; "currency substitution" is the more appropriate term for references to other foreign currencies in the region.

Types of Dollarization

Unofficial Dollarization
Unofficial dollarization occurs when people hold much of their financial wealth in foreign assets even though foreign currency is not legal tender in their country of residence.[2] Unofficial dollarization occurs in stages that correspond to the textbook function of money as a store of value, means of payment, and unit of account. In the first stage, which economists sometimes call "asset substitution," people hold foreign bonds and deposits abroad as stores of value. In the second stage of unofficial dollarization, people hold large amounts of foreign currency deposits in the domestic banking system (if permitted) and later foreign notes, both as a means of payment and as stores of value. Wages, taxes, and everyday expenses such as groceries and electric bills continue to be paid in domestic currency, but expensive items such as automobiles and houses are often paid in foreign currency. In the final stage of unofficial dollarization, people think in terms of foreign currency, and prices in domestic currency become indexed to the exchange rate. Such informal dollarization is a response to economic instability and high inflation, which cause residents to seek to diversify and protect their assets from the risks of devaluation of their own currencies.

Measuring the extent of unofficial dollarization is difficult. Accurate statistics on how much people hold in foreign bonds, bank deposits, or notes and coins is usually unavailable. However, estimates of the extent to which notes of the U.S. dollar and a few other currencies circulate outside their countries of origin give a rough idea of how widespread unofficial dollarization is. Researchers at the Federal Reserve System estimate that foreigners hold 55 to 70 percent of U.S. dollar notes, mainly as

$100 bills.[3] The amount of dollar currency in circulation is currently about $480 billion, which implies that foreigners hold roughly $300 billion.[4]

Semiofficial Dollarization

More than a dozen countries have what might be called semiofficial dollarization, or officially bimonetary systems. Under semiofficial dollarization, foreign currency is legal tender in the country and may even dominate bank deposits, but it plays a secondary role to domestic currency in paying wages, taxes, and everyday expenses such as grocery and electric bills. Semiofficially dollarized countries retain a domestic central bank or other monetary authority and have corresponding latitude to conduct their own monetary policy.

Official Dollarization

Official dollarization, also called "full dollarization," occurs when foreign currency has exclusive or predominant status as full legal tender. That means that foreign currency is not only legal for use in contracts between private parties, but used by the government in payments. If domestic currency exists, it is confined to a secondary role. It may be issued only in the form of coins having small value, for example. Under this official form of currency substitution, a government forfeits its right to print money, declaring the U.S. dollar or some other strong international currency, such as the euro or yen, legal tender. The country closes its central bank and gives up control of monetary policy. Some dollarized countries do not issue domestic currency at all, whereas others, such as Panama, issue it in a secondary role.[5]

Many countries have used foreign currency at some point in their history. In the United States, for example, foreign coins were legal tender until 1857. Today, twenty-nine countries or territories officially use a foreign currency as their predominant currency; for thirteen of these, the currency of choice is the U.S. dollar. Of the total, fifteen are territories that

are not independent, such as the U.S. Virgin Islands. With minor exceptions, territories use the currency of their "mother" country. Independent officially dollarized countries use either the currency of a large neighbor or, in the case of Pacific Ocean islands, the currency of their former colonial power. Of the fourteen officially "dollarized" countries that are independent, Panama, with a population of 2.7 million and a gross domestic product (GDP) of $10 billion (2000 figures), is several times larger in population and economy than all the rest combined.

Dollarization in Latin America

The idea of official dollarization would have been unthinkable in Latin America five or ten years ago, when market liberalization was sweeping the continent. Since then, hopes of economic revival have gone largely unrealized. During the past thirty years, Latin America has been plagued by financial instability, partly blamed on inflationary and unstable currencies. The crises have periodically seen severe crashes, such as the peso collapse in Mexico in late 1994,[6] and across the continent central banks have consistently failed at their job of stabilizing the local currency, setting off massive inflation. Now, political leaders, mostly of the Right, see the dollar as a way of bringing order to the chaos by forcing even soft-money radicals to obey the hard-money discipline of America's Federal Reserve. They are willing to dollarize even if it means swallowing their national pride and entrusting monetary policy to the United States.

"It is like castration," according to Sebastian Edwards, an economics professor at the University of California, Los Angeles, and the former chief Latin American economist at the World Bank. "You can teach abstinence to kids, or you can castrate them. Castration seems like a drastic last resort. Yet dollarization is being embraced with a religious fervor."

Unofficially and Semiofficially Dollarized Countries

As of January 2005, dollarized countries could be categorized as follows:

Unofficially dollarized—U.S. dollar: Most of Latin America and the Caribbean, especially Argentina, Bolivia, Mexico, Peru, and Central America; most of the former Soviet Union, especially Armenia, Azerbaijan, Georgia, Russia, and Ukraine; various other countries, including Mongolia, Mozambique, Romania, Turkey, and Vietnam.

Semiofficially dollarized—U.S. dollar: Bahamas, Cambodia, Haiti, Laos (also Thai baht), Liberia.

Officially dollarized—U.S. dollar: Ecuador, El Salvador, Panama.

Unofficially dollarized—other currencies: some former French colonies in Africa (French franc); Balkans (German mark); Macau and southern China (Hong Kong dollar); Belarus (Russian ruble).

Semiofficially dollarized—other currencies: Bhutan (Indian rupee); Bosnia (German mark, Croatian kuna, Yugoslav dinar); Brunei (Singapore dollar); Channel Islands, Isle of Man (British pound); Lesotho (South African rand); Luxembourg (Belgian franc); Montenegro (German mark, Yugoslav dinar); Namibia (South African rand); Tajikistan (use of foreign currencies permitted—Russian ruble widespread).

Anastasia Xenias

See Also Balance of Payments and Capital Flows; Currency Crisis and Contagion; Exchange Rate Movements

Endnotes

1. For a more detailed discussion, see, for example, Ronald McKinnon 1982; Marc Miles 1978; and Lance Girton and Don Roper 1981.

2. A currency designated as "legal tender" is legally acceptable as payment for all debts, unless the parties to the payment have specified another currency; that is, the currency *may be* used in transactions. Legal tender differs from "forced tender," which means that people must accept a currency in payment even if they would prefer to specify another currency.

3. Porter and Judson 1996, 899.

4. The term "unofficial dollarization" covers cases where holding foreign assets is legal as well as cases where it is illegal. In some countries, it is legal to hold some kinds of foreign assets, such as dollar accounts with a domestic bank, but illegal to hold other kinds, such as bank accounts abroad, unless special permission has been granted. In general, unofficial dollarization can include holding foreign bonds and other nonmonetary assets, generally abroad; foreign-currency deposits abroad; and foreign notes (paper money) in wallets and mattresses.

5. Panama has a unit of account called the "balboa" that is equal to the dollar and issued in coins but not notes. In practice, there is no difference between the balboa and the dollar; the balboa is simply the Panamanian name for the dollar.

6. Inter Press Service, October 6, 2000.

References

Girton, Lance, and Don Roper, "Theory and Implications of Currency Substitution," *Journal of Money, Credit & Banking* 13, no. 1 (February 1981): 12–30.

McKinnon, Ronald I. "Currency Substitution and Instability in the World Dollar Standard," *American Economic Review* 72, no. 3 (June 1982): 320–333.

Miles, Marc. A. "Currency Substitution, Flexible Exchange Rates and Monetary Independence," *American Economic Review* 68, no.3 (June 1978): 428–436.

Porter, Richard, and Ruth Judson. 1996. "The Location of U.S. Currency: How Much Is Abroad?" *Federal Reserve Bulletin,* vol. 82, no. 10, 883–903.

Economic Integration

The term "economic integration" commonly refers to increased economic interaction between two or more countries resulting from the removal of barriers on the movement of goods and services, factors of production (such as labor and capital), and information and ideas. Economic integration can thus occur in each of these areas—that is, through trade in goods and services, through movements of labor and capital, and through the exchange of information and ideas. The extent of integration that takes place, and the welfare implications of the integration, vary depending on the forms of integration that emerge.

Economists have proposed several theories of trade in goods and services, traditionally considered the key mechanism for integrating economic activities across countries. The simple Ricardian model of comparative advantage illustrates how countries can gain from international trade in goods. The key insight here is that a country can gain by devoting more of its resources to the production of the goods that it is best at producing, and exchanging them for other goods through international trade. Another model of trade, known as the Heckscher-Ohlin model, posits the differences in the endowments of different factors of production between countries as the basis of trade. This model demonstrates that the gains from trade do not necessarily accrue to everyone in the economy. Trade can produce winners and losers, even though the country as a whole gains from it. Other models look at trade based on economies of scale and love of variety. All of these insights about the gains from trade in

goods and services apply as well to the other two main forms of economic integration—integration through the movement of labor and capital and through the exchange of information and ideals. However, these forms also raise new issues. Also, significant strides toward economic integration have been made worldwide, and it is a central issue in the current debate on globalization.

International Trade in Goods

Ricardian Theory of Comparative Advantage

The theories of nineteenth-century British economist David Ricardo illustrate the desirability of economic integration through a simple model that shows how countries can gain by integrating their goods market, or simply by eliminating all barriers to trade in goods.

Suppose there are only two countries in the world: North and South. Each makes two goods, bread and cloth. Each has 100 labor hours per day, and labor is the only required input. The technology for producing the two goods in the two countries, along with other relevant information, is summarized in Table 1.

North could make 100 loaves of bread a day if it devoted all its labor to bread production, or it could make 100 yards of cloth if it devoted all its labor to cloth production. These numbers imply that it requires one hour of labor to produce a loaf of bread or a yard of cloth in North. Using all its labor, North could produce any combination of bread and cloth on the solid

Table 1: Illustration of Ricardian Comparative Advantage

	North	South
Total amount of labor, hours per day	100	100
Productivity		
Yards of cloth per labor hour	1	0.5
Loaves of bread per labor hour	1	0.9
Labor hours to make		
1 yard of cloth	1	2
1 loaf of bread	1	1.11
Autarky		
Production and consumption of cloth	55	30
Production and consumption of bread	45	36
Price of cloth in terms of bread	1	1.8
Price of bread in terms of cloth	1	0.55
Post-trade		
Production of cloth	100	0
Production of bread	0	90
Consumption of cloth	65	35
Consumption of bread	50	40
Price of cloth in terms of bread	1.43	1.43
Price of bread in terms of cloth	0.7	0.7

line in Figure 1a, which is the production possibility frontier (PPF hereafter) of North. To keep the focus on real values rather than looking at dollar prices (dollars per yard of cloth or per loaf of bread), one must look at the relative price, defined as the price of one good in terms of another. The numbers imply that one loaf of bread will exchange for one yard of cloth in North. Therefore, the relative price of bread in terms of cloth is one, and vice versa. Exactly how much of each good is produced in North depends on the demands for bread and cloth in North. Suppose demand is such that North produces and consumes 45 loaves of bread and 55 yards of cloth in autarky, that is, when it is not trading with South. This is point A_N on its PPF.

The technology for South is as follows. It could either make 90 loaves of bread or 50 yards of cloth a day by devoting all its labor to one or the other activity. These numbers imply that it requires 1.11 hours of labor to produce one loaf of bread and 2 hours of labor to produce one yard of cloth. These numbers clearly show that South has lower productivity in both

bread and cloth production: Each labor hour produces 0.5 yard of cloth or 0.9 loaf of bread in South. The numbers also imply that one loaf of bread will exchange for 0.55 yards of cloth. So, the relative price of bread in terms of cloth is 0.55. Alternatively, the relative price of cloth in terms of bread is 1.8: One yard of cloth exchanges for 1.8 loaves of bread. The PPF for South is the solid downward sloping line in Figure 1b. Assume that in autarky South produces and consumes 36 loaves of bread and 30 yards of cloth, given by point A_S on its PPF in Figure 1b.

Now suppose that the two economies are allowed to trade with each other. Do they want to trade? What is the pattern of trade? What are the gains from trade?

Since a yard of cloth sells for one loaf of bread in North, while it sells for 1.8 loaves of bread in South, North will be happy to exchange some cloth in return for bread. The flip side of this is that a loaf of bread exchanges for 0.55 yards of cloth in South but can fetch one yard of cloth in North. Therefore, South will be willing to exchange bread in return for cloth.

Figure 1: Comparative Advantage and Gains from Trade

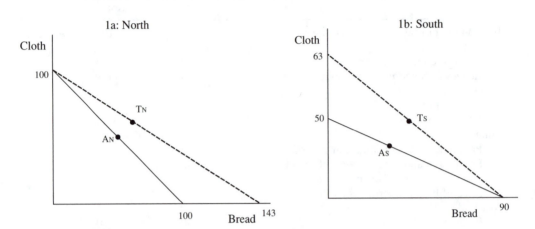

This is the Ricardian theory of comparative advantage. Even though North has higher productivity in both bread and cloth, South still has a comparative advantage in the bread production. In South, bread is cheap in relation to cloth; in North, bread is expensive in relation to cloth. Therefore, given the opportunity to trade, North will like to sell cloth to South in exchange for bread.

The rate at which the two goods will exchange for each other in the post-trade situation will depend on the demand conditions; however, it must fall within the range of the two price ratios that prevailed in each country before trade began: The price of cloth in terms of bread must be between 1 and 1.8. The gains from trade for both countries can be easily demonstrated by the numbers. Suppose North offers South the following deal: Give me 50 loaves of bread in exchange for 35 yards of cloth. The implied price of cloth in terms of bread is 1.43, while the price of bread in terms of cloth is 0.7. If South accepts this deal, then in the post-trade situation North can make itself better off by devoting all of its labor to cloth production. If North does so, it produces 100 yards of cloth, out of which 35 yards are exported to South in exchange for 50 loaves of bread. Therefore, North consumes 65 yards of cloth and 50 loaves of bread, which is clearly

preferable to its pre-trade consumption of 55 yards of cloth and 45 loaves of bread. The post-trade consumption point of North is given by T_N in Figure 1a, which lies to the northeast of A_N. What about South? South can now devote all its labor to bread production and thus produce 90 loaves of bread. Since South has to export 50 loaves of bread to North, it consumes 40 loaves of bread as well as the 35 yards of cloth that it imports from North. The post-trade consumption point of South is given by T_S in Figure 1b, which lies to the northeast of its autarky consumption point A_S. Therefore, international trade has the potential to make both countries better off.

In general, if the post-trade relative price of cloth is 1.43 in terms of bread, then North can consume anywhere on the dashed downward sloping line in Figure 1a, if it devotes all its resources to cloth production and exchanges some cloth for bread in the international market. The area between the dashed line and the solid line captures the expansion in the North's consumption opportunities as a result of trade. The same is true for South in Figure 1b. That is, upon opening to trade, a country can enhance its consumption opportunities and welfare by specializing in the production of a good in which it has a comparative advantage. This is how a country gains from economic integration in general and international trade in particular.

Apart from showing how countries can gain from trade, this example also shows that even if a country has lower productivity in all goods, it can still have a comparative advantage in some goods. This is a very powerful result, and the failure to grasp it lies behind a lot of misconceptions about trade. For example, it is commonly argued that many poor countries do not have a comparative advantage in anything. This is clearly wrong, as can be easily seen from the numerical example. Despite having a lower productivity in both bread and cloth, South is a relatively cheaper source of bread.

The basic insight of gains from trade due to the Ricardian comparative advantage, which arises from differences in technology across countries, carries over to other more general models of trade as well. One limitation of the simple Ricardian model is the assumption of a single factor of production: labor. The Heckscher-Ohlin model of trade generalizes the theory of comparative advantage to the case with many factors of production.

Heckscher-Ohlin Model of Trade

Named after two Swedish economists, Eli Heckscher and Bertil Ohlin, the Heckscher-Ohlin model studies the pattern of production and trade that arises when countries have different endowments of factors of production, such as labor, capital, and land. In contrast to the Ricardian model, where the pattern of comparative advantage, and consequently the pattern of trade, is determined by technological differences, in the Heckscher-Ohlin model it is determined by variations in the availability of different factors of production.

To understand the role of resources or endowments in trade, again assume that the world consists of two countries, North and South, each of which produces two goods, bread and cloth. In contrast to the Ricardian model, there are two factors of production: labor and capital. Both cloth and bread use both labor and capital; however, cloth production re-

quires more capital per unit of labor. That is, cloth production is more capital intensive in relative terms, and hence bread production is more labor intensive. Assume that each country has access to the same technology for producing the two goods. The only difference between the two countries comes from the fact that North is better endowed with capital than South. To be more precise, assume that North has more capital per unit of labor than South, which makes North relatively abundant in capital and South relatively abundant in labor.

Now, if North is capital abundant compared to South, then capital is going to be cheaper in North. Since cloth production uses more capital per unit of labor than bread production, it is going to be relatively cheaper to produce cloth in North, and hence in the pre-trade situation, the relative price of cloth in terms of bread is going to be lower in North than in South. Since the relative price of cloth is lower in North compared to South, North has a comparative advantage in cloth production. Therefore, upon opening up to trade, North will export cloth to South and import bread from it. By doing so, both countries can gain from trade just as in the Ricardian model.

The result is known as the Heckscher-Ohlin theorem. The statement of the theorem is as follows: *Countries tend to export goods that are intensive in the factors with which they are abundantly endowed.* In the example, North is abundantly endowed with capital, and hence it exports cloth, which uses capital more intensively than bread does; South is abundantly endowed with labor, and hence it exports the labor-intensive good, bread.

After trade begins, the relative price of cloth, which is exported by North, rises compared to the pre-trade situation. As North produces more cloth to meet the export requirement, the relative demand for capital increases in the North because cloth is more capital intensive. This leads to an increase in the reward of capital and a decrease in the reward of labor. Therefore, in North, capital owners gain from trade, whereas labor owners lose. The opposite happens in South. This important result shows that in a multifactor world, trade is likely to produce some winners and some losers. How can this result be reconciled with the gains from trade established in the Ricardian case? The implication in the Heckscher-Ohlin model is that the gains from trade do not accrue to everyone automatically. Since the country as a whole gains from trade, the winners from trade can compensate the losers and still be better off. However, in the absence of such redistribution, the potential losers from trade will have an incentive to restrict trade.

Given these two theories of trade, it is time to ask the next logical question: What determines the pattern of trade in the real word? Is it the differences in technologies or endowments? Empirical evidence on this issue is mixed. Both technological differences and endowment differences have been found to affect the pattern of international trade.

Trade Based on Economies of Scale and Love of Variety

According to the trade theories emphasizing comparative advantage, the similarity of industrialized countries in factor endowments and technologies suggests little reason for trade among them. Yet there is a lot of trade among the industrialized countries: It represents about half of world trade. Furthermore, a large part of this trade consists of intra-industry trade (IIT) in which a country both exports and imports goods in the same product category. For example, the United States exports cars to Europe and imports cars from Europe. Since the traditional trade theories cannot do a very good job of explaining IIT, trade theorists came up with newer models of trade based on economies of scale in production and love of variety in consumption. Much IIT involves trade in differentiated products—exports and imports of different varieties of the same basic product. One key factor driving this trade is that people love to have a wider choice of products. Another factor is that many industries are characterized by economies of scale in produc-

tion: Production is more efficient (average cost of production is less) the larger the scale at which it takes place. These two factors together imply that larger markets can support a wider variety of items at a lower price. Therefore, in the presence of economies of scale in production, economic integration through trade, by creating a larger market, benefits consumers.

Dynamic Gains from Trade

Gains from trade include not just the relatively static gains discussed thus far, however. Countries engaging in trade also enjoy dynamic gains. Theories of dynamic gains take into account a country's long-run economic growth prospects and how they are affected by economic integration.

There are two sources of economic growth: accumulation of factors of production, and technological progress. In terms of Figure 1, these changes will lead to an outward expansion of the PPF. International trade can affect economic growth by altering the incentives to factor accumulation and by affecting the pace of technological progress. Even though there is a wide agreement among economists on the subject of static gains from trade, the question of dynamic gains is far from settled. Theoretical models do not predict an unambiguous impact of trade on growth; however, most of the empirical work in this area has found that freer trade tends to lead to greater growth.

The Extent of Economic Integration through Trade

In addition to devising different theories of how trade occurs and how it benefits the parties engaging in it, economists are interested in the quantitative importance of trade for the world economy and its evolution through time. One measure of trade's quantitative importance for the world economy is the ratio of exports to gross domestic product (GDP) for the world as a whole, presented in Table 2.

The table shows that the first spurt in trade occurred in the late nineteenth century. It was driven primarily by the reduction in transport

Table 2: Merchandise Export as a Percentage of World GDP.

1820	1870	1913	1929	1950	1998
1.0	4.6	7.9	9.0	5.5	17.2

Source: Years 1820 and 1929 from Angus Madison, *Monitoring the World Economy, 1820–1992* (Paris: Organisation for Economic Co-operation and Development (1995); other years from Madison, *The World Economy: A Millennial Perspective* (Paris: Organisation for Economic Co-operation and Development, 2001).

costs due to the invention of steam-powered iron ships during the second half of the nineteenth century. The advent of railroads, and the reduction of tariffs and other trade restrictions by many countries, were other contributory factors. The interwar period, particularly the period after 1929, experienced a collapse of world trade. This collapse partly reflected the worldwide depression of economic activity and partly the huge increase in tariffs and other trade restrictions during this period, the Smoot-Hawley tariff of 1930 by the United States being the most infamous one. Since World War II, there has been a remarkable expansion in world trade driven mainly by continuing improvements in the technology of transportation and communication and a very substantial and progressive reduction in government-imposed restrictions on trade.

International Trade in Factors of Production (Capital and Labor)

Factor movements include labor migration, the transfer of capital via international borrowing and lending, and the subtle international linkages involved in the formation of multinational corporations. Movements of labor and capital are not radically different from the movement of goods, however, in economic analyses.

Labor Migration

International factor movements can sometimes substitute for trade, so it is not surprising that international migration of labor is similar in its causes and effects to international trade based on differences in resources. Labor moves from countries where it is abundant to countries where it is scarce. This movement raises total world output, but it also generates strong income distribution effects—just as trade did in the Heckscher-Ohlin model discussed earlier—that hurts some groups. A numerical example can be used to illustrate the economic effects of migration. Again assume two countries, North and South, that now produce a single good, rice, using two factors of production: land and labor. To fix ideas, assume that each country has the same amount of land. Table 3 describes a relationship between the amount of labor used and the output of rice in each of the two countries.

In Table 3, the column labeled "Marginal Output" shows the increase in total output resulting from the addition of an extra worker. Now, suppose that South has 7 workers while North has only 3 workers. Given the information in the table, the total output of rice is 490 in South and 270 in North. Output per worker is 70 in South and 90 in North. If workers in each country are paid according to the marginal output, then the wage of a worker in South is 40, while the wage in North is 70. Therefore, workers in South will have an incentive to migrate to North. What happens if free migration is permitted? Workers will keep moving to North until wages in the two regions are equalized, which means that the marginal output of an additional worker must be the same in both regions. This happens when two workers move from South to North so that the marginal output and hence the wage of workers in each region becomes 60. World output increases from 760 in the premigration situation to 800 in the postmigration situation. Also,

Table 3: Output and Input

Number of Workers	Total Output	Marginal Output	Output per Worker
1	100	100	100
2	190	90	95
3	270	80	90
4	340	70	85
5	400	60	80
6	450	50	75
7	490	40	70
8	520	30	65
9	540	20	60
10	550	10	55

the workers who originally resided in South experience an increase in wages from 40 to 60. However, the workers who originally resided in North experience a reduction in wages from 70 to 60. Therefore, even though the world as a whole experiences an increase in output, the workers in North become worse off as a result of migration.

Throughout most of historical time, human migration has remained the predominant mechanism of interaction and integration of different societies. Ironically, during the present time this channel of economic integration is the one that faces the strongest barriers. Data from the United States—known as the country of immigrants—summarized in Table 4 show that the immigration rate per thousand of population is significantly lower now than it was prior to World War I. Similarly, the share of foreign born in total population is lower than it was in 1910, even though it increased in the past three decades after reaching a low of 4.7 in 1970. The late nineteenth and early twentieth centuries saw great economic integration through all channels, including migration. Many Europeans left their native countries and immigrated to the New World. This trend had a substantial impact in reducing wage gaps between the host and source countries.

The transportation costs of migration have continued to decline since World War I. The economic incentives to migrate from Europe may have declined owing to the narrowing of the income gap between the United States and Europe, but the economic incentives for migration to both of these areas from developing countries are huge. The reason for the lower immigration rates has to do with government policies restricting immigration. The United States did not have any significant restrictions on immigration until the Chinese Exclusion Act of 1882. However, the wage-depressing effect of immigration was the principal driving force behind restrictions. For example, the restriction on Chinese immigration was imposed partly in response to political opposition from California and other western states that were facing downward pressure on wages owing to the import of Chinese laborers for railroad construction and other work. General restrictions on immigration from other countries did not come until the National Origins Act of 1924. In recent times, even though the barriers to the movement of goods and capital have come down significantly, economic integration through migration remains stifled.

Movement of Capital

The movement of capital takes place via international borrowing and lending, which are broadly classified into the following categories.

I. Private lending and investing
  A. Long term
    (1) Portfolio investment (purchases and sales of securities, such as

Table 4: Immigration to the United States

	Immigration Rate/ 1000 Population	Foreign-Born as a % of Population
1870	6.4	13.9
1890	9.2	14.6
1910	10.4	14.6
1930	3.5	11.5
1950	0.7	6.9
1970	1.7	4.7
1990	2.6	7.9
2000	4.1	10.4

Source: U.S. Department of Commerce, Bureau of the Census, Statistical Abstract of the United States (Washington, DC: various years).

bonds and stocks, in amounts that do not imply any direct management control or influence on the businesses issuing the securities)

(2) Loans (to a foreign borrower, maturity more than a year)

(3) Direct investment (lending to, or purchasing shares in, foreign enterprises largely owned and controlled by the investor)

B. Short term (short-term loans or purchase of foreign bonds with maturity of less than a year)

II. Official lending and investing (by a government or multilateral organization such as the World Bank, International Monetary Fund [IMF]; both long term and short term)

By its very nature, the movement of capital involves an intertemporal transaction because it involves a payment today to acquire something that is expected to return a payment or a series of payments sometime in the future. This kind of exchange can be viewed as a kind of international trade, but one that involves trade of present consumption for future consumption rather than trade of one good for another at a single point in time. Instead of exchanging bread for cloth today, intertemporal trade lets the parties exchange bread today for the promise of income with which to buy bread tomorrow. Due

to this intertemporal dimension, capital mobility involves problems that international trade in goods does not have, such as the uncertainty of future payments, a lack of information with which to estimate expected future payments, and adverse incentives to default on future obligations. Carrying out intertemporal exchanges across borders is even more difficult because the parties to the transaction live under different legal systems, their behavior is guided by different institutional and cultural factors, and they have different degrees of access to information that will enable them to judge the future value of an asset.

To understand the economics of intertemporal trade and gains from it, again assume two countries, North and South, which now exist for two periods: present and future. Consumers in each country consume a single good, in this case simply called "Consumption." Since the economies exist for two periods, there are effectively two goods in the model: present Consumption and future Consumption. Each country has a given amount of resources to devote to the production of present Consumption and future Consumption. The countries may have different preferences between present Consumption and future Consumption and/or different technologies for production, which will form the basis of comparative advantage. To fix ideas, assume that North has a comparative advantage in present Consumption and

South has a comparative advantage in future Consumption. Following the logic of the theory of comparative advantage, North should export present Consumption and import future Consumption, while South should import present Consumption and export future Consumption. Exporting present Consumption is lending, whereas importing present consumption is borrowing. In order to be a lender a country needs to produce more than it consumes today, so that it can lend the surplus amount. So, the model is very similar in spirit to the models of comparative advantage discussed earlier, and hence the gains from this intertemporal trade are similar to the gains from trade posited in those models.

The interesting question to ask is what determines the pattern of borrowing and lending or, alternatively, what gives South a comparative advantage in future Consumption. The tradeoff between present and future Consumption in a country depends on the investment opportunities and the preference of consumers between present Consumption and future Consumption. Suppose North and South have identical intertemporal preferences, but South has more attractive investment opportunities. Given this situation, South wants to devote fewer resources to present Consumption and more to investment activities that would increase the capital stock of South and lead to greater production of output in the future. Therefore, with identical intertemporal preferences, a country with relatively better investment opportunities is going to be a borrower in the international capital market. Alternatively, if countries have identical investment opportunities, but different intertemporal preferences, then the country with a greater preference for present Consumption will have a higher relative price of present Consumption, and hence it will import present Consumption, that is, will borrow in the international capital market. Now it can be shown that the price of present Consumption in terms of future Consumption is $1+r$, where r is the real rate of interest. When a country borrows a dollar today, it has to pay

$1+r$ next year. So, the tradeoff is one dollar of present Consumption exchanges for $1+r$ dollars of future consumption. Therefore, the price of present Consumption in terms of future consumption is simply $1+r$. If r_S is the real rate of interest in South, and r_N the real rate of interest in North, then saying that North has a comparative advantage in present Consumption implies that the relative price of present Consumption is lower in North: $r_N < r_S$. Therefore, the country with a lower real rate of interest is going to be a lender, and the country with a higher real rate of interest is going to be a borrower.

One category of international investment—direct foreign investment—is mainly undertaken by multinational firms. Two elements are supposed to be crucial in explaining the existence of multinationals: location motive, that is, the factor that leads the firm to locate its operations in different countries; and internalization motive, the factor that leads it to integrate these activities into a single firm.

The quantitative importance of international investments in the world economy is demonstrated by the ratio of foreign assets to the world GDP over the past several decades, as summarized in Table 5. The table shows that the extent of borrowing and lending was huge between 1870 and 1914, just as in the case of merchandise trade. There was a significant slowdown in capital movement during the interwar period, and it was not until 1980 that

Table 5: Foreign Assets as a Percentage of World GDP

1870	6.9
1900	18.6
1914	17.5
1930	8.4
1945	4.9
1960	6.4
1980	17.7
1995	56.8

Source: Maurice Obstfeld and Alan Taylor, *Global Capital Markets: Integration, Crisis, and Growth* (Cambridge: Cambridge University Press, 1999).

the ratio of foreign assets to the world GDP reached its pre–World War I level. However, in the past couple of decades, there has been a huge expansion of international capital flows.

Unlike growth in trade of goods, increased mobility of capital is not an unmixed blessing, and it has been implicated in many recent financial crises in developing countries. There are five main reasons why increased capital mobility can lead to or deepen financial crises. First, governments or banks may engage in excessive lending or borrowing. Second, events beyond the control of a country, such as increases in foreign interest rates, can shift flows away from developing country borrowers and make repaying debts more difficult. Third, the borrowing country may overuse short-term loans and bonds in its borrowing habits. The borrower may then experience difficulties if foreign investors refuse to refinance or rollover the debt. Fourth, debts denominated in foreign currency can become very expensive to pay off if the local currency depreciates unexpectedly. Finally, financial crises have elements of self-fulfilling panics, where investors fearing default stop lending and demand quick repayment. If many lenders do this at once, the borrowers cannot repay and a default and crisis occurs. For these reasons, many economists now advocate restrictions on private capital flows, particularly short-term credit flows, for countries with weak financial systems to reduce the likelihood of financial crises.

International Flow of Ideas and Knowledge

Another important channel of economic integration is through the exchange of economically relevant information and technology. International trade and movements of people and capital facilitate the flow of ideas and knowledge across borders. Provided that channels of communication remain open, there will be an exchange of ideas and knowledge across borders even in the absence of trade in goods and factors of production. The recent and continuing advances in communications technology are going to be a driving force in fostering deeper global economic integration in the future.

The Extent of Economic Integration in the World

Complete economic integration is a far-fetched idea for the world as a whole; however, several groups of countries have made progress in this direction. Below is a list of successive stages of economic integration that some groups of countries have achieved.

1. Free trade areas: Member countries remove trade barriers among themselves but keep their separate barriers against trade with the outside world. An example of this form of economic integration is the North American Free Trade Area (NAFTA), comprising Canada, the United States, and Mexico, which formally began in 1994.

2. Customs unions: In addition to removing internal trade barriers, members adopt a common set of external barriers. For example, the European Economic Community (EEC) was a customs union from 1957 to 1992. A southern common market, Mercosur, comprising Argentina, Brazil, Paraguay, and Uruguay, which started in 1991, is also a customs union.

3. Common markets: Members allow full freedom of factor flows (migration of labor and capital) in addition to having a customs union. The EEC was not a common market until the late 1980s owing to barriers on the movement of labor and capital. In 1992, it became a common market and the name changed to the European Community (EC).

4. Monetary unions: In addition to the features of a common market, member countries also have a permanently fixed

exchange rate for each others' currencies (or a single currency), and a single monetary authority conducts unionwide monetary policy. Twelve European Union countries are members of the European Monetary Union, which was established in 1999 and has a single currency, the euro. The European Central Bank conducts unionwide monetary policy.

5. Economic unions: Member countries unify all their economic policies, including monetary, fiscal, and welfare policies, as well as policies toward trade and factor migration. This is the highest stage of economic migration. Belgium and Luxembourg have had economic union since 1921, and the European Union is on the road to becoming an economic union.

Gains from trade suggest that if two or more countries form a free trade area or a customs union it must necessarily improve the welfare of the member countries. However, as was first pointed out by Jacob Viner in 1950, the creation of a customs union or a free trade area by a group of countries in a multicountry world has two opposing effects on welfare. Since the member countries eliminate trade barriers on each other's goods, there is *trade creation* among members, which is welfare improving. However, since member countries keep their trade barriers intact on nonmembers, the goods coming from nonmembers are discriminated against as they incur a higher tariff. This may result in what is called *trade diversion*, that is, some goods that were earlier imported from a lower-cost nonmember country are now imported from members. For example, Mexico's access to the U.S. market becomes tariff-free under NAFTA, but India's is not, so the United States shifts from cheaper imports from India to more expensive imports from Mexico, which causes welfare losses for the United States. The net effect of a customs union or a free trade area on welfare depends on the relative strengths of trade creation and trade diversion effects, an empirical issue.

The difference between a free trade area and a customs union is that in the former, each country has its own set of tariffs against nonmembers, whereas in the latter, all members have a common external tariff against nonmembers. The requirement of common external tariffs makes the customs union a politically difficult proposition compared to the free trade area. However, the administration of free trade areas is a nightmare because, in order to get a preferential treatment within the union, each good has to satisfy the rules-of-origin requirement. In the absence of such rules of origin, nonmembers will have an incentive to export all goods to the union through the member country with the lowest external tariff.

Even though a customs union may potentially be welfare worsening due to trade diversion, any move from a customs union to a common market is likely to be welfare improving by equalizing the returns to factors of production within the union. So, the additional gains from a common market are the same as the gains from labor migration and capital inflows mentioned earlier.

Monetary unions have both advantages and disadvantages. The advantage comes from the reduction of transaction costs and exchange rate risks. The disadvantage comes from the fact that by joining a monetary union a country gives up the ability to run an independent monetary policy to mitigate domestic imbalances and the ability to use exchange rate changes to mitigate external imbalances. In the case of economic shocks that affect member countries differently, monetary policy cannot be used to mitigate the effects of an adverse shock for a particular member country. Countries can use national fiscal policies to offset the effects of internal imbalances; however, fiscal policy changes have to go through a political process, which can cause delays. A unionwide fiscal policy, a feature of full economic union, can mitigate the problem by shifting some tax revenues from the growing countries to the recession countries through lower taxes and larger expenditures in the latter. Having a full economic union would eliminate the disadvantages of a monetary union.

Concluding Remarks

Improvements in transportation and communications technologies have played a key role in the increased economic integration of the past several decades. These improvements have reduced the costs of transporting goods, services, and factors of production and of communicating economically useful knowledge and technology. In addition, countries have generally favored taking advantage of the gains from economic integration. This can be most clearly seen in the desires of many East European countries to join the European Union, and of many small countries, such as Singapore and Chile, to enter into free trade agreements with the United States.

The protests and demonstrations at recent meetings of the World Trade Organization (WTO)—a multilateral institution facilitating trade agreement among countries—in Seattle and Cancun have shown that globalization has many detractors. The main groups opposed to unfettered economic integration are nongovernmental organizations (NGOs), including environmental groups and labor rights activists. These groups demand the incorporation of labor and environmental standards in trade agreements, which essentially means that the WTO should allow the use of trade sanctions to enforce higher labor and environmental standards in countries with lower standards. Most economists feel that economic integration through free trade should be kept separate from the issue of enforcing higher labor and environmental standards. The issue of standards should be dealt with through other multilateral institutions, such as the International Labour Organization (ILO), and in the context of multilateral environmental agreements such as the Kyoto Protocol, the Montreal Protocol, and so on. The main reason for the economists' reluctance to tie trade with labor and environmental standards is the fear that the use of trade sanctions to enforce these standards will become a tool for disguised protectionism.

Despite the current controversies, economic integration has been an important source of economic prosperity throughout history. Societies that cut themselves off from economic interaction with the rest of the world tend to stagnate.

Priya Ranjan

See Also Andean Community; APEC (Asia Pacific Economic Cooperation); Australia-New Zealand Closer Economic Relations Agreement (ANCERTA); Caribbean Community and Common Market (CARICOM); Central American Common Market (CACM); Common Market of the South (MERCOSUR); Common Market for Eastern and Southern Africa (COMESA); Commonwealth of Independent States (CIS); Council of Arab Economic Unity (CAEU); East African Community (EAC); Economic Community of Central African States (CEEAC); Economic Organization of West African States (ECOWAS); European Economic Area (EEA); European Union (EU); Gulf Cooperation Council (GCC); Latin American Free Trade Association; League of Arab States; South Asian Association for Regional Cooperation (SAARC); Southern African Development Community

References

Madison, Angus. 1995. *Monitoring the World Economy, 1820–1992.* Paris: Organisation for Economic Co-operation and Development.
———. 2001. *The World Economy: A Millennial Perspective.* Paris: Organisation for Economic Co-operation and Development.
Obstfeld, Maurice, and Alan Taylor. 1999. *Global Capital Markets: Integration, Crisis, and Growth.* Cambridge: Cambridge University Press.

Economic Sanctions

Economic sanctions are policies of an economic nature adopted by one government to induce policy changes by another government.[1] Examples include (but are not limited to) boycotts; embargos; subsidies; imposition of tariffs, quotas, or other import and export controls; denial of licenses; most-favored-nation treatment, national treatment, or membership in a trade agreement; suspension of aid or loans; freezing or seizure of assets; and blacklisting. In spite of their demonstrated costs, risks, unintended consequences, and ineffectiveness, economic sanctions continue to be employed by governments and international organizations as key policy instruments, and they continue to grow in number and scope. Their use runs counter to the trends of trade liberalization and globalization, however, and should be disciplined by enlightened self-restraint and international agreements.

History and Proliferation of Economic Sanctions

Economic sanctions have a venerable history, stretching back to Athens's attempt in 432 B.C. to curb Megara's trade. They were employed in the Roman conquest of Jerusalem, in a variety of wars during the Middle Ages, and in the American Revolution and American Civil War, the Franco-Prussian War, modern colonial and postcolonial conflicts, World Wars I and II, and the Cold War.[2] Debate continues on whether military measures such as siege, blockade, and interdiction qualify, with Geoff Simons arguing

the case for inclusion and most others inclined to exclude purely military measures and to focus on economic measures.

Economic sanctions appear to have proliferated during the twentieth century. From 12 cases in the period 1914 to 1945 (0.4 sanctions per annum), the number rose to 41 in the next quarter-century ending in 1969 (1.6 sanctions per annum). The count rose to 67 during the next twenty years (3.4 sanctions per annum) and peaked at 50 during the period 1990–1998 (6.3 sanctions per annum).[3] Within these totals, the proportion of multilateral sanctions grew when compared with unilateral sanctions. Whereas the League of Nations imposed only 7 notable sanctions from 1921 to 1939, the United Nations imposed 18 from 1945 to 2000. All but 5 of these took place in the 1990s, confirming the observation that sanctions are increasing in frequency.[4] During the decade 1990–2000, the UN Security Council passed 25 economic sanctions resolutions, imposing penalties on Iraq, Yugoslavia, Somalia, Libya, Liberia, Cambodia, Haiti, Angola, Rwanda, Sudan, Sierra Leone, Afghanistan, and Ethiopia/Eritrea.[5]

Within these broad trends, sanctions proliferate or attenuate with political and international events and in response to particular controversies. They have tended to rise with wars, economic depressions, or alleged political provocations, notably by the regimes of southern Africa, Israel, and the Communist countries. Particular leaders have backed sanctions for particular purposes. For example, U.S. President Jimmy Carter stimulated sanctions against human rights violations in the 1970s; Ronald Reagan encouraged trade sanctions against Asian partners, particularly Japan, in the 1980s; and in the 1990s Bill Clinton championed sanctions against Serbia's, Iraq's, and North Korea's military policies, often working through the United Nations.

Thus, economic statecraft or economic coercion, as economic sanctions are sometimes called,[6] should be regarded as equal in significance to diplomacy and military strategy in modern international relations. This is particularly true to the extent that the multilateralization of diplomacy, the rising risks and costs of military intervention, and the delegitimizing of interstate war by the UN Charter are recognized and acted upon by leaders of governments. Because economic sanctions stand midway between diplomacy and war, they provide leaders with a nonlethal but nevertheless concrete and visible set of instruments, easy to apply and difficult to ignore, by which to manage their relations with other states.

Objectives of Economic Sanctions

The broad category of economic sanctions linked to policy objectives may be divided into two streams: those based on economic policy objectives and those based on political-military policy objectives.

In the first category, the initiating government wishes to change the economic behavior of the target government through the imposition or threat of sanctions. For example, the initiating government may want to pressure the target government to lower trade barriers or subsidies, open investment opportunities, begin speedier repayment of debts, or curb illegal practices such as intellectual piracy or export of illicit goods. A subcategory of this stream is the policy area known as trade remedies—most notably, but not exclusively, practiced by the United States—in which antidumping penalties, countervailing duties, and "safeguard" levies are imposed on trade

partners in response to alleged unfair trading practices such as dumping, subsidizing, and market-disrupting export surges. The United States is also notorious for its use of Section 301 of the Trade Act of 1974 to bring pressure to bear on partners accused of unfair or unreasonable trade practices that restrain U.S. exports. Typically, these sorts of sanctions are exclusively economic in nature and guided by well-established legal and administrative precedents.

In the second category, the initiating government wishes to alter the political behavior of the target government. For example, the initiator may use sanctions to force an end to the target government's curbing of civil liberties, violation of human rights, threats or launching of military action such as cross-border aggression, or development or transfer of weapons of mass destruction and long-range missiles. Sanctions in these cases are often mixed, with economic penalties accompanying diplomatic pressure and military actions, including threat, blockade, interdiction, and attack. These mixed economic-diplomatic-military sanctions are also less routinized than purely economic trade sanctions inasmuch as they are initiated by political bodies such as cabinets and the UN Security Council, which apply criteria derived from international law, security requirements, and power politics to emerging and often unpredictable crises in the international arena.

U.S. Economic Sanctions

The United States is the country most active in imposing economic sanctions, including trade remedies, and therefore it is widely criticized by trade liberals and by sanctioned or potentially sanctioned governments. By 1998, the United States had no fewer than fifty-one laws and regulations authorizing unilateral economic sanctions in force, each of them legitimized by an act of Congress or a presidential executive order.[7] They are listed in Table 1.

Table 1: U.S. Laws and Regulations Authorizing Unilateral Economic Sanctions in Effect in 1998 (slightly abridged)

Antiterrorism Act of 1987
Antiterrorism and Effective Death Penalty Act
Arms Export Control Act
Atomic Energy Act
Bretton Woods Agreements Act
Burmese Sanctions Regulations
Chemical and Biological Weapons Control and Warfare Elimination Act
Cuban Assets Control Regulations
Cuban Liberty and Democratic Solidarity Act ("Helms-Burton Act")
Department of Commerce, Justice and State ... etc. ... Appropriations Act of 1990
Department of Defense Appropriations Act of 1987
Export Administration Act of 1979
Export-Import Bank Act
Federal Republic of Yugoslavia Sanctions relating to Kosovo
Fisherman's Protective Act of 1967
Foreign Assistance Act of 1961
Foreign Operations, Export Financing ... Appropriations Act of 1997
Foreign Terrorist Organizations Sanctions Regulations
Hickenlooper Amendment
India: Presidential Determination of May 13, 1998
Inter-American Development Bank Act
Internal Revenue Act
International Development Association Act
International Emergency Economic Powers Act
International Financial Institutions Act
International Monetary Fund Act
International Security and Development Cooperation Act
Iran and Libya Sanctions Act
Iran-Iraq Arms Nonproliferation Act of 1992
Iranian Transactions Regulations
Lacey (environmental protection) Act of 1981
Libya Sanctions Regulations
Magnuson-Stevens Fishery Conservation and Management Act
Marine Mammal Protection Act
Narcotics Control Trade Act
Narcotics Trafficking Sanctions Regulations
National Defense Authorization Act
North Korea: Relevant Foreign Assets Control Regulations
Nuclear Nonproliferation Act of 1978
Nuclear Proliferation Prevention Act
Pakistan: Presidential Determination of May 30, 1998
Spoils of War Act
Sudanese Sanctions Regulations
Tariff Act of 1930
Terrorism Sanctions Regulations
Trade Act of 1974
Trade Expansion Act of 1962
Trading with the Enemy Act of 1917

Note: Each of the above authorizes the curtailment of trade, aid, and financial flows. U.S. trade remedies acts, principally sections 202 and 301 of the Trade Act 1974, regarding antidumping, countervailing duties, import surge injury safeguards, fair trade, and intellectual property protection are additional to this list.

Source: Overview and Analysis of Current U.S. Unilateral Economic Sanctions: Investigation No. 332–391, Publication 3124 (Washington, DC: U.S. International Trade Commission, August 1998), available at http://www.usitc.gov/wais/reports/arc/w3124.htm (cited September 25, 2003).

Objections to Economic Sanctions

The principal objection to the employment of economic sanctions is their negative effect on the initiating government's own economy. That is, sanctions imply a curtailment of some economic activity, whether trade, investment, or movement of people, money, or ideas. They may be regarded as the antithesis of globalization. To the extent that a given bilateral transaction is economically beneficial to the government, commercial producers and marketers, or private consumers of a sanctioning country, that country will be less well off as a result of sanctions that interrupt that transaction.

There are exceptions. Some sanctions are applied in the expectation that they will produce a beneficial consequence for world economic transactions. For example, some trade sanctions may succeed in lowering a partner's import or investment barriers or reduce market-distorting subsidies.[8] These are characterized as trade remedies by the U.S. government even though they reduce net trade in the short run. In the political realm, they provide an opportunity for critics to castigate the United States as a protectionist country.[9] Thus the sanction may be treated as an investment with a positive long-term return. Governments must weigh the costs as well as the benefits, discounted by future uncertainties, expected as a result of their sanctions policies.

Governments must also weigh the political risks of their economic sanctions at home and their diplomatic acceptability abroad. U.S. sanctions regarding Communist China before 1979, pertaining to the Soviet pipeline during the Reagan administration, and against Cuba, Libya, and Iran up to the present have not only constrained U.S. producers and contractors from doing lucrative business abroad but also enraged European governments, particularly insofar as U.S. government policy constrained the choices of foreign branches of U.S. firms and even foreign commercial interests.[10]

A second objection is the lack of discrimination of many economic instruments and consequent harmful effects on innocent people. The outstanding example was the UN Security Council boycott and embargo of trade with Iraq from 1990 to 2003 to induce nuclear disarmament. Although the policy permitted oil to be sold for food and medicine, the regime of Saddam Hussein deliberately misapplied the oil-for-food exception, channeled funds to regime elites, neglected the infrastructure of Iraq, and impoverished its people. Ironically, Saddam blamed the UN and Western governments for Iraq's deterioration, attempting speciously but not without some success to legitimate his authoritarian regime as a "protector" against Western and Zionist hostility. Other Arab governments, Western liberals, and international humanitarian agencies joined the criticism of the sanctions. Sanctioning government leaders agonized over this unwanted consequence and deliberated how to recast sanctions to bring more direct pressure to bear on Saddam's regime. So-called "smart sanctions" were applied, such as restrictions on overseas travel by regime leaders and their families.[11] But the Iraq sanctions will be seen in retrospect as a well-intentioned policy that missed its target.

A third objection to the use of sanctions is their inefficacy. That is, they don't always work. Even when they do, their benefits may be outweighed by the economic and political costs and risks to the initiating governments and their producers, traders, and people and the detrimental effects on the innocent populations of the target governments. More often than not, the target countries ignore them, or evade them by diverting trade to other partners, without changing the targeted policies. As will be shown below, the picture is not encouraging to those who would advocate economic sanctions. Some estimates of success run as low as one-third, with corresponding nil or negative effects in two-thirds of cases.[12] Success rates vary by the category of behavior targeted by economic sanctions. Economic policies of targeted governments are more often successfully changed through sanctions than diplomatic and military policies, which often prove unsusceptible to economic coercion. When economic sanctions are reinforced by diplomatic and military pressures, and when they are applied by powerful and rich countries to small countries, the success rate rises. But numerous cases of multiple sanctions applied by the United States, even to small trade partners or political adversaries over a period of many years, have not ended in success.

Critics and Assessors of Sanctions

Observations regarding costs to the sender, political risks to leaders, collateral injury to innocent populations, and general lack of efficacy have mobilized numerous critics of U.S. sanctions policy. Among them are Geoff Simons cited above, Robert Pape,[13] Richard Haass,[14] and Thomas Weiss et al.[15] They are joined by American spokespeople for trade and commercial interests; free-enterprise think tanks such as the Cato Institute, Heritage Foundation, and American Enterprise Institute; and sanctioned governments and enterprises abroad. Nevertheless, economic sanctions continue to be widely employed by governments and international organizations, and they show no signs of disappearing as significant policy instruments in international relations. Empirical research on this policy sector continues in an attempt by scholars to assess and improve it—or definitively repudiate it.

Lessons from Case Studies

Research on economic sanctions falls into two categories: case studies and comprehensive surveys. These categories, in turn, are subdivided by their degree of qualification and statistical grounding. Case studies lend themselves to accounts involving political, diplomatic, and military elements and are characterized by qualitative analysis and policy-relevant conclusions. They provide vivid illustrations of the causes,

instruments, and outcomes of sanctions in their wider political and international setting. A well-known example is a 1998 volume edited by Richard N. Haass on *Economic Sanctions and American Diplomacy,* which presents reviews of U.S. sanctions of China, Cuba, Haiti, Iran, Iraq, Libya, Pakistan, and former Yugoslavia.[16] Haass concludes with lessons and recommendations to U.S. policymakers (summarized in Table 2). A wider net, capturing 115 historical and contemporary examples, was cast by Gary Clyde Hufbauer and Jeffrey J. Schott, assisted by Kimberly Ann Elliott, in their solid 1983 study *Economic Sanctions in Support of Foreign Policy Goals.*[17] The Hufbauer series of studies under the auspices of the Institute of International Economics underpins the widely cited estimate that economic sanctions are effective only one-third of the time.

Findings of Econometric Assessments

Comprehensive surveys, particularly those based on statistics and econometric analysis, lend themselves to more precise assessments of the effects of economic instruments, not only on the target economy but, equally important, on the economy of the initiating government. They rely on statistics of transactions, primarily commodity trade, but also incorporate trade in services and investment, where possible, and effects on the growth rates of manufacturing, jobs, GDP, and other comprehensive indicators. They are dependent not only on figures collected for other purposes but also on historical data series, so their policy implications are only as sound as the plausibility of the extrapolation of their findings to the future.

The most widely cited recent econometric study was one conducted by Gary Clyde Hufbauer and his associates at the Institute of International Economics in Washington, DC, in 1997.[18] The authors compiled data on U.S. exports and imports regarding eighty-eight partner countries in the years 1985, 1990, and 1995

Table 2: U.S. Sanctions: A Summary of Lessons Learned and Recommendations

Lessons Learned from Case Studies of U.S. Sanctions

1. Sanctions alone are unlikely to achieve desired results if the aims are large and time is short.
2. Under the right circumstances, sanctions nevertheless can achieve (or help to achieve) various foreign policy goals ranging from the modest to the fairly significant.
3. Unilateral sanctions are rarely effective.
4. Sanctions often produce unintended and undesirable consequences.
5. Sanctions can be expensive for American business, farmers, and workers.
6. Authoritarian, statist societies are often able to hunker down and withstand the effects of sanctions.
7. Military enforcement can increase the economic and military impact (although not necessarily the political effect) of a given sanction.
8. Sanctions can increase the pressures to intervene with military force when they are unable to resolve the crisis at hand.

Recommendations Distilled from Case Studies of U.S. Sanctions

1. Economic sanctions are a serious instrument of foreign policy and should be employed only after consideration no less rigorous than what would precede any other form of intervention, including the use of military force.
2. Multilateral support for economic sanctions normally should constitute a prerequisite for their introduction by the United States.
3. Secondary sanctions or boycotts are not a desirable means of bringing about multilateral support for sanctions and should be avoided.
4. Economic sanctions should focus to the extent possible on those responsible for the offending behavior or on penalizing countries in the realm that stimulated sanctions in the first place.
5. Sanctions should not be used to hold major or complex bilateral relationships hostage to a single issue or set of concerns.
6. Humanitarian exceptions should be included as part of any comprehensive sanctions.
7. Any use of sanctions should be as swift and as purposeful as possible.
8. Policymakers should prepare and send to Congress a policy statement not unlike the reports prepared and forwarded under the War Powers Act before or soon after a sanction is put in place.
9. All sanctions embedded in legislation should provide for presidential discretion in the form of a waiver authority.
10. The federal government should challenge the right of states and municipalities to institute economic sanctions against companies and individuals operating in their jurisdiction.
11. U.S. intelligence capabilities must be reoriented to meet the demands created by sanctions policy.
12. Any sanctions should be the subject of an annual impact statement.

Source: Richard N. Haass, ed., *Economic Sanctions and American Diplomacy* (Washington, DC: Council on Foreign Relations, 1998), pp. 197–210.

and, employing the standard "gravity model," analyzed them with regard to the severity or absence of economic sanctions toward those countries. Their findings were, in brief:

1. Sanctions reduced bilateral trade with sanctioned countries by an average of one-quarter to one-third, but by as much as 90 percent in some cases.
2. Sanctions reduced U.S. exports to twenty-six target countries by as much as $19 billion.
3. Sanctions reduced U.S. export-related jobs by 200,000.
4. Sanctions wiped out $1 billion in wage premiums among those employed in the high-tech export sector.

Criticism of the methodology of the Hufbauer study led Hossein Askari and his associates in 2003 to collect annual rather than snapshot data, refine the categories of sanctions, separate the effects on exports from those on imports, and consider third-country and regional effects in addition to bilateral effects. These and other refinements to the assumptions, methodology, and analysis of the gravity model were applied to data from 1980 to 1998. The basic equation was as follows:

Trade = function of economic size, income effect, geographic distance, sanctions, and influence of trade blocs

The regression calculations showed that sanctions had reduced U.S. exports overall by an average of $15.563 billion per year since 1989, with losses of more than $18 billion in 1997 and $23 billion in 1989.[19] Aggregate export losses were highest in the figures for the former Soviet bloc countries, including Russia, plus China, which together accounted for an average annual loss of around $10 billion. Losses to a collection of a dozen "rogue states," including Iran, Iraq, North Korea, Cuba, and Vietnam, amounted to more than $5 billion in 1998. Askari et al. also found sharp reductions in imports from those countries. But they also found evidence of export diversion by the sanctioned countries to the European market, which suggested that U.S. unilateral sanctions were being evaded. Overall, Askari et al. concluded that their findings independently confirmed those of the Hufbauer et al. study, and improved upon it in certain respects.

Conclusion

Case studies and statistical assessments revealing the flaws of sanctions policies are relatively recent and seem to have had little effect on policymakers. But there is hope that more numerous, credible, and persuasive studies will follow to inform a new generation of political leaders, empowering them to fend off protectionist interests and their legislative allies and thus to resort to sanctions less often and with more caution than current leaders. Another factor inducing less abuse of sanctions is the deepening of globalization and the widening of trade liberalization agreements. These parallel developments reveal the self-harm and futility of interventions to constrain legitimate economic intercourse and give strength to those leaders who would seek other means to achieve their diplomatic and military policy objectives that do not harm economically vulnerable members of society.

As Haass recommended, international economic problems should be dealt with through economic policies that are appropriate and proportionate to the sector. By the same token, diplomatic and military problems should be dealt with by diplomatic and military means, not by falling back on palliative, provocative, or muddled economic sanctions in lieu of making clear hard choices. The WTO and parallel regional, minilateral, and bilateral trade negotiations have the potential to elevate and at the same time regulate international economic relations for mutual benefit, making economic sanctions redundant, inappropriate, or unlawful in the long term.

Stephen Hoadley

See Also National Government Policies

Endnotes

1. Economic sanctions may also be initiated by groups of governments or intergovernmental organizations and directed at more than one target government or at nongovernment entities such as firms, churches, rebels, or secessionists. This wider conception was proffered by Dianne E. Rennack, E*conomic Sanctions: Legislation in the 106th Congress* (Washington, DC: Congressional Research Service, Library of Congress, 2000), as follows: "Economic sanctions are coercive measures imposed by one country, or coalition of countries, against another country, its government or individual entities therein, to bring about a change in behavior or policies." Harold S. Sloan and Arnold J. Zurcher generally concurred but added the aims of enforcing international law in their *A Dictionary of Economics,* 4th rev. ed. (New York: Barnes and Noble, 1964), 111. For simplicity, this entry assumes the bilateral government-to-government case unless otherwise specified (for example, UN Security Council sanctions).

2. Geoff Simons, *Imposing Economic Sanctions: Legal Remedy or Genocidal Tool?* (London: Pluto, 1999).

3. Calculated from figures provided by Hossein G. Askari et al., *Economic Sanctions: Examining Their Philosophy and Efficacy* (Westport, CT: Praeger, 2003), 3.

4. From tabulation presented by Askari et al., *Economic Sanctions.* The number has grown with sanctions against Afghanistan, Sierra Leone, and Liberia, among others, and with the economic measures instituted since September 11, 2001, to combat terrorism.

5. David Cortright and George A. Lopez, eds., *Smart Sanctions: Targeting Economic Statecraft* (Lanham, MD: Rowman and Littlefield, 2002), 4–5.

6. David A. Baldwin, *Economic Statecraft* (Princeton, NJ: Princeton University Press, 1985); Miroslav Nincic and Peter Wallensteen, eds., *Dilemmas of Economic Coersion: Sanctions in World Politics* (New York: Praeger, 1983). Economic sanctions do not preclude an initiating government from employing diplomacy or military suasion as reinforcement, as long as its policy instruments are primarily economic. Likewise, the policy changes desired in the target government are assumed to be mainly economic in nature, but they can equally well be directed at changes in another sector, such as political or military behavior.

7. *Overview and Analysis of Current U.S. Unilateral Economic Sanctions: Investigation No. 332–391* (Washington, DC: U.S. International Trade Commission Publication 3124, August 1998), http://www.usitc.gov/wais/reports/arc/w3124.htm (cited September 25, 2003).

8. But the effects of safeguard levies or negotiated voluntary export restraint agreements can impact negatively on consumers even as they may give relief to producers of the initiating country.

9. Anne O. Krueger, *American Trade Policy: A Tragedy in the Making* (Washington, DC: American Enterprise Press, 1995); Jagdish Bhagwati and Hugh T. Patrick, eds., *Aggressive Unilateralism: America's 301 Trade Policy and the World Trading System* (Ann Arbor: University of Michigan Press, 1990); Richard Boltuck and Robert E. Litan, eds., *Down in the Dumps: Administration of the Unfair Trade Laws* (Washington, DC: Brookings Institution, 1991).

10. The Soviet pipeline sanctions, the Iran-Libya Sanctions Act, and the Helms-Burton Act regarding investment in Cuba were also condemned by otherwise friendly European governments as illegitimate extraterritoriality. Successive U.S. presidents in the national interest were obliged to waive applications of these acts, which then retained symbolic effect only.

11. Cortright and Lopez, *Smart Sanctions.*

12. Hufbauer, et al. "US Economic Sanctions: Their Impact on Trade, Jobs, and Wages."

13. Robert A. Pape, "Why Economic Sanctions Do Not Work," *International Security* 22 (Fall 1997): 90–136, and "Why Economic Sactions Still Do Not Work," *International Security* 23 (Summer 1998): 66–78.

14. Richard N. Haass, "Sanctioning Madness," *Foreign Affairs* 76, no. 6: 74–95.

15. Weiss, Thomas G., David Cortright, George A. Lopez, and Larry Minear. *Political Gain and Civilian Pain: Humanitarian Impacts of Economic Sanctions* (Lanham, MD: Rowan and Littlefield, 1997).

16. Richard N. Haass, ed., *Economic Sanctions and American Diplomacy* (Washington, DC: Council on Foreign Relations, 1998). In a similar vein is Zachary Selden, Economic Sanctions as Instruments of American Foreign Policy (Westport, CT: Praeger, 1999).

17. Their studies were repeated, deepened, and updated to become the two-volume work *Economic Sanctions Reconsidered: History* and *Current Policies and Economic Sanctions Reconsidered: Supplemental Case Histories,* both with second editions published in 1990 by the Institute of International Economics in Washington, DC.

18. Hufbauer, et al. "US Economic Sanctions: Their Impact on Trade, Jobs, and Wages."

19. Askari, et al., *Economic Sanctions,* 169.

References

Askari, Hossein G. et al., *Economic Sanctions: Examining Their Philosophy and Efficacy.* Westport, CT: Praeger, 2003.

Baldwin, David A. *Economic Statecraft.* Princeton, NJ: Princeton University Press, 1985.

Bhagwati, Jagdish, and Hugh T. Patrick, eds., *Aggressive Unilateralism: America's Trade Policy and the World*

Trading System. Ann Arbor: University of Michigan Press, 1990.

Boltuck, Richard, and Robert E. Litan, eds., *Down in the Dumps: Administration of the Unfair Trade Laws.* Washington, DC: Brookings Institution, 1991.

Cortright, David, and George A. Lopez, eds., *Smart Sanctions: Targeting Economic Statecraft.* Lanham, MD: Rowman and Littlefield, 2002.

Haass, Richard N. "Sanctioning Madness," *Foreign Affairs* 76, no. 6.

Haass, Richard N. ed., *Economic Sanctions and American Diplomacy.* Washington, DC: Council on Foreign Relations, 1998.

Hufbauer, Gary Clyde, Kimberly Ann Elliott, Tess Cyrus, and Elizabeth Winston. "US Economic Sanctions: Their Impact on Trade, Jobs, and Wages," Working Paper. Washington, DC: Institute of International Economics, 1997.

Krueger, Anne O. *American Trade Policy: A Tragedy in the Making.* Washington, DC: American Enterprise Press, 1995.

Nincic, Miroslav, and Peter Wallensteen, eds., *Dilemmas of Economic Coersion: Sanctions in World Politics.* New York: Praeger, 1983.

Pape, Robert A. "Why Economic Sanctions Do Not Work," *International Security* 22, Fall 1997.

____. "Why Economic Sanctions Still Do Not Work," *International Security* 23, Summer 1998.

Rennack, Dianne E. *Economic Sanctions: Legislation in the 106th Congress.* Washington, DC: Congressional Research Service, Library of Congress, 2000.

U.S. International Trade Commission, *Overview and Analysis of Current U.S. Unilateral Economic Sanctions: Investigation No. 332–391.* Washington, DC: U.S. International Trade Commission Publication 3124, August 1998. http://www.usitc.gov/wais/reports/arc/w3124.htm (cited September 25, 2003).

Selden, Zachary. *Economic Sanctions as Instruments of American Foreign Policy.* Westport, CT: Praeger, 1999.

Simons, Geoff. *Imposing Economic Sanctions: Legal Remedy or Genocidal Tool?* London: Pluto, 1999.

Sloan, Harold S., and Arnold J. Zurcher *A Dictionary of Economics,* 4th rev. ed. New York: Barnes and Noble, 1964.

Weiss, Thomas G., David Cortright, George A. Lopez, and Larry Minear. *Political Gain and Civilian Pain: Humanitarian Impacts of Economic Sanctions.* Lanham, MD: Rowan and Littlefield, 1997.

Emerging Markets and Transition Economies

The term "transition economies," in a broad sense, includes all economies in transition from centrally planned to market systems. This group includes all ex-socialist countries in central Eastern Europe, all countries on the territory of the former Soviet Union, and several Asian countries, including China, Cambodia, Laos, Mongolia, and Vietnam. This definition has been used by the World Bank and the International Monetary Fund (see, for example, World Bank 1996 and IMF 2000).

In a narrower definition, used by the EBRD (European Bank for Reconstruction and Development) and the IMF (see, for example, EBRD 2001 and IMF 2000, 194), the term applies only to countries that are both transitioning from a centrally planned system to one based on market principles and in the process of restructuring a sizable industrial sector that has become largely obsolete. Under this definition, the Asian countries would be excluded because most of them are largely rural and low-income economies for whom the principal challenge is economic development as such (IMF 2001, 194).

Based on the EBRD classification, in the narrower definition the group includes twenty-seven countries that may be divided into three regional subgroups (EBRD 2001):

- *Central Eastern Europe and Baltic States (CEEBS).* This subgroup includes Croatia, Czech Republic, Estonia, Hungary, Latvia, Lithuania, Poland, Slovak Republic, and Slovenia.
- *South Eastern Europe (SEE).* This subgroup includes Albania, Bosnia and Her-

zegovina, Bulgaria, FR (former Republic of) Yugoslavia, FYR (former Yugoslavian Republic of) Macedonia, and Romania.
- *Commonwealth of Independent States (CIS).* This subgroup includes as full or associate members all countries of the former Soviet Union except for the Baltic states: Armenia, Azerbaijan, Belarus, Georgia, Kazakhstan, Kyrgyzstan, Moldova, Russian Federation, Tajikistan, Turkmenistan, Ukraine, and Uzbekistan.

Transition economies are also a subgroup of the nations considered "emerging markets." This term, introduced by the International Finance Corporation (IFC) in the mid-1980s, has also been interpreted to mean different things. Under a broad interpretation that has been used by the IMF (see, for example, IMF 1997a, 61), the term "emerging markets" includes all low- and middle-income countries that are not classified as "advanced economies" as well as some that are: that is, "developing countries," "transition economies," and also some "advanced economies" such as Hong Kong, the Republic of Korea, Singapore, and Taiwan.

In many contexts, especially in international finance and on international capital markets, the term is used in a significantly narrower sense. The IFC, for example, defines an emerging market as a country with a stock market that is in transition and increasing in size, level of activity, and sophistication. More specifically, a stock market has to meet two general criteria to be classified as "emerging": "(i) it is located in a low- or middle-income country as defined by the World Bank, and (ii) its investable market capitalisation is low relative to its most recent GDP figures" (IFC 1999, 2).

Transition—What Is It?

At the end of the 1980s and the beginning of the 1990s, socialist countries in Central and Eastern Europe embarked on a process known as a transition from a centrally planned to a market economy. In standard economic theory, there is no claim that market economies are necessarily better than planned ones. This means, in pure theory, that a perfect planning system can be as efficient in allocation of resources as a decentralized, competitive market mechanism. Why, then, did countries in the region consider a market system a better allocation mechanism than a planned system at the time when the communist regimes collapsed? The main reason seems to be the huge failures that took place in the planning system. The failures on political issues (for example, the lack of freedom and democracy) were compounded by failures on economic efficiency issues (for example, the impossibility of getting enough information about the economy to make appropriate adjustments and the suppression of individual incentives).

In response to these failures, countries of the region rejected central planning and embarked on a process—transition—toward a decentralized market system underpinned by widespread private ownership. Transition encompasses two closely interrelated processes. The first is a major change in the coordination and allocation system; the second involves a change in efficiency. "Transition" therefore means that fundamental reforms must penetrate to the rules of the economy and society as a whole as well as to the institutions that shape behavior and guide organizations.

The long-term goal of transition is the same as that of market economic reforms in emerging markets elsewhere: to build a vibrant market economy capable of delivering long-term growth and better living standards. What distinguishes transition economies from reforms in other emerging markets is their starting point as centrally planned economies and, consequently, the depth of the required changes. As economists Christopher Allsopp and Henryk Kierzkowski have pointed out, "Transition needs to involve the dismantling of one (politically discredited) system and its replacement by another . . . the political, legal and institutional changes required to go with this are large" (Allsopp and Kierzkowski 1997, 5).

The Legacy of the Central Planning System

In the first half of the twentieth century, countries containing about one-third of the total population in the world abandoned the market economy and started building up an alternative economic and political system based on the principles of communism and socialism. At the beginning, the achievements of the central planning system were considerable. They included growth in gross domestic product (GDP), industrialization, the provision of basic health care and education, jobs for the entire population, and relatively equally distributed incomes.

Among the many negative legacies of the now-defunct central planning system, the single most important one was the absence of market-generated signals about relative scarcities of outputs and inputs. This led to highly distorted relative prices and output structure. Central planning commissions simply could not get enough information to substitute for that supplied by prices in a market economy. As a consequence, enterprises emphasized plan fulfillment rather than profitability and had no incentive for innovation and for reducing the technological gap vis-à-vis advanced market economies. In order to facilitate control, production and employment were concentrated in large firms with a monopolistic or oligopolistic position on the market. Product markets were distorted by price and trade control, while labor markets were distorted by highly administrated wage structures and actual prohibition of dismissals. Financial markets were almost nonexistent, with financial flows simply implementing the demands of the plan. The system was also characterized by an absence of well-defined property rights, commercial legislation, and market-oriented institutions, both inside and outside the government. Distorted price structures led socialist countries toward relative autarky of their economies within their protected Council of Mutual Economic Assistance (CMEA). This policy bias disregarded potential gains from global international trade and made it difficult for these countries to identify their international comparative advantages.

After having initially narrowed the development gap with advanced market economies through forced industrialization, the relative performance of the centrally planned economies, in terms of per capita income and international competitiveness, deteriorated in the period after World War II. Several socialist countries, including Yugoslavia, Hungary, and Poland, introduced reforms aimed at stalling this relative decline. Their common characteristic was that they wanted to achieve this objective by reforming the planning system and by decentralizing the decisionmaking process. On this issue, Alan Gelb and Cheryl Gray wrote, "Major lessons of reform socialism in Central and Eastern Europe were negative. Efforts to increase efficiency and productivity through decentralisation and heavier reliance on market forces met with only limited success in the absence of ownership reform or capital market" (Gelb and Gray 1991, 4).

The serious inefficiencies of these central planning systems became increasingly evident with time. After posting relatively high annual economic growth rates during the 1950s, the economies of the region decelerated in the 1960s through the 1980s, and in 1990 they actually contracted. This trend took place in spite of the fact that socialist countries traditionally

had high investment rates, usually above 30 percent. Social indicators worsened as well during the 1980s, confirming the troubled state of the system.

There have, however, been positive legacies of the socialist systems. Human capital endowment, with respect to the level of education and health standards, was and still is relatively high in these countries in comparison with other emerging economies at their level of economic development. Incomes were significantly more evenly distributed than in capitalist countries, as work and thus income was guaranteed as part of a comprehensive social safety net.

Macroeconomic Developments

The macroeconomic developments of transition economies over the past dozen years have differed significantly, both across individual countries and across subgroups of the region. Macroeconomic developments are those involving general patterns in such areas as output level and structure, inflation, fiscal position, employment, and poverty and income equality.

Output Level and Structure

All countries in this transition experienced a substantial decline in recorded output in the early years of their transition. The initial output loss reflected: (1) the introduction of price and exchange rate liberalism, resulting in a significant cut of domestic purchasing power; (2) the general collapse of the former system of enterprise linkages and finance; and (3) the breakdown of the socialist trading bloc.

At the beginning of the transition, the difference in initial conditions and policies led to a much greater decline of GDP in the CIS than in the CEEBS. Another difference between these two subgroups of countries, with respect to output development over the recent decade, is that in the CEEBS, output since 1989 has followed a U-shaped pattern, with the lowest point being reached in 1992 or 1993. By 2001, the aggregate output of the subgroup surpassed its 1989 level by 10 percent. In contrast, the output pattern in the CIS was on a downward trend until 1998. Consequently, the GDP for this subgroup of countries was in 2001 at only 62 percent of its pre-transition level (EBRD 2002, 17).

Not all sectors of the economy were equally hit by the transformation from centrally planned to market-based systems. Trade liberalization, the new power of consumer preferences, and the cutback in defense spending are only some of the reasons that industrial growth rates were even more disappointing than the GDP rates. Sharp declines in the industrial-sector output in the early 1990s, accompanied by a strong performance in the services sector, have resulted in a dramatic shift in the economic structure of transition economies.

Inflation
The countries of the region had experienced significant inflationary pressures already in the pre-transition period. Therefore, it is not surprising that inflation exploded in the early years of transition. The size of price increases amounted to over 100 percent, and in some countries to even more than 1,000 percent a year. In most countries, the initial jump of inflation was a result of a combination of factors, including price liberalization, the sharp drop in output, and large fiscal and quasi-fiscal deficits. As there were actually no alternative sources of finance, large budget deficits were financed almost exclusively by monetary sources, and a result was a rapid growth of inflation. By the mid-1990s, however, most countries of the region had succeeded in drastically cutting inflation.

There is no doubt that disinflation has been one of the most remarkable achievements of the first decade of transition. It has been, however, confirmed very quickly that macroeconomic stability is not sustainable if it is not accompanied by appropriate structural-adjustment measures. The experiences of some CIS countries have clearly demonstrated that weak

macroeconomic foundations, especially large fiscal deficits and problems in the banking sector, combined with the negative implications of the Asian and especially Russian crisis, have contributed to the recent revival of inflation in these countries.

Fiscal Position
An important source of inflationary pressures in transition economies has been significant fiscal deficits. They peaked in 1992, when combined government deficits of CEEBS countries amounted to 5.1 percent of GDP, while those of the CIS and SEE countries rose to 17.6 and 10.1 percent of GDP, respectively (EBRD 2001, 62). Since then, government deficits by and large have been on a downward trend throughout the region. The exceptions were years 1998 and 1999, when some countries registered a deterioration of their fiscal position due to a combination of internal factors, such as adjustment to the European Union, and external factors, including the Russian and Kosovo crises.

Fiscal imbalances of transition economies, particularly strong in the early transition period, have been caused by developments on both the revenue and expenditure sides. A decline in taxes collected from the contracting state sector, administrative problems associated with the introduction of VAT (Value-added tax), and generally poor tax administration are the main explanations for the overall revenue fall in government budgets in almost all transition economies during the early 1990s. In some countries, especially in the CIS, large tax arrears have become a form of implicit subsidization of inefficient companies and have further reduced the already shrinking revenue base. On the expenditure side, transition has exposed governments in the region to new challenges, though these challenges were different for different groups of countries. In the more advanced countries of the CEEBS, relatively generous safety-net provisions were introduced early in the transition period, when many countries of the subgroup used pension schemes as a policy instrument to reduce the negative social implications of large-scale lay-offs. As a consequence, pension systems have entered into extensive deficits and with time have become a growing fiscal burden. In the countries of the CIS, where a safety net was practically nonexistent, the main issue on the expenditure side continues to be how to reduce subsidies to enterprises.

Employment

Transitions from centrally planned to market economies have been associated with major changes in the level of employment. Prior to transition, open unemployment was almost nonexistent in the region. The situation reversed dramatically thereafter, when, following the output collapse in early 1990, registered unemployment grew throughout the region and in many countries exceeded the 15 percent mark.

The revival of output growth in more advanced countries of the region over the past few years has so far not led to a significant revival of registered employment. Unemployment therefore remains uncomfortably high, which can at least partially be explained by the continuing process of labor shedding. Persistent high unemployment in the region is in contrast with initial expectations that fast-growing private-sector development would be able to absorb a significant proportion of the labor force previously employed by the state sector. The evidence for some CEEBS countries shows that the subgroup is increasingly facing the problem of structural unemployment where people who have become unemployed have no or little prospects to reenter the labor force.

Poverty and Income Inequality

Although extreme poverty is still less pronounced in transition economies than in other countries at similar income levels, it has increased sharply during the past decade. The increase was much greater than many expected at the start of the transition process and was more pronounced in the countries of the CIS,

that is, in countries where the reform process has stalled and where privatization, accompanied by poor targeting of safety-net measures, has permitted a concentrated accumulation of wealth. Poverty in the region increased not only because of the fall in output but because of greater inequality in the distribution of wealth. Income inequality, measured using the Gini coefficient, increased in all transition economies, although this increase has been much smaller in the CEEBS subgroup than in the CIS. In the latter, the average Gini coefficient almost doubled between the 1987–1990 period and the 1996–1998 period (from 28 to 46), while for CEEBS this coefficient increased from 23 to 33 during the same time span (World Bank 2002, 8).

Structural Adjustment and Institutional Changes

If the major objective of macroeconomic policies is to create a stable environment, then the major objective of microeconomic policies and structural reforms is to actually accomplish the transition and to make a transition economy a viable and competitive long-term actor on the internal market. Macroeconomic reforms alone, although necessary, do not automatically supply the responses needed for a comprehensive transformation to a market economy. These reforms, namely, do not deal systematically with the structural weaknesses of a country's economy, with the lack of entrepreneurial cadres and managerial and supervisory personnel, and with the inadequacies in the technological, financial accounting, and marketing realms.

The major components of the structural reforms and institutional changes that have been carried out in transition economies include: (1) adjustment of the legal and regulatory system; (2) financial-sector reform; and (3) enterprise-sector reform, including privatization, promotion of SMEs (Small and Medium-sized Enterprises), and enterprise restructuring. As in areas of macroeconomic stabilization, there are huge differences among individual transition economies in terms of the progress achieved in these areas. Countries that have already carried out a comprehensive macroeconomic stabilization program, primarily the CEEBS, are typically also countries that are now in a more advanced stage of transition. In contrast, countries that have been late with the introduction of macroeconomic measures are lagging behind also with structural transformation processes.

Adjustment of the Legal System

Aware that appropriate legislation is a necessary condition for an efficient transition from a centrally planned to a market economy, all countries in the region started at the outset of the transition with a comprehensive reform of their legal and regulatory systems. Although the design of a fully operational legal and regulatory framework takes time and makes heavy demands on scarce human resources, many of the transition economies have already gone a long way in drafting laws in all areas fundamental to economic transformation. A large majority of the countries has by now adopted property, contract, security, bankruptcy, competition, and company legislation. Although passing the legislation is an important step forward, experiences gathered over recent years increasingly show that this is of limited relevance if not accompanied by all the necessary by-laws as well as by effective implementation and enforcement.

Financial-Sector Reform

Transition to a market economy has required a drastically changed role for the financial sector in transition economies. The main challenge in this area has been and still is to overcome the legacy of the past and at the same time to design and develop an efficient system of financial markets and institutions. There are at least three reasons why financial-sector restructuring has been of strategic importance for transition economies: (1) Without an active financial market mechanism, their economies, having abandoned planning, have no alternative allocation mechanism; (2) through intermediation of financial institutions, resources can be channeled directly to enterprises and to the real sector in general; and (3) efficient financial institutions help impose a hard budget constraint on enterprises.

Taking into account the dominance of banking in the overall financial system within countries in transition, as well as at the nexus of nonperforming loans and enterprise-sector losses, the banking sector has been in the forefront of financial-sector reforms. Introduction of market reforms has forced banks to start their transition from passive distributors of credit to professional bankers. As in other market economies, banks in countries in transition are now required to actively meet their clients' financial needs, on the one hand, and on the other to adhere to capital adequacy criteria and new accounting rules regarding the provisioning of debt.

In spite of various difficulties, including the high concentration of the sector, the high share of nonperforming loans, and high transaction costs, transition economies have gone a long way in transforming their banking systems. The transformation has been implemented through a combination of policy measures. In addition to the replacement of the original mono-bank system with the two-tier banking system across all countries of the region, government policies in this area have typically included reforms in prudential regulation and supervision, recapitalization and privatization of state-owned banks, and the entrance of new private banks. Countries across the region differ not only in terms of the design of these policies but even more in terms of their implementation. The transition countries that have been strong performers in banking-sector restructuring share a number of features. Of particular importance are effective domestic and foreign entry and exit regulations, which facilitate the entry of foreign banks and thereby foster competition and encourage the development of new banking products. All of these countries have addressed the problem of bad debt in a rather early stage of their transition. There have, however, been two completely different approaches applied in dealing with this problem. Some countries have opted for a centralized, or top-down, approach, with a special workout agency established to handle bad debts taken over from banks, while others have followed a decentralized, or bottom-up, approach, leaving banks and enterprises to directly negotiate solutions.

Enterprise-Sector Reform
This segment of structural transformation is clearly at the very heart of the transition process and, in general, involves processes associated with the transition from a public-dominated to a private-dominated economy. These processes include: (1) introduction of financial discipline and competition in the enterprise sector; (2) private-sector development through both privatization of state-owned firms and promotion of new private firms; and (3) restructuring of enterprises in both the pre- and post-privatization periods.

- *Introduction of financial discipline.* The decade of transition was characterized by a sharp deterioration of enterprises' liquidity position as their sales were drastically reduced, or even stopped, owing to the opening of the markets to foreign competition, while the banks became, in a changed environment, much more reluctant to extend new loans. As a result, enterprises increasingly fell behind in payments to each other for goods and services and to the government for taxes and social security programs. In addition to curtailed bank lending, sharply reduced government subsidies, made either through direct or indirect budget transfers or through subsidized energy and/or other input prices, have been an important element of the financial discipline imposed on the enterprise sector.

- *Privatization of state-owned enterprises.* In contrast to market economies where a mixed economy has prevailed and where privatization has meant an enhancement to already-existing market rules in economic activity, for countries in transition privatization has become one of the crucial tests for the commitment of new governments to the establishment of a market-based economic system and a political system based on private property rights and individual freedoms. Practically all countries of the region have pursued privatization on two parallel tracks. The first, called "small-size privatization," refers mainly to privatization of retail outlets, transport equipment, and service enterprises. This segment of privatization has typically not been politically controversial and has received strong popular support, as procedures were relatively transparent and positive effects strikingly visible on a relatively short run. As a result, "small-scale privatization" has been more or less completed throughout the region.

  In contrast, so-called "large-scale privatization," that is, privatization of former state-owned enterprises, has proved to be more complicated than expected, and as a consequence the advances in this area have generally been much slower and also less uniform across the countries of the region. The slower pace of large-scale privatization has been typically caused by one or more of the following: (1) a high capital requirement; (2) major restructuring needs; (3) restitution problems; (4) regulatory and governance weaknesses; and (5) political sensitivity or even resistance. Countries have applied a wide range of methods for privatizing their large and middle-sized companies. Some countries—Hungary is the most notable but not the only case—have been successful in selling their enterprises to strategic, often foreign, investors. Others, such as Slovenia, Croatia, and Macedonia, have relied more on internal ownership transformation in the form of management buyouts. To help bring about massive and rapid privatization in an environment lacking prospective strategic buyers, voucher privatization has also been extensively used in the region.

- *Promotion of SME development.* Countries in the region have made significant progress in the SME sector since the transition began. Laws setting up a legal framework for small businesses have been adopted, and the countries have actually witnessed an impressive growth and development of their SMEs. The process has been marked especially by the surge of new small firms created, either in the form of start-ups, mainly in the trade and service sectors, or through spin-offs of large state-owned enterprises. In spite of the fast development of the SME sector throughout the region over recent years, entrepreneurs still face several kinds of difficulties and barriers. Some of them are common to all countries of the region, while others are more country specific. The most important barriers to even faster development of SMEs include inadequacies in the area of business regulation, lack of financial resources, and poor access to specialized training aimed at quality improvement, management, and technology counseling.

- *Enterprise restructuring.* In the world of constant changes and globalization, enterprise restructuring is centrally concerned with improving the efficiency with which an enterprise adapts itself to changing constraints and opportunities in an international environment. Firms throughout the world must continuously restructure in order to maintain their international competitiveness and therefore profitability, challenged by both increasing global competition and rapid technological change. For countries in

transition, enterprise restructuring is even more important. For them, it does not mean simply maintaining enterprise profitability, but transforming a highly distorted economy with many loss-making firms into a viable market economy in which most industrial enterprises are internationally competitive and profitable. Enterprise restructuring in countries in transition involves activities at both the policy and enterprise levels.

Countries in the region have achieved slower progress in enterprise restructuring than in many other areas of transition because of the complexity of the tasks involved. According to the EBRD, none of the countries in transition has reached a standard and performance typical for advanced countries in this area. Nevertheless, significant progress in enterprise restructuring has been made in a number of the CEEBS countries. Better enterprise-restructuring results in all these countries can be attributed to both their overall advancement in transition and their efforts toward early accession to the European Union. All other countries in the region have been considered less successful in restructuring their enterprise sectors (see EBRD 2001, 14).

Trade and Integration into the Global Economy

The pre-1989 socialist countries of Central and Eastern Europe were largely characterized by a deliberate isolation from other parts of the world economy. All segments of their international economic cooperation were predominantly occupied with intra–Soviet bloc transactions, and economic ties with countries outside the region were rather weak.

The change of political regime and the beginning of the transition process was a starting point on the region's path toward global economic integration. The economic transition of the countries of Central and Eastern Europe and their integration into the global economy are, in fact, two sides of the same coin. There would have been no economic transition for these countries to a market economy without their participation in the international markets for goods, services, capital, and labor. Moreover, the competitiveness of products from ex-socialist countries on international markets would not have been effectively established without dismantlement of the centrally planned economic systems that had over several decades proved to be economically inefficient and thus inferior to the market-led type of economy.

Trade Integration

Before transition, international trade was almost exclusively an intra-CMEA affair for these countries. Trade with other countries of the CMEA region accounted for more than 80 percent in the former Soviet Union and around 50 percent for Central European countries (Brenton and Gros 1997, 67–68). Trade within the region was distorted in several other ways as well. For example, trade flows were handled exclusively by the state-owned trading organizations.

Since the start of transition, trade has become an increasingly important part of transition economies. The ratio of foreign trade (average of exports and imports) to GDP increased throughout the region as a result of both strong growth of foreign trade, on the one hand, and the decline of GDP, on the other. The liberalization of external trade led to another important foreign trade pattern in transition economies, namely, a sizable change in the geographic composition of the trade, consisting mostly of the geographical reorientation of trade flows away from the CMEA and toward Western market economies, especially those of the European Union. The CEEBS have achieved by far the most in shifting away from trade with former CMEA countries and integrating themselves into the global trading system, roughly doubling the share of advanced coun-

tries in their total exports and imports in the ten-year period between 1986 and 1995, each from 35 percent to almost 70 percent (IMF 1997b, 98). Several factors contributed to the success of the CEEBS in reorienting their trade. These countries benefited from their geographical proximity to EU markets, and they had better initial conditions. They also more rapidly stabilized their economies and started the process of industrial restructuring. In addition, they have made significant strides toward institutionalizing their access to export markets in advanced countries.

A less favorable geographical position, slower progress in macroeconomic stabilization and industrial restructuring, and a lack of institutional trade arrangements with Western partners hampered Russia and other countries of the CIS in reorienting their trade flows. They continue to be highly dependent on trade links with other transition economies. To a large extent, this reflects the dependence of most CIS states on Russia rather than an intensification of their trade with other transition economies.

Financial Integration

In the pre-transition period, centrally planned economies were largely excluded from the global financial system, as most of them were not members of multilateral financial institutions and many of them, owing to considerable debt service problems, had no access to international capital markets. Besides, equity financing was never applied in socialist countries, and the decentralized system of bond financing was not in line with the centrally planned economy.

The reintegration of the region into the global financial system started at the outset of the transition process, when practically all countries of the region rapidly joined the three key multilateral finance institutions, namely the IMF, the World Bank, and EBRD. This institutional integration was accompanied by radical change both in the volume and composition of capital inflows to the region. In the early transition years, capital flows were dominated by flows from official Western government sources, multilateral and bilateral; more or less all transition economies were their recipients. These official flows aimed at supporting and protecting profound political and economic changes in the region have paved the way for an increasing flow of funds from private sources. In the early post-transition period, private-sector funding sources took a rather cautious attitude toward the region, as the country and commercial risks were perceived to be unacceptably high. Later on, when the economic performance of the countries improved and the process of transition progressed, private capital started to enter the market, first slowly, then with great speed. In contrast to some degree of uniformity of official flows in the early transition period, private capital quickly began to differentiate across countries. The perception of investment and lending risk has been closely correlated with the progress of transition.

Total capital flows to the region rose from around $3 billion in 1989 to over $60 billion in 1997 (EBRD 1998, 78). Owing to the Russian financial crisis, the total volume of capital inflows to the region has declined since then. Within the structure of capital flows to the region, the share of private flows has increased sharply, from less than 25 percent in 1993 to 84 percent in 1997. Although most CEEBS have practically ceased to rely on official financing, there are other countries, especially in the CIS and SEE subgroup, that still do not fulfill the criteria required for entering international capital markets.

Foreign direct investment (FDI) represents by far the most important source of private capital for the region. The FDI inflow trend was continuously upward after 1989 and reached $25 billion in 2001. The surge of FDI to the region has been caused by a combination of factors, including the strong interest that Western companies have in spreading their operations to new markets, improved macroeconomic performance in many countries in the region, and reduction of barriers in trade among the countries themselves and with advanced countries, especially EU members. Geographical distribution of FDI inflows has been very uneven. The CEEBS attracted some two-thirds of total 1989–2000 inflows, and even within this subgroup of countries, there is a big concentration, as Hungary, Poland, and the Czech Republic alone accounted for more than half of total inflows (EBRD 2001, 68).

Variations in the Progress of Transition

The most comprehensive analytical tool for assessing the overall progress achieved by an individual country in the transition process has been developed by EBRD. EBRD's rating system—published in its annual publication *Transition Report*—focuses on eight elements of a market economy: (1) small-scale privatization; (2) large-scale privatization; (3) enterprise governance and restructuring; (4) price liberalization; (5) trade and foreign exchange liberalization; (6) competition policy; (7) banking reform; and (8) capital markets. Progress in each of these areas represents an improvement in how well markets, enterprises, and financial institutions function, and the progress is measured against the benchmark set by industrialized countries. The measurement scale for each individual indicator ranges from 1 to 4+, with 1 representing little or no change from the old regime, and 4+ representing a standard that is in place in a mature market economy.

This overall transition indicator provides a summary measure of overall progress in reform across the region. Two major patterns emerge from EBRD's annual *Transition Reports*:

First, the data show *clustering of countries within particular geographical subgroups.* The average transition indicator score tends to decline the further east the subgroup of countries is located. The subgroup in the west, CEEBS, had the highest average transition indicator scores in the region, amounting to more than 3 in 1999. Countries in the other two subgroups,

SEE and CIS, had lower scores, indicating less progress achieved in the transition process. The data also show that the variation among individual countries within each of the three subgroups increases from west to east. There are a wide range of structural, political, and geographical factors that have contributed to the differences among the subgroups of countries with respect to their achieved progress in transition reforms. Among others, these factors include: (1) large differences in initial structural and macroeconomic imbalances; (2) political environment, including wars in SEE; (3) policy choices made with respect to the timing and sequencing of reforms ("shock therapy approach" versus "gradualist approach"); and (4) geographical proximity to the West (countries closer to the European Union have benefited from the process of integration arising from trade with Western countries and from strengthened political cooperation with this group of countries). The EU accession process has proved an extremely powerful instrument for speeding up the process of transition.

Second, the data reveal *persistent disparity across different areas of transition reforms.* Progress in areas in which the task of the state was to withdraw from all economic responsibilities has been particularly fast. By their nature, reforms that involve liberalization—that is, elimination of government-imposed restrictions on prices, trade, and the market for foreign exchange—are reforms that made rapid progress early in the transition. Areas of reforms in which transition requires redistribution of assets—that is, small- and large-scale privatization—have on average moved steadily over the period, with small-scale privatization moving much faster than privatization of large-scale company assets. The third set of reform areas are those that involve the building and/or rebuilding of institutions—that is, enterprise restructuring, banking-sector reform, the introduction of competition policy, and the establishment of securities markets and non-bank financial institutions. It is in these areas of institutional reforms that progress has been

slowest. This is not surprising, since institutional reforms inevitably take time because they require not only the enactment of new laws but also the capacity of the authorities to enforce the legislation (Stern 1998, 5).

Policy and Institutional Challenges for the Future of Transition

In 1989 and immediately thereafter, there was a broadly shared belief that transition to market economy would be a rather short and simple process. Based on a set of policy measures agreed upon by influential international financial institutions, political bodies, and professional economists, the so-called "Washington consensus" was accepted as a common wisdom of policies that would move transition economies from stabilization to growth. This set of policy measures, which also paved the way for the integration of transition economies into the global economic environment, also stressed the importance of liberalization, privatization, and the opening of transition economies and financial discipline (Kolodko 1999, 5).

After twelve years of experience, it has become obvious that transition is a highly complex, difficult, and lengthy process. There is no doubt that substantial progress has been made by the countries in the region in transforming their economies from centrally planned to market based. However, the advancement in transition has been unevenly distributed both across the countries of the region and across different areas of transition. There seems to be a growing consensus among numerous analysts that the region as a whole is now approaching the end of the first phase of transition. The analysts also agree that, while the process of change in the first phase of transition has been remarkable, the tasks have been in many respects more straightforward than those that follow.

The main challenges of the new, second phase of transition are to make these new market economies function more efficiently and to build on the foundations established in the first phase. The main objective is sustainable economic growth. The agenda for the new phase of transition should also incorporate issues that have not been addressed properly during the first phase, as confirmed by recent developments in the world, especially by the financial crises in Asia and Russia. Last but not least, there are some important issues for transition economies that have been either missing or have been largely underestimated in the first decade of transition. These issues—including institution building, redesign of the role of the state, improvement of corporate governance in the enterprise and financial sectors, investment in both education and infrastructure, and reduction of poverty and social inequality—must find an appropriate place in this new agenda. True, more attention has been given to these issues since the mid-1990s, and especially in the past three years, but much more has to be done on these issues in the future.

Mojmir Mrak

See Also Commonwealth of Independent States (CIS)

References

Aghion, Philippe, and Olivier Blanchard. 1994. "On the Speed of Adjustment in Central Europe" In Olivier Blanchard and Stanley Fischer, eds., *NBER Macroeconomics Annual 1994*. Cambridge, MA: MIT Press.

Allsopp, Christopher, and Henryk Kierzkowski. 1997. "The Assessment: Economics of Transition in Eastern and Central Europe." *Oxford Review of Economic Policy* 13, no. 2: 1–22.

Aslund, Anders. 1994. "Lessons of the First Four Years of Systematic Change in Eastern Europe." *Journal of Comparative Economics* 19 (August): 22–39.

Brenton, Paul, and Daniel Gros. 1997. "Trade Reorientation and Recovery in Transition Economies." *Oxford Review of Economic Policy* 13, no. 2: 65–76.

European Bank for Reconstruction and Development. *Transition Report 1998*. 1998. London: EBRD.

_____. *Transition Report Update 2002*. 2002. London: EBRD.

Gelb, Alan, and Cheryl Gray. 1991. *The Transformation of Economies in Central and Eastern Europe*. Policy and Research Series 17. Washington, DC: World Bank.

International Finance Corporation. *Emerging Stock Markets Factbook*. 1999. Washington, DC: IFC, 1999.

International Monetary Fund. *International Capital Markets*. 1997a. Washington, DC: IMF.

_____. "Transition: Experience and Policy Issues." 2002. Pp. 84–137 in *World Economic Outlook*. Washington, DC: IMF.

_____. *World Economic Outlook*. 1997b. Washington, DC: IMF.

Kolodko, Gregorz. 1999. *Ten Years of Post-Socialist Transition: Lessons for Policy Reforms*. Policy Research Working Paper 2095. Washington, DC: World Bank.

Stern, Nicholas. 1998. *The Future of the Economic Transition*. Working Paper 30. London: EBRD.

Stiglitz, Joseph. 1999. "Whither Reform? Ten Years of Transition." Pp. 27–56 in *Annual World Bank Conference on Economic Development*. Washington, DC: World Bank.

World Bank. *Transition—The First Ten Years: Analysis and Lessons for Eastern Europe and the Former Soviet Union*. 2002. Washington, DC: World Bank.

_____. *World Development Report 1996*. 1996. Washington, DC: World Bank.

Exchange Rate Movements

The exchange rate is the price of one nation's currency in terms of another nation's currency. This is often called the "foreign exchange rate," in that it is the price determined in the foreign exchange market when people buy and sell foreign exchange. The "numeraire" (or standard) of the international monetary system is the U.S. dollar. Exchange rates are thus normally quoted in terms of U.S. dollars. There are various possible exchange rate regimes. At the two extremes are fixed rates and floating rates, and in between the two extremes are a variety of possibilities, including "crawling peg" systems and managed (or "dirty") floats where the government intervenes to try to influence the value of the exchange rate.

The exchange rate can be used as a tool of economic policy to affect trade, inflation, interest rates, and growth in gross national product (GNP). Economists remain divided as to the macroeconomic benefits of different exchange rate regimes. Typically, fixed exchange rates have been associated with lower inflation, whereas flexible exchange rates have been associated with higher inflation but also higher levels of income growth. Currency crises remain a problem, sharpened by technology and globalization of capital. Since 1945, global trends in exchange rates have shifted from a preference for fixed rates in the immediate postwar period, to flexible rates in the 1970s and 1980s, to various forms of fixed rates and currency unions beginning in the 1990s, with economic and monetary union in the European Union as the most prominent example. Politics plays a role in a country's choice of exchange rate regime, with political parties, presidential versus parliamentary systems, economic size, openness, and industrial versus agricultural production, as well as the political voice of various sectors, typically influencing government decisions to a certain degree.

Determining Exchange Rates, Equilibrium, and Movements

Each country has a currency in which the prices of goods and services are quoted—the dollar in the United States, the euro in Germany, the pound sterling in Britain, the yen in Japan, and so on. A foreign exchange rate is the relative value between two currencies, or the quantity of one currency required to exchange one unit of currency for another, quoted as the price of the foreign currency in terms of home currency or as the price of home currency in terms of foreign currency. A hard currency—money that can be readily converted to other leading world currencies—is one in which investors have confidence, such as that of an economically and politically stable country. A soft currency is a currency that is not acceptable in exchange for currency of other countries, due to unrealistic exchange rates. Purchasing power parity (PPP) states that exchange rates between different currencies are in equilibrium when their purchasing power is the same in the two countries. In other words, the exchange rate between two countries should be equal to the ratio of the two countries' relative price levels. If the price level of one country increases (due to inflation), its currency depreciates to maintain PPP. The basis for PPP is the "law of one price," which states that in the absence of transportation costs and other transaction costs, competitive markets will equalize the price of an identical good in two countries when the prices are expressed in the same currency.

For example, a television set that sells for 750 Canadian dollars (CAD) in Toronto should cost 500 U.S. dollars (USD) in Boston when the exchange rate is 1.50 CAD/USD. If the price of the TV in Toronto were only 700 CAD, consumers in Boston would prefer to buy the TV set in Toronto. If this process (called "arbitrage") is carried out on a large scale, the U.S. consumers buying Canadian goods will bid up the value of Canadian dollars. The Canadian goods will become more costly to them. This process continues until the prices are equalized. One key problem with PPP is that it is based on impractical assumptions. It does not take into account different tastes and preferences across countries, trade barriers, the existence of nontradable goods, lack of competition, transportation costs, or other transaction costs. It also does not address daily market information. Exchange rate movements in the short term are news-driven. Announcements about interest-rate changes, economic growth, political scandals, and other factors drive exchange rates in the short run. PPP, by comparison, describes economic forces that equalize exchange rates in the long run of four to ten years.

Demand for anything depends not only on the price of that product but also on the prices of all other products. The same is true for currency: Demand, for a currency, is reflected in appreciation or depreciation of the exchange rate. Appreciation of the exchange rate is a more or less permanent increase in the value or price of the local currency in terms of an international standard or numeraire. For example, an appreciation of the euro in terms of dollars means that it "costs" more dollars to acquire the same amount of euros as in the previous time period, or fewer euros to acquire the same amount of dollars as in the previous time period. The appreciation of a nation's money is shown by an increase in the exchange rate, generally caused by a growing, expanding, and healthy economy, which increases demand for that country's currency and assets. Conversely, depreciation of the exchange rate is a more or less permanent decrease in value or price of the local currency in terms of an international standard or numeraire. The depreciation of a nation's money is seen as a decrease in the exchange rate. For example, in a yen depreciation against the dollar, the price of yen in terms of dollars declines, so that it "costs" fewer dollars to acquire the same amount of yen (or more yen to get the same amount of dollars). The exchange rate "overshoots" if in response to a shock it initially jumps above its long-run equilibrium and then adjusts back slowly.

Whereas appreciation and depreciation are market-determined exchange rate movements, revaluation and devaluation are policy-determined exchange rate movements. Revaluation is the act of increasing the price (exchange rate) of one nation's currency in terms of other currencies. This action is taken by a government if it wants to raise the price of the country's exports and lower the price of the country's imports. The procedure for revaluation is for the national monetary authority to buy the nation's currency and/or sell foreign currencies through the foreign exchange market in order to decrease supply and increase demand of domestic currency while increasing supply of foreign exchange. Devaluation is the act of reducing the price (exchange rate) of one nation's currency in terms of other currencies. This action is usually taken by a government to lower the price of the country's exports and raise the price of the country's foreign imports, which ultimately results in greater domestic production, higher exports, and lower imports. A government devalues its currency by actively selling it and buying foreign currencies through the foreign exchange market. Both revaluation and devaluation are achieved through foreign exchange intervention.

Types of Foreign Exchange Intervention

Foreign exchange intervention is the process of foreign exchange transactions conducted by monetary authorities with the aim of influencing market conditions and the value of the home currency exchange rates. Intervention usually either aims to promote stability by countering disorderly markets or in response to special circumstances. There are various types of foreign exchange intervention. "Entrustment Intervention" refers to intervention that is conducted in overseas markets with funds of local monetary authorities; an example would be the Federal Reserve Board of the United States intervening to support the dollar in the London market. "Reverse-Entrustment Intervention" refers to cases in which monetary authorities need to intervene in a country's foreign exchange market but request that country's authorities to conduct the operation on their behalf. For example, if the United States needed to support the dollar in terms of yen in the Tokyo market, the central bank of Japan could conduct interventions on behalf of the United States upon request. Concerted or Coordinated Intervention refers to cases where two or more countries jointly intervene by using their own funds simultaneously or in succession. For example, the Plaza Agreement in 1985 (a G5 meeting) and the Louvre Accord in 1987 (a G7 meeting) were held for the discussion of multilateral intervention to depreciate the overvalued U.S. dollar.

Foreign exchange intervention may or may not change the monetary base. When it does change the monetary base, it is called "nonsterilized intervention"; when it does not, it is referred to as "sterilized intervention." When a monetary authority buys foreign exchange, its own monetary base increases by the amount of the purchase. When it sells foreign exchange, its monetary base decreases by the amount of the sale. In order to prevent the money stock from increasing (or decreasing), the monetary authorities can sterilize the effect of the exchange market intervention by selling (or buying) short-term domestic assets through the banking system, leaving the monetary base of the country unchanged. Since sterilized intervention does not affect the money supply, it does not affect prices or interest rates and so does not influence the exchange rate. Instead, sterilized intervention affects the foreign exchange market through two routes: the portfolio-balance channel and the signaling channel. The portfolio-balance channel assumes that risk-averse investors diversify across assets denominated in different currencies. For example, sterilized purchases of yen raise the dollar price of yen. Risk-averse investors must be compensated with a higher expected return to hold the relatively more numerous U.S. bonds, thus the yen price of the U.S. bonds falls (the dollar price of yen rises). The signaling channel assumes that intervention affects exchange rates by providing the market with new relevant information as to the intentions of the risk-averse investors regarding the exchange rate and their expectations regarding economic indicators. Because private agents may change their exchange rate expectation after intervention, the exchange rate will be expected to change as well.

All interventions occur in the foreign exchange (FX or Forex) markets, where there are primarily two types of transactions, spot and forward. An agreement to buy or sell currency immediately at the current exchange rate is known as a "spot transaction." By convention, spot transactions are settled two days later. An agreement to buy or sell currencies for settlement at a future date at least three days later (but typically longer), at predetermined exchange rates, is known as a "forward transaction." Both the spot and forward markets can be used for intervention, and the two may be used simultaneously. A transaction in which a currency is bought in the spot market and simultaneously sold in the forward market is known as a "currency swap." Although a swap itself will have little effect on the exchange rate, it can be used as part of an intervention. Some central banks use swaps to sterilize spot interventions by conducting the forward leg of the swap in the opposite direction to the spot market intervention. The options market is also used for intervention. In this market, a call (put) option confers the right, but not the obligation, to purchase (sell) a given quantity of an asset on a given date. Usually, the option contract specifies the prices for which the asset may be bought or sold, called the "strike" or "exercise price." Monetary authorities seeking to prevent depreciation or devaluation of their currency may sell put options on the domestic currency or call options on the foreign currency. There are also many ways of indirectly influencing the exchange rate without conducting any transactions in Forex markets. These methods, known as "indirect interventions," involve capital controls (taxes or restrictions on international transactions in financial assets) or exchange controls (the restriction of trade in currencies).

Fixed to Floating: Forms of Exchange Rate Regimes

A fixed exchange rate is one where the value of the domestic currency is pegged (or fixed) at a certain level against another currency, a basket (or group) of currencies, or a commodity such as gold, and remains exactly the same from day to day. Governments hold large amounts of foreign exchange reserves in order to actively intervene to maintain the value of the currency. Monetary and fiscal policies also must be directed to keeping the rate constant. A flexible exchange rate is one where the external value of a currency is more or less determined by market supply and demand. Although it is customary to speak of fixed and flexible exchange rates, regimes actually span a continuum, ranging from hard pegs to currency boards, adjustable pegs, crawling pegs, or target zones; to managed (or "dirty") floats with heavy, light, or no intervention; to independently floating. Regimes can be classified according to either a publicly stated commitment of the central

bank (a de jure classification) or the observed behavior of the exchange rate (a de facto classification).

A country that claims to have a pegged exchange rate might, on the one hand, have frequent changes in parity. On the other hand, a country might experience very small exchange rate movements, even though the central bank has no obligation to maintain parity. Arguments in favor of a purely floating exchange rate regime are: (1) Laissez-faire: The exchange rate is a market price and as such should be determined by private demand and supply without government interference; and (2) Policy flexibility and independence: Exchange rates adjust more easily to new economic developments than wages and prices and can quickly equilibrate the trade balance by altering the relative price of imports and exports, while government policy remains free to pursue other economic goals. The arguments in favor of a purely fixed exchange rate rest on stable expectations: (1) Exchange rate volatility is low, which reduces investment risk, resulting in larger international trade, lending, and borrowing; and (2) A nominal anchor provides lower inflation expectation, yielding a lower actual inflation rate.

Forms of Fixed Exchange Rates

Establishing a fixed exchange rate between one national currency and another national currency (usually that of an industrial power) is often referred to as a "hard peg." The U.S. dollar is frequently used for a hard peg, but increasingly the euro and yen are being used. A nation that uses a hard peg relinquishes its control of the exchange rate and relies on the actions of the anchor nation or on conditions in the gold market. When the peg is to a single currency, fluctuations in the anchor currency against other currencies imply fluctuations in the exchange rate of the economy in question against those currencies. When the peg is to gold, the currency is valued in terms of gold; that is, the pegging nation fixes the price of gold in terms of national currency and maintains the convertibility of national currency into gold at that price. A gold standard defined the international monetary system in the nineteenth century and part of the twentieth century.

The case for a single-currency peg is stronger if the peg is to the currency of the country's dominant trading partner. A case against a single-currency peg can be made if a significant portion of the country's debt is denominated in currencies other than the anchor currency. By pegging to a currency basket instead, a country can reduce the vulnerability of its economy to the swings of a single country. Such a system characterizes regional monetary arrangements. An example of a regional monetary arrangement is the exchange rate mechanism (ERM) of the European Monetary System (EMS) that preceded the euro. The ERM set an initial fixed central value for the exchange rate of a member currency against the European Currency Unit (ECU). That exchange rate was then allowed to fluctuate in a target zone band by a set percentage up or down around that central value. If the currency approached the upper or lower limit, then the government would intervene, either by buying and selling the currency or foreign exchange or by changing the level of interest rates. An increase in interest rates would help raise the demand for the currency and raise its value, whereas a decrease in interest rates would help lower the demand for a currency and thus lower its value.

A currency board is an extreme form of a hard peg in which a country fixes its exchange rate and guarantees the peg by maintaining a 100 percent backing of its money supply with foreign exchange reserves. Under such a system, the central bank ceases having an independent monetary policy and issues currency solely in exchange for foreign assets, specifically the reserve currency. The country is importing the counter-cyclical monetary policy and the exchange rate policy from the anchor country; however, the central bank of the anchor country sets the interest rate according to its own needs without regard to the needs of the follower country. If the follower country suffers shocks positively correlated with the domestic shocks of the anchor country, mimicking its policy is not very costly. If the shocks are negatively correlated, then the follower country imports the opposite economic policy from that which it would need, amplifying the width of its economic cycle and potentially prolonging a crisis. This system may prohibit the printing of money to finance fiscal deficits, but it does not encourage fiscal adjustment. Because of the high level of reserves necessary and the parity commitment, a currency board arrangement may encourage the debt financing of unsustainable deficits. Argentina adopted this approach from 1991 to 2001, when it was abandoned in the midst of a severe crisis. Hong Kong has successfully maintained a currency board from 1983.

A crawling peg is an exchange rate arrangement whereby the exchange rate could be adjusted according to such preset criteria as relative changes in the rate of inflation. The basic idea behind a crawling peg system is that there exists an exchange rate that equilibrates the international demand and supply for a given currency. However, because political or economic uncertainties might generate undesirable fluctuations in the supply and demand over short periods, the movement of the exchange rate should be controlled. To accomplish this, countries hold the exchange rate within a predetermined range against a specified anchor during any business day by intervention, but allow the rate to change from day to day by small amounts. The crawling peg is distinct from an adjustable peg system. The adjustable peg is what characterized the Bretton Woods system. All countries maintained a hard peg to the U.S. dollar at a fixed rate within small fluctuations of 1 percent, but they could occasionally alter the rate, typically through a government announcement.

Nations may decide to forgo a national currency and the exchange rate altogether by entering into a currency union with one or more states. By joining a currency union, a country relinquishes its national currency and adopts the currency of another state or group of states as its own. For example, eleven members of the European Union in 2002 decided to form a currency union and create a new regional currency among them, the euro. Luxembourg used the Belgian franc as its national currency prior to the euro.

Ecuador and El Salvador decided to eliminate their national currency completely and adopt the U.S. dollar. As the national currency disappears, the exchange rate also disappears. There are a number of advantages to having a regional common currency. In a regional currency area, it is no longer necessary to change the domestic currency into a foreign currency. Transaction costs can be reduced in international trade and investments. Foreign exchange risks caused by fluctuations in relative currency values are no longer an issue. Credible commitment to the peg is not in question. There are also disadvantages, however. For example, all concerns regarding fixed exchange rates apply, and the country also loses all seignorage revenue. In the economic theory defining the rationale for such a system, a currency union is known as an "optimum currency area." In its basic form, the theory argues that if economic shocks among countries are similar, and capital and goods move freely and significantly among them, then the countries would benefit from a currency union.

Forms of Flexible Exchange Rates

A floating exchange rate, also called "independently floating," is one that is determined through the unrestricted interaction of supply and demand in the foreign exchange market. There is no government intervention, so the government is not trying to manipulate currency prices to achieve some change in the exports or imports, and the external value of the currency is allowed to find its own value against other currencies. The value of the cur-

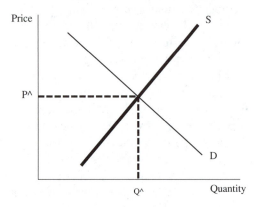

Figure 1:
The Supply and Demand Model

rency then rises or falls according to changes in supply and demand. This relationship can be represented by the graph in Figure 1.

A managed float, also called a "dirty float," is an exchange rate system with periodic central bank intervention to reduce fluctuations and change the direction of the value of the national currency. A managed float is similar to a floating exchange rate in that the exchange rate is free to move up and down, but as in a fixed exchange rate regime, the system is subject to government control and intervention if the rate moves beyond certain boundaries. With a managed float, the government intervenes in the foreign exchange market and buys or sells whatever currency is necessary to keep the exchange rate within desired limits. If it wants to try to raise the exchange rate or prevent it from falling further, the government intervenes by selling foreign exchange and buying local currency. This will raise the demand for the currency and help support the value of the exchange rate. The logic behind a managed float is that an unrestricted movement of exchange rates is usually pretty healthy; however, serious problems in the balance of payment and balance of trade result if the rate floats too far up or down. The graph in Figure 2 illustrates a managed float of British pounds sterling and U.S. dollars.

Figure 2: Government Interventions in the Foreign Exchange Market

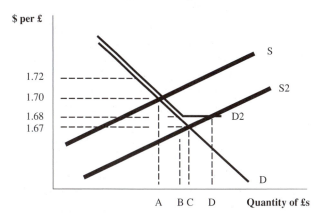

For example, if the government of the United Kingdom wants to intervene to prevent the exchange rate from falling below the threshold (for example, of $1.68) then it will have to buy all sterling offered at the rate it wants to maintain. This is shown by D2, where the demand curve becomes perfectly elastic at that rate. This is because the government will buy any sterling offered. A shift in supply from S1 to S2 will therefore only allow the exchange rate to fall to $1.68 rather than to the $1.67 that would be the case without intervention.

The Role of the Central Bank

Under a fixed exchange rate regime, central bank operations in the foreign exchange market are largely passive, with the central bank automatically clearing any excess demand or supply of foreign currency to maintain a fixed exchange rate. When there is an increase in the demand for foreign currency, the central bank purchases the local currency against foreign currency. Under this system, both the stock and the flow of the monetary base must be fully backed by foreign reserves. Hence, any change in the monetary base must be matched by a corresponding change in reserves, and the central bank is passive in intervening in the mar-

ket. Under a flexible exchange rate regime, central banks retain discretion to intervene in the foreign exchange market, but, as they are not obligated to maintain an exchange rate parity, they typically refrain from frequent interventions.

Exchange Rates and Economic Performance

Getting the exchange rate "right" is essential for economic stability and growth. Casual observation and formal econometric analysis suggest the existence of an empirical link between financial turmoil, economic problems, and currency crashes. Globalization can amplify the costs of inappropriate policies. When capital inflows accelerate, if the exchange rate is prevented from rising then inflationary pressures build up and the real exchange rate appreciates through higher domestic inflation. Sterilization prevents domestic interest rates from falling in response to the inflows and hence typically results in the attraction of more capital, pushing exchange rates up further. When capital outflows accelerate (capital flight), the opposite happens. New technologies make it increasingly difficult for governments to control either inward or outward international capital flows when they wish to do so. To fix the exchange rate and maintain it at a set level, a government must be willing to buy and sell currency in the foreign exchange market in whatever amounts are necessary. If the exchange rate is fixed too low, then a government needs to sell its currency in the foreign exchange market and may end up expanding the money supply too much, causing inflation. If the exchange rate is fixed too high, then export sales suffer. However, central bank reserves are only a fraction of the highly mobile capital available on global markets, and speculators possess an almost infinitely elastic supply of resources with which to test a government's resolve.

The exchange rate may be a useful weapon when a nation needs to adjust its external terms of trade and when domestic wages and prices are sticky. Exchange rate realignment can swiftly accomplish what might otherwise require a painful period of recession or inflation. However, an exchange rate is not helpful when internal relative prices are what need to change. In general, a fixed exchange rate (or a greater degree of fixity) is preferable if the disturbances affecting the economy are predominantly monetary—such as changes in the demand for money—and thus affect the general level of prices. A flexible rate (or a greater degree of flexibility) is preferable if disturbances are predominantly real—such as changes in tastes or technology that affect the relative prices of domestic goods—or external, originating abroad. Often, however, real world economies experience a combination of these conditions, with one or the other predominating over various (possibly short) periods. Selecting the appropriate exchange regime and deciding when to change it thus demand considerable skill.

A fixed rate constrains the monetary authority's choice of interest rate and exchange rate. A flexible exchange rate provides greater room for maneuver in a variety of ways. Most important, it leaves the authorities free to allow inflation to rise—which is also a way, indirectly, to increase tax revenue (through the "inflation tax"). The danger here is that it will probably be harder to establish that there is a credible policy to control inflation under floating exchange rates, and expectations of higher inflation often become self-fulfilling. Conversely, there is a strong link between fixed exchange rates and low inflation so long as the peg is credible. A mere declaration of a pegged exchange rate is insufficient to reap the full anti-inflationary benefits. Countries that change their parity frequently, although declaring a pegged exchange rate, experience higher inflation and higher inflation variability than countries that stick to their peg. In part, low inflation is associated with fixed exchange rates

because countries with low inflation are better able to maintain an exchange rate peg.

But there is also evidence of causality in the other direction: Countries that choose fixed exchange rates achieve lower inflation. This results from a discipline effect and a confidence effect. A pegged exchange rate provides a highly visible commitment to greater policy discipline and thus raises the political costs of loose monetary and fiscal policies. To the extent that the peg is credible, it instills confidence in stable policies, and there is a stronger readiness to hold domestic currency, which reduces the inflationary consequences of a given expansion in the money supply. There is also a link, albeit weaker, between the exchange rate regime and the growth of output. Pegged exchange rates, by enhancing confidence, can engender a greater demand for the domestic currency and foster higher investment, so that pegged rates are associated with higher investment. But they are also correlated with slower productivity growth.

While short-run effects of exchange rates are quite visible, economists remain divided as to which form of exchange rate regime is ultimately preferable in the long run and even whether the exchange rate regime has any effect at all on macroeconomic fundamentals and long-run equilibrium. Some argue that neither of the two main exchange regimes, fixed or flexible, ranks above the other in terms of its implications for macroeconomic performance. Although in previous years inflation appeared consistently lower and less volatile in countries with pegged exchange rates, in the 1990s the difference narrowed substantially. Output growth also does not seem to differ across exchange rate regimes, and misalignments and currency "crashes" are equally likely under fixed and flexible exchange rate regimes. There is also no clear-cut distinction between managed float and float within a crawling band in terms of macroeconomic outcomes. Some have concluded that exchange rate uncertainty has only a very small effect on trade, which may be attributed to financial instruments such as hedging that can eliminate risk at relatively low cost. The effect, then, of exchange rates is uncertain in the long run, though exchange rate uncertainty takes its toll in the short run.

In globalization, uncertainty has led to increasing monetary cooperation among states in order to stabilize adverse effects and secure benefits. Monetary cooperation is the cooperation among monetary authorities of different countries, often through forums, to prevent and cure the monetary problems among them and help stabilize further economic growth. There are various forms for monetary cooperation: information exchange among central banks; policy cooperation at the macro level; resource provision; banking supervision and financial regulation; and monetary integration, with a common currency, common fiscal policies, and common foreign exchange arrangements in a given region. One monetary problem that countries hope to solve through monetary cooperation is the problem of exchange rate or currency crises.

Risk, Volatility, and Crises

Exchange risk, or currency risk, is the risk that a business's operations or an investment's value will be affected by changes in exchange rates. For example, if money must be converted into a different currency to make a certain investment, changes in the value of the currency relative to the U.S. dollar will affect the total loss or gain on the investment when the money is converted back. This risk usually affects businesses, but it can also affect individual investors who make international investments. Exchange risk is higher under conditions of exchange rate volatility.

Exchange rate volatility is often attributed to three factors: volatility in market fundamentals, changes in expectations due to new information, and speculative "bandwagons." Volatility in market fundamentals, such as the money supply, income, and interest rates, affects exchange rates because the level of the exchange rate is a function of these fundamentals. For example, large changes in the money supply can lead to changes in the level of the exchange rate. Changes in the level of the exchange rate, in turn, imply exchange rate volatility. Changes in expectations about future market fundamentals or economic policies affect exchange rate volatility because when market participants receive new information, they alter their forecasts of future economic conditions and policies. Exchange rates based on these forecasts will also change, thereby leading to exchange rate volatility. For example, news about a change in monetary policy may cause market participants to revise their expectations of future money supply growth and interest rates, which could alter the level and hence the volatility of the exchange rate. Volatility is also affected by the degree of confidence with which these expectations are held. Exchange rate volatility tends to rise with increases in market uncertainty about future economic conditions and to fall when new information helps resolve market uncertainty. Finally, exchange rate volatility can be caused by speculative bandwagons, or speculative exchange rate movements unrelated to current or expected market fundamentals. For example, if enough speculators buy dollars because they believe the dollar will appreciate, the dollar could appreciate regardless of fundamentals. If speculators then think that the market fundamentals will not be sustained, active selling by the same speculators could cause the dollar to depreciate. Fluctuation in the value of the dollar arising from such speculative forces will contribute to exchange rate volatility. Most of the governmental exchange rate interventions in recent years have aimed to stabilize disorderly exchange rate markets. Unfortunately, many studies have revealed that intervention could not have smoothed exchange rate movement. Making interventions large, coordinated between two or more countries, spread out over several days, and publicized increases their chances for success.

Exchange rate crises, or currency crises, are characterized by large, out of the ordinary changes in the exchange rate in a very short period of time caused by large and swift movements in markets in cases where government intervention is usually ineffectual. With the rapid development of international trade and international investment (including direct investment, portfolio investment, and bank lending), economies of different countries are increasingly integrated. Therefore, financial crises occurring in one country are said to be more globally or regionally "contagious" than in earlier times.

One well-known example of a currency crisis that illustrates the dangers is what is now known as the Asian financial crisis. It started in early July 1997, when Thailand had to devalue its currency, the baht, about 20 percent against the U.S. dollar as a result of intense pressure in the foreign exchange market. In the process, interest rates shot up as the outflow of short-term capital intensified. The previously inflated stock and real estate markets collapsed, leading to Thailand's worst recession in the postwar period, with sharply rising unemployment and business failures. The crisis quickly spread to neighboring countries in the Southeast Asian region. The devaluation of the baht made Thai exports cheaper, pressuring other currencies to follow suit. In particular, Indonesia's rupiah came under vicious attack and had to be devalued by about 90 percent over a period of just a few months while again interest rates rose sharply as capital flight accelerated. South Korea had invested heavily in the Southeast Asian countries in general, and in Indonesia, in particular.

In this so-called "Asian contagion" process, South Korea, Indonesia, and Thailand almost became bankrupt as nations and had to rely on financial assistance from the International Monetary Fund (IMF) and other major countries. The crisis spread to create currency and financial problems in Russia, Eastern Europe, and Latin America. Exchange rates played a role in triggering the crises. By the end of 1996,

all of the Southeast Asian currencies were overvalued, as they were pegged to the rapidly appreciating U.S. dollar against the Japanese yen and the Chinese yuan in 1995–1996. In particular, the Thai baht, which was first hit by speculation in the crisis, had been almost completely pegged to the dollar for more than ten years.

In the European currency crisis of 1992, long-term forces pushed the German mark and British pound apart, but each had a fixed exchange rate commitment within the ERM. Speculators gambled that the link could not be maintained and sold pounds in huge quantities, forcing the pound to withdraw from the ERM, float, and fall in value. Other currencies in the ERM came under speculative attack at the same time, resulting in massive interest rate increases, unprecedented government interventions (and losses) in the currency markets, and realignments within the EMS. In the Mexican peso crisis in 1994, the peso dropped 20 percent in one day and 50 percent over several months when allowed to float.

Recent exchange rate crises are not all alike. Earlier crises, such as those in Mexico (1976 and 1982) and Argentina (1975 and 1981), seemed to be due to ongoing expansion of domestic credit. Domestic credit growth depletes foreign exchange resources until near exhaustion. A speculative attack exhausts the supply of reserves, reducing real money demand to its post-collapse equilibrium, with higher interest rates due to higher monetary growth. This model has focused attention on inconsistent government policies as the reason exchange rate regimes fail. Inconsistent fundamentals imply an inevitable collapse.

The exchange rate crises in the ERM in 1992–1993 and in Mexico in 1994 did not seem to follow this pattern, however. In these crises, governments had not been pursuing steady domestic credit creation to finance deficits. Therefore, to explain these recent crises, a second-generation exchange rate crisis model was developed. This approach focuses on the optimizing decision of government to maintain or abandon the fixed exchange rate when private-sector behavior affects the net benefits of pegging. Exchange rate crises can be caused by shocks to macroeconomic policy variables, including a change in expectations or a speculative attack itself. These models focus on the role of government choice in setting policy and in the potentially self-fulfilling nature of expectations. The most recent round of crises in Southeast Asia (1997–1998) has led to the development of additional models that emphasize the role of financial fragility in generating exchange rate crises, relating these crises to bank runs on the central bank's reserves. Others attribute the crises to a combination of moral hazard and a change in expectations about the willingness of governments to stand behind bank loans.

Whether central banks should defend their currencies against a speculative attack has emerged as a key and controversial aspect of the policy response, and this choice is increasingly governed by possible effects on the financial sector. Some have called for monetary expansion and depreciation in response to adverse shocks, reaffirming the validity of prescriptions derived from the conventional Mundell-Fleming analysis. Others have argued that in the presence of sizable dollar debts, a sudden depreciation may do more harm than good. One useful way of thinking about exchange regimes is that sharp devaluations and appreciation can occur with both fixed and flexible exchange rates, but the daily standard deviation around the mean is smaller in fixed-rate systems.

Fixed to Flexible to Fixed

The shift from fixed to more flexible exchange rates has been gradual, dating from the breakdown of the Bretton Woods system of fixed exchange rates in the early 1970s, when the world's major currencies began to float. At first, most developing countries continued to peg their exchange rates—either to a single key

currency, usually the U.S. dollar or the French franc, or to a basket of currencies. By the late 1970s, they began to shift from single-currency pegs to basket pegs, such as to the IMF's Special Drawing Right (SDR). In 1975, for example, 87 percent of developing countries had some type of pegged exchange rate. By 1996, this proportion had fallen to well below 50 percent.

For most countries it is folly to try and recapture the "lost innocence" of fixed exchange rates. As a number of examples show, a fixed exchange rate is very costly for a government to maintain when its promises not to devalue lack credibility. At the same time, developing and maintaining credibility has become increasingly difficult. A careful examination of the genesis of speculative attacks suggests that even broadband systems à la EMS pose difficulties, and that there is little, if any, comfortable middle ground between floating rates and the adoption of a common currency. Efforts to reform monetary institutions should focus directly on restraining domestic inflation. The exchange rate should be used as an indicator but virtually never as the central target for monetary policy. Fixed rates are impossible; most economists recommend either having a free-floating currency with an inflation target or joining a currency union.

According to the "unholy trinity" explained by the Mundell-Fleming model, governments cannot simultaneously maintain the objectives of capital mobility, fixed exchange rates, and monetary policy autonomy. Only two out of the three can hold at once. Whether a country has fixed or flexible exchange rates will depend partly on which two of these three objectives they value more and which one they are willing to sacrifice. Importers prefer an overvalued exchange rate that reduces the costs of foreign products. Exporters prefer undervalued exchange rates that make their goods cheaper. Banks and large corporations are likely to favor exchange rate stability.

Policymakers representing constituents harmed by nominal exchange rate instability propose exchange rate institutions to improve their constituents' welfare. Exchange rate systems evolve as the costs of exchange rate stability rise above the benefits. Labor-capital conflict over the distribution of income enters the political arena as conflicting monetary policy preferences. Ties to trade unions and capital interests are represented by parties. Parties of the left tend to accommodate shocks and generate inflation; right-wing parties tend to prefer monetary policy and fixed exchange rates. Instability in exchange rates disrupts business in trade-oriented sectors, with companies unable to plan correctly because of unpredictable changes in income and expenses.

Despite shared interests in currency stability and monetary cooperation, states do experience conflicts over exchange rates. States often prefer a low value for their own currency relative to others because a low value promotes exports. In any case, policymakers adopt exchange rate systems in order to achieve politically determined domestic monetary objectives, and they face a formidable challenge in attempting to balance the complex factors involved in doing so.

Anastasia Xenias

See Also Balance of Payments and Capital Inflows; Currency Crisis and Contagion; International Financial Markets; International Monetary Fund (IMF)

References

Argy, Victor, and Paul de Grauwe, eds. 1990. *Choosing an Exchange Regime.* Washington, DC: International Monetary Fund.

Eichengreen, Barry. 1995. *International Monetary Arrangements for the 21st Century.* Washington, DC: Brookings Institution.

Frieden, Jeffrey A. 1991. "Invested Interests: The Politics of National Economic Policies in a World of Global Finance." *International Organization* 45 (Autumn): 425–451.

Friedman, Milton. 1953. "The Case for Flexible Exchange Rates." In *Essays in Positive Economics.* Chicago: University of Chicago Press.

Funabashi, Yoichi. 1988. *Managing the Dollar: From the Plaza to the Louvre.* Washington, DC: Institute for International Economics.

Henning, C. Randall. 1994. *Currencies and Politics in the United States, Germany and Japan.* Washington, DC: Institute for International Economics.

Krugman, Paul. 1989. *Exchange Rate Instability.* Cambridge, MA: MIT Press.

Mundell, Robert A. 1961. "A Theory of Optimal Currency Areas." *American Economic Review* 51: 657–665.

Mussa, M., et al. 2000. "Monetary Policy Arrangements with Floating Exchange Rates." In *Exchange Rate Regime.* Washington, DC: International Monetary Fund.

Obstfeld, Maurice. 1985. "Floating Exchange Rates: Experience and Prospects." Brookings Papers on Economic Activity 2, pp. 369–450.

Taylor, M. 1995. "The Economics of Exchange Rates." *Journal of Economic Literature* 33, no. 1: 19–21.

Webb, Michael C. 1995. *The Political Economy of Policy Coordination: International Adjustment since 1945.* Ithaca, NY: Cornell University Press.

Fiscal Policy

Fiscal policy concerns the behavior of national governments in raising the money they need to fund the vital aspects of public policy for which they are responsible. Edwin Seligman, who dedicated his scholarly career to the science of finance, first used the term "fiscal policy" to emphasize the need for government to implement some redistribution of income through taxing and spending.[1] Later, John Maynard Keynes and the Keynesians modified the term's meaning to suggest "the manipulation of taxes and public spending to influence aggregate demand."[2]

The goals of the modern theory of fiscal policy extend beyond stabilization to the idea that fiscal tools can help to redistribute and allocate resources. Nowadays, however, theory and practice are far apart, as fiscal policy is undergoing a serious crisis owing to economic globalization, which is an increasing part of the world's economic activity, now carried out across borders,[3] and imposing further constraints on governments' sovereignty to fulfill an allocative, distributive, regulative, and stabilizing role in their national economic systems. These constraints originate from the incongruence of the dynamic transjurisdictional mobility of production factors and the static institutions of governance based on geographic criteria. National governments therefore have to balance external and internal pressures when formulating fiscal policies and must consider the issues of efficiency, equity, and feasibility within a complex global environment with fuzzy borders

Technological changes and market forces have induced a dematerialization of the tax base, which gives rise to a *fuzzyfication* of the national border. Historically, taxation has been based on territorial and residential principles, but the dematerialization is now undermining the practical rule of these principles. The *exit option*[4] of mobile factors[5]—capital, services, and skilled labor—implies that governments' sovereignty and autonomy has been significantly reduced. The formulation and implementation of macroeconomic fiscal policies are no longer a purely national affair because domestic policies can influence the economic activity of other national economies. The restrictions on internal fiscal sovereignty, coupled with external pressure, push governments to "race to the bottom." In this race, each national government is forced to shift the tax burden from highly mobile factors (capital, enterprises) to less mobile factors (individuals, unskilled labor, older people) in order to collect enough revenue, while cutting social security public expenditure.

Under these constraints, the welfare state becomes obsolescent. Each national government has to reform the social security system and improve public-expenditure efficiency in order to limit the effects of economic globalization, which include, for instance, the erosion of national control over the management of economic and social affairs[6] in the interest of citizens, especially for democratic governments.

In a different analysis, Dani Rodrik[7] underlined that the relationship between a country's vulnerability to international markets and the size of its tax-based social programs is positive and could be implied by the negative "race to the bottom"; that is, countries with greater global market vulnerability typically have higher taxes and more social spending.[8]

Tax Sovereignty and Globalization

Economic globalization has jeopardized the basic idea of economic and political governance based on geographic jurisdiction. In this context, one of the main problems for national governments comes from the incongruence of the dynamic transjurisdictional mobility of production factors and the static institutions of governance. The conflict between the modern concept of multinational enterprises and the very old idea of a nation-state means that the latter can no longer satisfy the needs of the present-day complex world. Nowadays, governments are formally still the sovereigns of a particular territory, but they are losing their internal sway—represented by monopoly force within their territory—and their external sovereignty as defined by relations among states in the international system.

In other words, the national system of taxing asset transactions and corporate earnings loses its autonomy as more enterprises become multinational and put aside national characteristics while assuming a global breadth with other countries having a higher degree of economic cohesiveness.

Unfortunately, the loss of autonomy caused by the framework of a globalized market reduces the role of governments and increases the emphasis on private markets, making life harder for policymakers. The state's ability to control the results of policy tools is reduced, making it difficult to achieve policy objectives. Economic globalization has increased the fiscal constraints facing states, and thus their ability to raise revenue; this has started a cumulative process of causation between liberal policies, fiscal constraints, and welfare reduction. Trade and investment liberalization—coupled with transportation and telecommunications cost reduction—weakens the tax base and makes it

difficult to sustain a large share of public sector expenditures within the economy.

Microeconomic and Macroeconomic Effects of Globalization

The process of global economic integration increasingly exposes private agents and governments to international competition. It is possible to differentiate between microeconomic and macroeconomic effects. At the microeconomic level, global competition leads to a lowering of both price markups and excess wages, whereas at the macroeconomic level, as new countries (competitors) enter the world's market, global economic integration leads to new and fiercer competition. The increased openness to trade and capital flows, due to liberalization and deregulation, augments the locational or infrastructural competition between regions and countries and in turn forces governments to reduce inefficiencies. This is because the unitary cost of tax augmentation, or the marginal cost of the rise of revenue, will increase in terms of *legitimacy;* the effect will be a *nonlinear,* regressive redistribution of taxes and expenditures.

Effects of Globalization on Public Budget

Economic globalization often implies some additional costs for public budgets because of the need for additional spending and reductions in total revenue. The additional spending is required to help society adjust to the rapid economic changes that are taking place and to respond to the challenges brought about by resource migration. The cumulative effects of these costs pose a dilemma to public authorities about whether to cut public expenditure—which could jeopardize social cohesion and weaken the government's ability to raise revenue—or cut the tax rate. Moreover, each government competing within the global market has to implement policies that are attractive to its tax base. This can be accomplished by cutting taxes on capital gains, for example. However, if these cuts lead to a dealignment of different rates on capital income, domestic allocation becomes less efficient. Thus, internal resources tend to reproduce and evolve slowly.

To contain this allocation inefficiency, governments could maintain high and progressive tax rates on labor incomes, but they should sacrifice comprehensive income taxation. The significant reduction in the progressiveness of labor income taxation implies significant revenue losses; therefore, governments have to simultaneously reach four goals—competitiveness, allocative efficiency, horizontal equity (comprehensive income taxation), and progressivity—if a given revenue level is to be maintained. This is not an easy task, because public institutions seem to change more slowly than enterprises, due to technology and market innovation, and sometimes no change is adequate for neutralizing the effects of the "fiscal termites,"[9] and especially the effects of economic globalization on public budgets.

Direct Effects. The direct effects of globalization include:

- erosion of the tax base, as in the case of loss of revenue from tariffs, with a weakening of administrative abilities to collect information about global revenue, tax loopholes, e-commerce, intracompany trade, offshore financial centers, derivatives and hedge funds, growing foreign activities, and foreign shopping; and
- an increase in public expenditures, due, among other things, to an increase in public goods demands[10] that regard risks not adequately covered and that are linked to rapid economic change, and the need to bring welfare provisions into line with these new demands.[11]

Indirect Effects. Economic globalization also affects the public budget indirectly, imposing on national governments to provide:

- additional resources for firms, such as tax investment incentives for firms that local-

ize their activities in a given place, financial aids, and subsidies to business; and
- social adjustments, such as labor mobility subsidies.

Fiscal Competition

Because enterprises possess both potential mobility and exit options, national authorities must formulate and implement active competitiveness policies in the global framework in order to fulfill two aims: provision of public goods[12] and reduction of the fiscal burden. Each government tries to attract mobile capital[13] from other locations and to keep domestic mobile capital (human capital as well as financial and real capital and investment) from moving outward. In other words, globalization induces stronger locational competition among countries for mobile capital and in the meantime leads to a widespread cutback[14] and to a social protection redesign.

To attract mobile capital, the competition policies could require each country to lower its source-based capital taxes to the Nash equilibrium.[15] Furthermore, for countries wanting to operate generous programs, competition would jeopardize their ability to do so and might even lead, through a downward spiral, to levels that no country would consider best. Assaf Razin and Efraim Sadka (1991) gave a second-best scenario for efficiency if residence-based capital taxes and wage taxes are available.

Worldwide competition policy thus limits government autonomy and imposes additional constraints to tax and redistributive policies. A potential incompatibility might arise between certain types of national welfare arrangements and increasingly integrated product markets, compounding the effects of technological change on patterns of employment.

Implications for the Welfare State

Economic globalization might significantly influence welfare state policies because, by modifying the width of the public sector, it changes the determinants of global tax policy and internal income distribution.

Although the literature traditionally takes a negative approach to this subject, worldwide competition may also have positive effects, since it could reduce the monopoly power of institutions and limit the waste of public resources. Unfortunately, sometimes asymmetries of power and technological and financial capacity between rich and poor countries have produced very different consequences. In particular, the withdrawal of strategic public investments (in physical infrastructure), the reduction of social spending, and the dismantling of public social security systems weaken society and foster increased violence and further concentration of income within and across countries. As a consequence, fiscal policy in a globalized framework has to consider the complexity and the economic consequences of the capital-labor relationship: It has to avoid allowing welfare systems to disappear or go below a certain minimum level as economic global fluctuations occur.

The standard neoclassical approach to calculating the social welfare function no longer works because it was based on the notion that governments possessed an absolute or at least partial fiscal autonomy, which implies that the best allocation of resources between public and private sectors derives from an optimization, based on the hypothesis of a substantial invariance of tax base to fiscal policy. A more recent approach solves the optimization problem using either the fitness landscape[16] or the dynamic evolutionary approach.

Conclusion

This framework shows that state reforms are required to meet the challenges of globalization. They must be equitable, efficient, and sustainable fiscal policies capable of improving the balance between competitiveness and equity while not inhibiting economic progress.

A widespread feeling among analysts high-lights the need for a new adaptive institutional framework to permit a more efficient public management of global interdependence. As a consequence of economic globalization, national state fiscal policy has to evolve toward a multilayer, pluralistic sovereignty having a variable geometry. In this way, each functional or spatial jurisdiction will be able to address the structurally complex aspects of public policy for which it is responsible.

Maria Alfano

See Also National Government Policies; National Tax Rules, and Sovereignty

Endnotes

1. Edwin Seligman was a professor of economics at Columbia University in the early part of the last century. As highlighted by Tanzi 2004a, "This was the genesis of the 'redistribution branch' of [Richard] Musgrave's famous trilogy" which also includes stabilization and allocation (Musgrave 1959, 5).

2. Tanzi 2004a.

3. This, of course, implies serious problems in applying traditional tax principles based on territorial and residential criteria. The territoriality principle recognizes the right of each country to determine tax institutions within its territory (Abedian and Biggs 1998, 13).

4. Habermas 1999, 50.

5. The mobility of the production factor allows owners of firms to "vote with their feet" on the implementation of fiscal policies: "Footloose capital that is, as it were, exempt from the obligation to stay at home in its search for investment opportunities and speculative profits can threaten to exercise its exit options whenever a government puts burdensome constraints on the conditions for domestic investment in the attempt to protect social standards, maintain job security, or preserve its own ability to manage demand" (Habermas 1999, 50).

6. This effect of globalization seems mainly due to an increasing interconnectedness between nations, which restricts national sovereignty and democratic control over the political agenda and tends to eliminate social correctives to the market economy.

7. Rodrik 1998.

8. Therefore, in this case there is no apparent tendency for globalization to undermine the safety nets. Tanzi 2004b highlights the link between globalization and public spending, which cannot be restricted to the role that each state should play to protect individuals from economic risks that could be increased due to globalization. In fact, that connection must also be considered in

terms of the role that each state plays that might be affected by globalization.

9. "Fiscal termites" are parts of the evolving ecosystem of globalization; see Tanzi 2001, 34.

10. For example, the need for upgrading low-skilled groups through extended schooling, vocational training, and education.

11. For example, the need for health and pension schemes, which face growing cost pressures, and the need to shift the cost burden for such programs through changes in taxation or social insurance systems. Moreover, governments must determine how much of these costs should be borne by companies and the risks caused by fluctuations in demand when the costs are transferred to workers.

12. Locational competition means that countries have to provide good infrastructure (better infrastructure than competing countries) to attract mobile production actors. Good infrastructure increases the incentive for foreign direct investors to invest in the country and improves the chances of domestic firms attracting foreign mobile production factors or keeping their own productive factors from moving outward.

13. Governments feel pressured by the (globalization-driven) locational competition to promote international competitiveness through macroeconomic stability, particularly by lowering taxes, government debt, and inflation; as is highlighted in economic literature, governments play an important role in creating the conditions for attracting foreign direct investment (FDI) and in maximizing the FDI contribution to growth and development.

14. Increased competition in product markets, in combination with rapid technological change, has led to a significant decline in the demand for low-skilled labor in the exposed sectors, forming the most important challenge to social and employment policy.

15. A Nash equilibrium, named after John Nash, is a set of strategies, one for each player, such that no player has incentive to unilaterally change her action. Players are in equilibrium if a change in strategies by any one of them would lead that player to earn less than if she remained with her current strategy.

16. Kauffman and Levin 1987.

References

Abedian, Iraj, and Michael Biggs. 1998. *Economic Globalization and Fiscal Policy.* Cape Town: Oxford University Press.

Habermas, Jürgen. 1999. "The European Nation-State and the Pressures of Globalization." *New Left Review* 235: 46–59.

Held, David, and Anthony McGrew, eds. 2002. *Governing Globalization.* Cambridge: Polity.

Kauffman, S. A., and S. Levin. 1987. "Towards a General Theory of Adaptive Walks on Rugged Landscapes. *Journal of Theoretical Biology* 128: 11–45.

Musgrave, Richard. 1959. *The Theory of Public Finance.* New York: McGraw Hill.

Razin, Assaf, and Efraim Sadka. 1991. "International Tax Competition and Gains from Tax Harmonization." *Economics Letters* 37: 69–76.

Razin, Assaf, and Efraim Sadka, eds. 1999. *The Economics of Globalisation.* Cambridge: Cambridge University Press.

Rodrik, Dani. 1998. "Why Do More Open Economies Have Bigger Governments?" *Journal of Political Economy* 106 (October): 997–1033.

———. 2002. *Feasible Globalization.* Working Paper, Harvard University, May.

Tanzi, Vito. 2001. "Globalization and the Work of Fiscal Termites." *Finance and Development* 38, no. 1 (March): 34–37.

———. 2004a. "Fiscal Policy: Theory versus Reality." Notes for speech delivered at the Congress of the International Institute of Public Finance, Bocconi University, Milan, August 25.

———. 2004b. Globalization, Social Protection and Public Finance. Proceedings of the 16th SIEP Conference, October 7–8.

Foreign Direct Investment and Cross-border Transactions

The commonly accepted goal of a multinational enterprise (MNE), sometimes called a multinational corporation (MNC) or transnational corporation (TNC), is to maximize shareholder wealth. Thus, MNEs, like other firms, enact strategies to improve cash flows, increase market share, and enhance shareholder wealth. To reach its stated sales and profit targets, however, the MNE has gone beyond local investment to invest in a foreign country. The foreign market may have offered better opportunities (market size, liberalized economy, market prospects, and so on); the home market (also called a local market or the company's market of origin) may have become too saturated; or globalization and competition pressures may have played a role in the decision. Thus, when a company is planning to become multinational, its management must decide which market(s) to enter, when to enter, and which entry modes to implement. All the possible obstacles that the enterprise will face in the foreign market must be considered, and the various incentives offered by the host country (recipient country) must also be taken into account.

Foreign Involvement and Entry Modes

The choice of a market entry mode is the most crucial part of an international business strategy. Companies employ different modes to cope with international markets that differ in the level of control that the entrant attains over the local operations and the resources that are required for the entry. Firms entering a foreign market can choose among an array of possible organizational modes.

In general, there are five main ways to become involved in the economic activities of a foreign country. The first is to engage in foreign trade, that is, to either import goods from a foreign country or export them to a foreign country (directly or indirectly). The second way is to engage in foreign direct investment (FDI), and the third is to engage in indirect (portfolio) investment. (See page 89 for the other two methods.) Portfolio investment is the mere transfer of money capital that allows the investor to participate in the earnings of a company. It is differentiated from direct investment by the intent of the investor. In portfolio investment, the goal is short term and focused on making a quick return on the money invested, and the investor has no intention of interfering with ownership rights, management, and voting equity. In direct investment, the primary goal is the beneficial influence (enlargement of market share, elimination of competition, strategic alliance, and so on) of the investment for the investor-company, which is expected to lead eventually to increased profits. Another difference between the two is the percentage of the financial capital involvement. What is considered FDI is different throughout the world owing to different regulations concerning the percentage of ownership in the operations in question.

There are six types of FDI projects:

1. Wholly owned subsidiary: 100 percent ownership of the assets by a sole company. It involves the internal transfer of capital technology, know-how, and rights to production of the parent firm to the subsidiary and full ownership of the subsidiary by the parent firm.

2. Joint venture: a commitment, for more than a very short duration, of funds, facilities, and services by two or more legally separate interests to an enterprise involving doing business in common, the sharing of profits, the sharing of business risk and losses, and longevity of cooperation. A special kind of joint venture is the contractual joint venture, where a local firm and a foreign firm form a joint venture (but without creating a separate entity) of limited (long term or short term) time in order to conclude a certain project.

3. Greenfield investment: the establishment of an entirely new entity, including building production facilities and an organizational structure as well as distribution channels, human resources, and so on.

4. Brownfield investment: the acquisition of an existing establishment, followed by the development of entirely new production facilities (Estrin et al. 1997, 23).

5. Other forms of acquisition: direct acquisition or privatization of a state-owned company (SOE), acquisition majority holding, or even an acquisition stake.

6. Merger and Acquisition (M&A): the merger of two or more companies. Usually one is larger than the other(s), and the larger company has as its main purpose the dismantlement and restructuring of the small company or companies. The banking sector is a pioneer in M&A. Major banks or enterprises merge in order to survive in a time of high levels of information, strong competition, and pressures from global integration (Bitzenis, Aristidis, 2004a).

The fourth way to become involved in foreign activity is employed by MNEs when they perceive a strong need to complement and reinforce their knowledge through collaboration with other MNEs in order to cope with the pressures of intense global competition and increasingly complex and rapid technological development. Collaboration can be achieved through participation in a strategic alliance. An alliance is a form of weak contractual agreement or even minority shareholding between two parent companies and usually falls short of the formation of a separate subsidiary. Several European telecommunications companies have built alliances as the basis for international expansion.

The fifth path for foreign involvement concerns agreements that do not involve money transfers on the part of the foreign partner. Instead, the foreign partner contributes knowledge and experience around the investment project in return for a reward, either financial or other (strategic). Such involvement may include licensing agreements, franchising, management contracts, and turnkey projects. In turnkey projects, the foreign company starts the facilities from scratch in the host country, and the company operates for a short period of time and then hands management over to the local company. A management contract may be negotiated, if it is considered necessary. This arrangement involves the transfer of know-how and requires the foreign company to train the local workers and the local managerial staff (Buckley and Casson, 1985, 26–33).

Each company must find its own way to fully exploit the potential of its investment. A firm's foreign strategy may involve creating an offshore company in a country where certain aspects about the relationship of MNEs and government, such as taxation, are favorable, for example, in order to minimize taxes. Typical "tax havens" are Cyprus, Bermuda ($7.7 billion FDI outward stock), Cayman Islands ($20 billion FDI outward stock), and Virgin Islands ($23.7 billion FDI outward stock). A "fade-out," or planned divestment agreement, may also be applied in all kinds of FDI agreements that involve a local partner. In a fade-out, the agreement states that the foreign company agrees to liquidate the investment by selling its stakes after a certain period of time.

The expansion of a company's operations across the same level of production, either in the same sector or in a different sector from the one in which the company is already active, is referred to as "horizontal integration." The purpose of horizontal integration is mainly to expand the company's market share and eliminate competition, or, if applied to a different sector, to employ the company's expertise in the specific level of production (raw materials supply, production, distribution channels, and so on) in order to exploit an opportunity.

"Vertical integration" is the acquisition of control of other stages of a product's passage from raw material to retail sale. For example, a producer of a certain product may expand to the retail stage (forward integration), or expand from the retail stage to the production stage (backward integration). This can be done either within a country or internationally. As in the case of horizontal expansion, the company will search for the most cost-effective site that simultaneously fulfills the quality requirements. The new location may offer easier access to production factors such as physical resources or skilled labor, if the integration is backward, or may present only limited competition in an atmosphere suitable for a new company, for both backward and forward integration. Vertical integration is a common form of FDI because the foreign investments may be structured so that each location offers advantages suitable for a particular stage of production and its corresponding requirements for inputs and processes.

Difficulties in Defining Foreign Direct Investment

Despite the difficulties involved in defining FDI, some generally accepted characteristics are common to all FDIs and have been defined by several sources. According to the International Monetary Fund (IMF), "Direct investment is a category of international investment made by a resident entity in one economy (direct investor) with the objective of establishing a lasting interest in an enterprise resident in an economy other than that of the investor (direct investment enterprise)" (IMF 1993). "Lasting interest," in this case, implies the existence of a long-term relationship between the direct investor and the enterprise and a significant degree of influence by the direct investor on the management of the direct investment enterprise. Direct investment involves both the initial transaction between the two entities and all subsequent capital transactions between them and among affiliated enterprises, both incorporated and unincorporated (IMF 1993).

Several authors have proposed definitions for FDI or commented on existing definitions. As Thomas L. Brewer has pointed out, the IMF's definition emphasizes the investor's "lasting interest" in the foreign company and its "significant degree of influence" over the foreign company (Brewer 1994, 117). Klaus Meyer wrote, "FDI is defined as investment in equity to influence management operations in the partner company" (Meyer 1998, 125). Ray Barrell and Nigel Pain said, "There are many different operational definitions of FDI, but all aim to encompass the desire of a home country firm to obtain and manage an asset in a host country" (Barrell and Pain 1997, 64). And Giorgio Ragazzi wrote, "A Foreign Direct Investment is the amount invested by residents of a country in a foreign enterprise over which they have effective control" (Ragazzi 1973, 471).

The issue of control and influence is obviously a very important part of the FDI definition, but it does need some clarification. The fact is that, depending on the host country, when an entrepreneur or a company acquires more than 10, 20, or even 25 percent of a foreign company, it is considered an FDI. But does such a small percentage ensure control for the investor? The ownership rights issue is a very complicated subject nowadays. Who has control over the decisions affecting the company is determined by the elaborate enactment of each company, which varies greatly, enough to forbid assumptions and generalizations. Sometimes a person owning only 10 percent of a company can have management control (if, for example, the given company's shares are divided among many shareholders through the stock market), but another person, who owns more than 50 percent of a company, may have little or no management control. In another scenario, someone with more than 50 percent of the shares may have management control and yet not be able to make important decisions (for example, if the agreement of all parties dictates that in order for a decision to be valid, two-thirds of the owners must agree). Thus, not all investments of more than 10 or 25 percent aim and lead to control.

Through the years, many theorists have studied the concept of investing abroad, and foreign direct investment in particular. Nevertheless FDI eludes simple definition because it involves much more than a simple monetary transaction aiming at profit. The complications begin with the very first step economists might take: measuring and comparing FDI flows among several countries. This is because each country may have different standards for a foreign investment to be considered direct. The IMF and the Organisation for Economic Cooperation and Development (OECD) (1999) have recommended that the minimum equity stake for an investment to qualify as direct should be 10 percent. The international manuals generally agree that owning 10 percent or more of the ordinary shares or voting power (for an incorporated enterprise) or the equivalent (for an unincorporated enterprise) establishes a direct investment relationship—the so-called "10 percent rule." The differences, though, among countries are distinct. For example, in the United States, Canada, and Australia, the minimum is 10 percent; in France and Germany it is 20 percent (or 25 percent, according to Brewer [1994, 117]; and in New

Zealand it is 25 percent. It is obvious that the requirements differ across states (Dunning 1993, 12).

Moreover, the components included in FDI measurement are difficult to measure. The following components should be used in FDI when reporting to the IMF:

- Equity capital: the value of the initial investment
- Reinvested earnings: all earnings of the affiliate company that are reinvested on the initial investment
- Other capital: the transfer pricing between the mother company and the affiliate (short- and long-term capital)

A problem arises because many countries in their records leave out at least one, if not two, of these components. As Brewer pointed out, "The reinvested earnings component of FDI is particularly problematic. It is the most difficult component to measure because the data are not collected from foreign exchange records, but are based on surveys of the firm" (Brewer 1994, 117). Consequently, this component is left out in many national FDI records.

Another problem that often arises is the failure of many countries to record cross-border real estate transactions. A significant number of countries exclude all cross-border purchases and sales of real estate in reporting FDI flows, and many additional countries exclude "noncommercial" real estate transactions from the statistics.

A third problem appears when incremental rather than accumulated ownership is used to define FDI. For example, if an investor purchases 5 percent of the share in an enterprise as a portfolio investment, and subsequently acquires another 7 percent of the shares of the enterprise, only the 7 percent is recorded as direct investment. In other words, shares previously classified as portfolio investment are not reclassified in the balance of payments (BOP) as an FDI when the 10 percent threshold is reached.

There are several sources from which one may find data on FDI. The primary sources of information are the company itself and the governments of the home and the host country. The secondary sources are the international and regional economic agents. Some of them are the United Nations, especially the United Nations Conference on Trade and Development (UNCTAD) and the United Nations Economic Commission for Europe (UNECE) and its Economic Analysis Division (EAD); the International Monetary Fund (IMF); the Organisation for Economic Co-operation and Development (OECD); the European Bank for Reconstruction and Development (EBRD); the Economist Intelligence Unit (EIU); the WIIW (Vienna Institute for International Economic Studies); the World Bank; the EU's Eurostat;the industrial and commercial trade associations; and academic scholars.

In general, one should be careful when using statistical data on FDI because of several inaccuracies. Sometimes the deviations are so significant that the FDI outwards (outflows) are not so close when measured as inwards (inflows). Such deviations also exist when the data are derived from two different sources regarding the same variable. According to the Polish research department PAIZ, Poland had received $6.06 billion in 2002, while at the same time, according to UNECE, Poland had received less than $4 billion.

Table 1: FDI Inflows in Poland

1990	10
1991	117
1992	284
1993	580
1994	542
1995	1132
1996	2768
1997	3077
1998	5130
1999	6474
2000	8293
2001	6995
2002	4119
TOTAL	39521

Source: United Nations Economic Commission for Europe (UNECE), http://www.unece.org/ead.

Global capital flows can be examined by looking at either capital outflows (flows coming from the source home country—outward FDI) or capital inflows (flows received by the recipient host country—inward FDI), which theoretically should be equal in magnitude. In practice, recorded world capital inflows tend to be larger than world capital outflows.

Since there is little anyone can do about those inaccuracies, a researcher should always remember that all estimates are only as good as the data on which they are based.

Decisive Factors and Obstacles for Undertaking an FDI Project

Empirical studies regarding the determination of FDI worldwide have shown that the majority of foreign investors have undertaken FDI projects to service domestic demand in the host country, especially to overcome natural or policy-induced barriers to trade. Most investors further emphasize that their focus is to invest in countries with large markets and promising growth prospects. At the same time, investors with efficiency-seeking investments prefer low labor-force costs, and those engaged in extractive activity note that foreign investments will be driven largely by the availability of natural resources. However, investors engaged in efficiency-seeking activities cite the importance of the availability of skilled labor and wage-adjusted labor productivity.

Generally, investors prefer sound macroeconomic fundamentals (stable exchange rate, low inflation, and sustained growth) and the availability of infrastructure as well as a stable and favorable tax regime and stable institutional and regulatory factors and policies, mentioning at the same time the importance of free trade agreements and regional trade integration schemes. Most of the investors claim the importance of infrastructure (electricity, water, transportation links, and telecommunication), rather than their costs, in influencing FDI location decisions.

One of the most important factors a company considers before undertaking FDI is the minimization of risk for their investment. When a country has an unstable legal system (with frequent changes), lacks appropriate laws, and insufficiently enforces the ones it does have, the risk increases. From the economic point of view, if the exchange rate is volatile and the country suffers macroeconomic instability (inflation), and from the political point of view, if the country suffers political or social instability (for example, a high level of strikes), the risk of investing in this country is also increased. Especially in transition economies, when the transition process is delayed (because of unclear property rights; delays in resolving problems; slow progress in privatization, banking reform, or liberalization; existence of a mafia; corruption and bureaucratic red tape; and so on), then the economic and political instability is enforced, and the risk again increases. Moreover, a significant number of investors observe that recent financial crises have highlighted the underlying risks of investing in emerging and transition markets. Potential investors must pay attention to issues relating to political and macroeconomic stability, the legal framework, corruption, and bureaucracy (Bitzenis Forthcoming).

The Impact of FDI on the Parties Involved

FDI has a significant impact on the host country, especially when the country is in the midst of a transition process, as well as on the home country and on the MNE itself. Foreign firms may influence the productivity and growth of the domestically owned firm; may change the nature and evolution of consideration; and may alter financing, marketing, and technological and managerial practices. However, foreign direct investment significantly affects the host country in many aspects, both directly and indirectly. The effects of FDI in the host country may be either positive or negative, de-

pending on the way it is handled by the local government and industry. The effects of FDI may be seen either in the short run or in the long run. The short-run effects may be different from the long-run effects in terms of maturing conditions. For example, the unemployment rate may increase in the short run by acquisitions but decrease in the long run if the company expands production. Magnus Blomström and Ari Kokko (1995) concluded that MNEs may play an important role for productivity and export growth in their host countries, but that the exact nature of the impact of FDI varies among industries and countries, depending on country characteristics and the policy environment.

The Impact of FDI in the Host Country

According to economic theory and empirical evidence, there are four groups of areas in a host country that may be affected by FDI: resources (technology and capital); employment; growth and productivity; and balance of payments and trade.

Resource Transfer Effects (Technology and Capital). MNEs play a major role, especially in developing countries, in applying and transferring new technology. Technology can stimulate economic development (growth) and industralization. It can be incorporated in a production process, in a product, in research development, and in skills development (management skills, labor force skills, and entrepreneurship). The technology transfer may lead to an increase in the efficiency of the local firms (efficiency spillover). In some cases, the countries do not absorb the technology provided by the MNE and cannot use or develop it locally without depending on the foreign company. This still results in short-term benefits from the technology transfer, but the country will probably fall behind in later years. Often, the technology transfer is speeded up, and the local firms become interested in the new technology. If the MNE is by far more efficient than the other firms in the industry, its presence does not positively affect the efficiency rate of the whole industry. When the technology transfer occurs through employee and management training, the people of the host country become familiar with previously unknown technologies, and the upgrades in their skills may be transferred through them to the rest of the industry. The technology spillover is more likely to be significant when the gap between the technology level of the MNE and that of the local industry is large. The managers who initially work for an MNE subsidiary may later transfer the new skills to the host economy.

The entrance of foreign firms affects the structure of the host economy and the performance of the local firms, and there is a spillover effect for related industries. Other companies of the same industry may "steal" managerial techniques from the MNE, improving, in this way, their own organizational structures. The "ownership structure" of MNEs may provide an example of a new structure for the other firms in the industry. The entrance of MNEs may also trigger the development of related industries that recognize the opportunity to provide necessary services or inputs for the MNE at a profit. The services sector, in particular, gains by the presence of MNEs, because their operations necessitate the existence of banks, insurance companies, financial consultants, and financial intermediaries, thus providing incentives for those industries to seek improvement and development. It should be noted that the effects of FDI are stronger in a small market of a developing country than in an already big market of a developed country.

Different researchers have expressed different opinions about the significance of FDI spillovers in a host country. Several empirical studies on different countries have supported the assumptions that FDI has significant positive effects on the productivity of labor in the related industries of the MNE and generally on productivity levels and growth rates. Other studies have found no evidence of consistent, significant spillovers of FDI in any industry or country. Foreign firms seem to positively influence large local firms in terms of growth rate and multifactor productivity, especially in low-technology industries. The weaker firms in an industry cannot keep up with large MNEs, cannot absorb the technology transferred, and cannot afford the higher rate of competition; therefore, the entrance of a large foreign firm may lead to their elimination or their further weakening. The technology spillover is only valuable when the local firms are strong enough to absorb them and when there is not a large productivity gap between the foreign firm and the local industry (Kokko 1994).

The host country also gains from the capital transfer and from the company's own capital sources (funds that have been invested or will be invested). The revenue from the taxation of profits of foreign companies is then available to finance the budget or other deficits of the host country, to cover and repay government debts, or generally to improve the BOP position of the host country.

Employment Effects. The employment effects of FDI on the host country may be positive or negative. Although MNEs may provide the country with new job positions (especially in the case of green-field FDI), they may have a negative effect on the employment rate when they invest in capital-intensive production or participate successfully in a privatization program. In the latter situation, the MNE may decrease the number of job positions in order to increase efficiency. The effect on the employment rate may be positive if the MNE is aiming at exploiting the low labor costs in the host country to create a labor-intensive industry (for example, textiles companies). FDI may also increase the total real wages of the labor force, especially in transition (developing) or less-developed countries. However, the entrance of large-sized MNEs that are strong financially in a host country may create problems for local companies owing to the increased competition. Thus, a few of them may close down (having a negative employment effect). Furthermore, an indirect positive employment effect occurs when the establishment of MNEs in a specific industry creates a favorable environment for related industries to emerge and operate.

Growth and Productivity. FDI has an effect on the gross domestic product (GDP) of a country because MNEs may add to the number of production sites or cause an increase in the productivity rate. The "competitive pressure" increases, motivating higher efficiency in host country companies. That is, local firms are pressured by foreign competition to seek more efficient methods in their operations. FDI may bring about changes in supporting industries as well. Thus, it is expected that lower prices for products will result from the increased competition, although sometimes the opposite appears. The demands of an MNE, in terms of quality of goods and services from local producers, may influence those producers to pursue better operations, such as improved time of delivery, stock control, supply networks, and the like. The host country gains by the creation of "external economies" (Blomström et al. 1994). However, negative effects may also appear, especially when the MNE acquires greater economic power, when private monopolies are created in the host country, when the MNE threatens the national sovereignty of the host country, and when there is a loss of economic independence of the host government. The highly developed and sophisticated MNE and the increased competition may result in the elimination of local firms that are small and weak, if they fail to keep up with the MNE. The local government may block FDI through buyouts in order to encourage "green-field" investments that encourage competition rather than foreign acquisition of local firms that eliminate competition for the MNEs. Finally, FDI and the participation of MNEs in a host country may increase consumer choice, improve the quality and variety of products, modernize the infrastructure, increase the wages, and/or boost production, the GDP, the GDP per capita, and the living standards.

Balance of Payments (BOP), Trade, and Capital Balance Effects. FDI provides significant financial assistance to host countries, and these capital inflows can be utilized in covering the BOP deficit or the interest payments of international debt. Although foreign companies tend to export rather than only to serve the local market, the evidence demonstrates that they also tend to import much of their inputs and that, on average, they have a negative effect on the trade balance. The effect on the trade balance may be positive (current account) if the FDI is a trade substitute (an MNE stops exports to the host country and moves to FDI) or aims at establishing an export base (the MNE starts exports to the home country or to a third country). However, the initial capital inflow of the FDI has a one-time positive effect on the BOP of a host country, although the outflow of an MNE's earnings (repatriation of profits) to the parent company, or to any other MNE's foreign subsidiary, has a negative effect on BOP.

The Impact of FDI in the Transition Process

Foreign ownership may be of great help in the transformation of a state-owned firm to an efficient "market" firm; it may also put pressures on the government to proceed on various issues. For example, it may pressure the government to establish a legal framework concerning companies' rights and obligations. It may make it clear that the government needs to proceed into reforms in order to stop the monopolies, that it should eliminate government subsidies, that it must accelerate the competitive pressures in the market, and that it should enforce hard budget constraints and consequently bring the "fair play" rules of an open market to bear. The foreign ownership will certainly reform the objectives of a firm from output and rent-for-the-state maximizing to profit maximizing. The foreign firm will contribute to legal reform because it does not jeopardize its investment by relying on bluer laws and regulations. It may also contribute to minimizing the exploitation of state bureaucracy, or at least the dependence on it, although MNEs are known to be able to receive favorable government treatment. FDI assists the transition of the country as a whole to a market system because the capital invested helps to stabilize the economy. Thus, apart from the financial help, FDI aids in the clarification of property rights, the reallocation of resources, and the establishment of profit orientation. FDI also helps the effective corporate governance system and brings about technological, management, and employment advancement. Therefore, it provides significant assistance for the transition process from a planned to a market economy.

The Benefits and Costs of FDI for Home Countries

FDI "produces" costs and benefits to the home country. The benefits of FDI outflows to the home country are threefold. First, the capital account of the home country's BOP benefits from the inward flow of foreign earnings (repatriation of profits). FDI can also benefit the current account of the home country's BOP if the MNE receives exports from its home country of capital equipment, intermediate goods, complementary products, and so on. A second benefit occurs when the MNE boosts employment (for example, when the MNE imports raw materials that are produced into goods in the home market). Third, benefits accrue when the home-country employees of the MNE learn valuable skills from their exposure to foreign markets that can subsequently be transferred to others in the home country (superior management techniques, superior product and process technologies, entrepreneurship, and the like).

Negative effects also relate (or accrue) to the home country's BOP, which may suffer in three ways. First, the capital account of the BOP suffers from the initial capital outflow required to finance the FDI. Second, it suffers if the purpose of the foreign investment is to serve the home market with imports from a low-cost foreign production location (creating an export base). Third, it suffers if the FDI is a substitute for direct exports. With regard to employment

effects, a problem also arises when FDI has been seen as a substitute for trade (increasing the home country's unemployment rate).

The Impact of FDI on the MNE

In general, a company investing abroad aims to increase its corporate profitability. Thus, it wishes to reduce costs and to increase sales and profits, and it will therefore invest only when real returns are positive or when other gains from the investment are feasible. The company has to establish a relationship with the government in the host nation and must take into account the favorable or unfavorable infrastructure of the host country, the difficulties in establishing ownership structure, the stability of the legal framework, the difficulties of financing its own operations, the problems involved in creating a human resources strategy in a different cultural environment, and the importance of positive or negative financial indicators in the host country. The company has to work out many different issues that are essential for the operation of the new subsidiary. Finally, the MNE must consider state bureaucracy, corruption, and the different mentality of the workers and consumers, who may have been born and raised in a different business environment, such as those created by the communist regimes of transition economies. In general, more often than not the cultural differences and the language gap are significant drawbacks for foreign managers.

Cross-border Transactions under Globalization

FDI can play a key role in improving the capacity of the host country to respond to the opportunities offered by global economic integration, a goal increasingly recognized as one of the key aims of any development strategy or effort to bring about an increased growth rate. It can be argued that there was a continuous increase of FDI flows up to 2000 and then a significant decrease. Global flows of FDI fell sharply in 2001 and 2002 in the largest decline in three decades: The FDI flows shrank by half in 2001 and by another quarter in 2000. This decline followed a historical boom when, in 1999–2000, FDI flows worldwide exceeded $1 trillion annually (WIR 2003).

World FDI inflows grew rapidly and faster than world GDP and world exports during the 1980s and 1990s. In particular, world FDI inflows over the period 1991–2000 increased 4.8-fold as compared to the previous ten-year period and surpassed the 4.5-fold increase attained between the 1970s and 1980s. From an all-time high of $1392 trillion billion in 2000, world FDI inflows fell by around 50 percent to $651 billion in 2002.

The dramatic increase in FDI over the 1990s was based on eight main factors: (1) globalization and economic integration; (2) technological improvements in communications, information processing, and transportation; (3) new organizational structures and restructuring processes adopted by companies in order to become more competitive and effective; (4) the changing framework of international competition and the deregulation of key sectors, such as telecommunications, which led to the liberalization of capital flows among countries; (5) the sharp increase in investments in the high-tech and telecommunication sectors in the advanced economies; (6) the increase in M&A cross-border transactions; (7) the liberalization occurring in developing and transition countries, which were abolishing their barriers and obstacles in order to receive decisive inward FDI flows; and (8) the abolishment of monopolies, elimination of tariffs and quotas, and increased free trade transactions that complemented FDI flows.

But there were also reasons for the dramatic decrease in FDI flows after the year 2000. The first is the slowdown in the world economy, which has reduced world demand and accelerated the global restructuring process of major MNEs in sectors characterized by excess capacity. Especially from 2001 onward, the decline reflects the terrorist attacks of September

11, 2001, in New York City and Washington, DC. The decline in 2001, which was most evident in developed countries, was also a result of a decisive drop in cross-border M&As. The economic recession, especially in the United States and the European Union, has intensified competitive pressures, thus forcing companies to search for cheaper locations (this is a reason for the stable FDI flows to the CEE [central Eastern Europe] region). The picture is not totally bleak, however. The issue of lower demand (the economic recession resulted in lower GDP per capita) can be offset by lower prices and lower production costs. The downward trend may result in increased FDI flows in activities that benefit from relocation to low-wage economies (for example, increases of Japanese FDI outflows to China and EU outflows to the CEE region). In general, there has been a redistribution of FDI toward developing countries, where growth has reportedly been higher than in developed countries. The rise in developing countries' shares may also reflect the further liberalization of their FDI regimes and the openness of their borders, which have been reinforced by the growth in the number of bilateral investment promotion and protection treaties.

Cross-border M&As

In recent years, cross-border M&A activities have risen significantly. Europe was an increasingly active player in the M&A market throughout these years, though Central and Eastern Europe remained out of favor for cross-border M&As. Actually, the increase in FDI flows was primarily due to the rise in M&A activities. For example, in 1999 the four largest cross-border M&As in which German investors participated accounted for more than half of the German total investments abroad (outflows) (WIR 2000). The value of international cross-border M&A activities attained record levels in the peak year of 2000, when it reached more than $865 billion (WIR 2001). The importance of cross-border M&As can be seen by the following example. In 2002, Vivendi, a

French company, acquired USA Networks for around $11 billion; thus it spent an amount almost equal to the total (stock) FDI inflows received by Greece over the past three decades. Just one cross-border transaction nearly equaled three decades of FDI inflows.

In other statistical milestones, the United Kingdom overtook the United States as the most active source (purchaser) of M&A investment. In terms of inflows, the United States has remained the most attractive location (seller). The telecom industry is still the most important sector for M&A, closely followed by the chemicals sector. The sale of state-owned companies to foreign investors has represented a large share of the source of FDI, particularly among new members to the OECD and in some emerging economies. For example, the most attractive location for FDI (inflows) in 2001 and 2002 was the United States, with $185 billion and $173 billion, respectively; within the European Union, it was the United Kingdom, with $68 billion and $53 billion, followed by Germany, with $48 billion and $46 billion, respectively. In the peak year 2000, the United States was again first, with $324 billion, followed by Germany with $247 billion and the United Kingdom with $180 billion. The countries with the highest levels of FDI outflows in 2001 were the United Kingdom with $111 billion, followed by the United States with $96 billion, France with $59 billion, and Germany with $57 billion. In 2002, the United States was first, with $78 billion, followed by the United Kingdom with $69 billion, Germany with $45 billion, and France with $33 billion. In the peak year 2000, the United Kingdom was first with $382 billion, followed by France with $168 billion and the United States with $159 billion, and only $58 billion from Germany. The preferred sectors and industries for cross-border M&As (either sales or purchases) over the past decade have been transport, telecommunications, finance, and business services followed by food, beverages and tobacco, chemicals, petroleum and nuclear fuel, and electrical and electronic equipment (WIR 2003, 2002).

Specific M&A deals have brought cross-border transactions to some of the world's leading countries in recent years. For example, two deals, Vodafone-Airtouch ($60.3 billion) and Zeneca-Astra ($34.6 billion), made the United Kingdom the world's most acquisitive country for cross-border M&As in 1999. At the same time, the United States was the leading country for inward M&A deals in 1999 due to two major transactions, including Vodafone-Airtouch and Scottish Power–Pacificorp ($12.6 billion) (WIR 2000). In 1997–2002, the ratio of FDI flows over M&A transactions ranged from 27 percent to 62 percent (the peak year was 2000, when 62 percent of total world FDI inflows were cross-border M&A transactions). Thus, M&A deals constitute the most important driving factor behind overall FDI flows; at least one-third (up to two-thirds) of the total FDI flows may be due to M&A cross-border deals in any given year.

Trends in FDI

Regarding the regional distribution of FDI inflows for the period 1986–1990, more than 80 percent went to the advanced economies, whereas the developing countries absorbed less than 20 percent of world inflows. This trend changed dramatically in the period 1991–1998, when only 61–66 percent went to the advanced economies and 31–35 percent went to the developing countries. However, in the period 1999–2000 flows returned to the trend of the 1980s: The advanced countries absorbed 80 percent of total FDI inflows and only 18 percent was absorbed by the developing countries. In 1986–2001, Asia and the Pacific absorbed between 10 and 20 percent of the world inflows, Latin America and the Caribbean absorbed between 5 and 12 percent, and FDI inflows into Africa and the Middle East and into the CEE region remained level at less than 2.5 to 4 percent of world inflows, respectively. The share of the FDI inflows in the transition economies in 2001 reached 3.7 percent, surpassing that in developing Asia, excluding China, which had a much longer history of hosting FDI (Table 2).

Table 2: Distribution of World FDI Inflows, 1986–2001 (percentage)

Region	1986–1990	1991–1992	1993–1998	1999–2000	2001
Developed countries	82.4	66.5	61.2	80.0	68.4
Western Europe	38.4	46.0	33.7	51.9	45.7
European Union	36.2	45.3	32.1	50.2	43.9
Japan	0.2	1.2	0.3	0.8	0.8
United States	34.6	12.7	21.7	22.6	16.9
Developing countries	17.5	31.2	35.3	17.9	27.9
Africa	1.8	2.2	1.8	0.8	2.3
Latin America and the Caribbean	5.0	11.7	12.3	7.9	11.6
Asia and the Pacific	10.6	17.4	21.2	9.2	13.9
Central and Eastern Europe (CEE)	0.1	2.2	3.5	2.0	3.7
Least developed countries	0.4	1.1	0.6	0.4	0.5

Source: World Investment Report (WIR), *Transnational Corporations and Export Competitiveness,* United Nations Conference on Trade and Development (New York and Geneva: United Nations, 2002).

Cumulated FDI inflows in the developed countries were concentrated in the United States, with over $1.3 trillion FDI inflows, followed by China (Hong Kong included) with approximately $900 billion, the United Kingdom with $600 billion, and Germany and France with less than $500 billion each. In the developing countries, FDI inflows were concentrated in a handful of countries, such as China, Brazil, Argentina, and Mexico. China emerged as a popular destination of FDI in the early 1990s and became the second-largest FDI recipient in the world after the United States. Other main destinations of international investment within Asia in the 1990s were Singapore, Malaysia, Thailand, Indonesia, and the Philippines. The four largest economies of Latin America— Mexico, Argentina, Brazil, and Chile—have been constantly receiving over 70 percent of the total inward FDI in Latin America since the 1970s. This trend remained unchanged in the 1990s. For the countries in transition in Central and Eastern Europe and the Commonwealth of Independent States (CIS), FDI only began to take off as they moved toward more market-based economies in the early 1990s. However, two-thirds of the total inflows to these transition economies are concentrated in Poland, Hungary, the Czech Republic, and Russia (WIR 1999, 2000, 2003).

Western Europe supplied over 40 percent of world FDI outflows in 1980 and close to 55 percent in the 2000s. It was followed by the United States, with a share of 38 percent in 1980 and 19 percent in the 2000s, and Japan, with a share of less than 4 percent in 1980 and less than 5 percent in the 2000s (OECD 2002, 2003, 2004; WIR 2003). However, only a limited number of countries became net providers (having more outflows than inflows) of direct investment to the rest of the world: the United Kingdom ($400 billion), Japan ($270 billion), France ($250 billion), and the United States ($120 billion). In terms of net inflows (inflows overcome outflows), China has the largest ($475 billion), followed by Brazil ($180 billion), Mexico ($140 billion), and Ireland ($120 billion). Among the top twenty countries with the largest net inflows, five are Asian economies: China, Malaysia, Singapore, Thailand, and Indonesia.

Finally, there are regional concentrations of FDI: Greek MNEs in the Balkan region; the Austrians in Slovenia and Croatia; the Nordic countries (Sweden, Norway, and Finland) in the Baltic region (Estonia, Lithuania, and Latvia); Germany, France, and the United Kingdom in the ex-Visegrad countries (Poland, Hungary, the Czech Republic, and Slovakia); the United Kingdom, France, Germany, and the Netherlands in advanced economies such as Belgium; Spain in Latin America; the United States in Canada and Mexico; Japan in China and in the whole Southeast Asian region; and so on (Bitzenis 2004c).

A Universal Model of FDI Theories

What stands out from a review of the literature on FDI from 1937 up to the present is the relativity of each theory of FDI; there is no theory that dominates the decisionmaking processes of companies undertaking FDI projects. Some of the FDI theories may be viewed as static, whereas others may be considered dynamic. The static theories study only the factors leading up to the decision about whether to engage in FDI; the dynamic ones also consider the evolution of the foreign company, its interactions within the industry, and its interaction with the host country (Aristidis 2003).

Market conditions are always changing, and the changing character of international boundaries and globalization theory, as well as the creation of the European Union, the Economic and Monetary Union, and other organizations, will definitely create new challenges and opportunities for a company seeking value-adding activities internationally that are different from the ones studied up to now. Authors of theories on FDI have drawn conclusions about why companies have undertaken FDI in certain time periods, but one might also argue that no theory can be general and applicable to all countries or time periods. Since every country offers different motives and incentives for investment and has different obstacles that change through time, firms considering becoming MNEs must look at their specific circumstances and choose the country that maximizes their possibility of success. Each investment plan will be different. Even when two countries hold the same properties, an MNE must base its investment decision on an evaluation of all the factors in relation to its corporate priorities and needs. FDI policies and decisions require all the parties—countries, MNEs, and industry leaders—to carefully ex-

amine all the options, and always in relation to the time period in which they are living.

It is more than possible that the world will become more globalized with the passage of time. Globalization pressures, liberalization, economic integration, and the constant increase of MNEs will facilitate a constant increase in world FDI flows, on the one hand; on the other, these flows will most likely continue to be concentrated in specific regions that offer unique opportunities. The investment opportunities that countries and regions "have to offer," however, will change through time, and MNEs will have to continue to evaluate these opportunities to develop optimal plans (Bitzenis 2004b).

Aristidis P. Bitzenis

See Also Balance of Payments and Capital Inflows; Industrial Location and Competitiveness; International Joint Ventures; Strategic Alliances

References

Barrell, Ray, and Nigel Pain. 1997. "The Growth of Foreign Direct Investment in Europe." *National Institute Economic Review* 162: April, 63–75.
Bitzenis, Aristidis. 2003. "Universal Model of Theories Determining FDI; Is There Any Dominant Theory? Are the FDI Inflows in CEE Countries and Especially in Bulgaria a Myth?" *European Business Review* 15, no. 2: 94–104.
———. 2004a. "Why Foreign Banks Are Entering Transition Economies: The Case of Bulgaria." *Global Business and Economics Review Journal* 6, no. 1 (June): 107–133.
———. 2004b. "Is Globalisation Consistent with the Accumulation of FDI Inflows in the Balkan Countries? Regionalisation for the Case of FDI Inflows in Bulgaria." *European Business Review* no. 4 (July).
———. 2004c. "Political Instability, Historical Links and Geographical and Cultural Distance as Explanatory Variables for the Low Western Investment Interest in Bulgaria." *Eastern European Economics* (November/December).
———. Forthcoming. "Decisive Barriers That Affect Multinationals' Business in a Transition Country." *Global Business and Economics Review Journal.* Special Issue: The Political Economy of Transition.

Blomström, Magnus, and Ari Kokko. 1995. "Policies to Encourage Inflows of Technology through Foreign Multinationals." *World Development* 23: 459–468.

Blomström, Magnus, Ari Kokko, and Mario Zejan. 1994. "Host Country Competition and Technology Transfer by Multinationals." *Weltwirtschaftliches Archiv* 130: 521–533.

Brewer, Thomas L. 1994. "Indicators of Foreign Direct Investment in the Countries of Central and Eastern Europe: A Comparison of Data Sources." *Transnational Corporations* 3, no.2: 115–126.

Buckley, Peter J., and Mark Casson. 1985. *Economic Theory of the Multinational Enterprise.* London: Macmillan.

Dunning, John H. 1993. *Multinational Enterprises and the Global Economy.* Addison Wesley.

International Monetary Fund. 1993. *Balance of Payments Manual,* 5th ed. Washington, DC: IMF.

International Monetary Fund/Organisation for Economic Co-operation and Development. 1999. "Report on the Survey of Implementation of Methodological Standards for Direct Investment." DAFFE/IME(99)14. Paris: OECD.

Kokko, Ari. 1994. "Technology, Market Characteristics, and Spillovers." *Journal of Development Economics* 43, no. 2: 279–293.

Meyer, Klaus. 1998. *Direct Investment in Economies in Transition.* Cheltenham, UK: Edward Elgar.

Organisation for Economic Co-operation and Development. 2002. *Trends and Recent Developments in Foreign Direct Investment.* September, pp. 1–27.

———. 2003. *Trends and Recent Developments in Foreign Direct Investment.* June, pp. 1–20.

———. 2004. *Trends and Recent Developments in Foreign Direct Investment.* June, pp. 1–24.

Polish Information and Foreign Investment Agency, http://www.paiz.gov.pl (cited April 1, 2004).

Ragazzi, Giorgio. 1973. "Theories of the Determinants of Direct Foreign Investment." *International Monetary Fund Staff Papers* 20, no. 2: 471–498.

United Nations Economic Commission for Europe, Economic Analysis Division, http://www.unece.org/ead (cited June 5, 2004).

World Investment Report. 1999. *Foreign Direct Investment and the Challenge of Development.* United Nations Conference on Trade and Development, United Nations, New York and Geneva.

———. 2000. *Cross-Border Mergers and Acquisitions and Development.* United Nations Conference on Trade and Development, United Nations, New York and Geneva.

———. 2001. *Promoting Linkages.* United Nations Conference on Trade and Development, United Nations, New York and Geneva.

———. 2002. *Transnational Corporations and Export Competitiveness.* United Nations Conference on Trade and Development, United Nations, New York and Geneva.

———. 2003. *FDI Policies for Development: National and International Perspectives.* United Nations Conference on Trade and Development, United Nations, New York and Geneva.

Global Economic Growth

The development of a global economy, initiated by the Industrial Revolution of the mid-eighteenth century but with roots that go back further, accelerated with the technological leaps of the twentieth century, which have revolutionized industry and generated increases in living standards. Although Great Britain was the first center of the Industrial Revolution and the dominant world economic power, new technologies spread rapidly throughout Western Europe and to the United States.

With industrialization, world trade expanded considerably. In the nineteenth century, the nature and geographical patterns of world trade changed with the export of manufactured goods throughout the world and the import of raw materials, especially from colonies. The export of textiles became the engine of economic growth, followed in the second half of the nineteenth century by heavy manufactured goods such as iron, steel, and coal. As a result, a new international division of labor emerged. Economic growth changed pace over the period. In the second half of the nineteenth century, the growth was faster than it had been in the first half. In 1870, Great Britain produced about 30 percent of the world's industrial output. The new industrializing United States produced almost 25 percent of the total figure, and Germany produced 13 percent. By the beginning of the twentieth century, growing international commerce and investment, dominated by Europe and the United States but with increasing impact on local economies, had participated in the evolution of a global economy. The main characteristics of

the period that helped to produce an integrated economy on a global scale were the adoption of the gold standard system, an open international trading system, and economic leadership by Great Britain. The gold standard was a monetary system in which most major currencies were convertible into gold and could be exchanged on this basis. Most nations adopted the gold standard between 1870 and 1910. It was a system that allowed money to cross borders very easily, that equilibrated processes in international trade, and that removed barriers to international investment and finance. A major problem with the gold standard was that the world's supply of money would depend on gold discoveries, and any unusual increase in the supply of gold would lead to an abrupt rise of prices.

The growth of the global economy before 1914 involved the development and increasing role of the multinationals. Companies from the 1870s onward started to expand their activities over national borders. For example, in the late nineteenth and early twentieth centuries, the United States emerged as a major industrial nation with the support of modern multinational enterprises that had production facilities outside the country, such as Standard Oil of New Jersey, Singer, International Harvester, Western Electric, and Ford Motor Company by 1914. However, the major source of overseas investments was still Great Britain.

The global economy was based on the gold standard until the start of World War I. As a consequence of the war, international trade was disrupted, and most of the world's major currencies, except the U.S. dollar, had to cease trading openly. When the war ended, the attempt to recreate the global economic structure that prevailed before the war became a vain effort. The 1920s and 1930s were chaotic for the international monetary system. Most countries, such as Great Britain in 1925, also tried to return to the gold standard but later found it necessary to abandon gold.

The Great Depression, which began with the crash of the New York Stock Exchange in October 1929, had profound effects on international finance and trade. It created high unemployment levels and low production and investment levels in both the United States and Europe. With the devaluation of most currencies, the global economy disintegrated into a group of currency blocs. Many countries imposed high tariffs on imported goods. For example, the Smoot-Hawley Tariff Act of June 1930 in the United States increased U.S. tariffs to historic levels. U.S. imports from Europe were characterized by a decline, decreasing from US$1.33 billion in 1929 to US$390 million in 1932. U.S exports to Europe declined from US$2.34 billion to US$784 million during the same period. Higher tariffs and a dysfunctional international monetary system contributed to a drastic decline in international commerce. As a result, world trade fell by two-thirds between 1929 and 1934. Unemployment rose to 22 percent in the United Kingdom. French production represented 72 percent of the 1929 level by 1932. In July 1932, world industrial production was 38 percent lower than it had been in June 1929. Moreover, the balkanization of the global economy into exclusive currency blocs is viewed by some historians as a major cause of World War II. According to this theory, Germany and Japan pursued military expansion because they could not trade for the primary resources they needed for their expanding industrial economies. In the mid-1930s, some nations, particularly the United States, Great Britain, and France, made an effort to revitalize the global economy by negotiating new trade and monetary agreements. Those efforts, however, had not brought any positive results by the time of the outbreak of the war in 1939.

World War II produced the same effects as World War I on international commerce and devastated the global economy. The postwar reconstruction period started with actions to shape a new global economic system. This new beginning reflected the new political realities of the postwar period, particularly the political division between the West (led by the United States) and the East (the Soviet-dominated nations of Eastern Europe). The so-called "Third World," or developing world, a heterogeneous but impoverished group of nations, many of whom at that time were still under colonial domination, were neutral in this East-West alignment. The Soviet bloc would control the boundaries around itself and its European satellites. The postwar international economy came to be dominated by two systems: the capitalist market economies of the West, and the Soviet economy.

The economic and political domination of the United States had a strong influence on the economic order built after 1945 in the West. After World War II, of all the major industrial nations, the United States experienced the most phenomenal economic growth. It consolidated its position as the world's richest country. The U.S. gross national product (GNP) was US$200 billion in 1940, reached US$300 billion in 1950, and surpassed US$500 billion in 1960. The institutional basis of this new order was set up formally at a conference at Bretton Woods in New Hampshire in July 1944 with representatives from forty-four countries. Agreements from the Bretton Woods conference (official title: United Nations Monetary and Financial Conference) resulted in the establishment of two major international institutions: the International Monetary Fund (IMF) and the International Bank for Reconstruction and Development (World Bank). It was the first time a formal agreement at the international level had set up the rules for the international monetary system.

The main objective of the Bretton Woods

system was to ensure the stabilization and regulation of international financial transactions between and among nations on the basis of a fixed currency exchange rate in which the U.S. dollar would play the central role. Under Bretton Woods, the exchange rate of IMF members was fixed in terms of gold or the dollar. In that period, only the dollar was convertible into gold, at a rate of US$35 per ounce. The aims of the World Bank were to raise and channel the funds required for postwar reconstruction and to promote economic and industrial development. These two institutions still play a central role in the management of the global economy The other major pillar of the postwar international economic order was free trade. In 1947, the General Agreement on Tariffs and Trade (GATT) was set up. The purposes of GATT were to reduce tariff barriers and to prohibit other types of trade discrimination. According to the Most Favored Nation clause, every member state was to receive the same treatment in terms of access to foreign markets as any other member state. Another series of negotiations were held in an attempt to create an International Trade Organization (ITO) that would oversee the liberalization and policing of trade relations. However, the negotiations were not successful, and the ITO never came to be set up.

The free trade principles in action in the capitalist world started to break down as European nations and Japan emerged as potential economic challengers to U.S. economic hegemony. The IMF, the World Bank, and the GATT formed the international institutional framework in which the rebuilding of the world economy took place. The GATT came to an end in 1994 with the conclusion of the Uruguay Round, which aimed to correct the failings of the GATT. The World Trade Organization (WTO), which incorporated the GATT, the new General Agreement on Trade in Services (GATS), and other agreements, provided the new institutional structure and a mechanism for management of trade disputes. These institutions reflected a greater role of the state in the economy and in the management of social

welfare. Globalization was well under way, though it is important to note that the reconstruction of the international economy after World War II was not truly global, in the sense that many countries did not participate.

Western powers built up European economies in large part in order to resist the model of communism in the Soviet Union. The Marshall Plan (European Recovery Program), signed by President Harry S. Truman on April 3, 1948, provided aid to European nations to help them rebuild their economies. U.S. aid to Europe amounted to more than US$74 billion by the end of the1950s. Similar aid was given to Japan. It was hoped that this assistance would enable Europe to avoid the errors of the post–World War I era and to rebuild its economies on an integrated, non-Communist basis. Western Europe after the war experienced a period of prosperity for about fifteen years. West Germany, France, and Italy experienced high economic growth rates, and the standard of living reached unprecedented levels. France attained an 8 percent annual growth rate by the end of the 1950s, continued to a slower rate in the 1960s, and returned to an annual growth rate of 7 percent in the early 1970s.

Partly as a result of the aid, this period was one of rapid growth and low unemployment for most of the industrialized world. The economic miracle of Japan proved that non-Western states could be major world powers. Many Eastern bloc countries participated in the Council for Mutual Economic Cooperation (COMECON) but were still largely outside the global economy. The number of countries participating in the international monetary system expanded, particularly as a result of the decolonization process. The process began between 1947 and 1948, when independence came to the Indian subcontinent (India, Pakistan, Sri Lanka); this trend continued, with independence for most Southeast Asian colonies between 1948 and 1957 and most African colonies in between 1956 and 1966. The economic conditions and strategies of the developing countries during this period were very diverse. Many states were involved in developing industrial policies, including policies on import substitution, and some implemented them with apparent success. The general growth in the world economy in the 1960s and early 1970s generated greater demand for raw materials and primary products that were exported by the less developed countries.

The beginning of the 1970s saw two major changes in the structure of the global economy. The international monetary system created at Bretton Woods for fixed exchange rates collapsed. The United States, which had suffered an acceleration in the rate of inflation during the1960s, lost its competitive edge and ran fiscal and balance of payments deficits. U.S. debts accumulated and exceeded the country's gold stock, and its monetary policy did not respond appropriately to changes in the economic environment. The dollar started to grow weaker, and, owing to the increasing pressures of an overvalued dollar, the U.S. government suspended the convertibility of the dollar into gold. In response, other countries dropped the dollar, giving rise to fluctuating exchange rates. The international gold standard was replaced by a system in which major currencies could trade freely in an international market.

Another major change came about with the oil shock of 1973. The Organization of Petroleum Exporting Countries (OPEC) imposed selective oil-supply embargoes and restricted oil exports in response to Western support for Israel during the Yom Kippur War. The sensitivity of prices to supply shortages became very apparent; prices increased 400 percent in six short months. This situation had an impact on economic growth, and most industrialized countries entered into recession. At the same time, the major petroleum-exporting countries, particularly those located near the Persian Gulf, became wealthy. "Petrodollars" from global oil transactions gave a boost to the new international capital market developing in response to the collapse of the Bretton Woods agreements, and the capital openness of the global economy gave many developing countries, oil exporters

and nonexporters alike, access to loans. Many of the less developed countries borrowed large sums of money when interest rates were low. This resulted in impressive growth rates in many developing economies during the decade. The 1970s brought many changes in international economic relationships; although many developed countries went through a period of economic stagnation, the developing world experienced rapid industrialization.

In 1979, a second oil crisis began, leading to further recession, rising unemployment, and the intensification of "stagflation." With the higher interest rates of the 1980s, it became impossible for the primary debtor countries to pay the interest on their loans; the international debt crisis that ensued had serious consequences for many developing countries and some of the world's biggest banks. The debt crisis gained international recognition when Mexico, in August 1982, declared it would suspend all payments on US$80 million in foreign debt. Brazil was also hit hard by the debt crisis; there, the crisis marked the end of a long period of strong growth that began after the 1929 international stock market crash. Other countries in Latin America (Venezuela, Argentina, and Chile) were affected by the debt crisis as well, along with other developing countries in the world. By late 1983, twenty-seven nations, owing US$239 billion, had to reschedule debt repayment. The 1980s also qualifies as the lost decade because high levels of poverty resulted in huge social costs. Africa's economic annual growth rate was, on average, only 1.8 percent during the period 1980–1990, well below the annual average growth target of 4 percent set by the World Food Conference in 1974.

Even through the crisis of the 1970s and the 1980s, however, average income per capita increased steadily around the world. In general, the global economy has been characterized by steady integration. The world economy has been in continual expansion since 1950, and international trade has grown faster than output, accounting in the 1990s for 25 percent of world gross domestic product (GDP). Despite the fact that in some parts of the world economic growth slowed for a significant period of time, taken as a whole global economic activities and output have increased continuously. A World Bank study showed that per capita income in wealthier countries was 11 times greater than in the poorest countries in 1870; 38 times greater in 1960; and 52 times greater in 1985. The industrialized economies still dominate economic activity, accounting for US$22.5 trillion of the US$27.7 trillion global GDP in 1993.

There are noticeable variations in the average economic growth rates of countries by region. Between 1985 and 1995, East Asia had the fastest growth of GNP per capita, with more than 7 percent. In two other regions of the developing world, the average annual growth rate showed negative figures: –1.1 percent in sub-Saharan Africa and –0.3 percent in the Middle East and North Africa. The highest decrease in GNP per capita (–3.5 percent) was registered in the Eastern European and Central Asian countries that undertook a transition from a planned to a market economy following political and economic collapse. India and China, however, have shown positive growth rates: In India, the GNP per capita has grown by 3.2 percent a year, and China has seen an unprecedented 8.3 percent a year during the 1990s.

Many economists believe that the contemporary global economy is entering a new stage of its evolution as it enters a period of "postindustrialization" (or "deindustrialization"). The importance of the agricultural sector as a proportion of the total economy has long been in decline as countries developed economically, while, until recently, the share of industry increased. In many low- and middle-income economies, this situation is still prevalent; however, industry is becoming less important in developed, high-income economies. Between 1980 and 1995, agriculture's share of low-income economies decreased from 34 percent to 25 percent; industry's share increased from 32 percent to 38 percent. Industrial production began to move out of Europe and the United States in the 1970s as the newly industrialized economies (NIEs) of the Pacific Rim

(South Korea, Taiwan, Singapore, Hong Kong) started exporting to developed countries on a large scale, a situation that has changed the nature of the NIE economies. South Korea, for example, in 1960 derived 75 percent of its national income from agriculture; in 1962, it started its first five-year development plan, and by 1990 it was the eighth largest industrial country, with only 10 percent of its GNP from agriculture. Developed economies meanwhile are more and more dominated by services. Today about three-quarters of the industrial nations' economy is generated by the service sector, and the importance of services in the global economy is growing (from 53 percent in 1980 to 63 percent in 1995).

International developments and issues have been influential in the U.S. economy; indeed, the acceleration in the pace of globalization has meant that one economic event anywhere in the world is more likely to have a significantly greater global impact than it would have in earlier times. The debt crisis of the mid-1980s, and later the Asian crisis, threatened the liquidity and the solvency of U.S. financial institutions. The international trade agreements of the 1990s, such as the North American Free Trade Agreement (NAFTA), the Uruguay Round of GATT, and the agreement establishing the WTO, contributed to both international trade and trade liberalization. Increasing homogenization of economic policies worldwide has extended markets and reinforced capitalist relations on a global scale. The intensification of European economic integration, the breakdown of central planning in Communist-dominated Eastern Europe, and the breakup of the USSR into countries in transition have all affected global relations in crucial ways.

In 1997, the IMF reclassified some newly industrializing countries (NICs) as advanced economies (for example, Hong Kong, Taiwan, Korea, and Singapore). However, the volatility of the global economy was demonstrated in 1997 when speculation against the currencies of some NIEs (Thailand, Indonesia, and Malaysia) produced a series of devaluations, stock market crashes, bank failures, and IMF rescue packages. These events constituted the most serious shock to the global economy since OPEC's price rise in 1973. This financial crisis, also known as the Asian crisis, spread to other countries in the region, including Korea and the Philippines, and in the world, such as Russia and Brazil. It has been followed by an economic recession that has been severe and of long duration and that has had a significant impact across the world.

Different theories have been advanced regarding the exact causes of the Asian financial crisis. Among the most popular are the "crony capitalism" and "financial panic" hypotheses. The first hypothesis cites the close relations between government and business in Asian countries to suggest inefficient allocation of financial capital. Financial institutions, according to this theory, acted as if lenders had implicit government guarantees and extended excessive loans to borrowers. The lack of regulation in terms of quantity and quality of lending, as well as the lack of transparency in the financial and corporate sectors, therefore contributed to the crisis. The other hypothesis evokes the irrational panic among speculative investors who bet on Thailand having to devalue its currency, given its trade deficits. According to this theory, "contagion" spread the crisis rapidly in the region after the devaluation of the baht because investors worried that other countries in the region were facing similar circumstances: fixed exchange rates, low foreign exchange reserves, trade deficits, and high inflows of short-term capital.

The economic recovery of most of the countries that experienced the crisis has been mixed, but more rapid than anticipated. In 2001, the Thai economy grew at a rate of 1.9 percent, compared to a 4.6 percent growth rate in 2000. The slowdown in the Thai economy resulted from the adverse impact of the sluggish world economy. Exports, which accounted for more than 60 percent of Thailand's GDP, contracted by 6.9 percent as a result. South Korea's economy was hit by the collapse of the won in 1997 and entered into recession in 1998 with a real GDP growth rate of –6.7 percent; a year

earlier the GDP growth rate was 5.5 percent. However, South Korea has been recovering strongly; the GDP growth rate reached 10.9 percent in 1999, then slowed to 9.3 percent in 2000 and 3.1 percent in 2001. Indonesia's economy began to grow again in late 1999; its real GDP growth rate was expected to increase to 4.8 percent in 2000. The Malaysian economy achieved a recovery in 1999, when real GDP growth rose to 5.4 percent; the rate reached 8.3 percent in 2000. Stronger economic growth in Malaysia led to a decline of the unemployment rate to 3 percent of the labor force in 1999 from 3.2 percent in 1998.

Japan was not swept into the Asian crisis; however, its economy was sluggish throughout the 1990s, the so-called "lost decade." During this time Japan maintained its position as the world's second-largest economy. In 1998, Japan, along with the rest of the Asian economies, recorded negative growth. Japan's economy, however, had been stagnant since its financial bubble burst in the early 1990s. Moreover, despite the increase in the economic power of the European Economic Community (EEC), Europe was still not performing as well economically as the United States and Japan. Steps were taken to stimulate technological improvements and increase productivity and competitiveness through the removal of some economic restrictions within the EEC. The establishment of the euro in 1999 was the most important innovation in the international monetary system since the collapse of the Bretton Woods system and the advent of floating exchange rates in 1973. The introduction of the euro has contributed to the emergence of a new economic player, the euro area, which represents the largest trading partner in the world economy, accounting for 19 percent of world exports.

By the end of 2000, new signs of a slowdown in global economic growth were appearing. Globally, the growth in output decreased from 4 percent in 2000 to 1.3 percent in 2001. The sluggish economy was exacerbated by the terrorist attacks of September 11, 2001, in the United States. The global economic slowdown forced U.S. manufacturing capacity utilization to levels equal to the 1982 recession; moreover, the slowdown has been expanding to Europe, South America, and parts of Asia. Foreign direct investment (FDI) have fallen more than 50 percent worldwide, from US$1.49 trillion to US$735 billion (in part because of the decline in cross-border mergers and acquisitions). This slowdown in the economies of advanced countries was induced by several factors, including the tighter fiscal policies of 1999–2000, the collapse of the technology bubble in 2002, and higher oil prices in 1999–2000. The euro area during the period 1998–2000 experienced rates of economic growth averaging more than 3 percent. The high rates of growth reflected the new economy and the euro-integration and macro-stability dividends.

During the same period, new shocks occurred that certainly affected the economy, including the Enron scandal and other corporate scandals; severe tension in the Middle East; and financial crises in some emerging markets. The crisis in Argentina in 2002 was the result of a failure to tighten fiscal policy at the end of the 1990s because of political constraints. Asia has shown signs of recovery as a result of increased trade, a rebound in information technology, and a rise in domestic demand. China arrived at the forefront of the world stage; its entry into the WTO in 2000 and its hosting of the Olympics Games in 2008 will further stimulate its economic growth and accelerate its integration into the global economic market. After China, India continues to be one of the fastest-growing nations and is increasing its integration into the world economy, although its economic growth declined in 2002 to 4.4 percent, from 5.6 percent in fiscal 2001. The economic growth of Africa was positive in 2001. Because Africa has not yet been well integrated into the global economy, it may not be as affected by events in other countries as other regions. The slowdown of the global economy has continued since 2003 with the uncertainties of the U.S.-led invasion of Iraq, the outbreak of SARS (Severe Acute Respiratory Syndrome), and other major events.

Despite the great economic advances that have been achieved in the second half of the twentieth century, the world economy has entered a new century with an increasing globalization of economic activity, new economic problems, and the challenge of ensuring economic growth with equity. Concerns about the long-term future of the world economy now focus on environmental degradation and sustainability.

Nathalie Cavasin

See Also International Productivity; Technology and Technical Change

References

Asian Development Bank. 2002. *Annual Report 2002.* Manilla: Asian Development Bank.

Breslin, Shaun, ed. 2002. *New Regionalisms in the Global Political Economy: Theories and Cases.* New York: Routledge.

Dicken, Peter. 2003. *Global Shift: Reshaping the Global Economic Map in the 21st Century.* London: Sage.

Foreman-Peck, James. 1998. *Historical Foundations of Globalization.* Northampton, MA: Edward Elgar.

Gardner, Richard. 1980. *Sterling-Dollar Diplomacy in Current Perspective: The Origins and the Prospects of Our International Economic Order.* New York: Columbia University Press.

International Monetary Fund. 2003. *World Economic Outlook: Growth and Institutions.* Washington, DC: International Monetary Fund.

Kindleberger, Charles. 1973. *The World Depression, 1929–1939.* London: Penguin.

Paehlke, Robert C. 2003. *Democracy's Dilemma: Environment, Social Equity, and the Global Economy.* Cambridge: MIT Press.

Stiglitz, Joseph. 2002. *Globalization and Its Discontents.* New York: Penguin.

World Bank. 1997. *The World Development Report, 1997: The State in a Changing World.* New York and Oxford: Oxford University Press.

———. 2000. *The World Development Report, 2000: Entering the 21st Century.* New York and Oxford: Oxford University Press.

———. 2002. *The World Development Report, 2002: Building Institutions for Markets.* New York and Oxford: Oxford University Press.

———. 2003. *The World Development Report, 2003: Sustainable Development in a Dynamic World: Transforming Institutions, Growth, and Quality of Life.* New York and Oxford: Oxford University Press.

Industrial Location and Competitiveness

Studies of industrial location look at why certain countries or regions specialize in specific industries. That is, what determines industrial location, how is industrial activity measured, and what factors determine how it changes over time? In answering these questions, economists have proposed that industrial location is determined by a combination of two main factors: the extent of location advantages, and the intensity of firm competition relative to the size of the market. Technology, factor endowments, geography, and scale economies are influential for determining location advantages, whereas agglomeration, variety, proximity, and market access are important for determining the intensity of firm competition relative to the size of the market. This implies that what appears to be a minor change in the balance of the forces determining industrial location may sometimes turn out to have drastic consequences for the global distribution of manufacturing activity. Both the ongoing process of globalization and local interactions between producers, consumers, and firms are also important factors for determining competitiveness and the location of industrial activity.

Who Produces (and Exports) What? Revealed Comparative Advantage

Analysts of industrial activity use a standard measure to determine empirically which countries hold particularly strong positions in the production of specific goods. It is based on the idea that a country's actual export flows "reveal" the country's strong sectors. Based on the work of Bela Balassa, a twentieth-century economist, it is known as the Balassa index, and a Balassa index value is also known as a country's "revealed comparative advantage."

The Balassa index depends on detailed analyses of export data. Many countries are, for example, producing and exporting cars. To establish whether a country, say Japan, holds a particularly strong position in the car industry, Balassa argued that one should compare the share of car exports in Japan's total exports with the share of car exports in a group of reference countries. The Balassa index is therefore essentially a normalized export share. So if Japan's normalized export share for cars is higher than 1, Japan is said to have a revealed comparative advantage in the production of cars. Economists generally use the exports of the member countries of the Organisation for Economic Co-operation and Development (OECD) in twenty-eight manufacturing sectors as the reference group.

Figure 1 illustrates the evolution of the Balassa index in the period 1970–1996 for the two sectors with the highest Balassa index for Japan and Finland. The Balassa index is above 1, as it should be for the strong export sectors. Apparently, Japan has a revealed comparative trade advantage for electrical machinery and professional goods. Note the fairly small value of the highest Balassa index for Japan (about 2) compared to Finland (about 11). This can be attributed to the fact that Japan has a much larger industrial base than Finland and exports a wider variety of goods, which makes it more

Figure 1: Two Top Revealed Comparative Advantage Sectors, Japan and Finland

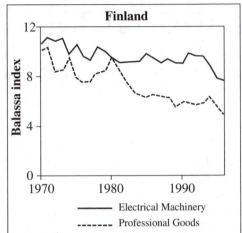

Source: Unless otherwise specified, all information, figures, and tables in this entry are taken from Charles Van Marrewijk, *International Trade and the World Economy* (Oxford: Oxford University Press, 2002).

difficult to achieve high values for the Balassa index. Finland's highest-ranking sectors are paper and paper products and wood products. This corresponds with the easy availability of factor inputs, that is, wood from the large Finnish forests, as discussed below.

In general, sectors with a high revealed comparative advantage tend to sustain this advantage for a fairly long time. Tobacco, for example, is always the sector with the highest Balassa index in the United States. The same holds for footwear in Italy and paper and paper products in Finland. Changes over extended

periods of time are, however, also possible. Table 1 gives an overview of the sector with the highest Balassa index in 1996 for the twenty OECD countries. In general, the highest Balassa index for large countries is lower than those for small countries. Note that paper and paper products constitute the highest-ranking sector for Finland and Sweden, both of which have extensive forests. Also note that the labor-intensive footwear industry is the highest-ranking sector for Spain, Portugal, and Italy. A closer look at changes in the distribution of the Balassa index shows that:

Table 1: Revealed Comparative Advantage in Manufacturing (1996)

Australia Nonferrous metals	*Finland* Paper & products	*Italy* Footwear	*Portugal* Footwear
Austria Wood products	*France* Beverages	*Japan* Electrical machinery	*Spain* Footwear
Belgium Other manufacturing	*Germany* Industrial chemicals	*Netherlands* Tobacco	*Sweden* Paper & products
Canada Wood products	*Greece* Wearing apparel	*New Zealand* Food	*United Kingdom* Beverages
Denmark Furniture & fixtures	*Iceland* Food	*Norway* Nonferrous metals	*United States* Tobacco

Figure 2: Growth in World Trade and World GDP

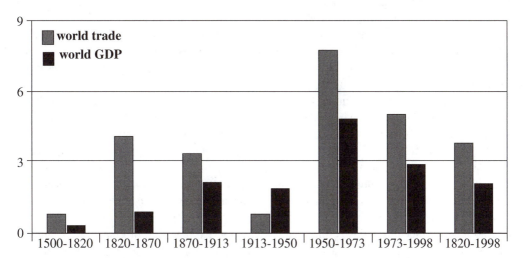

Source: A. Maddison, *The World Economy: A Millennial Perspective* (Paris: Organisation for Economic Co-operation and Development, 2001).

- The mean value of the Balassa index is slowly increasing over time. This points to an increase in international specialization.
- There is a positive relationship between employment and industries with a high Balassa index.
- There is no clear-cut relationship between labor productivity and sectors with a high Balassa index.

Two questions now come to the fore: Why do countries tend to specialize in certain industries, and why are those industries found in particular locations? The answers to these questions are related to the process of globalization.

Globalization and Trade

The trend toward increased interaction with distant markets and competition from foreign firms has been in progress for at least 500 years, although not monotonically. During the nineteenth and early twentieth centuries, for example, declining shipping rates and declining levels of protectionism resulted in a highly global world economy as measured by world trade as a percentage of world gross domestic product (GDP). This reached a peak of about 8.7 percent just before World War I, not to be matched again for another sixty years as a result of the inward-looking behavior and protectionist tendencies associated with the two world wars and the Great Depression.

Similarly, there were very large capital and migration flows before 1913. Net capital flows were as high as 10 percent of GDP for investor or recipient. In the period 1870–1910, no less than 10 percent of the world population migrated to other countries, mostly to the New World. The migration flows are now more restricted than in the nineteenth century, whereas capital flows can move more freely than ever before.

Figure 2 illustrates that world trade flows have been increasing more rapidly than world production for the past 500 years, with the exception of the period 1913–1950. As a consequence, merchandise exports as a share of GDP rose gradually, although not monotonically, from about 1 percent in 1820 to more than 17 percent in 2000.

After World War II, many trade restrictions that had hampered the globalization process were relaxed under the guidance of what is now known as the World Trade Organization (WTO). Similarly, transportation costs declined considerably. The cost of ocean freight transport, for example, declined by 70 percent between 1920 and 1990, and the cost of air transport declined by 84 percent between 1930 and 1990. But it was not only commodity trade that increased: Thanks to technological breakthroughs in the information and communication industry, more and more services that used to be nontradable became internationally tradable. These technological advances not only stimulated trade of existing commodities but also created new products. All factors combined to greatly stimulate world trade in goods and services, suggesting that the world economy is becoming a truly integrated economy.

From a historical point of view, world trade has clearly become more important than in the past, but is the world economy now fully integrated? The answer is no, as the following example illustrates. How much would a U.S. citizen spend on foreign commodities in a fully integrated world without any trade barriers whatsoever? The U.S. share in world GDP is roughly 25 percent. If a U.S. citizen were completely indifferent about whether the goods she was purchasing were domestic or foreign, she would spend 25 percent on domestically produced goods and 75 percent on foreign goods. In reality, the current share of U.S. spending on foreign goods is only about 12 percent, so the globalization process may still have some way to go.

Technology Differences

At the end of the eighteenth century and the beginning of the nineteenth, two British economists, Adam Smith and David Ricardo, pointed to a fundamental force determining the location of industrial activity: technology differences leading to differences in relative production efficiency (comparative advantage).

International trade is not simply an extension of the local market by adding international markets: It affects the industrial composition of countries. The theory of comparative advantage explains how countries gain from trade even if a country imports commodities that it could produce more efficiently itself, or exports goods to countries that could produce them more efficiently themselves. The key insight of Ricardo is a generalization of the concept of opportunity costs of production. In the case of, for example, shoes and wine, the opportunity cost of shoes is the amount of wine a country must forgo in order to produce more shoes (the price of shoes in terms of wine). A country that is more efficient in producing both types of goods relative to another country might still direct all its resources to shoes if it is relatively more efficient in producing shoes than wine. For a country that prefers to consume both goods, the most efficient way to get wine is to internationally trade shoes for wine, instead of giving up some of the production of shoes and produce the wine itself. So, simply comparing the efficiency of wine producers in different countries gives the casual observer the wrong answer, as he would probably predict that the country would export wine instead of shoes.

The relatively inefficient trading partner gains as well from international trade. A comparison of relative efficiencies in the two hypothetical countries—the inefficient country and its efficient trading partner—would show that the opportunity cost of shoes in terms of wine is higher in the less efficient country (the price of shoes in terms of wine is higher than in the efficient country). This less efficient country directs all its resources to the production of wine. By internationally trading wine for shoes, it gets the shoes cheaper than it would by producing them itself. Comparing absolute productivity differences in one industry across different countries thus produces a misleading conclusion. Sometimes workers and managers in certain industries claim that foreign competition is "unfair"; they feel that they are at least as productive as their foreign counterparts but face "too much competition," and they conclude that this means that some unfair trading practice is to blame. However, they could be unaware that other industries have the comparative advantage in their country (and are even more productive compared to the trading partners).

These fundamental principles on competitiveness have important consequences for the industrial structure of a country. The relatively more efficient country will, in this example, specialize in the production of shoes, and the relatively inefficient country will specialize in the production of wine. The industrial structure of both countries is very different in autarky than under free trade: In autarky, they will both have a shoe industry and a wine industry, whereas under free trade the countries will specialize in one of the two industries. Whether this specialization will be complete depends on many factors, such as the relative size of the trading partners. But the key insight here is that relative and not absolute efficiencies determine the international location of industries. In an actual example, that of trade between the European Union and Kenya, the productivity of Kenya is lower in both food products and chemical products: Value added per person in the food sector is $233 in Kenya compared to $45,341 in the EU, and for chemical products the value added per person is $452 in Kenya compared to $154,537 in the EU. Still, Kenya has a net export surplus of food to the EU, and the EU has a net export surplus of chemical products to Kenya, because in relative terms Kenya is more efficient in food products, whereas the EU is relatively more efficient in chemical products. But how did these differences in comparative advantage come about? This is another issue that has captured the attention of economists.

Factor Endowments

At the beginning of the twentieth century, two Swedish economists, Eli Heckscher and Bertil Ohlin, pointed at another force determining the location of industrial activity: differences in availability of factors of production. Heckscher

and Ohlin observed that different goods were produced using different intensities of the factors of production. The production of textiles, for example, uses labor intensively, whereas the production of machines uses capital intensively. India, for example, has a large supply of labor, so this factor of production tends to be relatively cheap there. Similarly, Germany has a large supply of capital, so this factor of production will be relatively cheap there. Consequently, textile production, which is labor intensive, tends to be relatively cheap in India, whereas production of machinery, which uses more capital, tends be relatively cheap in Germany. Thus, India will export textiles to Germany and import machines from Germany. As the intensity of international competition increases (owing to lower transport costs and removal of other trade barriers), India will increasingly specialize in the production of labor-intensive textiles, and Germany will increasingly specialize in the production of capital-intensive machines.

If differences in the availability of factors of production determine, in part, where an industry will locate, then obviously it becomes important to identify the factors of production that vary enough to make a difference for comparative advantage. For instance, is the ratio of labor supply to capital that much higher in India compared to Germany, for example, to make labor-intensive products more profitable than other kinds of products? Such questions are not always easy to answer because the factors of production are complex; in this example, one must aggregate many different varieties of capital and labor into one measure. The construction of a consistent data set that can be compared for a large number of countries is complicated and time consuming. Figure 3 illustrates the distribution of the capital stock per worker for the sixty countries for which data are available in the most widely used data set (Summers and Heston, 1988). Swiss workers had the highest capital stock per worker available ($73,459). Workers from Sierra Leone had the lowest capital stock per worker ($223). One would therefore expect Switzerland to pro-

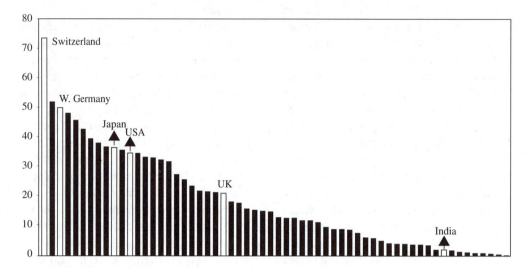

Figure 3: Capital Stock per Worker x $1000 (1990)

duce mostly capital-intensive goods and Sierra Leone to produce labor-intensive goods.

To empirically verify the prediction of specialization in accordance with the availability of factors of production, one needs to identify categories of goods and factors of production. This is done, for example, on the Web site of the International Trade Center (ITC, http://www.intracen.org), the joint organization of the United Nations Conference on Trade and Development (UNCTAD) and the WTO. To classify international trade flows, the ITC distinguishes five factors of production and 257 final goods. It aggregates the 257 final goods into five broader categories based on the intensity of the five factors in the production process, namely (1) primary products; (2) natural-resource-intensive products; (3) unskilled-labor-intensive products; (4) technology-intensive products; and (5) human-capital-intensive products.

For example, the ITC classifies 31 goods as unskilled-labor-intensive manufacturing products, incorporating pipes, various textiles, and clothing, glass, pottery, ships, furniture, footwear, and office supplies. For the 151 countries for which the ITC provides data, total exports of unskilled-labor-intensive manufactures in 1998 were equal to $610 billion, some 13 percent of all exports. China, which exports the

equivalent of $78 billion in such products annually, is the world's largest unskilled-labor-intensive manufactures exporter (of, for example, shoes, and wearing apparel), followed by Italy, with a value of $48 billion (including furniture, footwear, and sweaters).

Despite the fact that unskilled-labor-intensive manufactures represent a sizable 43 percent of Chinese exports and 24 percent of Italian exports, neither country makes it to the top ten list of world exporters of unskilled-labor-intensive manufactures in relative terms, the majority of which are located in Asia. The top three are Nepal (carpets), Bangladesh (clothing and textiles), and Pakistan (cotton and textiles). The dependence on the exports of unskilled-labor-intensive manufactures for these countries is high, ranging from 89 percent for Nepal to 62 percent for tenth-ranked Albania. Figure 4 shows the relative dependence of countries on the exports of unskilled-labor-intensive manufactures. These are clearly concentrated in Southeast Asia and Central Europe.

Dynamics of Industrial Location

Explanations of the location of industrial activity based on technology differences, the avail-

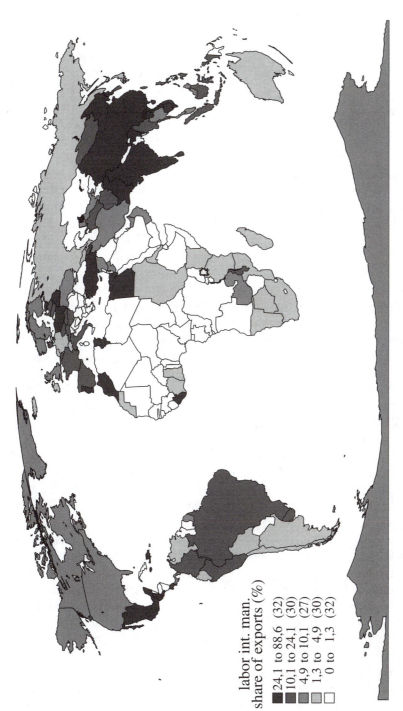

labor int. man.
share of exports (%)

24,1 to 88,6 (32)
10,1 to 24,1 (30)
4,9 to 10,1 (27)
1,3 to 4,9 (30)
0 to 1,3 (32)

Figure 4: Unskilled-Labor-Intensive Manufacturing: Share of Exports, 1998

Figure 5: Dynamics of the Location of Industrial Production

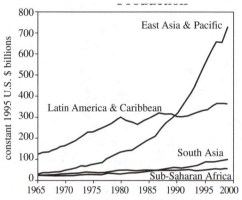

Source: World Bank development indicators CD-ROM (2001).

ability of factors of production, and the ongoing process of globalization, especially as the pace of the latter increases with the elimination of trade barriers, reductions in transport costs, and technological improvements, suggest that fundamental shifts in the structure of global industry should be in progress. This is indeed the case, as illustrated in Figure 5 for four of the seven global regions identified by the World Bank: (1) East Asia and the Pacific (including China and Indonesia); (2) Latin America and the Caribbean (including Brazil and Mexico); (3) South Asia (SAS, including India); and (4) sub-Saharan Africa (including Nigeria and South Africa). Measured in constant 1995 U.S. dollars (corrected for inflation), these four regions produced a total of $173 billion in manufactures in 1965. This amount increased more than seven times (by about 6 percent per year) to reach $1.23 trillion in 1999.

The distribution of the production of manufactures for the four regions changed drastically in this period. The increases in the sub-Saharan and Latin American regions were modest, or about 3.4 percent per year in both cases, rising from $16 billion to $49 billion in sub-Saharan Africa and from $117 billion to $361 billion in Latin America. As is well known, most countries in these regions did not actively promote international trade and specialization throughout most of this period. The

South Asia region, with its increasingly outward-looking development strategy, saw its production level of manufactures rise more substantially, from $15 billion to $93 billion, about 5.5 percent per year. The East Asia and Pacific region, with its predominantly outward-looking development strategy throughout most of the period, experienced very rapid growth and saw its production level of manufactures rise more than twenty-eight times in thirty-four years, from $26 billion to $730 billion, or about 10.4 percent per year.

The spectacular rise of the production of manufactures in the East Asia and Pacific region demonstrates the power of the forces underlying the globalization process and the speed at which changes in industrial location can take place. It does not indicate, as is frequently suggested, that manufacturing activity disappears in the developed countries. For example, the European countries now forming a monetary union produce about twice as many manufactures as the entire East Asia and Pacific region. Moreover, this level is still rising, although slowly. Instead, the developed countries are increasingly shifting their economic structure toward producing a wide range of services. A related aspect of international economic interactions that deserves our attention is that more than 75 percent of the world trade flows are to and from the high-income countries (Western Europe, North America, and Japan). Indeed, the majority of flows are from one high-income country to another high-income country. For example, the intra–West European trade flows alone account for more than 27 percent of world trade. As it is hard to see how differences in technology and factor abundance can fully explain these large trade flows, one must examine other forces underlying the global economic structure.

**Intra-Industry Trade,
Scale Economies, and Variety**

The international trade flows between similar high-income countries are not only very large,

Table 2: Intra-Industry Trade Index, Manufacturing Sector, 1995 (3-digit level, %)

Country	World	OECD 22	NAFTA	East Asia Dev.	Latin America
Australia	36.6	17.5	16.0	39.2	41.6
Bangladesh	10.0	3.5	1.7	3.4	8.0
Chile	25.7	10.1	11.5	3.6	47.8
France	83.5	86.7	62.7	38.7	22.9
Germany	75.3	80.1	61.2	36.2	22.8
Hong Kong	28.4	20.2	25.2	19.9	13.6
Japan	42.3	47.6	45.7	36.1	7.0
Malaysia	60.4	48.5	57.9	75.0	10.4
UK	85.4	84.0	72.5	46.6	38.6
USA	71.7	74.0	73.5	41.4	66.0

they are also characterized by intra-industry trade. In other words, many countries simultaneously export and import very similar goods and services; intra-industry trade is trade within the same industry or sector. Germany, for example, exports many cars to France and simultaneously imports many cars from France. Why does Germany do this? Intra-industry trade is measured using the Grubel-Lloyd index, which ranges from zero (if a country only imports or only exports a particular good) to one (if a country's exports of a good are exactly as high as its imports of that good). Table 2 summarizes the extent of intra-industry trade in 1995 for a selection of countries.

Take the United States as an example. Averaged over all countries, no less than 71.7 percent of U.S. trade can be categorized as intra-industry trade. This trade, however, is unevenly distributed. U.S. intra-industry trade with the Asian newly industrialized countries (41.4 percent intra-industry trade) and with Latin America (66 percent intra-industry trade) is lower than its intra-industry trade with the countries of the North American Free Trade Agreement (NAFTA) (73.5 percent) or the OECD countries (74 percent). Similarly, underlying the high overall level of intra-industry trade for France (83.5 percent) is a low level of intra-industry trade with Latin America (22.9 percent) and Southeast Asia (38.7 percent) and a high level of intra-industry trade with NAFTA countries (62.7 percent) and OECD countries (86.7 percent). Table 2 also illustrates low intra-industry trade levels for developing

nations (for example, 10 percent for Bangladesh). All of this leads to the conclusion that intra-industry trade is more prevalent among developed nations and that similar developed nations are largely engaged in trading similar types of goods with each other.

Obviously, the goods and services produced by firms in the same industry are not, in fact, identical. Everyone acknowledges that a Volkswagen Golf is not the same as a Peugeot 206. They are similar products delivering similar services, produced using similar technologies, such that they are classified in the same industry, but they are not the same. That is, one must distinguish between goods and services that are imperfect substitutes, as consumers demand many different varieties of similar, but not identical, products in the same industry. In addition, one must explain why the domestic industry does not provide an arbitrarily large number of varieties to cater to the preferences of consumers. Going back to the Germany-France car example, it is clear that Volkswagen has the ability and technology available to produce a car virtually identical to the Peugeot 206, and is thus able to fulfill demand for that type of product. Large initial investment costs, spread over several years, would be required, however, before such a new type of car could be designed, developed, tested, and produced. These large investment costs, giving rise to increasing returns to scale, are the primary reason for Volkswagen, or other German car manufacturers, to produce only a limited number of different varieties. This example also implies that a car manufacturer, being the only producer of a particular variety, has considerable market power, which it takes into consideration when maximizing profits. In short, intra-industry trade flows occur because of: (1) consumer preferences, that is, the demand for different varieties of similar products; (2) increasing returns to scale in production, which limit the diversity in production that the market can provide; and (3) a market structure of imperfect competition consistent with the phenomenon of increasing returns to scale. These aspects, and their interaction, also explain why proximity of demander and supplier is important and why clustering of economic activity is so prevalent.

Proximity and Clustering

Economic activity is clearly not randomly distributed across space. Clustering of people and firms, at various levels of aggregation (continents, countries, regions, cities, and even neighborhoods or sections within cities), is the rule and not the exception. Clustering certainly holds for industrial or manufacturing production, also for specific industries. Examples are the car-manufacturing cluster around Detroit, the film industry in Hollywood, the tapestry industry in Belgium, the financial district in London, or the fashion industry in Paris. The question arises as to why location matters. Basically, two answers exist. The first answer is that natural advantages account for the clustering phenomenon. This answer is essentially based on (geographic) technology advantages and factor abundance, as explained above. Special circumstances—such as whether a region is landlocked or near a coast—can also influence the productivity of the factors of production. To a large extent, these natural advantages and disadvantages are givens, that is, they are not manmade. The second and somewhat more complicated explanation for the clustering phenomenon is that it is caused by the interactions between economic agents. More spe-

cifically, clustering arises as a result of positive external economies of scale that lower a single firm's average costs of production if the industry-wide output increases.

The nineteenth-century British economist Alfred Marshall gave three examples of external economies of scale: (1) an increase in industry-output increases the stock of knowledge for every single firm, lowering the costs and increasing the output of the individual firm; (2) a large industry-wide output supports the existence of a local market for specialized inputs; and (3) a large local market makes labor-market pooling possible. These positive externalities imply that firms (in an industry) want to be located close together; therefore, there is a supply-side concentration force. But because of the costs of transporting goods and services, for example, firms also want to be located close to a large market; therefore, there is a demand-side clustering force. Both types of clustering forces are "endogenous," that is, determined by the economic interaction between consumers, workers, and firms. The exact location is then not so important and could be largely determined by chance or historical accident. New York City, for example, was initially an attractive location for business activity because of its natural harbor. However, for the past 150 years or so, it has been an attractive location in which to establish a firm or to which to migrate simply because it is a large agglomeration that provides all possible intermediate goods and services, a well-connected large market, and all sorts of specialized (labor) inputs.

Interaction

Although it is useful to identify the two main reasons for economic clustering (natural advantages and external economies of scale), the distinction between them is not razor-sharp; the determinants are not independent of each other. There is one main difference between them, however: Natural advantage or disadvantage predetermine a location's production structure, which is not the case with external economies of scale. It was not destined that Seattle or Silicon Valley should become home to a relatively large part of the U.S. aircraft or computer industry, respectively. A small initial advantage can be enough to set in motion a process of self-reinforcing economies of scale. Industrial location is then historically determined, or path-dependent. Only a large shock (like Boeing's decision to relocate its headquarters) or a substantial change in transportation costs (due to globalization or economic integration at large) could lead firms to decide to relocate and thereby bring about a change in the spatial distribution of economic activity.

Natural advantage is a very strong determinant, and in many cases the predominant force. A landlocked country will, on average, be engaged in less trade than a country that has coastal areas. Since trade constitutes a vital transmission mechanism for information or knowledge spillovers, firms will find that their competitiveness is hurt when they locate in a landlocked country. Empirical research estimates, for example, that almost 20 percent of the concentration of U.S. industries can be explained by natural advantages. The impact of natural forces is aptly illustrated in Figure 6, which measures GDP according to four climate zones (tropical, desert, highland, and temperate) and distance to a coastal area (near = less than 100 km from the coast; far = more than 100 km from the coast). The figure shows not only that different climate zones lead to different per capita income levels, but also that within each climate zone a landlocked region is disadvantaged relative to a region along the coast.

Economics literature that emphasizes geographical forces in determining a consistent framework for how firms make industrial location decisions is referred to as "geographical economics." (See, for example, the work of Paul Krugman.) This branch of economics focuses attention on whether or not the ongoing process of globalization, measured as a decrease in

Figure 6: Impact of Geography on Income Level

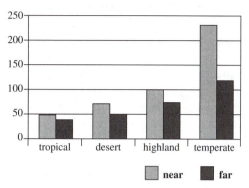

Source: J. D. Sachs, A. D. Mellinger, and J. L. Gallup, "The Geography of Poverty and Wealth," *Scientific American,* March 2001, 62–67.

the costs of interaction (transport costs, trade restrictions, cultural barriers, technological change, and so on), tends to reinforce a core-periphery pattern in location.

To benefit from external economies of scale and to minimize interaction costs, manufacturing firms have an incentive to locate where demand is relatively high or where the supply of their inputs is abundant, that is, they want to locate where other firms and workers have chosen to locate. A core-periphery pattern is, however, not inevitable. If the costs of interaction are either very low or very high, an equal spatial distribution (spreading) of manufacturing activity results. For an intermediate range of interaction costs, a core-periphery pattern results. The geographical economics literature therefore strongly suggests that the ongoing process of globalization will initially favor the establishment of core-periphery patterns in industrial location, as illustrated in Figure 6. As the globalization process continues, however, and the costs of interaction fall below some critical level, firms will start to relocate from the core to the periphery as the advantage of being close to large markets dwindles. This return to a spreading pattern of industrial location would lead to more rapid increases in real income in the disadvantaged locations.

Since, on a global scale from the late nineteenth century onward, the actual changes in the distribution of economic activity among countries and in the degree of economic integration match the predictions of the geographical economics literature quite well, this may be good news for the future of the currently disadvantaged climate zones and landlocked regions; however, the time frame within which these positive changes may occur is more likely to be measured in centuries than in decades.

Steven Brakman
Harry Garretsen
Charles Van Marrewijk

See Also Foreign Direct Investment and Cross-Border Transactions; International Joint Ventures; National Government Policies

References

Brakman, Steven, Harry Garretsen, and Charles van Marrewijk. 2001. *An Introduction to Geographical Economics.* Cambridge: Cambridge University Press.

Fujita, Masahisa, Paul Krugman, and Anthony Venables. 1999. *The Spatial Economy: Cities, Regions, and International Trade.* Cambridge: MIT Press.

Krugman, Paul. 1991. *Geography and Trade.* Leuven: Leuven University Press.

Marrewijk, Charles van. 2002. *International Trade and the World Economy.* Oxford: Oxford University Press.

Summers, Robert, and Alan Heston. 1988. "A new set of international comparisons of real product and price levels estimates for 130 countries, 1950–1985," *Review of Income and Wealth* 34(1), March 1–25.

———. 1991. "The Penn World Table (Mark 5): An expanded set of international comparisons, 1950–1988," *Quarterly Journal of Economics* 106(2), May, 327–368, http://www.nuff.ox.ac.uk/Economics/Growth/summers.htm.

Inequality

In general usage, "inequality" refers to the uneven distribution of social and economic resources among different groups of people. It is commonly used to describe the imbalances in economic opportunities, benefits, or results between rich and poor, skilled and unskilled workers, women and men, whites and minorities, or developed and developing countries. Beyond this simple definition, however, it is an incredibly complex term that has given rise to multiple meanings depending on the context and who is using the term. There is much debate over exactly what constitutes equality/inequality, how to measure it, and how it has developed over time.

Concepts of equality and inequality are usually treated as relational: That is, either concept is analyzed in terms of how the lives of one group or individual compare to other groups and individuals during the same time period. Although it is true that the poor in the modern world are better off compared to the economically disadvantaged of 500 years ago, most economists believe it is more useful to compare the relative positions of rich and poor in the same historical context. Following from this, there is ample evidence that inequality within and among nations is a chronic feature of the modern world. In recent decades, the internationalization of trade, rapid technological innovation, the reorganization of work, and shifting political policies at the national and international level have all contributed to the deepening of inequalities in many areas of social and economic life.

Equality/Inequality: A Brief History of a Contested Concept

American political philosopher Ronald Dworkin has recently argued, "Equality is the endangered species of political ideals" (Dworkin 2001, 172–177). Nowadays, many politicians have rejected the ideal that citizens should share equally in their nation's wealth and resources. For most of the past two centuries, however, concepts of equality constituted a core value in the dominant trends of political thought. Notions of equality first emerged in the modern world from the series of great political struggles against the hierarchical monarchies of the old order in Europe. In the American and French revolutions of the eighteenth century, for example, successful mass movements and political forces rallied around the concepts of *liberty, equality,* and *fraternity* in contrast to the traditionally accepted idea that only certain people (kings and aristocrats) could rule based on tradition or supposedly God-given right. In this epoch, equality was loosely defined as government by consent of the people, or democracy. What constituted the *people* and *democracy* in this vision, however, was highly limited: Political equality was gradually granted to white men with property, whereas slaves, workers, women, and colonized peoples had few political rights. Nevertheless, from this time forward the notion that human beings were political subjects solely by virtue of their humanity was central to political thought and the development of democratic government. In the past two centuries, political struggles have determined what kind of political equality is desirable and to whom it should be applied.

Just as the political revolutions of the eighteenth century were implementing concepts of political equality, so too were the economic transformations of the period prompting critiques of social and economic inequality. In the eighteenth century, the economic system of capitalism—production for profit on the basis of wage labor—developed in Europe, and in the next century it spread around the world. Capitalism revolutionized production and transformed many aspects of economic and social life. Wealth was created on a scale never before seen, but this revolutionary economic system also brought great disparities between the tiny minority who controlled the means of production (capitalists) and the vast majority whose only resource was their labor (workers). Soon many political thinkers, economists, and social movements began to raise demands for equality in the economic sphere. These struggles would eventually center on the extent to which the state should establish equitable social and economic conditions through the redistribution of income and social policies.

Broadly speaking, three distinct intellectual currents in relation to social and economic equality developed in the eighteenth and nineteenth centuries, and to a greater or lesser extent these still dominate discussion today. Classical economic theorists in the neoclassical or utilitarian tradition and their modern-day supporters hold up the unregulated market as the essence of freedom and reject broader notions of relational equality. They believe that economic inequities are natural results of the business cycle and are even valuable for the market and society in the long run as they improve efficiency in production and labor markets. Proponents of classical economics (generally known today as neoliberals and/or libertarians) also view inequalities as a reflection of individuals' free choices over the use of their talents and resources. Differences in

wealth and income are not regarded as problems that need to be solved by political intervention. Indeed, these thinkers maintain that state interference in the natural workings of the market cause inequalities themselves. Contemporary proponents of this view have had great influence on governments in North America and Britain since the 1980s.

Liberal egalitarian theorists, in contrast, reject the idea that inequality is a natural and desirable state of affairs, believing that some sort of economic equality is socially just and essential for social stability and political democracy. Modern egalitarian liberals, including many theorists in the social democratic tradition, aim to reconcile political liberty and economic equality. The most influential theorists in this school of thought, such as John Rawls and Ronald Dworkin, believe that it is impossible to attain justice without at least some measure of equality. Egalitarian liberals accept the capitalist market economy, arguing that it is compatible with both individual freedom and adequate equality if there is sufficient state regulation to balance the two ideals. Therefore, they support redistribution of income to even out standards of living. In general, such thinking is behind the more or less interventionist government policies (industrial policies, monetary and market regulation, social policies, and progressive taxation) of most democratic countries.

Radical or Marxist thinkers constitute the final dominant tradition of thinking on equality. Radical thought originated in critiques of the unrealized equality promised by the French and American revolutions and was most clearly developed by Karl Marx in the second half of the nineteenth century. Marxists uphold the principles of justice and freedom of egalitarian liberalism but maintain that they cannot be genuinely attained within capitalism. According to Marxist analysis, disparities of income, wealth, and power are not side issues that can be made compatible with the market economy. Workers enjoy legal and political freedoms, but their effective lack of economic power inherently puts them at a disadvantage with the capitalists who control production. As the early twentieth-century Marxist Rosa Luxemburg argued, "The hard core of social inequality and lack of freedom [is] hidden under the sweet shell of formal equality and freedom." Social and economic equality can thus only be achieved in a socialist society where production for profit is abolished. Marxist thinking on equality informed many of the socialist revolutions and radical movements of the twentieth century.

Political and economic thinkers also diverge considerably on the question of "Equality of What?" *Simple equality* refers to everyone having the same level of goods and services and is generally rejected by most thinkers, since human beings are recognized as incredibly diverse. Treating people equally in one area, for instance, may lead to considerable inequalities in other areas. For example, equal treatment of nations with considerable differences in economic and political power may result in preferential treatment to those countries that are better able to take advantage of a particular policy. The dominant trend in contemporary thinking among academics and policymakers, therefore, focuses on some sort of *substantive equality,* which takes into consideration the vast differences among social groups and the larger economic, social, cultural, and political context.

Measuring Inequality

Given the contested nature of equality/inequality, it comes as little surprise that the measurement of these concepts is also highly debated. Most studies of inequality rely on official government statistics that measure concrete economic variables such as income or gross domestic product per capita. However, the scope and precision of such numbers has varied over time and by country, and the actual variables and units of analysis being measured may result in different measurements of inequality. Income, for instance, refers strictly to the money that comes from employment, whereas wealth includes income as well as ownership of savings, stocks, and property. Studying the incomes or wealth of individuals, families, or households may lead to different conclusions about inequality because familial arrangements differ from one region or country to the next and fluctuate over time and place.

Poverty lines that measure those families, households, or individuals who fall below a predetermined amount of income per year also vary widely. Until recently, the U.S. Census Bureau used a limited definition of poverty that only included cash income and expenses based on national averages. Recently this agency has experimented with alternative measures that include most potential sources of cash and government transfers as well as adjustments for regional differences in housing and medical costs. Many European countries employ the following standard: Families are in poverty if their income is less than 50 percent of the national median income. In any case, academic institutes, national governments, and international institutions such as the Organisation for Economic Co-operation and Development (OECD) utilize a variety of different methods, all of which have disadvantages and advantages depending on the particular question being explored.

Probably the two most common measurements used nowadays are: (1) the ratio between the richest and poorest in a country; and (2) the Gini index. The Gini index measures the extent to which the distribution of income or consumption expenditure among individuals or households within an economy differ from a perfectly equal distribution. The numbers are meaningless on their own and only make sense in terms of comparisons over time or comparisons of two societies at a particular time. A Gini index of 0 would represent perfect equality, and an index of 100 would reflect perfect inequality. Those countries with numbers closer to 0 are therefore considered more equal, as Table 1 exhibits. A simpler but in some ways more effective measure is the ratio between rich and poor. Usually the richest 10 or 20 percent are compared to the poorest 10 or 20 percent to show the difference between the most affluent and disadvantaged in a society.

The most common measurements of poverty still only use strict economic variables. In 1990, however, the United Nations introduced a broader measure, called the index of human development. This is an important innovation that attempts to measure not only income or wealth but also various "quality of life" indicators such as literacy, health care, education, and access to technology. Similarly, the UN's gender empowerment measure is a pioneering attempt to measure women's participation in the political and economic arenas.

Social and Economic Inequality on a World Scale

In general, most developed and developing countries saw increases in the standard of living from the 1940s to the 1970s. In the advanced capitalist countries, this period was characterized by growing international trade, rapid industrial development, full employment, and an expanding welfare state. Developing countries in Asia, Africa, and Latin America also enjoyed growth, but at a pace and scale much below the economic powerhouses of Japan, North America, and Western Europe.

Yet in the past two decades of the twentieth century, a period of expanded international trade, researchers have noted that by almost any measure, the gap between rich and poor has grown substantially on a world scale. According to the 1999 United Nations Human Development Report (UNHDR), the ratio of the income of the richest fifth of the world's population to that of the poorest fifth increased from 30 to 1 in 1960 to 60 to 1 in 1990. By 1997, it was 74 to 1. The 2003 UNHDR observed that the richest 1 percent of the world's population (around 60 million people) earned as much income as the poorest 57 percent, while the income of the richest 25 million Americans was equal to that of 2 billion of the world's poorest

people. The wealthiest billionaires in the world in 1996—Microsoft chief Bill Gates; the Walton family, who control Wal-Mart; and the Sultan of Brunei—had incomes worth more than thirty-six of the least developed nations put together.

Much of this disparity results from the gap in wealth and income between the advanced Western countries and developing nations. To give some idea of the extent of the change over time, the 2003 UNHDR report notes that in 1820, the per capita income of Western Europe was three times that of Africa; by the 1990s, it had risen to thirteen times as high. The UN study documents fifty-four countries whose per capita income dropped from 1990 to 2001 owing to a deadly mix of famine, HIV/AIDS, wars, and failed economic policies. The majority were in African countries, but there were also numerous representatives from the former Communist countries of Eastern Europe, such as the Russian Federation and the Ukraine; traditionally oil-rich nations such as Saudi Arabia and Kuwait; Latin American nations, including Nicaragua, Paraguay, and Ecuador; and Haiti and Jamaica in the Caribbean. Overall, there are more than 1.3 billion people in the world who live under the UN's poverty line index.

There were some success stories in the 1990s. There was a drop from 30 percent to 23 percent in the number of people worldwide living on less than a dollar a day, largely as a result of income increases in China and India, the world's two most populous countries. Some African countries, such as Benin, Ghana, Mauritius, Rwanda, Senegal, and Uganda, improved their position in the rankings, as did Bangladesh, China, Laos, Malaysia, Nepal, and Thailand. Brazil, Bolivia, and Peru also bettered their situation as a result of social policy initiatives. Although there has been some progress in some developing countries over the past decade, the gap in wealth and incomes between the developed and developing world remains high and has not changed substantially. Table 1 shows some of the contrasts between what the UN labels high-, medium-, and low-development nations.

Table 1: Various Measurements of Social and Economic Inequality between and within Selected Nations

Country and UN Human Development Rank	Survey Year	Ratio of Richest 20% to Poorest 20%	Gini Index	Life Expectancy at Birth in 2001	Education Index	Highest Gross Domestic Product Per Capita 1975–2001 ($US)	Year of Highest Gross Domestic Product Per Capita
High Human Development Countries							
1 Norway	1995	3.7	25.8	78.7	0.99	29,620	2001
3 Sweden	1995	3.8	25.0	79.9	0.99	24,180	2001
4 Australia	1994	7.0	35.2	79.0	0.99	25,370	2001
5 Netherlands	1994	5.5	32.6	78.2	0.99	27,190	2001
7 United States	1997	9.0	40.8	76.9	0.97	34,592	2000
8 Canada	1997	5.4	31.5	79.2	0.97	27,130	2001
13 United Kingdom	1995	7.1	36.0	77.9	0.99	24,160	2001
17 France	1995	5.6	32.7	78.7	0.96	23,990	2001
18 Germany	1998	7.9	38.2	78.0	0.96	25,350	2001
55 Mexico	1998	17.0	51.9	73.1	0.86	8,581	2000
Medium Human Development Countries							
63 Russian Federation	2000	10.5	45.6	66.6	0.93	10,326	1989
65 Brazil	1998	29.7	60.7	67.8	0.90	7,360	2001
69 Venezuela	1998	17.7	49.5	73.5	0.84	7,619	1977
74 Thailand	2000	8.3	43.2	68.9	0.88	6,763	1996
75 Ukraine	1999	4.3	29.0	69.2	0.93	9,303	1989
78 Jamaica	2000	6.9	37.9	75.5	0.83	4,174	1975
99 Sri Lanka	1995	5.3	34.4	72.3	0.82	3,273	2000
104 China	1998	8.0	40.3	70.6	0.79	4,020	2001
111 South Africa	1995	33.6	59.3	50.9	0.83	13,510	1981
127 India	1997	5.7	37.8	63.3	0.57	2,840	2001
Low Human Development Countries							
144 Pakistan	1998–1999	4.8	33.0	60.4	0.41	1,890	2001
145 Zimbabwe	1995	12.0	56.8	35.4	0.79	2,780	1998
146 Kenya	1997	9.1	44.5	46.4	0.73	1,079	1990
152 Nigeria	1996–1997	12.8	50.6	51.8	0.59	1,084	1977
156 Senegal	1995	7.5	41.3	52.3	0.38	1,525	1976
158 Rwanda	1983–1985	4.0	28.9	38.2	0.63	1,643	1983
160 Tanzania	1993	6.7	38.2	44.0	0.61	520	2001
169 Ethiopia	2000	24.8	57.2	45.7	0.38	811	1983
170 Mozambique	1996–1997	7.2	39.6	39.2	0.43	1,140	2001
175 Sierra Leone	1989	57.6	62.9	34.5	0.41	1,070	1982

Source: Adapted from United Nations Development Programme, *Human Development Report 2003* (New York: United Nations, 2003).

Social and Economic Inequality within Countries

Inequality is not simply a global problem *between* so-called First and Third World nations. Income disparities *within* many countries have also escalated. The transition to market capitalism in the former Soviet Union has seen some of the most rapid increases in inequality ever. In the Russian Federation, the income share of the richest 20 percent is eleven times that of the poorest. Between 1987–1988 and 1993–1995, the Gini index rose from 0.24 to an astonishing 0.48. Developing countries in Southeast Asia (Bangladesh, Bhutan, North Korea, India, Myanmar, Nepal, and Sri Lanka) have witnessed economic growth in the past decade, but it too has been unevenly distributed. More than a third of the population of India lives below the country's own national poverty line, while in Bangladesh and Nepal close to half the population is classified as poor.

Even in the richest countries, income inequality has been growing. Incomes have risen rapidly for the top 20 percent of the population in most of the developed countries in the past three decades. Although there is much debate over what has happened to the middle-income groups in the population, it is clear that their share of income has declined in relation to the very rich. For the bottom 20 percent of the population, poverty rates, as measured by subsistence on family income amounting to 50 percent of the national median, remained the same or rose slightly in most European and North American countries during the 1980s and 1990s. Overall absolute income has been rising, so it is possible that some of the poor have seen real income increases in the past two decades. Yet there is evidence from many developed countries that a large proportion of the poor have become even poorer in recent decades, including those who rely on social assistance or poorly paid jobs, live in state housing, or are recent immigrants. Much of this disparity is related to changes in work and

employment: There are consistently high levels of unemployment and underemployment and fewer well-paid jobs with decent benefits and stability. As Michael Storper summarized, there has been a "combination of decline and stagnation at the bottom, moderate growth and relative loss in the middle and big growth at the top" (Storper 2000).

There has been some variation in the developed countries: The most unequal countries in terms of income and wealth are the United States, Israel, Australia, Italy, Portugal, and Greece. In the middle are Canada, the United Kingdom, and most continental European countries. The least amount of income inequality occurs in Japan, Belgium, and the Scandinavian countries. The 1989 Luxemburg Income Study (http://www.lisproject.org), which measured the distribution of income and poverty in twelve developed countries, and a follow-up study conducted by the OECD, found Sweden to have the lowest level of poverty and income inequality and the United States to have the highest. The 2003 UNHDR confirms that these two countries still occupy the top and bottom positions among developed countries.

Adequate educational levels, health care, and literacy may mitigate measurements of income and wealth. Although incomes may be relatively inequitable in Australia, for example, the country is still ranked as the fourth best country on the 2003 UNHDR. The United States consistently ranks among the top countries in the world in terms of gross domestic product per capita, but the high concentration of wealth at the top of society skews average figures, putting it in eighth place on the UN human development rankings. Table 1 illustrates some of these processes for selected nations.

All countries also demonstrate variations between men and women and dominant ethnic groups and minorities. In addition to noneconomic forms of discrimination, there is overwhelming evidence of economic disparities in most variables in both developed and developing countries between the majority group and many indigenous, immigrant, ethnic, or linguistic minorities. Native peoples in all North and South American countries are desperately poor in relation to the dominant ethic group. Many depressed economic regions, such as the Maritime Provinces of Canada, several southern U.S. states, and the northeastern states of Brazil, exhibit substantially lower incomes than the economically successful regions of these countries. Globally, more than 70 percent of the poor population is female, and in virtually every nation women make substantially less than men for the same work.

The United States:
A Case Study in Inequality

In the post–World War II economic boom, the United States consolidated its position as the richest and most influential country in the world. By the mid-1960s, the country peaked in terms of income equality measured by the Gini index even though it remained a highly polarized society in many other aspects. However, from the late 1960s onward, an upward trend toward more income inequality has occurred. In fact, the United States is more unequal now than at any time since World War II.

Without a doubt, the strong economy of the 1990s benefited the richest Americans, but the middle and lower income groups enjoyed little or no growth in incomes. The richest 5 percent made ten times as much income as the poorest 5 percent in 1979. By 1995, the ratio was 25 to 1. Another interesting measure is to compare the distribution of income between the average corporate executive and the average worker. In 1965, corporate executives made twenty times more than the average production worker; by 1989, the ratio had almost tripled to 56 to 1. By 1997, the figure was 116 to 1. Between 1989 and 1997, the salary, bonus, and stock plans of the average executive grew by 100 percent. Needless to say, the middle-income sections of the population did not keep pace, and low-income earners suffered, at best, stagnation, and,

at worst, a decline in their economic positions. On average, real wages for American workers were only slightly higher in 1993 than in 1973, and this can probably be accounted for by the increase in two-income families. Although there may have been some improvement since the late 1990s, many ordinary Americans are just trying to catch up from the losses of the 1980s and 1990s, a process reflected in the fact that the average American now works one and a half weeks more than they did thirty years ago. Finally, many of today's poor—disproportionately single mothers, blacks, Hispanics, and public housing residents—are relatively poorer now than twenty years ago owing to the widening of the overall income disparity and reductions in social services.

Interestingly, black households have improved their relative position since the 1980s as a result of income gains and corresponding declines for many white workers. The gap nevertheless remains substantial. The black poverty rate is at an all-time low, but black household incomes still remain an abysmal 63 percent of white households. By the same token, women have improved their position vis-à-vis men. Average incomes for all women were 54 percent of men's in 1996, a considerable increase over the 39 percent figure in 1985. In addition to entrenched discrimination, part of the reason for women's lower incomes is that fewer women work, and among those who do, fewer work full time for the whole year. Domestic work in the home, which women do much more than men, is also not paid. The narrowing of the income gap has much to do with the overall decrease in men's incomes.

Globalization and Inequality

The term "globalization" is almost as fiercely disputed as "equality." Nicola Yeates offered a useful definition, writing that globalization is "the emergence of an extensive network of economic, cultural, social and political interconnections and processes which routinely transcend national boundaries" (Yeates 2001). There is intense debate among researchers about the actual consequences of globalization. Economists and politicians in the neoliberal tradition are ardent supporters of globalization, arguing that the long-term benefits of increased internationalization of trade, finance, and politics outweigh any potential negative consequences. They maintain that the new global order rules out any attempt to regulate the system through state intervention because companies will simply move their operations to a more profitable part of the world. Any inequalities that do exist are explained as a result of individual differences: The wealthy benefit from having skills that are highly valued, whereas the majority suffer from their lack of marketable talents.

Liberal and radical critics of inequality also disagree over the effects of the global integration of economics and politics. The most pessimistic commentators, known as the hyperglobalists, claim that globalization has created a more open world economy with stiff competition within industries and among countries and growing overall sensitivity to international economic fluctuations. Formerly state-owned and/or managed sectors have been privatized or substantially deregulated, leaving them open to the pressure of market forces. In the pessimistic view, global financial markets have grown so powerful that banks and financial institutions exert a decisive influence on the monetary and social policies of governments, forcing states to reduce social investment. In this climate, multinational companies have been able to negotiate positive investment, production, and taxation benefits from states as well as to force through extensive changes in the organization of work. The resulting shift in labor-market, macroeconomic, and industrial policies has effectively led to the end of full employment and put downward pressures on wages, working conditions, and benefits. Manufacturing jobs that traditionally offered high wages and benefits have restructured, leading to contracting out of production and services

to low-wage companies or sometimes even the transfer of production to other countries with lower wages and benefits. The jobs that have been created have tended to be in low-paid, insecure positions, often in the services sector, that offer few opportunities for long-term advancement. The same process has seen unions lose much of their power so that they have been unable to challenge reforms to labor rights that weaken the bargaining position of workers. Above all, hyperglobalists argue that the traditional nation-state has become largely obsolete owing to the growing power of multinational corporations and international financial bodies such as the International Monetary Fund and the World Bank.

Critics of the pessimistic account rarely dispute the fact that global economic integration has accelerated or that inequalities have increased, yet they do not believe that it is globalization of trade and finance per se that is responsible. Some researchers emphasize technological change, such as the automation of production, and organizational changes in the labor process, which have created a wage and benefits gap between a relatively small sector of highly skilled workers and a larger sector of semiskilled labor whose living standards have not kept up with economic growth. In this account, the reorganization of work probably accounts for much of the growing inequality between rich and poor. Low unemployment used to offset the gap between rich and poor. In the new economy of the twenty-first century, however, this is no longer the case. Having a full-time job no longer necessarily means a secure existence.

Others argue that an increase in inequality has resulted chiefly from shifting political strategies that have been determined by national domestic concerns. They argue that a strong ideological transformation among economists, political parties, and policymakers in favor of the corporate agenda and the weakening of traditional social movements and trade unions has occurred, prompting governments to actively reduce social protections. According to this argument, governments have shifted their ideological and political priorities and now accept the existence of income inequality and high unemployment, reject structural causes of poverty, and promote a more or less socially conservative social policy agenda that stresses individual morality. Globalization is regarded more as a consequence of this political shift than the cause.

The Future of Inequality

The 2003 UNHDR observes that there have been some improvements in a number of poor countries, especially in the area of social programs, but many more countries declined in the 1990s than in previous decades. The overall trend indicates that social and economic inequalities will increase because of immense changes in work, trade, finances, and politics that favor rich countries on a global scale and the already affluent within nations. The exact outcomes will nonetheless be determined by national and international political struggles over the real and perceived gains and losses of globalization.

Sean Purdy

See Also Labor Markets and Wage Effects; National Government Policies; Bank for Reconstruction and Development (World Bank); International Monetary Fund (IMF)

References

Callinicos, Alex. 2000. *Equality.* Cambridge: Polity.
Dworkin, Ronald. 2001. "Does Equality Matter?" In Anthony Giddens, ed., *The Global Third Way Debate.* Cambridge: Polity.
Haveman, Robert, and Edward Wolff. 2001. "Who Are the Asset Poor? Levels, Trends and Composition, 1983–1998." Institute for Research on Poverty, Discussion Paper 1227–01, April.
Held, David, Anthony McGrew, David Goldblatt, and Jonathan Perraton. 1999. *Global Transformations.* Cambridge: Polity.
Henwood, Doug. 2003. *After the New Economy.* New York: New Press.
Oxley, Howard, Jean-Marc Burniaux, Thai-Thanh Dang, and Marco Mira d'Ercole. 1997. "Income Distribution and Poverty in 13 OECD Countries." *OECD Economic Studies* 11, no. 29, pp. 55–94.
Luxemburg, Rosa. 1900. *Reform or Revolution.* London: Militant Publications.
Storper, Michael. 2000. "Lived Effects of the Contemporary Economy: Globalization, Inequality, and Consumer Society." *Public Culture* 12, no. 2, special issue on "Millenial Capitalism," pp. 375–409.
Yeates, Nicola. 2001. *Globalisation and Social Policy.* London: Sage.
United Nations Development Programme. 1999. *Human Development Report 1999.* New York: United Nations.
———. 2003. *Human Development Report 2003.* New York: United Nations.

International Financial Markets

Global financial market activity consists of the transactions and financial flows that occur within bond, equity, derivatives, banking, and exchange rate markets around the world. The importance of the globalization of financial markets lies in the fact that the financing process is an integral part of both commercial and non-profit-making activities. In addition, the finance process is affected by other sectors, such as economic activity, politics, and differing country cultures. The surge in financial market activity during recent years may be attributed to deregulation and technological improvements, which now allow access to worldwide markets at reasonable transaction and information costs. The trading activity taking place on organized exchanges and over-the-counter (OTC) markets is undertaken by participants who differ in terms of their foreseen investment horizons, return objectives, and tolerance to risk.

Globalization of financial markets has brought about higher efficiency and competition, yet one should not overlook the fact that the potential for the spreading of financial crises is higher in a global marketplace. It is therefore important to ensure that adequate systems are in place to deal with such eventualities, both at international and national levels as well as in individual organizations. Other concerns about the globalization of financial market activity center on whether the current system is in fact channeling long-term funds to finance real business activities, especially in the case of less developed countries.

A General Overview

Over the past few decades, financial market activity around the world has been stimulated by a combination of improved technology, deregulation, and financial innovation. This has resulted in the integration of different financial markets across the globe—the globalization of financial markets. In a wider context, this process has been coupled with corresponding patterns in trade, labor, and political and cultural ideas. For the purpose of this discussion, examples and illustrations are largely drawn from bond, equity, and derivatives markets, given that financial services and exchange rate activities are being treated in separate sections of this book.

Traditionally, investors tended to shy away from holding foreign financial assets owing to inherent country and exchange rate risks as well as exchange controls. Gradually, private investors started to delegate the management of their portfolios to financial institutions, such as through participation in collective investment schemes. This helped to overcome the barriers of risk management, as investments were more likely to be backed by technical knowledge, and the higher amounts of managed funds implied a wider scope for diversification benefits. Countries started to realize that controls on financial flows were becoming less effective—and indeed these had to be gradually dismantled if new financial investment was to be attracted. This resulted in a deregulation process in several countries, especially in the 1980s, which furthered the scope of cross-border financial flows and the resulting globalization of financial markets.

Advances in communications and transaction-processing technologies led to a shift away from physical trading floors to computerized trading systems. This resulted in controlled transaction costs, given that automated execution systems, such as electronic communication networks (ECNs), reduce the required interaction between counterparties as well as execution time. Technology has also led to a higher degree of information accessibility and to more efficient computation of elaborate calculations that are necessary in the assessment of risk and in the pricing of some products, such as derivatives. The value of the latter instruments depends on the price of an underlying asset such as a basket of stocks, a financial variable such as an interest rate, or a physical commodity such as oil.

In this way, globalization is the integration of domestic activity with that of other countries. Local transactions have to be viewed in the context of a larger global market that is present irrespective of whether transactions with foreign economies occur.

Global Market Participants

Trading participants in financial markets are spread across the world, and these differ in terms of their home currencies, transaction costs, risk-management policies, and time zones. Market participants are likely to have different objectives; some portfolio investors may have set long-term investment horizons, whereas day traders aim to profit from the price differentials of a financial asset prevailing during different times of the day. Trading on securities, derivatives, and currency markets takes place on organized exchanges or OTC. In the latter case, the counterparty is typically a bank or a financial institution. In addition, trades also differ according to whether they are

spot transactions, which are settled immediately, or transactions settled at a future date agreed upon in advance, such as derivative contracts.

One of the major impacts of globalization of financial markets is that it offers financial managers a higher degree of flexibility in obtaining funds for their companies. For example, a company may issue securities overseas, or it may borrow on the home markets, if it would like to exploit its local goodwill, and then "swap" the debt into another currency if it prefers to do so. Swaps are derivative contracts that enable financial managers to control risks by altering their exposure to changes in interest rates, exchange rates, or other variables.

Trading on Global Financial Markets

During the 1980s, governments and large companies started to take a more active approach to financing their activities by emphasizing the issuing of quoted securities rather than borrowing money from banks. This disintermediation trend was partly fueled by the fact that banks had to limit the expansion of their loan portfolios in order to comply with new capital adequacy requirements.

Large bond issues became more common, with London becoming the major venue for international bond issues. Such bonds were issued either with short-term maturities or with longer maturities, such as twenty-five years. In this way, banks diversified their roles in the company financing process—from direct lenders to underwriters and/or guarantors. In their underwriting role, banks undertake to purchase any portions of the security issue that remain unsubscribed, whereas when acting as guarantors, banks agree to compensate the bond holders in case the borrower defaults on its obligations.

Stocks and bonds are traded around the world almost twenty-four hours a day on different exchanges; trading begins in London within a couple of hours of the closing of exchanges in Tokyo, and trading activity in New York commences prior to the closing in London. Equity holding has become more widespread among households, whereas traditionally this was mainly restricted to wealthy individuals and institutions. One possible reason for this is that households are becoming aware of the importance of saving up for their retirement.

The increased number of companies raising funds through public offerings means that it is important for these financial instruments to be accessible to a wide variety of investors. Therefore, large companies and multinationals often list their equity on different exchanges or tap overseas sources of funds by floating primary issues on foreign exchanges.

Derivative contracts are intended for the usage of larger companies and portfolio managers in controlling financial risks, such as exchange rate and interest rate risk. Despite this, the reputation of derivatives has been tarnished because they can also be used for heavy speculative activities. Indeed, in some cases derivatives were (partly) responsible for large losses incurred by financial institutions such as Britain's Barings Bank in 1995. Apart from OTC contracts, a number of standardized derivatives are traded on various exchanges. These include interest rate futures of various maturities, which are traded on exchanges such as the Chicago Mercantile Exchange and the Singapore International Monetary Exchange; bond futures, where the underlying instruments are typically government bonds; and futures on commodities such as agricultural products, petroleum, and precious metals, which are traded on various exchanges, including the Chicago Board of Trade.

In contending with this new business, exchanges sought to modernize their trading systems, partly because they had to compete with other trading mechanisms, such as OTC markets and electronic trading systems (Island and Instinet, for example). Overall, there was a ten-

dency to shift from physical trading floors in favor of electronic systems. Exchanges also sought to lengthen their period of activity through after-hours sessions.

Exchanges modified their roles in this changing environment as well, and today they are trading a wide variety of products. One example of a new market developed by exchanges is the trading of derivatives that have quoted securities or stock price indices as their underlying asset. Exchanges are also involving themselves more actively in the clearing of transactions, that is, the process of settling transactions through the delivery of assets or cash after execution.

The competition between exchanges is often considered a mixed blessing. Competition instigates market reform, which can result in reduced transaction costs. However, there are concerns that, as trading splits among different exchanges, the liquidity associated with large volumes of transactions occurring at the same venue may dissipate away. Despite this, one should note that traders can make informed decisions about the optimal venue that will result in the best deal, and they can transact on the exchange that they choose at the touch of a button or a phone call. In this way, it might be misleading to think about different trading venues as completely separate entities—if liquidity moves away from one venue, traders may move accordingly.

A significant part of trading activity and cross-border business financing tends to be intermediated within definite areas called financial centers, such as New York, London, and Tokyo. In such centers one finds a concentration of financial institutions and exchanges as well as high volumes of trade in currencies, international securities, and derivatives.

The Effects of Globalization on Financial Market Structure

Globalization has radically reshaped the financial markets in terms of structure and relationships between different players. As exchanges compete for business and borrowers seek finance, institutions often lay particular importance on establishing themselves in the United States, given that U.S. securities markets provide access to a large tap of funds. This may be due to the fact that issuing public securities was historically popular among U.S. businesses, whereas European and Japanese businesses relied more on bank finance. U.S. institutions have also emphasized the possibility of overseas expansion, as deregulation trends minimized barriers to entry. Such factors resulted in considerable merger and takeover activity. As financial institutions establish their presence overseas, there are potential benefits resulting from the transfer of innovative business and risk-management methods, even if such developments may prove to be difficult for those entities facing new competitors. The latter typically go through processes of modernizing their operations and revising the portfolio of the services they offer.

Another factor resulting from such trends is the likely increase in competition as the number of financial institutions in a country increases. This is particularly important in those countries where the financial services industry tended to operate as an oligopoly dominated by a few large firms. Overseas expansion should enhance competition, yet as institutions consolidate through merger activity, one should reassess the possibility of the global industry becoming dominated by a handful of major players. In addition, overcoming the cultural differences in cross-border merger activity may also prove to be a challenge.

A related concern associated with the industry becoming concentrated is that the failure of a large player may have excessive repercussions on the global industry, as this might compromise the repayment of obligations to a large number of counterparties. This is particularly possible in derivatives activity, where a significant portion of OTC contracts has clustered with the select major players.

Merger and acquisition activity among financial institutions has wider implications for management teams. In particular, when management policies are deemed unsatisfactory, the share price of the particular institution is likely to fall, making it a more attractive takeover possibility. In other words, mediocre management teams are more likely to be replaced. Similarly, in an increasingly efficient and globalized securities market, shareholders cannot be neglected; this explains why management teams emphasize the generation of shareholder wealth, which entails generating profits in order to boost the value of the company's shares, and the distribution of attractive dividends.

One might question the role of smaller institutions in such an environment. It was traditionally believed that small institutions could barely survive competition from larger ones. Gradually, the potential for smaller institutions to adapt quickly to change and their role in satisfying the needs of smaller markets (niche markets) became more apparent. However, these ideas conveyed a "large or small" philosophy with little role for medium-sized institutions. Nowadays it is being realized that mid-sized institutions can also survive, if they focus on their own strengths and formulate successful business strategies.

Such arguments also apply to the securities markets. Although these markets are dominated by the big names, such as the New York Stock Exchange, Nasdaq, and the London Stock Exchange, the role of smaller stock exchanges should not be overlooked. Smaller exchanges should serve as a means through which medium-sized companies can tap funds. Such businesses may find the marketing campaigns and the fees involved in listing on major exchanges to be prohibitive and therefore conclude that it might be more practical for them to list on smaller exchanges in their own region. Likewise, large companies are not likely to list on distant exchanges unless the additional liquidity and access to capital make it worth the effort and cost. Another important role of smaller exchanges is the gathering and provisioning of market information. Such information is now required on a global basis, as fund managers increasingly diversify their portfolios and seek the best risk-return combinations.

Smaller exchanges are also targeting cross-listing possibilities from companies already listed on larger exchanges. Through the use of appropriate technology and infrastructure, the securities listed on smaller exchanges may be accessible internationally, and this may reduce the traditional disadvantages of remoteness from the major financial centers. In this respect, the infrastructure of exchanges (especially the smaller ones) should be able to interact with that of other exchanges. Compatibility between systems is gaining importance as exchanges seek to interconnect trading systems and develop a global market structure based on transparency. Smaller exchanges should also be on the alert to spot and to take advantage of opportunities when they come along. These opportunities may be in the form of proposed mergers or agreements aimed at closer cooperation.

Flexibility and Efficiency on International Financial Markets

The advantages of a global financial market include the efficient allocation of worldwide savings toward the best investment opportunities in terms of their return-risk combination. For any given level of risk, investors select the business opportunity with highest expected returns, whereas for any given level of expected return investors allocate their funds toward the lowest-risk projects. In an ideal market, the owners of financial capital select the best investment opportunities according to these criteria, irrespective of whether the funds are financing local or overseas activity. In this way, the companies having the most efficient business proposals would be the first to obtain funding.

This degree of flexibility is not only afforded to the owners of financial capital but also to borrowing companies. Large firms may borrow funds in whatever currency they require and then swap the debt to another denomination, as discussed above. Today, most companies face no regulatory impediment from seeking to obtain financial services from overseas institutions, and in this way there is greater flexibility in shopping around for the best deal—whether in the form of issuing securities or bank finance. Despite this, one should note that smaller businesses might still shy away from overseas funding sources on the grounds that information search costs might be high. In addition, different languages and business practices may compromise the success of some overseas transactions.

Another change in the structure of financial markets relates to the increased importance of institutional investors. Individual investors tend to entrust the management and investment of their savings to financial institutions on the grounds that they might not have the time and expertise to manage their portfolios themselves. Institutional investors therefore hold large portions of the financial assets of industrialized countries. Portfolio managers invest in international financial assets for diversification benefits, possible capital gains from exchange rate movements, and higher overseas growth rates. This enhanced role of institutional investors may be considered a positive feature, as long as these entities endeavor to allocate their clients' funds efficiently. Large fund-management companies may also realize transaction cost savings and exercise significant voting powers and management influence in the companies in which they have invested. Such advantages are not likely to be realized by the typical individual investor. The expectations of institutional investors have also instigated innovation in various areas, such as new risk-management products and more efficient trading systems.

Other Implications of Global Financial Markets

Information is an important component in the global financial system. The Internet gives investors access to the latest news, security trading prices, and financial announcements, in most cases in real time. Therefore, the overall level of information has increased. Yet, one may argue that asymmetric information still characterizes financial markets; for example, some market participants have access to insider knowledge, and scandals such as Enron and WorldCom in 2002 showed how published information may not always reveal the true financial standing of an entity. Information asymmetries may be even more pronounced in a global financial system, where funds typically pass through different institutions and markets while on their way from the owner to the ultimate borrower. This implies that financial institutions and investors may be indirectly exposed to counterparties whom they do not even know.

In this way, risk management becomes more important in a global financial market. Risk-management methodologies have become more sophisticated, and financial institutions typically manage their own risks and offer derivative products to help other firms in managing their risks. When financial institutions take on the risks of their clients, some of these risks might net out, given that they may be symmetrically opposite positions—say, having to pay interest in yen to one client, but receiving interest in yen from another client. Financial institutions also seek to reduce or hedge any remaining positions that they deem excessive. Exchanges that trade derivatives manage counterparty risk by asking customers to deposit money in margin accounts. Risk management may actually turn out to be a complex activity, because extreme events that impact on the value of financial assets are difficult to forecast. In addition, risk-management techniques are far from perfect; for example,

most of them are based on the assumption that liquidity is available on the markets, and this might not hold in times of market stress, such as the U.S. stock market crash of October 1987.

Globalization of financial market activity is also relevant to other aspects of economic activity. For example, countries should strive to attract financial investment, which is a precondition if the economy is to develop at a faster rate, especially if direct foreign investment is lacking. In this respect, active and transparent financial markets are important for economic growth. Globalization is also likely to affect the monetary policy of the country. For example, in setting their interest rate targets, central banks need to take account of the rates offered in other countries, and similarly, if they target money supply growth, this is likely to affect the exchange rate, which impacts on cross-border investment prospects.

Financial Crises and Contagion

The potential for contagion of financial problems across businesses and financial institutions is higher in a global marketplace than when trade is limited to fewer trading partners or stays within regional boundaries. Financial crises emanating from one economy may spread to other countries, as witnessed in the Southeast Asian crisis originating in Thailand in 1997. This crisis spread to other regional economies and also to the United States through higher risk premiums on corporate debt. There are different explanations as to why financial crises can spread. For example, it may be the case that as a financial crisis appears in one country, international investors reassess their portfolio decisions about investments in a number of other countries that may be prone to similar problems. Following this, some investors withdraw their funds from such markets, causing liquidity problems. An alternative explanation is that countries experiencing a crisis may devalue their currencies in the hope of improving their balance of payments position. When this happens, neighboring countries follow suit in order to avoid losing their competitiveness, and this results in a series of competitive devaluations. Such processes may be amplified through currency attacks by speculators.

As soon as the prospect of a financial crisis becomes evident, flows of funds to the countries that may be affected tend to reduce drastically, as investors rush to sell their financial assets in order to repatriate their money and invest it in less risky markets. This worsens the situation of borrowing economies, propagating the crisis. The process may go on as investors subsequently shy away from other financial systems, either because they tend to become more cautious, or because they may have to sell other financial assets in order to raise cash to make up for the money they lost elsewhere.

The extent to which different international markets are correlated, and the potential for contagion, are still debated issues. However, one may assume that the potential for contagion is higher in a globalized financial system than in an (unrealistic) situation where markets are insulated from one another.

When analyzing the potential causes of crises in the financial systems of developing economies, one may mention a variety of factors. In the case of the Latin American crisis of the 1980s, one may speak of a combination of shortcomings on the part of the borrowing and lending countries as well as a range of external factors. For example, the borrowing countries at times were inefficient in their use of funds. The lending banks might have been inattentive to the fact that they were highly exposed to this group of countries, or perhaps they took for granted official support from various institutions. In addition, a drop in the price of oil at the beginning of the 1980s, increasing interest rates, and an appreciating U.S. dollar worsened the prospects of less developed countries. In the case of the Asian financial crisis, one may mention factors such as insufficiently diversi-

fied economies, high exposure to foreign currency borrowing, and inadequate loan-management processes on the part of commercial banks. Although some of these factors have improved, other shortcomings may take longer to overcome, and the issue of adequate regulation and supervision of financial systems and institutions is always at the fore.

Reforming the International Financial System

Given that the global financial system may undergo problems when a crisis occurs, efforts are being directed at reforming the system. International institutions at the forefront of these developments include the IMF, the Basle Committee of Banking Supervisors, and the International Organization of Securities Commissions. In addition, countries also establish their own safety nets, such as the lender of last resort function of central banks and local regulatory and supervisory functions. The objectives of financial reform include strengthening the international monetary and financial systems as well as devising ways for them to operate with a higher degree of transparency and efficiency. Institutions such as the IMF have an important role in such developments; however, the stabilizing function of this institution is at times criticized on the grounds that funds are typically provided to countries in crisis only if they implement deficit-cutting polices, when an expansionary fiscal policy might be desirable to revitalize the economy. Yet it is important to note that often it is not easy to arrive at the "correct" solution to a problem, given that this is likely to involve a complex interlinking of various factors, including exchange rate management, regulatory policies, and negotiations with creditors.

In order to secure continued inflows of financial capital, less developed countries (and indeed all countries) must inspire confidence in their financial systems. This entails the presence of institutions whose roles include administration of sound monetary policy and supervision of the financial system. Other structural reforms might also be needed in a wider context to encourage competition, invest in education, and reevaluate country debt-management policies. Developed countries might also contribute to the expansion of less developed economies by promoting trade with these countries and, in some cases, by renegotiating or forgiving debts.

Some of the salient trends in the extensive area of financial reform include an emphasis on what governments, international organizations, and financial institutions can do to prevent problems from occurring. Some of the recommendations that economists have suggested include: monitoring the factors that may lead countries to a crisis, updating national regulatory and supervisory functions continuously, establishing sound risk-management processes for financial institutions, implementing international standards, and enhancing the degree of transparency within countries.

Other Challenges of
Financial Market Globalization

The globalization of financial markets is at times questioned on account of the policies adopted in developed economies. One concern is whether business managers, in their quest to satisfy shareholders, are focusing on the generation of short-term profits to the detriment of long-term objectives. Indeed, the pressure to generate returns has, in extreme cases, led companies to inflate or invent profit figures, as witnessed in the scandals of Enron and World-Com.

Another concern is that a large portion of the international flows of funds no longer represents the transfer of real resources for productive investment, but rather financial capital in search of quick profits, which tends to be volatile in nature. In particular, the rise in the activity of foreign exchange and securities markets was not matched by an equivalent increase in world output. Despite this, there is not much that countries can do to mitigate the hastiness with which fund managers reallocate their portfolios. Indeed, an understanding that investors will be able to withdraw funds quickly is a precondition for attracting financial capital. It is also argued that most of the daily transactions on securities markets represent investors or fund managers who are exchanging claims on the capital of companies, rather than investors wishing to finance business activity. One possible concern about such trends is that financial capital is diverted from long-term productive uses to speculation. Again, this highlights how important it is that countries and businesses continue to inspire investor confidence if they are to replace outflows of short-term financial investment with other inflows.

The increased number of day traders on the markets during recent years has led to concerns about whether such traders have increased volatility. For example, Internet stocks have often been the target of speculative trading, and this led to high volatility, excessive valuations, and ultimately a crash in the prices of these stocks in 2000. Volatility in the flows of financial capital may bring about uncertainty and instability in financial markets through the resulting shocks in variables such as interest rates and exchange rates. This would have further repercussions on real business activity as firms' costs of borrowing money and buying foreign goods change.

The financial crises experienced in recent decades have exposed the risks inherent in the globalization process. As capital flows become more volatile, these risks increase. In addition, less salient risks arise from the interaction of different cultures; at times, the less developed economies lag behind. The solution to such problems is not likely to be the reversal of the globalization trend, given that this would also withdraw the inherent opportunities in the process. Yet, it is important to devise policies that lead to more resilient economies and financial systems as well as ensuring that the benefits of globalization are distributed in an equitable manner among nations.

Silvio John Camilleri

See Also Balance of Payments and Capital Inflows; Currency Crisis and Contagion; Dollarization; Exchange Rate Movements; Financial Services; International Monetary Fund (IMF)

References

Chorafas, Dimitris N. 1992. *An Introduction to Global Financial Markets.* Berkshire, UK: McGraw-Hill.

Clark, Gordon L. 2000. *Pension Fund Capitalism.* Oxford: Oxford University Press.

Eichengreen, Barry. 1996. *Globalizing Capital: A History of the International Monetary System.* Princeton, NJ: Princeton University Press.

Grabbe, J. Orlin. 1986. *International Financial Markets.* New York: Elsevier Science.

Johnson, Hazel J. 2000. *Global Financial Institutions and Markets.* Malden, MA: Blackwell.

Kenen, Peter B., ed. 1995. *Understanding Interdependence: The Macroeconomics of the Open Economy.* Princeton, NJ: Princeton University Press.

Leyshon, Andrew, and Nigel Thrift. 1997. *Money/Space: Geographies of Monetary Transformation.* London: Routledge.

Martin, Ron, ed. 1999. *Money and the Space Economy.* West Sussex, UK: John Wiley and Sons.

Singh, Kavaljit. 2000. *Taming Global Financial Flows: A Citizen's Guide.* New York: St. Martin's.

Stiglitz, Joseph E. 2002. *Globalization and Its Discontents.* New York: W. W. Norton.

Valdez, Stephen. 2000. *An Introduction to Global Financial Markets.* New York: Palgrave.

International Indebtedness

International indebtedness refers to money owed by governments on a global scale to private and public banks and international financial institutions such as the International Monetary Fund (IMF) and the International Bank for Reconstruction and Development (World Bank). Nations rely on bank loans to finance social and economic development projects as well national defense and military campaigns.

The advanced capitalist countries in North America, Europe, and Japan have substantial national debts, but their relatively strong economic and political position in the international economy has allowed them to weather the severe global economic and financial storms of recent years. In many poor nations, however, spiraling external debt has meant economic and social devastation. Beginning in the 1980s, heavily indebted countries in Africa, Latin America, and Asia found it increasingly difficult to pay off their debts owing to falling export prices for the products they sold in international markets, a decline in the value of their currencies in relation to the U.S. dollar, and economic mismanagement and corruption by national elites. The IMF and the World Bank, effectively controlled by the United States and its closest allies, negotiated "rescue" packages for many developing countries but dictated stringent conditions, such as the necessity of paying a high proportion of national income toward debt repayment, cutting state spending on social and economic programs, and further integrating their economies in the world market. This program has resulted in deepening poverty and inequality in much of the developing world. International debt is therefore not a simple economic fact; it is closely related to ideology and politics on an international level and needs to be viewed in the context of the rise of global integration in trade and finance in addition to shifting international political strategies by the dominant states.

Debt, National Governments, and the International Financial System in Historical Context

Until the twentieth century, national states had few debts. In the eighteenth and nineteenth centuries, governments in Europe and the United States did borrow from private banks to pay for wars, but usually the debts were small and short term. A glance at the ratio of U.S. government debt to gross domestic product (GDP) during that period shows moderate borrowing during wartime and almost complete repayment during peacetime. In the 1830s, U.S. President Andrew Jackson even paid off the entire national debt. Government borrowing was largely unregulated: State officials simply sought out the best deals with private domestic or international lenders for short-term loans.

As international trade and domestic industrialization increased in the late nineteenth and early twentieth centuries, however, the leading states began to more actively intervene in economic and social life to ensure prosperity and growth. Financial markets and credit blossomed as the growing profits from industrial development were channeled through banks and other lending institutions. Gradually, nations began to use debt financing to partially or fully bankroll major state projects such as the building of highways, railroads, and power plants. The two world wars also saw a massive increase in state borrowing, and relatively high debt levels were maintained after hostilities ended in most developed nations. Yet sustained economic growth, a steady rise in taxes, and international financial regulation in the post–World War II period allowed governments in most developed countries to adequately manage their debt levels.

Much of the stability in world financial markets from the 1940s to the 1970s resulted from international regulation consciously established by the leading states after World War II. There was a generalized belief in policy circles in most Western countries that the postwar capitalist economy was likely to revert back into marked economic instability like that experienced in the 1930s unless significant steps were taken to control key aspects of the economy. In addition to social welfare spending and domestic economic regulation, the United States and Britain also wanted to construct an international monetary system that would favor the growth of international trade. Thus, the Bretton Woods international monetary system (named after the town in New Hampshire where the agreement was negotiated) and its key components, the IMF and the World Bank, were created in 1946.

The Bretton Woods system had two major objectives. The first was to provide stability in the price of international currencies, making it easier and less risky for businesses to conduct international trade. It accomplished this by fixing currencies to gold—a form of money separate from the currency of any nation. The price of the U.S. dollar, the most powerful currency, was fixed to gold, and other national currencies, such as the English pound, the French franc, and the German mark, set their currencies in relation to the U.S. dollar. No country was allowed to unilaterally change currency

prices. The IMF was responsible for managing negotiations between countries in the changing of currency prices and for providing loans to member states that were having difficulties with imbalances between the products they exported and imported. The World Bank was established during the same period to provide member countries with economic reconstruction and development funds. A second major aim of Bretton Woods was to prevent private financial operators from freely moving money around the world in the search for speculative gains. Private banks were allowed to move funds to finance trade and productive investment, but states were given the right under this system to control the activities of financial institutions so that investment in goods and services was prioritized.

Critics of the massive debts owed by developing countries still use the term "Bretton Woods" to refer to the current international monetary system, and the IMF and the World Bank are certainly still key players in the global political economy. Yet the Bretton Woods system was transformed significantly by the early 1970s under pressure from growing multinational corporations and international banks as well as through conscious political changes initiated by the administration of U.S. President Richard Nixon in response to concerns about growing economic competition with Japan and European nations.

By the late 1960s, U.S. political and economic leaders increasingly asserted that the Bretton Woods arrangements were restricting their global economic and political interests. Massive military spending in the 1950s and 1960s during the Korean and Vietnam wars had created a structural deficit in external payments; that is, the United States was spending much more money than it had, forcing it to borrow from both domestic and international lenders. The states that were in surplus with the United States were demanding their right according to the Bretton Woods agreements to transfer their surplus dollars into gold. By the late 1960s, however, U.S. gold reserves were quickly depleting. Moreover, powerful multinational companies and international banks resented the restrictions that prevented them from easily transferring money to other countries to make profits. Rather than taking the necessary steps to ensure the maintenance of the system, the U.S. government decided to break from Bretton Woods altogether and establish what Peter Gowan has aptly called the "Dollar–Wall Street regime."

In August 1971, the U.S. government unilaterally decided to withdraw from the gold standard and use the dollar itself as the world standard. The fixed exchange rates of Bretton Woods were abandoned, and a floating exchange rate system was introduced based on whatever values the U.S. government deemed appropriate. President Nixon also used the economic and political power of the United States in the Middle East to force the countries in the Organization of Petroleum Exporting Countries (OPEC) to quadruple oil prices in 1973, which harmed the main competitors of the United States in Japan and Europe, who depended on oil from the region. This move also produced windfall profits for oil producers that were subsequently deposited in private U.S. banks. Finally, the restrictions on the flow of finance capital were substantially reduced in several key areas, allowing banks and other financial institutions to shift money across national borders with fewer obstructions. Part and parcel of this latter process was the increased involvement of the IMF and the World Bank in new and broader types of lending to developing countries.

The general significance of the Dollar–Wall Street regime in relation to international indebtedness may be summarized as follows:

1. The U.S. government could now effectively control the direction of world monetary policy by unilateral changes to the value of the dollar. The floating exchange rate set up was a useful tool that allowed the United States to avoid the adjustments that would have otherwise

been required by the country's status as a debtor nation. If the United States had continued under the fixed exchange rate system, it would have had to pay for its indebtedness through unpopular domestic austerity measures, as many heavily indebted, poor nations were forced to do in the 1980s and 1990s.

2. Since the dollar became the dominant world currency, most nations and businesses in the world turned to U.S. banks and lending institutions centered on New York's Wall Street to finance investment. The great bulk of international financial market activity continues to occur on Wall Street and its satellite, the City of London.

3. As the main source of the world's credit, the U.S. financial system could now play an even more central role in world trade. A large proportion of the goods bought and sold in world markets are sold in dollars. U.S. companies importing or exporting are far less affected by changes in the value of the dollar than other countries, especially developing nations.

4. The successive reduction of state regulations in international and national financial markets since the 1970s has allowed the big commercial banks to lend money to whatever country or business they want with few restrictions. In 1970, 90 percent of international financial transactions were related to investment in trade and long-term development; by 1995, 95 percent of such transactions were purely short-term, speculative ventures unrelated to the production of goods and services.

5. The role of the IMF and the World Bank has shifted in this new international financial regime. They became auxiliary players responsible for "policing" countries suffering financial troubles and organizing "bailouts" of countries unable to pay their debts. As Gowan argued, when a U.S. bank faces default in the do-

mestic economy, it is rescued by U.S. tax-payers, who foot the bill for government bailouts. When a U.S. bank has trouble collecting abroad, however, the population of the borrowing country ends up bailing out the bank through austerity programs enforced by the IMF and World Bank.

The dollar and Wall Street do not have a complete monopoly in global financial markets. Other currencies, such as the British pound, the German mark, and the Japanese yen, have also been significant, as have non-U.S. banking centers, but the dollar and U.S. commercial banks have dominated international financial markets since the 1970s. By 1995, over 75 percent of all international bank loans were negotiated in the U.S. dollar, and it served as the currency in half of all world trade.

Rich Nations and International Debt

Contrary to popular belief, the accumulated debt of a handful of rich nations absolutely dwarfs the money owed by developing nations. In 1999, for example, the debt of developing countries (including the former Eastern bloc) was estimated at $2.32 trillion, or about 7 percent of total world debt. At the same time, the public debt of Canada was $600 billion, that of France was $750 billion, and Japan weighed in with a national debt of $2 trillion. The most heavily indebted nation was the United States, at $5 trillion, representing over half the country's GDP. Yet this represented only slightly more than the 47 percent of GDP in debts that the United States had in 1939. Belgium enjoys one of the most successful economies in the world, yet its accumulated debt equaled 130 percent of GDP in 1995.

Unlike the developing countries, the rich countries have not experienced social and economic devastation. This is understandable given that in the first instance the rules have been largely orchestrated in favor of the United States and its allies. Moreover, the developed countries have relatively healthy economies and have maintained respectable rates of economic growth through the postrecession 1990s. Consequently, their credit rating is high, enabling them to borrow money at relatively low interest rates. Until recently there was actually a general assumption in the international financial community that debt was a healthy feature of strong economies and that it contributed positively to economic development. In fact, there is no automatic link between economic success and the state of the national debt.

Nevertheless, the 1980s and 1990s witnessed a concerted campaign among supporters of neoliberal economics in the developed countries to pay down the annual deficit and the accumulated debt. (The "deficit" is the shortfall between government revenues and expenses in any given year; the sum total of the deficits up to the present become the "accumulated debt.") It was argued that high deficits and debts were a drain on economic resources and affected international competitiveness. Most rich countries regularly run deficits; the United States, for instance, has had a budget deficit every year since 1970. Couched in technical arguments about the economic necessity of cutting deficits, the debate was really about the appropriate role of the federal government in the economy and society. There is little convincing evidence that the high debt levels of any developed country really affect their creditworthiness or international economic competitiveness. In domestic politics, however, the campaign against deficits and debts has been quite successful in the Anglo-Saxon countries in eroding popular support for the notion that the government should actively maintain high levels of internal social and economic investment. Consequently, social programs such as welfare, education, and health care have been significantly reduced, resulting in increasing socioeconomic inequality within many wealthy countries.

Poor Nations and International Debt: The Borrowing Years

Governments in most poor countries shared in the widespread international optimism of the post–World War II years that growing international trade would bring rising national incomes and improvements in social and economic structures. They believed that what was needed first and foremost was heavy capital investment to overcome the structural obstacles of underdevelopment and colonialism, such as poor infrastructure in communications, power and water supplies, urban facilities, health care, and education. Lacking internal sources of finance, developing nations looked to the banks of the Western world to finance development. From the lenders' point of view, the poor countries appeared to be safe risks with substantial opportunities for profit: From the 1950s to the 1970s, commodity prices were high, contributing to economic growth in many developing countries. By and large, incomes grew and economic development occurred during these years. In addition to Western aid and loans from the IMF and World Bank, African, Latin American, and some Asian nations enthusiastically sought loans from private banks to finance ambitious development projects. In 1970, the total external debt load of developing countries was US$62 billion; by 1980, it had multiplied by seven times, to US$481 billion. By 1996, the figure stood at US$2 trillion, more than thirty-two times the 1970 level. Western lenders eagerly maintained, in the words of Citicorp chairman Walter Kriston, that unlike individuals, "A country does not go bankrupt."

It is crucial to emphasize that international banks and Western governments saw development loans and aid as both economically and politically profitable. Economically, the rise in oil prices sparked by the OPEC crisis of 1973 provided Western banks with huge quantities of money that they were keen to expand by lending to poor countries at low interest rates with generous payment provisions. Demand for credit was low during this period in the industrial nations, forcing commercial banks to seek borrowers in the developing world. Politically, development aid by Western governments and World Bank loans were consciously regarded as tools to counter potential radical social challenges from the poor "South," a strategy Walden Bello in 1999 called "containment liberalism." World Bank lending rose from an average of US$2.7 billion a year in the early 1970s to US$12 billion by 1981. Antipoverty programs funded by the loans formed part of an economic modernization scheme to develop poor countries while leaving in place authoritarian governments friendly to Western interests. It comes as little surprise that the largest recipients of World Bank loans were Indonesia, the Philippines, and Brazil, all ruled by military dictatorships during this era. As Karin Lissakers puts it, foreign loans were "the glue that held together fragile political coalitions of urban workers, a growing middle class of mostly public sector employees, and the military. . . . Foreign money enabled governments to survive without resolving fundamental political and economic inequities in their countries" (Lissakers 1991).

Poor Nations and International Debt: The Crisis Years

In the 1980s and 1990s, most developing countries in Latin America, Eastern Europe, Africa, and Asia became trapped by escalating debt levels and came to depend on the IMF and World Bank to reschedule their debts and maintain lines of commercial credit. The price they paid for the support of these international institutions was austerity programs that forced governments to slash already low levels of social security, shift their production to one or more export cash crops to sell on the international market, and devote a large percentage of their export earnings to debt repayment. By any measure, social and economic inequality has deepened considerably in the developing world. In Africa, in particular, high debt levels, in combination with economic restructuring, natural disasters, and the HIV/AIDS pandemic, have led to an unparalleled human tragedy.

There were some "success" stories in the economic development of poor countries during the early part of the 1970s. Sustained economic growth was experienced in several Latin American countries, such as Brazil, and in numerous sub-Saharan African nations, including Kenya, that compared favorably with growth rates in the rest of the world. Much of this growth was what Giovanni Arrighi in 2002 termed "perverse": fragile, short term, and unequally distributed among the population. Yet it disproves the prominent argument that "character flaws" among certain peoples in the Third World were responsible for underdevelopment.

Still, the tables turned in the 1980s against those countries that had borrowed heavily from Western banks. As recession in the industrial countries began in the early 1980s, the prices of raw materials from developing countries sunk to their lowest level since the 1930s. Many poor countries were dependent on one or two commodities to gain foreign exchange, so the steep decline in prices hampered their ability to pay off not only the debt itself, but also the mounting interest rate charges. In addition, many developing countries were harmed by technological advances in the West, such as artificial substitutes for sugar, which undercut the export products that they relied on. Since many of the loans had variable interest rates and were pegged to the U.S. dollar, the steady increase in interest rates and the value of the U.S. dollar struck a hard blow against the borrowing nations, which found themselves in the unenviable position of negotiating new loans to pay off old ones.

The debt crisis was severely exacerbated by mismanagement and outright theft by government officials in some developing countries, many of whom were not elected and ruled only with the military and financial support of Western nations. Loan and aid money was stolen to personally enrich economic and mili-

tary elites, who frequently transferred the wealth abroad. This "capital flight" occurred regularly in the weeks and months preceding the financial crises of the 1980s and 1990s. In 1980–1982, capital flight reached 70 percent of borrowing for eight leading debtor states. According to the World Bank, capital flight in Venezuela exceeded its foreign debt by 40 percent in 1987. Similar capital flights were repeated in Mexico in 1994 and Brazil in 1998. According to Susan George, more than US$418 billion of funds borrowed by Third World countries flowed back to the rich countries in the 1980s (George 1977). Between 1997 and 2002, this figure reached US$700 billion. Thus, the population as a whole in the developing world became responsible for paying back mounting debts and interest costs that they never benefited from in the first place.

By the mid-1980s, more than seventy debtor nations in the Third World were forced to renegotiate their loans to private and state banks under the sponsorship of the IMF and World Bank. In the 1990s and early 2000s, countries facing financial crises because of their inability to pay back their loans, including Mexico, Brazil, Indonesia, South Korea, Malaysia, Russia, and Argentina, were also subjected to a variety of new loans, loan repayment schemes, (reduced) aid proposals, and bailout packages (collectively referred to as structural adjustment programs, or SAPs) that were intended not only to guarantee repayment to the lenders but also to restructure economies to further integrate them into the new global economy dominated by Western countries. The SAPs came with strict conditions, such as: (1) radical reductions in government social and infrastructure spending; (2) wage cuts to reduce inflation and make export products cheaper and more competitive; (3) liberalization of imports from the rich countries and incentives to encourage more export production for the world market; (4) removal of restriction on foreign investment in industry and financial services; (5) the devaluing of local currencies in relation to the dollar to make exports more competitive; and (6) the wholesale privatization of state companies and deregulation of key economic sectors. In addition to acceptance of these conditions, poor countries also had to agree to monitoring and enforcement by the IMF and World Bank, which had the power to withhold loans if the economic policies of the borrowing nations went off track.

In terms of ensuring the repayment of loans, the new loan arrangements have been successful. Western lenders have seen a steady flow of funds from repayment. These repayments have scarcely dented the overall level of the debts, however, because the amounts are so large in relation to the economic activity occurring in most poor nations. Taking on new loans to pay for old ones has contributed to a "debt spiral" in which countries get deeper and deeper into debt. Most countries barely manage to pay the debt service and interest charges, let alone the debt principal. In the sixteen countries of sub-Saharan Africa, the US $200 billion debt amounted to 110 percent of national income in 1994. Debt servicing alone was $10 billion per year, which was about 20 percent of export earnings, or 7 percent of national income. The average citizen in Tanzania or Zambia, for instance, owed external creditors twice what they earned in 1994. In Uganda, full debt service charges were equivalent in the same year to seven times the value of annual export earnings. In 1996, Nicaragua paid over half its national revenue just to service the debt. Overall, the developing world now spends US$13 on debt repayment for every US$1 it receives in grants. In combination with the negative consequences of SAPs, debt repayment continues to be an unmanageable drain on the ability of poor countries to invest in productive and social services and build healthy, environmentally sustainable economies. Table 1 presents the most recent figures available, which clearly illustrate the crushing burden of debt in relation to economic activity in many of the most heavily indebted poor countries.

Proposed Solutions to the Debt Crisis

The destitute state of many poor debtor nations provoked concerted protest both within the Third World and in the West by the 1990s. Even Western politicians and former World Bank economists, such as Joseph Stiglitz, have harshly criticized the human tragedies caused by debt repayment, assigning blame in particular to the SAPs created by the IMF, the World Bank, and the Western nations that control them. Three main solutions have been proposed. First, some governments and IMF reports have recommended rescheduling of the debts, that is, changing the terms of repayment and allowing more time to pay. This proposal has largely been rejected because many countries are still unable to generate the type of economic recovery required for long-term repayment. The Heavily In-debt Poor Countries (HIPC) initiative launched by the rich nations through the IMF and the World Bank in 1996 called for the voluntary write-off of debt by lending institutions. Aimed at the poorest nations whose debt averaged more than four times their annual export earnings, it has been heavily criticized for abolishing parts of the national debt of some countries in order to ensure repayment of the largest portion. Furthermore, it does not aim to help countries develop their economies to reach a stage where they may actually repay their debts.

The third solution proposed for the debt crisis is debt forgiveness. Supported by many charities, churches, and social movements, such as Jubilee 2000, it has even gained the support of some Western politicians, such as British Deputy Prime Minister Gordon Brown. The debt-forgiveness movement points out that the levels of Third World debt are insignificant compared to the economic resources of the rich nations and that debt forgiveness is the only rational and just solution to the crisis. They argue that there are historical precedents: In the chaotic years of the Great Depression of the 1930s, for example, Britain, France, and Italy actually defaulted on loans to the U.S. gov-

Table 1: Key External Debt Returns for Selected Developing Countries
(average percentages, 1999–2001)

Country	Total External Debt (EDT) to Exports of Goods and Services (XGS)	EDT as % of Gross National Income	Total Debt Service as % of XGS	Interest Service as % of XGS
Argentina	375	50	67	30
Bangladesh	178	33	8	2
Bolivia	327	59	38	11
Brazil	337	43	81	24
Central African Republic	766	84	12	4
Chad	462	73	10	2
Chile	164	55	28	8
Democratic Republic of Congo	1,121	257	2	2
Ecuador	198	102	22	10
Egypt	140	30	9	4
Ethiopia	598	91	19	6
Gambia	415	120	9	1
Honduras	210	88	14	3
Hungary	93	64	42	14
India	131	21	12	5
Indonesia	205	99	23	9
Malaysia	41	56	6	2
Mexico	89	29	27	7
Mozambique	569	125	11	1
Nicaragua	702	306	37	6
Paraguay	86	37	11	4
Peru	284	53	23	14
Philippines	114	67	17	7
Poland	129	39	32	5
Russian Federation	140	63	16	7
Sierra Leone	1,100	178	89	12
Sudan	710	156	3	0
Tanzania	500	75	11	3
Turkey	207	65	40	11
Uruguay	227	49	35	15
Venezuela	113	30	25	9
Yugoslavia	379	123	4	2
Zambia	626	178	14	4

Source: World Bank, *Global Development Finance* (Washington, DC: World Bank, 2003).

ernment, but Washington "forgave or (forgot)," as the *Wall Street Journal* noted at the time. In any case, how the debt crisis plays out in the future will depend on the outcomes of the social and political struggles both within and among rich and poor countries over trade, finance, and economic development strategies.

Sean Purdy

See Also Currency Crisis and Contagion; International Monetary Fund (IMF); Foreign Aid

References

Arrighi, Giovanni. 2002. "The African Crisis: World Systemic and Regional Aspects." *New Left Review,* no. 15 (May/June) pp. 5–36.

Adelman, Morris Albert. *OPEC: The Genie Out of the Bottle: World Oil since 1970.* Cambridge, Mass.: MIT Press, 1995.

Bello, Walden, with Shea Cunningham and Bill Rau. 1999. *Dark Victory: The United States and Global Poverty.* London: Pluto.

Chomsky, Noam. 1999. "The People Always Pay." *Guardian,* January 21, 1999.

Chossudovsky, Michel. 1997. *The Globalization of Poverty: Impacts of the IMF and World Bank Reforms.* New York: St. Martin's.

Danielsen, Albert L. *The Evolution of OPEC.* New York: Harcourt Brace Jovanovich, 1982.

George, Susan. *How the Other Half Dies: The Real Reasons for World Hunger.* 1977. Montclair, NJ: Allanheld, Osmun.

Global Issue, www.globalissues.org.

Gowan, Peter. 1999. *The Global Gamble: Washington's Faustian Bid for World Dominance.* London: Verso.

Lissakers, Karin. 1991. *Banks, Borrowers, and the Establishment: A Revisionist Account of the International Debt Crisis.* New York: Basic.

Rocha, Geisa Maria. 2002. "Neo-Dependency in Brazil." *New Left Review,* no. 16 (July/August) pp. 5–33.

Sinclair, Timothy J. 2000. "Deficit Discourse: The Social Construction of Fiscal Rectitude." In Randall D. Germain, ed., *Globalization and Its Critics: Perspectives from Political Economy.* London: Macmillan.

Watkins, Kevin. 1994. "Debt Relief for Africa." *Review of African Political Economy* 21, no. 62 (December) pp. 599–609.

Williams, Gavin. 1994. "Why Structural Adjustment Is Necessary and Why It Doesn't Work." *Review of African Political Economy* 21, no. 60 (June) pp. 214–225.

World Bank. 2003. *Global Development Finance.* Washington, DC: World Bank.

International Joint Ventures

An international joint venture (IJV) is formed when a parent company located abroad establishes an affiliate firm in a host country with a local firm as a partner. The joint venture is established when both the parent and the host firm are able to benefit from their strategic positions and comparative advantages. IJVs are a relatively recent feature of foreign direct investment (FDI). This form of industrial organization flourished after World War II. Recent experience, however, has shown that the mutual advantages of the partners may often erode over time, leading to termination of the relationship. In many cases, the affiliate firm may end up being wholly owned by the parent company.

In the less developed countries such as China, the nations of Eastern Europe, and Russia, a very large volume of FDI is still in the form of IJVs. China, which has the highest number of joint ventures in the world, encouraged this form of industrial organization right after it began implementing its liberalization policies in 1978. Eastern Europe and Russia have also subsequently encouraged joint ventures with limited success. Large firms such as General Electric, General Motors, Ford, Toyota, Unilever, Coca-Cola, and others have used IJVs as a major part of their global corporate strategy. In the more developed world there are several noteworthy joint ventures as well: Coca-Cola and Nestle have a joint venture in Japan; Proctor and Gamble and Fater have joint productions in Italy; and Whirlpool and Philips have jointly owned affiliates in Europe.

International joint ventures did exist in the nineteenth and early twentieth centuries, but they were not very popular forms of foreign direct investment at the time. IJVs evolved primarily in the post–World War II era as many newly independent countries adopted policies that protected domestic firms ("infant industries") from international competition. As these state and privately owned firms grew in size and started taking advantage of scale economies and efficiencies arising from learning-by-doing, it was clear that these "infants" needed some help in order to grow up: Substantial transfer of technology from abroad was necessary. Consequently, under the watchful eye of the host governments, these firms started forming alliances with globally recognized foreign firms. Multinational companies also realized that, given market saturation in the more developed countries and the protective nature of many developing country markets, joint ventures were a viable area for future growth.

Firm-Specific Advantages

Joint ventures should be seen in the context of transactions cost and contract theory/property rights literature. This literature demonstrates that fundamental imperfections in market conditions may induce certain forms of collusion. There are benefits and costs to both parties when they collude. On the benefits side, a joint venture seeks to reduce the underlying high transaction costs that both firms must bear if they invested independently. However,

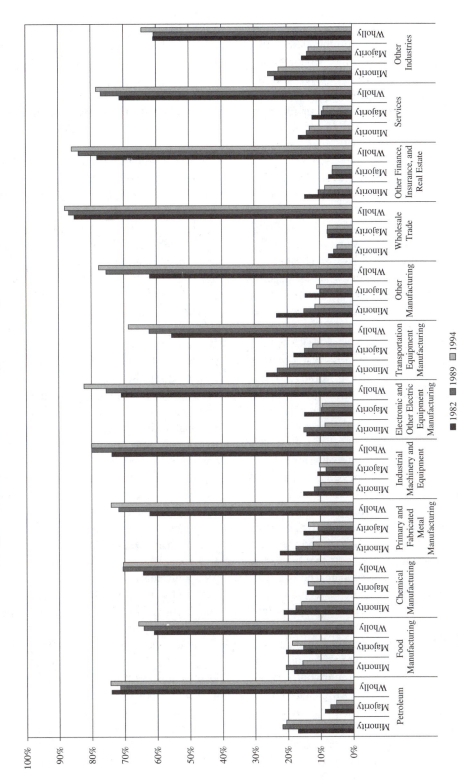

Figure 1: The Use of Ownership Forms by Industry, 1982, 1989, 1994

■ 1982 ■ 1989 ▨ 1994

Note: The bars represent the share of affiliates with minority, majority, and whole ownership by U.S. parents by industry for 1982, 1989, and 1994.
Source: Mihir A. Desai, C. Fritz Foley, and James R. Hines, Jr., "International Joint Ventures and the Boundaries of the Firm," NBER Working Paper, 2002.

this form of industrial organization also gives rise to "moral hazard" and other strategic problems that joint ownership entails. In other words, a joint venture is formed if both the parent and the local partner firm perceive a need to have a mutually beneficial affiliate that unleashes the forces of synergy and mutual complementarity that more than offset the increased costs associated with shared control of the affiliate firm.

More specifically, IJVs are established when certain local firms have ownership-specific advantages with respect to local inputs and are more efficient (compared to the foreign firms) in carrying out day-to-day operations in the local area. The local firms have an advantage in gathering relevant information at all stages of planning, production, and distribution. In many cases, the local firms possess better knowledge of local laws, are able to train the local workers better, and almost certainly have better access to political sources that help them overcome formidable legal hurdles and bureaucratic roadblocks in the host country. Investments are thus more secure and high yielding if channeled through the local firms. For the local firm, an international alliance creates the possibility of acquiring superior process and product technologies and managerial know-how, and it provides access to larger financial resources abroad. The local firms also benefit from skilled-worker training programs and facilities of the parent firm and the international distribution networks that the parent firm may share with the affiliate. The local firm is sometimes able to "co-brand" its products to benefit from the reputation of the multinational enterprise.

In addition, both the parent firm and the local partner benefit from internalization of production: In some cases, input coordination may be better between jointly owned firms than between separately owned firms. IJVs also have a better ability to price-discriminate in various markets and are able to reduce import tariffs on intermediate goods. Some economists have attempted to classify these factors

under three categories: ownership-specific advantages, location-specific advantages, and hierarchical or internalization-specific advantages.

Role of the Government and the Market Environment

Historically, domestic content laws and legal ownership limitations have been one of the most important reasons behind IJV formation. The governments of China and India, for example, specifically prohibited 100 percent foreign ownership in many sectors. Given these laws, many multinational firms found that a joint venture with a local firm was the only way of getting a foothold in the local market.

There are at least three important extra-firm exogenous factors that may encourage formation of joint ventures. First, political risk is considered to be one of the most important considerations behind IJV. Historically, some governments in less developed countries have nationalized a number of wholly owned multinational affiliate firms. IJV reduces political risks associated with asset nationalization. A host country is less likely to threaten asset nationalization if some of the assets are owned locally. A joint venture thus serves as an *insurance* against possible takeover attempts by a future government.

Second, IJVs may be formed simply to avert stiff competition. If a local firm in a near-monopoly market teams up with a foreign firm, both firms avoid a possible fallout from a duopolistic market-share rivalry, and they also create an entry-deterrence for a third international firm that is contemplating entry into the local market. When a monopolistic input-seller forms a joint venture with a monopsonistic input-buyer, possible problems of bilateral monopoly are also avoided.

Third, the local government may not be a neutral player in the IJV game: There is evidence that governments sometimes create import tariff barriers, foreign ownership limits,

Table 1: Hazard Rates of Manufacturing Joint Ventures Located in the United States (Based on a Survey of 92 U.S. Firms)

	Age							
	1	*2*	*3*	*4*	*5*	*6*	*7*	*>7*
Total terminations	5.4	9.2	15.2	10.4	13.3	11.8	16.6	35
Dissolution	4.3	3.4	3.8	4.5	6.7	5.9	7.1	12
Acquisition	1.1	5.7	11.4	6.0	6.7	5.9	9.5	22
Number at risk	92	87	79	67	60	51	42	31

Notes: Hazard rate is the ratio of terminated joint ventures surviving to that age. Rates are computed relative to numbers at risk in the relevant age group and will not sum to one horizontally. The last row shows the number of initial joint ventures minus previous terminations and those still alive but younger than column age.

Source: Bruce Kogut, "The Stability of Joint Ventures: Reciprocity and Competitive Rivalry," *Journal of Industrial Economics* 38, no. 2 (1989): 183–198.

and domestic content laws to encourage or discourage formation of IJVs. Import tariffs discourage exports from abroad and encourage domestic production but create well-known deadweight losses. If domestic production is carried out by foreign capital, deadweight loss from import tariffs may be offset by the surpluses from capital flow and productivity gains for the domestic firm. A government may increase import tariffs to maximize such gains.

Joint Ventures and National Welfare

Since a joint venture reduces cost (from technology transfer) but increases market power (from collusion), the net welfare effect on the host country is ambiguous. Consider a sector that historically enjoyed near-perfect competition. A collusive joint venture in this sector would probably increase price because of collusion, but it would also decrease costs. The net welfare effect is positive if the cost-reducing effect offsets the market-concentration effect and the new producer surplus plus consumer surplus exceeds the consumer surplus prior to formation of the joint venture.

From the global perspective, the overall welfare effects are also predictable. If joint ventures are established in the host country to avoid high tariffs on importables, much of new investment may be investment-diverting and not investment-creating. The investment-creating effect must outweigh the investment-diverting effects for world welfare to rise.

Future of Joint Ventures

There is some doubt whether phenomenal growth of joint ventures would continue in the long run. In an integrated world, with better-coordinated government policies and fewer policy distortions, joint ventures would be set up based mainly on firm-specific organizational advantages, and not on government-dictated domestic control laws and tariff structures. If IJV synergy is based on organizational learning for both the parent and the local firm, it is possible that after a few years both firms will exhaust all avenues of learning from each other, and one firm may start free riding on the other's contribution. Since the inputs provided by both firms have "intangible" qualities (how does one quantify the value of local political connections and knowledge of local cultures?), one party may not be able to verify the quality of the other's input. This may lead to a phenomenon known as moral hazard: the risk that an IJV will break down if both the partners cannot monitor each other's input quality. Indeed, many IJVs have collapsed after a few years. As Table 1 shows, joint ventures located in the United States have displayed a propensity to break down within a short period of time.

An International Finance Corporation study (Miller et al. 1996) corroborated this view. The study showed that parent firms and their affiliates often develop serious disagreements about input valuation. This, of course, is the flip side of intangible qualities of their respective contributions. How does the parent firm value the affiliate's reputation, access to the local political power base, and appropriateness of technology? How does the affiliate decide the optimal equity structure, debt-equity ratio, dividend policy, future investments, and many other fundamental issues if the partners' contributions are hard to assess? Should an IJV export goods to a third-country market where the parent firm has a wholly owned subsidiary? Moreover, since an IJV is an independent entity, the shareholders of both the parent and the local firm must deal with an additional layer of complexity: Shareholders of the parent firm and the shareholders of the affiliate may develop contradictory interests. For example, the local firm may lose profit if the foreign firm uses transfer pricing techniques. Essentially, the problem is that of having two masters. A divided loyalty of the affiliate may harm both the local and foreign firms.

As a result of these problems, Mihir A. Desai et al. (2002) have noted that the trend now is an increasing ownership of the affiliate firm by the parent firm. In all twelve industries studied, the authors showed that wholly owned affiliates have become more popular over time (see Figure 2). At the same time, there was also a distinct shift away from minority or even majority ownership patterns. Wholly owned subsidiaries are apparently becoming more popular once again. A rapid pace of globalization may actually decrease the extent of firm-level international alliances. Would a local and a global firm play cooperative or noncooperative games in the long run? In a world with fewer cross-border restrictions, the future of joint ventures is as unpredictable as the future of collusion in uncontrolled oligopolistic markets.

Dipankar Purkayastha

See Also Foreign Direct Investment and Cross-Border Transactions; Industrial Location and Competitiveness; Strategic Alliances

References

Desai, Mihir A., C. Fritz Foley, and James R. Hines Jr. 2002. "International Joint Ventures and the Boundaries of the Firm." NBER (National Bureau of Economic Research) Working Paper.

Kogut, Bruce. 1989. "The Stability of Joint Ventures: Reciprocity and Competitive Rivalry." *Journal of Industrial Economics* 38, no. 2:183–198.

Miller, Robert R., Jack D. Glen, Frederick Z. Jaspersen, and Yannis Karmokolias. 1996. "International Joint Ventures in Developing Countries: Happy Marriages?" International Finance Corporation Discussion Paper 29.

Figure 2: Formation of Joint Venture

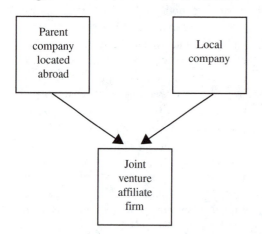

International Migration

International migration defines a change of residence—temporary or permanent, legal or illegal—that crosses national boundaries. Sociocultural practices and political and economic structures in migration receiving countries often differ substantially from a migrant's country of origin. Further, the increased scope and scale of international migration during the latter half of the twentieth century has served as a driving force fueling economic globalization and socioeconomic change. As compared to historical experience, more recent patterns of international migration exhibit far greater variety in the sources and destinations of human movement. These highly visible and sometimes massive movements of people have long been the subject of academic scrutiny, and this interdisciplinary research addresses the myriad and often interrelated aspects of international migration: types of migration (location choice, length of stay), push and pull factors, migration policies, remittances, and the domestic effects of international migration.

Scope and Scale of International Migration

Between 1965 and the end of the twentieth century, world population nearly doubled, rising from 3.3 billion to more than 6 billion people (Table 1). In the same period, the volume of international migrants rose from 75 million to 175 million, an increase of 133 percent. As a percentage of world population, international migrants increased gradually through the latter half of the century to 2.9 percent owing to a reduction in global population growth rates and renewed acceleration of international migration.

Between 1970 and 1995, Mexico was the largest source of international migration, sending more than 6 million people, primarily to the United States (Table 2). Mexican emigration has been motivated by economic factors, whereas other major labor-sending countries have had additional catalysts for emigration, such as revolution and civil war. These include

Table 1: Migrants and World Population, 1965–2050 (in millions of people)

Year	World Population	No. of Migrants	%
1965	3,333	75	2.3
1975	4,066	84	2.1
1985	4,825	105	2.2
2000	6,057	175	2.9
2050	9,000	230	2.6

Source: United Nations, *Statistical Yearbook 2001* (Geneva: United Nations Population Data Unit, Population and Geographic Data Section, 2002).

Table 2: Top Migration-Sending Countries, 1975–1995 (in millions of people)

Country	Net Number of Emigrants
Mexico	6.0
Bangladesh	4.1
Afghanistan	4.1
Philippines	2.9
Kazakhstan	2.6
Vietnam	2.0
Rwanda	1.7
Sri Lanka	1.5
Colombia	1.3
Bosnia and Herzegovina	1.2

Source: United Nations, *Statistical Yearbook 2001* (Geneva: United Nations Population Data Unit, Population and Geographic Data Section, 2002).

Table 3: Top Migration Destination Countries, 1970–1995 (in millions of people)

Country	Net Number of Immigrants
United States	16.7
Russian Federation	4.1
Saudi Arabia	3.4
India	3.3
Canada	3.3
Germany	2.7
France	1.4
Australia	1.4
Turkey	1.3
United Arab Emirates	1.3

Source: United Nations, *Statistical Yearbook 2001* (Geneva: United Nations Population Data Unit, Population and Geographic Data Section, 2002).

Table 4: Top Countries, Migrants as a Percentage of Total Population, 2000

Country	Percent
United Arab Emirates	73.8
Kuwait	57.9
Jordan	39.6
Israel	37.4
Singapore	33.6
Oman	26.9
Estonia	26.2
Saudi Arabia	25.8
Latvia	25.3
Switzerland	25.1

Source: United Nations, *Statistical Yearbook 2001* (Geneva: United Nations Population Data Unit, Population and Geographic Data Section, 2002).

Afghanistan (4.1 million), Kazakhstan (2.6 million), and Rwanda (1.7 million).

The United States is the most common destination for international migrants, having taken in 16.7 million migrants between 1970 and 1995, as much as the next five largest migration host countries combined (Table 3). Although Western industrialized countries dominate the list of top migration destinations, Saudi Arabia, India, Turkey, and the United Arab Emirates are also important recipients of international labor, hosting a total of 9.3 million migrants between 1970 and 1995.

Measuring international migrants as a percentage of total population brings forth a substantially different list of countries (Table 4). Middle Eastern countries, small in population and wealthy in valued natural resource endowments, attract relatively large quantities of international workers to fulfill the needs of service, retail, and manufacturing sectors. These predominantly Muslim countries also experience substantial migration within the region. Nearly three-fourths of the population of the United Arab Emirates is foreign born, followed by 57.9 percent in Kuwait and 39.6 percent in Jordan. Approximately one-fourth of the populations of Estonia and Latvia are immigrants, primarily from the Russian Federation and the former Soviet Union.

Historical Overview

Although not exhaustive of the motivations or reasons for international migration, the history of international migration can be divided into four distinct types or phases: mercantile migration, forced migration, industrialization migration, and postindustrial migration (Hirschman et al. 1999; IOM 2003; Massey et al. 1998).

Mercantile Migration

The colonial expansion of European powers between 1500 and 1800 dominated global immigration flows. The nascent colonial powers, primarily in Western Europe, sought new sources of productive inputs to fuel expanding commercialism and consumption by a growing middle class and thus undertook to make use of vast and seemingly unused resources, particularly in Asia, Africa, and the Americas. The global volume of European migrants to colonized areas is unknown; however, their numbers were sufficient to transform the socioeconomic structures of the colonized areas, imparting European culture, language, religion, and institutional infrastructure. These expansions primarily include the British influence in North America, Africa, and South Asia; the Iberian presence in Central and South America; and the French colonization of West Africa and the Caribbean. On a smaller scale, German colonization efforts focused on North America, Africa, and the Pacific Islands, whereas Dutch colonies were scattered in North and South America, Africa, and East Asia.

International migrants were of three general varieties. The most significant in number were settlers seeking to escape religious or ethnic discrimination or depressed economic conditions in Europe. Particularly in Britain and France, migration was employed as a method to alleviate poverty by conscripting paupers and wards of the state to migrate as settlers to colonized areas. In order to maintain colonial authority, an important, although relatively small, number of public administrators and military officials also inhabited colonized areas. However, of greatest economic significance were the entrepreneurial migrants who sought to capitalize on the trade potential between the colonies and the home country. These migrants promoted large-scale exports of agricultural products and natural resources via plantation production systems that absorbed large quantities of land and minimized production costs through economies of scale and, in some cases, the use of indentured or slave labor. Such plantations were common and most successful in India, East Africa, and the Americas.

Forced International Migration

Forced international migration involves the involuntary dislocation of people across national boundaries. Although forced migrations occur for numerous reasons, such displacements of people have most commonly occurred in the context of slave trade and colonialism, with the most significant levels of activity during the seventeenth, eighteenth, and early nineteenth centuries. The large acquisitions of capital, in the form of land and natural resources in colonized areas, generated an immediate labor shortage, since the technological capacity of the time required substantial labor input in the productive process.

The importation of slaves to colonized areas provided a cost-effective means of solving a labor-shortage problem without disrupting the social hierarchy of the colonial power. Much of the work associated with the establishment of colonies was physically demanding and required relatively low skills; it was thus considered socially inappropriate for many of the early colonizers to perform it. The slave trade, particularly to the Americas, constituted an expansion of the active slave trade among warring African nations. Upon the arrival of Europeans, many African chiefs found it lucrative to sell or trade enemy slaves. Global population in 1800 was approximately 1 billion people; in all, nearly 12 million African slaves were brought to the New World between the sixteenth and nineteenth centuries.

From a social perspective, slaves made up a separate lower class in the receiving country. Indeed, as pieces of property, slaves were afforded few rights, and issues of the integration or assimilation of these immigrants—common issues today—were not relevant. Until the abolition of slavery (in approximately the mid–nineteenth century), these groups remained officially apart from the host country society.

The economic role of slaves, however, was of major importance. The slave system classified those individuals as property, much like land or equipment, and they had value arising from their direct labor power. Land tended to be abundant in colonized areas, often given freely by the colonial authority, such that it held little value as an asset. As the scarce resource in the productive process, slaves had a relatively high value in comparison to other inputs, and they were often used as collateral in the extension of credit. Slave prices were thus highly monitored, and the property rights of owners over slaves were clear and enforced.

Industrialization Migration

The advent of the Industrial Revolution sparked a wave of migration that began in the early nineteenth century and lasted until the Great Depression, with a substantial reduction of migration flows during World War I. The Industrial Revolution marks the beginning of unprecedented increases in productive capacity resulting from the widespread application of new technology, primarily in Western Europe and its former New World colonies. The majority of these "industrial" migrants were skilled Europeans seeking to take advantage of the new and expanding job opportunities.

Demographically, the period of the Industrial Revolution is typified by a large surge in urbanization as production facilities organized around resource and distribution channels, thus attracting labor to available jobs in growing urban centers. The attraction of labor—or any productive resource—is, however, a general concept; thus migration during industrialization occurs both internally and internationally and, in either case, primarily to urban destinations. Population growth also accelerated in the nineteenth century as birth rates rose and death rates fell owing to improvements in medical technology.

The period of industrialization is also characterized by nationalism and revolution. For example, the Ottoman and Russian empires collapsed during this period, splitting into distinct, ethnically defined nations and motivating minority groups within the new nations to emigrate to escape nationalistic discrimination. During the early part of the twentieth century, Eastern European Jews, in particular, constituted over 70 percent of all international migrants to the United States.

Most European migration occurred from southern countries to the more industrialized north. The experience of the United States during this time period is unique. On the path of industrialization, the United States attracted a large share of immigrants to its urban centers, primarily on the East Coast, and many neighborhoods emerged in large cities where ethnically similar immigrants would cluster. However, with a large western expanse, the United States offered substantial opportunities for frontier and farm community settlement. The country thus not only attracted international migrants but also saw major flows of east-to-west internal migration within the United States itself.

International migration during industrialization tended to be permanent household migration. Most migrants left their countries of origin without a strong expectation of returning in the near future, and migration often occurred as a family unit. One notable exception to the pattern was the migration of Chinese men to the western United States. Leaving their families behind, these immigrants provided labor during the Gold Rush and western railroad expansion. Socially, migrants clustered together in the destination country, retaining many of their cultural practices and traditions, but direct ties to the home country were typically weak.

Government attempts to limit immigration appeared in the United States and elsewhere in the 1880s. Recent large waves of migrants from, for example, Eastern Europe had brought many people to U.S. shores who had ethnic and religious backgrounds different from the mainstream Euro-American culture, and they were predominantly low-skilled workers. In 1882 alone, more than 780,000 immigrants entered the United States. Anti-immigrant sentiments were escalating. Congress thus passed several pieces of legislation barring entrance to political offenders and "lunatics" (1882), polygamists and those "afflicted with dangerous diseases" (1891), and Asians and illiterates (1917), the latter by overriding a presidential veto. Australia and the major countries of Western Europe enacted similar restrictions during this time period.

Postindustrial Migration

After World War II and during a new wave of industrialization, especially in the 1960s, worldwide migration began a period of acceleration; however, the patterns and characteristics of this period of migration, which persisted into the twenty-first century, differ substantially from those of earlier episodes. With the advent and growth of the commercial travel industry, the feasible range of source and destination countries for international migration expanded such that, by the end of the twentieth century, foreign enclaves and influences were common in nearly every part of the world.

There has been a turnaround in both the sources and destinations of migration in the postindustrial era. The countries of the Western Hemisphere, with the exception of the United States, and other formerly colonized nations worldwide have experienced surges of emigration. But whereas migrants in the nineteenth century were seeking economic opportunities in rapidly industrializing countries, the push-pull factors in more recent years have centered on political realities. Even 150 years after independence from colonial rule, many countries remain unable to establish political, institutional, or economic stability, and government corruption has often been identified as a key motivator for emigration. Many international migrants from such countries as Afghanistan, Burundi, El Salvador, Iraq, and Somalia have been refugees fleeing from revolution, civil war, or totalitarian regimes. More

generally, countries with relatively low levels of per capita gross domestic product (GDP) exhibit greater income inequality than wealthier countries, suggesting a socioeconomic structure for poorer countries whereby the owners of productive capital constitute a wealthy minority with political power, and the bulk of the population supplies labor at relatively low wages. This lack of social or economic mobility for large portions of a country's population provides a strong "push" factor for international migration as workers search abroad for more highly valued uses for their labor power.

The postindustrial period is also characterized by strong "pull" factors to France, Germany, England, Spain—former migration-sending countries—and especially the United States. Countries that successfully adopted the technological advances of the Industrial Revolution experienced growth in living standards unprecedented in human history. This economic revolution and its widespread social consequences initiated a persistent and growing worldwide gap in real income and living levels. As a result, Alfred Sauvy's (1952) concept of First, Second, and Third World countries remains intuitively understood, even in the absence of a specific context. Taken together, the forces repelling people from their home countries and the relative abundance of opportunities in foreign locations offer a broad macroeconomic context for postindustrial international migration.

The growth of industrialization in Western countries provided opportunities for low-skilled immigrants in the agricultural, service, and industrial sectors of the economy. The typical migrant in the postindustrial period arrives in the destination country with lower skill levels than earlier migrants. Migrants today also have lower literacy rates. Although most migrants continue to be young men, beginning in the 1970s a marked feminization of migration has occurred as women began to explore the global labor market, filling many jobs in the entertainment, service, agricultural, and industrial sectors. In 2000, female international migrants numbered approximately 80 million, nearly half of the total.

Migrants in the twenty-first century enter receiving countries that have begun to manifest the social and economic effects of previous migration. Migrants tend to arrive into a network of ethnically similar communities, and often they obtain employment and a place to live through these networks. The networks reduce the transaction costs associated with international migration and, for some, improve the probability of economic success in the host country.

The existence of transnational migration networks has also stimulated the growth of temporary or seasonal migration. Transnational migrants are those able to maintain active participation in two geographically distinct cultures, a near impossibility when migration is undertaken on a permanent basis. As exemplified by patterns of Mexican emigration, many migrants engaged in agricultural work annually flock to the United States during the harvesting season and return home in autumn, often having accumulated enough income to sustain their extended families for several months. Among other similar examples, Turkish immigrants to Germany also tend to engage in medium-term temporary migration, often staying as many as seven years in Germany before returning.

Other countries, such as the Philippines and Indonesia, have more formalized temporary migration programs whereby the issuance of international visas is expedited and job placement in the host country is facilitated. Despite the growth of such programs, unofficial outmigration from those countries has continued to grow.

Issues in International Migration

Why Does International Migration Occur?
Despite the relatively low cost of travel and the existence of transnational migration networks, the personal, social, and national upheaval as-

sociated with international migration remains large, begging a deeper understanding of the motivations behind migration. Further, as countries seek to manage their migration flows, a consistent and coherent analytical framework is necessary for the implementation of appropriate policies. Although there is no "grand theory" of international migration, the conclusions from several perspectives yield a rich set of analytical tools (Djajiae 2001; Taylor 1996).

The Dual Economy Approach. Economic development through industrialization requires substantial labor power, which is typically abundantly available from the declining traditional agricultural sector, according to analyses based on the concept of the dual economy by, for example, W. Arthur Lewis (1954). The traditional sector is oversupplied with labor such that the marginal productivity of any individual is very low; thus, any person's labor could be redirected to the modern industrial sector without affecting total production in the traditional sector, highlighting the importance of migration. Wages remain low, and thus profits become high, in the modern sector, while chronic underemployment in the traditional sector is reduced. The result is mutually beneficial, as the modern sector expands while not harming output in the traditional sector, making better use of labor resources. Although not explicitly a model of international migration, the dual-economy perspective explains the basic impetus of the industrial migration waves.

The Neoclassical Approach. Pioneered by Gustav Ranis and John C. H. Fei (1961), studies based in the neoclassical tradition typically conceive of aggregate quantities of individuals as factors of production in the process of generating national output. International migration thus shares many of the characteristics associated with international capital flows. In the theory's purest sense, differences in the price of labor between countries motivate international migration. Such disparities represent disequilibrium in the international labor market, and migration is the natural adjustment tool. The outflow of labor from the sending country creates relative scarcity, and the price of labor rises. Similarly, the host country experiences an inflow of labor and commensurate downward pressure on the price of labor. The net effect represents one of the most basic results of economic theory: The allocation of resources to their most valued use equalizes rates of return. Migration thus promotes productive efficiency in both the sending and host countries, and at the same time it enforces international wage parity.

Other neoclassical approaches focus on the individual as the primary agent in the decision to migrate (Todaro 1969). The potential migrant is postulated as a rational actor—maximizing his or her own well-being—who engages in a benefit-cost analysis, and for whom international migration constitutes one of a menu of "investment" options. Migration as investment is a natural association because it typically requires a substantial initial cost with the expectation of future gain. The migrant, or potential migrant, thus estimates his or her expected net return from migration as compared to remaining at home based on: (1) expected wage differentials between the home and host countries; (2) the probability differentials of obtaining employment between the home and host countries; (3) the probability of deportation, if migration would occur illegally; and (4) the cost of the migration itself. Migration then occurs when the expected net return is positive and outweighs that of other investment options.

Taken together, the macroscopic and individual approaches imply that migration would eventually cease as international wage parity emerges and individuals no longer have economic incentives to migrate.

Household Approaches. As an expansion of the neoclassical approach, household approaches posit that individuals make decisions in the context of a family unit or household that seeks to maximize and secure the well-being of all its members as measured by both the quantity of household income and its lack of variation (Hirschman et al. 1999). In developing economies, large portions of the population may have very few options for financial savings, and other methods of smoothing income streams over time against both cyclical and structural variations are required.

A common and successful solution has been for the household to incur the expense of sending a migrant abroad with the expectation that the migrant would regularly send remittance income to the nonmigrating household. Ideally, employment in the destination country, and thus the stream of remittances, would be countercyclical to income variations in the home country. Especially if international migration is to occur illegally, the cost of migration may be large—in the case of households in El Salvador, for example, sometimes as much as annual household income—and many households incur debt to finance international passage for a migrant. Further, the typical migrant is a young, economically active male, and the immediate loss of that income to the sending household is not trivial. While economically significant, the remittance income also confers a social obligation on the migrant that motivates the maintenance of ties to the home country.

International Remittances

International remittances—money sent to the country of origin by an international migrant—are an integral aspect of international migration (Djajiae 2001, IOM 2003). When international migration is undertaken as part of a household strategy to increase income and reduce income risk by diversifying the sources of income, remittances are not windfall income to the receiving household, but rather, the expected return on the household's migration investment. Remittances also play a key role in the formation and maintenance of transnational migrant networks, providing the migrant an avenue for remaining active in the home country while residing abroad.

Table 5: Top Remittance-Receiving Countries, 2000 (in thousands of U.S. dollars)

Country	Remittances
India	11,585,699
Mexico	6,572,599
Turkey	4,560,000
Egypt	3,747,000
Spain	3,414,414
Portugal	3,131,162
Morocco	2,160,999
Bangladesh	1,948,999
Jordan	1,845,133

Source: World Bank. *World Development Indicators* (Washington, DC: World Bank, 2004).

Table 6: Top Remittance-Receiving Countries, Percentage of GDP, 2000

Country	% GDP
Jordan	19.6
Cape Verde	16.1
Albania	14.4
Yemen Republic	13.7
El Salvador	13.3
Serbia and Montenegro	13.2
Bosnia and Herzegovina	12.3
Jamaica	10.6
Dominican Republic	8.6
Ecuador	8.3

Source: World Bank, *World Development Indicators* (Washington, DC: World Bank, 2004).

The volume of income generated by the cycle of migration and remittances has proven to be of major significance to many countries. Although India receives the largest amount of remittances (over $11.5 billion in 2000; Table 5), other countries experience a larger overall impact from remittances. Remittances in El Salvador—some $1.7 billion annually—amount to 12–15 percent of GDP (Table 6), surpassing the value of the country's primary export, coffee. They dictate the direction of the Salvadoran economy, providing funds for savings and investment, supplying a constant source of foreign exchange, and, most of all, supporting current consumption at the household level. Similar patterns are evidenced in many parts of the world, including Western Samoa, Jordan, the Philippines, and Sri Lanka.

Negative economic effects have also been registered as a result of migration and the large volume of remittance income it can generate. Most remittance income is sent in the currency of the migrant's host country; thus the remittance-receiving household must transact in the foreign exchange market to utilize it. This creates an artificial overvaluation of the receiving country's exchange rate, as a shortage of domestic currency is created by the excess supply of foreign currency. The overvalued exchange negatively impacts the country's export sector

as its goods become relatively more expensive abroad.

Large sustained remittance flows have also caused "Dutch Disease" effects (Corden and Neary 1982). The increase in national income from remittances raises overall expenditures, but, for a small economy, only domestically produced goods and services increase in price, since small economies have almost no effect on the world prices of traded goods. Thus, as prices and profits rise in the domestic sector, investment and productive resources flock to it, leaving the traditional sector (typically agriculture) forced to pay higher wages and lacking in new investment. The resulting "Dutch Disease" is the unbalanced economic growth that occurs when the domestic sector booms while the traditional sector lags.

The success of international migration and remittances as a form of household investment has also had important social effects. For many Salvadoran households, remittance income more than doubles income from other sources, thus alleviating deep poverty, but also reducing incentives to augment productivity in the home country. Further, many young Salvadorans believe that emigration is the only avenue to achieve economic success, and the country has experienced a significant "brain drain" where young people, including many professionals, choose to emigrate, further exacerbating the lack of skilled workers. The experience of other labor-sending countries suggests that the Salvadoran experience is not unusual.

The Feminization of International Migration

Although women have always been an integral part of international migration, traditionally migrating as part of a household unit, the independent migration of women has risen in recent decades. In 2000, the number of women migrants totaled approximately 80 million, nearly half of all international migrants worldwide. The gender mix of migrants varies by region: Migrants from Latin America remain predominantly male, for example, whereas the majority of Asian migrants are female. However, policies concerning immigration do not usually deal with the migration of women per se and instead focus most commonly on limiting the volume of immigration and designing effective border-control regimes. Even policies that address the rights and obligations of immigrants, whether legal or illegal, do not usually take account of issues related to gender.

Immigrants in general are hesitant to seek legal enforcement of their rights, but women abroad are more susceptible to human rights abuses because a significant percentage of female employment opportunities arise in unregulated manufacturing settings or the entertainment and sex industries. Female migration has nonetheless risen as women take advantage of the social and financial independence gained through migration, as well as the increased social status acquired in the home community via remittance income. In Sri Lanka, female migrants have become primary contributors to household income, sending over $600 million annually in remittances. Philippine and Moroccan migration and remittance patterns emulate the Sri Lankan case on a smaller scale. The female role in international migration has increased worldwide, however.

Impact of International Migration on the Receiving Country

Immigrants provide labor to the receiving economy and typically occupy positions of low status, performing predominantly physical labor requiring few specific skills. Low immigrant wages thus tend to reduce production costs in the agricultural, service, and industrial sectors of the receiving economy. At the same time, immigrants are participants in the receiving economy and contribute to consumption expenditures and, to a lesser extent, savings.

Immigrants also impose costs on the receiving country. Explicit costs occur primarily in the distribution of public resources (access to schools, health facilities, and other public services) to immigrants, many of whom, owing to illegal immigration, do not necessarily contribute to the source of public funds. In the United States, illegal immigrants are more likely to pay federal taxes than state or local taxes; however, most public benefits are provided by state funds. It is estimated that it cost approximately $17 billion to provide public services to illegal immigrants in the United States in 2000. Despite the passage of California's Proposition 187 in 1994 barring illegal immigrants from receiving public health or education services, California spent approximately $3 billion providing services to illegal immigrants in 2000.

Other countries have also found their public institutions strained by the influx of immigrants. Traditionally homogeneous in its ethnic composition and generous in its public assistance programs, Sweden experienced significant immigration from West Africa during the late twentieth century. Similar to migrants around the world, immigrants to Sweden had on average greater need for public assistance, largely owing to lower incomes and higher rates of fertility. By 2000, funds for public assistance had dwindled, and political tension was strong. More recently, like many countries with longer histories of multiethnic immigration, Sweden has embarked on assimilation and integration programs.

The implicit costs of immigration are a source of controversy. As immigrants enter a country in significant numbers, they are believed to compete with native workers for jobs, thus depressing wages and harming native incomes. Opponents to this view contend that immigrants are employed in low-status jobs that native workers would find unsuitable and that there is, therefore, no direct labor competition. Evidence is mixed. In the United States, immigration has not been found to be associated with higher unemployment rates overall, suggesting that broad economic growth has been able to absorb the influx of labor. Although there is no clear consensus on the effect of immigration on the wages of low-skilled native workers, the wages of high-skilled workers exhibit a slightly positive association with immigration. As the use of low-skilled labor rises, capital inputs must also rise in order to maintain the productivity of labor. High-skilled labor "manages" capital inputs and is therefore complementary to capital such that a rising demand for capital translates to increased wages for high-skilled labor.

International migration also changes the sociocultural structure of the receiving country. Immigrants bring religions, values, and cultural practices that may clash with the mainstream of the receiving society, and those differences have often led to discrimination, both formal and informal, against immigrants. Over time and in the aggregate, the degree and character of immigrant integration into the mainstream society is loosely tied to the economic success of the immigrant group. Although Latin Americans make up the vast majority of immigrants to the United States and collectively register a strong economic impact, most remain at the lower income levels, and their representation, for example, in higher education and political spheres remains disproportionately low. Similar situations exist worldwide, including, for example, West Africans in France and Indians in East Africa.

Impact on the Sending Country

Emigration from a developing country—typical of the postindustrial period—has been welcomed by governments as an effective method to reduce chronic unemployment or underemployment. Further, remittance income from migrants often serves to alleviate the most severe instances of poverty and, particularly when transnational migrant networks are strong, provides investment capital to the developing economy.

However, the costs of emigration are not trivial. In countries such as El Salvador and Western Samoa, where remittances are large as a percentage of GDP, the combined exchange rate and Dutch Disease effects transform the fundamental economic structure of the country. The traditional agro-export sector declines in economic importance in favor of services and industry, causing a realignment of labor usage and additional urbanization.

Urbanization and structural transformation, however, necessitate skilled labor that may be less available as a result of the brain drain associated with emigration. When artisans, craftsmen, and skilled professionals emigrate (often to jobs of lower status), the remaining skilled workers enjoy a wage premium because of their relative scarcity, but the aggregate effect is a reduction in productivity associated with less efficient management of capital resources and a slower adoption rate of new technology. This also depresses the return to capital and reduces the flow of investment.

The social effects of international migration on the sending country can be profound. Like public assistance benefits, remittance income is associated with economic dependency such that individuals elevate their reservation wage to account for external remittance income. The reservation wage is the minimum wage an individual must receive before being willing to enter the labor market. Migration and remittances are thus particularly associated with a reduction in the labor-force participation of young people as well as an increase in drug use, teen pregnancy, and youth gangs. Within a particular community, income inequality also increases between households that receive remittances and those that do not. Households that receive remittances may substantially improve their daily quality of life as compared to their community as a whole. This "relative deprivation" may spark jealousy and animosity within the community, but it also motivates further out-migration from the community to correct obvious income imbalances.

Emigration necessarily involves some form of separation. Parents leave behind spouses and children, and emigration of a nuclear family leaves behind an extended family. Such costs are nonquantifiable but significant to the extent that nonmigrants, particularly children, benefit from the family unit in terms of psycho-emotional development and the inculcation of values and ethics. Similarly, the migrant incurs the psychological cost of separation such that the true value of economic gain from migration is reduced.

International Migration in the Twenty-First Century

Although international wage parity has not become a large-scale reality and the economic incentives to migrate internationally are no less than in the past, the age of global terrorism will affect patterns of international migration. Legal restrictions and barriers to immigration from predominantly Muslim countries into the United States and other Western countries have been enacted, slowing dramatically the outflow of migrants from those regions. Further, the use of active military force against terrorism suggests that such restrictions on migration will remain in force.

Beyond the explicit costs of more tightly controlling international migration flows, one of the major long-term costs will be reduced economic growth rates for developing countries. Although the brain drain out of develop-

ing countries is significant, it is also the case that migrants often participate in higher education abroad and return to their home countries to apply their acquired skills. This type of migration is an important mechanism for the transfer of technology from more developed to less developed regions. India, China, and Japan provide notable examples. To the extent that such transfers are diminished by the new restrictions, productivity growth in those and similar countries will be lessened. At the same time, China continues to liberalize its economy, and as it integrates more thoroughly into the world economy, Chinese migrants overall are expected to increase their presence in global migration flows.

Political and economic instability will continue to be major motivators for emigration. Afghanistan and the former Soviet republics will remain important labor-sending countries, as will several African countries, including Sudan, South Africa, and Congo. Latin Americans will continue to dominate migration to the United States; however, the flow may diminish. Immigration controls to the United States affect all immigrants, and the enforcement of anti-immigrant policies increases the risks associated with international migration. Finally, policymakers in Mexico, El Salvador, Western Samoa, the Philippines, and other countries are gradually adopting the belief that migration and remittances provide only a second-best, temporary solution to domestic problems. To the extent that such countries are able to improve the domestic opportunities for natives via transparent and credible policies that stimulate sustainable economic growth, migration outflows would be expected to diminish.

Paul A. Rivera

See Also Labor Markets and Wage Effects; Population Growth

References

Borjas, George J. 1994. "The Economics of Immigration." *Journal of Economic Literature* 32, no. 4: 1667–1717.

Corden, Max W., and J. Peter Neary. 1982. "Booming Sector and De-Industrialization in a Small Open Economy." *Economic Journal* 92 (December): 825–848.

Díaz-Briquets, Sergio, and Sidney Weintraub, eds. 1991. *Determinants of Emigration from Mexico, Central America, and the Caribbean.* Boulder: Westview.

Djajiae, Slobodan, ed. 2001. *International Migration: Trends, Policies and Economic Impact.* New York: Routledge.

Hirschman, Charles, Philip Kasinitz, and Josh DeWind, eds. 1999. *The Handbook of International Migration: The American Experience.* New York: Russell Sage Foundation.

International Organization for Migration. 2003. *World Migration 2003: Managing Migration—Challenges and Responses for People on the Move.* Geneva: IOM.

Lewis, W. Arthur. 1954. "Economic Development with Unlimited Supplies of Labor." *Manchester School of Economic and Social Studies* 22: 139–191.

Massey, Douglas S., Joaquin Arango, Ali Kouaouci, Adela Pelligrino, and J. Edward Taylor. 1998. *Worlds in Motion: Understanding International Migration at the End of the Millennium.* International Studies in Demography. New York: Oxford University Press.

Papastergiadis, Nikos. 2000. *The Turbulence of Migration: Globalization, Deterritorialization and Hybridity.* Malden, MA: Polity.

Ranis, Gustav, and John C. H. Fei. 1961. "A Theory of Economic Development." *American Economic Review* 51: 533–565.

Sauvy, Alfred. 1952. "Trois Mondes, Une Planète." *L'Observateur,* no. 118.

Stalker, Peter. 2000. *Workers without Frontiers: The Impact of Globalization on International Migration.* Boulder: Lynne Rienner.

Stark, Oded, and J. Edward Taylor. 1989. "Relative Deprivation and International Migration." *Demography* 26, no. 1: 1–14.

Taylor, J. Edward, ed. 1996. *Development Strategy, Employment, and Migration: Insights from Models.* Paris: Organisation for Economic Co-operation and Development.

Todaro, Michael P. 1969. "A Model of Labor Migration and Urban Unemployment in Less Developed Countries." *American Economic Review* 59: 138–148.

United Nations. 2002. *Statistical Yearbook 2001.* Geneva: United Nations Population Data Unit, Population and Geographic Data Section.

World Bank. 2004. *World Development Indicators.* Washington, DC: World Bank.

International Productivity

Productivity, a key measure of economic performance, relates an increase in output to the rise of inputs. There are various concepts of productivity, ranging from physical labor productivity (for example, tons of steel produced per worker hour) to total factor productivity (for example, growth in real gross domestic product [GDP] over a composite input measure of labor and capital).

Applications

International comparisons of productivity have many analytical applications. At the macroeconomic level, productivity measures can be linked to improvements in the standard of living. For example, a measure for labor productivity (output per hour) can be reconciled with a per capita income measure (output per inhabitant) through the use of labor-market indicators reflecting the intensity of use of labor (hours worked, labor force participation, and the like). Macroeconomic measures of productivity estimates are also an important ingredient for quantifying the contribution of factor inputs (labor, capital, and so on), technology, and other variables to differences in growth or levels of GDP across countries. Finally, macro measures of productivity are an important input for the analysis of economic convergence between countries.

At the meso level, productivity studies focus on the comparative performance of sectors and industries. Such studies provide an important tool for analyzing the strengths and weaknesses of a country's industrial structure, assessing the competitive strength of individual industries and exploring the causal factors behind productivity gaps between and among countries. Industry measures of productivity are also used for comparisons of unit labor costs across countries. At the micro level, productivity is a measure of significant interest to examine firm dynamics—for example, how the entry and exit of firms impacts the productivity performance of a sector of the economy. Finally, productivity studies are also useful for individual firms and companies, particularly when such comparisons can be narrowed down to plants producing a comparable range of clearly specified products or services. This approach allows economists to determine benchmarks for the efficiency of particular projects or production processes within and among countries.

Productivity in the Short and Long Term

It is important to consider the time period over which productivity trends can be usefully analyzed. Productivity can behave quite differently in the short term versus the long term. In the short term, productivity measures may be volatile, as they are strongly related to the business cycle. Labor productivity typically behaves in a pro-cyclical manner, showing an acceleration in the upward phase of the cycle and a slowdown in the downward phase. Following a peak in GDP growth, the slowdown of growth may not be immediately matched by declining employment, and capital may be left idle before it is discarded. When a recession occurs, productivity may increase again as firms begin to lay off workers and scrap capital. But this rise may be offset by a reduction in consumption by dismissed workers, so that GDP contracts further.

In an international comparative framework, the dynamics of output and input growth over the business cycle are very dependent on the flexibility of labor and capital markets. In the long term, the structural factors that affect productivity growth come more to the forefront. Policies to enhance productivity, either in the field of technology and innovation or in the field of market reforms or other institutional changes, only show effects in the longer term.

International Productivity Comparisons at the Macro Level

International comparisons of productivity have a long history. Perhaps the first international comparison was made by Samuel Pepys, a naval administrator in seventeenth-century England. In a diary entry for February 13, 1665, while en route between the Netherlands and England, he wrote: "And coming home, did go onboard Sir W. Petty's *Experiment*—which is a brave roomy vessel—and I Hope may do well. So went on shore to a Dutch house to drink some Rum, and there light upon some Dutchmen, with whom we had a good discourse touching Stoveing and making of cables. But to see how despicably they speak of us for our using so many hands more to do anything than they do, they closing a cable with 20 that we use 60 men upon" (Pepys 1665).

Various studies have documented the rise of productivity in eighteenth-century England since the times of the Industrial Revolution and the explosive growth of productivity in the New World, particularly in the United States during the late nineteenth century. These productivity growth spurts were linked to a rapid growth in capital intensity and an acceleration in technological change. The rise of electricity as a major general-purpose technology was an important source of productivity growth in many advanced countries during the early twentieth century. After World War II, a clear pattern of productivity catch-up was observed for Europe and Japan relative to the United States. This catch-up process was partly driven by the legacy of the two world wars, which had led Europe and Japan to fall seriously behind American performance. But the postwar period was conducive to international technology diffusion and institutional innovations, and both regions adopted and adapted to new technologies. For example, Japan, which had lagged behind in productivity during the prewar years, had one of the fastest productivity growth rates during the postwar period. The "golden age" of productivity catch-up vis-à-vis the United States had already halted for most advanced countries by the early 1970s.

From the late 1970s to the late 1980s, productivity growth in most countries, including the United States, was dismal. The slowdown was surprising in light of major changes in the technological paradigm of the twentieth century, which shifted the emphasis from electricity to information technology. The slow growth in productivity led Nobel Prize winner Robert Solow to coin the term "productivity paradox." He wrote: "You can see the computer age everywhere but in the productivity statistics" (Solow 1987). However, since the mid-1990s, the United States has experienced a substantial acceleration in productivity growth. These gains have often been attributed to the explosive growth of the production of information and communication technologies (ICT). In contrast, many other countries, in particular the nations of Europe, have experienced much slower productivity growth due to differences in industry structure and slower adoption of ICT relative to the United States.

Meanwhile, productivity growth in many countries that are not members of the Organisation for Economic Co-operation and Devel-

Table 1: Rate of Growth of GDP per Hour Worked, 1870–1950

	1870–1913	1913–1950
Western Europe	1.55	1.56
Austria	1.75	0.89
Belgium	1.24	1.42
Denmark	1.94	1.65
Finland	1.80	2.27
France	1.74	1.94
Germany	1.56	0.75
Italy	1.66	1.96
Netherlands	1.23	1.31
Norway	1.64	2.48
Sweden	1.75	2.76
Switzerland	1.80	2.71
United Kingdom	1.22	1.67
Australia	1.96	1.54
Canada	2.25	2.30
Japan	1.99	1.80
United States	1.92	2.48

opment (OECD) has remained relatively slow, with the most notable exception of many of the countries of East Asia. Even after the economic and financial crisis of the 1990s, many countries in the region—and nowadays China, in particular—have continued to show rapid productivity growth. Finally, under the impact of transition, many economies in Central and Eastern Europe have shown accelerated labor productivity growth during the 1990s.

Productivity at the Industry Level

One must take an industry perspective to output, input, and productivity performance in order to fully understand the comparative productivity of countries. For example, the slowdown in productivity growth in the original fifteen nations of the European Union since the mid-1990s reflects an adjustment process toward a new industrial structure. This adjustment has proceeded more slowly in Western Europe than in the United States. Similarly, the rapid productivity catch-up taking place in

East Asian countries has been driven to a large extent by the manufacturing sector, and much less so by service industries. Productivity growth in agriculture has been an important source of structural change in many developing countries, but the underperformance in services, in particular in informal service industries, puts a drag on aggregate productivity growth. Thus, economists must go beyond an analysis of the aggregate numbers to ascertain the extent to which variations across countries may be explained by industry structure.

There are various approaches that may be taken in analyzing industry productivity growth. First, when a particular country realizes an improvement in productivity, it is important to pinpoint which industries have achieved superior performance and whether it is confined to only a few industries or the improvement is widespread across the economy. For example, some scholars have suggested that the improvement in U.S. productivity growth since the late 1990s has been confined to ICT-producing industries, such as computers, semiconductors, and software. Others have stressed the important productivity contributions of a small number of service sectors, in particular wholesale and retail trade and financial securities, which are intensive users of ICT. Similarly, one needs to understand whether the slowdown in EU productivity growth during the same period is due to a failure to match the United States in its best-performing industries, or due to problems in other industries.

Second, an industry analysis aids in understanding the forces underlying competitiveness. Under the influence of ongoing globalization in product, labor, and capital markets, the industry structures of open economies are under continuous pressure from competitive forces. Traditional protection mechanisms provided by national governments are less and less effective. As a result, firms in "old" industries are under strain to adjust or disappear altogether, whereas firms in "new" industries face an uphill struggle to open up new markets and develop capabilities to face off against compet-

**Table 2: Rate of Growth of GDP per Hour Worked, 1950/1960–2003
(approximately 100 countries)**

	1950–1973	1973–1995	1995–2003
"OECD[1], of which"	3.9	2.0	1.9
"European Union-15[2], of which:"	4.6	2.6	1.5
France	5.0	2.7	2.1
Germany[3]	5.8	2.7	1.9
UK	2.8	2.3	2.0
USA	2.5	1.2	2.4
Japan	7.0	2.7	2.2
Central and East Europe[4]	3.8	1.2	3.9
(former) USSR[5]	3.4	-1.2	3.7
	1960–1973	1973–1995	1995–2003
Asia[6], of which	2.2	3.6	4.0
East Asia	5.5	4.7	3.6
China	1.3	4.2	6.1
Southeast Asia	3.2	3.0	0.7
South Asia	1.8	2.4	3.2
Latin America	2.8	0.9	0.1
Middle East	6.5	-0.8	0.8
Africa	2.5	0.1	1.2
World	3.2	1.1	1.6

Notes: For country coverage, see http://www.ggdc.net/dseries.shtml. Regional growth rates are weighted at gross domestic product (GDP) in purchasing power parity (PPP). In many cases, hours per person employed for low-income countries were assumed constant at 2,200 hours per year. In several Central and Eastern European countries, they were estimated at 2,000 hours per year.

[1] Organisation of Economic Co-operation and Development (OECD) figures are supplied as of pre-1994 membership.
[2] EU-15 data are calculated as of pre-2004 membership.
[3] Figures for Germany for 1990 onward include East Germany.
[4] Figures for Central and Eastern Europe from 1990 onward include Slovenia.
[5] Figures for the former Soviet Union since 1990 include Russia and the countries that were formerly part of the USSR.
[6] Figures for Asia exclude Japan.

Sources: Groningen Growth and Development Centre, http://www.ggdc.net/dseries/shtml; Maddison, Angus. 1995. *Monitoring the World Economy 1820–1992.* Paris: OECD (Organization for Economic Cooperation and Development): Maddison, Angus. 2001. *The World Economy:A Millennial Perspective.* Paris: OECD.

itive pressures of incumbents or other new entrants.

Finally, the upsurge of opportunities for new technological applications may have very different implications for industries. Indeed, the absorptive capacity for ICT differs greatly across industries and has very different impacts on output, employment, and productivity performance. For example, in most manufacturing industries, ICT has largely contributed to a rationalization of production processes, raising productivity through the use of fewer inputs, in particular unskilled labor. In many service industries, the introduction of ICT has had, in addition, an impact on "product" innovation, in turn implying increased use of high-technology inputs. Indeed, some service industries (in particular finance and some business services) are among the most intensive users of ICT in the economy. The impact of ICT on the

Table 3: Average Annual Growth of GDP per Hour Worked of ICT-Producing, ICT-Using, and Non-ICT Industries in the European Union, Japan, and the United States, 1979–1995 and 1995–2000

	1979–1995			1995–2002		
	EU-15	Japan	U.S.	EU-15	Japan	U.S.
Total Economy[1]	2.3	3.6	1.2	1.8	2.5	2.5
ICT-producing Industries	7.0	13.6	7.2	8.7	19.1	9.3
ICT-producing Manufacturing[2]	12.1	19.2	15.1	16.7	30.8	23.5
ICT-producing Services	4.4	6.4	2.4	5.9	6.2	2.7
ICT-using Industries	2.2	5.0	1.6	1.8	2.0	4.9
ICT-using Manufacturing	2.6	4.1	0.8	2.3	0.7	2.6
ICT-using Services	2.0	5.3	1.9	1.7	2.1	5.3
Non-ICT Industries	1.9	1.9	0.4	1.1	1.1	0.2
Non-ICT Manufacturing	3.2	3.3	2.3	2.1	1.4	1.2
Non-ICT Services[1]	0.8	0.9	-0.3	0.5	0.8	0.2
Non-ICT Other	3.4	2.4	1.4	2.1	1.5	0.4

Notes: Industry groupings into the ICT-producing category are from the Organisation for Economic Co-operation and Development (OECD). The distinction between ICT-using industries and less intensive ICT users is based on the share of ICT capital services in total capital services from nonresidential capital. See Ark, Bart van, Robert Inklaar, and Robert H. McGuckin. 2003. "Changing Gear: Productivity, ICT and Service Industries in Europe and the United States." Pp. 56–99 in J. F. Christensen and P. Maskell, eds., *The Industrial Dynamics of the New Digital Economy.* Cheltenham: Edward Elgar.

[1] "Total Economy" figures and "Non-ICT Services" data exclude real estate.
[2] The figures in this row are based on U.S. hedonic price deflators for ICT production (adjusted for national inflation rates) instead of actual national accounts deflators.

Source: Groningen Growth and Development Centre, "60-Industry Database," http://www.ggdc.net.

composition of labor in services is twofold. On the one hand, the rationalization of processes and the introduction of more knowledge-intensive services have strengthened the skill-bias of service innovation in favor of very highly skilled workers. On the other hand, adaptations to information technology since its introduction may also have facilitated the increased use of labor with lower skill levels. An industry-level analysis aids in understanding the impact of input use and technology adoption on productivity growth.

Productivity at the Firm Level

Compared to macroeconomic and industry-level studies, much less is known about the mechanisms underlying productivity development at individual firms or the differences between firms within sectors. In most productiv-

ity studies, differences among companies within a given industry are simply averaged out. Still, these differences can provide valuable information for the study of productivity. First, the world's most innovative and productive companies can be assumed to be at the technological frontier of the specific industry they are in. Knowledge about the productivity gap between the average firm (or each individual firm) and the most productive firm in an industry in a particular country or region may thus lead to insights about the potential for productivity advances, given the current state of technology. Second, the reallocation of resources (labor and capital) between high- and low-productivity firms and between entering and exiting firms in a particular industry can be an important source of productivity growth. When high-productivity companies are successful in rapidly gaining market share at the expense of lower productivity companies, this results in a higher average productivity within a particular industry.

Economists are beginning to better understand how firm dynamics contribute to productivity growth owing to greater availability of longitudinal firm-level data (Bartelsman and Doms 2000). For example, it appears that a large part of the productivity differential between American and European manufacturing firms during the 1990s can be explained by much faster productivity growth among the top quartile of firms with the highest productivity levels. These firms also exhibited much faster employment growth in the United States than in the European Union. In contrast, among the firms in the lowest quartile of productivity levels, the European firms appear to show faster employment growth than the American firms. Although there are large differences between countries, the evidence suggests that although the entry rate of new firms is not all that much larger in the United States than in Europe, the potential for new entrants to grow in terms of employment and output is much less in Europe. It is well known that larger firms tend to exhibit faster productivity growth due to large capital-intensity and scale advantages.

In addition to the index-number approach to productivity measurement described here, more studies are now making use of econometric methods, such as data-envelopment analysis or stochastic frontiers, to measure productivity and efficiency at the firm level (Coelli et al. 1998). Such approaches are particularly useful for benchmarking purposes.

Concepts of Productivity

The literature distinguishes many different measures and concepts of productivity, each of which has its own particular meaning and use. The first distinction is between physical productivity and volume productivity. Physical productivity is the quantity of output produced by one unit of production input in a unit of time. For example, when a laborer in the ce-

ment industry in Country A produces 100 tons of cement per year on average, compared to 200 tons per laborer in Country B, the physical labor productivity in the cement industry in Country A is half that of Country B. Nowadays, the use of physical units of output for productivity measurement is mostly restricted to analyses of the efficiency of particular production processes for specified products or for closely related groups of products over time. In comparisons of productivity at the firm or industry level, the heterogeneity of output and the large variety of products make physical units an anachronistic device. Moreover, it is often difficult to allocate inputs to a single output. In services, the use of physical units is often not possible at all.

In practice, economists are more likely to use figures on total values than quantities of outputs and inputs. For the construction of the growth rate of volume productivity, the change in values needs to be corrected for price changes. For example, a change in production values in the car industry needs to be adjusted for the increase in sales prices of cars to obtain a real output measure. Similarly, a real input measure for energy use must take account of changes in the value of energy inputs, that is, the rise in energy prices. International comparisons of productivity growth are very sensitive to the use of adequate deflators. For example, in comparing the growth of productivity in the computer industry, it is of crucial importance to use price deflators that are properly adjusted for rapid quality changes in that industry. For comparisons of productivity levels across space, value measures need to be corrected for differences among countries in relative prices. This correction can be made through the use of purchasing power parities (PPPs), which specify the ratio of the price for a good or service, or for a bundle of goods and services, between two countries.

Broadly speaking, productivity measures can be classified in two ways: as single-factor productivity measures (relating a measure of output to a single measure of input) or as total-

Table 4: Overview of the Main Productivity Measures from the OECD Productivity Manual

| | Type of Input Measure | | | |
	Single-factor productivity measures		Total factor productivity (TFP) measures	
Type of output measure	Labor	Capital	Capital and Labor	Capital, Labor, and Intermediate Inputs (energy, materials, services)
Gross output	Labor productivity (based on gross output)	Capital productivity (based on gross output)	Capital-labor MFP (based on gross output)	KLEMS total factor productivity
Value added	Labor productivity (based on value added)	Capital productivity (based on value added)	Capital-labor MFP (based on value added)	—

Note: See, for example, OECD (Organisation for Economic Co-operation and Development). 2001. *Measuring Productivity.* Paris: OECD and D. W. Jorgenson, F. M. Gollop, and B. Fraumeni, *Productivity and U.S. Economic Growth.* 1987. Cambridge: Harvard University Press, for an exposition in mathematical terms.

Source: OECD 2001, 13.

factor productivity (TFP) measures (relating a measure of output to a bundle of inputs). The specific measure used depends in the first instance on the focus and purpose of the comparison. Labor productivity, the most widely used measure, is mostly quantified in terms of value added over employed persons or value added over total working hours. TFP distinguishes between contributions to GDP from inputs and those from efficiency improvement. TFP can be measured as output relative to a capital-labor combination or output relative to a capital-labor-energy-materials-services combination of inputs (Table 4). The factor inputs can be measured either homogeneously (for example, total hours worked and total capital services), or with an adjustment for changes in composition of labor (gender, education level, and age) and capital (machinery and structures, ICT capital, non-ICT capital). In practice, these adjustments are quite important, in particular for capital. For example, the rapid rise of ICT capital has created large substitution effects be-

tween ICT capital and non-ICT capital and between ICT capital and low-skilled labor (that is, skill-biased technological change). A failure to identify these effects separately transfers those substitution effects to the TFP residual.

TFP growth is often interpreted as a rise in efficiency or technological change, but one must be cautious when making such assumptions. When the index-number approach is applied, TFP is quantified as a residual measure obtained from the growth output minus the growth rates of the weighted inputs. This is done on the assumption that each input gets paid its marginal product, so that the weights can be derived from the share of compensation of each input in total output. In the likely case that this assumption does not hold—for example, because labor markets do not pay a wage according to the productivity of the last worker added to the labor force—the identity of TFP, efficiency, and technical change breaks down. In practice, measured TFP then includes everything that is not otherwise measured, including the growth of unmeasured intangible inputs (which positively affects measured TFP growth) and the effects of imperfect market competition that create mark-ups on prices beyond the "normal" returns to inputs (and therefore reduce measured TFP growth). There is a substantial literature that aims to interpret differences in TFP residuals across countries not only due to market imperfections but also due to differences in historical, institutional, or policy-related factors (Maddison 1989; Hulten et al. 2001).

Another distinction that is of particular relevance at the industry or firm level is that between productivity measures that relate gross output to one or several inputs and measures that use value added to capture movements in output (see Table 4). At the macroeconomic or industry level, value-added measures are more widely available, and, lacking information on intermediate inputs, most desirable, as they avoid double counting of output. But at the level of industries or firms, gross output is a preferred concept, as it allows a similar treatment of factor inputs and intermediate inputs and imposes fewer restrictions on substitutions between factor inputs and productivity.

Measurement Issues

The most comprehensive sources for productivity measurement, either at the level of the total economy or for individual industries, are the national accounts. National accounts include measures of value added at basic prices at both the aggregate and industry levels. These measures are constructed on the basis of international conventions concerning measurement of output and inputs laid down in the United Nations System of National Accounts (SNA). Unfortunately, in practice, the implementation of SNA conventions in national accounts statistics is not the same across countries. There are still differences between European countries and the United States concerning measures of nominal GDP (for example, as regards the

treatment of military expenditures and financial intermediation services) and real GDP (for example, the use of appropriate deflators for ICT products). There are also differences among countries on whether aggregate GDP is primarily measured from the income or the output side. However, at the aggregate level, the impact of such differences on the GDP measure is small, and the effects in part offset each other. An assessment of past adjustments to real GDP growth rates suggests a margin of uncertainty of no more than plus or minus 0.1 percent (Van Ark 2004). To adequately handle the measurement of gross output (in addition to value added and intermediate inputs), an input-output framework is needed, but those input-output models are not yet available on a systematic basis for all countries.

Although national accounts cover the value of factor inputs, data on the volume of factor inputs (labor and capital) often need to be derived from other sources. Labor input estimates are mostly based on figures from labor-force survey or enterprise statistics. In particular, the measurement of working hours presents a major problem for international productivity comparisons. Information on labor quality is also mostly derived from labor-force surveys, but owing to comparability issues, it is usually not possible to make international comparisons for more than three skill categories (pre-primary, primary, and lower secondary education; upper secondary education; and tertiary education).

The contribution of capital to output growth needs to be estimated on the basis of the capital services that each asset produces. Measures of capital services are not directly available from the national accounts or any other official statistics. Series on capital formation by asset type can in principle be obtained from national accounts, and estimates of the gross and net capital stock can then be constructed by cumulating investments and by applying a retirement or depreciation profile. Although the exact shape of the depreciation profile is an important factor, the actual age of the asset has a much bigger impact on the estimate of the growth rates and levels of capital. Differences in asset lives between countries are difficult to verify, and in most cases the statistical basis for the variation in asset lives and retirement patterns across countries is weak, since statistical offices collect such information only infrequently. To obtain a volume series of capital services, two additional steps need to be taken. First, the stock needs to be estimated in terms of "standard efficiency units" (the productive capital stock). This requires the use of a particular age-efficiency profile that reflects the fact that older assets are usually less efficient than newer ones. Second, the productive capital stock for different assets needs to be aggregated on the basis of an estimate of the user cost of capital, which reflects the rental price of a capital good.

It is difficult to precisely assess the accuracy (that is, the extent to which these measures describe reality) of all these variables. At the level of international comparison, informed guesstimates of accuracy are the best that can be achieved. Such guesses need to be based on assessments of the revisions that have been carried out in various countries, sampling errors of underlying survey statistics, and counterfactual experiments. In terms of comparisons of growth rates, it is unlikely that measurement errors affect labor productivity growth by more than 0.2 percent in either direction, and for TFP growth, by more than 0.25 percent either way. Users of such estimates should therefore be cautious in interpreting country rankings of productivity growth. Differences within the range of roughly 0.4 percent (for labor productivity growth) or 0.5 percent (for TFP growth) are insufficient for reaching conclusions on differences in productivity rankings. The level of uncertainty concerning productivity estimates and differences across countries is high, and it is likely to be higher for low-income countries (Ark 2004).

At the industry level, uncertainties about the quality of the productivity estimates may differ from the aggregate and will, for example, generally be larger for service industries than for manufacturing. For many advanced countries, one can observe a striking difference between higher growth rates of labor productivity in "measurable" sectors of the economy (agriculture, mining, manufacturing, transport and communication, and public utilities) and those in "unmeasurable" sectors (construction, trade, the financial sector, "other" market services, and government) over past decades. This may at least partly be related to larger measurement problems in services (Griliches 1994).

The current methodology of splitting the change in output value into a quantity component and a price component is difficult to apply to many service activities, as often no clear quantity component can be distinguished. In many service industries, information on inputs (such as labor income) has been used as a very imperfect proxy for output. Moreover, changes in the quality of services are difficult to measure. These problems are not new, but the increased use of ICT may have led to quality changes and higher productivity growth in services that previously were not envisaged. To measure those aspects of quality change, multiple dimensions of a service need to be taken into account, including, for example, the service concept, the client interface, and the service delivery system. This implies that the real output of a particular service cannot be measured on the basis of one exclusive quantity indicator. Some statistical offices have undertaken changes in measurement methods toward a range of volume measures (for example, in financial services, health services, and other government services). Even though such changes in measurement methods have not exclusively led to upward adjustments of real output, on balance the bias is probably toward an understatement of the growth in real service output.

Comparisons of Productivity Levels

Most of the work on productivity has focused on measurement, comparisons, and analysis of productivity *growth*. Only limited efforts have

Table 5: Level of GDP per Hour Worked, 1950/1960–2003, in 1990 U.S. Dollars

	1950	1960	1973	1995	2003
United States	100.0	100.0	100.0	100.0	100.0
European Union-15,[1] of which:	43.5	51.3	70.8	91.8	85.4
France	46.9	60.9	82.8	114.1	111.1
Germany[2]	36.3	54.7	77.6	91.8	88.3
UK	62.5	58.8	66.9	85.2	82.5
Japan	19.2	26.6	54.1	74.3	73.0
Central and Eastern Europe[3]	18.7	23.5	25.3	25.3	28.4
(former) USSR[4]	27.2	30.6	33.4	19.4	21.6
Asia[5], of which		6.1	5.8	9.7	11.1
East Asia		13.9	20.2	43.7	48.1
China		5.1	4.3	8.3	11.2
Southeast Asia		9.3	10.0	14.9	13.1
South Asia		6.0	5.5	7.1	7.6
Latin America		36.4	37.2	34.8	29.0
Middle East		24.9	41.6	26.3	23.2
Africa		7.7	7.6	6.0	5.4

Notes: For country coverage, see http://www.ggdc.net/dseries.shtml. Regional levels are weighted at gross domestic product (GDP) in 1990 purchasing power parity (PPP). In many cases, hours per person employed for low-income countries were assumed constant at 2,200 hours per year. In several Central and Eastern European countries, they were estimated at 2,000 hours per year.

[1] EU-15 data are calculated as of pre-2004 membership.
[2] Figures for Germany for 1990 onward include East Germany.
[3] Figures for Central and Eastern Europe from 1990 onward include Slovenia.
[4] Figures for the former Soviet Union since 1990 include Russia and the countries that were formerly part of the USSR.
[5] Figures for Asia exclude Japan.

Sources: Groningen Growth and Development Centre, http://www.ggdc.net/dseries/shtml; Maddison 1995, 2001.

been undertaken to measure comparative productivity *levels* between countries. This is mainly because level comparisons, unlike growth comparisons, need to be corrected for differences in relative price levels across countries. This requires the use of data on purchasing power parity, that is, the ratio of the price for a good or service, or for a bundle of goods and services, between two countries. PPP measurement is much more complex than measurement of a time series of prices. For the aggregate economy, PPPs are constructed on a regular basis by international agencies such as the OECD and Eurostat. They are also made available through the Penn World Tables published by the Center for International Comparisons at the University of Pennsylvania. Most studies of comparative productivity levels therefore focus on the aggregate economy.

Comparative measures of productivity levels are important for international economic analysis. They are an essential ingredient for testing catch-up and convergence hypotheses, for example, which, in their simplest version, suggest that a country with a low starting level of productivity, compared to a country at the productivity frontier, will exhibit relatively rapid productivity growth in the subsequent period. The follower country can raise productivity through the diffusion and exploitation of technological and institutional innovation from the country that is characterized by best practice. Productivity levels also shed light on the debate concerning comparative productivity performance among OECD countries. For example, labor productivity levels in several advanced European countries were higher than in the United States for most of the last two decades of the twentieth century. However, such high productivity levels are related to a relatively low intensity of labor to capital in many European countries and therefore to lower comparative levels of per capita income.

Industry-of-origin comparisons, like productivity comparisons for the aggregate economy, aid economists in understanding the determinants of differences in economic performance across countries and regions. The relative productivity standings in agriculture, industry, and services are important for structural growth analysis. They also strengthen analyses of the locus of technical progress, especially when supplemented by micro-oriented investigations of variances in performance across industries and between average and best-practice firms. Finally, these studies shed further light on the relation between productivity and competitiveness at the industry level.

The measurement of productivity levels by industry requires industry-specific measures of relative prices. Since PPPs for the aggregate economy, as compiled by Eurostat and the OECD, are based on final expenditure components (consumption, investment, and government expenditure), they cannot be directly applied to output by industry. As there is considerably more specialization across countries in terms of production than in terms of expenditure, it is more difficult to find sufficient accurate product matches on the basis of which industry PPPs can be obtained. In addition, for productivity comparisons by industry, measures of PPPs for intermediate inputs, labor input, and capital input are also required. Two alternatives have been explored to arrive at producer output and input price relatives: (1) reallocating existing expenditure PPPs to industry groups and "peeling off" transport, distribution, and tax margins, or (2) calculating unit value ratios based on output values and quantities from business statistics. In practice, a mixed approach that makes use of both unit value ratios (mainly for agriculture, mining and manufacturing, and some service sectors, such as distribution and transportation and communication) and "peeled" expenditure PPPs (for most service industries) is considered the most practical and desirable method.

Future Directions

International comparisons of productivity have become considerably more sophisticated over time. At the macroeconomic and industry levels, the measurement of productivity has greatly improved through the availability of higher quality and more detailed data from national accounts and related statistical sources. Still, substantial problems, in particular concerning the measurement of service output, remain. Given the increased importance of services in the economies of advanced countries, these issues require urgent attention from economists and statisticians. Although labor productivity remains a straightforward performance measure that is useful in relation to labor-market indicators and per capita income measures, total factor productivity will be the workhorse for future international comparisons.

The improved measurement of intermediate and factor inputs to output growth, in particular ICT capital, has created more sensible measures of total factor productivity. Also, the number of countries for which TFP measures can be obtained is gradually increasing. Nevertheless, TFP growth is obtained as a residual by deducting the change in weighted factor inputs from output growth, and TFP residuals will be affected by the changes in unmeasured inputs. Various types of intangible capital inputs, such as research and development and organizational capital, form an important category of unmeasured inputs. TFP residuals will also be affected by deviations from the standard neo-classical assumptions concerning perfect markets and the like. The index-number approach to TFP measurement can be complemented by an econometric approach to relax some of these assumptions. Finally, even when TFP measures are fully cleaned up for unmeasured inputs, the residual will only represent that part of technology that is costless and not embodied in any of the input measures.

In addition to international comparisons of productivity growth, studies on relative levels of productivity would help to shed further light on important issues, such as catch-up and convergence, structural change, and competitiveness. It will also be important to further develop adequate measures of relative price levels between countries by industry in order to obtain sensible measures of comparative productivity. Finally, important directions for future research include micro-measurements of productivity by firm, especially those supported by increased availability of longitudinal databases on outputs and inputs by firm.

Bart van Ark

See Also Global Economic Growth; Labor Markets and Wage Effects; Technology and Technical Change

References

Ark, B. van. 2004. "The Measurement of Productivity: What Do the Numbers Mean?" Pp. 28–61 in G. Gelauff et al., eds., *Fostering Productivity: Patterns, Determinants and Policy Implications*. North Holland: Elsevier.

Ark, Bart van, Robert Inklaar, and Robert H. McGuckin. 2003. "Changing Gear: Productivity, ICT and Service Industries in Europe and the United States." Pp. 56–99 in J. F. Christensen and P. Maskell, eds., *The Industrial Dynamics of the New Digital Economy*. Cheltenham: Edward Elgar.

Bartelsman, E. J., and M. Doms. 2000. "Understanding Productivity: Lessons from Longitudinal Microdata." *Journal of Economic Literature* 83, no. 3: 569–594.

Coelli, T., D. S. Prasada Rao, and G. E. Battese. 1998. *An Introduction to Efficiency and Productivity Analysis*. Boston: Kluwer Academic.

Gordon, Robert J. 2004. *Productivity Growth, Inflation, and Unemployment: The Collected Essays of Robert J. Gordon*. Cambridge: Cambridge University Press.

Griliches, Zvi. 1994. "Productivity, R&D, and the Data Constraint." *American Economic Review* (March): 1–23.

Hulten, C. R., E. R. Dean, and M. J. Harper, eds. 2001. *New Developments in Productivity Analysis*. Chicago: University of Chicago Press.

Jorgenson, D. W., F. M. Gollop, and B. Fraumeni. 1987. *Productivity and US Economic Growth*. Cambridge: Harvard University Press.

Maddison, A. 1989. *The World Economy in the Twentieth Century*. Paris: Organisation for Economic Co-operation and Development, Development Centre.

Organisation for Economic Co-operation and Development. 2001. *Measuring Productivity*. OECD Manual. Paris: OECD.

Pepys, Samuel. 1665. The Diary Volume VI. London: Latham and Matthews.

Solow, Robert M. 1987. "We'd better watch out." *New York Times Book Review* (July 12): 36.

Labor Markets and Wage Effects

Wages reflect labor-market trends, state policy, and union protection. These factors have significantly influenced the status of workers worldwide over the past thirty years. From the mid-1970s to the first decade of the new millennium, regional global labor markets have grown more integrated with the ascendancy of free-market policies. These neoliberal economic policies that support the deregulation of state functions have reduced wages through accelerating regional and global labor competition. Wages and employment have also been buffeted by the privatization of state property, government functions, and social responsibilities throughout the nations the world. No country that participates in the global economy is immune from deleterious effects of neoliberal policies that increase labor competition, and thus reduce wages. In the postwar era, from the 1940s through 1970, wages tended to grow steadily as a result of strong state regulation, more effective labor-market protection, and the larger and more robust unions that reflected the workers movements of the mid-twentieth century.

Labor Capital Competition

Labor markets are products of an ineluctable process of historical change in which capital is constantly seeking greater profits through technological change, economic restructuring of work, and geographic relocation to lower-cost areas. Capital accumulation is always at least a step ahead of labor movements, which must seek to preserve the gains of the past or call for new demands on economic systems in response to the lowering of wage and working standards. Therefore, evaluation of labor markets must presuppose a continual process in which capital constantly tries to restructure the economic terrain to enhance profitability, while organized labor (or the labor movement writ large) opposes changes that alter the old balance of power and reduce the standards of workers. Certainly, capital will always seek ways to expand profitability; one cannot presume, however, that labor will always successfully defend against new forms of economic activity that erode the power of workers.

To properly understand the vicissitudes of contemporary labor markets in the current age of global capitalism, one must take a historical approach that identifies the ways that work and labor are transformed over time. When economists recurrently invoke the term "new economy," they imply that national labor markets are being swept away by globalization. The idea that globalization is a new phenomenon that has suddenly appeared on the scene fails to account for the historical nature of capitalism, which has always expanded to new areas of the world in search of higher profits. What is termed "globalization" today in not a novel feature in the world economy, but a process that is rapidly accelerating at a faster pace than in the past. The recent expansion of global labor markets is part of a universal process that began centuries ago.

At the dawn of the twenty-first century, political economists began to call attention to the emergence of a "new economy," as if the terms and conditions of the global economy were completely changing all at once. The global economy of the twenty-first century does break with a steadier and predictable past wherein nation-states controlled the flow of capital, industry, and labor, providing secure jobs and a modicum of income for all. But the global economy is not new. What is different is the expansion of economic interchange, which profoundly influences established labor markets throughout the world. The stylish formulation of "the new global economy" does not take into account the fact that capital continually seeks to expand profitability by restructuring itself and changing the balance of power with labor. Since the late eighteenth century, capital has ineluctably pressed forward for change, most often prevailing over labor's efforts to protect a more predictable past. In 1942, political economist Joseph Schumpeter coined the term "creative destruction" to portray the process of perpetual change under capitalism that undermines established labor markets to increase profitability.

So what many economists call new is in fact only an acceleration and expansion of the scope of capital mobility in a process that has profoundly altered the conditions of labor through most of the world. For much of the past century, workers and growing national labor movements called upon their governments to defend worker interests through regulation and enforcement of labor-management relations and provision of social-welfare programs. Unions could count on national labor laws to protect workers from employer abuse and guarantee them the right to join unions of their choice. Although the labor movements that emerged contrasted greatly, through much of the developed world they could count on standards to regulate wages and hours. The industrial unions that expanded so dramatically in Europe and North America during the twentieth century established wage and work standards in exchange for labor peace. However, employers always maintained control over the

work process and determined how to invest profits. Though most workers in any part of the world did not have an easy time joining unions, democratic rights in the private workplace were significantly stronger during the mid- to late twentieth century than they are today.

The recent decline of state regulations protecting workers is not a new phenomenon growing out of globalization, but a gradual process that began in the late nineteenth and twentieth centuries. Global trade flows undermining workers' interests even continued during the heyday of labor power from the 1940s through the 1970s; however, the process accelerated over the next three decades and has now shifted labor and capital flows. The United States, once the leading manufacturer, is now the world's leading importer of fabricated goods, largely produced by the low-wage workers of the South, that is, the less developed nations of Asia, Latin America, and Africa.

The promotion and ascendancy of neoliberal capitalism on a global scale has significantly eroded worker rights and the ability of unions that are organized on a national basis to defend workers in their respective countries. Under neoliberal capitalism, the capacity of national governments to regulate the flow of capital, labor, and goods is reduced significantly in the global economy. To actively participate in trade, national governments must comply with new rules set out by international institutions that significantly compromise the power of labor in both the advanced economies of the North and the less developed ones of the South. These conditions that are imposed on national governments create significant uncertainties for workers around the world. As labor markets erode and unemployment rises in the North, new entrants that manufacture goods at lower cost appear in the South. While jobs are lost in the North, as a rule, the jobs that emerge in the South pay workers significantly lower wages, even in countries with much lower costs.

Globalization has significantly compromised wages, labor standards, and worker rights throughout the world; meanwhile, unions have become increasingly unable to control capital flows across national boundaries, and their bargaining power with employers has been severely eroded. The twenty-first century brand of globalized deregulated capitalism provides legal protections for multinational corporations while threatening worker and environmental standards. In this context, state power to protect noncorporate interests is severely marginalized. As trade and tariff restrictions that once protected labor unions on a national basis are broken down by the rise of global and regional trade blocs, workers no longer have the same capacity to appeal to state leaders for protection and relief. Since worker rights are not adequately incorporated into these global and regional agreements, labor, in most cases, finds itself sitting outside the table.

National labor unions the world over now debate how best to participate in a more hostile global economy dominated by large corporations. Some argue that their nation-states must engage in protectionist policies, including trade restrictions and higher tariffs on goods, to protect workers in their home countries. However, the emerging position among union leaders throughout the world is that the rapid flow of capital to the low-cost South, made possible by new information and communication technologies that allow corporations to relocate industry and services to host countries, cannot be stopped. Most nations believe that opting out of the global system is not an option, since they depend on foreign trade and do not want isolation from the rest of the world. Nonetheless, the scope and intensity of the current round of globalization is giving rise to higher levels of unemployment, underemployment, and displacement and the proliferation of low-wage jobs.

Labor Markets and Global Trade

Most labor organizations representing workers across industrial sectors do not believe that the tangible benefits of global trade outweigh the

huge costs to workers and their families. But since labor is not as strong as capital today, they must counter corporate-dominated globalization with demands for greater rights for workers. Labor unions have been formulating strategies on how best to address these issues, defend workers in their own nations, and increase labor standards throughout the world. This new labor approach takes a global perspective on labor rights, asserting that workers in all countries, rich and poor, must be paid decent wages and assured of a safe and healthy environment in which to work.

This objective of labor standards and rights is one that will take, at the very least, decades to attain—that is, if it can be attained. Since the global institutions that govern economic exchange do not take labor rights into account when determining terms of trade, a growing number of unions are debating how to pragmatically respond to the assault on workers' rights throughout the world. More and more, the labor movement is opposing the growing penetration of global trade organizations, since workers stand to gain little from more liberalized trade. Even in the best of worlds, if labor unions were allowed to actively participate in international organizations, they would be just one voice demanding labor standards in organizations dominated by exponents of corporate interests.

The lack of a role for defenders of labor interests in the more powerful global trade organizations significantly undermines labor rights. In the past three decades, the power of the World Trade Organization (WTO), the International Monetary Fund (IMF), the World Bank, and regional trade blocs have expanded dramatically, and, wittingly or not, these organizations have significant influence over labor flows across national boundaries and the conditions under which people work. National labor unions have declined as workers in unions have lost jobs that were relocated to lower-cost regions. As unions lose members, their influence over labor policy erodes significantly. The relaxation of trade policies is therefore inimical to the interest of unions; in particular, unions have been impacted by the growth of regional trade blocs and free trade zones such as the North American Free Trade Agreement (NAFTA), Mercosur (the South American trade bloc), and the European Union. In the Western Hemisphere, negotiations are under way for the creation of the Free Trade Area of the Americas, a trade bloc that would encompass North and South America.

Unions are now pursuing strategies for building solidarity across borders by supporting labor movements across national boundaries, and a broader international labor movement is emerging that may be able to defend the interests of workers in the advanced northern countries as well as in the undeveloped world of the South. However, many national and international labor organizations no longer believe they can advance the interests of workers in the current globalized system of predatory capitalism typical of the late twentieth century. A growing number of labor activists believe that unions should opt out of the system and call for a new system of trade that protects workers, the poor, peasants, and the global environment.

Wages and the WTO
(World Trade Organization)

The economic and political priorities of WTO member governments that are dominated by multinational corporations greatly outweigh any interest in reducing violations of core labor standards. Only governments can make formal complaints to the WTO; labor unions and human rights organizations can only encourage member states to do so. Since the WTO sanctions governments and not transnational corporations for labor rights violations, companies face few penalties and no real financial consequences.

A pressing question for labor movements in developed countries, according to Keith Ewing

(2000), is how they can demand compliance with international labor standards when their governments have not ratified or complied with many of these conventions and are in breach of their provisions. Ewing argued that the most pressing need is to advance the rights of workers and the poor throughout the world, and that better labor standards must be achieved for workers in countries of both the North and the South. To raise standards, labor unions must understand how hostile global corporations regularly violate worker rights and freedoms. Moreover, social clauses for labor must both protect jobs in rich countries and promote economic development in poorer countries.

How effective have the efforts to build a labor rights movement that encompasses the needs of workers in the South been? In the wake of the formation of the WTO, an international campaign emerged to establish the importance of labor rights in clauses, agreements, and conventions. However, thus far, the efforts have not successfully defended the core labor standards undermined by global agreements. Absent international labor rights campaigns for development-related demands and increasing union and social movement involvement in the South, efforts to improve the conditions of workers in the South will likely fail. International labor solidarity is necessary to complement lobbying efforts, with increased membership mobilization and protest activity, if any progress is to be made in this area. Ewing argued further that, rather than exclusively focusing on low-wage countries, greater attention must be paid to violations of labor rights in the United States.

In the Third World countries of Africa, Asia, and Latin America, although most trade unionists support the notion of labor rights as human rights, efforts to incorporate standards into the WTO, which is controlled by transnational corporations in northern governments, have not been successful. Arbitrary WTO labor standards have contributed to massive unemployment and would inevitably contribute to protectionism. Thus, other mechanisms to advance worker rights and protections without the threat of trade sanctions must be advanced by supporters of equality.

Labor Markets and International and State Regulations

In the North and South, government regulations that protected workers for half a century have been eroded as corporations have restructured their operations to save costs. On the job, workers can no longer count on the government to enforce its own regulations covering wages, hours, and safety in their work environments. More and more, corporations are outsourcing work tasks to subcontractors that offer manufactured goods and services at significantly lower cost. The outsourcing of work is producing low-wage jobs that do not even pretend to provide for the basic living requirements of workers and their families. The changes in the nature of the job are taking place concurrently with the erosion of the state social safety nets that people have relied on in the past to provide unemployment insurance, income support, medical benefits, and social security.

The decline in government social services for working people has had profound implications for the capacity of corporations to more freely shift capital, industry, and labor the world over. Globalization has accelerated the transformation of once stable labor markets in countries throughout the world. More precisely, globalization has created transnational linkages between countries and regions and reduced the power of governments to maintain old labor markets.

The acceleration of the flow of goods, capital, industry, technology, information, and workers spurred by advances in telecommunications and transportation has undermined established laws that protected labor standards in nations where labor movements formerly

defended workers and social safety nets. Thus, the regulatory capacity of labor markets by weaker states has declined as more powerful countries have permitted the erosion of regulatory standards that defended worker labor power. The rights of labor to organize are diminishing, as is welfare state protection through the social wage, the basket of government programs that defended workers from the effects of joblessness and poverty and that ensured reasonable levels of health care and education.

Corporate Economic Power and Wages

Government efforts to establish regional and international alliances and institutions, such as the North American Free Trade Agreement, the European Community, and the World Trade Organization, have been a major factor in globalization in recent decades. These efforts seek to break down trade barriers. But the growth of trade translates into a growing capacity and willingness among corporations to shift manufacturing industries from higher-wage to lower-wage countries as a means to expand profitability. Consequently, corporations once situated in one nation have become multinational firms with reduced loyalty to workers. The increased capital flows and the development of new industry in less developed and Third World countries that result from the establishment of multinational firms contribute to economic growth, but not necessarily to improved conditions for workers. For example, the massive shift of apparel firms from industrialized countries to less developed ones has created joblessness in advanced economies; it has also expanded the number of jobs in the less developed countries that are now the primary producers of garments, but the conditions for these workers have not necessarily improved, and these workers have few options, as job opportunities in older sectors of the economy have declined. The same trends can be seen in steel, automobiles, electronics, and toys and trinkets.

Transnational Labor

Besides affecting the flow of capital to low-cost labor markets, globalization affects the growth of labor mobility. In the 1990s, the great demand for cheap labor to fill essential jobs in the North spurred the expansion of low-wage migration from the South. With globalization, however, the labor flows are no longer largely limited to low-wage labor. As the populations of the North age and the number of available workers declines, there is a growing demand for high-skilled labor that is spurring a new kind of international migration. Table 1 demonstrates the sizable growth of international migration.

Wages and Regional Labor Markets

Over the past thirty years, most nation-states have steadily withdrawn from labor-market intervention and the provision of social welfare, and unions have weakened in response to the erosion of trade protection. Thus, deregulation is the dominant trend of the past twenty years. The changes in regional labor markets reflect the overall trend of the shift in production and services from North to South.

North America
The North American Free Trade Agreement of 1994 between Canada, Mexico, and the United States sharply reduced trade barriers in the region and dramatically accelerated the flow of labor and capital, leading to significant labor-market changes. The agreement has accentuated the differences in wages and facilitated the transfer of manufacturing from the United States to Mexico. The loss of high-wage jobs in the United States to Mexico has reduced wage growth in the manufacturing sector. Unions have been able to restrain the decline in wages;

Table 1: Foreign-Born Labor in Economically Advanced Countries

Foreign-Born Labor Force	As Percentage of Labor Force 1990	1998
Austria	7.4	9.9
Belgium	…	7.9
Denmark	…	3.1
France	6.2	6.1
Germany	7.1	9.1
Ireland	2.6	3.4
Italy	…	1.7
Japan	0.2	1.0
Luxembourg	45.2	55.0
Netherlands	3.1	2.9
Norway	2.3	2.8
Portugal	1.0	1.8
Spain	0.6	1.1
Sweden	5.4	5.2
Switzerland	18.9	17.5
United Kingdom	3.3	3.6
Australia	…	24.6
Canada	18.5	18.5
United States	9.4	10.8

Notes: Ellipses indicate that data is not available. Foreign labor force, data for other countries refer to noncitizens. Data relate to 1996.

Source: Organisation for Economic Co-operation and Development/SOPEMI, *Trends in International Migration* (Paris: OECD/SOPEMI, 1999).

however, the disappearance of jobs in manufacturing has sharply reduced the influence of organized labor, especially in the steel, machinery, and automobile industries.

The main labor-market trends are the growth of service-sector employment and the "casualization" of employment. Indeed, employment continued to grow in the United States during the economic expansion of the 1990s mainly as a result of the creation of jobs in the service sector. Most of the new job growth has been in health care, education, communications, high technology, and support services. Wage growth has been restrained by the expansion of low-wage jobs in the retail, food services, hospitality, and building service industries. Unions have targeted service-sector workers for organizing but, with the exception of health care and education, have yet to gain a presence to significantly influence wages. For example, the growth of large all-purpose retail chain stores has put significant pressure on unionized workers in the supermarket industry. In Canada, unions remain significantly stronger than in the United States.

The growth of casual labor is a new phenomenon. Today, the notion of a job as a means of providing for one's essential needs is becoming obsolete for many workers. Casual labor refers to nonstandard jobs such as day labor, temporary work, seasonal work, part-time work, and the fundamental redefinition of norms established in the 1930s about the value of work. The lifetime job has become an anachronism, and corporations typically do not pay workers enough to meet basic living needs for themselves and their families. The restructuring of the economy has forced people to work extra hard and to rely on more people for income to maintain what is conventionally considered a middle-class lifestyle.

Latin America and the Caribbean

During the past two decades, dependence on the U.S. market has increased substantially in Latin America and the Caribbean. By the 1990s, much of Latin America had adopted neoliberal policies favored by the United States, opening financial and labor markets to international capital forces, and some of the countries—most notably Argentina—were considered by proponents of free markets as models for the developing world. But the region suffered major setbacks at the beginning of the twenty-first century as countries were unable to maintain a stable balance of trade. The financial crisis in Argentina led to the devaluation of that nation's currency and declines in employment security and living standards. Throughout the region, severe austerity programs have been imposed by governments in response to demands by the IMF, leading to the growth of unemployment and political unrest.

Brazil, with one of the highest global levels of wage inequality between rich and poor, has restrained its budget deficits and adhered to international financial strictures that have placed great strains on the majority of the population, which is living in poverty. In October 2002, Luiz Inácio Lula da Silva, leader of the Workers Party, was elected president of Brazil after promising to improve the conditions of the peasantry and working class. However, under pressure from international financial institutions, the government remains wedded to neoliberal policies that have benefited the affluent without improving the lives of the poor. Thus, although Brazil has not experienced a financial collapse equivalent to that of Argentina, and despite the rhetoric of helping the poor, poverty and inequality have not been stanched. The region as a whole suffers from the rise of poverty; wage jobs in the informal sectors do not provide the basic needs for workers and their families. Instead, new jobs paying poverty wages and unregulated by the state have increased over the past decade. High unemployment and underemployment among significant sectors of the population are a defining feature of the Latin American and Caribbean region.

Europe

Western and Northern European workers continue to have the most wage protections in the world stemming from their comprehensive social welfare policies. The protections include long-term unemployment benefits, worker retraining programs, and health benefits and pensions. The social safety net is in large part due to the strength of the labor unions in Europe. Unions continue to bargain on an industrial and labor-market basis, as opposed to enterprise-level bargaining, which is prominent in North America. Consequently, unionized workers have become accustomed to steady and equal wage growth. Since the early 1990s, private-sector corporations have sought to establish enterprise-level bargaining to gain competitive advantages. Although some erosion of industrial bargaining has occurred, on the whole the industry-level model remains the norm. In the public sector, state governments have sought to curtail wages and benefits for public-sector employees. Despite several inroads, including cuts in wages and benefits, the trade unions in the region have successfully challenged most of these efforts to extract concessions from workers.

The continuing regional integration of the European Union and its labor market has resulted in growing interdependence and an enlarging of the trade bloc to include countries of Central and Eastern Europe. Continental Western European countries have eliminated their national currencies and replaced it with a common currency—the euro—that accentuates the labor-market wage differences in the region. The United Kingdom has retained the pound as its currency, however, and has not adopted the euro—reflecting the uneven integration of member states. EU member states are required to reduce budget deficits through curtailing spending, and most have initiated efforts to reduce social benefits to conform to the new policies. The EU has eliminated labor-market barriers that in the past prevented citizens from working in other countries of the region. Meanwhile, national immigration laws have limited the number of workers from outside the bloc who are permitted to work in the region.

Expansion of the European Union will further erode trade restrictions across the continent. Countries in Central and Eastern Europe seek to join the bloc in the hope of promoting trade and increasing living standards. However, the EU plans a gradual process of integration that will have the effect of reducing wages and benefits as workers in high-wage Western Europe come into greater competition with workers in lower-wage Eastern Europe. The gradual integration may have the effect of even further accentuating wage differences among member states.

East and Southeast Asia
In the post–World War II era, Japan, with its advanced and extensive industrial base, has maintained dominance in East Asia. Up until the 1980s, the Japanese economy, devastated by the war, benefited from government economic and technical support for industrial development and export promotion. In the 1980s, however, Japanese workers, guaranteed lifetime employment at relatively high wages, began to encounter intense regional competition from the export-promotion economies known as the four tigers: South Korea, Hong Kong, Singapore, and Taiwan, which produced goods at significantly lower cost. In subsequent years, production shifted to even cheaper labor markets in the Philippines, China, and Southwest Asia. Indeed, trade restrictions, tariffs, and even lower wages in the United States made it cheaper to shift production of durable manufacturing goods to North America.

The 1997 financial crisis in East Asia severely eroded the "economic miracle" in the countries of the Pacific Rim. Virtually every country in the East Asia region faced economic decline and currency devaluation, leading to growing unemployment and declining wages. In the ensuing five years, the region has only slowly recovered as national governments imposed structural adjustment policies that eroded living standards by reducing social benefits, demanding wage concessions from workers, and devaluing currencies.

In the 1990s, Indonesia, South Korea, Malaysia, and Thailand, considered models of economic growth, were under threat from nations in the region with even lower labor costs, including Cambodia, Myanmar, Vietnam, and of course China, where new foreign investment contributed to the growth in the garment and electronics industries. The typical garment worker is an adolescent girl or young woman employed at a wage below the local poverty line.

The most notable labor-market trend in East Asia is the growing competitiveness of China. Despite the fact that the government maintains its facade as a socialist state, since the mid-1970s public officials and economic leaders have begun a slow but sure shift from publicly owned enterprises toward privately owned industries. Privatization in China accelerated in the last two decades of the twentieth century and the country is now seeking to compete in global consumer markets. Privatization and the opening of the economy to foreign investment have had profound economic effects on the country's population by exacerbating inequality between rich and poor. As the government focuses investment on industrial and commercial development, the standard of living in urban areas has increased substantially. However, the focus on urban development has dramatically increased poverty in the nation's rural regions. The growth of rural poverty has forced large segments of the population into urban areas; those who can find work are employed in marginal positions in the informal sector, when they can find work at all.

South Asia

The economies of South Asia, most notably India, Pakistan, and Bangladesh, are marked by the divide between urban and rural regions. Although most of the region is mired in poverty, the advance of new technology has spurred economic growth in major urban centers. Perhaps most notable is the development of Bangalore, India, as a technology and communications center. Advances in Internet technology have made it easier for work to be outsourced by corporations to employees paid a fraction of the wages in the global North. Not all new job growth is among high-skilled workers. Increasingly, transnational corporations are outsourcing communications to the region through the development of calling centers that service the needs of consumers in North America and Western Europe. Workers in the region suffer from high underemployment, poverty-wage jobs, and youth unemployment.

Middle East and North Africa

The dominant industry of the Middle East and North Africa is oil. However, the petroleum industry employs comparably few workers. Several industries related to oil have grown in importance, including tertiary service jobs in the building of infrastructure, transportation, and finance. The region is affected by significant problems, not least of which are the ongoing Palestine-Israel conflict and the growing U.S. military presence. Political instability and ongoing military involvement has created high levels of unemployment and underemployment, exacerbated by rapid population growth. In response, oil-producing countries are reducing their reliance on foreign guestworkers from the Arab world, intensifying unemployment in sending countries.

Africa

With few exceptions, the African continent has been mired in economic decline since the 1980s. Countries in the region suffer from severe balance of trade shortfalls and in many cases must comply with IMF restrictions that impose structural adjustment policies that necessitate reductions in essential social services (education, health care, and housing). Civil war and political turmoil have also limited economic growth—most notably in the Democratic Republic of the Congo, the Ivory Coast, Liberia, Rwanda, and Sierra Leone. Although the continent has some bright spots (for example, Ghana and Uganda), industrial production has on the whole declined. The falling value of natural resources on international commodity markets—traditionally a major staple of national economies—is intensifying the region's problems. The rising AIDS crisis has placed greater stress on national economies, as high death rates among workers during their most productive years diminishes the workforce and significantly increases health-care and child-care costs.

Immanuel Ness

See Also International Productivity; International Labor Organization (ILO); Labor Rights and Standards

References

Baldwin, Robert E., and L. Alan Winters, eds. 2004. *Challenges to Globalization: Analyzing the Economics.* Chicago: University of Chicago Press.

Bales, Kevin. 2000. *Disposable People: New Slavery in the Global Economy.* Berkeley: University of California Press.

Bhagwati, Jagdish. 2004. *In Defense of Globalization.* Oxford: Oxford University Press.

Elliott, Kimberly Ann, and Richard B. Freeman. 2003. *Can Labor Standards Improve under Globalization?* Vienna: Institute for International Economics.

Ewing, Keith, and Tom Sibley. 2000. *International Trade Union Rights for the New Millennium.* Institute for Employment Rights.

International Labour Organization. 2000. *World Labour Report: Income Security and Social Protection in a Changing World.* Geneva: ILO.

———. 2001. *The World Employment Report 2001: Life at Work in the Information Economy.* Geneva: ILO.

———. 2002. *2001 Labour Overview: Latin America and the Caribbean.* Geneva: ILO.

Lee, Eddy. 1998. *The Asian Financial Crisis: The Challenge for Social Policy.* Geneva: International Labour Organization.

Mishel, Laurence, and Paula B. Voos, eds. 1992. *Unions and Economic Competitiveness.* Armonk, NY: M. E. Sharpe.

O'Higgins, Niall. 2001. *Youth Unemployment and Employment Policy: A Global Perspective.* Geneva: International Labour Organization.

Organisation of Economic Co-operation and Development/SOPEMI. 1999. *Trends in International Migration.* Paris: OECD/SOPEM.

Ozaki, Muneto, ed. 1999. *Negotiating Flexibility: The Role of the Social Partners and the State.* Geneva: International Labour Organization.

Portes, Alejandro, and Manuel Castels. 1991. "World Underneath: The Origins, Dynamics, and Effects of the Informal Economy." In Alejandro Portes, Manuel Castels, and Lauren A. Benton. *The Informal Economy: Studies in Advanced and Less Developed Countries.* Baltimore: Johns Hopkins University Press.

Richards, Peter. 2001. *Towards the Goal of Full Employment: Trends, Obstacles and Policies.* Geneva: International Labour Organization.

Sassen, Saskia. 1988. *The Mobility of Labor and Capital: A Study in International Investment and Labor Flow.* Cambridge: Cambridge University Press.

———. 1991. *The Global City: New York, London, Tokyo.* Princeton, NJ: Princeton University Press.

Schumpeter, Joseph. 1942. *Capitalism, Socialism, and Democracy.* New York: Harper.

Stalker, Peter. 2000. *Workers without Frontiers: The Impact of Globalization on International Migration.* Geneva: International Labour Organization.

Stiglitz, Joseph E. 2003. *Globalization and Its Discontents.* New York: W. W. Norton.

Tajgman, David, and Karen Curtis. 2000. *Freedom of Association: A User's Guide to Standards, Principles and Procedures of the International Labour Organization.* Geneva: International Labour Organization.

Torres, Raymond. 2001. *Towards a Socially Sustainable World Economy: An Analysis of the Social Pillars of Globalization.* Geneva: International Labour Organization.

Money and Monetary Policy

"Globalization" is a broad term representing a wave of different phenomena. To understand the effect of globalization on a particular feature of an economy—in this case monetary policy—it is first necessary to identify what aspects of globalization are relevant to that feature. Globalization affects monetary policy because it increases the mobility of capital around the world, that is, the increased integration and sophistication of international financial markets are making it increasingly easier and less costly to sell assets in one country and buy assets in another, and this greater capital mobility influences the effectiveness of monetary policy. Although greater capital mobility also has the undisputed benefit of promoting a more efficient allocation of world capital by more deftly directing it where it will be most productive, it is the compromising effect that increased capital mobility has on monetary policy that is addressed here. To explain exactly why the degree of capital mobility matters, it is helpful to start with some basics about money and monetary policy.

Liquidity

Money is the medium of exchange that finances almost every purchase of a good or asset, and it is requisite for the operation of anything more than a primitive, barter economy. It circulates around an economy as people receive it (in exchange for some good, service, or asset) and then spend it. A meaningful measure of the quantity of the medium of exchange in an economy is the nominal money supply divided by the price level. This measure is referred to as the level of "real balances." The term "liquidity" is used to characterize the quantity of real balances in an economy. For example, either a greater nominal money supply or a lower price level increases real balances and, therefore, increases the level of liquidity.

Although an economy's real balances constitute the amount of the medium of exchange that actually exists, they do not necessarily equal the amount that is required in order for the economy to function at its peak, sustainable level of output. The given size and structure of the economy, as well as the tastes of the economic agents, determine a minimum amount of real balances that are necessary to accommodate the economic activity when all resources are efficiently employed at their maximum sustainable level, or "full-employment" level of output. Any level of liquidity less than the minimum level will hinder economic activity in general owing to the scarcity of the medium of exchange to carry out transactions. But it is interesting to note that the slower economy will put resources out of work that would be productive if the economy were at full employment, and the increase in unemployed resources will push input prices down, which in turn will lower output prices. The lower price level will increase the level of real balances. Therefore, too little liquidity in the economy will bring about equilibrating forces that increase real balances.

An excessive amount of liquidity in the system, that is, more real balances than are needed to permit the economy to function at its full-employment level, will cause increased activity as the excess liquidity circulates around the economy like a hot potato. Not only can this stimulate output to rise above its long-run equilibrium level, but it will also generate inflation. Thus, a surplus of liquidity will cause prices to rise, which will bring the level of real balances down until the surplus disappears.

Although the optimal level of liquidity will eventually be attained owing to the equilibrating forces that drop prices when liquidity is too scarce and raise them when there is excess liquidity, the speed of the price adjustments is a subject of serious and important debate in economics. On one side of the debate are economists who believe that prices are "sticky" and move so slowly that changing the nominal money supply can accelerate the adjustment of real balances and the economy back to full employment. These economists advocate "activist" (or "discretionary") monetary policy, that is, they recommend changing the money supply to address, if not prevent, recessions and economic booms. On the other side of the debate are economists who think that prices are flexible and will adjust before talented human beings can perceive actual liquidity problems and appropriately adjust the nominal money supply. These economists do not advocate activist monetary policy but instead prefer to adhere to some predictable, long-term trend or rule in determining how much money to issue. Some of these economists even maintain that prices are "perfectly flexible" and adjust instantaneously and, therefore, that monetary policy has no effect on real balances or the real economy, that is, they maintain that money is "neutral." For example, classical and real-business-cycle theories assume price flexibility that assures money neutrality and aggregate output that does not deviate from its full-employment level. Any variations in output that appear, like a business cycle, are due to changes or shocks to the productivity of the underlying economy.

Monetary policy clearly influences prices and the rate of inflation regardless of the flexi-bility of prices. Although the rate of inflation can influence the level of real output (that is, money can fail to be "supraneutral") even when prices are perfectly flexible, any such effects are small compared to the possible effects of monetary policy when prices are not perfectly flexible. The remaining discussion addresses the relationship between globalization and monetary policy assuming that prices are sticky.

Confidence

Given the importance of having a sufficient level of real balances to achieve full-employment output, it is evident that a major goal of monetary policy is to maintain that minimum level of liquidity. A second yet related concern of the monetary authority that determines a country's monetary policy is that people have confidence in the currency's future worth. As part of being an effective medium of exchange, money needs to be a dependable "store of value." After all, who would accept money in an exchange if they believed it could devalue before they had the opportunity to spend it? As uncertainty about the money's future worth increases, the less desirable it is to accept, which only handicaps its effectiveness as a medium of exchange. Perhaps more important, the price of bonds denominated in the questionable currency falls as promised future receipts in terms of the money are less valuable; reductions in confidence will raise interest rates.

A principal source of reduced confidence in money is expected inflation. Inflation is simply a reduction in the purchasing power of money; therefore, expected inflation makes receiving and holding money less appealing. Past experience has demonstrated that one of the more dependable indicators of coming inflation is current inflation. Monetary authorities have learned the effect that current inflation tends to have on expected inflation, and they are mindful that excess liquidity can increase inflation, which will spark fears of future inflation and hurt confidence in money.

In the discussion on liquidity above it was noted that increased liquidity raises bond prices and lowers interest rates. This is true if, as was implicitly assumed, the level of confidence in the money is not affected by the change. Here it is acknowledged that increased liquidity can lead to expected inflation, which will diminish people's confidence in the money and raise interest rates. The net effect of an increase in the money supply on interest rates depends on the relative strengths of the two influences.

If an economy were closed to any interaction with other economies, then confidence in its money would be buoyed by the mere lack of substitutes. The fact that any transaction beyond barter would require the currency, and that any asset would carry a market price in terms of the currency, helps assure people that the money will be worth something in the future. This is not to imply that confidence cannot be dented. High enough inflation would give people an incentive to avoid holding their wealth in cash and other forms of money and assets that do not keep pace with inflation. Interest rates would rise as bonds would become relatively less attractive compared to other assets such as equities, real estate, and commodities such as gold or antiques. In addition, the resources used to carry out cash-management practices that limit the time that wealth is held in money represent a cost to the economy (called "shoeleather costs"), since those resources are diverted from the production of other goods and services.

Confidence and Exchange Rates

The problems accompanying reduced confidence in a country's money are much worse for an open economy, where foreign assets serve as substitute instruments for maintaining people's wealth, than in a closed economy. In the case of the open economy, people can protect their wealth from inflation and the reduced purchasing power of the domestic currency by selling their domestic assets to purchase and hold foreign assets. The existence of different currencies leads to foreign exchange markets where the laws of supply and demand determine the relative prices of currency, which, of course, are known as exchange rates. Inflation in one of the currencies will cause its exchange rate to fall. There are two reasons for this correlation. First, inflation will make the country's goods relatively more expensive, thus making its exports more expensive and its imports relatively cheaper. The associated decrease in demand for the currency and increase in its supply causes its exchange rate to drop. It is not surprising that the loss in purchasing power of a currency due to inflation is matched by a fall in the currency's exchange rate.

Second, and more important, because domestic inflation will cause the exchange rate to fall for the reason just described, there will be an incentive for capital to move from assets denominated in the domestic currency to assets denominated to foreign currencies before the value of the domestic currency can fall. There is essentially a rush to sell the currency before it depreciates, but, of course, this capital flow increases the supply of the currency in the foreign exchange markets and assures that the exchange rate does fall. The greater the mobility of capital, the more rapidly this shift in assets can occur, and the faster and farther the exchange rate will fall.

This reveals the self-fulfilling nature of expectations regarding the exchange rate when capital is mobile. The mere belief or fear that a currency will depreciate will cause people to transfer their assets from that currency, and the associated increase in supply of the currency in the foreign exchange market causes the depreciation. Even simple rumors that manage to cast doubt on a currency's credibility can lower its exchange rate. As globalization reduces the costs and barriers to capital flows, the self-fulfilling reactions occur more dependably and rapidly.

The possible volatility of a "floating" or flexible exchange rate that is left free (by the government) to rise or fall in response to the forces of supply and demand for the currency engenders uncertainty about what the exchange rate will be at any particular future date. In other words, it reduces confidence in the currency. This uncertainty accompanying floating exchange rates is referred to as "exchange rate risk," which, like almost all forms of risk, will generally dissuade economic agents from going ahead with economic activity. Uncertainty will promote agents pausing and waiting for more information before acting, and therefore it often causes economic activity to slow. Perhaps the most tangible indicator of the reduced activity is a higher interest rate as investors require higher expected returns as premiums to compensate them for accepting the greater risk. Again, the higher interest rate reduces investment and consumption. Uncertainty about the future value of a particular currency can also discourage the formation of trade relationships with exporters or importers from that country.

The damaging nature of exchange rate risk under a floating exchange rate with respect to both international capital and trade flows has led to the concept that governments should intervene in foreign exchange markets to stabilize the exchange rate. Essentially, a government can try to improve confidence in its currency by following a policy whereby it augments the demand or supply of its currency, whichever is necessary to dampen, if not prevent, movements in the exchange rate. A "fixed" exchange rate is a policy in which the government agrees to honor a particular exchange rate, thus purchasing any excess supply or supplying any excess demand prevailing at that exchange rate from the private participants in the foreign exchange market. There are less extreme policies that governments might take that are designed to stabilize, if not rigidly fix, the exchange rate (for example, crawling pegs, wide bands, managed floats). One difficulty with fixing or stabilizing an exchange rate that would otherwise be depreciating is that the government must own sufficient foreign cur-

rency to purchase its own currency in the foreign exchange markets. A currency board is a monetary agency designed—and with sufficient foreign reserves—to honor the government's chosen fixed exchange rate.

The Tradeoff between Liquidity and Confidence

One might initially think from reading the above that the ideal amount of real balances in an economy is just the minimum necessary to meet the liquidity requirement for full employment, without any excess liquidity that would spur inflation and compromise confidence in the money. Unfortunately, it is not quite that simple. The problem is that the level of confidence depends on expectations of future conditions and not just on the current level of liquidity. Therefore, it is possible that people's confidence in a currency can become shaky because of uncertainty about the future, even though no excess liquidity currently exists. In this case, they will still want to protect their wealth and sell assets denominated in the seemingly shaky currency to buy assets denominated in a more trustworthy currency, which includes selling the questioned currency in the foreign exchange markets. Without government intervention, the increased supply of the suspected currency will cause the exchange rate to drop, which will validate the doubts that precipitated the capital outflow in the first place. This depreciation will only make the concept of exchange rate risk more salient to economic agents, and it could give the currency a lingering reputation of not meriting confidence.

If the government chooses to defend the credibility of its currency (and has accumulated sufficient foreign currencies, or "foreign reserves"), it will purchase its own currency in the foreign exchange markets to dampen or prevent the fall in the exchange rate. Although credibility might be saved by this policy, the purchasing of domestic currency in the foreign exchange markets contracts the outstanding money supply and therefore reduces liquidity. It is possible (and some would argue it has occurred many times) that defending the reputation of currency by reducing liquidity will contract the economy along with the money supply. This analysis demonstrates how a country's exchange rate policy is inseparable from its monetary policy.

Monetary Policy and the Tradeoff between Liquidity and Confidence

The ongoing tradeoff facing those who conduct monetary policy is that increasing the money supply increases liquidity, but the increase can threaten higher inflation that will undermine confidence. The benefit of increased liquidity is a short-run boost to output. Even if an economy is already operating above its full employment level, added real balances can increase output even further (along with the greater inflation as the economy rebounds farther back to full employment). More practically, monetary policy is used to accelerate the return of output to its long-run equilibrium faster than price adjustments would accomplish it. Not only is expansionary monetary policy employed in recessions, but contractionary monetary policy is used to tame booms and prevent the associated increase in prices, which, as pointed out above, can reduce confidence in the currency. But even though most economists agree that changes in liquidity will have short-run consequences, mainstream economic theory maintains that it does not affect the long-run level of output.

The benefits of confidence, in contrast, contribute to the economy in both short-run and long-run ways. The perceived safety of the currency makes bonds denominated in the currency more desirable and increases their prices, that is, interest rates fall, promoting more investment and consumption over the short run. Confidence also benefits the underlying real economy more generally by maintaining a safe, less risky environment for economic actors that makes them more likely to invest, consume, work, and employ their resources. Thus, the economy will produce more than when a backdrop of uncertainty clouds the economic landscape and complicates people's economic decisions. By influencing the full-employment level of output, altering the degree of confidence will also affect short-run activity. But the combined short-run benefits of preserving confidence by contracting the money supply are often smaller than the harmful short-run effects of the lost liquidity. Still, many maintain that the short-term pain is worth the long-term gain from having a credible currency with a sound reputation. Thus, the tradeoff between liquidity and confidence can be cast as a tradeoff between short-run and long-run output.

Economists are inclined to favor the growth of long-run output and therefore tend to advocate monetary policy that preserves confidence in the currency. The cost of more variable short-run output that creates larger swings in the business cycle is obviously undesirable, but it is generally preferred by many economists to sacrificing growth. However, politicians and government leaders are more intent on keeping their supporters—and not economists— happy. There is much evidence to suggest that the recent short-run behavior of the economy has much to do with a politician's popularity and likelihood of reelection. Therefore, those people who are actually in charge of conducting monetary policy often prefer a monetary policy that focuses on liquidity, even though these same people may publicly pay homage to the importance of confidence and the short-run sacrifices that might be necessary to achieve greater long-run growth.

Thus, financial markets observe those who conduct monetary policy as if they were watching someone on a diet. The long-term benefits of a diet are known, and dieters will claim that the benefits are worth the short-run discomfort of not eating everything that is desired and easily available. But maintaining a diet takes a great amount of discipline because it only takes one moment of weakness for the diet to be broken. Similarly, those who are conducting monetary policy when a recession occurs may be torn between maintaining the credibility of the currency, or increasing liquidity to help alleviate the short-run misery (and increase the probability of them staying in power). Choosing to preserve credibility requires repeatedly making the decision not to increase liquidity.

The degree of confidence in a currency depends on people's expectations regarding the *possible* future behavior of monetary policy officials, but, unfortunately, looking at their past behavior does not provide certainty regarding their future actions. Just as one may doubt the willpower of a successful dieter when a piece of chocolate cake is about to be put before him, there is often uncertainty about the monetary policymakers' commitment to credibility when a recession is seemingly on its way, if not already present. Argentina, plagued by this kind of problem, fixed its currency (the peso) to the dollar in 1990 and honored the same exchange rate for over ten years. But still by the ninth, tenth, and eleventh year confidence in the currency was clearly lacking.[1] Argentina dutifully sacrificed liquidity to honor the fixed exchange rate, but the economic hardship that existed, in part because of the low levels of liquidity, only fueled fears that the government would yield to political pressures, expand the money supply, and let the exchange rate drop. Thus, a kind of vicious cycle was in place: Reduced confidence in a currency with a fixed exchange rate led to reduced liquidity that harmed the economy, which then generated fears that the government would concede and increase the money supply (that is, a further loss of confidence). In Argentina's case, more than a decade of demonstrating its commitment to assuring the peso's value (relative to the dollar) was insufficient to establish confidence, as people still questioned the Argentine government's future resolve.[2]

Argentina's quandary led some economists to recommend a policy of dollarization, in which Argentina would retire its own peso and adopt the U.S. dollar as its only legal tender. This extreme policy would at least finally give Argentina a working money with credibility, but, of course, at the cost of permanently forfeiting the power to influence liquidity.[3]

The difficulty in constantly determining the appropriate monetary actions that is part of an activist monetary policy is compounded by the self-fulfilling nature of suspected exchange rate movements that are facilitated by capital mobility. Activist monetary policy itself generates uncertainty about how and when the monetary authorities anticipate or experience shocks to fundamentals, as well as uncertainty about how they perceive and then react to possible changes to the level of confidence in the currency. Uncertainty regarding what the monetary officials might do only makes asset owners more jittery and more ready to transfer their wealth to assets denominated in different currencies. The greater the ease of such transfers, the larger the wave of capital flows in reaction to concerns about potential monetary policy as well as to shocks of all other kinds. These larger waves have more dramatic effects on the exchange rate, which only heighten exchange rate risk, which in turn only makes wealth holders even more cautious.

Monetary Policy Options Given the Tradeoff

Globalization and the corresponding increase in capital mobility has essentially eliminated monetary policy as an effective countercyclical policy tool for many countries. For example, if a country were to increase the money supply hoping to counter a recession, then it risks engendering fears of a depreciation of the currency, and capital would flee the country. Not only would this movement in capital bring about the feared depreciation, it would also cause interest rates to rise (that is, domestic asset prices would fall now that they were less desirable), and this would have adverse effects on investment as well as consumption activity. All in all, the costs of active monetary policy have grown to be much larger than the benefits for many countries.

There are serious concerns about the variability of exchange rates in general and the associated exchange rate risk. The volatility of exchange rates is not just because of monetary policy actions; other types of shocks and doubts afflicting assets denominated in a particular currency will also cause capital flight and self-fulfilling depreciations of the currency. Many economists have endorsed the idea of capital controls to impede the flow of capital and stabilize exchange rates.[4] They do not dispute that increased capital mobility allocates capital around the world more efficiently, but they believe that reducing exchange rate risk is worth the loss of this particular benefit. Examples of capital controls include taxes on exported factor income, required domestic deposits with foreign ownership of domestic capital, and even taxes on foreign exchange transactions (for example, the Tobin tax). Of course, one argument for capital controls is that they undo many of the effects of globalization and partially restore the usefulness of monetary policy: Altering liquidity has less of a deleterious impact on confidence when capital is prevented from fleeing the country.

An alternative policy to impeding capital flows is to join with other countries and share a currency in a monetary union. This is what many countries of Europe have done through the creation of the European Central Bank and the euro. As was pointed out above, a closed economy's currency would benefit from the lack of substitute currencies to hold wealth in. Therefore, knowing that all transactions will ultimately take place using that currency gives it an inherent degree of credibility. Similarly, larger, stronger economies provide a larger base of activity that employs their respective currencies and gives reason to believe the currency will be of value in the future. Confidence in the U.S. dollar is bolstered by the large amount of economic activity within the United States and around the world where payments are in dollars. Small countries do not have the same advantage in maintaining confidence in their currencies. However, a group of small countries can form a monetary union with a single currency that serves as the medium of exchange for all the economic activity of the member countries. Of course, sharing a currency means that the corresponding monetary policy must be shared as well. For example, since Germany and Ireland belong to the same monetary union, it is impossible to conduct expansionary monetary policy for Germany that does not also affect Ireland.

Conclusion

The central benefit of activist monetary policy—that is, the decision to add liquidity to promote more economic activity in the face of a slowdown—has remained relatively unaffected by the increased capital mobility that has accompanied globalization. However, the downside of activist monetary policy—that is, the self-fulfilling consequences of diminished confidence in a currency due to the mere possibility of future monetary policy–induced inflation and depreciation of the currency—has been exacerbated by greater capital mobility. Globalization has made confidence in a currency increasingly vulnerable when exchange rates are flexible, and if countries attempt to fix or stabilize their exchange rates, then the level of liquidity can be compromised.

The mutual exclusivity of activist monetary policy (which enables policymakers to effectively alter the level of liquidity), fixed exchange rates (which maintain the credibility of the currency), and capital mobility constitute the "inconsistent trinity." Any two of these highly desirable characteristics can coexist, but governments are forced to decide which of the three to sacrifice. It would seem that most governments of small countries claim—whether credibly or not—to be forgoing monetary policy/liquidity management. They do not dare

inhibit capital flows from increasing investment and assisting growth, and lost confidence
in the currency will not only keep foreign
savers from investing domestically, but domestic savers as well. However, a currency that
serves a large amount of economic activity,
such as the U.S. dollar, has an inherent advantage in maintaining confidence. Therefore, the
U.S. government sacrifices less in terms of confidence by adjusting the level of liquidity and
still benefits somewhat from activist monetary
policy. This is one reason why many members
of the European Union were willing to join a
monetary union and replace their respective
traditional currencies with the more widely accepted euro.

Stephen Elwood

See Also National Government Policies

Endnotes

1. Throughout these years the interest rates on U.S.
dollar loans/deposits in Argentine financial institutions
remained significantly lower than interest rates on Argentine peso loans/deposits.

2. This is not to imply that Argentina's problems did
not have other causes, including questionable fiscal policies.

3. Another cost of dollarization would be the loss of
seigniorage that the Argentine government would otherwise accrue from providing the domestic currency.

4. The fact that many top economists advocate some
sort of capital controls is remarkable: The idea that raising transaction costs to impede market activity could
raise social welfare runs completely counter to bedrock
economic intuitions.

References

Browning, Martin, and Annamaria Lusardi. 1996.
    "Household Saving: Micro Theories and Micro Facts."
    Journal of Economic Literature 34 (December):
    1797–1855.
Greenspan, Alan. 1998. "The Globalization of Finance."
    Cato Journal 17, no. 3 (Winter): 243–250.
Obstfeld, Maurice. 1998. "The Global Capital Market:
    Benefactor or Menace." *Journal of Economic
    Perspectives* 12, no. 4 (Fall): 9–30.
Smithin, John. 1999. "Money and National Sovereignty in
    the Global Economy." *Eastern Economic Journal* 25,
    no. 1 (Winter): 49–61.
Volcker, Paul. 2002. "Globalization and the World of
    Finance." *Eastern Economic Journal* 28, no. 1
    (Winter): 13–20.

Monopolies and Antitrust Legislation

Monopoly

The term "monopoly" refers to the artificial exclusive right or privilege to control, own, buy, or sell something. A monopoly is formed in expectation of enlarged profits, wages, or other benefits not possible in a market of free, unrestricted competition. Such rights and privileges of a monopoly serve as imitation property rights, which have been in existence from the beginning. An example is a free man's monopoly over his labor; another example is a slave master's monopoly over the slave's labor. People who own their own property can dictate when to buy, sell, work, and develop the land. A firm has a monopoly over what it produces and sells.

Firms that have a monopoly often exercise illegitimate control, that is, they assume the right to dictate production levels and prices independently of the market mechanism of supply and demand. Their power derives from either a grant by the state or from some other means of force. Such monopolies lead to artificially adjusted prices, inefficiencies in production, unsatisfied consumer demand, and a reduced division of labor; in a globalized market, these negative effects can have global effects. The monopolistic market works contrary to the motives of achieving economic growth and prosperity.

Monopolistic Market Structures

In a capitalist society, the microeconomic model of pure or perfect competition is the targeted ideal. The purely competitive market is characterized by easy entry into an industry. Many firms producing homogeneous goods (that is, goods that are identical or easily substituted) must compete with each other for business. Each controls a small, nearly equal share of the industry's market. The market's supply-and-demand mechanism, based on consumer preferences, production costs, and the like, drives the prices for goods. Firms that cannot keep up with the market's level of efficiency are eliminated; they may be unable to adjust their prices for fear of losing business. If an overambitious firm attempts to engage in "predatory pricing," driving prices down to force competition out of the market, it will be hurt in the long run. It cannot maintain prices below cost for long before it begins to suffer, too. Easy entry allows a new firm to purchase the capital of the dying firm, in order to compete with the suicidal firm.

In contrast to the purely competitive market, the monopolistic market is controlled by one monopolizing firm. It may gain market control from other firms because of superior levels of efficiency, exclusive access to important resources, or other means. This firm acts as the sole supplier of a good, unthreatened by the production of any close substitutes. In the absence of competition, the firm acts as a "price setter" rather than a "price taker." Prices are determined by the monopoly's profit-optimizing plans. This usually requires artificially limiting the supply by decreasing the levels of production or barring consumer access to goods. As a result, consumer demand remains unmet, since consumers are forced to pay too much for too little compared to what the market would naturally permit.

The monopolist's success serves as a primary attraction to competition. Difficult or impossible entry into the market keeps rival firms from attempting to share in these artificially large profits. If another firm is able to enter the market to compete with the monopolistic firm, then the monopoly collapses, and output and prices return to the market levels. A purely monopolistic market is rare. More common are similar structures that are able to function much like a monopoly but contain more than one firm. These structures are the "oligopoly" and the "monopolistic competition" forms.

The oligopolistic market is characterized by a small number of dominant firms and large monopolistic-like barriers to entry. In the case of a balanced oligopoly, the market power is equal. Threat from competition discourages firms from price setting, just as in the purely competitive market. In the case of an unbalanced oligopoly, one firm is more dominant than the others and acts as a monopolistic price setter, and the other dominant firms must act as "price takers" in a competitive environment.

In monopolistic competition, a number of firms compete with each other but individually have more control over price than in a purely competitive situation. Product heterogeneity, real or imaginary differentiation, such as that through brand recognition, plays a large role in allowing the firms to control prices. For firms in both the oligopoly and the monopolistic competition structures, advertising is the crucial means for increasing market power.

Market Monopolizing Techniques

Attempts to increase market control in a competitive market structure rarely produce long-lasting success. A monopolizing firm can use various means to control prices and competitors, such as mergers. A vertical merger unites the firm to its own supplier. This sort of merger can reduce a firm's production costs, lowering the prices of goods. By gaining control over

production resources, a firm can exclude competition from accessing these resources cheaply. Competitors are forced to raise their prices above the market rate and risk being thrown out of business.

Another merger type is the horizontal merger, a merger between two firms producing identical or substitute goods. Unlike the vertical merger, this one can potentially increase a firm's market share and result in price setting. Because mergers allow firms to share information, they can also lead to greater production efficiency and lower costs. The conglomerate merger can save a firm from competition. Merging with a firm in a different industry serves as insurance against cyclical recessions in the industry. However, the resulting product diversification can cause the firm to spread resources too thin, increasing inefficiencies in production.

In addition to merging, firms may attempt to act as a monopoly through collusion. The dominant firms in an oligopoly can negotiate prices to maximize their profits and act collectively as one price setter. Such agreements are unusually inadequate because of the game that results. Firms must predict each other's reactions to the monopolistic price-setting attempts. If one firm cheats on the cartel, the formal written agreement, the other firms are not protected by law and are subject to losses from artificially raising their prices.

Product differentiation arises naturally from differences in firms' methods of production. Market power is secured if a firm can increase the perceived product heterogeneity of goods produced by other firms. This is a central goal of a firm in a monopolistic competition structure. Through means of advertising and other nonpricing competitive methods, this real or imaginary product differentiation can influence consumers and establish more concrete price-setting allowances. If the firm cannot influence the consumers in this manner, monopolistic pricing attempts will fail. If product differentiation succeeds, there are positive results. The consumers gain greater satisfaction because firms are able to meet their preferences perfectly with the large variety of goods available. The high profits encourage firms to enter the market, increasing competition and driving the prices back down.

Firms may also take three direct actions on prices: price discrimination, predatory pricing, and price maintenance. Price discrimination involves charging different prices to different consumers. This allows the monopolizing firm to increase its profits and satisfy the individual needs of its consumers. Predatory pricing, a suicidal technique in an easily entered market, involves selling below costs to force out competition. Price maintenance is an agreement with a firm's supplier that allows it to buy at a lower price than its rivals.

All of these monopolistic techniques can serve as positive mechanisms in the economy, increasing efficiency and lowering costs. They are unable to completely restrict competition in the long run. Because of this uncertainty, most monopolies can only find success by obtaining state consent to their operations and legal means to keep their competition at bay.

Nature of State Support

State-supported monopolies exist for many reasons. The government may wish to control an industry outright through "socialization" or "nationalization." It may wish to regulate an industry to avoid a privatized monopoly. It may also wish to save a failing domestic industry from foreign competition in hopes of boosting its own economy.

In the United States, examples of state-sanctioned monopolies include the Federal Reserve System's exclusive right to print currency and the U.S. Postal Service's exclusive right to deliver first-class mail. Another state-supported monopoly is created by the body of U.S. labor law that allows union activity. A craft or industrial union or other workers organization may create a market consisting of a single seller of labor and use legal means of barring nonaffiliated workers from participating in the labor market.

To enforce a particular monopoly, a state may exclude competition from entering the market. This is primarily done though licensure, which allows participation by those who meet a set of standards and refuses it to others. Licensure, which is required to participate in occupations such as medicine, is different from certification, which acknowledges proper training. Licensure restricts the number of individuals who are allowed to participate in an industry regardless of qualifications. Licensure artificially reduces the service labor force and the ability of firms to enter the markets.

A state may also regulate a patent registry, which constitutes another form of monopoly. Through the patent system, the government grants an individual or firm an exclusive right to manufacture and sell a particular innovation or technology. Although this law can sometimes ensure that the inventor reaps the benefits of new ideas, the patent laws discriminate against those who develop the innovation simultaneously yet were unable to register first. Similarly, copyright laws may promote research and development, but they are not cost effective for consumers because more efficient firms may be barred from entering the market.

To force out competition and increase market control, a state may impose restrictions that artificially change the prices of goods. Price caps prevent firms from increasing prices when costs are too high or supplies are too low. Such restrictions keep new firms from entering the market because the entrants would not be able to compete with the extreme levels of efficiency required to remain in the business and make a profit.

In the past, the state established fair-trade laws to protect small firms from the predatory pricing techniques of large firms. These survive in price floors imposed on certain industries, such as housing. These minimum prices allow firms to realize monopolistic profits independently of oligopolistic collusion. Proper resource allocation suffers because inefficient firms are able to remain in business, earning an artificially high profit.

Another type occurs in the case of a "natural monopoly." This refers to the monopolizing firm that can produce more goods because government subsidies enable it to produce at a loss. The state can choose which firms or industries to subsidize. Nonsubsidized firms are then forced out of the market, while others agree to sell at artificially low prices. New firms are barred from entry because they are not able to produce at a loss without state subsidies. Subsidized firms that remain in an unprofitable industry are inefficient because the market cannot correct for deficiencies. Surpluses and shortages are the results.

Besides preventing firms from entering a monopolized market, the state may restrict consumer access to goods, creating an unnaturally large demand to support monopolistic prices. An example is farming, where farmers are paid not to produce so that prices will not fall below subsistence level. Excess supply may be destroyed or left to waste rather than taken to market.

On an international scale, a state may attempt to create domestic monopolies. This is done by eliminating foreign competition through trade restrictions, including tariffs (taxes on imported goods), quotas (limits on amounts allowed), and embargoes (bans on foreign trade). The protective tariff artificially raises the price of foreign-made goods, allowing domestic firms to sell at above-competitive prices. This enables failing domestic firms to compete with more efficient foreign firms, securing domestic jobs in the short run but hurting consumers and the whole economy in the long run.

Costs of Monopolization

When the monopolistic firm, with or without the support of the state, attempts to override the market's supply-and-demand mechanism by artificially adjusting prices, only inefficiency can result. The monopoly can survive only because of the manipulation of state power and market regulation. Whereas a free market encourages efficient and cheap production, the

monopoly encourages wastefulness. Whereas the free market promotes greater access to goods, the monopoly fails to satisfy consumer demand, producing too much or too little than the market dictates. The state may attempt to control trade to benefit its own economy, hurting it in the long run. Rather than promoting international trade as a benefit to society, an industry that advocates this approach acts as a victim.

When inefficient industries are protected from foreign competition, the market cannot dictate proper resource allocation, and the whole society loses. Workers are resources that are withheld from more productive industries when protected industries are not allowed to fail. Consumers are forced to pay high prices for goods. The countries involved cannot benefit from the increased levels of efficiency that accompany an international division of labor. Gains from one country's comparative or absolute advantages in production are lost in the regulations. Trade restriction leads to lower quality in goods and greater costs. All economic benefits are short term or mere delusions.

Antitrust Legislation

The term "antitrust legislation" refers to legislation against business practices that are regarded as unfair, unethical, or anticompetitive. A "trust" is a combination of firms or corporations for the purpose of reducing competition and controlling prices throughout a business or industry. Trusts are generally prohibited or restricted by antitrust legislation. The term "trust" came from the practice of collective shareholding that led to domination of an industry's firms. It now refers to monopolistic firms in general. Since monopolies are generally considered inefficient and hurtful to the economy, a state may enforce antitrust or antimonopolistic laws that promote competition in commerce by prosecuting a suspected monopolist alleged to be in violation of these laws. State-supported monopolies do not lie under the jurisdiction of antitrust policies; a state is usually concerned about maintaining a balance of market power only in the private sector. Deregulation is the primary method used to abolish state-protected monopolies.

Although working to secure a competitive market, antitrust policies can be very inefficient and costly. Justice is not executed quickly, dragging out in long and involved court cases. Monopolistic practices transform with the times, and their original definitions may become meaningless and obsolete. Practices that are not explicitly identified in the purely competitive market model are automatically dismissed as anticompetitive even if the practices prove otherwise. In addition, much antitrust legislation is subject to judicial interpretation. There has been a continuous shift between a focus on monopolistic actions and a focus on the firm's size or market share.

Under antitrust policies, firms cannot explicitly behave in a monopolistic manner. Mergers are prohibited if the action would drastically widen their market shares. Oligopolies cannot legally collude on prices, nor are their cartels and other monopolistic contracts enforced by law. The strictest and most all-encompassing antitrust legislation policies are found in the United States. However, many other countries and global organizations have felt the need to include them in their legislation.

Antitrust in the United States

In colonial America, trusts and other informal agreements were not outlawed but remained unenforced by law. Provisions for trade and commerce were made through the individual colonial charters and private land grants from the kings of England. The Articles of Confederation, passed in 1777, declared in Section IV that the "people of each State . . . shall enjoy therein all the privileges of trade and commerce" without the earlier restrictions and taxes imposed on them.

After the American Revolution ended in 1783, politicians worked to reorganize the economic functions of the newly independent states. They desired a unifying law of commerce to facilitate trade between the states and with other countries. This opinion was expressed by statesman Alexander Hamilton in support for the Union:

> An unrestrained intercourse between the States themselves will advance the trade of each by an interchange of their respective productions, not only for the supply of reciprocal wants at home, but for exportation to foreign markets. The veins of commerce in every part will be replenished, and will acquire additional motion and vigor from a free circulation of the commodities of every part. Commercial enterprise will have much greater scope, from the diversity in the productions of different States. . . . The speculative trader . . . will acknowledge that the aggregate balance of the commerce of the United States would bid fair to be much more favorable than that of the thirteen States without union or with partial unions. (Hamilton 1787)

With the ratification of the Constitution of the United States in 1788, Section 8 of Article I gave Congress the authority to "regulate Commerce with foreign Nations, and among the several States, and with the Indian Tribes." This law did not affect monopolies until the case of *Gibbons v. Ogden* in 1824, a dispute concerning a state-granted monopoly on steamboat traffic. The U.S. Supreme Court ruled against state-licensed monopolies that conflicted with the provisions made in the Constitution, namely that states had a right to govern internal but not interstate commerce.

In the case of *Munn v. Illinois* in 1877, the Supreme Court endorsed state antimonopoly policies, deciding that the regulation of private property may be "necessary for the public good." This was an early decision against the monopolistic practices of private railroads. A later decision, in the case of *Wabash, St. Louis & Pacific Railroad Company v. Illinois* in 1886, further extended federal control over commerce.

In 1887, the Interstate Commerce Act was passed to regulate the railroad businesses. The act dealt with monopolistic practices such as unreasonable pricing, price discrimination, and collusions to divide market shares and established the Interstate Commerce Commission (ICC) to hear complaints against the unfair actions of the railroad companies and carry out the necessary investigations. Railroads were forced to report to the commission annually and were subject to fines for committing monopolistic offenses.

Congress passed the Sherman Anti-Trust Act in 1890, forbidding the formation of trusts and other collusive behavior in interstate commerce. Jurisdiction was given to the Anti-Trust Division of the U.S. Department of Justice. The act imposed fines and imprisonment for violators and allowed victims of monopolistic practices to sue for damages. An attempt to monopolize was made a felony, and trusts were forced to dissolve. Successful cases were brought against the Northern Securities Company (1904), the Standard Oil Company (1911), and the American Tobacco Company (1911). The principle of the "rule of reason" used in these and later cases required that the prosecution prove the firm used monopolistic power to eliminate competition. A large market share was considered inadequate proof, as was shown in later cases.

Although it served as a major breakthrough for federal antitrust legislation, the Sherman Anti-Trust Act was vague and subject to interpretation. The case of the *United States v. E. C. Knight Company* of 1895 affirmed that federal jurisdiction lay only with monopolies in commerce and not in manufacturing. The Clayton Anti-Trust Act of 1914 was far more direct in regulating monopolies in general. The act outlawed predatory pricing, price discrimination, exclusive deals, and stock ownership in competing firms. It also established rules regarding the firms' conduct toward labor unions.

Also passed in 1914, the Federal Trade Commission Act established an administrative watchdog for the economy. Like the ICC, the Federal Trade Commission (FTC) had the responsibility of investigating charges brought against firms for monopolistic practices. The FTC promoted written agreements from firms pledging not to violate antitrust laws.

The Webb-Pomerene Act of 1918 exempted exporting firms from the antitrust policies and penalties as long as monopolistic practices were not used against domestic competition. In 1936, the Robinson-Patman Act (also called the Anti-Chain-Store Act or Anti-Price Discrimination Act) prohibited predatory pricing, price maintenance, and price discrimination in the retail markets. It protected smaller retail stores from the monopolizing schemes of larger chain stores by forcing manufacturers to sell on equal terms.

Under the administration of President Franklin D. Roosevelt, the Agricultural Adjustment Act passed in 1933, forming the Agricultural Adjustment Agency (AAA) under the Department of Agriculture. This agency introduced subsidized farming and regulated crop production to decrease food production. Another agency, the Commodity Credit Corporation, made loans available to farmers and stored excess supplies of crops to artificially raise food prices. The act was repealed in 1936, but its work was carried on by later legislation and federal agencies.

Following the Robinson-Patman Act, another protective act for small retail stores was the Miller-Tydings Act of 1937. This act exempted fair-trade practices from the penalties of the Sherman Anti-Trust Act. This practice involved minimum price setting, designed to keep larger retailers from predatory pricing. Following this act was the Wheeler-Lea Act of 1938, which extended FTC authority against public deception, also called false advertising.

In 1945, the Supreme Court ruled against Alcoa in the *United States v. Aluminum Company of America* despite the fact that it was not found guilty of any monopolistic practices. This ruling began the era of the "per se" criterion, in which prosecuted firms were considered monopolies *per se* because of their size.

In 1950, Congress passed the Celler-Kefauver Merger Act (also called the Anti-Merger Act) to cover a loophole left open by the earlier Clayton Anti-Trust Act. The act prevented anticompetitive mergers that would enlarge market shares but continued to allow smaller firms to buy out competition.

In 1975, Congress passed the Consumer Goods Pricing Act. This act repealed the Miller-Tydings Act and barred firms from making price maintenance agreements with their suppliers. The Hart-Scoss-Rodino Anti-Trust Improvement Act of 1976 expanded federal authority to scrutinize corporate mergers. One result was that the American Telephone and Telegraph Company (AT&T) was dissolved in 1982.

The year 1982 also ended the long trial of the *United States v. IBM,* when the "rule of reason" triumphed over the "per se" criterion a second time. Although the International Business Machines (IBM) Corporation was accused of holding a monopolistic market share, no evidence of monopolistic practices was found.

In 2002, the final decision in the *United States v. Microsoft Corporation* found the company in violation of antitrust policies. This ruling brought about questions concerning the effectiveness of antitrust legislation and the apparent double standard used in prosecuting. As antitrust legislation continues to battle the problem of interpretation, policymakers must ask themselves a question that has important implications for antitrust law: When do "competitive" practices became "anticompetitive"?

Antitrust on a Global Scale

Free trade and competition bring long-term economic benefits to all economies. Trade increases income and living standards and stimulates growing economies. It also promotes efficiency, not only in production but also in the use of irreplaceable resources. In an effort to preserve domestic competition in their economies, countries such as Germany and the Netherlands have joined the United States in passing antitrust legislation.

In 1995, the U.S. Department of Justice and the FTC issued the "Anti-Trust Enforcement Guidelines for International Operations" for firms to apply to foreign commerce. These agencies have also formed agreements with individual countries such as Canada, Israel, and Mexico to standardize antitrust policies and preserve competition. These agreements allow the dissemination of knowledge and ease of investigation in antitrust cases.

Equal efforts have been made to preserve global competition. Many countries participate in agencies that were created to regulate global and regional trade and commerce. The General Agreement on Tariffs and Trade (GATT) was established in 1947 and reorganized as the World Trade Organization (WTO) in 1995. The purpose of the GATT was to promote unrestricted trade between countries by setting international regulations on protective barriers. It also authorizes the creation of free trade areas and customs unions that permit unrestricted trade among members only as a means of opening protectionist economies. Serving as a mediator, the WTO encourages countries to move away from monopolistic practices.

Antitrust regulation goes against a natural mercantilist instinct. Struggling economies desire to keep capital, jobs, and currency "in house" in hopes of a last chance at survival. Although global antitrust legislation may be seen as an invasion of state supremacy, the efforts of many countries have led to a promising battle against international cartels such as the Organization of Petroleum Exporting Countries (OPEC).

Jennifer Vaughn

See Also National Government Policies; National Tax Rules, and Sovereignty; Political Systems and Governance

References

Casler, Stephen D. 1992. *HarperCollins College Outline Introduction to Economics.* New York: HarperResource.

Hamilton, Alexander. 1787. "Federalist No. 1: The Utility of the Union in Respect to Commercial Relations and a Navy." *Independent Journal.*

Hazlitt, Henry. 1996. *Economics in One Lesson.* San Francisco: Fox and Wilkes.

Heilbroner, Robert L. 1999. *The Worldly Philosophers: The Lives, Times, and Ideas of the Great Economics Thinkers.* 7th ed. New York: Touchstone.

Heilbroner, Robert L., and Aaron Singer. 1999. *The Economic Transformation of America: 1600 to the Present.* 4th ed. Fort Worth, TX: Harcourt Brace College.

Legrain, Philippe. 2002. *Open World: The Truth about Globalisation.* London: Abacus.

Soto, Hernando de. 2003. *The Mystery of Capital: Why Capitalism Triumphs in the West and Fails Everywhere Else.* New York: Basic.

Sowell, Thomas. 2000. *Basic Economics: A Citizen's Guide to the Economy.* New York: Basic.

Varian, Hal R. 1999. *Intermediate Microeconomics: A Modern Approach.* 5th ed. New York: W. W. Norton.

National Government Policies

National government policies are initiatives by governments that are attempting to exert leadership or intervene more subtly in their domestic affairs. In the realm of economics, it is commonly agreed that sovereign governments can take on three important tasks in their efforts to influence socioeconomic outcomes. Governments can, through the manipulation of a wide variety of policy instruments, (1) shape the allocation of a country's resources; (2) pursue macroeconomic stabilization; and (3) prioritize the distribution of a nation's wealth.

Despite general acknowledgment of governments' tremendous potential to affect the course of economic events, views on how and to what extent governments are expected to intervene in the economy tend to change in the minds of the political and economic elites across time. The global consensus on the normative role of the state as an advocate for economic development, in particular, is closely related to the prominent ideas upheld by the leading economies in the international system in distinct historical times. Joan E. Spero and Jeffrey A. Hart (2003), for example, have argued that after World War II three major international economic systems developed—periods in which assertions on the optimum role of the state also evolved. They are the Bretton Woods system (from World War II to 1971); the period of interdependence (from 1971 to 1989); and the contemporary era of globalization (from 1989 to the present).

Government Policies during the Bretton Woods System

Named after a vacation resort in New Hampshire, the Bretton Woods system was created by a United Nations monetary and financial conference that took place there in July 1944. Representatives of forty-four countries got together in an effort to establish a new economic order capable of promoting economic, political, and military stability in the international system (Spero and Hart 2003). At that time, world leaders believed that the absence of strong international institutions was one of the causes of World War II.

Two important organizations that were created during that conference include the International Monetary Fund (IMF) and the International Bank for Reconstruction and Development (IBRD, also known as the World Bank). The General Agreement on Tariffs and Trade (GATT, whose rules are today upheld by the World Trade Organization, WTO) was also signed during the occasion. All of those initiatives had the ultimate aim of establishing world order. The 1944 conference also addressed concerns with the reconstruction of Western Europe and Japan, which were badly damaged by the war. However, the conference had initially underestimated the damages in the warring countries. A few years later, the U.S. government realized the need to sponsor aid programs, in part with the goal of promoting capitalism and democratic regimes throughout the world. The Marshall Plan, instituted in 1947, was one of these initiatives.

The Bretton Woods system affected the domestic policies of nations in many ways, particularly those not aligned with the Communist bloc, and it would also change the way in which they related with one another. In 1947, the U.S. dollar became the main currency used in international transactions. The dollar, in turn, had a fixed parity to the value of gold ($35 an ounce). Currencies of many states were fixed against the U.S. dollar, which thus served as the reference for exchange rate transactions. One of the purposes of this initiative was to encourage monetary stability as well as predictability by laying out a more practicable environment for international trade and financial transactions in general.

One of the primary participants of the Bretton Woods conference was the economist John Maynard Keynes, who led the UK delegation. At that time, this British economist's theories on macroeconomic policy enjoyed great influence in the United States. Keynes was very skeptical, in particular, of the ability of the market alone to solve socioeconomic problems such as unemployment. Many of his contemporaries, however, had defended the manipulation of interest rates as a means to facilitate the access of producers and financial investors to capital in times of economic hardship. Monetarist economists argued that the extra capital injected into the economy would serve as a suitable "fuel" to generate jobs. Keynes, however, believed that national governments could be more effective in solving the problem of unemployment if they also sponsored projects that created jobs—even at the cost of higher public spending. In many respects, the agreements signed at Bretton Woods reflected Keynes's economic views.

Overall, the post–World War II period can be characterized not only as a time in which the leading economies, especially the United States, were concerned with promoting international integration, but also as a period in which governments were expected to play an active role in the economic welfare of their domestic markets.

State-Led Development Strategies

The idea that a government should be at the forefront of a country's economic development was prominent among developing nations in the post–World War II era. It was during this period that most countries in East Asia, Latin America, and Africa embraced import-substitution industrialization (ISI) programs. As the name indicates, ISI was an attempt by developing countries to industrialize their economies through import substitution. To that end, governments offered a package of subsidies to their local industries, which oftentimes were government owned. The ISI policy prescriptions included: (1) high import tariffs on consumer goods; (2) low or negative tariffs on imports of machinery and intermediary inputs; (3) cheap credit (frequently at negative real interest rates) to industrial firms; (4) preferential exchange rates for industrial producers; and (5) public investment in infrastructure (for example, transportation and power) and in the so-called "basic industries" (for example, steel) (Weaver 1980).

Another trait of the ISI countries was their tendency to transfer income from agricultural exports in order to subsidize industrial development in urban areas. Economist Michael Lipton (1976) denounced this practice as the "urban bias" because the policies favored industrial producers and labor at the expense of farmers and workers in rural areas. ISI policies consisted of a tightly staged program aimed at speeding up the modernization of developing countries. A major source of the philosophical inspiration for ISI came from the "dependencist theory." This school of thought asserts that developing countries have been historically engaged in very unfavorable economic relations with the developed world. Dependencists believe that Third World countries run the risk of being deprived of imports from industrial countries if they do not attempt to promote their local industries.

ISI policies became widely adopted in Third World countries for several reasons. First, past international crises (such as the Great Depression and major wars) had brought havoc to the developing world, which suddenly found itself deprived of imports from industrial nations. Dependencists believed that developing nations were predestined to experience balance of payments problems because of declining terms of trade; that is, their ability to use earnings from agricultural (or other primary) exports to pay for high value-added (mostly manufactured) imports from industrial nations would diminish (Hirschman 1971). Another source of inspiration for ISI was the economic success of the Soviet Union. Policymakers throughout the developing world—even those who were proponents of capitalism—were persuaded by the apparent efficacy of a centrally planned economy. Indeed, they were convinced of the important role of the state in leading the boom of industrialization that took place in the Soviet republics during the first few decades of the twentieth century.

Despite widespread enthusiasm over ISI policies, levels of economic success among governments that pursued those policies tended to vary across time, regions, and countries. Particularly, there existed a major distinction between the ISI policies adopted in Latin America (for example, Argentina, Brazil, and Mexico) and Africa (for example, Botswana, Gabon, and Kenya) and those adopted in East Asia (for example, South Korea and Taiwan). Whereas the Latin American and African governments tended to overtax their exporting sectors in order to finance urban industrialization, their East Asian counterparts understood from the beginning the importance of promoting exports as a means of obtaining foreign revenues as well as stimulating higher productivity in local industries. The result was that East Asian countries were able to enjoy sustainable economic growth for a longer period of time.

By the mid-1960s, ISI was already showing signs of exhaustion as an economic strategy. The unprecedented industrial growth that countries experienced as a result of import substitution could not solve the unemployment problem in those economies. If, on the one hand, industrialization created a demand for high-skilled labor, on the other hand the jobs that this economic strategy produced were not nearly plentiful enough to meet the needs of their labor markets. In fact, ISI marked the beginning of an extraordinary rural exodus in which people sought better job opportunities in the urban centers. As mentioned earlier, ISI policies did not address the economic problems of the rural population. Instead, they heavily penalized the rural sector in favor of high-capital-intensive industries. This phenomenon also spurred increasing levels of inequality within developing countries. The East Asian experience of economic development nevertheless proved to be very different from that of the Latin American and African nations.

One last important feature of ISI economies was that they tended to borrow heavily from international capital markets to finance the development of their industrial sector. The post–World War II period was indeed an era characterized by cheap money: Developing countries had access to foreign capital at very low interest rates. Those years of heavy borrowing would set the stage for what Spero and Hart (2003) identified as the period of global interdependence.

The Period of Interdependence

The 1960s and 1970s marked the beginning of a surge in capital mobility across national borders. This new world order was mostly a product of technological innovations, internationalization of production, and government policies. An important economic policy change in this period was the return to the flexible exchange rate system, motivated mostly by the end of the U.S. dollar's pegged rate to gold. In response to a shortage in the U.S. gold stock, the administration of President Richard Nixon decided unilaterally to end the dollar convertibility to gold on August 15, 1971. The new international economic environment would have a major impact on national government policies in many countries, limiting the influence of those policies in this increasingly interdependent financial system.

What made the period of economic interdependence distinct from the first twenty-five years or so after the end of World War II was that the composition of capital flows became concentrated on portfolio investment, as opposed to foreign direct investment (FDI). This change had significant effects, especially on smaller economies, which became more vulnerable to sudden fluctuations in capital flows.

Technological innovations and the deregulation of financial markets were two of the fundamental novelties that allowed for increased capital mobility. Large amounts of money could be transferred from one country to another almost instantaneously, thanks to revolutionary advances in telecommunications, information processing, and computer technologies (Spero and Hart 2003). Financial markets in general thus became highly sophisticated. In addition, national governments started liberalizing their capital accounts, not only reducing restrictions on the entrance and exit of foreign capital but also creating policies that attracted international investors seeking higher rates of return on their financial investments. In many respects, the years of economic interdependence were a transitional phase between two very distinct eras, namely, (1) the post–World War II period, in which national governments were expected to have a strong hold on the country's economic matters; and (2) the era of globalization, when greater faith was placed in the efficiency of market forces as a source of development.

The liberalization of capital markets, along with the adoption of floating exchange rate systems, reduced governments' options in using fiscal and monetary policies to influence economic outcomes. In his elucidating study, Jeffrey A. Frieden (1991) explained this phenomenon by portraying the international economic system as "before capital mobility" (BCM) and "after capital mobility" (ACM). In the BCM world, if a government wanted to adopt expansionary policies (à la Keynes), the most frequent way to pursue them would be by reducing interest rates. Low interest rates would make access to capital easier for producers, who in turn would become likely to hire more workers, who would also contribute to the increased production of goods. Low interest rates can help the economy by stimulating consumption. Hence, the implementation of a particular monetary policy tool, the reduction of interest rates, was believed to be a useful instrument for governments to lead the country into a virtuous economic cycle.

However, in the ACM world, the composition of international financial flows has changed. Before capital mobility, countries could easily finance development projects, thanks to ample access to foreign loans at very low interest rates. In addition, multinational corporations (MNCs) played an important role in transferring large sums of capital across countries through FDI. In the ACM period, however, portfolio investment became the major source of foreign capital, and the stakes in attracting it have significantly increased.

One way to attract foreign investors is to award high returns on their capital. This means that countries are now expected to offer not only positive real interest rates but also internationally competitive ones. Otherwise, governments run the risk of seeing investments leave their countries in favor of more profitable financial markets elsewhere. As a result, the ability of governments to manipulate interest rates to promote expansionary policies has been somewhat diminished in the ACM world.

In countries with liberalized capital accounts—that is, with full capital mobility—

governments have the alternative option of using exchange rate policies to expand the money supply in their domestic markets. For example, if a government decreases the value of its domestic currency, it can both increase the competitiveness of the country's exports and stimulate internal consumption of goods produced domestically. Unfortunately, exchange rate devaluations have not always been successful in boosting economic activity.

The Mundell-Fleming model presents a heuristic way of understanding changes in policy preferences in an economic environment before and after capital mobility. The model basically predicts that a country can enjoy only two of the following scenarios: a fixed exchange rate, monetary policy autonomy, and/or capital mobility. Suppose that a government chooses to have a fixed exchange rate system and an autonomous monetary policy, where interest rates are set according to its preferences. These policies can only be sustained by closing the country's capital account. Otherwise, foreign investors would immediately react to the government's setting of interest rates and its exchange rates policies, making the country susceptible to currency speculative attacks that could destabilize its exchange rate.

Although already highly interdependent, the international economic system had not appreciated the full extent of the effects of an ACM world until the late 1980s. Only after the end of the Cold War and the rise of the United States as the world's single superpower did the international system witness the victory of capitalism and the remarkable spread of its ideals and practices.

National Policies after Globalization

With the collapse of the Soviet Union and the subsequent transformation of the East European Communist bloc, a large pool of countries underwent market-based reforms. There already existed a consensus among most of the former Communist countries, also called "transitional economies," that communism had failed as an economic system. Since then, these countries have pursued thorough economic reforms with the goal of diminishing the control of states over the economy and making their societies more market friendly.

One characteristic of transitional societies was that economic liberalization reforms took place alongside political democratization. The end of Soviet rule also represented, in many states, a revival of the ideals of ethnic and national sovereignty. All in all, most of the former Communist states have undergone sweeping changes in their governments with new leadership taking control of their political and economic fates Therefore, when the transitional countries adopted capitalism, many had very high expectations that this new economic system would also lead to freer and more democratic societies. This optimistic environment certainly helped some of the newly empowered leaders in those states to execute comprehensive marked-based reforms at a very fast pace (Nelson 1995).

In contrast, Latin America—and to a certain extent Africa—did not enjoy the same initial broad public consensus for market reforms and economic liberalization. Specifically, the democratization of Latin America in the 1980s was not associated with the rejection of the state-led economic strategy. According to political economist Joan Nelson, there was a widespread belief among the newly elected civilian leadership in the mid-1980s that "Latin American economies were fundamentally sound but had been mismanaged" by former governments. Nelson argued that this was particularly true in some of the countries that had been under military dictatorship, such as Brazil, Bolivia, and Argentina (1995, 48).

Despite the initial reluctance of some developing economies to adopt economic liberalization, by the mid-1990s very few countries were not yet participating in this new global economic paradigm, as Table 1 indicates.

Table 1: Economic Liberalization Reforms

Developing Countries	Start Date	Transitional Economies	Start Date
Greece	1959	Hungary	03/1990
Portugal	1960	Slovenia	10/1991
Taiwan	1963	Poland	06/1989
Jordan	1965	Czechoslovakia	06/1990
Ireland	1966	Bulgaria	06/1990
South Korea	1968	Estonia	08/1991
Indonesia	1970	Latvia	08/1991
Chile	1973	Lithuania	08/1991
Botswana	1979	Albania	03/1991
Morocco	1984	Kyrgyzstan	10/1991
Bolivia	1985	Croatia	10/1991
Gambia	1985	Moldova	08/1991
Ghana	1985	Kazakhstan	12/1991
Costa Rica	1986	Macedonia	11/1991
Guinea	1986	Georgia	08/1991
Mexico	1986	Belarus	08/1991
Guinea-Bissau	1987	Ukraine	08/1991
Guatemala	1988	Uzbekistan	08/1991
Guyana	1988	Armenia	09/1991
Jamaica	1988	Azerbaijan	10/1991
Mali	1988	Russia	12/1991
Philippines	1988	Romania	05/1990
Uganda	1988	Tajikistan	09/1991
El Salvador	1989	Turkmenistan	10/1991
Paraguay	1989		
Tunisia	1989		
Turkey	1989		
Benin	1990		
Uruguay	1990		
Argentina	1991		
Brazil	1991		
Colombia	1991		
Ecuador	1991		
Honduras	1991		
Nepal	1991		
Nicaragua	1991		
Peru	1991		
South Africa	1991		
Sri Lanka	1991		
Cameron	1993		
Kenya	1993		
India	1994		

Source: Data for transitional economies are based on Joel S. Hellman, "Competitive Advantage: Political Competition and Economic Reform in Postcommunist Transitions" (San Francisco: American Political Science Association, 1996), and data for developing countries are based on Jeffrey D. Sachs and Andrew Warner, "Economic Reform and the Process of Global Integration," in *Brookings Papers on Economic Activity* (Washington, DC: Brookings Institution Press, 1995).

Policy Prescriptions

As alluded to earlier, the era of globalization (1989 to the present) will challenge the role of the state as the primary actor for advancing economic development. Greater reliance on market forces and free trade will constitute the two philosophical pillars of the new economic order. Trade liberalization is one of the market-based (or neoliberal) policies that has been greeted with enthusiasm, even among skeptics of this economic agenda. In essence, free trade entails the end of protectionism in all countries. Historically, both developed and developing nations have had records of practicing some form of trade protectionism.

The strongest theoretical motivation for free trade is that it improves the welfare of all nations that participate in it, regardless of their individual levels of economic development. Free trade allows countries to specialize in the production of goods in which they have comparative advantage. This means that countries will have an incentive to specialize in the production of goods in which they are relatively more productive than the rest of the world. In addition, trade liberalization promotes the free flow of international goods, greatly benefiting consumers everywhere because they will be able to have access to an enormous variety of internationally produced goods (something unthinkable in a closed economy) and will be able to pay for them at very competitive prices.

Unfortunately, the gains for producers and workers in countries that engage in free trade are not always clear-cut, nor are the predictions as to which societal groups will win and lose during a trade liberalization program. However, there are a few trade models in economics that attempt to answer exactly these questions. Two of the most famous ones are the Ricardo-Viner and the Stolper-Samuelson models, which predict that social cleavages against and for trade liberalization will occur through either sectoral or class interests, respectively.

For example, the sectoral model (Ricardo-Viner) asserts that social groups' alignment will reflect the interests of different industrial sectors. More specifically, support for or opposition to trade liberalization will occur, correspondingly, between export-oriented and trade-competing industries. Hence, the main prediction of the sectoral model is that producers and labor in specific industries will be politically aligned in the fight for the trade policy of their preference, according to whether those industries are internationally or domestically oriented.

The class model (Stolper-Samuelson) predicts that group coalitions will form on the basis of class interests. This means that labor and producers in the same industry, for instance, may share different policy preferences. In addition, the model predicts which group will support trade liberalization as a function of each country's factor endowments. That is, social groups that control an economic factor that is abundant in a country will tend to support free trade in the long run, as opposed to an interest group that utilizes a scarce economic factor in its production.

Take the United States as an example. This country is considered relatively abundant in both financial capital and human capital (that is, skilled labor). According to the Stolper-Samuelson model, capital owners and skilled labor will support free trade policies because they are very competitive internationally. Free trade is likely to make them wealthier. This is not true, though, for low-skilled laborers in the United States, who will be competing with workers of poorer countries. The fear among the believers in the Stolper-Samuelson model is that eventually there will be a "race to the bottom" among workers everywhere, and that employers will be forced (or willing) to reduce wages and other benefits in order to be more competitive in the international market, and thus ultimately will provide more jobs.

The predictions of both of these models with regard to the social consequences of trade liberalization are still highly disputed among scholars and policymakers. In fact, there has been international evidence in support of both models. Therefore, the final word has yet to be declared on which model best predicts the effects of trade liberalization on income distribution. The distributional effects of trade liberalization explain in part why one does not see a completely integrated international economic system, with nations freely trading goods among one another. Governments do respond to societal pressures—even in nondemocratic environments—and the trade policies that they pursue take into account the interests of individuals or groups in the society.

Some of the most common tools through which governments can enact protectionist policies include import tariffs, quotas, licenses, and other nontariff barriers (NTBs). Notice that although the trade models mentioned above do not always predict the winners and losers of trade liberalization, protectionist policies, such as import tariffs and licenses, clearly benefit specific economic groups within a country. Using the United States as an example again, a high import tariff on steel will promptly protect the U.S. steel industries, including producers and labor, from foreign competition. Therefore, the incentives for groups to mobilize in favor of trade protectionism are enormous in practically every country, because the gains from trade protectionism tend to be high and very concentrated. The losses that consumers suffer from that particular policy, however, tend to be relatively small and highly dispersed. In the end, a country's welfare is damaged by trade protectionism. That is why proponents of economic globalization defend free trade as a means of improving the allocation of a country's resources and, ultimately, the allocation of the world's resources.

Neoliberals do acknowledge, though, that import tariffs are valuable as a source of revenue collection. They maintain that the ideal government approach would be to set low import tariffs, with a pattern of spread as close as possible to a flat tariff system across industries to reduce the chances for economic favoritism of one group over another.

Another government policy that affects trade performance is the exchange rate regime. Devaluation of a country's currency normally helps the exporting sector because the country's goods become cheaper in the international market. Thus, exporters win twice with a low exchange rate: They are both able to sell more of their products and to receive more domestic currency during exchange conversions. This policy preference also tends to benefit the import-competing sectors, because their products become cheaper than imports under a low level of exchange. However, importers and consumers in general will benefit from a strong, or overvalued, domestic currency because their purchasing power is strengthened at an international level.

Neoliberal economists argue that most countries will gain if they set their currency slightly below the real rate of exchange. This will help the exporting sector, which in turn can bring more foreign revenues to the country. Conversely, they caution that if the domestic currency is too undervalued, it can create inflationary pressures. In addition, a policy that promotes the weakening of the domestic currency is likely to become politically unpopular among consumers.

The Role of the State

Another set of policy prescriptions defended by the neoliberal school has to do with the spending priorities of the state. In this respect, the era of economic globalization is very distinct from the post–World War II period, and even more so from the economic strategies pursued by the ISI countries. Neoliberal economists have a propensity to be very skeptical of governments' motives, as well as competence, for leading a country's economic development. They argue that an all-encompassing state is likely to produce many distortions during policymaking, in addition to being very vulnerable to corruption. These are some of the reasons why neoliberals defend that states should be "lean," so that they can concentrate on a few policies and, hopefully, execute them well.

John Williamson (1990) in his celebrated piece on the so-called "Washington Consensus," a term that he coined, explained that the role of government in the economy can be reduced in many ways. Deregulation of the domestic market (for example, through eliminating red tape), privatization of state-owned enterprises (SOEs), and reduction of public spending all lead to a smaller degree of government intervention in the economy. Nevertheless, neoliberals do acknowledge that there are policy areas in which the government should step in, given that the private sector has a poor record in taking care of them. Examples of selective areas where the state can perform well include basic health and education services. Neoliberals also favor state investment in a country's infrastructure, as private initiatives are not always forthcoming in this area.

Despite the supremacy of neoliberal ideals in the era of economic globalization, an increasing number of voices have questioned the efficacy of these policies in alleviating poverty around the world. Even more disturbing is the neoliberal record with regard to income inequality, which since the end of the Cold War has been increasing not only within developed and developing countries but also between developed and developing societies. One of the most ardent critics of the neoliberal strategy is Nobel laureate in economics Joseph Stiglitz, who has become internationally popular for his analyses on the competence of the IMF in fostering macroeconomic stability in the international system.

Monica Arruda de Almeida

See Also Antidumping and Countervailing Duties; Economic Sanctions; Fiscal Policy; Industrial Location and Competitiveness; Inequality; Monopolies and Antitrust Legislation; Subsidies; U.S. Trade laws

References

Frieden, Jeffrey A. 1991. "Invested Interests: The Politics of National Economic Policies in a World of Global Finance." *International Organization* 45 (Autumn): 425–451.

———. 1998. "The Politics of Exchange Rates." In Moisés Naím, *Mexico 1994: Anatomy of an Emerging-Market Crash.* Sebastian Edwards Publisher: Washington, DC: Carnegie Endowment for International Peace.

Gilpin, Robert. 1987. *The Political Economy of International Relations.* Princeton, NJ: Princeton University Press.

Hellman, Joel S. 1996. "Competitive Advantage: Political Competition and Economic Reform in Postcommunist Transitions." Manuscript. San Francisco: American Political Science Association.

Hirschman, Albert. 1971. *A Bias for Hope: Essays on Development in Latin America.* New Haven, CT: Yale University Press.

Keynes, John Maynard. 1936. *The General Theory of Employment, Interest and Money.* Amherst, NY: Prometheus.

Lipton, Michael. 1976. *Why Poor People Stay Poor.* Cambridge: Harvard University Press.

Nelson, Joan. 1995. "Linkage between Politics and Economics." In *Economic Reform and Democracy.* Baltimore: Johns Hopkins University Press.

Sachs, Jeffrey D., and Andrew Warner. 1995. "Economic Reform and the Process of Global Integration." In *Brookings Papers on Economic Activity.* Washington, DC: Brookings Institution Press.

Spero, Joan E., and Jeffrey A. Hart. 2003. *The Politics of International Economic Relations.* 6th ed. Toronto: Thompson Wadsworth.

Stiglitz, Joseph E. 2002. *Globalization and Its Discontents.* New York: W. W. Norton.

Weaver, Frederick Stirton. 1980. *Class, State, and Industrial Structure.* Westport, CT: Greenwood.

Williamson, John. 1990. "What Washington Means by Policy Reform." In *Latin American Adjustment: How Much Has Happened?* Washington, DC: Institute for International Economics.

National Tax Rules and Sovereignty

Introduction

It has become commonplace to observe that economic globalization has reduced the sovereignty of nations.[1] A particular aspect of this more general phenomenon is the question of how globalization reduces national sovereignty in taxation. This loss of sovereignty may take several forms, among them market-induced pressures to lower taxes and difficulty in applying existing tax rules. By making it difficult to sustain revenue yields without placing increased tax burdens on consumption and labor, such developments may lead to calls for limits on the activities of tax havens, new rules governing the taxation of international flows of income (generically, a "GATT for taxes"), or even a new institution (a "World Tax Organization") to enforce such rules, all of which, ironically, would also entail loss of national sovereignty.

The tax rules that have traditionally governed international economic relations were created for a world of relative autarky and were generally appropriate for that world. In the increasingly globalized world that exists at the beginning of the twenty-first century, however, the traditional tax rules have come under strain and national sovereignty in taxation has been eroded. Two initiatives are under way at the Organisation for Economic Co-operation and Development (OECD) to deal with the effects of globalization, but many economists have observed a need for new multilateral rules and institutions.

Limits on National Sovereignty

National sovereignty in taxation may be defined as the ability of a nation to pursue whatever tax policy it chooses, unfettered by external influences. Of course, complete sovereignty is impossible, except perhaps for a country that is totally isolated from external influences, such as Burma. Four general types of limitations on the exercise of national sovereignty in the taxation of income from capital exist.[2] They are market-induced voluntary limits; negotiated limits; externally imposed limits; and administrative limits.

Market-Induced Voluntary Limitations on Sovereignty

In a world where capital is highly mobile, market forces may limit a nation's choices in the taxation of income from capital in a number of ways. In other words, the nation voluntarily makes unilateral choices that it might not make in the absence of market-induced pressures on its tax system. These choices generally have to do with the location of economic activity or financial investment, the shifting of the tax base, the tax structure, and the relative immunity of destination-based sales taxes to tax competition.

Taxation and the Location of Economic Activity. Source-based taxes that are substantially heavier than the international norm may, all else being equal, discourage economic activity and investment.[3] As a result, a nation may choose lighter taxation of income from capital than in the absence of such market-induced limitations on its sovereignty. Indeed, there may be convergence of taxation across nations. (Governments may also compete in offering tax incentives to attract investment, as has happened in countries in transition from socialism since the early 1990s. In that case, convergence would not occur.) For these purposes, the relevant tax rate is presumably the marginal effective tax rate (METR) on income from capital, the fraction by which taxation reduces the before-tax rate of return, rather than the statutory rate.[4] Thus, it can be said that tax competition imposes market-induced limitations on effective tax rates. In the extreme case, there could be a "race to the bottom" that eliminates taxation of income from capital.[5]

Taxation and the Location of Financial Investment. The "economic activity" that may be repelled by high taxation is not only "real" activity; financial investment may be repelled. Thus, for example, a nation enacting a withholding tax on interest not matched by similar taxes elsewhere may become an unattractive place to invest, unless it provides other benefits, such as bank secrecy. In short, there may be market-induced limitations on the taxation of financial investment.[6]

Taxation and the Shifting of the Tax Base. Even if constrained not to impose taxes on income from capital that creates a METR that dramatically exceeds the international norm, a nation might appear to retain substantial sovereignty, since different tax structures (combinations of statutory rates and other provisions) can produce the same METR. For example, an income tax with a comprehensive definition of income and a low statutory tax rate can produce the same METR for a given industry as an income tax with a higher statutory tax rate and generous investment incentives, such as accelerated depreciation and investment credits.

If, however, a nation's statutory tax rates are substantially higher than the international norm, multinational corporations may shift taxable income out of that nation and shift deductions into it, most commonly through the manipulation of transfer pricing and thin capitalization (and the choice of where to borrow). These shifts need not involve reallocation of economic activity and real investment; they may affect only where income is taxed (or not taxed). Thus, Canada's Technical Committee on Business Taxation concluded: "After the mid-1980s, when several countries, including the United States and the United Kingdom, reduced their corporate income taxes significantly below Canada's general corporate rate, multinationals tended to shift income out of, and deductions into, Canada for tax reasons."[7] To avoid loss of tax revenues, a nation may thus be forced to impose lower statutory rates on income from capital than otherwise; in other words, there may be market-induced limitations on statutory tax rates.

The Choice of Tax Structure. If a nation faces market-induced limitations on both the effective tax rates and the statutory tax rates that it can apply to income from capital, other decisions on tax policy may be constrained. For example, revenues from taxing capital income may be lower than in the absence of tax competition; the tax burden may be shifted from capital to labor; use of progressive taxation to achieve redistributional objectives may be abandoned (or at least curtailed); or greater reliance on schedular taxation may replace global taxation of income, as in the separation of the taxation of income from capital and the taxation of other income found in the dual income taxes imposed in the Nordic countries.[8] In short, there may be market-induced limitations on tax structure.[9]

The Relative Immunity of Destination-Based Sales Taxes to Tax Competition. Because sales taxes and excises commonly follow the destination principle (so that imports are taxed, but exports are not), market-induced limitations on such taxation are relatively minor. If, contrary to fact, nations levied origin-based sales taxes (taxing exports, but not imports), there would be a market-induced pressure to reduce rates and provide exemptions to avoid reducing the competitive position of producers in the taxing nation.[10] This can be seen in the "tax wars" waged by the states of Brazil, which (on internal trade) have long imposed the world's only origin-based value-added tax (VAT).

This description of destination-based taxation depends on an assumption that is invalid in the special cases of cross-border shopping and sales of digital content by remote vendors—that taxes on imported goods can be collected at the border (or at the post office).[11] The OECD and the European Union have been investigating methods of taxing digital content on a destination basis to prevent both loss of revenue and unfair competition with local merchants selling competing goods.[12]

Negotiated Limitations on National Sovereignty

Not all voluntary limitations on national sovereignty in taxation are market induced; nations sometimes agree voluntarily to negotiated limits on their exercise of sovereignty. The General Agreement on Tariffs and Trade (GATT) is the most extensive system of negotiated limits on taxing power and the only important multinational tax agreement, aside from those between the EU member states. The GATT, which pertains primarily to import duties and export subsidies, demonstrates a key point that has analogous implications in other contexts: that the potential gains from free trade are so great—and the potential harm from widespread resort to "beggar-thy-neighbor" tariff policies and retaliation so enormous—that nations agree to forgo the national benefit that might result from unilateral departures from free trade.

Most developed countries have extensive networks of bilateral tax treaties with other countries. The purpose of these treaties, which generally apply only to taxes on income and capital, is to limit the double taxation of income, create greater certainty for investors, assure nondiscrimination (based on taxation of their investors by the treaty partner that is no less favorable than that accorded investors from the host country), and provide exchange of information between tax authorities that can be used to prevent tax evasion. As with the GATT, countries enter into tax treaties to gain these benefits, which they believe justify the acceptance of limitations on their taxing powers. Two features of almost all (non-EU) international tax agreements other than the GATT are worth noting: They are bilateral treaties, and they do not apply to VAT and other sales taxes or to excises.

Most tax treaties between developed countries are based on the OECD Model Tax Convention on Income and on Capital. (By comparison, treaties among developing countries generally follow the United Nations Model Convention.) Among the topics covered by the OECD Model are the primacy of source-country taxation of business profits (achieved via foreign tax credits or the exemption of foreign-source income allowed by the home country); the requirement of a permanent establishment for the imposition of source-country tax on business profits; the use of separate accounting and the arm's length approach for calculating the income of affiliated entities; the primacy of residence-country taxation of interest, dividends, and royalties; the withholding tax rates that source countries apply to interest, dividends, and royalties; exchange of information; and procedures for resolving disputes. Tax treaties ordinarily do not constrain the tax rates that can be levied on business profits or other aspects of calculating taxable income.

Tax treaties commonly do not cover sales taxes. This is understandable because a destination-based sales tax—by far the predominant type of sales tax—involves primarily transactions that occur within the taxing country: essentially production, distribution, and importation for domestic consumption and rebate of tax on exports; thus, there is no reason for other countries to get involved.[13] The difficulty of taxing direct sales of digitized content that cross national borders may require increased international cooperation in tax administration.

If origin-based taxation were the international norm, it is more likely that tax treaties would be required to regulate sales taxation. Treaties might be needed, for example, to specify the minimum conditions under which non-resident entities are obligated to collect tax and the calculation of transfer prices used to determine the division of value added between countries when products cross international borders. (Under an origin-based VAT, it is necessary to value the products that cross international borders because the exporting country taxes the value up to the point of export and the importing nation taxes only the value added after importation.)

Externally Imposed Limitations on Sovereignty
The limitations on taxing power considered to this point are induced by market forces or accepted in negotiations intended to provide mutual benefits to parties to treaties and other international agreements. The third type of limitation on sovereignty is not voluntary but imposed externally under threat of retaliatory action. Though there is little or no history of such limitations actually being imposed, they deserve examination because of the recent OECD project on harmful tax competition.[14]

Some corporations regularly divert income to tax havens in order to reduce taxes, as do some wealthy individuals. Tax havens, typically small countries with little other economic base, eagerly participate in this activity, as they gain modest amounts of employment and perhaps a small amount of revenue from doing so. Unlike normal tax competition, a tax haven does not merely cause the location of economic activity (or even the tax base) to shift; rather, it creates a "black hole" that can swallow part of the tax base of both source and residence countries. Income is shifted from source countries (or is exempt there), but is not taxed currently by residence countries because of deferral (in the case of corporations) or difficulties in gaining information (especially relevant for individuals). Besides causing a loss of tax base, revenue, and tax equity in non–tax haven countries, this "poaching" creates market-induced limitations on taxing powers of the type discussed above.

The OECD has recently undertaken an effort to identify the key characteristics of tax havens and examine the preferential tax regimes of OECD member countries in an effort to determine whether the latter could have similar harmful effects. The intent is to encourage offending countries to mend their ways. If that approach should fail to bring about results, the OECD apparently intends to propose that its members undertake joint efforts to put pressure on these countries to make needed changes.

Limitations on Administrative Independence
"Administrative independence," or what Sijbren Cnossen has called "operational independence," refers to the ability of a country to administer (or operate) its tax system with little or no assistance from the tax authorities of other countries.[15] Sovereignty in taxation is clearly greater the higher the level of administrative independence.

Traditionally, source countries (those where income is derived) have had greater administrative independence than residence countries, especially with regard to some forms of income. Thus, for example, residence countries may have difficulty imposing tax on the worldwide income of residents without obtaining information from source countries on interest payments. Tax havens take advantage of this fact by shielding interest flows from the tax authorities of residence countries. By comparison, source countries can easily impose tax on such income.

The commercial development of the Internet has reduced the administrative independence of both source and residence countries imposing income taxes and of countries imposing destination-based sales taxes. It has become more difficult to impose both source-based income taxes and destination-based sales taxes; it has become easier to invest in tax havens; and it has become easier to manipulate the residence of corporations. Greater international cooperation may be required to offset the reduction in the administrative independence of individual countries.

Conflicts in Sovereignty

Exercise of sovereignty in taxation by one country or group of countries can constrain the sovereignty of others. First, a low-tax regime such as Ireland's, for example, can create pressures ("tax competition") that induce other countries to reduce their level of taxation (but see the qualification in note 3). Second, the shift to a comprehensive income tax with low statutory rates can create pressures on other countries to follow suit to avoid loss of tax base, as happened following the U.S. reduction in tax rates in 1986.[16] Third, the exercise of sovereignty by tax havens can limit the tax policy options of other countries. Conversely, if in an effort to defend their own sovereignty the OECD member countries force tax havens to change their laws, this will interfere with the sovereignty of tax havens.

Tax Rules

Over the years, the countries of the world have constructed a complex system of international agreements governing taxation. The most important components of this system are the GATT; bilateral treaties based primarily on the OECD Model; and the European Union's directives, which increasingly resemble agreements regulating taxation within a federation. (The Sixth Directive, which regulates the application of VAT within the Union, is especially important. There are also a few EU agreements on income taxation.) In addition, the tax laws of both source and residence countries apply to international income flows.

Indirect Taxation

For the reasons given above, there has not been much need for international agreements governing indirect taxation, aside from the GATT, which limits border tax adjustments to the amount of domestic indirect taxes (and prohibits them for direct taxes). (The EU member states have, however, agreed to coordinate indirect taxation in an effort to create a single market.) The advent of electronic commerce may create a need for greater international cooperation in this area.

Income Taxation

The situation is very different in the case of income taxation, where tax treaties are quite prevalent, especially among developed countries. The rules contained in tax treaties and domestic laws can be described in the following general terms, despite the many variations among treaties.[17]

Reconciling Source and Residence Taxation. In addition to taxing income arising within their borders, many countries tax the worldwide income of their residents. This creates the possibility for duplicative taxation of the same income by source and resident countries. To prevent double taxation, residence countries that tax worldwide income generally allow foreign tax credits for the income taxes paid to source countries.[18] Although some countries do this unilaterally, many do so only in the context of a tax treaty in order to gain reciprocal benefits, including exchange of information. By comparison, some countries rely almost entirely on source-based taxation, thus effectively exempting foreign-source income. In either case, there is a need to determine the geographic source of income; this is necessary in the case of countries with worldwide taxation and foreign tax-credit regimes because foreign tax credits are normally limited to the domestic tax that would be paid on foreign-source income.

Residence. Both source and residence-based systems of taxation require rules for determining whether a country has taxing jurisdiction. Residence-based taxation requires knowledge of the place of residence of the entity receiving income. Article 4 of the OECD Model defines a resident as "any person who, under the laws of that State, is liable to tax therein by reason of his domicile, residence, place of management or any other criterion of a similar nature." Since a given entity might be deemed to be a resident under the laws of both states that are party to a treaty, the OECD Model provides a "tie-breaker" rule: The entity "shall be deemed to be a resident only of the State in which its place of effective management is situated."

Permanent Establishment. Under the OECD Model, the existence of a permanent establishment (PE) is the minimal connection required for source-based taxation of business profits. Article 5 of the OECD Model defines the term "permanent establishment" as "a fixed place of business through which the business of an enterprise is wholly or partly carried on." The OECD Model states that a PE includes a place of management, branch, office, factory, workshop, mine, oil or gas well, quarry, or any other place of extraction of natural resources. The OECD Model also excludes from the definition of a PE, inter alia, "the use of facilities solely for the purpose of storage, display or delivery of goods or merchandise belonging to the enterprise" and "the maintenance of a fixed place of business solely for the purpose of carrying on, for the enterprise, any other activity of a preparatory or auxiliary character." A PE exists where

an agent (other than an independent agent) "is acting on behalf of an enterprise and has, and habitually exercises, . . . authority to conclude contracts in the name of the enterprise."

Business Profits/Transfer Pricing. Under Article 7 of the OECD Model, the profits to be attributed to a PE (and thus taxed in the source country) are "the profits which it might be expected to make if it were a distinct and separate enterprise engaged in the same or similar activities under the same or similar conditions." Implicit in these words, in conjunction with those of Article 9,[19] is the arm's length standard for determining transfer prices. The OECD's *Transfer Pricing Guidelines* elaborate on the application of the transfer pricing rules.[20] Traditionally, comparable uncontrolled prices, cost plus (a margin), resale value (minus a margin), and unspecified "other" methods have been used to examine transfer prices for individual transactions. More recently, analysis of the functions performed, risks undertaken, and assets employed have been examined.

Royalties. Article 12 of the OECD Model provides that, except where the property giving rise to royalties is "effectively connected" to a PE in the source country, royalties are to be taxed in the country of residence of the owner of the royalties. For this purpose, royalties are defined as "payments of any kind received as a consideration for the use of, or the right to use, any copyright of literary, artistic or scientific work including cinematograph films, any patent, trade mark, design or model, plan, secret formula or process, or for information concerning industrial, commercial or scientific experience."

Interest and Dividends. Articles 10 and 11 of the OECD Model govern the taxation of interest and dividends. Contrary to the situation with regard to business profits, the OECD Model accords primacy in taxation to the country of residence of the recipient. Even so, the OECD Model provides for the source country to impose withholding taxes on these forms of income, which are not to exceed 5 percent on dividends on direct investment (direct ownership of 25 percent or more of the capital of the payer); 15 percent on other (portfolio) dividends; and 10 percent on interest.

Mutual Agreement Procedure. Where a taxpayer believes that taxation violates the terms of a relevant tax treaty, the taxpayer can initiate a mutual agreement procedure by appealing to the competent authority of his or her country of residence. According to Article 25 of the OECD Model, the competent authority "shall endeavour . . . to resolve the case by mutual agreement with the competent authority of the other Contracting State, with a view to the avoidance of taxation which is not in accordance with the Convention."

Exchange of Information. Article 26 of the OECD Model provides that the tax authorities of treaty partners may exchange the information required for the implementation of the treaty or the domestic tax laws of each country.

Deferral. When a parent corporation resident in a country that taxes worldwide income receives dividends from a foreign subsidiary, the parent includes the dividends in its income for tax purposes and generally takes credits for the corporate tax and withholding taxes the subsidiary has paid to the host country. Until the dividends are received, income taxation in the country in which the parent is resident is normally deferred.

Tax havens and CFC legislation. Deferral is one of the building blocks that make tax havens possible for corporate income. (Other building blocks include the use of thin capitalization and transfer pricing to shift income from source countries to entities resident in tax havens. Also, treaties do not require countries to provide information that is not obtainable

under their laws or to supply information when doing so would be contrary to public policy. This exception creates a substantial loophole for countries whose laws provide for bank secrecy.) In an attempt to nullify the advantages of tax havens for corporations, more than twenty countries have unilaterally enacted "controlled foreign corporation" (CFC) legislation under which certain types of low-taxed income derived by foreign subsidiaries of resident corporations are treated as if distributed currently.[23]

Taxation in a World of Relative Autarky

Most of the existing tax rules were formulated in—and for—a world that no longer exists. Vito Tanzi wrote: "The tax systems of many countries came into existence or developed when trading among countries was greatly controlled and limited and large capital movements were almost non-existent."[22] Limitations on the exercise of national sovereignty in taxation were relatively minor and innocuous in that world.

The Way Things Were

At the risk of oversimplification, the post–World War II world, that is, circa 1950, for which existing tax rules were created can be described in the following general terms:[23]

- international trade consisted primarily of tangible products;
- most international trade occurred between unrelated entities;
- telecommunications services were provided either by a state monopoly or a regulated public utility—in either case, providers of telecommunications services operated only in one country;
- communications were relatively slow;
- a physical presence was generally required for the conduct of business, including the provision of almost all services;

- intangible assets were relatively unimportant;
- although international investment existed, capital was relatively immobile internationally;
- the country of residence of a given corporation was unambiguous;
- almost all investment occurred in the country of residence of the investor, and almost all investment in corporations was by those living in the entity's country of residence;
- interest and dividends were readily distinguishable;
- tax havens were, at most, a minor nuisance; and
- the United States was the undisputed economic and political leader of the (non-Communist) world. (The European Union had not yet been created; indeed, the countries of Europe and Japan were still recovering from the physical and economic devastation of World War II.)

Implications of the Way Things Were

These characteristics of the world economy had important implications for both the nature and adequacy of tax rules and the limitations on the taxing powers of countries. (Some of the terminology used here may not have been current in the 1950s.)

The GATT could reasonably cover only trade in goods; coverage of services and intangible products was hardly necessary. Indeed, it would not have seemed inappropriate to apply the origin principle to services, since telecommunications was the only important service that crossed international borders, and it was controlled by local monopolies.

It was also relatively straightforward in the postwar era to apply income tax rules to international transactions. A PE could be defined in a straightforward way, and the existence of a PE was a bright line test of a source country's jurisdiction to tax business profits. The arm's length standard provided a clear way to divide the income of affiliated entities. Transfer pricing was less important than now, except in a few industries (for example, oil), and transfer pricing methodologies were less sophisticated than they are now. "Comparable uncontrolled prices" was an adequate test of transfer prices in most cases, and either cost plus (a margin) or resale price (minus a margin) provided a satisfactory fallback test in many others; little resort to "other" methods of determining arm's length prices was needed. Because almost all financial investment occurred at home, there was little need for exchange of information. There was also little need for antiabuse legislation to deal with tax-haven investment.

It was a world in which countries could, for the most part, structure their taxes with only domestic considerations in mind; they could achieve substantial operational independence in taxation and were not much constrained by the fear of losing economic activity or their tax base to other countries with lower taxes, especially since the foreign tax credits allowed by the United States created an umbrella over rates below the U.S. rate. Tax havens were not much constrained in their attempts to sell their advantages; nor did they pose much threat to the revenues of other countries. Countries could exercise considerable sovereignty in taxation, although sovereignty was somewhat constrained—albeit voluntarily—by the GATT and tax treaties, of which there were still relatively few.

Taxation in a Globalized "Electronic" World

Globalization, epitomized by the advent of electronic commerce, has changed the world dramatically, placing strains on the present tax rules and creating new and significant limitations on taxing powers.

The existing body of international tax rules, as reflected both in national law and in treaties, is based in large part on the supposition that international trade consists of the physical shipment of tangible goods or the physical movement of persons to perform services at different locations. The challenge posed by the development of the Internet and related means of communication is that in many cases this is simply no longer true.[24]

The Way Things Are

The world economy differs significantly from the one described above. Today, the major characteristics are as follows:

- a substantial amount of international trade consists of services and intangible products;
- most international trade occurs between related entities;
- a physical presence may no longer be required for the conduct of business, especially trade in intangibles, digital content, and services that can be digitized;
- intangible assets are vital to the modern corporation—often there is no external market for their services;
- in many countries, telecommunications services are provided by privately owned and unregulated public utilities that operate across national boundaries;
- much communication is instantaneous;
- capital is highly mobile internationally;
- because of the development of financial derivatives, interest and dividends are no longer readily distinguishable;
- the country of residence of a given corporation can be ambiguous or easily changed;
- many investors invest outside their country of residence, and substantial investment in corporations comes from outside the entity's putative country of residence;
- tax havens pose a significant threat to tax revenues and to the equity and neutrality of the tax systems of non–tax haven countries;[25] and
- although the United States is the only remaining superpower, with the ascendance of the European Union, it is no

longer the undisputed economic and political leader of the world.

Implications of Globalization and Electronic Commerce

Indirect Taxation. The implications of globalization and electronic commerce for indirect tax rules are relatively minor.[26] First, the GATT has been modified to apply to services. Second, efforts are under way in several venues (for example, the European Union) to convert the taxation of services to the destination principle.[27]

The implications for the administration of indirect taxes are somewhat more ominous, but still probably not extremely important.[28] The problems relate primarily to consumer purchases of digital content (for example, music, videos, books, and games). Since such products do not stop at the customs house or post office, it is impossible to use traditional methods to collect destination-based taxes on them. (Tangible products do still stop; thus, although the volume of taxable transactions crossing borders may increase, the nature of the administrative problem does not change.) This problem is aggravated by the possibility of using untraceable money to pay for digital content. Even so, the OECD has said that "end-to-end virtual transactions are currently a small part of e-commerce and a fractional non factor in commerce overall."[29] Of course, the problem will grow in magnitude as commerce in digitized products becomes more important.

The problems are likely to be even less serious in the case of business purchases of digital content. Under a credit-method VAT, registered traders are allowed a credit for the tax paid on their purchases. Thus, in principle, it does not matter (except for the timing of tax collection) whether tax is collected on imports, since the failure to collect tax simply reduces the amount of credits, with no effect on the amount of tax ultimately collected. Alternatively, the VAT can be "reverse-charged" (self-assessed) and remitted by registered business purchasers; this is the approach followed in the European Union for trade between member states.[30]

Income Taxation. Globalization and the advent of electronic commerce potentially have a much greater impact on income taxation. The range of issues under discussion extends from such fundamental issues as the long-standing primacy of source-based taxation of business profits to such minutia as whether a Web site constitutes a PE. The issues include such basic questions as the classification of the types of income, the conceptual foundation for determining jurisdiction to impose source-based taxation, the definition of a PE, the choice between the arm's length standard and formula apportionment, transfer pricing methodologies, identification of the residence of corporations, the problem of tax havens, and the need for greater international cooperation.

Source vs. residence taxation. In recognition of the undeniable difficulties involved in implementing source-based taxation, the U.S. Treasury Department has suggested that primacy in taxation should shift to residence countries: "The growth of new communications technologies and electronic commerce will likely require that principles of residence-based taxation assume even greater importance. In the world of cyberspace, it is often difficult, if not impossible, to apply traditional concepts to link an item of income with a specific geographical location. Therefore, source-based taxation could lose its rationale and be rendered obsolete by electronic commerce."[31]

According primacy to residence-based taxation would have the considerable advantage of reducing the importance of the distinctions between business profits, royalties, and income from services—distinctions that make little economic sense and are difficult to implement in a world of electronic commerce in digital content.[32] Some, however, have found the U.S. Treasury suggestion to be technically naive, as well as self-serving and politically unrealistic. Developed countries and developing countries have long disagreed on whether source or residence countries should have the primary right to tax international flows of income. Even some advanced countries may be unwilling to agree

with a shift to the primacy of residence-based taxation of electronic commerce.

Residence is not the unambiguous and immutable concept the U.S. Treasury Department implies it is. The place of incorporation, the test used by the United States, can be changed. Most countries use the place of effective management, not the place of incorporation, as the test of residence. The place of effective management, however, may be quite ambiguous under certain circumstances and can be manipulated.[33] In short, as Richard L. Doernberg and Luc Hinnekens noted: "The same forces that question the permanent establishment concept, and other source-based taxation concepts, also call the adequacy of the residence concept into question—particularly the residence of a company. If the definition of residence is artificial and easily manipulated, granting exclusive authority to residence countries is not a good solution."[34] Deferral implies that residence countries do not tax foreign-source income until it is distributed. Given the tax advantages of deferral, this might be a long time, indeed; residence-based taxation might thus be tantamount to no taxation at all in many cases.

Tax havens further aggravate the problems of placing primary reliance on residence. In the absence of source-based taxation, the incentive to use tax havens to avoid or evade home-country taxes—and the need for antiabuse legislation, such as CFC rules, and other defensive measures—would be even greater.

PE as the test of source-based jurisdiction to tax. There are at least three ways one can justify the existence of a PE as the minimal requirement for jurisdiction to impose source-based taxation. First, the benefit principle has been offered as a rationale for the PE test; unless a company has a PE, it is not likely to benefit significantly from public services. At a conceptual level, however, the presence of a PE would not be required under the benefit or entitlement theories of taxation.[35] The advent of electronic commerce leads some, especially in countries providing markets for electronic commerce, to suggest that the PE threshold may be too high—that some entities with less of a presence in the country should be subject to income tax. Even so, the second and older justification for the PE test must be confronted: It may not be administratively feasible to implement an income tax imposed on an entity that lacks a PE. Finally, even if the threshold for jurisdiction to tax were lowered, it seems unlikely that market countries would gain much revenue under standard transfer-pricing methodologies.[36]

Web sites and servers as PEs. In the past several years, considerable ink has been spilled over the question of whether Web sites and servers should constitute a PE. The OECD recently amended the commentary on Article 5 of its Model Treaty to clarify this issue:

Regarding web sites: The OECD states that a web site cannot, in itself, constitute a permanent establishment, . . . a web site hosting arrangement typically does not result in a permanent establishment for the enterprise that carries on business through that web site and . . . an ISP will not, except in very unusual circumstances, constitute a dependent agent of another enterprise so as to constitute a permanent establishment of that enterprise.

Regarding servers: The OECD states that in many cases, the issue of whether computer equipment at a given location constitutes a permanent establishment will depend on whether the functions performed through that equipment exceed the preparatory or auxiliary threshold, something that can only be decided on a case-by-case analysis.

Regarding human intervention: The OECD states that human intervention is not a requirement for the existence of a permanent establishment.[37]

Transfer prices. As noted earlier, the majority of international trade involves transactions between corporate affiliates, and many of the transactions are in intangible products. This means that implementation of the arm's length standard is far more important than before and that the traditional methods of valuing such

transactions are much less reliable.[38] As a result, two additional methods of determining transfer prices have been added to the OECD *Transfer Pricing Guidelines:* "profit split" and "comparable profit." Electronic commerce further accentuates the problems of transfer pricing.[39] To reduce the possibility of nasty surprises (rejection of transfer prices and unexpected tax liabilities), the tax authorities of some countries have begun to enter into advance pricing arrangements (APAs) with taxpayers that specify the transfer pricing methodology that will be found acceptable.

Not only has it become more difficult to implement the OECD guidelines, but if different countries do not all accept the same determination, there is also a substantial risk that disagreement will cause double taxation. (Undertaxation is, of course, also a possibility.) The OECD Model provides for appeal to the competent authority, which is to "endeavour" to resolve problems. The competent authorities involved in a dispute, however, are under no obligation to reach a satisfactory and timely resolution.

Transfer pricing issues are probably the single most important source of conflicting claims to tax.[40] To deal with this problem, the OECD has created the mutual agreement procedure (MAP). Under a MAP APA, a taxpayer simultaneously enters into APAs with more than one taxing jurisdiction.[41] In theory, the APA approach should provide the taxpayer with greater certainty, avoid the risk of inconsistent rulings by the tax administrators of various countries, assure tax administrators that the taxpayer is not telling a different story in each country, and reduce costs for both taxpayers and tax authorities. The MAP, however, suffers from the same weaknesses as any approach that relies on competent authorities to "endeavour" to resolve issues—relief for the taxpayer is not guaranteed, since the procedure does not require the competent authorities to reach a settlement.[42] This has led to suggestions for binding arbitration.

Formula apportionment. Some observers believe that it would be advisable to abandon separate accounting and the arm's length method and to shift to using formula apportionment to divide the income of multinational corporations among the countries in which they operate. This approach is used by the states of the United States and the provinces of Canada, and a profit split approach is employed to apportion profits from global trading. This is not the place for a detailed examination of formula apportionment or its advantages and disadvantages relative to separate accounting and arm's length pricing.[43] Suffice it to say that the only sensible way to implement formula apportionment would be on a worldwide basis; otherwise, problems of arm's length pricing would remain. (Indeed, if different apportionment formulas were applied to different industries, arm's length pricing would be required to divide the income of multinationals engaged in more than one industry.) Unless all countries adopted the same definitions and apportionment formulas, there would be considerable risk for over- and undertaxation, as well as considerable complexity. (This is not to say that there is not a substantial amount of over- and undertaxation and complexity today, owing to inconsistencies in the tax systems of various countries.) This degree of uniformity would require unparalleled international cooperation.

Taxation of interest. Interest expense incurred in the course of business is generally deductible. Thus, interest goes untaxed unless it is taxed by the creditor's country of residence.[44] For administrative reasons, residence countries have difficulty taxing international flows of interest income received by individuals, unless the residence countries have the assistance of source countries, which generally is not forthcoming.[45] As Joel Slemrod wrote, "Although it is not *desirable* to tax capital on a source basis, it is not administratively *feasible* to tax capital on a residence basis" (emphasis in original).[46] The difficulty in taxing interest income undermines the ability to tax other forms of capital income. Thus, Sijbren Cnossen wrote, "This weak spot in the CT [corporate tax] bucket can only be repaired by taxing in-

terest on the basis of the source principle."[47] Similarly, a multilateral agreement to *require a minimum withholding tax on interest,* and perhaps on dividends, would constitute an important reform in the taxation of international capital flows because it would tax interest before it reaches the haven.[48] Although this would undermine tax havens, such an agreement is unlikely because it would represent a significant departure from the rules enshrined in the OECD and U.S. model tax conventions and numerous bilateral treaties.

In theory, evasion of residence-based taxation on interest income could be addressed through greater international cooperation in tax administration. As Tanzi wrote, however, "It seems naive to assume . . . that enhanced exchange of information among countries independent in their tax affairs is the instrument that will allow countries to cope with the exponential growth of foreign source income that accompanies the increasingly deeper integration of the world's economies."[49]

Taxation of dividends. At the end of World War II, most developed countries used the classical system for taxing corporate equity income; that is, they taxed corporate profits and then taxed dividends when received by the shareholders.[50] By 1980, most of these countries (but not the United States or the Netherlands) provided some kind of relief from the double taxation of dividends. In theory, an exemption for dividends paid, application of a lower rate on distributed corporate-source income (the split-rate system), and a shareholder credit for the corporate tax attributed to dividends (the imputation or withholding method) are economically equivalent ways of doing this. Although an exemption for dividends paid (or split-rate system) is administratively simpler than the shareholder credit, the latter was almost universally preferred because it allowed the benefits of dividend relief to be denied to foreign investors (and to tax-exempt organizations). In recent years, the European Court of Justice has found that an EU member state's denial of the benefits of dividend relief to residents of other EU member states is inconsistent with the European Community (EC) Treaty. As a result, the EU member states are returning to the classical system. The implied double taxation of income from equity-financed corporate investments means that there will be an increased incentive to use debt finance and increased pressure on the taxation of interest.

OECD Coordination Efforts

The OECD recently assumed the leadership in international efforts to modify the tax rules applicable to international transactions. Among other issues, the OECD has taken steps to deal with harmful tax competition and the taxation of electronic commerce.

The European Union is also involved in various efforts to coordinate the tax policies of EU member states. In addition to harmful tax competition and the taxation of electronic commerce, the EU member states are studying the possibility of coordinating their corporate income taxes.[51] Besides being of interest in its own right, the EU experience may be relevant for what it reveals about the likelihood of various proposals gaining acceptance in the wider community of nations. (It should be noted that the EU adoption of tax measures requires unanimous agreement.) Space, however, prevents consideration of these activities, some of which, in any event, involve issues that resemble questions of fiscal federalism more than simply issues of international taxation.

Harmful Tax Competition
In order to combat harmful tax competition, the OECD has undertaken to "develop measures to counter the distorting effects of harmful tax competition on investment and financing decisions and the consequences for national tax bases."[52] It has concentrated on geographically mobile activities, such as financial and other service activities, including the provision of intangibles.

The OECD has noted: "Tax havens serve three main purposes: they provide a location for holding passive investments ('money boxes'); they provide a location where 'paper' profits can be booked; and they enable the affairs of taxpayers, particularly their bank accounts, to be effectively shielded from scrutiny by tax authorities of other countries."[53] Tax havens are especially attractive to certain highly mobile activities such as financial services. To remain competitive, some countries that would not generally be considered tax havens—including some OECD member countries—have created "preferential tax regimes" that resemble those found in tax havens to attract these activities. Tax havens and preferential tax regimes create what the OECD calls "harmful tax competition." As a result, other countries lose revenue and can exercise less sovereignty over taxation.

Among the adverse effects the OECD highlights are:

- distorting financial and, indirectly, real investment flows;
- undermining the integrity and fairness of tax structures;
- discouraging compliance by all taxpayers;
- reshaping the desired level and mix of taxes and public spending;
- causing undesired shifts of part of the tax burden to less mobile tax bases, such as labor, property, and consumption; and
- increasing the administrative costs for tax authorities and the compliance burdens of taxpayers.[54]

The legislation of a tax haven commonly provides more than merely little or no taxation. The OECD uses "four key factors" to identify a tax haven:

1. there is no tax or only a nominal tax on the relevant income;
2. there is no effective exchange of information with respect to the regime;

3. the jurisdiction's regime lacks transparency—for example, the details of the regime and/or its application are not apparent, or there is inadequate regulatory supervision or financial disclosure; and

4. the jurisdiction facilitates the establishment of foreign-owned entities without the need for a local substantive presence, or the jurisdiction prohibits these entities from having any commercial impact on the local economy.[55]

In the case of "harmful preferential tax regimes" found in the OECD member countries, the OECD has used essentially the same criteria, except that the fourth is replaced by the following: "The regime is 'ring-fenced'" from the domestic economy.[56] The OECD also indicates that the following "other factors" may be evidence of harmful preferential tax regimes: an artificial definition of the tax base, failure to adhere to international transfer-pricing principles, exemption of foreign-source income, negotiable tax rate or tax base, existence of secrecy provisions, access to a wide network of tax treaties, a regime promoted as a tax-minimization vehicle, and a regime that encourages purely tax-driven operations and arrangements.[57]

The OECD recognizes that the considerations facing tax havens are quite different from those facing OECD member countries with preferential regimes: "In the first case, the country has no interest in trying to curb the 'race to the bottom' with respect to income tax and is actively contributing to the erosion of income tax revenues in other countries. For that reason, these countries are unlikely to cooperate in curbing harmful tax competition. By contrast, in the second case, a country may have a significant amount of revenues which are at risk from the spread of harmful tax competition and it is therefore more likely to agree on concerted action."[58]

The OECD compiled a list of potentially harmful preferential tax regimes of the member countries, and the members agreed to both "standstill" and "rollback" provisions. Most potentially harmful tax regimes were eliminated by April 2003.[59] In addition, the OECD identified almost fifty countries that it categorized as tax havens.[60] Tax havens that did not agree to eliminate harmful practices were included in a "List of Uncooperative Tax Havens" published in 2004 and can now be subjected to common defensive measures by the OECD member countries.[61] Finally, nonmembers that are not tax havens now cooperate in efforts to eliminate potentially harmful tax regimes.[62]

At a meeting held in Barbados in January 2001, "OECD and Commonwealth countries . . . agreed on a way forward in efforts to achieve global co-operation on harmful tax practices through a dialogue based on shared support for the principles of transparency, non-discrimination and effective exchange of information on tax matters."[63] A Working Group created at the meeting was given the task of finding "a mutually acceptable political process by which these principles could be turned into commitments" that could "replace OECD's process in the context of its Memorandum of Understanding" and examine how to continue the dialogue begun in Barbados.

U.S. Treasury Secretary Paul O'Neill said in 2001 that he will "reevaluate" U.S. participation in the OECD's efforts to combat harmful tax competition. He seemed to believe that the OECD project is based on a suspicion of low tax rates, the notion that it is appropriate to interfere in the tax policy of other countries, and a perceived need to harmonize world tax systems and stifle tax competition.[64] In fact, there is little basis for any of these beliefs. The OECD has stated: "It is not intended explicitly or implicitly to suggest that there is some general minimum effective rate of tax to be imposed on income below which a country would be considered to be engaging in harmful tax competition."[65] The OECD has also stated that "the project . . . is not intended to promote the harmonisation of income taxes or tax structures generally within or outside the OECD, nor is it about dictating to any country what should be the appropriate level of tax rates."[66] Most OECD member countries that have preferential systems that are "ring-fenced" seem to be willing to give them up in order to gain the benefits of eliminating tax havens. Many economists believe that it seems a bit far-fetched to say that this voluntary action of member countries involves external interference.

There is no doubt that the OECD initiative, if successful, would involve encroachment on the fiscal sovereignty of tax havens. This seems to be similar in nature to interference in sovereignty to accommodate money laundering and the drug traffic.

Economist Brian Arnold offered an appropriate appraisal of the harmful tax competition project: "There is no reason for governments to give up their corporate taxes just because multinational corporations operate globally. Governments must operate multilaterally on the same global basis. Such multilateral action in the tax area has historically been difficult, if not impossible. Governments have been reluctant to relinquish their sovereignty concerning tax policy. Globalization, however, has rendered this selfish attitude obsolete. International cooperation with respect to taxation is critical, and the harmful tax competition initiative is an important first step on a long journey."[67]

Taxation of Electronic Commerce

Following high-level multinational meetings in Turku, Finland, in 1997 and Ottawa, Canada, in 1998, the OECD created five Technical Advisory Groups (TAGs), composed of representatives of the OECD secretariat, member countries, and business, to investigate particular aspects of the taxation of electronic commerce.[68] Two of the TAGs have concentrated on consumption taxation, and two on income taxation; the fifth, on "professional data assessment," has dealt primarily with tax administration. The following are thumbnail sketches of the activities of the TAGs that are concerned with consumption taxes and income taxes.[69]

Consumption taxes. The Consumption Tax TAG has investigated implementation of the decision taken in Ottawa that taxation should occur at the place of consumption. In concentrating on the taxation of sales to households and unregistered traders, it has examined collection options.[70]

Technology. In an extension of the work of the Consumption Tax TAG, the Technology TAG has been involved in "examining the technological implications of the various collection models considered for collecting consumption taxes on cross-border electronic commerce transactions and the reliability of systems and trails for audit purposes."[71] Some of the approaches being examined may require international cooperation, and some may be stymied by existing nontax agreements—for example, those dealing with privacy.

Business profits. The Business Profits TAG has investigated the attribution of profits to a PE engaged in electronic commerce, especially whether servers and Web sites should be treated as PEs, and the suitability of "effective management" as the test of a PE in the world of electronic commerce. The TAG also plans to take a closer look at the conceptual foundation for using a PE as the test of jurisdiction to tax electronic commerce and to examine transfer pricing of electronic commerce transactions.[72]

Income characterization. The Income Characterization TAG has examined the distinctions between business profits and royalties, which are treated differently under the OECD Model.[73]

The OECD Initiatives Compared

The OECD initiative on harmful tax competition involves a clear conflict in the exercise of fiscal sovereignty by tax-haven countries and by other countries; the latter group wishes to impose limits on the fiscal sovereignty of the former group in order to avoid market-induced restrictions on their own fiscal sovereignty. In addition, the OECD member countries with preferential tax regimes appear to be willing to accept limitations on the exercise of their own sovereignty in order to gain the benefits expected to result from a multilateral effort to prevent harmful tax competition.

The OECD initiative on the taxation of electronic commerce is quite different. To the extent that it involves income taxation, it seeks to determine whether the provisions of the OECD Model are adequate to deal with electronic commerce and how the provisions or their interpretation need to be modified. In other words, it would provide the background for negotiated constraints on tax sovereignty. In the case of consumption taxes, the thrust is to examine how best to implement consumption taxes on digitized products. There is, of course, no model treaty on consumption taxes, and only a few treaties deal with consumption taxes.

Are New International Tax Institutions Needed?

Vito Tanzi, Jack Mintz, and others have raised the possibility of a "GATT for taxes," or General Agreement on Taxes (GATaxes), which has been described as "a multilateral agreement on the ground rules for the taxation of international flows of income from business and capital."[74] A World Tax Organization (WTaxO), analogous to the World Trade Organization, would perhaps be needed to oversee the implementation of such an agreement. Tanzi, former head of the Fiscal Affairs Department of the International Monetary Fund, wrote: "There is no world institution with the responsibility to establish desirable rules for taxation and with enough clout to induce countries to follow those rules. Perhaps the time has come to establish one."[75] Mintz wrote: "For the development of a 'globalized corporate income tax,' it would be useful to create a formal body such as a World Tax Organization or provide powers to

an existing international organization that would facilitate mutual co-operation for developed and developing countries."[76]

The coverage of a GATaxes and the mandate of a WTaxO might be either quite broad—involving substantial harmonization of world tax systems—or quite limited—to cover only the international aspects of taxation or only the "tax haven" problem.[77] The implications of these options for national sovereignty are quite different.

A General Agreement on Taxes/ World Tax Organization

Regarding the function of an international tax organization, Mintz has suggested that "the purpose of the co-ordinating body would not be to collect taxes but instead put a mechanism in place to achieve global co-operation in tax policy," and one of the responsibilities he would assign to the organization would be to "develop a code for a 'model' corporation income tax."[78] There are, however, serious conceptual caveats, as well as overwhelming political obstacles, to the creation of a GATaxes and a WTaxO with broad powers. First, as Tanzi noted: "Unlike trade, for which the obvious reference point is free trade, it would be very difficult to agree on the instructions to give such an agency."[79] Some tax policy experts might advocate international adoption of a comprehensive income tax patterned after the Schanz-Haig-Simons model. Others, however, might prefer an international consensus to employ another standard, such as some type of cash-flow tax or the "comprehensive business income tax" examined by the U.S. Department of the Treasury in 1992, which would implement source-based taxation of interest by allowing no deduction for interest expense.[80]

Second, there is little reason to believe that countries will soon engage in the massive surrender of national sovereignty over tax policy implied by this option. (If they did, the most likely result would be a system that looked, in the words of the old joke, like a camel, "a horse designed by committee.") U.S. Treasury Secretary O'Neill's stance against the OECD initiative on harmful tax competition, though wide of the mark, suggests that there would be vigorous American opposition to such an agreement. Finally, if ever there were international agreement on a particular system, the tyranny of the status quo would likely take over, and further change would proceed at a glacial pace, if at all. Once made, mistakes would plague the international world of finance forever.

An Agreement on International Taxation
Even limited narrowly to international flows of income, a GATaxes/WTaxO arrangement would entail substantial surrender of national sovereignty over taxation, as well as vexing conceptual questions. Given the ever-widening network of treaties, however, most of which conform substantially to the OECD Model, multilateral adoption of a system based on that model might involve less surrender of sovereignty than it would seem at first glance, at least for those countries that already participate in the treaty network. But would the rich countries that make up the OECD want to share power to revise the OECD Model with poor nations? (The UN Model Convention and the OECD Model, while generally similar, are not identical; the former accords more taxing power to source countries.) The many developing countries and countries in transition that do not now have extensive treaty networks might not wish to participate in such an organization if it meant accepting the terms of the OECD Model. In any event, the lack of success in harmonizing direct taxes within the European Union suggests that multilateral agreement even in this limited sphere is not likely to come quickly.

Combating Tax Havens
It appears that the current OECD initiative on harmful tax competition strikes a reasonable balance between a laissez-faire attitude, under which tax havens could thrive and continue to undermine national tax policies, and an overly

harmonized system, in which all countries would lose substantial amounts of fiscal sovereignty.

Concluding Remarks

Globalization and the advent of electronic commerce have increased the power of market forces, the difficulty of administering a tax system without assistance from other countries, and the potential for sheltering income in tax havens. These developments have thus reduced the sovereignty that countries can exercise over tax policy. It seems almost certain that part of the response will be increased international cooperation in administering income taxes and perhaps in combating tax havens. Much of this may be facilitated by the OECD. It does not, however, seem likely that this cooperation will extend to the creation of either a "GATT for taxes" or a World Tax Organization.

The author has benefited substantially from comments on an earlier draft, especially by Joann Weiner.

Charles E. McLure, Jr.

See Also Fiscal Policy; Monopolies and Antitrust Legislation; U.S. Trade laws

Endnotes

1. In *The Lexus and the Olive Tree* (New York: Random House, 1999), 104, Thomas L. Friedman wrote: "When your country recognizes . . . the rules of the free market in today's global economy, and decides to abide by them, it puts on what I call the Golden Straitjacket. . . . If your country has not been fitted to one, it soon will." He went on (p. 105) to list the characteristics of the Golden Straitjacket. Interestingly, he did not list limits on the power to tax.

2. Globalization also limits national sovereignty in the taxation of labor income. Given the substantially greater international mobility of capital and the correspondingly greater potential for loss of sovereignty, this article focuses on the limitations on sovereignty in the taxation of capital.

3. The issue is substantially more complicated than this paragraph suggests. Even if the description is accu-

rate for a world of pure source-based taxation—and it probably is not—it need not accurately describe a world in which residence countries tax the worldwide income of potential investors and allow foreign tax credits for taxes paid to source countries, since source-based taxation may be largely absorbed by foreign tax credits. But excess foreign tax credits and the deferral of tax on income of foreign subsidiaries of domestic corporations until it is repatriated (unless countered by defensive measures, such as accrual taxation of controlled foreign corporations) imply that tax systems based on worldwide taxation with foreign tax credits may actually function more like source-based systems. See the section on "Tax Rules" in this entry for more information, and for an excellent explanation of the above, see Joel Slemrod, "Tax Policy toward Foreign Direct Investment in Developing Countries in Light of Recent International Tax Changes," in Anwar Shah, ed., *Fiscal Incentives for Investment and Innovation* (New York: Oxford University Press, for the World Bank, 1995), 289.

4. The meaning and methodology of METR calculations are explained in Mervyn A. King and Don Fullerton, eds., *The Taxation of Income from Capital* (Chicago: University of Chicago Press, 1984). Ironically, the King-Fullerton analysis, which has spawned a vast literature, does not treat the issues that arise in an open economy satisfactorily; for that, see Robin M. Boadway, Neil Bruce, and Jack M. Mintz, "Taxation, Inflation and the Effective Marginal Tax Rate on Capital in Canada," *Canadian Journal of Economics* 17, no. 1 (1984): 62.

5. See Roger H. Gordon, "Can Capital Income Taxes Survive in Open Economies?" *Journal of Finance* 47, no. 3 (1992): 1159.

6. The Ruding Committee concluded: "Recent experience suggests that any attempt by the EC to impose withholding taxes on cross-border interest flows could result in a flight of financial capital to non-EC countries." Commission of the European Communities, *Report of the Committee of Independent Experts on Company Taxation* (Luxembourg: Commission of the European Communities, 1992), 201. Even so, in 1998, the Commission of the European Communities proposed the "coexistence model," under which the member states could opt for either transmission of information on interest payments or a withholding tax on such payments. See *Proposal for a Council Directive to ensure a minimum effective taxation of savings income in the form of interest payments within the Community,* COM (1998) 295 final. More recently, the EU member states agreed to exchange information instead of adopting withholding taxes. See "Conclusions of the European Council," Santa Maria Da Feira, June 19–20, 2000, Para. 42 and Annex IV, available at www.google. com/search?hl=en&safe=off&q=ecofin+brussels+ November+2000&spell=1.

7. *Report of the Technical Committee on Business Taxation* (Ottawa: Technical Committee on Business Taxation, 1998), 1.9.

8. See Peter Birch Sorensen, "From the Global Income Tax to the Dual Income Tax: Recent Tax Reforms in the Nordic Countries," *International Tax and Public Finance* 1, no. 1 (1994): 57.

9. Tanzi wrote: "It is conceivable that they [trends he has identified] will make it difficult for countries to maintain their present levels and structures of taxation. For example, in a highly integrated world, where capital will be able to move freely between countries, it will become increasingly difficult to maintain high tax rates on capital income. Such rates would simply stimulate capital to emigrate from the high-tax to the low-tax countries." Vito Tanzi, "Forces That Shape Tax Policy," in Herbert Stein, ed., *Tax Policy in the Twenty-First Century* (New York: John Wiley, 1988), 277.

10. A well-known theorem states that, if generally applied, origin- and destination-principle taxes are equivalent, except for the equilibrium exchange rate. The theorem, however, is not very helpful as a guide to tax policy or to the understanding of political economy. First, the conditions required for its validity may not hold. See, for example, Martin Feldstein and Paul Krugman, "International Trade Effects of Value-Added Taxation," in Assaf Razin and Joel Slemrod, eds., *Taxation in a Global Economy* (Chicago: University of Chicago Press, 1990), 263. More important for present purposes, domestic producers competing with untaxed foreigners in both foreign and domestic markets are not likely to be persuaded by the theorem; they are likely to prefer destination-based taxation, which obviously puts them on a level playing field vis-à-vis competitors in both markets. See Watanabe Satoshi, "Indirect Taxes and Electronic Commerce," *State Tax Notes* 19, (December 11, 2000), p. 1575.

11. Until recently, telecommunications, like other services in the European Union, were taxed wherever the provider had its place of business. This, in effect, created origin-based taxation.

12. See the following reports: OECD, "Consumption Tax Aspects of Electronic Commerce," in *Taxation and Electronic Commerce: Implementing the Ottawa Framework Conditions* (Paris: OECD, 2001), 17; Report by the Consumption Tax Technical Advisory Group (TAG), December 2000, available at www.oecd.org/daf/fa/e_com/ ec_7_CT_TAG_Eng.pdf (hereafter "OECD, Consumption Tax TAG"); and Report by the Technology Technical Advisory Group (TAG), December 2000, available at www. oecd.org/daf/fa/e_com/ec_8_TECH_TAG_Eng.pdf (hereafter "OECD, Technology TAG"). See also Commission of the European Communities, *Proposal for a Regulation of the European Parliament and of the Council amending Regulation* (EEC) No. 218/92 on administrative cooperation in the field of indirect taxation (VAT), COM (2000) 394 final.

13. An exception is the need to specify that (1) the tax applied to imports cannot exceed the tax on domestic products; (2) rebates of tax on exports cannot exceed the

tax actually collected at the prior stages in the production/distribution process; and (3) such border tax adjustments are allowed only for indirect taxes. Since the GATT includes these specifications, there is no need for bilateral treaties in this area.

14. Two other externally imposed limitations on sovereignty deserve mention. First, if the existence of a tax treaty is seen as a "seal of approval," developing countries may conclude treaties that might not otherwise be desirable, giving away benefits in exchange for little other than the existence of the treaty. (This might better be classified as a market-induced limit on sovereignty.) Second, limitations on the availability of foreign tax credits may limit the policy options of other countries. For example, in the mid-1990s, when the United States refused to indicate that a consumption-based direct tax might be creditable, Bolivia was forced to abandon consideration of such a tax. For the case that foreign tax credits should be allowed for a cash-flow tax, see Charles E. McLure, Jr., and George R. Zodrow, "The Economic Case for Foreign Tax Credits for Cash Flow Taxes," *National Tax Journal* 51, no. 1 (March 1998): 1.

15. See Charles E. McLure, Jr., "Substituting Consumption-Based Direct Taxation for Income Taxes as the International Norm," *National Tax Journal* 45, no. 2 (June 1992): 145; and Sijbren Cnossen, "Company Taxes in the European Union: Criteria and Options for Reform, *Fiscal Studies* 17, no. 4 (November 1996): 67.

16. See the earlier quotation from the *Report of the Technical Committee on Business Taxation.* See also Vito Tanzi, "Tax Reform in Industrial Countries and the Impact of the U.S. Tax Reform Act of 1986," *Bulletin for International Fiscal Documentation* 42, no. 2 (1988): 51; Vito Tanzi, "The Response of Other Industrial Countries to the U.S. Tax Reform Act," *National Tax Journal* 40, no. 3 (September 1987): 339; and John Whalley, "Foreign Responses to U.S. Tax Reform," in Joel Slemrod, ed., *Do Taxes Matter: The Impact of the Tax Reform Act of 1986* (Cambridge: MIT Press, 1990), 286.

17. See OECD, Committee on Fiscal Affairs, *Model Tax Convention on Income and on Capital* (condensed version of April 29, 2000). Treaties commonly also provide for nondiscrimination (prohibiting the taxation of foreign persons that is more burdensome than that applied to nationals of the state) and cover capital taxes, but (in some instances, including, notably, treaties with the United States) do not cover subnational taxes.

18. Articles 23 A and 23 B of the OECD Model deal with the issues discussed in this paragraph. Bird and Mintz wrote, "The fundamental significance of treaties is that the countries involved admit that other countries are in some sense *entitled* to impose tax" (emphasis in original) and that "tax treaties can be seen as international agreements on how to allocate income among those jurisdictions with which the taxpayer arguably has a suffi-

ciently strong connection for them to assert their right to tax." Richard M. Bird and Jack M. Mintz, "Sharing the International Tax Base in a Changing World," prepared for a CESIfo conference on Public Finance and Public Policy in the New Millennium, University of Munich, January 12–13, 2001.

19. The relevant part of Article 9 provides: "Where . . . conditions are made or imposed between the two enterprises in their commercial or financial relations which differ from those which would be made between independent enterprises, then any profits which would, but for those conditions, have accrued to one of the enterprises, but, by reason of those conditions, have not so accrued, may be included in the profits of that enterprise and taxed accordingly." Articles 11 (Interest) and 12 (Royalties) also contain provisions that specify the use of the arm's length approach.

20. OECD, *Transfer Pricing Guidelines for Multinational Enterprises and Tax Administrations* (Paris: OECD, 2001).

21. For a masterful discussion of CFC legislation and its relationship to the OECD initiative on harmful competition, see Brian J. Arnold, "Controlled Foreign Corporation Rules, Harmful Competition, and International Taxation," *Report of the Proceedings of the World Tax Conference: Taxes without Borders* (Toronto: Canadian Tax Foundation, 2000), 17:1.

22. Vito Tanzi, "The Impact of Economic Globalization on Taxation," *Bulletin for International Fiscal Documentation* 52, no. 8/9 (1998): 338, 339.

23. Since tax rules have evolved over time, it is difficult to pick a single date for a snapshot of "the way things were." The basic business practices and methods of taxation, if not the current form of the tax rules, were in place shortly after World War II; thus, 1950 seems to provide a reasonable time frame. The term "relatively" is used to describe the situation relative to now.

24. David R. Tillinghast, "The Impact of the Internet on the Taxation of International Transactions," *Bulletin for International Fiscal Documentation* 50, no. 11/12 (1996): 524.

25. Arnold, in "Controlled Foreign Corporation Rules," 17:4, wrote: "The increasing use of tax havens is one of the most important phenomena of the last half-century."

26. See generally OECD, *The Economic and Social Impact of Electronic Commerce: Preliminary Findings and Research Agenda* (Paris: OECD, 1999); and Charles E. McLure, Jr., "Taxation of Electronic Commerce: Economic Objectives, Technological Constraints, and Tax Law," *Tax Law Review* 52, no. 3 (Spring 1997): 269. The statement in the text is applicable primarily to sales tax systems that are conceptually sound, such as the VATs levied by the EU member states. Electronic commerce may have more important implications for subnational taxation in countries with flawed systems of sales taxation. The implications

for state corporate income taxes are discussed in Charles E. McLure, Jr., "Implementing State Corporate Income Taxes in the Digital Age," *National Tax Journal* 53, no. 4 (December 2000): 1287.

27. See Commission of the European Communities, Proposal for a Regulation of the European Parliament.

28. For a more detailed discussion, see Charles E. McLure, Jr., "Taxation of Electronic Commerce in Developing Countries," prepared for presentation at "Public Finance in Developing Countries: A Conference in Honor of Richard Bird," held in Stone Mountain, Georgia, April 5–6, 2001. For convenience, business purchasers that are not registered for VAT are lumped together with consumers.

29. OECD, Technology TAG, Para. 7.

30. OECD, "Consumption Tax Aspects of Electronic Commerce," 38. Substantial amounts of revenue from state sales taxes in the United States and provincial sales taxes in Canada are derived from sales to business. In principle, states and provinces should be able to employ audits to assure the payment of tax on taxable business purchases of digital content. (Most digital content is, however, exempt under the laws of many states and provinces, which apply primarily to tangible products.) Since out-of-state vendors are not responsible for collecting tax unless they have a physical presence in the state, this entails "direct pay," a procedure analogous to reverse charging under VAT.

31. U.S. Department of the Treasury, *Selected Tax Policy Implications of Global Electronic Commerce* (1996), available at www.ustreas.gov/taxpolicy/internet.html.

32. OECD, "Treaty Characterisation Issues Arising from E-Commerce," in *Taxation and Electronic Commerce: Implementing the Ottawa Framework Conditions* (Paris: OECD, 2001), 85. This report attempts to clarify these distinctions.

33. See OECD, Committee on Fiscal Affairs, "Impact of the Communications Revolution on the Application of 'Place of Effective Management' as a Tie Breaker Rule," in *Taxation and Electronic Commerce: Implementing the Ottawa Framework Conditions* (Paris: OECD, 2001), 143. For a more detailed discussion of the problems with residence-based taxation, see Reuven S. Avi-Yonah, "International Taxation of Electronic Commerce," *Tax Law Review* 52, no. 3 (Spring 1997): 507.

34. Richard L. Doernberg and Luc Hinnekens, *Electronic Commerce and International Commerce* (The Hague: Kluwer Law International, for the International Fiscal Association, 1999), 306.

35. Charles E. McLure, Jr., "Source-Based Taxation and Alternatives to the Concept of Permanent Establishment," *Report of the Proceedings of the World Tax Conference: Taxes without Borders* (Toronto: Canadian Tax Foundation, 2000), 6:1. On the history of the concept of "permanent establishment," see Michael J. Graetz and Michael M. O'Hear, "The 'Original Intent' of U.S. International Taxation," *Duke Law Review* 46, no. 5 (1997): 1021.

36. Regarding the attribution of profits to servers considered to be PEs, the OECD Business Attribution TAG concluded: "The activities of the permanent establishment are very unlikely to warrant it being attributed with a significant share of the profit associated with the distribution activities of the enterprise conducted through the server." OECD, "Attribution of Profit to a Permanent Establishment Involved in Electronic Commerce Transactions," Discussion Paper from the Technical Advisory Group on Monitoring the Application of Existing Treaty Norms for the Taxation of Business Profits, in *Taxation and Electronic Commerce: Implementing the Ottawa Framework Conditions* (Paris: OECD, 2001), 104.

37. OECD, "Clarification on the Application of the Permanent Establishment Definition in E-Commerce: Changes to the Commentary on the Model Tax Convention on Article 5," in *Taxation and Electronic Commerce: Implementing the Ottawa Framework Conditions* (Paris: OECD, 2001), 79.

38. See generally Charles E. McLure, Jr., "U.S. Federal Use of Formula Apportionment to Tax Income from Intangibles," *Tax Notes International* 14, no. 10 (March 10, 1997): 859; Peyton H. Robinson, "The Globally Integrated Multinational, the Arm's Length Standard, and the Continuum Price Problem," *Transfer Pricing* 9, no. 13 (November 1, 2000); and Stanley I. Langbein, "The Unitary Method and the Myth of Arm's Length," *Tax Notes,* February 17, 1986, 625.

39. For a provocative example of the problems that electronic commerce can cause, see Frances M. Horner and Jeffrey Owens, "Tax and the Web: New Technology, Old Problems," *Bulletin for International Fiscal Documentation* 50, no. 11/12 (1996): 516.

40. Robert E. Culbertson and Alexandre S. Drummond, "Is the Country That Developed the Advance Pricing Agreement Finally Ready to Take Arbitration Seriously?" *Report of the Proceedings of the World Tax Conference: Taxes without Borders* (Toronto: Canadian Tax Foundation, 2000), 13:2.

41. OECD, Committee on Fiscal Affairs, extract from the Annex: *Guidelines for Conducting Advance Pricing Arrangements under the Mutual Agreement Procedure (MAP APAs),* October 1999, available at http://www.oecd. org/daf/fa/tr_price/guidelines.pdf.

42. See, for example, Paras. 26 and 45 of the OECD Commentary on Art. 25 (mutual agreement procedure) of the OECD Model.

43. See, for example, Reuven S. Avi-Yonah, "Slicing the Shadow: A Proposal for Updating U.S. International Taxation," *Tax Notes,* March 15, 1993, 1511; Jerome R. Hellerstein, "Federal Income Taxation of Multinationals: Replacement of Separate Accounting with Formulary Apportionment," *Tax Notes,* August 23, 1993, 1131; Louis M. Kauder, "Intercompany Pricing and Section 482: A Proposal to Shift from Uncontrolled Comparables to For-

mulary Apportionment Now," *Tax Notes,* January 25, 1993, 485; Langbein, "The Unitary Method," 39; and Jack M. Mintz, "The Role of Allocation in a Globalized Corporate Income Tax," WP/98/134 (Washington, DC: International Monetary Fund, 1998); *Finanzarchiv* 56, no. 3/4 (1999): 389.

For a contrary view, see Eric J. Coffill, and Prentiss Willson, Jr., "Federal Formulary Apportionment as an Alternative to Arm's Length Pricing: From the Frying Pan to the Fire," *Tax Notes,* May 24, 1993, 1103. For an analysis of using formula apportionment as the international norm, see Joann M. Weiner, "Using the Experience in the U.S. States to Evaluate Issues in Implementing Formula Apportionment at the International Level," OTA Paper 83, U.S. Department of the Treasury, April 1999, available at www.ustreas.gov/ota/ota83.pdf. McLure, "U.S. Federal Use of Formula Apportionment," provides further references to the literature on both sides of this issue.

On the use of separate accounting and formula apportionment in the European Union, see Charles E. McLure, Jr., and Joann M. Weiner, "Deciding Whether the European Union Should Adopt Formula Apportionment of Company Income," in Sijbren Cnossen, ed., *Taxing Capital Income in the European Union: Issues and Options for Reform* (Oxford: Oxford University Press, 2000), 243; and Joann Weiner, "EU Corporate Tax Reform" (xerox, 2001). A system that might be appropriate for use in the European Union might not be suitable as the international standard.

44. Royalties are generally accorded the same tax treatment as interest in source countries, but individuals receive far smaller amounts of royalties than of interest. By comparison, dividends generally are not deductible.

45. See Vito Tanzi, *Taxation in an Integrating World* (Washington, DC: Brookings Institution, 1995), 84–89; and Bird and Mintz, "Sharing the International Tax Base."

46. Joel Slemrod, "Comments," in Tanzi, *Taxation in an Integrating World,* 144. See also Tanzi, 84–89.

47. Cnossen, "Company Taxes in the European Union," 80.

48. Charles E. McLure, Jr., "Tax Policies for the XXIst Century," in *Visions of the Tax Systems of the XXIst Century* (The Hague: Kluwer, 1997), 37.

49. Tanzi, *Taxation in an Integrating World,* 89.

50. See generally Mitsuo Sato and Richard M. Bird, "International Aspects of the Taxation of Corporations and Shareholders," *International Monetary Fund Staff Papers* 22, 384 (July 1975); Charles E. McLure, Jr., *Must Corporate Income Be Taxed Twice?* (Washington, DC: The Brookings Institution, 1979); U.S. Department of the Treasury, *Integration of the Individual and Corporate Tax Systems: Taxing Business Income Once* (Washington, DC: U.S. Government Printing Office, 1992); and Cnossen, "Company Taxes in the European Union."

51. See Weiner, "EU Corporate Tax Reform."

52. Ministerial Communique of May 1996, quoted in OECD, Committee on Fiscal Affairs, *Harmful Tax Competition: An Emerging Global Issue* (Paris: OECD, 1998), Foreword.

53. Ibid., Para. 49.

54. Ibid., Para. 30.

55. Ibid., Para. 52.

56. Ibid., Para. 59.

57. Ibid., Paras. 69–79.

58. Ibid., Para. 43. The OECD notes (Para. 80): "Governments may find themselves in a 'prisoners dilemma' where they collectively would be better off by not offering incentives but each feels compelled to offer the incentive to maintain a competitive business environment."

59. Ibid., Para. 140 and Box III. Both Luxembourg and Switzerland abstained on the approval of the report and the adoption of the recommendation; see ibid., Annex II.

60. OECD, Committee on Fiscal Affairs, "Towards Global Tax Co-operation: Progress in Identifying and Eliminating Harmful Tax Practices," Para. 16, Report to the 2000 Ministerial Council Meeting and Recommendations by the Committee on Fiscal Affairs, available at www.oecd.org/daf/fa/harm_tax/Report_En.pdf). In addition, a few tax-haven countries agreed to "advance commitments" to eliminate their harmful practices and thus were not included on the list of tax havens.

61. For the possible defensive measures being considered, see ibid., Para. 35.

62. Ibid., Para. 34.

63. OECD, "OECD, Commonwealth Agree to Work towards Global Co-operation on Harmful Tax Practices," press release dated January 10, 2001, available at www.oecd.org/media/release/nw01-03a.htm.

64. U.S. Treasury Department, press release of May 10, 2001.

65. OECD, *Harmful Tax Competition,* Para. 41.

66. OECD, "Towards Global Tax Co-operation."

67. Arnold, "Controlled Foreign Corporation Rules," 17:22–23.

68. For background to the Ottawa meeting, see OECD, Committee on Fiscal Affairs, "Electronic Commerce: Taxation Framework Conditions," Report by the Committee on Fiscal Affairs, as presented to Ministers at the OECD Ministerial Conference, "A Borderless World: Realising the Potential of Electronic Commerce," Ottawa, October 8, 1998, in *Taxation and Electronic Commerce: Implementing the Ottawa Framework Conditions,* 227.

69. See *Taxation and Electronic Commerce: Implementing the Ottawa Framework Conditions,* including summaries of the reports of the TAGs. The work of the TAGs is described and discussed more fully in McLure, "Taxation of Electronic Commerce in Developing Countries."

70. See OECD, "Consumption Tax Aspects of Electronic Commerce," and OECD, Technology TAG.

71. See "Main Findings of the Technology Technical Advisory Group (TAG), in *Taxation and Electronic Commerce: Implementing the Ottawa Framework Conditions,* 188.

72. See generally OECD, Committee on Fiscal Affairs, "Report by the Technical Advisory Group on Monitoring the Application of Existing Treaty Norms for the Taxation of Business Profits (Business Profits TAG)," December 2000, available at www.oecd.org/daf/fa/e_com/ec_5_BP_TAG_Eng.pdf; OECD, "Clarification on the Application of the Permanent Establishment Definition in E-Commerce"; and OECD, "Attribution of Profit to a Permanent Establishment Involved in Electronic Commerce Transactions," 102.

73. See OECD, "Treaty Characterisation Issues Arising from E-Commerce."

74. McLure, "Tax Policies for the XXIst Century," 36.

75. Tanzi, *Taxation in an Integrating World,* 140.

76. Mintz, "The Role of Allocation in a Globalized Corporate Income Tax," WP/98/134, 36.

77. Tanzi suggested the possibility of creating an International Revenue Service "to collect taxes that could not be collected by separate governments. . . . Such an international institution might also collect information on taxpayers for the benefit of the member tax administrations." See Tanzi, "Forces That Shape Tax Policy," 277. This proposal is not likely to gain popularity soon.

78. Mintz, "The Role of Allocation in a Globalized Corporate Income Tax," WP/98/134, 36.

79. Tanzi, *Taxation in an Integrating World,* 9. Tanzi (p. 66) also quoted Hinnekens: "In the disarray of this 'fin de siècle,' tax policymakers turn for guidance to the tax theorists, but find that little thought has been given to the shape and form of a comprehensive tax system that is up to the challenge of the new regional and global scene." See Luc Hinnekens, "Territoriality-Based Taxation in an Increasingly Common Market and Globalization Economy: Nightmare and Challenge of International Taxation in the New Age," *EC Tax Review,* 1992, 157.

80. U.S. Department of the Treasury, *Integration of the Individual and Corporate Tax Systems.* These possibilities are examined in McLure, "Tax Policies for the XXIst Century."

Nontariff Barriers

Nontariff barriers (NTBs) are restrictions on international trade, usually imposed by an importing country, that operate through means other than tariffs. The most common NTBs, quotas and voluntary export restraints (VERs), place a ceiling on the quantity or value of a good traded. The restriction makes the good artificially scarce, raises its domestic price to consumers, and allows domestic producers of the good (and any foreign exporters not covered by the restriction) to charge higher prices. Quotas are administered by the importing country; voluntary export restraints are administered by the exporting country. This difference affects which interest groups gain or lose from the two policies and by how much. Both types of policies harm import-country consumers, help import-country producers, and reduce total world welfare. Quotas and VERs are most prevalent in agricultural products, textiles, and apparel. The General Agreement on Tariffs and Trade (GATT) and its successor, the World Trade Organization (WTO), have discouraged members from using quotas and VERs. Despite this discouragement, use of VERs spread rapidly during the 1980s and 1990s. The 1994 Uruguay Round Agreement, however, did impose some discipline on WTO member countries' imposition of new VERs.

Quota Effects in a Small Country's Competitive Market

Consider the market for a small country's import good, good X. In Figure 1, the downward-sloping line $D^{domestic}$ represents the total quantity of good X that residents demand at each price. The upward-sloping line $S^{domestic}$ represents the quantity of good X that the country's X producers supply at each price. The horizontal line S^{world} represents the supply of good X produced in the rest of the world. This world supply curve is horizontal because the import country is small; this means that the country's residents can buy as much of good X as they want in world markets without affecting the world price, P^{world}. The world supply curve lies below the intersection of $D^{domestic}$ and $S^{domestic}$ because good X is the country's import good; that is, the world price of good X is less than the domestic price that would prevail with no trade, $P_{nt}^{domestic}$, reflecting the country's comparative *dis*advantage in good X. With no restrictions on trade, the country consumes X_0 units of good X, produces X_1 units, and imports $(X_0 - X_1)$ units. Consumers pay a domestic free-trade price, $P_{ft}^{domestic}$, equal to the world price, P^{world}.

The net benefits that import-country consumers get from their ability to participate in the market for good X is called "consumer surplus," measured by the area under the demand curve and above the price consumers pay for the good. With free trade, consumer surplus is area ABC. The net benefits that domestic producers get from their ability to participate in the market for good X is called "producer surplus," the area above the domestic supply curve and below the price that producers receive for the good. With free trade, domestic producer surplus is area CEF. Total surplus, the net bene-

Figure 1: Quota Imposed by a Small Country in a Competitive Market

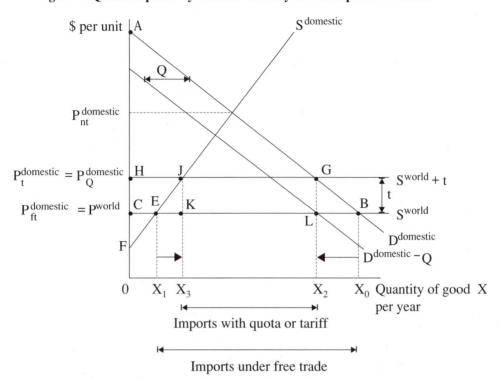

Note: Under free trade, the country consumes X_0 units, produces X_1 units domestically, and imports $(X_0 - X_1)$ at a price of $P_{ft}^{domestic} = P^{world}$. Total domestic surplus equals (ABC + CEF). Under an import quota set at Q, the country consumes X_2 units, produces X_3 units domestically, and imports $(X_2 - X_3)$ units; the domestic price is $P_Q^{domestic}$. Area JGLK represents the quota rents, which may go to foreign firms, domestic importers, or the government or be exhausted by rent-seeking activities, depending on how the quota is administered. Total domestic surplus is at least (JKE + GBL) less than under free trade, and may be as much as (JKE + GBL + JGLK) less if the quota rents go to foreign firms or are lost in rent seeking. Under an equivalent tariff set at t, the country consumes X_2 units, produces X_3 units domestically, and imports $(X_2 - X_3)$ units; the domestic price is $P_t^{domestic}$. Total surplus is (JKE + GBL) less than under free trade.

fits all domestic participants receive from the X market, equals the sum of consumer and producer surpluses, or (ABC + CEF).

Let the import-country government impose a quota on X imports: No more than Q units per year can enter the country, and $Q < (X_0 - X_1)$, which makes the quota binding. The total demand facing domestic firms at each price, represented by the line $D^{domestic} - Q$, equals the total quantity domestic consumers demand minus quantity of imports (the quota, Q). Consumption falls to X_2, domestic production rises to X_3, and the country imports $X_2 - X_3 = Q$ units. The new domestic price with the quota is

$P_Q^{domestic}$. Consumer surplus falls to area AGH, and domestic producer surplus rises to area HJF.

Who gains and who loses from the quota? Domestic consumers lose area HGBC of consumer surplus, which can be divided into four parts: (1) Domestic producers of X gain area HJEC of producer surplus; (2) area JKE is a deadweight loss caused by the fact that the quota causes units X_1 through X_3 to be produced domestically (at an opportunity cost represented by the height of $S^{domestic}$ for each unit) when those units could have been produced abroad at lower opportunity cost (represented by the height of S^{world}); (3) area GBL is a deadweight loss caused by the fact that the quota, by raising the domestic price of good X, causes consumers to cut consumption from X_0 to X_2 units, even though each unit between X_2 and X_0 would provide more benefit to the consumer (measured by the height of the $D^{domestic}$ curve for each unit) than the opportunity cost of production (represented by the height of S^{world}); (4) area JGLK represents the quota rents, or the difference between the new domestic price and the world price ($P_Q^{domestic} - P^{world}$) multiplied by the quantity of imports.

Who captures the quota rents depends on how the government administers the quota. To restrict imports to the quota limit, the government must establish a system of import licensing. If the government auctions the licenses to import good X, firms will willingly pay up to JGLK for those licenses, and the rents go to the government. If licenses are allocated on a first-come, first-served basis and importers are free to buy good X for P^{world} on the world market, import it, and sell it at $P_Q^{domestic}$, the quota rents go to importers. If firms in exporting countries receive the licenses to sell Q units of good X in the domestic market, those foreign firms capture the rents. If the government allocates the import licenses through a political lobbying process, firms may expend economic resources to capture the rents, thereby turning them into additional deadweight losses (Krueger 1974). The quota's effects on the importing country's welfare include a loss for consumers (HGBC), a smaller gain for domestic producers (HJEC), deadweight losses because of the distorted production and consumption decisions (JKE and GBL), plus the effects generated by the allocation of the quota rents (JGLK), which depend on the license-allocation system.

Governments can define quotas in terms that limit either the volume (quantity) or the value (price times quantity) of imports. Volume quotas are easier to administer, since they do not require tracking import prices. But volume quotas can have an additional detrimental effect on consumers. When applied to goods available in a range of qualities and prices (for example, automobiles or apparel), volume quotas give exporters an incentive to cut back most on exports of lower-quality, lower-priced goods. This puts additional upward pressure on price and harms consumers, especially low-income individuals who would buy lower-quality, lower-priced versions of the good.

Governments that impose a quota can also choose between global and country-specific quotas. Global quotas impose a single ceiling on imports, regardless of source. Country-specific quotas discriminate between exporting countries by assigning individual exporting countries or groups of exporting countries specific ceilings, often based on the countries' historical market shares. By influencing the sources of imports, this choice can affect who receives the quota rents.

Quotas, like other import restrictions, create an incentive for smuggling of the restricted goods, because smugglers can capture part of the quota rents. The welfare effects of smuggling are ambiguous. To the extent that the illegal activity voids the harmful effects of the quota by making available more of the imported good, smuggling eliminates the quota's deadweight losses. But illegal activities such as smuggling use up real resources, contribute to corruption, and erode the public's support for law, all of which reduce welfare.

Comparison of Quota with Tariff

In a competitive market, for any import quota there is an import tariff (that is, a tax on imports) that generates the identical effect on price, consumption, domestic production, and imports. This result is known as "the equivalence of tariffs and quotas" (Bhagwati 1965). In Figure 1, imposition of an import tariff of t per unit shifts the world supply curve up by the amount of the tariff. Domestic consumers must pay $P_t^{domestic}$, which equals the world price plus the tariff, for each unit they import. A tariff of t reduces consumer surplus by

HGBC, raises domestic producer surplus by HJEC, and causes deadweight losses of JKE and GBL, just as the quota does. The difference between the tariff and the quota lies in area JGLK. In the case of the quota, this area represents the rents generated, and which groups capture the rents depends on how import licenses are allocated. In the case of the tariff, area JGLK represents the revenue raised by the tax, which goes to the domestic government.

The equivalence of tariffs and quotas provides a useful benchmark, but once dynamic market conditions and different market structures are taken into account, many additional differences in the two policies' effects appear. These fall into four main categories. First, if domestic demand increases or domestic supply decreases, price rises more under a quota than under an "equivalent" tariff (a result called "dynamic nonequivalence"). This occurs because the quota is the more restrictive policy: A tariff allows consumers to import more in response to changed market conditions, as long as they pay the tariff, whereas a quota prohibits additional imports regardless of market conditions. So domestic producers seeking protection from foreign competition may prefer a quota if they anticipate worsening comparative disadvantage, but quotas cause larger welfare losses, both for the imposing country and for the world, than tariffs.

Second, with a single or only a few domestic producers, a quota, unlike a tariff, facilitates the firm or firms acting as a monopolist or cartel. A tariff limits domestic firms' ability to raise price to a ceiling of the world price plus the tariff. Under a quota, domestic firms' ability to raise price faces no such constraint, because imports cannot rise no matter what price domestic firms charge.

Third, the quota allows any one of several groups to capture its rents, depending on how the government administers the quota or allocates the import licenses. These groups have incentives to engage in lobbying or rent-seeking activity to convince the government to allocate in their favor. Such activities can both alter

who captures the quota rents and lead to additional deadweight losses if interest groups use up real resources in rent seeking.

Finally, quotas are more likely than tariffs to be applied to only some trading partners, thereby discriminating among alternative sources of supply. If low-cost-producer trading partners are subject to quotas, the restriction can shift production to higher-cost foreign producers.

In addition to being applied separately, as alternative means to protect a domestic industry, quotas and tariffs can be used together. If a country imposes a quota and also a tariff, the tariff can allow the import-country government to capture the quota rents. Another way of pairing the two policies is a "tariff-rate quota." Under this system, imports up to a certain level or quota face a low (or zero) tariff, and imports above the specified level face a much higher (often prohibitive) tariff.

Quota Effects in a Large Country's Competitive Market

Figure 2 depicts the effects of an import quota of Q imposed by a large country; that is, a country important enough in the market for good X that the country's trade policies affect the world price. The import country's large size implies that the world supply curve is upward sloping. The quota's effects match those of the small-country case with one addition: The quota reduces the world price of good X. In other words, the large importing country, by imposing the quota, can force foreign suppliers to accept a lower price for the good, P_Q^{world}. Out of total quota rents of area JGNM, part (area KLNM) come from foreign producers. This introduces the possibility that the quota-imposing country may gain in net welfare from the quota if: (1) a domestic interest group captures the rents, and (2) area KLNM is larger than the quota's deadweight welfare loss (area JKE + GBL). All the importing country's gains (KLNM) come at the expense of the exporting

Figure 2: Quota Imposed by a Large Country in a Competitive Market

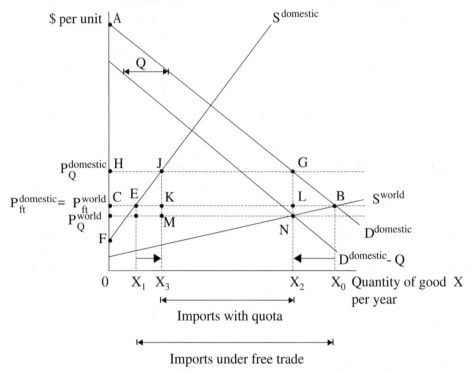

Note: Under free trade, the country consumes X_0 units, produces X_1 units domestically, and imports $(X_0 - X_1)$ at a price of $P_{ft}^{domestic} = P_{ft}^{world}$. Under an import quota set at Q, the country consumes X_2 units, produces X_3 units domestically, and imports $(X_2 - X_3)$ units; the domestic price is $P_Q^{domestic}$. Area JGNM represents the total quota rents, which may go to foreign firms, domestic importers, the government, or be exhausted by rent-seeking activities, depending on how the quota is administered. The portion of the rents represented by JGLK is paid by domestic consumers of good X; the portion represented by KLNM is paid by foreign producers who must accept the lower world price, P_Q^{world}, for their product. The quota's effect on total domestic surplus depends on which group captures the quota rents and on how the size of the rents paid by foreign producers (KLNM) compares with the size of the two deadweight losses (JKE + GBL).

country; thus, the quota's net effect on world welfare is negative even when the quota-imposing country is large.

Voluntary Export Restraints

Under a voluntary export restraint, one or more exporting countries agree to restrict "voluntarily" their exports of a product to another country. In effect, a VER is a quota administered by the exporting country. The restricted country usually agrees to a VER only under threat of a more severe restriction on its exports (for example, a quota or a high tariff)

should it fail to agree. VERs typically are negotiated on a bilateral basis, and GATT/WTO discipline against such measures has been less than completely effective. Among the industries most affected by VERs are textiles and apparel, automobiles, steel, and consumer electronics products.

VER agreements (often called "orderly marketing agreements") may be negotiated between governments, between the import and export countries' industries, or between the import-country government and the export-country industry. The agreements often are kept secret because of their illegality under the GATT/WTO (in the case of government-to-government enforced agreements) and their ambiguous status under countries' antitrust and anticollusion laws (in the case of firm- or industry-enforced agreements). For example, if private foreign firms collude to restrict exports to the United States, the firms can be liable to either criminal prosecution or civil treble-damage suits under U.S. law (Jackson 1997, 204); the United States therefore typically negotiates export-restraint agreements with foreign governments to avoid falling under these laws. Because many VER agreements have not been reported to the GATT/WTO (although the 1994 Uruguay Round Agreement on Safeguards now requires such reporting), it has been difficult even to estimate the prevalence of the restraints. This secrecy, lack of transparency, lack of legal scrutiny, discrimination among suppliers, and tendency to facilitate collusive behavior places VERs near the top of most economists' lists of harmful trade policies.

The main effect of a VER system is to grant quota rents to foreign firms. In Figure 1, the foreign government is made responsible for ensuring that no more than $(X_2 - X_3)$ units of good X are exported. The government allocates export licenses to firms, who can then produce the good at a cost equal to the world price and export it to the VER-imposing country where the good can be sold for the higher price $P_Q^{domestic}$. The export-license scheme effectively prevents competition among exporting firms because no firm could export more than its allocated quantity even if it cut its price; exporting firms thus capture the quota rents of area JGLK. Exporting firms are definitely better off under a VER, in which case they earn the quota rents, than under a quota, in which case they do not. This is why export countries often agree to VERs. In fact, in the competitive case, exporting firms may end up better off with the VER than under free trade, if the restraint is loose enough that the quota rents foreign firms gain more than offset the lost opportunity to export more than the amount allowed under the VER, and if no unrestrained exporters exist to fill the void left by the restrained exports. If

the exporting firm is a monopolist, a VER cannot make the firm better off, because even under free trade the firm would restrict exports to the level that maximizes its profit. Note that any shift of quota rents from import-country consumer surplus to export-country producer surplus as a result of a VER is just a transfer; VERs have negative welfare effects for the world as a whole, even if market conditions are such that exporting firms gain.

Use of VERs grew rapidly during the 1980s and 1990s, a trend that started with agreements negotiated by the United States and spread to other developed and, later, developing countries. The restrictions were never technically legal under the GATT. But export countries, if threatened with trade restrictions that would harm them even more than a VER (usually either a quota or a high tariff in the form of an antidumping duty or countervailing duty), had little reason either to resist agreeing to a VER or to file a complaint with the GATT.

In the United States, quotas other than those in dairy products historically have been administered as VERs, so the quota rents go to foreign producers. This lessens the likelihood of retaliation by trading partners. For example, in the case of the 1981 U.S. VER on Japanese automobile exports, estimates suggest that Japanese auto firms felt little effect, since their quota rents offset the lost export volume. However, in comparison with a tariff that allows the same quantity of imports, a VER imposes a far larger loss of welfare on the import country owing to the loss of quota rents, which under a tariff would go to the import-country government as tariff revenue. For example, economists Gary Clyde Hufbauer and Kimberly Ann Elliott estimated that in 1990 the U.S. quota on machine tools cost U.S. consumers a total of $542 million, of which $385 million was a net loss to the United States in the form of lost quota rents and the deadweight losses caused by the quota. This translated into a cost to U.S. consumers of $348,000 for each job maintained in the U.S. machine-tool industry through the quota (Hufbauer and Elliott 1994, 9, 13).

Data and Measurement Issues

Nontariff barriers and their effects are harder to measure than are tariffs. The primary source of detailed information on nontariff barriers is the United Nations Conference on Trade and Development (UNCTAD) Database on Trade Control Measures. Information in the database is far from perfect, however; the NTB measures included are better suited for studying change over time in a single country's use of NTBs than for comparing different countries' uses of such policies. The difficulties in quantifying NTBs contribute to difficulties in international negotiations to lower them because measurement ambiguities allow countries to overstate others' NTBs while understating their own.

Most empirical measures of NTBs estimate either the frequency of their application in particular industries or the extent of trade covered by them. The two main measures for quotas and VERs are frequency ratios and coverage ratios. Both are calculated based on tariff lines, or the detailed classifications of goods that countries use to organize their trade statistics. Each tariff line refers to a specific good (for example, U.S. tariff line 8542.13 refers to metal oxide semiconductors). The frequency ratio calculates the percentage of a country's tariff lines affected by nontariff barriers. For example, if out of 8,800 tariff lines, 2,200 contain items covered by nontariff barriers, the frequency ratio is 2,200/8,800 = 0.25, or 25 percent. One disadvantage of the frequency ratio is that it fails to capture the relative importance of the different tariff lines in the country's trade. The coverage ratio corrects this problem by weighting the various tariff lines by the amount of imports, so that high-volume items affected by NTBs receive more weight in the calculation than do low-volume items.

The frequency ratio and the coverage ratio share important weaknesses. First, neither accounts for the restrictiveness of NTBs, but merely for their presence or absence. An import quota of ten cars per year enters the frequency ratio in the same way as a quota of 1 million

cars per year, even though the former clearly has much more harmful welfare effects. The coverage ratio also suffers from this problem, because the tariff lines covered by the most restrictive NTBs have, by definition, the lowest levels of imports; therefore, those lines receive small weights in the coverage-ratio formula. Second, the coverage ratio can fall in response to a tightening of NTBs, giving a perverse indication that trade policy has become less rather than more restrictive. For example, suppose a country moves from a quota of 1 million automobiles to a prohibitive quota of zero autos. The weight attached to the tariff line for autos goes to zero as imports fall to zero, so the coverage ratio falls—despite the shift toward tighter protection. Calculating coverage ratios using domestic-production weights rather than import weights eliminates this perverse result, but the production-weighted measure still suffers from the weakness that the weights used are themselves affected by changes in NTBs.

Another measurement technique often applied to quotas is the tariff equivalent, or implicit tariff; this is the tariff rate that would have the same effects on price, consumption, production, and imports as does the quota. In the small-country case illustrated in Figure 1, both the domestic price with the quota in effect ($P_Q^{domestic}$) and the world price (P^{world}), which will remain the effective price in countries following free-trade policies, can be observed. The difference between these two prices measures the tariff equivalent of the quota, or the tariff rate that would generate the same effects. In the large-country case (Figure 2), the original world price is not observable once the quota is in effect, so calculating the tariff equivalent requires econometric techniques to estimate world prices using information about demand and supply elasticities. Using tariff equivalents to estimate quotas' effects will not produce reliable results if demand or supply conditions change during the period under study because, as noted earlier, market prices and quantities respond differently to changes in market conditions under tariffs and quotas.

Figure 3: Quota Imposed by a Large Country in a Monopoly Market

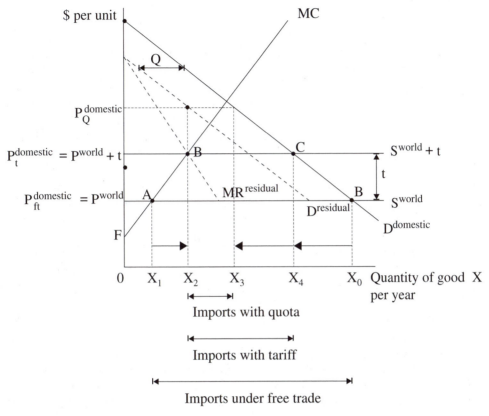

Note: Under free trade, the country consumes X_0 units, produces X_1 units domestically (at point A), and imports $(X_0 - X_1)$ at a price of $P_{ft}^{domestic} = P^{world}$. Under an import quota set at Q, the domestic monopoly firm faces the residual demand curve, $D^{residual}$, and its marginal revenue curve, $MR^{residual}$. The country consumes X3 units, produces X_2 units domestically (at point B), and imports $(X_3 - X_2)$ units; the domestic price is $P_Q^{domestic}$. Under a tariff set at t to generate the same level of domestic production as the quota, the country consumes X_4 units (at point C), produces X_2 units domestically, and imports $(X_4 - X_2)$ units; the domestic price is Ptdomestic, which equals the world price plus the tariff. The quota results in a higher price and lower consumption than does the tariff because the quota, by blocking all imports above the quota regardless of the price charged by the domestic firm, allows the domestic firm to exploit its monopoly power.

Quotas in Monopoly Industries

When the domestic industry in a small country consists of a single monopoly firm and the foreign industry is competitive, three results hold concerning imposition of an import quota: (1) A quota allows the domestic firm to exploit its monopoly power, whereas the firm would be forced to act competitively under free trade; (2) a quota may cause the domestic firm to produce either more or less output; and (3) a quota results in a higher domestic price than does a

tariff designed to lead to the same level of domestic output. All three effects follow from the fact that the quota alters the shape of the demand curve facing the firm. The firm always maximizes profit by producing the output at which marginal cost (the change in total cost when the firm changes its output by a small amount) equals marginal revenue (the change in total revenue when the firm changes its output by a small amount). By altering the demand curve that the firm faces, an import quota changes the outcome of this profit-maximizing process, allowing the firm to exploit its market power at consumers' expense.

Consider first how free trade disciplines a potential domestic monopoly firm from behaving as a monopolist. In Figure 3, the downward-sloping line $D^{domestic}$ represents the total quantity of good X that residents demand at each price. The upward-sloping line MC represents the domestic firm's marginal cost. The horizontal line S^{world} represents the supply of good X produced in the rest of the world. The small country's residents can buy as much good X as they want in the world market without affecting the world price, P^{world}, so any attempt by the domestic firm to charge a price above P^{world} would result in zero sales. In other words, with free trade the domestic firm must take its price as given and equal to the world price. The demand curve facing the domestic firm is *horizontal* at P^{world} out to the intersection with $D^{domestic}$ and then becomes coincident with the $D^{domestic}$ line. For a price-taking firm, P = MR, so throughout the range in which the firm must act as a price taker, MR = P^{world}. The profit-maximizing firm produces X_1 at point A, where MC = MR. Consumers buy X_0 units of good X, of which the domestic firm produces X_1 units and $(X_0 - X_1)$ units are imported. Consumers pay a domestic free-trade price, $P_{ft}^{domestic}$, equal to the world price, P^{world}. Under free trade, the domestic monopolist cannot exploit its monopoly power. It must act as a price taker, as if it were just one of many firms in a competitive domestic industry, because consumers have the alternative of buying imports.

An import quota allows the domestic monopolist to exploit its market power. With the quota in effect, consumers no longer can buy all the imports they want at the world price. Now the domestic firm faces a residual demand curve equal to consumers' overall demand for good X, $D^{domestic}$, minus the quota amount, Q; so, at each price above the world price, the residual demand curve, $D^{residual}$, lies Q units to the left of $D^{domestic}$. (For prices below the world price, $D^{residual} = D^{domestic}$, because

consumers would not purchase imports at a price above that available on domestic X. This range of prices is not of interest because the point of the quota is to restrict imports consumers would otherwise buy.) Assuming that the firm must charge the same price for all units it sells, its marginal revenue curve is $MR^{residual}$. This marginal revenue curve lies below the residual demand curve because the firm must lower its price to sell an additional unit; therefore, the marginal revenue (change in total revenue) from selling another unit of output is less than the price for which that unit is sold. The firm maximizes profit by equating MC and MR at point B and charges the monopoly price, $P_Q^{domestic}$, from the residual demand curve. At that price, domestic consumers buy X_3 units of X, of which X_2 are produced by the domestic monopolist and $(X_3 - X_2)$ units are imported.

Figure 3 illustrates the case in which the quota causes the monopolist to increase its output relative to that under free trade ($X_2 > X_1$). However, domestic output under the quota (X_2) can be either greater or less than domestic output under free trade (X_1). This is true because the quota has two counteracting effects on the domestic firm's choice of output: The quota gives the domestic firms more of the market by limiting imports, but the quota also allows the firm to exploit its monopoly power by restricting output in order to raise price. Either effect can dominate. The fact that an import quota facilitates monopoly behavior by the domestic firm means that even a quota set at the free-trade level of imports (for example, $X_0 - X_1$ units in Figure 3) causes the domestic firm to reduce output and raise price above the free-trade level; even such a just-binding quota allows the potential monopolist to become an actual monopolist.

When the domestic industry consists of a potential monopolist, quotas have more restrictive effects than a tariff designed to generate the same level of domestic output. In Figure 3, the per-unit tariff that would cause the domestic firm to choose to produce X_2 is t. With a tariff of t, domestic consumers would consume X_4 at point C and import $(X_4 - X_2)$; domestic price would be $P_t^{domestic}$. The quota causes a larger fall in consumption and allows the domestic firm to charge a higher price than does the tariff. This occurs because the tariff protects the domestic firm only to the extent of allowing it to charge a price higher than the world price by the amount of the tariff. The quota, in contrast, rules out imports in excess of Q regardless of the price charged by the domestic monopolist. The quota, therefore, causes a larger loss of welfare for the imposing country and for the world than would the tariff.

Treatment of Quotas and VERS in the GATT and WTO

There are strong economic arguments against use of import quotas: They facilitate monopoly behavior by severing the link between domestic and foreign prices; they often discriminate among trading partners; they cause markets not to respond to changing demand or cost conditions; they are opaque to consumers and voters; and the contest to capture the quota rents can lead to both rent seeking and corruption. These same characteristics that make quotas undesirable from the perspective of a country's overall economic welfare make them desirable from the perspective of the industry seeking protection.

Framers of the GATT envisioned the following approach to trade liberalization: Limit quotas and other NTBs, then negotiate tariff levels down over time. Import quotas had proliferated during the 1930s and were a widespread trade-policy practice during the early postwar years, so GATT rules written during those years prohibited use of quotas (GATT Article IX). In principle, GATT allowed only tariffs as means to restrict trade and ruled out other measures that countries could use to circumvent their promises to lower tariffs and move toward free trade. Nonetheless, governments continue to use quotas to protect domestic producers, es-

pecially in the agriculture, textiles and apparel, and steel sectors. And GATT largely exempted developing countries from the quota prohibitions.

GATT rules prohibited quotas by developed countries with three major exceptions. First, quotas were allowed in markets for agricultural commodities in which governments used price-support programs, as long as the imposing country also took steps to restrict domestic production. A major loophole opened in 1955 when the United States won a GATT waiver from this rule for Section 22 of the U.S. Agricultural Adjustment Act. The waiver allowed the United States to use quotas on agricultural goods, such as dairy products, peanuts, and sugar, for which the country used price supports and no domestic-production limits. In 1990, U.S. import quotas on dairy products, peanuts, and sugar cost U.S. consumers an estimated $498,000 for each job retained in the dairy-product industry, $136,000 for each job maintained in the peanut industry, and $600,000 for each job kept in the U.S. sugar industry (Hufbauer and Elliott 1994, 13).

Second, GATT rules allowed quotas for balance-of-payments (BOP) purposes; that is, to lower a country's imports to a level consistent with its exports (GATT Articles XII, XIII, and XIV). In this case, rules required nondiscriminatory application, but in practice countries often applied country-specific quotas based on exporters' historical market shares. Developing countries continued to use the BOP exception as justification for long-term import quotas even after the international monetary system shifted to more flexible exchange rates in the early 1970s, removing the economic rationale for BOP-motivated quotas.

Third, GATT member countries could impose nondiscriminatory import quotas under the safeguard or escape-clause provision, which allows a country temporarily to suspend its GATT obligations if imports increase to an extent to cause or threaten serious injury to the domestic industry (GATT Article XIX). In practice, few countries used this particular protectionist route for two reasons: Industries seeking protection often wanted discriminatory protection directed against certain trading partners, and GATT rules required a country that imposed a quota for safeguard reasons to compensate the exporting countries harmed by the policy (for example, by lowering tariffs on other products). To achieve protection that was discriminatory and avoid the GATT requirement to pay compensation to trading partners, governments negotiated VERs.

The 1994 Uruguay Round Agreement transformed the GATT into the WTO and introduced further discipline on members' use of quotas and VERs. In agriculture, the agreement prohibits new quotas, requires existing quotas to be replaced with tariffs (a process called "tariffication"), and requires countries to commit to a schedule of future tariff reductions on agricultural products (Uruguay Round Agreement on Agriculture). A country claiming a need to restrict imports for balance of payments reasons now must report the move to the WTO and publish a timetable for the removal of the restrictions; and quotas may be used only with a rationale for why other less-trade-distorting measures, such as tariffs, are not feasible (Uruguay Round Understanding on the Balance-of-Payments Provisions of the General Agreement on Tariffs and Trade 1994). Under post-1994 WTO safeguard rules (Uruguay Round Agreement on Safeguards), if a quota is imposed as a safeguard measure (that is, for temporary relief when increased imports harm or threaten a domestic industry), the quota cannot reduce imports below the average level for the previous three years and may not last more than four years (or a maximum of eight years, if nondiscriminatory and if extended on the basis that injury continues and the domestic industry is adjusting). Exporting countries may not demand compensation for the first three years of a safeguard-motivated import quota. Safeguards in a given industry cannot be reintroduced within two years, or for the life of the earlier safeguard measure, whichever is longer; this limits the potential for

long-term protection in the guise of temporary safeguard actions. The agreement also prohibits VERs as safeguard measures, although a footnote that permits export-country-administered quotas when all parties agree provides a significant loophole for countries to continue to use VERs.

Nontariff Barriers in Textile and Apparel Products

Like agriculture, the textile and apparel industries have existed largely outside GATT discipline on NTBs. Developing countries began to demonstrate comparative advantage in labor-intensive and low-technology basic textile and apparel products during the late 1950s. Developed-country textile and apparel industries responded to the increased competition by demanding protection. The first restraint was a Japanese VER on cotton textile exports to the United States, negotiated in 1955. Quotas imposed only on developing-country exporters violated GATT rules against discrimination, so developed countries asked for and received a GATT exemption for their protectionist policies in textiles and apparel. Over the next forty years, a global web of bilateral quotas and VERs was negotiated that severely restricted textile and apparel exports from developing countries to developed ones. The protection gradually became tighter, covered a growing range of products (cotton fabric, wool, synthetic fibers, vegetable fibers, and silk blends), and was extended to cover more exporting countries. In 1974, the growing protectionist system was named the Multi-Fiber Agreement (MFA); it operated as an umbrella framework within which individual import-country/export-country pairs negotiated bilateral quotas and VERs. By the early 1990s, the fourth Multifiber Agreement encompassed the United States, members of the European Union, and Canada, plus five other developed-country importers and thirty-seven developing-country exporters.

Within developed countries, the burden of this textile and apparel protection was borne disproportionately by low-income consumers because the volume-based import restrictions caused exporters to cut exports of low-quality, low-priced products most. Economists Hufbauer and Elliot estimated that each U.S. apparel job saved by the MFA cost domestic consumers $138,000, and each textile job cost consumers $202,000 (Hufbauer and Elliott 1994, 13). The main pressure for change, however, came from export countries who demanded phasing out of the MFA in return for concessions on other items to be included on the Uruguay Round trade-negotiation agenda. The Uruguay Round Agreement on Textiles and Clothing (ATC) replaced the Multi-Fiber Agreement. The ATC requires that trade in the textile and apparel sectors gradually be brought under WTO rules. In particular, new quotas and VERs no longer are permitted, and existing ones must be phased out after a ten-year transition period (1995–2004); high tariffs, however, will remain in place for many textile and apparel products. The rule changes apply only to WTO members; member countries may continue to apply ATC-noncompliant policies to exports by WTO nonmembers.

Import countries (for example, the United States and members of the European Union) will gain from elimination of the MFA, especially since its VERs allocate most quota rents to foreign exporters. Export countries with small quota allocations relative to their comparative-advantage-based abilities to export textiles and apparel (for example, China and Indonesia) also will gain. Export countries that enjoy large quotas relative to their comparative advantage (for example, Korea, Taiwan, and Hong Kong) may lose as they face competition for newly allowed exports from lower-cost producers, as may some exporters not restricted under the MFA (for example, in sub-Saharan Africa) who filled the gaps left by restricted exporters. Import countries that did not restrict imports under the MFA (for example, Japan) may also lose from its elimination because they

have enjoyed low-priced imports as a result of the blockage of MFA-restricted import markets for those products.

Export Quotas

An export quota restricts the quantity of a good that can be exported within a set period of time. VERs are, in effect, export quotas that a country implements at the insistence of its importing trade partners rather than for its own policy purposes. To ensure compliance, the export-country government will need to impose an export-licensing system. As with import quotas, who captures the rents from an export quota depends on how it is administered. Licenses may be allocated on a first-come first-served basis, auctioned, or allocated on the basis of historical export market shares or on political criteria. In a simple, static, competitive-market context, export quotas and export tariffs are equivalent; but as in the case of import quotas, equivalence disappears if market conditions change or if markets are not competitive.

An export quota reduces the exporting country's domestic producer surplus, increases domestic consumer surplus, causes deadweight losses by interfering with efficient production and consumption decisions, and generates quota rents. The net welfare effect of an export quota on a small country is negative. Except for VERs, imposed at the instigation of importers, the primary reasons for export quotas include: (1) national-security or other similar reasons to prevent a particular good (for example, weapons or supercomputers) from becoming available in other countries; (2) political pressure from domestic consumers for lower prices on a particular good (for example, food or oil); or (3) political pressure for lower prices from firms that use a good as an input (for example, raw materials such as logs, oil seeds, or raw hides). If the exporting country is large, an export quota may allow the country to gain by forcing up the world price, which transfers income from foreign consumers to domestic firms or export-license holders (the International Coffee Agreement provides one example). However, regardless of the exporting country's size, an export quota lowers welfare for the world as a whole because it leads to inefficient levels of production and consumption; any gain for a large exporter comes entirely at the trading partners' expense.

Beth V. Yarbrough and
Robert M. Yarbrough

See Also Agriculture; Clothing, Textiles, and Apparel; Dumping and Countervailing Duties; Protectionism; Tariffs; Technical Barriers to Trade; Transport Manufacturing: Aircraft/Automobiles/Shipbuilding; U.S. Trade Laws; World Trade Organization (WTO); U.S. Trade laws

References

Bhagwati, Jagdish N. 1965. "On the Equivalence of Tariffs and Quotas." Pp. 52–67 in Robert E. Baldwin et al., eds., *Trade, Growth, and the Balance of Payments.* Chicago: Rand McNally.

Bowen, Harry P., Abraham Hollander, and Jean-Marie Viaene. 1998. *Applied International Trade Analysis.* Ann Arbor: University of Michigan Press.

Deardorff, Alan V., and Robert M. Stern. 1998. *Measurement of Nontariff Barriers.* Ann Arbor: University of Michigan Press.

Francois, Joseph F., and Kenneth A. Reinert, eds. 1997. *Applied Methods for Trade Policy Analysis: A Handbook.* Cambridge: Cambridge University Press.

Grossman, Gene M., and Kenneth Rogoff, eds. 1995. *Handbook of International Economics.* Vol. 3. Amsterdam: North-Holland.

Hoekman, Bernard M., and Michel M. Kostecki. 1995. *The Political Economy of the World Trading System: From GATT to WTO.* Oxford: Oxford University Press.

Hufbauer, Gary Clyde, and Kimberly Ann Elliott. 1994. *Measuring the Cost of Protection in the United States.* Washington, DC: Institute for International Economics.

Jackson, John H. 1997. *The World Trading System: Law and Policy of International Economic Relations.* 2d ed. Cambridge: MIT Press.

Krueger, Anne O. 1974. "The Political Economy of the Rent-Seeking Society." *American Economic Review* 64: 291–303.

Martin, Will, and L. Alan Winters, eds. 1996. *The Uruguay Round and the Developing Countries.* Cambridge: Cambridge University Press, for the World Bank.

Mshomba, Richard E. 2000. *Africa in the Global Economy.* Boulder: Lynne Rienner.

Organisation for Economic Co-operation and Development. 1997. *Indicators of Tariff and Non-tariff Trade Barriers.* Paris: OECD.

Trebilcock, Michael J., and Robert Howse. 1995. *The Regulation of International Trade.* London: Routledge.

United States Trade Representative. Various years. *National Trade Estimate Report on Foreign Trade Barriers.* Washington, DC: U.S. Government Printing Office.

Vousden, Neil. 1990. *The Economics of Trade Protection.* Cambridge: Cambridge University Press.

Yarbrough, Beth V., and Robert M. Yarbrough. 2003. *The World Economy: Trade and Finance.* 6th ed. Cincinnati: South-Western.

Protectionism

"Protectionism" refers to the imposition of barriers to international trade by government entities. These barriers usually involve either taxes on imports—that is, tariffs—or quantitative restrictions limiting the volume of legally allowable imports of particular goods—or quotas—to achieve various economic and political targets.

Historical Overview

Mercantilism may have been the earliest economic theory to advocate protectionism. According to J. Overbeek (1999), mercantilist views and practices prevailed among European writers and statesmen between the end of the seventeenth century and the late eighteenth century. As argued by Charles Wilson (1971, 8), the two major aims of mercantilism were the pursuit of power and the accumulation of treasure. The accumulation of treasure made power possible, and power led to more wealth. The most important and desirable form of wealth was treasure, or precious metals. This preoccupation with gold and silver led to a particular kind of trade policy. Countries that had no gold or silver mines, and that were deprived of colonies where precious metals could be found, had no option other than to acquire bullion through trade. A country therefore had to strive for a favorable, or positive, balance of trade (BOP). To achieve a positive BOP, many trade policies were designed to stimulate exports and hamper imports. From discouraging imports to protectionism is but one step; thus import pro-hibitions, quotas, tariffs, and other protectionist measures became part of the stock and trade of mercantilist policy and recommendations.

The nineteenth century was characterized by an increasing spread of nationalism. Overbeek has held that protectionism and nationalism tend to go hand in hand, as the writings of protectionist authors clearly show. Indeed, nationalism, which promotes a state of mind whereby individuals feel that their supreme secular loyalty belongs to the nation-state, and mercantilism were closely associated. However, during the nineteenth century new dimensions were added to mercantilism. From about 1800 to 1848, nationalism was a movement of national emancipation and constitutional rights. After 1848, however, hostile, sinister, despotic characteristics of nationalism became more apparent. Economic nationalism, a body of economic theories and policies aimed at making the nation as independent of foreign economic influences as possible, emphasizes self-sufficiency. It loosens the ties between the economic processes taking place within a nation and those occurring beyond that nation's boundaries. And according to Overbeek, mercantilism is essentially a regime of economic nationalism.

Both the old mercantilism of the pre-1750 period and the new mercantilism of the nineteenth century explained and justified the right of the state to control, regulate, and restrict internal and international economic activities. This right included the ability to implement protectionist measures such as tariffs, quotas, and export subsidies. By the early nineteenth century, mercantilism seemed to be a thing of the past—a historical curiosity even—but with the return of political nationalism a number of mercantilist ideas and policies returned. Proponents were able to prolong them well into the twentieth century. History has shown that the free trade period of the nineteenth century was to last only a few decades; free trade as a principle was unable to defend itself successfully against the attack of nationalist and statist ideas, which once again aimed at the subordination of the individual to the state and government interference in economic life. The nationalist neomercantilism of the nineteenth century differed from the old mercantilism in its principal aim of generating an influx of precious metals. However, in many other ways the two mercantilisms resembled each other. Both postulated a conflict of national interests; both sought greater self-sufficiency; both tended toward protectionism and colonial expansion. Moreover, the state had to be powerful in both the old and the new mercantilism.

In the interwar period, ideas of hegemony, domination, nationalism, collectivism, and oppression began to prevail in an extreme form in the Soviet Union, Italy, and Germany. In other countries, these ideas existed in less drastic varieties. Some degree of economic autarky was always part of these conceptions. In the world as a whole, protectionism continued to hold the upper hand until World War II. The total level of international trade shrank dramatically between 1930 and 1939.

During the first two decades following World War II, protectionism stayed silently on the sidelines, but the 1970s, as is well known, witnessed the rise of the so-called "new protectionism"—the rebirth of economic nationalism among typical welfare states. As Jan Tumlir (1985) pointed out, this neoprotectionism should be seen as a government's prime weapon against the threat posed by a relatively free world trade order. It did not develop in a vacuum. It was a symptom of the inherent contradiction between the interfering welfare state and an open trading system. Many other factors, however, did contribute to the rise of the

new protectionism, such as the fact that some countries, including the United States and the members of the European Community, faced increased competition both domestically and abroad. Japan, among others, proved a formidable rival. Increased competitive pressure tended to evoke a protectionist response.

This neoprotectionism has resulted in a proliferation of voluntary export restraints, so-called orderly market agreements, anti-dumping levies, subsidies to domestic industries, and other nontariff trade barriers. At present, protectionists in wealthier countries, who are always on the lookout for new reasons to impose trade barriers, are using arguments related to labor and the environment to back up demands for additional trade impediments. They argue that low trade barriers, the spread of technology, and cheap labor in emerging economies will combine to enable poorer countries to overwhelm the rich countries with their low-cost products, wiping out jobs in countries with historically high wages. The usual conclusion is that high tariffs and quotas are needed. Trade policy activists also claim that it is difficult for the more developed nations, which often have rigid environmental controls, to compete with Third World countries that have lax environmental policies. The proponents of free trade face the challenge of fighting policy proposals for managed trade. Managed trade consists of policies to establish and strengthen comparative advantage through temporary trade protection in certain areas at the expense of foreigners. The tools usually involve a combination of domestic market protections and subsidies. Managed trade, therefore, is a newer form of economic nationalism.

Debate about Free Trade and Protection

For hundreds of years, at least since Adam Smith's publication of *The Wealth of Nations,* the majority of economists have been strong supporters of free trade among nations. The original arguments for free trade began to supplant mercantilist views in the early to mid–eighteenth century. Many of these original ideas were based on simple exchange or production models that suggested that free trade would be in everyone's best interests, and surely in the national interest. During the nineteenth and twentieth centuries, however, a series of objections were raised suggesting that free trade was not in everyone's interest and perhaps not even in the national interest. The most prominent of these arguments included the infant-industry argument, the terms-of-trade argument, arguments concerning income redistribution, and, more recently, strategic trade policy arguments. Although each of these arguments might be thought of as weakening the case for free trade, each brought forth a series of counterarguments that have acted to reassert the position of free trade as a favored policy. The most important of these counterarguments focus on the theory of endogenous policy regime (Cheng et al. 2000a; Yang and Zhang 2000), the theory of endogenous comparative advantage (Yang 1994; Yang and Ng 1993), the likelihood of incomplete or imperfect information, and the presence of lobbying in a democratic system.

Research shows that the division of labor among countries helps to determine which trade policies governments choose. Tariff wars, tariff negotiations, and laissez faire regimes are all possible outcomes. When a high level of division of labor occurs, all countries prefer a tariff bargaining game that results in multilateral free trade. If a medium level of division of labor occurs, then it is possible for a unilateral protection tariff in a less developed country to coexist with unilateral laissez faire policies in a developed country. In any case, tariff negotiations are essential for achieving multilateral free trade. This research explains the policy transition of some European governments from mercantilism to free trade in the eighteenth and nineteenth centuries as well as policy changes in developing countries from protection tariff to tariff negotiation and trade liberalization (see Cheng et al. 2000a; Cheng et al. 2000; Yang and Zhang 2000).

What Forms Does Trade Protection Take?

Gains from trade may be generated by exogenous differences among countries in tastes, endowments, and technology. Gains can also be generated by increasing returns in the absence of such differences, especially through endogenous (or acquired) comparative advantage (Yang and Ng 1993; Yang 1994). Despite these advantages, trade protection is still common. It takes two main forms: tariffs and nontariff barriers.

Tariffs are a tax levied on imports to restrict their inflow by raising their price. Higher prices encourage domestic firms to expand production; thus, tariffs also serve as a domestic subsidy. Nontariff barriers include quotas, voluntary export restraints (VERs), and export subsidies. Quotas limit imports by specifying the maximum amount of foreign-produced goods that will be permitted into the country over a specified period of time. VERs are used in a similar fashion and involve an agreement by one country to limit exports to another. Like quotas, VERs restrict quantity, driving the price of the good upward. An export tax, for example, forces exporters to sell cheaply in the domestic market rather than incur the tax. Profits that would normally go to the importer would then go to the exporting country instead, causing competition for licensing in the exporting country. Richard Harris (1985), examining the VER against Japanese automobile exports to Europe and the United States in the 1980s, suggested that the term "voluntary" is often a misnomer. Such restraints are termed as such because exporting countries can theoretically modify or remove them at any time; however, VERs are often implemented in response to threats or pressures from the importing country (Jones 1994, 3).

Export subsidies allow exporters to expand overseas supply. This lowers the price paid overseas, increasing overseas demand, while raising the domestic price and lowering domestic demand. Welfare losses occur because the subsidies generate distorted impacts on consumer and producer behavior; however, the magnitude of these effects depends on the size of the country implementing the subsidy. The welfare losses of the subsidy are smaller for a small country than for a large one because a large country influences the price of its exports. A subsidy will raise the world supply of the exported commodity and lower the demand for it, thus worsening the terms of trade. This is an apparent paradox, since the worsening of the terms of trade actually promotes imports.

Comments on Protection Measurement

Despite the disadvantages associated with protection, governments continue to employ tariffs, quotas, and VERs. Reasons for doing so include assisting an infant industry, improving terms of trade, reducing unemployment, increasing fairness, ensuring income redistribution, retaliating against overseas protection, assisting a developing nation, promoting national security, and correcting for market failure (new protectionism).

Takumi Naito (2000) argued that industries take time to develop the necessary expertise and economies of scale to compete against established firms. Established firms typically enjoy advanced production techniques and better knowledge of market characteristics, and so they are able to earn profits even though their products are sold at lower prices. The high initial costs of establishing an enterprise may deter entrepreneurs from doing so at free trade prices. However, once that industry develops, the returns may be sufficiently high to compensate for any establishment costs. Consequently, a temporary shielding from foreign industries may reduce the initial costs suffi-

ciently to permit infant-industry development. Protection allows developing firms to sell their products at an internationally competitive price. Other economists have pointed out flaws in this argument, saying it does not make sense because a competitive financial market can utilize the opportunity of investment in an infant industry. What is really needed for infant industry to develop is a free and competitive financial market, not protection. Protectionist tariffs reduce trading efficiency and deter industrialization and globalization; the equilibrium degree of industrialization is an increasing function of trading efficiency due to the tradeoff between increasing returns and transaction costs (Sachs and Yang 2002; Yang and Ng 1993).

The terms-of-trade argument in favor of protection was developed by R. Torrens (1844). Torrens argued that some countries have a large enough share of the world market to affect world prices and that a tariff imposed by a "price maker" will lower the price of imports and generate more favorable terms of trade. As a result, tariffs, quotas, and VERs may be used to improve the bargaining position of a country versus other countries (Krauss 1979, 11). According to Jeffrey Sachs, Xiaokai Yang, and Dingsheng Zhang (2000), however, deterioration of a country's terms of trade and increases in its gains from trade may occur simultaneously if productivity gains generated by an expanding network of division of labor more than compensate for the deteriorations. P. Sen (1998) provided empirical evidence for this phenomenon from Singapore data.

The balance of trade is argued to benefit from protection by curbing imports. This argument is dubious, however, since it ignores a host of negative impacts, including increases in transaction costs, which reduce the equilibrium level of the international division of labor and aggregate productivity (Cheng et al. 2000a; Yang and Zhang 2000), distortions leading to welfare losses, and higher input costs (if inputs were imported). Likewise, it is true that in the short term, protection may preserve jobs, but this would occur at the cost of organization inefficiency, allocation inefficiency, higher prices to consumers, and a distortion of consumer choice. All of which accrue to lower welfare.

A frequently voiced counterargument to protection is the potential for retaliation. However, according to Wenli Cheng, Jeffrey Sachs, and Xiaokai Yang (2000a), as well as Yang and Zhang (2000), protectionism does not necessarily cause retaliation. They have shown that if the equilibrium level of division of labor is very high, a possible tariff war will generate Nash tariff negotiation, which will lead to a multilateral free trade regime similar to that which occurs under the WTO framework. If the equilibrium level of division of labor is high in the developed country, but low in the developing country, all gains from trade may go to the developed country. The developing country has an incentive to use tariffs to get a fairer division of gains from trade, whereas the developed country has no incentive to retaliate but prefers a unilateral free trade policy. Hence, unilateral protection in the developing country and unilateral free trade policy in the developed country may coexist. But these authors have shown that if the developing country can improve trading efficiency through institutional reforms and the development of better transportation infrastructure, it can get more gains from free trade than from tariffs.

M. B. Krauss (1979) recognized the income redistribution powers of trade protection; however, he argued that tariffs are often used to redistribute incomes when the government wants to hide income transfers. He wrote, "This kind of device is used when the redistribution has little to do with accepted standards of distributional equity in the economy, but amounts, more or less, to a 'payoff' to a particular group" (Krauss 1979, 9). Australian tariff protection for Toyota is an example. One may suggest that distributional equity does not require an increase in the real incomes of car manufacturers. Yet the government transfers income to Toyota by imposing import restrictions on foreign-produced cars. One could expect a transparent subsidy to Toyota from the government to raise the suspicions of taxpayers, who may question whether it is proper for Toyota to be treated as a welfare recipient.

The effect of protectionism relates to the Stopler-Samuelson (S-S) (1941) theorem, which states that tariffs can increase the relative price of labor-intensive goods and thereby increase wage rates relative to interest rates in the developed country importing the labor-intensive good. This theorem, however, has been proved wrong: Wages relative to interest rates may decrease, and the relative price of a labor-intensive good may increase at the same time, even if each country produces all goods (see Cheng et al. 2000b). Chang, Sachs, and Yang also showed that even if tariffs increase the relative price of a labor-intensive good and thereby increase wages relative to interest rates in the developed country, this will marginally decrease the level of international division of labor and thereby reduce wage rates inframarginally.

According to Yang and Zhang (1999), protection does not reduce inequality of income distribution, and the relationship between inequality of income distribution and international trade is not monotonic. As international trade increases, inequality of income distribution fluctuates. This prediction is verified by empirical evidence (Deininger and Squire 1996).

"Dumping" refers to the practice of exporting products at prices lower than domestic prices, production costs, or "fair" market values. A country may have an excess supply of a particular good that enterprises cannot sell domestically, and so they "dump" the product on the international market at an attractive price. The profits of other exporters are temporarily lowered. Free trade advocates sometimes suggest the term "dumping" is a misnomer, however. If foreign exporters are selling at a lower price, wealth is transferred from the producer to the consumer. Thus, foreign exporters are in fact making a gift to local consumers (Nieuwenhuysen 1989, 24). Furthermore, it is not always clear why overseas exporters are able to lower prices. They may actually be engaging in rational profit-maximizing behavior through price discrimination. Despite these arguments, countries continue to employ antidumping protection. Dumping is difficult to identify, and as countries have been pressed to lower their tariffs, protectionists increasingly have been employing antidumping procedures to curb imports.

National security may be improved through protection to vital industries in times of war. If Japan relied on imports of food from Australia, for example, and a war were to prevent these imports, Japan could suffer considerably, depending on the state of its domestic food-production industries. Similarly, a country may exercise export restraints to prevent the accumulation of arms or high-technology goods in other countries. In addition to the allocative inefficiencies that arise from stockpiling and other distorted behavior, national security and defense arguments are problematic because it may be difficult to identify which goods pose a threat to health or defense.

Some economists say that tariffs can generate much-needed government revenue. This argument is particularly relevant to low-income developing nations. When a country's citizens are poor and the potential for generating taxation revenue from domestic workers is limited, tariffs become a desirable source of income to fund the provision of essential services, education, and public goods. Developing countries may also borrow funds to provide these services. During recessionary periods, countries that have not implemented trade barriers, however, may suffer from credit shortages. Protection is argued to shield developing countries from this sort of external exposure. However, J. N. Bhagwati (1987, 33) asserted that countries that did not engage in import-competing strategies during the postrecession years of the late 1970s and early 1980s recorded high rates of growth even as they slowed down with the rest of the world.

Another argument relevant to developing (and developed) nations is that protectionism

attracts foreign investment. This view posits that industries will establish companies overseas rather than export to those same countries to avoid the loss of profits stemming from protectionist activities.

Markets, both domestic and international, are rarely perfect. The examination of market failures in the international market has generated a number of neoprotectionist arguments against free trade. D. Salvatore (1987, 1) refers to the new protectionist arguments as the revival of mercantilism; others compare these arguments to putting old wine in new wineskins (Bhagwati 1987, 31). The terms-of-trade argument discussed earlier demonstrated that protection in the presence of a market failure (monopoly power) could raise aggregate welfare in the economy. This argument can be extended to other international market failures, such as externalities, and the presence of imperfect information.

Externalities are costs or benefits to third parties (that is, other than the buyers or the sellers of a product) that are not reflected in the market price. Social and private interests diverge, and so private markets will not produce the socially optimal amount of an externality. Pollution is regarded as an externality because third parties are affected by decisions made between the polluter and the consumer of the polluter's output. A number of countries, including Australia, emit greenhouse gases from coal production at the expense of world welfare. A tariff on Australian exports of coal would raise the cost of producing coal in Australia and reduce the levels of production and pollution.

Conventional economic theory suggests that a monopoly will charge a price above marginal cost. Therefore, a country that imports a good produced by a monopoly is charged a monopoly rent. Taxation is commonly used to extract rents from domestic monopolists. J. A. Brander and B. J. Spencer (1987) extended this argument to suggest that tariffs are suitable for extracting rent from foreign monopolists. When a tariff is imposed on each unit of output imported from the foreign monopolist, this reduces the revenue of the monopolist and generates tariff revenue for the protected country.

The tariff represents a rise in the marginal cost of production for the monopolist. This leads to a fall in production and an increase in prices, which inevitably reduces the consumption of imports in the protected country. This represents a loss of domestic welfare that must be offset against the revenue gains of the tariff. If the gains exceed the losses, domestic welfare is enhanced. However, higher prices are charged to all the clients (countries) of the monopolist, reducing world welfare. Furthermore, the benefit of policies that aim to protect the domestic economy at the expense of the monopolist's country will depend on the extent to which the residents of the monopolist's country own the monopolist (Dixit 1987, 185). Also, potential for retaliation exists when national welfare is increased at the expense of other countries.

Natural monopolies also present a case for protection. A natural monopoly is a firm that experiences economies of scale sufficiently large to make room for only one profitable firm in the industry. If another firm were to enter, both firms would incur losses. However, the firm that establishes its position as the natural monopolist can extract super-normal profits. A. K. Dixit and A. S. Kyle (1985) and P. R. Krugman (1987) illustrated how an international natural monopoly creates the potential for governments to intervene. In the absence of government intervention, if two firms are competing for the position of natural monopolist, the first firm to enter the industry will win, and the other firm will not enter the industry. This situation can be turned around through government intervention that boosts the credibility of the "loser's" threat to enter the industry and survive. A small government subsidy that allows the loser to enter the industry and break even will force uncompensated losses upon the "winner." These losses will force the winner below its break-even point, and the subsidy to the loser sends a signal that the situation is not likely to improve. Assuming there is no retaliation, the winner exits the industry and the loser gains supernormal profits well in excess of the initial government subsidy.

A counterargument to new protectionist trade policy is known as the "second-best theory" (Lipsey and Lancaster 1956). It suggests that because a number of government policies aimed at deriving optimal equilibrium conditions are impractical, "second-best" policies are implemented that may result in welfare losses but, in sum, produce a net gain. A tariff on a foreign exporter that produces a negative externality such as pollution, for example, may send the exporter a mixed signal. That is, the exporter may simply view the tariff as a tax to protect industry and jobs. First-best policies, such as marketable pollution permits, benchmarks, or property right assignments, would address the externality more directly. In this case, the tariff is a second-best policy for correcting pollution, developed because the first-best solution was considered impractical.

Krugman (1987) highlighted the empirical difficulties associated with market-failure models. Externalities affect third parties via nonmarket mechanisms, and values outside of the market can be difficult to estimate. Will production of coal by Australia lead to $50,000 of external costs, or $50 billion? The answer to such questions is often unknown. Furthermore, a unifying theory of imperfect competition does not exist. Imperfectly competitive firms may exhibit a variety of behaviors (limit pricing, entry deterrence, strategic signaling, and collusion, for example).

Cost of Protection

According to the National Center for Policy Analysis, political pressure for trade protection has grown during the current economic expansion. Similarly, the United States enacted the infamous Smoot-Hawley Tariff in 1930. It may be that economists have not done a very good job of explaining either the benefits of free trade or the costs of protection.

A 1999 study from the Federal Reserve Bank of St. Louis estimates the cost of protectionism to the United States. St. Louis Fed economist Howard Wall calculated that U.S. exports would have been 26.2 percent higher in 1996 if other countries practiced free trade. He also found that U.S. protectionism hurt, costing consumers in the United States more than $100 billion. In a recent speech in Dallas, Federal Reserve Chairman Alan Greenspan said the ultimate cost of protection can be even higher if it blocks the flow of technology and new ideas that are the life's blood of economic progress.

Similarly, the benefits of free trade may not be as apparent as their perceived costs in terms of job displacement. However, the benefits are large. According to a new study by the Department of Foreign Affairs and Trade in Australia, a 50 percent reduction in world tariffs would increase the world economy by more than $400 billion per year, and complete elimination of tariffs would add $750 billion to the world economy annually.

Xiaokai Yang and Dingsheng Zhang

See Also Antidumping and Countervailing Duties; Nontariff Barriers; Subsidies; Tariffs; Technical Barriers to Trade; GATT; World Trade Organization (WTO); U.S. Trade Laws

References

Bhagwati, J. N. 1987. "Protectionism: Old Wine in New Bottles." Pp. 45–68 in D. Salvatore, ed., *The New Protectionist Threat to World Welfare*. New York: Elsevier Science.

Brander, J. A., and B. J. Spencer. 1987. "Tariffs and Extraction of Foreign Monopoly Rents under Potential Entry." In J. N. Bhagwati, ed., *International Trade: Selected Readings*. 2d ed. Cambridge: MIT Press.

Cheng, Wenli, Meng-chun Liu, and Xiaokai Yang. 2000. "A Ricardian Model with Endogenous Comparative Advantage and Endogenous Trade Policy Regimes." *The Economic Record* 76: 172–182.

Cheng, Wenli, Jeffrey Sachs, and Xiaokai Yang. 2000a. "An Inframarginal Analysis of the Ricardian Model." *Review of International Economics* 8: 208–220.

———. 2000b. "A General-Equilibrium Re-Appraisal of the Stolper-Samuelson Theorem." *Journal of Economics* 72:1–18.

Deininger, K., and L. Squire. 1996. "A New Data Set Measuring Income Inequality." *World Bank Economic Review* 10: 565–591.

Dixit, A. K. 1987. "International Trade Policy for Oligopolistic Industries." In J. N. Bhagwati, ed., *International Trade: Selected Readings*. 2d ed. Cambridge: MIT Press.

Dixit, A. K., and A. S. Kyle. 1985. "The Use of Protection and Subsidies for Entry Promotion and Deterrence." *American Economic Review* 75: 139–153.

Harris, Richard. 1985. "Why Voluntary Export Restraints Are 'Voluntary.'" *Canadian Journal of Economics* 18, iss. 4, pp. 799–809.

Jones, K. A. 1994. *Export Restraint and the New Protectionism: The Political Economy of Discriminatory Trade Restrictions*. Ann Arbor: University of Michigan Press.

Krauss, M. B. 1979. *The New Protectionism: The Welfare State and International Trade*. Oxford: Basil Blackwell.

Krugman, P. R. 1987. "Is Free Trade Passe?" *Journal of Economic Perspectives* 1: 131–144.

Lipsey, R. G., and K. Lancaster. 1956. "The General Theory of the Second Best." *Review of Economic Studies* 24: 11–32.

Naito, Takumi. 2000. "A Rationale for Infant-Industry Protection and Gradual Trade Liberalization." *Review of Development Economics* 4: 164–174.

National Center for Policy Analysis. N.d. "Cost of Protectionism," http://www.ncpa.org/oped/bartlett/jun799.html (cited May 25, 2002).

Nieuwenhuysen, J. 1989. *Towards Free Trade between Nations*. Oxford: Oxford University Press.

Overbeek, J. 1999. *Free Trade versus Protectionism*. Cheltenham: Edward Elgar.

Sachs, Jeffrey, and Xiaokai Yang. 1999. "Gradual Spread of Market-Led Industrialization." Harvard Center for International Development Working Paper 11.

Sachs, Jeffrey, Xiaokai Yang, and Dingsheng Zhang. 2000. "Globalization, Dual Economy, and Economic Development." *China Economic Review* 11: 189–209.

Salvatore, D. 1987. *The New Protectionist Threat to World Welfare*. New York: Elselvier Science.

Sen, P. 1998. "Terms of Trade and Welfare for a Developing Economy with an Imperfectly Competitive Sector." *Review of Development Economics* 2: 87–93.

Stopler, W. F, and P. Samuelson. 1941. "Protection and Real Wages." *Review of Economic Studies* 9: 58–73.

Torrens. R. 1844. *The Budget: On Commercial and Colonial Policy*. London: Smith, Elder.

Tumlir, Jan. 1985. *Protectionism: Trade Policy in*

Democratic Societies. Washington, DC: American Enterprise Institute.

Wall, Howard. 1999. "Using the Gravity Model to Estimate the Costs of Protection," Review, Federal Reserve Bank of St. Louis, 33–40

Wilson, Charles. 1971. *Mercantilism.* Historical Association.

Yang, Xiaokai. 1994. "Endogenous vs. Exogenous Comparative Advantage and Economies of Specialization vs. Economies of Scale." *Journal of Economics* 60: 29–54.

Yang, Xiaokai, and Yew-Kwang Ng. 1993. *Specialization and Economic Organization: A New Classical Microeconomic Framework.* Amsterdam: North-Holland.

Yang, Xiaokai, and Dingsheng Zhang. 1999. "International Trade and Income Distribution." Harvard Center for International Development Working Paper 18.

———. 2000. "Endogenous Structure of the Division of Labor, Endogenous Trade Policy Regime, and a Dual Structure in Economic Development." *Annals of Economics and Finance* 1: 211–230.

Strategic Alliances

Strategic alliances are cooperative agreements between firms. They range from formal joint ventures to various types of contractual agreements in which no equity ownership is involved. They may involve any stage of the value chain, for example, research and development, joint manufacturing, or distribution. Strategic alliances frequently involve cooperation between rivals in the same industry, but they have also been broadly defined to include supplier networks and other types of partnering arrangements between firms in different industries. They are distinguished from ordinary procurement relationships in that they are "strategic," that is, they are in some way significant to the long-term competitive position of the firm.

International strategic alliances are cooperative agreements between firms based in different nations. The rapid growth of strategic alliances since the late 1980s has been one of the most significant impacts of globalization on international business. As the number of strategic alliances has grown, trends in the types and purposes of these alliances have evolved as well.

Trends in International
Strategic Alliance Formation

Traditionally, multinational corporations (MNCs) from developed countries sought to establish joint ventures with partners in developing countries as a means to increase volume by penetrating overseas markets. The develop-

ing country partner would benefit from technology transfer while providing access to and in-depth understanding of local markets.

Two driving forces have changed this traditional pattern of cooperation. The first is globalization, which necessitates obtaining both local and global partners if companies are to compete successfully in global industries. The opening up of centrally planned economies in Eastern Europe and China and the expansion of regional integration schemes, such as the North American Free Trade Agreement (NAFTA) and the European Union, are among the changes in the global environment that accelerated the pace of globalization. Lower cross-national barriers to cooperation have made it possible for MNCs to bring together inputs from alliance partners located in a large number of different nations for the manufacture of a single product. For example, the auto industry consists of strategic alliances in so many different countries that it is increasingly difficult to define a product's origin of manufacture.

The second driving force is rapid technological change. Few companies have all the capabilities needed to take advantage of the opportunities resulting from information technology. Even the largest MNCs must find partners in order to remain on the cutting edge. Moreover, first-mover advantages accrue to the firms that take the lead in establishing strong interenterprise networks: Those that lag may find that all the best global partners have already been taken. Increased technological uncertainty also puts pressure on firms to learn as much as possible from alliance partners, rather than solely relying on partners to balance a firm's own weaknesses (Doz and Hamel 1998).

The result of these forces has been a shift to new types of alliances. First, a greater proportion of alliances occur between firms from industrialized countries, as opposed to alliances between firms based in developed and less developed countries. Second, the focus of alliances has shifted from the mass distribution of existing products to the creation of new products and technologies. Third, alliances tend to be established in large numbers during industry transitions, when industry boundaries are in flux and the keys to competitive advantage are in the process of being redefined (Bartlett and Ghoshal 2000).

Global trends toward deregulation and privatization of state assets have stimulated the above types of critical turning points in many industries, such as telecommunications and airlines (Culpan 2002). Alliances sometimes serve as temporary, rather than permanent, structures for managing these industry transition points.

Strategic alliances provide an alternative to mergers and acquisitions as a means to rapidly obtaining the critical capabilities that a firm lacks. Acquisitions often require the firm to purchase more assets than it actually needs. As a result, unwanted divisions must be sold off, overlapping divisions must be merged, and excess personnel must be fired. Consequently, mergers are generally also costlier than alliances and frequently fail to achieve their objectives.

Another drawback of acquisitions is that the purchase itself may destroy the desired advantage that the acquired firm originally had. Close contacts with a particular foreign government, for example, may be lost if the local company in question is merged with a firm based elsewhere, whereas these contacts could be maintained in a strategic alliance. Key personnel are often lost in an acquisition: Individuals possessing skills in high demand will often find jobs elsewhere rather than stick with a newly acquired firm under new management. Such personnel are more apt to remain as shared assets in a strategic alliance (Doz and Hamel 1998).

Alliances involving collaboration between two firms become even more complex as multiple alliances are formed or alliances with multiple partners are created. Strategic alliance concepts then overlap with the concepts of "networking" and "enterprise groups." Firms involved in various types of long-term exchange relationships may be viewed as nodes in complex networks, and the intensity of the relationships between particular exchange partners in a network may be examined in order to better understand the structure and competitive positioning within an industry. The term "enterprise groups" refers to multiple partner alliances in which firms recognize membership in the group and are often linked by minority ownership. The forms these groups take are often affected by national political environments, which shape their form via antitrust laws and business-government relationships, and by the organization of capital markets in a particular nation or region. Asian-based enterprise groups, such as the Japanese *keiretsu* and overseas Chinese enterprise groups, predate the wave of strategic alliances in the United States and Western Europe (Richter 2000).

Theoretical Foundations

Theoretical frameworks from a number of disciplines have been used to explain the existence and growth of strategic alliances. These include the resource-based theory of the firm, theories of organizational learning, transaction cost economics, and social exchange theory.

The resource-based theory of the firm provides one of the most important foundations for understanding strategic alliances. According to the resource-based view, the firm is a unique bundle of resources, capabilities, and competences that form the basis for competitive advantage. Resources may be tangible, such as physical and financial assets, or intangible, such as technology and reputation. They include human resources, which are characterized not only by expertise and training, but also by employee adaptability and commitment. Capabilities, such as research and development, manufacturing, marketing, and corporate management, build on a firm's resources. Distinctive competences are activities that a firm performs better than its competitors. Strategic alliances become necessary when no firm holds all the resources necessary to compete effectively. The alliances are therefore the means by which firms pool their resources and capabilities (Culpan 2002).

Theories of knowledge creation and organizational learning provide an important supplement to the resource-based approach by clarifying how firms in a strategic alliance learn from each other. Knowledge may be categorized as explicit or tacit. Explicit knowledge is easily documented and readily communicated. Tacit knowledge is less formal and is embedded in people's heads and in a firm's processes. Explicit knowledge may be easily transferred through market transactions. The transfer of tacit knowledge requires close working relationships and a high degree of trust.

Strategic alliances facilitate the transfer of tacit knowledge. Alliances expose people to new ideas from outside firms and may encourage them to challenge old programs in their own firms that are becoming obsolete. In some cases, certain types of knowledge may be available from only one source. If an acquisition is unfeasible, then a strategic alliance might be the only available means to obtain that tacit knowledge. One of the key challenges for firms involved in strategic alliances is ensuring that complex, tacit knowledge needed to develop critical new capabilities is absorbed from the alliance partner. Once individuals involved in an alliance learn these new capabilities, it is then essential that this knowledge is appropriately dispersed throughout the parent organization.

Transaction cost economics (TCE) also provides a foundation for understanding the nature and coordination of interfirm relationships. TCE posits that human beings are characterized by bounded rationality, and thus they cannot foresee all the possible consequences of a complex, long-term transaction. Since contracts cannot take all possible contingencies into account, there is a risk that a party to a transaction may act opportunistically, enhancing their own position at the expense of their partner's interest. It is thus in a firm's interest to carefully craft appropriate structures to govern complex transactions. Simple, one-shot transactions are most efficiently organized through markets. Transactions that involve investments in specialized assets, or that are characterized by high levels of uncertainty, require greater levels of safeguards to assure both parties that their interests are secure. At the extreme, a firm will internalize a transaction within the boundaries of its own hierarchy.

Strategic alliances represent a form of hybrid governance that falls in between the extremes of market and hierarchy. Technological changes, which have decreased the costs of communications, have lowered transaction costs and shifted preferences from complete internalization of transactions toward hybrid governance modes. In order to be successful, strategic alliances must be crafted in such a way that partners are confident that opportunism is not a threat and that trust is built up between alliance members. Transaction cost economics has been criticized in some contexts for emphasizing legal safeguards over interpersonal ties.

Social exchange theory provides a deeper understanding of the role and meaning of trust. The interpersonal relationships developed in an economic exchange may be of intrinsic value to the players, who may make decisions influenced by friendship rather than solely the self-interest of the organizations they represent. Trust may also be the outcome of habit, arising from repeated reliance on a particular partner, or from ignorance and gullibility, rather than calculated self-interest. It is thus important to distinguish between trust at the interpersonal and interorganizational levels. If an alliance depends solely on interpersonal relationships for its success, the loss of a few key personnel can cause alliance failure. Linkages need to be made between interpersonal trust developed between individuals working in firms in an alliance and interorganizational trust (Nooteboom1999).

When one firm trusts another to fulfill its role in an alliance, there are two key components: (1) competence—that is, the firm trusts that the partner is capable of completing obligations, and (2) intentions—that is, the firm trusts that the partner will act ethically and in good faith to hold up its end of the deal. If one partner's performance is poor, it is often difficult to distinguish whether failure was due to incompetence, to opportunism, or to circumstances outside the firm's control. In general, trust grows with positive experience. Those with bad alliance experiences in the past will approach a new alliance differently than those who have had good experiences (Nooteboom 1999).

Types of Alliances and Their Respective Advantages/Risks

Alliances may be generally categorized as "horizontal" or "vertical" alliances. Each type is characterized by different advantages and inherent risks.

Horizontal alliances, or alliances with firms in the same industry, take on many forms. They often involve joint manufacturing in one of the partners' home countries. In some cases, they may involve joint manufacturing in a third country. Alliances in research and development have become increasingly prevalent, as rapid technological change makes it impossible for even the largest companies to remain at the cutting edge without collaboration with other firms. When the boundaries separating industries break down—as, for example, those de-

marcating telecommunications, electronics, and entertainment—the imperative of establishing alliances becomes more intense if firms are to maintain viable competitive positions.

There are a number of distinct advantages to establishing alliances with rival firms. One is that an alliance can facilitate entry to a foreign market. A local partner can provide in-depth knowledge of its home market. It can advise a foreign partner how best to handle government requirements, and it can provide local contacts with suppliers, distributors, and government officials that substantially increase the odds of success of a new foreign entrant.

A second advantage is that alliance partners can share fixed costs and the risks of developing new technology. This is particularly important for smaller firms that may lack the resources to achieve economies of scale. The combination of globalization, entailing risks associated with political instability, economic downturns, and exchange rate fluctuations, with rapid technological change, involving huge investments in research and development that may not pay off, makes alliances that can help cope with the high costs of these uncertainties particularly desirable.

A third advantage of strategic alliances with rivals is that alliance partners can exchange complementary competencies. This goes beyond the concept of shared costs, where the need to invest in new technologies is lessened by relying on a partner to supply them. Organizational learning has become an increasingly central part of strategic alliances. Unlike market-based transactions, strategic alliances provide firms with the opportunity to acquire tacit knowledge from alliance partners that is not easily obtained from blueprints or other written documents. This knowledge, which is locked within people's heads or demonstrated by the processes they use, can become an important source of competitive advantage (Doz et al. 2001).

A fourth advantage of horizontal alliances is that they facilitate the establishment of global standards. As decades of research culminate in a marketable product, firms seek to establish the specifications of their in-house developed products as global standards. The standards chosen for videotapes, floppy disks, DVDs, and mobile phone technologies have had major competitive implications for firms in those industries. If another firm's specifications are chosen instead of one's own, it can obtain first-mover advantages while competitors spend years of additional innovation to make their products conform with their rival's standard. Firms that set up alliances to establish technological standards have a greater chance of seeing their own specifications accepted as the global norm.

The advantages of strategic alliances must be balanced with their risks. The greatest risk is that a partner will leave the alliance as a much stronger and more formidable competitor. If one firm in an alliance learns its partner's core technologies and managerial competences while the other firm merely relies on its partner to lower costs, the firm that learns the most may eventually drive its partner out of business. U.S. firms, in particular, have been criticized for not being as adept at organizational learning as their Japanese partners. Moreover, a number of American firms that established manufacturing ventures in developing countries later found themselves in jeopardy, after their low-cost manufacturing partners began penetrating developed-country markets on their own.

Another risk is that a firm will invest heavily in an alliance without achieving its long-run objectives. Firms have less control over alliances than acquisitions, and partners' goals may not be identical. A firm may exit from an alliance no better off than it started, having failed to penetrate key markets or develop targeted technologies that the alliance was designed to achieve.

Firms in collaboration with rivals must also be aware that alliances often are transformed into acquisitions or mergers. Weaker firms frequently get swallowed up by stronger partners. Sometimes an outright sale of a corporate division brings more value to stockholders than an alliance that is converted to a sale. This does not mean that strategic alliances that are transformed into mergers are necessarily failures. In certain cases, a strategic alliance allows a potential acquirer to learn more about the value of a target division from its parent before buying it. In other cases, as circumstances change, the strategic direction of one of the parents shifts, thus making it in both partners' interests for one to take over the alliance. Caution is required, however, as rival firms enter into an alliance to ensure that an unintended merger is not the inevitable outcome of a new horizontal strategic alliance.

Vertical alliances consist of collaborative agreements with customers, distributors, and suppliers. Alliances with customers may provide in-depth knowledge about current and future market needs, whereas alliances with distributors may yield a deeper understanding about the features peculiar to market channels in a particular foreign country. Access to these types of specific local knowledge may not only facilitate adaptation to cultural preferences in one country, but may also provide multinational corporations with new ideas for differentiating themselves globally (Doz et al. 2001).

Global supplier networks have generally been set up as a means to lower costs or access distinctive inputs: Each component is manufactured in the country with the lowest costs or most productive resources for that particular stage of the value chain. Alliances with suppliers may also provide access to new knowledge. If structured appropriately, such alliances may enhance an MNC's capabilities by allowing access to new technologies.

Vertical alliances have been criticized for hollowing out firms through outsourcing all manufacturing abroad. There is a risk that a firm will outsource all its core competencies, so that instead of becoming an agile, virtual firm it instead loses its competitive advantage to the firms to which it has outsourced. There are, however, instances where competitive position has been substantially enhanced. For example, U.S. industrial electronics firms established supply networks in East Asia, particularly Tai-wan, during the 1990s in such a way that American computer firms significantly improved their relative position vis-à-vis Japanese electronics firms as compared to the previous decade (Borrus et al. 2000).

Building and Managing Strategic Alliances

Because of the risks involved in strategic alliances, considerable attention has been given to methods of structuring and managing alliances to increase the chances of success. The initial choice of a partner in a strategic alliance is particularly crucial.

Complementary capabilities are one of the most important features to be sought from a potential alliance partner. Overlapping capabilities minimize the opportunities for learning and thus decrease the value of a strategic alliance. Both partners need to be capable of contributing in significant ways toward meeting the goals of the alliance.

Self-deception must be avoided: Two weak companies, rather than saving each other through the advantage of greater size, often sink together if neither has the capabilities needed for competitive success. In cases where the partner firms' capabilities are not balanced, the stronger partner will most likely take over the weaker one. Even where complementary capabilities appear to be balanced at the outset of an alliance, consideration should be given to the relative importance of these capabilities in the long run. The strengths needed for competitive success change over time as the alliance evolves and global conditions change. If the partner's capabilities can be expected to take on greater importance as the alliance evolves, a firm risks a possible future sale of its stake in the alliance.

A second characteristic to be kept in mind when seeking a partner is that both parties need to share the same vision about the direction in which the alliance should progress and

grow. MNCs with joint ventures in developing countries have frequently encountered this problem. If the local partner is interested in obtaining technology from the MNC in order to increase exports, while the MNC is interested in its partner's local knowledge in order to more deeply penetrate local markets, the alliance may eventually break down as neither party achieves its goals. Conflicts can also arise about the appropriate long-term scope for expansion once short-term goals have been successfully reached.

Another key to finding a good partner is to make sure that the potential partner has a reputation for fair play. Research concerning the firm's previous alliances, and direct input from people who have worked with the firm in the past, provide important insights as to whether an alliance is worth pursuing. An alliance in which trust is impossible has a slim chance of success.

One of the challenges in finding a compatible partner is that firms with complementary capabilities often have very different corporate cultures. Certain types of clashes, for example, are characteristic of strategic alliances between large and small firms. In research and development alliances, large firms often have resources that small entrepreneurial firms lack, whereas the smaller firms have a successful record of innovation in key fields where the large firms may be weak. Cooperation makes sense, but it can be difficult to implement owing to cultural differences. Large companies tend to have more formal decision-making processes and thus are viewed by small firms as slow and bureaucratic. Small firm decision-making tends to be rapid, unscheduled, and informal, and thus, large firms tend to view them as disorganized and sloppy (Doz and Hamel 1998). Corporate culture differences are further exacerbated in global alliances with differences in national culture. Conscious efforts must be taken to overcome these differences if an alliance is to succeed.

Partner selection becomes even more complex when a firm is involved in multiple alliances. If a firm is involved in alliances with firms that are direct rivals, each partner may be unwilling to share knowledge that it fears will be transferred without its consent to other alliance members. Care must be taken to avoid the potential for competitive conflict.

Once partners have been chosen, attention must be given to structuring an alliance to best assure that goals will be met while risks are minimized. One technique is to "wall off" sensitive technologies. This entails deciding upfront which technologies will be shared in an alliance and which represent key sources of competitive advantage that should not be leaked to a partner. Engineers working in these sensitive technologies should then not be included as alliance personnel, since knowledge is often diffused informally. Cross-licensing agreements are another technique for structuring an alliance to ensure that both partners benefit. Additional contractual safeguards may be used to minimize the risk of opportunistic behavior for both parties to an alliance. When partners make significant investments, in human capital as well as financially, in an alliance, it demonstrates credible commitment by both parties, thereby assuring both partners of each other's seriousness in achieving success (Hill 2000).

After the initial conditions of the alliance have been established, implementation issues remain: The alliance must be managed appropriately to ensure effective performance. Building trust between the partners over time is especially important. Successful implementation requires that each side bring in highly qualified team players who are a good fit with the needs of the alliance. No written contract can ensure that each partner will contribute its best people or that each side will be enthusiastic in pursuing alliance goals. Clearly, one of the worst breaches of good faith behavior would be to poach a partner's people from an alliance to work at one's own firm: Neither side would be willing to contribute the human assets needed for firm success if even this minimal level of trust were not achieved. Implementation gen-

erally is much smoother if those who are to take charge of alliance implementation are also involved in negotiations. Continuity of key personnel in an alliance should be sought, and mechanisms to ensure that the firms' understandings are maintained under turnover need to be in place (Lewis 1999).

Unlike the organization of activities within one hierarchy, where what the boss says goes, an alliance has joint leaders drawn from independent partners. When a problem arises, alliance partners must rely on trust, not authority, to solve it. Leaders designated by each partner must be carefully chosen, and a good working relationship between these joint leaders is highly beneficial to the alliance. In order to reinforce trust, alliance leaders need to be candid about the objectives they seek to achieve. Issues that both sides are unable to agree upon should not be hidden; rather, they mark the explicit boundaries of what the alliance is to accomplish (ibid.).

Attention must also be paid to organizational issues. When multiple units within one firm are all involved in the implementation of one alliance, it is important to make sure that all relevant internal units recognize the broader interests of the firm in their participation in the alliance, particularly when some units perceive that the alliance does not benefit all units equally. When two firms are involved in multiple alliances together, conflict-resolution mechanisms should be instituted at higher levels in each partner organization; otherwise, problems in one alliance could negatively affect other successful alliances. Partners with different organizational structures also need to pay attention to appropriate alignment in order to assure alliance success. For example, if two MNCs had an alliance in a country outside the national boundaries of both partners' headquarters, tensions could arise if one MNC were organized by country while the other MNC was organized by function or business line. While the MNC organized on a country-by-country basis might be extremely responsive to the alliance's needs, the MNC organized by function might be highly centralized and slow to respond to demands from the alliance. The latter would need to make organizational changes, for example, decentralizing decision-making for the alliance, in order to avoid difficulties for both sides (ibid.).

Strategic alliance success also requires that both partners are able to continuously learn from each other. Favorable initial conditions increase the chances of developing a long-term positive learning cycle among partners. If the conditions for trust are initially met, then the odds are higher that successful learning will occur early in the alliance. When each side evaluates progress on the alliance, each will be more apt to look at performance in a positive light. Each side makes constructive adjustments, successful learning continues, and positive reevaluations further enhance trust. On the flip side, if the conditions for trust are not met at the outset, successful learning may not be achieved in the early stages of the alliance. Negative evaluations by each side make each partner more defensive and less apt to adjust to its partner's needs in a constructive way. This makes successful learning even more difficult to achieve, and the alliance spirals downward into failure (Doz and Hamel 1998).

Eventually, most strategic alliances come to an end. Alliances between rivals, in particular, tend to be of shorter duration than vertical alliances, because rapid changes in the industry environment often require new competitive responses. Negotiating termination agreements up-front can facilitate an orderly breakup of an alliance. Termination agreements are sometimes viewed as a sign of a lack of trust in one's future partner or a lack of confidence in the venture itself. This interpretation can vary by country: Americans tend to be more legalistic than other cultures. However, though some companies have successfully managed alliances with only a brief agreement of understanding, this tends to work best with those firms that had substantial business dealings before an alliance was created. No matter how much effort is invested during an alliance to develop trust, trust cannot be counted upon when the time comes to exit the alliance (Lewis 1999).

Laura Whitcomb

See Also Foreign Direct Investment and Cross-Border Transactions; International Joint Ventures

References

Bartlett, Christopher A., and Sumantra Ghoshal. 2000. *Transnational Management: Text, Cases, and Readings in Cross-Border Management.* 3d ed. Boston: McGraw-Hill.

Borrus, Michael, Dieter Ernst, and Stephan Haggard, eds. 2000. *International Production Networks in Asia: Rivalry or Riches?* London: Routledge.

Cullen, John B. 2002. *Multinational Management: A Strategic Approach.* Southwestern.

Culpan, Refik. 2002. *Global Business Alliances: Theory and Practice.* Westport, CT: Quorum.

Doz, Yves L., and Gary Hamel. 1998. *Alliance Advantage: The Art of Creating Value through Partnering.* Boston: Harvard Business School Press.

Doz, Yves, Jose Santos, and Peter Williamson. 2001. *From Global to Metanational: How Companies Win in the Knowledge Economy.* Boston: Harvard Business School Press.

Hill, Charles W. L. 2000. *International Business: Competing in the Global Marketplace.* 3d ed. Boston: McGraw-Hill.

Lewis, Jordan D. 1999. *Trusted Partners: How Companies Build Mutual Trust and Win Together.* New York: Free Press.

Mockler, Robert J. 1999. *Multinational Strategic Alliances.* Chichester, England: John Wiley.

Nooteboom, Bart. 1999. *Inter-Firm Alliances: Analysis and Design.* London: Routledge.

Richter, Frank-Jurgen. 2000. *Strategic Networks: The Art of Japanese Interfirm Cooperation.* New York: International Business Press.

Subsidies

Government subsidies are grants given by governments to specific industries or enterprises for the purpose of keeping consumer prices at an acceptably low level or below the marginal cost of production. Unlike tariffs, which raise consumer prices, subsidies lower consumer prices; theoretically they can therefore be considered a type of negative tax, though they are not levied as such. They enable the government to subsidize the production of certain goods and/or services, usually food and energy, in order to make them affordable for consumers; to maintain the revenue level of the producers; or to favorize the export of such goods. Government subsidies thus fall into several categories, including production subsidies, consumer subsidies, export subsidies, and so on, and are financed mainly by tax revenues. In some cases, individuals may also offer such grants in order to promote religious, political, or social goals and ideas.

Subsidies are not always in the form of sums of money. The U.S. federal government, for example, subsidized private railway companies in the nineteenth century by allocating state-owned lands for their use, and in other cases publicly owned property has been designated for low-cost housing.

Subsidies maintain the price levels of the subsidized goods and services and are usually applied to common goods used on a large scale by all or most of the actors of the economy, consumers and producers alike. Often, an inflationary pressure would arise without the subsidies because demand for these common goods is always on a high level. The price elasticity of demand (that is, the change in demand that occurs in response to a price change) for a good or service can be represented by the following equation:

$$\varepsilon = \frac{\partial Q / Q}{\partial p / p}$$

The equation basically states that the price elasticity of demand is equal to the percent of change in quantity demanded divided by the percentage change in price. In the case of a subsidized good or service, the price elasticity is below 1, that is, the demand is inelastic. This elasticity may eventually become positive, as in the case of gasoline or in the case of a given good, such as bread or potatoes, if substitutes are not available.

Increases in price for these products will cause inflation or accelerate it because they make up a significant share of the consumer basket. The inflation rate can be calculated as a percentage variation in the price of some set of goods according to a commonly used index such as the Laspeyres index. In this index, the price of a "fixed basket," or "consumption bundle," whose overall size and composition are unchanged over time, is calculated for two time periods—for example, a base period in the past and the current period; the inflation rate is the rate of change over time. Formally then, we have:

$$L_p = \frac{\sum_i p_{1i} q_i}{\sum_i p_{0i} q_i}$$

The index measures the price change for a basket of goods over time. Inflation, especially high inflation, hits the economy as a whole; thus, subsidizing aimed at keeping prices low and stable can be viewed as an anti-inflationist measure and may form part of a general policy designed to fight inflation. But subsidizing on a large scale with huge sums of tax money can lead to increased taxation and subsequently to higher inflation. To counteract this, the state may fix prices, as former Soviet-type economies did, where price regulation led to repressed inflation. In the absence of profits, state companies could function only through regular subsidies. The same concept applied to consumers as well, and subsidies represented a major part of the state budget. The collapse of communism in Europe led to the abolition of planned economies of this type and yielded price liberalization. As a consequence, subsidies were reduced as shown in Table 1, inflation geared up, and state budgets became smaller. But the reduction in the state deficits did not

last for long. Cost levels started to rise dramatically, fueling an upward-crawling spiral of inflation, and reducing inflation is now among the key policy objectives of these economies after fifteen years of transition.

The Methods and Sources of Subsidies

The simplest form that subsidies take involves the direct outlay of government funds to target groups of producers. In some cases, governments prefer emitting coupons, paper-based entitlements for the use of some raw material at a subsidized price. These coupons are sometimes nominal, allowing only the recipient to make use of it, thus ensuring that the subsidy goes directly to the target group. Subsidies financed directly from the federal budget from tax revenues appear as expenditures and therefore place a burden on the national budget that is clearly defined. Some subsidies are hidden, however, because they do not enter national accounting records. This happens, for example, if the government offers a low-interest-rate loan or a loan guarantee or imposes a protective tariff on some imports, which is equivalent to paying a subsidy to the home producers of

Table 1: Subsidies Paid for Producers and Consumers and Their Ppercentage in GDP in Hungary, 1987–1995

Year	Producer Subsidies (billion HUF)	Consumer Subsidies (billion HUF)	Producer Subsidies of GDP	Consumer Subsidies of GDP
1987	150.7	66.7	12.3	5.4
1988	143.8	44.5	10.0	3.1
1989	115.7	44.1	6.8	2.6
1990	98.2	36.8	4.7	1.8
1991	64.3	42.3	2.8	1.8
1992	74.8	19.2	2.9	0.7
1993	76.8	21.7	2.5	0.7
1994	132.6	27.0	3.4	0.7
1995	132.4	32.5	2.7	0.6

Notes: annual inflation rate based on CPI was 16.8–29.1% in the nineties in focus. HUF stands for Hungarian Forints, the national currency denomination.
Source: Statistical Yearbook of the Hungarian Statistical Office, Erdos p. 85.

these same goods. This kind of subsidy is paid directly by domestic consumers in the form of higher prices.

Some subsidies may appear as tax deductions, others as loan guarantees favoring individual borrowers. Many countries, in an effort to eliminate conflicts of interest and interest-group pressures, allow only public authorities, through state-owned banks, to manage credit. Others operate on the opposite assumption— that public provision of a private good can lead to inefficiency and corruption.

Subsidizing Agricultural Producers

Most subsidies target agricultural producers because the provision of food, though often not profitable, is essential for the whole society. Agricultural subsidies make up most of such governmental expenditures in the developed countries and may reach more than 50 percent of crop value. In fact they represent transfers from the industrial and service sectors to the agricultural sector, since through the taxation and subsidization systems part of the income of those employed in the first two sectors, or of consumers in general, goes to farmers.

In most developed countries direct outlays of cash are often given to larger producers, whereas for the small farmers the use of coupons is preferred. The latter receive such coupons for gasoline, fertilizer, insecticide, and other chemicals on the basis of their estimated average production costs, livestock or crop variety and output, or simply the amount of agricultural land they own or rent. For instance, in Romania, each farmer receives $60 for synthetic fertilizer purchases for each hectare of land farmed, but only up to 5 hectares; larger Romanian landowners or producers need no such aid, in the government's view. Consumption of the subsidized good is limited to the producers so as to prevent farmers from purchasing an unlimited amount of low-cost gasoline and reselling it at a higher price. The amount that each producer is entitled to is cal-

culated on the basis of the average normative consumption for the necessary field operations. To counteract misuse, in some countries agricultural gasoline has a different color or scent to make it easily recognizable so that state controllers can discover unauthorized users and merchants. In other words, the consumption of subsidized goods such as agricultural gasoline is rationed, and if a farmer overuses machinery and his operating costs run high, he must bear the losses. Once he has used up his ration, he must buy gasoline at normal pump-station prices, which can also be seen as "taxing" his excess consumption. Thus the farmer's budget line will present a kink at the subsidized quantity limit.

Another type of subsidy rewards producers for the quantity of goods sold abroad. Export subsidies are aimed at keeping certain positions on relevant product markets, especially if the product forms a significant part of the country's gross domestic product (GDP), as with farm products in an agricultural country; in cases where the livelihood of many or most of the country's citizens depend on a product (for example, in countries relying on a cash crop, or a "banana republic," although this observation is also valid for countries with several main products but simple export structures); or in countries where there are strong pressure groups asking for export subsidies, as in the case of French farmers.

Special export subsidies may keep prices for some products lower on foreign markets than at home, since they are based only on the quantities sold abroad. This situation may lead to dumping on the target foreign market. Or the subsidized goods may be offered at the same price on the foreign market but of better quality than at home to give them a competitive advantage over the target country's producers. As a result, domestic consumers may begin to purchase more imported goods, which in turn may lead to bankruptcy for the home producers of similar goods. This is why antidumping measures and other trade barriers, such as tariffs, import quotas, and administrative barriers (for example, food safety regulations), are imposed. The debate between the United States and the European Union on the issue of genetically modified food provides an example.

The United States and other large agricultural producers have long blamed the EU for causing high consumer prices in the Union by heavily subsidizing domestic agricultural production. European consumers cannot have access to cheaper food from the United States, where production is more efficient, because those products cannot penetrate the European markets in desired quantities, despite worldwide agreements on free trade such as the General Agreement on Tariffs and Trade (GATT). Similar complaints lodged by Third World countries, especially the banana republics, asserted that the EU's subsidies of banana production in its overseas territories hurt poor countries; although the poor countries had lower production costs, they could not get their products on the European market because they did not have the financial ability to subsidize them. Therefore, as a gesture, the EU accepted preferential treatment for these countries, offering them a competitive advantage against other major exporters such as the United States. This move annoyed banana producers from Florida to Central America even more, and they exerted a strong pressure on the World Trade Organization (WTO) to set special principles regarding this crop. In retaliation, the EU imposed a ban on the import of genetically modified crops, arguing that these products present health hazards and are implicitly subsidized through U.S. government support for biotechnology and genetic research. Thus, disagreements over subsidies have led to trade wars between the United States and the European Union.

Such disputes have arisen even inside trade blocs such as the Central European Free Trade Association. Moreover, for years, despite its obligations from the international association treaty, the Central European Free Trade Agreement in 1991, Romania imposed high tariff rates (up to 45 percent) on Hungarian meat

and wheat flour imports under the pretext of protecting home producers of pork, poultry, and cereals. Romanian meat processors and bakeries were against these measures, pointing out that because they lacked sufficient domestic raw materials, domestic production could not meet home demand. Romanian officials, however, argued that the tariffs were necessary because Romania could not keep up with Hungary's subsidies: Whereas Hungary subsidized home production, Romania did not because of lack of funds. The trade gap was exacerbated by inefficiency on Romania's big state farms. The measure hit domestic consumers in Romania the most and allowed domestic producers to produce even more inefficiently than before and charge a monopoly-like price on the domestic market. This was clearly a policy failure: The government intervention created its own distortions of the market by failing to correct for existing market failure and even exacerbating it. Domestic meat processors and consumers alike exerted pressure on the government to change its policy, and in any case, the EU accession treaty made it compulsory to open up the market.

Subsidies in the Industry

Subsidies in the industrial sector tend to make it less expensive for producers to purchase raw materials or to maintain high levels of energy consumption. The most common method is direct subsidy via tax expenditures that allow producers to purchase materials or energy from suppliers at subsidized rates. The mining industry, for example, which is often in the public domain, is inherently inefficient: The revenue from sales of ore or coal is usually less than the cost of extracting and processing them. Many states cover the additional costs for the sake of maintaining the industry, whether for the sake of traditions, because of fear of social unrest, or simply to preserve a degree of industrial freedom by encouraging the maintenance of a home mining industry. The same principles apply to other raw material and energy industries. Such policies allow a country to exert control in key industries relevant to national security, keep it from being overly dependent on imports, and enable it to be free from pressure from exporters of strategic raw materials, including those for energy production such as oil and gas. The industrial sector and the whole economy are less vulnerable to supply shortages, price fluctuations, and events that could cause world markets to tumble.

Maintaining a traditional industry through subsidies may in fact constitute a subsidy for culture, national self-esteem, or international image. Subsidizing an industry in order to avoid social unrest reflects the government's inability to perform needed structural changes in the economy. In some cases, such policies aim at keeping supporters and voters on board, especially in the case of socialist, social-democrat, democrat, and labor ruling parties—in general, left-wing parties and coalitions. These populist governments have nevertheless had to revise their attitude toward subsidies from time to time and decrease them if they are faced with huge budgetary deficits, high inflation, or recession due to high taxation burdens. Measures adopted under pressure by the International Monetary Fund (IMF) or the European Union have at times provoked industry-wide strikes in highly unionized sectors, which can in turn lead to early elections or attempts to overthrow the government. The latter occurred, for instance, in 1999, when miners in Romania, fueled mainly by drastic mine-closure decisions of the Romanian government, started an uprising.

Another method of subsidizing certain industries is to place huge state orders, as in the case of the Romanian truck company "Roman." In the absence of foreign or internal private demand, the government rescued the company by ordering some 500 trucks for the national army. This was enough to allow the company to avoid closure, restructuring, or privatization. Such practices are found worldwide, especially

in the United States for weapon manufacturers, in Germany for the steel industry, in Europe for airplane manufacturers, and so on.

A more subtle way to subsidize industries or companies is to write off their debts toward the state, a method used on a large scale in the former Communist states. Most of the companies benefiting from this type of subsidy are large public ones, but many private companies also benefit. For example, their debt toward government-run national health insurance funds or social security funds may be written off from time to time. A less radical but not less efficient method involves the cancellation of penalty payments for delays of transfer for these fund contributions. Penalties may consist of fines or of a combination of fines and higher rates of interest on the sums forming the debt. Huge rescue packs for bankrupt state companies, consisting mostly of large transfers of cash into the accounts of heavily indebted companies—for example, national airlines such as Alitalia or Swissair—are a more direct way of subsidizing. These transfers are always associated with cancellation of debts. This also occurs with large state banks that fall into bankruptcy, such as Bancorex of Romania, which experienced a total loss of $3 billion. All these subsidies fuel inflation, however. Raising taxes is unpopular and also takes time, so the government that offers such remedies easily yields to printing money in order to cover the gaps.

Another method of subsidizing is to guarantee private credit or lending for investments of public interest, flagship companies of the economy, or infant industries. Small business development programs, for example, may ensure credit up to a certain limit for startup or development loans, which may also take the form of no-interest loans. Sometimes only a fraction of the "loan" has to be repaid, or the entrepreneur, which can be the state itself, has to contribute only a small fraction of the startup costs, usually between 10 and 50 percent, and the rest of the total investment value is provided for free by the state, an organization, the EU, or international banks. These are run through certain programs that impose strict rules that must be obeyed in order to benefit from the subsidy. The Special Accession Program for Agricultural and Rural Development (SAPARD) of the EU is an example. In loan guarantees, the state guarantees that it will repay the loan contracted by the favored company if it fails to meet its repayment obligations. This approach is preferred by foreign investors engaging in a large joint venture with a domestic company and by foreign suppliers for importers of high-value goods on commercial credit agreements.

Cross-subsidization occurs when a company uses profits from one product to offset losses from another product. In this case, the profits are redirected to avoid having to raise price levels for the losing product, because demand for the losing product is low. Subsidization may consist of securing a minimum price level for some industrial outputs, but the result is to raise price levels above the competitive market level. This will lead to increased production of the commodity, which in turn can create unwanted surpluses and encourage resource waste.

Subsidies for Consumers

Consumer subsidies are provided to encourage the consumption of some goods or services by offering them at lower prices that are mainly controlled. The amount of the subsidy equals the difference between the market price and the subsidized price, if consumption is constrained to a certain amount; otherwise it is even larger. Such subsidies can lead to overconsumption and produces excess waste, and therefore may constitute an environmental hazard. Domestic demand will be larger than its private optimum, and higher consumption could lead to shortages. Overproduction caused by overconsumption leads to the depletion of resources, making sustainable development less likely. Excessive domestic demand may also decrease foreign exchange revenues

from foregone exports and cause a trade balance deficit.

Consumer subsidies are usually given initially to protect consumer income levels and habits, but usually the main benefit is to the producers of the subsidized goods. Subsidized consumption comes at a price lower than the market rate; indeed, prices may not reflect all the costs of production and consumption. The producers themselves may also receive the consumer subsidies directly, if they consume subsidized products. It may happen that in the cost budgeting of such products, certain inputs or outputs have no price at all, which can be interpreted as a market failure, according to market economy principles. In efficient markets, private welfare is maximized when prices equal marginal private costs, and any deviation from this optimal level will lead to inefficiencies.

Some consumption subsidies are given for health care or education. Their forms are varied and range from direct subsidies to providers to tax deductions for consumers for their contributions to nonprofit organizations, for scholarship income, or for employee contributions to medical care or insurance programs. Some subsidies target specific age groups—for example, subsidized railway tickets, free admission to museums, or discounts on tickets to plays or other events for senior citizens or young people. Some subsidized services are rationed: For instance, youth or the elderly may be allowed a certain amount of free travel on a state railway system.

The consumption of subsidized goods may be unlimited in some cases—for example, when basic foods, such as bread, are subsidized for the poor. Even food rationing, however, may occur during wartime or periods of economic hardship. Direct subsidies such as food stamps in the United States, or food or meal tickets in other countries, are similar in that they are nontaxable. Buying subsidized import goods is beneficial for consumers even if it is the result of dumping, especially if it lasts indefinitely. Consumers may rightly consider this a case of foreign taxpayers contributing to their welfare, and the foreign production as a consequence of the existing comparative advantage in that industry.

The Role of Subsidies

Policymakers have four main goals in enacting subsidies: protection of domestic producers and consumers; correction of externalities; transfer of income from certain groups to other, perhaps disadvantaged, ones; and limitation of inflation. The protection of domestic producers is carried out through many methods, but mostly through imposition of tariffs, import quotas, voluntary export restraints (VERs), countervailing duties, and direct subsidies. Almost all governments use subsidies alongside tariffs and nontariff barriers to protect their infant industries. An infant industry, that is, one just being developed, cannot be profitable and efficient at the same time, because efficiency requires the existence of large-scale production that can yield low unit costs. The existence of such economies of scale is a precondition for profitable investments, given the high fixed costs of research and investment in production facilities before actual production can start. Thus, a start-up industry in a developing country needs protection from the competition exerted by well-established industries in foreign countries. Otherwise, the latter, producing at lower costs and with a high volume of output, could squeeze out the domestic industry before the domestic industry could acquire even a small market share. The home industry, in competitive disadvantage, needs subsidies to match its rivals' prices. The renewable energy sector is another example: It needs protection not only against foreign but also from domestic competitors that produce energy using fossil fuels.

Another role of subsidies is to provide the home industry with the necessary support to develop into a big player on the global market. An example is found in aircraft building. The EU subsidized its Airbus firm to challenge U.S.

supremacy in the industry, since Boeing already had the great advantage of being an older, established firm on the global market. The oligopoly setup is necessary if the new company is to make a profit, because the development and building costs are so high that very few firms can afford to enter the market. The market is not big enough to host many competitors, and in the case of perfect competition, profits would be driven down to zero or losses could occur. Subsidizing a future strong player pays the supporting state back many times over in the long run through increases in export revenues, the boost to domestic taxes, and emerging supplier networks. Such huge investments are useful for governments, and thus subsidies may play the role of tariffs, but without the risks of the latter in an atmosphere of free trade treaties and trade war dangers. The combination of subsidies with tariffs offers even better protection, as in the case of the Japanese victory over the U.S. entertainment electronics industry.

Externalities are the unwanted effects of one producer's activity on another producer's output levels. They are usually harmful (negative externalities) but sometimes beneficial (positive externalities). The most obvious example of a negative externality is that of a polluting firm that harms a neighboring firm's activity. The problem can be solved in economic terms by taxing the polluter and transferring these environmental tax revenues to the suffering producers in order to compensate them for their losses, in other words, by subsidizing them. Another remedy is to subsidize the polluting firm directly in order to reduce pollution levels. The cost of such subsidization is directly proportional to the level of pollution abatement reached; therefore, taxpayers may prefer the taxation alternative or the imposition of fines. This alternative is cheaper for the taxpayers compared to subsidization, but it does not reduce pollution levels significantly. Instead, it decreases output levels, making the products more expensive and the consumers worse off. Polluting firms gain little from pollution abatement, because benefits accrue to the neighbors; therefore, they have little incentive to invest in it. The efficient level of pollution abatement investment is where the marginal social benefit from fighting pollution equals the marginal social costs. Firms are better off receiving subsidies for pollution abatement because this enables them to reach higher output levels and hence higher profits. If both alternatives are feasible, the system of fines results in a Pareto-efficient allocation, whereas the subsidy system alone usually does not. In any case, taxing a firm or imposing a fine on it allows the government to use that money to compensate other firms or persons suffering from that activity, or, in this example, hit by the pollution.

In case of negative externalities, too much is produced or with too much pollution; in the case of positive externalities, the production is usually less than desired. Governments therefore subsidize the latter as well as the consumption of commodities considered beneficial to society (public education and cultural activities, for example). The implementation of any subsidy scheme requires adequate research and constant monitoring by a public authority, since individuals attempting to engage in research or monitoring would face high costs to carry out such activities and polluters are not willing to announce their pollution output level.

The Effects of Subsidies

Besides its beneficial effects on consumer prices and producer protection, subsidizing is blamed for the misallocation of goods because it distorts prices and costs, leading to the perturbation of the competitive equilibrium in the economy. In the presence of subsidies, markets cannot clear in the usual manner and the price mechanism cannot lead to a Pareto-efficient allocation of resources. A Pareto-efficient allocation is that in which nobody can get better off without somebody getting worse off. Of course, such an allocation can be the result of the per-

fect textbook competition, which does not mean at all that such an allocation is socially just or equitable. Subsidies are designed to reduce the level of this social injustice created by the free-market mechanism.

Many governments and home producers consider foreign subsidies a major threat to their industries, whereas those granted by the home government are considered a normal method of support. Producers complaining of unfair competition caused by foreign subsidized goods may call for their government to create a level playing field, that is, conditions promoting fair trade. The governments may argue that they are unable to compete with the seemingly unlimited resources of the foreign governments. As a result, countervailing duties may be imposed, sometimes even if the foreign subsidies are smaller than the domestic ones or not large enough to distort competition. The United States is one country that resorts to this method. Finally, any kind of governmental support may be labeled as a subsidy, and indeed, there are many forms of thinly disguised barriers to trade.

The World Trade Organization's Agreement on Subsidies and Countervailing Measures enables the least developed countries to compete with developed ones on the global market. Under the agreement, the poorer countries receive trade concessions and benefit from special provisions. The use of subsidies is disciplined, and counteractions are regulated. A member country can use the special dispute-settlement procedure to seek the withdrawal of a subsidy or the removal of its adverse effects, or it can launch its own investigation and if necessary charge a countervailing duty on subsidized imports that have negative effects on domestic producers.

In an eight-year period (1995–2003), 169 countervailing duties were reported to the WTO. Of the affected exporting countries, India was in the forefront with 39, followed far behind by Italy and the Republic of Korea (South Korea) with 13 and the EU with 11. The most protected markets proved to be those of the United States, the EU, and Canada, which reported in the same period having imposed 66, 42, and 12 such duties, respectively, against subsidized imports.

Alternatives to Subsidies

One alternative to subsidies would be direct income support. With this approach, the subsidy planner does not have to take existing consumption patterns into account. Granting subsidies without knowing the preferences of consumers, however, may result in the waste of resources. Another alternative would be heavier regulation of polluting industries. If this regulation is tough, then firms will spend more to comply; if it is loose, they will not comply. Under this approach, however, the government would not take proper account of firms' needs and obligations, which could be a drawback because technologies and managements differ. The regulation of pollution is a less efficient way to minimize it than subsidizing pollution-abatement activities, though it is less costly. In the case of regulation, there may be implementation problems and inadequate monitoring of each firm's polluting and pollution-abatement activity.

Laszlo Kocsis

See Also National Government Policies; Nontariff Barriers; Protectionism; Tariffs

References

Bannock, Graham, R. E. Baxter, and Evan Davis. 1987. *The Penguin Dictionary of Economics.* London: Penguin.

Dornbusch, Rudiger, and Stanley Fischer. 1988. *Inflation Stabilization.* Cambridge: MIT Press.

Erdõs, Tibor. 1998. *Infláció, különös tekintettel az 1990-es évek magyar gazdaságára* (Inflation, with special respect to the Hungarian economy of the nineties). Budapest: Akadémiai Kiadó.

Kornai, János. 1992. *The Socialist System: The Political Economy of Communism.* Oxford: Clarendon.

Krugman, Paul R., and Maurice Obstfeld. 1994. *International Economics: Theory and Policy.* New York: HarperCollins.

Lipsey, Richard G., and K. Alec Chrystal. 1995. *An Introduction to Positive Economics.* Oxford: Oxford University Press.

Maddala, G. S., and Ellen Miller. 1989. *Microeconomics: Theory and Applications.* New York: McGraw-Hill.

Pierce, David W., ed. 1986. *Macmillan Dictionary of Modern Economics.* London and Basingstoke: Macmillan.

Stiglitz, Joseph E. 1988. *Economics of the Public Sector.* New York: W. W. Norton.

Varian, Hal. 1990. *Intermediate Microeconomics. A Modern Approach.* New York: W. W. Norton.

World Trade Organization, http://www.wto.org.

Tariffs

Governments often use instruments such as taxes, subsidies, quotas, and many other measures on international transactions. One such instrument is a tariff, or a tax on imported goods. It is sometimes referred to as an "import duty." There are two kinds of tariffs that are levied on imports: (1) specific tariffs, a fixed charge for each unit of goods imported (for example, $3 per barrel of oil, or $0.50 per pound of sugar); and (2) *ad valorem* tariffs, levied as a percentage or fraction of the value of the imported goods (for example, a 25 percent tariff on trucks, or a 10 percent tariff on steel).

Most economists feel that ad valorem tariffs are preferable to specific tariffs for a number of reasons. Specific tariffs are less transparent, as the impact of the tariff depends upon the unit value of the imported commodity. Specific tariffs have a greater impact on cheaper products falling under the same tariff line. Finally, when prices change, so does the effect of specific tariffs. For instance, when prices of traded goods fall, if the specific tariff rate is not reduced, the level of protection will increase.

Tariffs are the oldest form of trade policy. In the past they have been used as a source of government revenue, but more recently they have been used to protect domestic industries from import competition. When a tariff is imposed, there are costs and benefits that affect not only the impacted sector but the rest of the economy as well. The importance of tariffs has declined over time as other forms of protection have been used to protect domestic industries.

Tariff dispersion refers to the extent of tariff peaks and troughs within a country's tariff structure. If there is a wide dispersion in the tariff structure, then there are relatively higher levels of economic inefficiency in the tariff regime. Uniform tariffs are more transparent and easier to administer than widely dispersed tariffs. Furthermore, it is easier to reduce uniform tariffs and more difficult to increase them than for nonuniform tariffs. A useful way to measure tariff dispersion is the standard deviation from the mean. Tariff dispersion varies significantly across countries, as the data in Table 1 show. Tariff dispersion is caused by tariff differences between broad categories of products. In most developed countries, tariffs on textiles and apparel are higher than for other commodities, resulting in greater dispersion. Tariff dispersion also results when a country's tariff structure has tariff peaks. Tariff peaks are tariffs that exceed a given reference level. Economists distinguish between national peaks, in which the reference level is three times the national average, and international peaks, where the reference level is 15 percent higher than an international average. Table 1 shows tariff peaks for selected countries.

Costs and Benefits of Tariffs

A tariff raises the price of a good in the importing country and may lower it in the exporting country. When domestic prices rise as a result of a tariff, consumers are worse off, but the protected industry gains. In addition, the government imposing the tariff gains revenue. When tariffs are imposed by "small" countries, there is

Table 1: Bound Tariffs on Industrial Products: Scope of Bindings, Simple Averages, Standard Deviations, and Tariff Peaks

Import Markets	Total Number of Tariff Lines	Share of Bound Tariff Lines	Share of Bound Duty-Free Tariff Lines	Share of Unbound Duty-Free Tariff Lines	Share of Non-Ad Valorem Tariff Lines	Simple Average Bound Tariff	Standard Deviation	Share of Tariff Lines with Duties More than 3 times the Average	Share of Tariff Lines with Duties about 15%
North America									
Canada	6261	99.6	34.5	0.1	0.3	5.2	5.0	5.8	5.8
United States	7872	100.0	39.4	0.0	4.2	3.9	5.6	7.5	3.5
Latin America									
Argentina	10530	100.0	0.0	0.0	N.A	31.0	6.7	0.0	99.7
Brazil	10860	100.0	0.5	0.0	0.0	30.0	7.4	0.0	97.4
Chile	5055	100.0	0.0	0.0	0.1	25.0	0.5	0.0	99.9
Colombia	6145	100.0	0.0	0.0	0.2	35.5	3.3	0.0	100.0
Costa Rica	1546	100.0	0.0	0.0	N.A	44.6	5.5	0.0	99.8
El Salvador	4922	100.0	0.0	0.0	0.0	36.9	8.1	0.0	100.0
Jamaica	3097	100.0	0.0	0.0	0.0	50.0	0.9	0.0	100.0
Mexico	11255	100.0	0.0	0.0	0.0	34.8	3.4	0.0	99.3
Peru	4545	100.0	0.0	0.0	N.A	30.0	0.0	0.6	100.0
Venezuela	5974	100.0	0.0	0.0	0.0	33.9	3.7	0.0	99.2
Western Europe									
European Union	7635	100.0	26.9	0.0	0.5	4.1	4.0	2.6	1.5
Iceland	5689	93.2	41.6	2.9	0.0	9.7	11.9	9.2	28.1
Norway	5326	100.0	46.5	0.0	2.6	3.4	6.2	10.6	0.3
Switzerland	6217	98.9	17.2	0.0	82.8	1.8	4.6	8.7	0.3
Turkey	15479	36.3	1.4	0.8	0.1	42.6	36.7	3.5	73.9
Eastern Europe									
Czech Republic	4354	100.0	14.0	0.0	0.0	4.3	3.1	1.2	0.9
Hungary	5896	95.4	10.4	0.2	0.1	7.4	5.4	2.0	3.1
Poland	4354	95.8	2.2	0.0	0.0	10.4	5.2	1.2	13.3
Romania	4602	100.0	5.8	0.0	0.0	30.8	9.8	0.0	90.1
Slovak Republic	4354	100.0	14.0	0.0	0.0	4.3	3.1	1.2	0.9
Asia									
Australia	5520	95.9	17.7	0.2	0.8	14.2	14.7	6.3	25.3
Hong Kong, China	5110	23.5	23.5	76.5	0.0	0.0	0.0	0.0	0.0
India	4354	61.6	0.0	0.4	1.1	58.7	33.3	0.1	97.8
Indonesia	7735	93.2	0.0	1.2	0.0	38.9	12.3	0.3	97.2

Table 1 (continued)

Import Markets	Total Number of Tariff Lines	Share of Bound Tariff Lines	Share of Bound Duty-Free Tariff Lines	Share of Unbound Duty-Free Tariff Lines	Share of Non-Ad Volorem Tariff Lines	Simple Average Bound Tariff	Standard Deviation	Share of Tariff Lines with Duties More than 3 times the Average	Share of Tariff Lines with Duties about 15%
Japan	7339	99.2	47.4	0.4	3.5	3.5	6.0	5.2	1.8
Korea, Republic of	8882	90.4	11.6	0.0	0.2	11.7	9.6	1.4	19.1
Macau, China	5337	9.9	9.9	90.1	0.0	0.0	0.0	0.0	0.0
Malaysia	10832	61.8	1.6	2.8	3.2	17.2	13.4	0.4	58.3
New Zealand	5894	100.0	39.4	0.0	2.5	12.7	15.7	4.0	39.5
Philippines	5387	58.6	0.0	0.0	4.1	26.1	12.0	0.0	82.7
Singapore	4963	65.5	15.2	33.8	0.2	4.6	4.8	0.5	0.2
Sri Lanka	5933	8.0	0.1	1.4	22.4	28.1	24.1	0.2	52.0
Thailand	5244	67.9	0.0	1.2	19.7	27.5	10.6	0.1	87.1
Africa									
Cameroon	4721	0.1	0.0	0.0	0.0	17.6	9.4	0.0	45.8
Chad	4721	0.4	0.0	0.0	0.0	17.8	10.0	0.4	45.8
Gabon	4721	100.0	0.0	0.0	0.0	15.5	4.8	1.1	1.3
Senegal	2818	32.3	0.9	0.0	N.A	13.8	5.3	0.0	79.2
South Africa	11677	98.1	7.7	0.3	1.3	17.7	10.9	0.1	46.4
Tunisia	5087	46.3	0.0	1.0	0.0	34.0	15.0	0.0	98.4
Zimbabwe	1929	8.8	3.0	44.7	NA	11.3	13.0	9.3	44.1

Notes: The data in all columns exclude petroleum. In Column 2, "Share of Bound Tariff Lines," all shares are expressed as a percentage of the total number of industrial tariff lines.
Source: World Trade Organization, IDB (Integrated Database), Loose Leaf Schedule and national custom charts.

Figure 1: Effect of a Tariff: Small Country Case

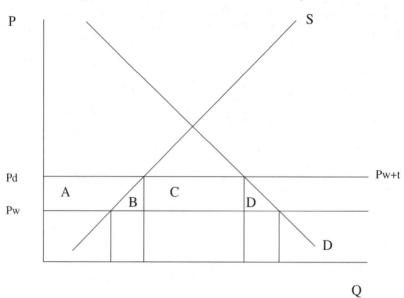

no effect on the foreign price of the good. This is because the country in question imports a very small share of the good so that its action has no effect on the world price of the good. However, when a tariff is imposed by a "large" country, one that can affect the quantity of the good traded, it causes the world price to fall.

Figure 1 illustrates the effect of a tariff on the industry or market being affected. When the country is small, the tariff raises the domestic price by the full amount of the tariff. The price of the domestic good rises from Pw to Pd, domestic production increases, and imports are reduced. The government receives tariff revenue. Consumers are worse off, since they are now paying a higher price and consuming less. Domestic producers are better off, since they are producing more at higher prices. Hence, the primary objective of the tariff is to protect domestic industries from import competition. In addition, the government receives tariff revenue. The overall effect of the tariff can be seen by evaluating the loss to consumers with the gains that accrue to domestic producers and the government. In Figure 1, the areas A + B + C + D denote the loss to consumers from paying higher prices and consuming less (also

known as the loss in consumer surplus, the difference between what consumers were willing to pay and what they actually pay). Domestic producers gain in the amount equal to A (also known as the gain in producer surplus, the difference between what producers receive and the minimum price they are willing to supply the good for), whereas government tariff revenue is equal to the area C. The tariff unambiguously reduces welfare by the area B + D. From the imposing country's point of view, a tariff leads to welfare losses or net social losses. The consumer loss is too large to be offset by the gain to producers and to the government. The area B is called the "production distortion loss" because the tariff leads domestic producers to produce more of the good at a distorted higher price. There is inefficiency in production, since extra resources are being used in domestic production that should be used in the production of other goods. The area D is called the "consumption distortion loss" because the tariff leads consumers to consume too little of the good at the distorted higher price.

Figure 2 illustrates the effect of a tariff when the country imposing the tariff is large. Now the tariff raises the domestic price from Pw to

Figure 2: Effect of a Tariff: Large Country Case

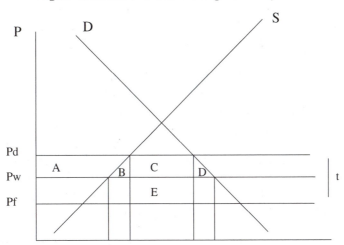

Pd but lowers the foreign price from Pw to Pf. Domestic production rises, while domestic consumption falls. Once again, the costs and benefits of the tariff can be expressed as sums of the areas in the figure. Consumers lose the areas A + B + C + D, and domestic producers gain area A. The government, however, gains area C + E in the form of tariff revenue. This additional gain in revenue for the large country's government, the area E, is referred to as the "terms-of-trade gain." Thus, the overall welfare effect of the tariff is ambiguous, since it depends on whether the areas B + D are greater than or less than the area E. In the case of a large country, there is a possibility that a tariff can be welfare improving. The analysis ignores the possibility of tariff retaliation, which could negate any welfare-improving effects.

From an economy-wide perspective, tariffs reduce welfare because they restrict trade and competition, prevent the attainment of scale economies and specialization, and result in inefficiencies in resource allocation. Finally, tariffs on imports can eventually penalize a country's own exports via a pass-through effect. As tariffs cause imports to fall, less foreign exchange is used to purchase them, and hence the demand for foreign currency declines. This causes a relative increase in the importing country's currency in the foreign exchange market, making exports more expensive. Furthermore, since tariffs cause higher domestic prices, those prices are "passed on" to other nontraded goods and services in the economy, causing higher economy-wide prices.

The Effective Rate of Protection and Tariff Escalation

A tariff on an imported good enables domestic producers to raise their prices for similar goods. Thus, the principal objective of a tariff is to protect domestic producers from the impact of low world prices. Clearly, the higher the tariff on a good, the higher the protection enjoyed by the domestic firms. However, the degree or extent of protection enjoyed is not evident from the nominal tariff rate alone. Although the nominal tariff rate indicates the nominal rate of protection enjoyed by domestic firms, the effective rate of protection (ERP) provides a better measure of the degree of protection enjoyed by an industry. The effective rate of protection is simply the increase in the value added to the product resulting from the tariff. A simple example illustrates this concept.

If the world price of cotton textiles is $100 per unit, and the value of inputs used to produce the textiles is $80 per unit, then, in the absence of any tariffs, domestic textile producers receive $20 per unit in added value (the difference between $100 and $80). This amount is the profit margin enjoyed in the textile industry. If the country imposes a 10 percent tariff on cotton textiles, the domestic price of textiles increases to $110, and with no tax on inputs, the value added to textiles in the domestic textile industry is now $30. The value added to the product increased from $20 to $30, a 50 percent increase. A nominal protection rate of 10 percent led to an effective rate of protection equal to 50 percent. The ERP will be higher the higher the nominal tariff rate, and higher the value of inputs per unit of the output. The ERP will be lower if there is a tax on inputs.

When effective tariffs are much higher on finished goods than they are on raw materials, this is known as "tariff escalation." When tariffs escalate with the stage of processing, the ERP also increases. The wide disparities between nominal tariffs on raw materials and processed goods imply that many developing countries are at a disadvantage when trying to export manufactured goods to the industrial countries. Table 2 shows the extent of tariff escalation for a selected group of World Trade Organization (WTO) members. The data show that tariff escalation differs significantly across countries. In the United States, tariffs are higher for semimanufactured goods than for raw materials.

Most tariffs are undertaken to protect the income of particular interest groups. Figures 1 and 2 illustrate the gains to domestic producers that result from tariffs. However, other arguments have been proposed to justify the use of tariffs. One argument has to do with the fact that when a tariff is imposed by a large country, it could lead to lower world prices and hence a terms-of-trade benefit for the imposing country. Although this is theoretically possible for small tariffs, as tariff rates are increased the costs begin to outweigh the benefits. A second argument often made with respect to developing countries is that temporary tariffs are needed to allow infant industries to grow and compete with well-established manufacturing in developed countries. The infant-industry argument is plausible and has been used by many governments. Economists often point to the dangers of using this argument, however. In particular, they argue that it is often difficult and costly to predict which industries will have the best chance to compete globally. Second, protecting manufacturing is futile unless it makes the industries competitive. The evidence suggests that several developing countries have protected their domestic industries for long periods with little or no improvement in the competitiveness of the industry.

Thus, there is very little economic rationale for tariff protection. There is a growing body of literature on the role of political processes that result in protectionist pressures (Baldwin 1985; Bhagwati 1988; Grossman and Helpman 1994; Stern 1987). These studies illustrate how electoral competition and collective action can result in protection for certain industries. Tariff protection has been argued to stem the loss of jobs in certain industries, to protect certain strategic industries (agriculture and defense-related enterprises, for example), and even to counter unfair trade practices of other countries. However, the negotiations achieved through several rounds of talks within the General Agreement on Tariffs and Trade (GATT) resulted in a substantial lowering of tariff rates across member countries.

GATT Rounds and Tariff Reduction

From 1948 to 1994, the GATT provided the rules for much of world trade and presided over periods that saw some of the highest growth rates in international trade. The original intention was to create a third institution handling international economic cooperation to join the "Bretton Woods" institutions now known as the World Bank and the International Monetary Fund (IMF). The complete

Table 2: Bound Tariffs on Industrial Products: Simple Average Tariff and Standard Deviation by Stage of Processing

Import Markets	Stage of Processing	Average Rate	Standard Deviation
North America			
Canada	Raw materials	1.6	3.0
	Semi-manufactures	4.8	4.5
	Finished products	5.7	5.3
United States	Raw materials	0.8	2.2
	Semi-manufactures	4.1	4.2
	Finished products	4.1	6.5
Latin America			
Brazil	Raw materials	33.3	5.9
	Semi-manufactures	26.6	8.1
	Finished products	32.3	5.8
Chile	Raw materials	24.9	1.2
	Semi-manufactures	25.0	0.0
	Finished products	25.0	0.5
Colombia	Raw materials	35.1	1.1
	Semi-manufactures	35.0	0.8
	Finished products	35.8	4.3
El Salvador	Raw materials	38.8	6.6
	Semi-manufactures	35.9	7.9
	Finished products	37.3	8.2
Jamaica	Raw materials	50.0	0.0
	Semi-manufactures	50.0	0.0
	Finished products	50.0	1.1
Mexico	Raw materials	33.8	5.8
	Semi-manufactures	34.8	3.0
	Finished products	34.9	3.5
Venezuela	Raw materials	34.0	4.0
	Semi-manufactures	33.9	3.7
	Finished products	33.9	3.7
Western Europe			
European Union	Raw materials	5.1	6.7
	Semi-manufactures	4.0	3.2
	Finished products	4.0	4.0
Iceland	Raw materials	1.7	6.1
	Semi-manufactures	2.7	4.8
	Finished products	15.4	12.6
Norway	Raw materials	0.1	0.6
	Semi-manufactures	3.0	4.1
	Finished products	4.0	7.3
Switzerland	Raw materials	1.0	7.3
	Semi-manufactures	2.0	6.6
	Finished products	1.8	2.5
Turkey	Raw materials	20.9	13.8
	Semi-manufactures	40.4	36.2
	Finished products	46.9	37.9

continues

Table 2: Bound Tariffs on Industrial Products: Simple Average Tariff and Standard Deviation by Stage of Processing (*continued*)

Import Markets	Stage of Processing	Average Rate	Standard Deviation
Eastern Europe			
Czech Republic	Raw materials	0.9	2.9
	Semi-manufactures	4.2	2.5
	Finished products	4.9	3.2
Hungary	Raw materials	5.3	6.4
	Semi-manufactures	5.4	3.6
	Finished products	8.9	5.8
Poland	Raw materials	6.2	8.4
	Semi-manufactures	9.3	2.7
	Finished products	11.6	5.4
Romania	Raw materials	31.2	8.2
	Semi-manufactures	31.9	8.4
	Finished products	30.1	10.6
Slovak Republic	Raw materials	0.9	2.9
	Semi-manufactures	4.2	2.5
	Finished products	4.9	3.2
Asia			
Australia	Raw materials	1.5	3.7
	Semi-manufactures	12.3	11.3
	Finished products	16.7	16.4
Hong Kong, China	Raw materials	0.0	0.0
	Semi-manufactures	0.0	0.0
	Finished products	0.0	0.0
India	Raw materials	41.3	14.7
	Semi-manufactures	52.4	30.2
	Finished products	65.1	35.3
Indonesia	Raw materials	39.5	3.3
	Semi-manufactures	38.0	6.1
	Finished products	39.5	15.6
Japan	Raw materials	2.2	3.2
	Semi-manufactures	4.0	3.6
	Finished products	3.4	7.6
Korea, Republic of	Raw materials	8.7	7.2
	Semi-manufactures	8.0	5.4
	Finished products	14.3	11.0
Macau, China	Raw materials	0.0	0.0
	Semi-manufactures	0.0	0.0
	Finished products	0.0	0.0
Malaysia	Raw materials	16.6	8.1
	Semi-manufactures	16.9	10.7
	Finished products	17.8	16.9
New Zealand	Raw materials	1.6	4.3
	Semi-manufactures	6.8	8.9
	Finished products	17.3	17.7
Philippines	Raw materials	19.0	11.5
	Semi-manufactures	23.4	9.5
	Finished products	29.1	12.8
Sri Lanka	Raw materials	25.0	22.3
	Semi-manufactures	25.7	23.4
	Finished products	30.5	24.6
Singapore	Raw materials	4.7	5.0
	Semi-manufactures	4.6	4.1
	Finished products	4.5	5.1
Thailand	Raw materials	17.9	13.4
	Semi-manufactures	26.9	8.0
	Finished products	29.3	10.7

continues

Table 2: Bound Tariffs on Industrial Products: Simple Average Tariff and Standard Deviation by Stage of Processing (*continued*)

Import Markets	Stage of Processing	Average Rate	Standard Deviation
Africa			
Cameroon	Raw materials	17.1	9.1
	Semi-manufactures	14.5	7.7
	Finished products	19.7	9.9
Chad	Raw materials	17.0	17.0
	Semi-manufactures	14.4	14.4
	Finished products	20.0	20.0
Gabon	Raw materials	15.0	0.0
	Semi-manufactures	15.1	2.4
	Finished products	15.9	6.1
South Africa	Raw materials	7.8	16.6
	Semi-manufactures	16.1	7.6
	Finished products	19.8	12.1
Tunisia	Raw materials	29.1	16.2
	Semi-manufactures	32.5	15.4
	Finished products	32.5	14.4

Source: World Trade Organization, IDB (Integrated Database), Loose Leaf Schedule and national custom charts.

plan was to create an International Trade Organization (ITO) as a specialized agency of the United Nations. The draft ITO Charter extended beyond world trade disciplines to include rules on employment, commodity agreements, restrictive business practices, international investment, and services.

Even before the charter was finally approved, twenty-three of the fifty participants decided in 1946 to negotiate to reduce and bind customs tariffs. With World War II only recently ended, they wanted to give an early boost to trade liberalization and to begin to correct the large legacy of protectionist measures that remained in place from the early 1930s.

This first round of negotiations resulted in 45,000 tariff concessions affecting $10 billion of trade, about one-fifth of the world's total. The twenty-three countries also agreed that they should accept some of the trade rules of the draft ITO Charter. The combined package of trade rules and tariff concessions became known as the General Agreement on Tariffs and Trade. It entered into force in January 1948, while the ITO Charter was still being ne-

gotiated, and those same twenty-three countries became founding GATT members (officially, "contracting parties").

Although the ITO Charter was finally agreed upon at a UN Conference on Trade and Employment in Havana in March 1948, ratification in some national legislatures proved impossible. The most serious opposition was in the U.S. Congress, even though the U.S. government had been one of the driving forces. In 1950, the United States announced that it would not seek congressional ratification of the Havana Charter, and the ITO was effectively dead. Even though it was provisional, the GATT remained the only multilateral instrument governing international trade from 1948 until the WTO was established in 1995.

For almost half a century, the GATT's basic legal text remained much as it was in 1948. There were additions in the form of "plurilateral" agreements (that is, with voluntary membership), and efforts to further reduce tariffs continued. Much of this was achieved through a series of multilateral negotiations known as "trade rounds." The biggest leaps forward in international trade liberalization have come

Table 3: A Round-by-Round Analysis of Tariff Reductions

Name of Round	Dates	Number of Participants	Tariff Cut (%)	Subject Covered
Geneva	1947	23	73	Tariffs
Annecy, France	1949	13		Tariffs
Torquay, England	1951	38	73	Tariffs
Geneva	1956	26		Tariffs
Dillon Round, Geneva	1960–1961	26		Tariffs
Kennedy Round, Geneva	1964–1967	62	35	Tariffs and antidumping
Tokyo Round	1973–1979	102	33	Tariffs, nontariff measures
Uruguay Round	1986–1994	130	40	Tariffs, nontariff measures, rules, services, intellectual property, dispute settlement, textiles, agriculture, creation of WTO

through these rounds, which were held under GATT's auspices.

In the early years, the GATT trade rounds concentrated on reducing tariffs. Then, the Kennedy Round in the mid-1960s brought about a GATT Anti-Dumping Agreement. The Tokyo Round during the 1970s was the first major attempt to tackle trade barriers that did not take the form of tariffs, as well as to improve the system. The eighth, the Uruguay Round of 1986–1994, was the latest and most extensive of all. It led to the WTO and a new set of agreements.

The Tokyo Round lasted from 1973 to 1979, with 102 countries participating. It continued GATT's efforts to progressively reduce tariffs. The results included an average one-third cut in customs duties in the world's nine major industrial markets, which brought the average tariff on industrial products down to 4.7 percent. The tariff reductions, phased in over a period of eight years, involved an element of "harmonization"—the higher the tariff, the larger the cut, proportionally.

GATT was provisional, with a limited field of action, but its success over forty-seven years in promoting and securing the liberalization of much of world trade is incontestable. Continual

reductions in tariffs alone helped spur very high rates of world trade growth during the 1950s and 1960s—around 8 percent a year on average. And the momentum of trade liberalization helped ensure that trade growth consistently outpaced production growth throughout the GATT era, a measure of countries' increasing ability to trade with each other and to reap the benefits of trade. The rush of new members during the Uruguay Round demonstrated that the multilateral trading system was recognized as an anchor for development and an instrument of economic and trade reform.

GATT's success in reducing tariffs to such a low level, combined with a series of economic recessions in the 1970s and early 1980s, drove governments to devise other forms of protection for sectors facing increased foreign competition. High rates of unemployment and constant factory closures led governments in Western Europe and North America to seek bilateral market-sharing arrangements with competitors and to embark on a subsidies race to maintain their holds on agricultural trade. Both these changes undermined GATT's credibility and effectiveness.

By the early 1980s, the General Agreement was no longer relevant to the realities of world trade. Trade had become far more complex, international investment had expanded, and trade in services had grown significantly. Agricultural trade was not covered by GATT rules, and even in the textiles and clothing sector, an exception to GATT's normal disciplines was negotiated in the 1960s and early 1970s, leading to the Multifibre Arrangement. Even GATT's institutional structure and its dispute settlement system were giving cause for concern.

These and other factors convinced GATT members that a new effort to reinforce and extend the multilateral system should be attempted. That effort resulted in the Uruguay Round, the Marrakesh Declaration, and the creation of the WTO.

The WTO and Tariffs

At the Uruguay Round, approximately 130 countries made tariff concessions. A country makes a tariff concession by submitting to the WTO a schedule of commitments of bound rates. The commitment represents the member country's legal obligation not to impose a tariff on any listed product at a rate higher than the specified bound rate. Table 1 summarizes the increase in bindings and the tariff reductions that were expected from the Uruguay Round commitments. The data show that the share of post–Uruguay Round industrial tariffs covered by bindings is above 95 percent for most developed countries and transition economies. For developing countries, the share varies between 10 percent and 100 percent. The Uruguay Round led to an agreement by the industrial countries to cut their tariffs by 40 percent, in five equal steps of 8 percent each, beginning in 1995. The WTO maintains a database that includes national tariff schedules for most countries, based on submissions to the WTO at the conclusion of the Uruguay Round. In the WTO, when countries agree to open their markets for goods or services, they "bind" their commitments. For goods, these bindings amount to ceilings on customs tariff rates. Sometimes

countries tax imports at rates that are lower than the bound rates. Frequently this is the case in developing countries. In developed countries the rates actually charged and the bound rates tend to be the same.

These official tariff rates cannot be raised unless a negotiated waiver is arranged. The duty that is actually applied to imported products, whether it is at the bound rate or at a lower rate, is called the "applied tariff rate." The applied tariff rate can change frequently depending upon the supply of the product, the demand for the product, and the political situation in the importing country. Some developing countries also apply a "ceiling binding," a single tariff rate for all agricultural products. Applied rates less than the ceiling binding may exist for specific items of interest to that country. Currently, the WTO has no mechanism requiring the notification of applied tariff rates. The members of Asia Pacific Economic Cooperation (APEC), including the United States, have agreed to maintain updated schedules of applied tariffs on the World Wide Web. The other members are Australia, Brunei, Canada, Chile, China, Hong Kong, Indonesia, Japan, South Korea, Malaysia, Mexico, New Zealand, Papua–New Guinea, Philippines, Singapore, Taiwan, and Thailand. The site can be found at www.apectariff.org.

A country can change its bindings, but only after negotiating with its trading partners, which could mean compensating them for loss of trade. One of the achievements of the Uruguay Round of multilateral trade talks was to increase the amount of trade under binding commitments. In agriculture, 100 percent of products now have bound tariffs. The result of all this is a substantially higher degree of market security for traders and investors.

The fundamental results of the Uruguay Round have been the 22,500 pages listing individual countries' commitments on specific categories of goods and services. These include commitments to cut and "bind" their customs duty rates on imports of goods. In some cases, tariffs have been cut to zero—with zero rates

Table 4: Uruguay Round Tariff Concessions Given and Received

	Bindings (% of 1989 imports)		Tariff Reductions Depth of cut	
	Pre-UR	Post-UR	% of Imports	(dT/(1+T))
Tariff concessions given, all merchandise				
Developed economies	80	89	30	1.0
Developing economies	30	81	29	2.3
All	73	87	30	1.2
Tariff concessions received, all merchandise				
Developed economies	77	91	36	1.4
Developing economies	64	78	28	1.0
All	73	87	33	1.3
Tariff concessions given, industrial goods				
Developed economies	85	92	32	1.0
Developing economies	32	84	33	2.7
All	77	91	32	1.3
Tariff concessions received, industrial goods				
Developed economies	79	93	37	1.5
Developing economies	72	86	36	1.2
All	77	91	37	1.4

also committed in 1997 on information technology products. Developed countries' tariff cuts were for the most part phased in over five years beginning 1 January 1995. The result was a 40 percent cut in tariffs on industrial products, from an average of 6.3 percent to 3.8 percent. The value of imported industrial products that receive duty-free treatment in developed countries jumped from 20 percent to 44 percent. There are also fewer products charged high duty rates. The proportion of imports into developed countries from all sources facing tariff rates of more than 15 percent declined from 7 percent to 5 percent. The proportion of developing-country exports facing tariffs above 15 percent in industrial countries fell from 9 percent to 5 percent.

Developed countries increased the number of imports with bound tariff rates from 78 percent of product lines to 99 percent. For developing countries, the increase was considerable: from 21 percent to 73 percent. Economies in transition from central planning increased their bindings from 73 percent to 98 percent.

Table 4 illustrates the tariff bindings for both developed and developing countries as a result of the Uruguay Round.

Table 5 shows the post–Uruguay Round averages of bound and applied rates. As the data show, developing countries agreed to larger cuts, but their tariffs, on average, are still considerably higher than those of developed countries.

A major accomplishment of the Uruguay Round was to negotiate an Agreement on Agriculture, which created a "tariffs-only" framework in which nontariff barriers were replaced by tariffs. Tariffs on all agricultural products are now bound. Almost all import restrictions that did not take the form of tariffs, such as quotas, have been converted to tariffs—a process known as "tariffication." About forty countries participated in this process, which covered twenty-two tariff lines. This has made markets substantially more predictable for agriculture. Previously, more than 30 percent of agricultural produce had faced quotas or import restrictions. At first, they were converted

Table 5: Post-Uruguay Round Tariff Rates, All Merchandise

	Bound Rate, Average Ad Valorem	Post-UR Bound Rate above Applied Rate	Applied Rate, Average Ad Valorem
Developed economies	3.5	19	2.6
Developing economies	25.2	37	13.3
All	6.5	22	4.3

Note: Column 2, "Post-UR Bound Rate above Applied Rate," shows percentage of 1989 imports.

Source: J. Michael Finger and Ludger Schuknecht. "Market Access Advances and Retreats: The Uruguay Round and Beyond," World Bank Working Paper 2232 (November 1999).

to tariffs that represented about the same level of protection as the previous restrictions, but over six years these tariffs have been gradually reduced. The market-access commitments on agriculture are being eliminated. Table 6 summarizes the Uruguay Round Agreement on Agriculture.

The Multi-Fiber Arrangement and an agreement to cut tariffs on textiles were other important accomplishments of the Uruguay Round. Most of the restrictions on textiles and apparel are being eliminated beginning in 2005. Although developed countries were expected to eliminate the restrictions in stages, most have postponed elimination until 2005. Developed countries' tariffs on textiles and clothing remain high when compared to other industrial goods.

Since the Uruguay Round, WTO members have agreed to further tariff reductions. The largest of these came under the Information Technology Agreement, signed in April 1997 by forty countries accounting for more than 92 percent of world trade in information technology (IT) products. The products it covered included computers, semiconductors, telecom equipment, software, and scientific instruments. Another post–Uruguay Round cut in tariffs was applied to pharmaceutical products and involved the United States, Canada, the European Union, and Japan. Other significant cuts in tariffs have been achieved through regional trade agreements such as the South Asian Association for Regional Cooperation

(SAARC) and the Association of Southeast Asian Nations (ASEAN).

Though much progress has been made with respect to tariff reductions through multilateral negotiations, improving market access across countries may require additional measures to be implemented. For instance, although an exporting country may take the situation to the WTO and its dispute settlement process if a member country levies a tariff rate above the bound rate, WTO members have no specific mechanism to monitor the implementation of tariff commitments. High agricultural tariffs still need to be reduced, and special attention needs to be paid to tariff escalation. Tariff peaks feature prominently in many industrial countries, affecting, for example, imports of leather, clothing and footwear, and vehicles, as well as a range of agricultural raw materials and processed foodstuffs. Furthermore, average tariffs remain relatively high in most developing countries, and in some cases they have increased in recent years as quantitative trade restrictions have been replaced by welfare-superior tariffs. Future efforts will likely focus on seeking deeper reductions in tariffs, particularly in textiles and agriculture; greater percentages of bound tariffs; reductions in the gap between bound and applied rates; and limitations on the use of mechanisms allowed under WTO rules for temporarily raising rates in extraordinary circumstances.

Ashish Vaidya

Table 6: Uruguay Round Agreement on Agriculture: Base Rates and Rates of Reduction

Pre–Uruguay Round Situation	Developed Countries		Developing Countries	
	Base Rate	Reduction	Base Rate	Reduction
Bound rate	Bound rate	36% unweighted average cut, with minimum 15% per tariff line	Bound rate	24% unweighted average cut, with minimum 10% per tariff line
Unbound rate	Applied rate in September 1986	36% unweighted average cut, with minimum 15% per tariff line	Ceiling binding	No reduction
Bound rate cum nontariff measures	Tariffication	36% unweighted average cut, with minimum 15% per tariff line	Tariffication	24% unweighted average cut, with minimum 10% per tariff line
Unbound rate cum nontariff measures	Tariffication	36% unweighted average cut, with minimum 15% per tariff line	Tariffication	24% unweighted average cut, with minimum 10% per tariff line *or*
			Ceiling binding	No reduction

Source: World Trade Organization, Market Access: *Unfinished Business. Post Uruguay Round Inventory and Issues* (Geneva: WTO, 2000).

See also Antidumping and countervailing duties; National Government Policies; Nontariff Barriers; Protectionism; Subsidies; GATT; World Trade Organization (WTO); U.S. Trade Laws

References

Baldwin, Robert. 1985. *The Political Economy of US Import Policy.* Cambridge: MIT Press.

Bhagwati, Jagdish. 1988. *Protectionism.* Cambridge: MIT Press.

Finger, J. Michael, Merlinda D. Ingco, and Ulrich Reincke. 1996. *The Uruguay Round: Statistics on Tariff Concessions Given and Received.* Washington, DC: World Bank.

Finger, J. Michael, and Ludger Schuknecht. 1999. "Market Access Advances and Retreats: The Uruguay Round and Beyond." World Bank Working Paper 2232, November.

General Agreement on Tariffs and Trade. 1993. *Overview of Developments in International Trade and the Trading System.* Annual Report by the Director General, Geneva.

Grossman, Gene, and Elhanan Helpman. 1994. "Protection for Sale." *American Economic Review* (September): 833–850.

Krugman, Paul, and Maurice Obstfeld. 2003. *International Economics,* 6th ed. Reading, MA: Addison-Wesley.

Stern, Robert, ed. 1987. *US Trade Policies in a Changing World Economy.* Cambridge: MIT Press.

World Trade Organization. 2000. *Market Access: Unfinished Business. Post Uruguay Round Inventory and Issues.* Geneva: WTO.

Technical Barriers
to Trade

Technical barriers to trade (TBTs) are regulations and standards imposed by individual countries on traded goods that may create obstacles to free multilateral trade. They include testing and certification procedures to assure, for example, high technical standards for particular types of equipment. These standards may make it difficult or more costly for firms to export to the country that has imposed the measures. Countries may have requirements for recycling certain materials (for example, components of refrigerator units or used cars) that may create extra costs for foreign firms. Most countries place restrictions on the quality of the ingredients used in food products, and many require the ingredients to be labeled on the product packaging. This type of barrier is relatively easy to overcome through compliance with the regulations, but other TBTs may be more difficult to surmount. Measures taken to protect the environment, for instance, may require technical expertise or preclude trade in certain items (for example, measures requiring automobiles to meet emissions standards, banning the use of certain materials, and so on). Although such restrictions may be justified in their own terms, the obstacles or barriers to trade that they create often come under sharp debate.

Main Types of Technical Barriers to Trade

Technical barriers to trade may be divided into a number of different types (WTO 2002a). First, and most important, are measures taken for the protection of human health and safety. These include standards for electrical equipment, regulations on the use of fire-retardant materials in the production of household furniture, and so on. They also involve regulations on food, drink, and tobacco products (such as requirements that harmful materials are not used, that labeling of contents is accurate, that weights and measures are correct, and so on). In the case of tobacco products, these restrictions include the statements printed on cigarette packages saying that cigarettes are damaging to human health. In addition, some countries require testing of products (for example, meat products) before imports are allowed into the country. These requirements are typically paid for by the importer and add to the costs of exporting for the foreign firm.

Second, measures can be taken for the protection of animal and plant life and health. For example, countries may have in place measures designed to protect an endangered species or certain rare plants. Thus, in some countries, products from various marine animals (for example, whales) are protected, and some fish may be protected if they are below a certain size. In many countries (especially developed countries), trade in specific animal products is banned (such as ivory, medical ingredients derived from endangered animals, and so on). Products made from plants or trees (for example, from the rainforests of South America) may also be banned.

Third, measures are frequently put in place to protect the environment. These include requirements on emissions from automobiles, safety measures governing the transport of dangerous materials, and restrictions against products known to generate environmentally harmful substances such as chlorofluorocarbons (CFCs). Increasingly, advanced industrial countries are becoming more aware of the environmental hazards associated with waste products, as well as of the need to recycle, and measures taken to deal with these concerns have also led to increased costs to producers (which, arguably, fall more heavily on foreign than on domestic firms).

Finally, regulations may be put in place to protect the public against deceptive practices or to provide quality control. For example, controls on labeling, on weights and measures, and so on fall into this category.

Problems with Technical Barriers

Regulations on traded goods may create obstacles to trade for several reasons. First, they may put importers at a disadvantage or require them to modify their product to meet the standard. A domestic firm may be able to meet the standard more easily, or the importer may have to engage in costly modification of production equipment to meet the standard. In the latter case, the importer may find it more costly to produce the modified product because it has to sacrifice economies of scale in production, or it may have to engage in costly research activity before it can modify its product. This can be a major problem if different countries use different standards or regulations, in which case costs may be considerably higher to meet multiple sets of standards. Second, product testing of imported products to ensure that the standards are met may be also costly and time consuming. If the tests do not apply to domestic products, the importer may be at a considerable cost disadvantage (and, indeed, these measures might be designed to have this effect).

Third, importers may have to pay for translators and local agents to keep them up-to-date about new or changed regulations in the differ-

ent countries in which they compete. Moreover, foreign firms have an even greater disadvantage when the disparity in regulations and standards between different countries is large. In some cases, foreign firms may conclude that the regulations are so complex that it is not worth exporting to some countries at all; in others, higher costs imply more limited trade than would otherwise be the case. In both cases, policy action may be required to overcome the barriers to trade that result from the regulations.

Policy Measures: The WTO Agreement

Though it was recognized early on that technical regulations could present barriers to trade just as more explicit barriers such as tariffs and quotas could, little progress was made in the early history of multilateral policy in this area. The 1947 General Agreement on Tariffs and Trade (GATT) only made passing reference to the problem, and no action was taken for a period of more than twenty years. At the end of the Tokyo Round of multilateral negotiations (1973–1979), however, thirty-two contracting parties signed an agreement on technical barriers to trade. The aim of this agreement was to provide for fair and unbiased treatment in the application of standards and testing, to encourage harmonization of standards where possible, and to remove any unnecessary barriers to trade.

Following the Uruguay Round of negotiations (1986–1994), which led to the establishment of the World Trade Organization (WTO), provisions on technical barriers to trade were clarified and extended. The Agreement on Technical Barriers to Trade (TBT Agreement) was one of the founding agreements of the WTO in 1995 and provided the basis of current world trade policy in this area.

Objectives of the Agreement
A number of objectives drove the TBT Agreement (WTO 2002a, 2002b; see also Qureshi

1996; Das 1999). First, although the agreement recognizes that countries have a right to set their own standards on human, animal, and plant life or health; protection of the environment; and protection of consumers, it requires contracting parties, where possible, to avoid unnecessary obstacles to trade. Second, it requires that signatories set standards that are fair and unbiased and to avoid creating standards and tests that discriminate against foreign firms. Third, the policy encourages the contracting parties to work toward the creation of international standards and regulations and to harmonize existing regulations. The policy also calls for transparency and information provision to make it clearer what standards and testing are required.

Provisions of the Agreement

The agreement is not mandatory but urges contracting parties, where possible, to reduce TBTs in the general interest of promoting multilateral trade. Article 1 states that the agreement applies to all products, including industrial and agricultural products, but excluding sanitary and phytosanitary standards. The agreement covers technical regulations, standards, and conformity assessment, where "technical regulations" refers to mandatory requirements of countries, "standards" refers to nonmandatory requirements, and "conformity assessment" refers to testing regulations and standards. Article 2 requires all member governments to treat imports fairly and equally with products of domestic origin and products from other countries. Members are also asked to ensure that regulations are not prepared with a view or effect of creating unnecessary obstacles to trade. Technical regulations should not be more restrictive of trade than is required to meet some other legitimate objective, and the risks associated with the achievement of that objective must be taken into account. The article also requires members to conform to relevant international standards if they exist and to participate in setting up international standards where they are not currently in

place. Member countries are required to make information available on new regulations at an early stage to allow exporting members to adapt their products to conform with the new regulations.

Article 4 requires standardization bodies within countries to comply with a Code of Practice in line with the requirements noted above. Articles 5 and 6 require members to allow, where possible, testing of products in the foreign country to reduce the problem of multiple testing. Article 9 requires that international and regional arrangements comply, where possible, with articles 5 and 6.

Article 10 requires each member country to set up a "national enquiry point" within its territory to provide information to foreign enterprises on its technical regulations and standards. Article 11 deals with assistance for members (primarily developing countries) in the preparation of technical regulations, in setting up national standardization bodies, and in participating in international standardization bodies. Article 12 allows for differential and more favorable treatment of developing countries and time-limited exceptions to the agreement.

Article 13 sets up a Committee on Technical Barriers to Trade (TBT Committee), of which all signatories are members. It must meet at least once a year and acts as a forum for members to consult on aspects of the agreement. Article 14 covers consultation and settlement of disputes and allows for the creation of expert groups to help in the technical aspects of such matters. Article 15 requires the TBT Committee to undertake an annual review of the implementation of the agreement. It also sets up a triennial review with the power to recommend changes to the agreement or its implementation. Any recommended changes to the agreement are considered by the Council for Trade in Goods.

Policy Review

The first two triennial reviews of the implementation of the TBT Agreement were in 1997 and 2000. The First Triennial Review, published on November 13, 1997, raised a number of issues, including the need to establish national arrangements for administering the agreement, the need to set up national enquiry points, and problems of developing countries. The second review (WTO 2000), published on November 13, 2000, developed some of these themes further. At the time of this review, 77 members out of a total of 139 had notified the WTO of steps taken to implement the agreement, and 103 had notified the WTO that they had set up a national enquiry point. In most cases, members that had not made these arrangements were developing countries. In addition, rules introduced to provide notification of changes in standards had only been followed patchily, as had rules on mutual recognition in testing products. In the latter case, the committee had been notified of only twenty-nine agreements, although the actual number of agreements may be higher. The committee urged members to consider such mutual recognition schemes further and, where appropriate, to make more use of supplier declarations on testing products in order to limit multiple testing of products and the higher costs associated with testing products away from manufacturing sites.

The second review, like the first one, recognized the special problems of developing countries in implementing the agreement. Developing countries, for example, were underrepresented on international standard-setting bodies. This was put down to a lack of technical capacity, the location of secretariats and meetings, financial and human resource constraints, and lack of translation of standards into their own language. In the case of conformity assessment it was argued that exporters in developing countries, especially small and medium-sized enterprises (SMEs), sometimes find it difficult to meet requirements set by other countries. This is due to limited resources, high costs, legal difficulties in obtaining foreign accreditation, and the difficulty of establishing an internationally recog-

nized accreditation body. The committee noted these issues and the need to establish methods of providing technical assistance to developing countries in this area. It noted also that some technical assistance was already taking place in training conformity assessment practitioners, in training these practitioners in the formation of accreditation bodies, and in the development of strategies to boost product quality to meet international standards.

Other Issues

Agricultural Products: Sanitary and Phytosanitary Measures

The TBT Agreement covers most products but does not cover food safety or animal and plant health regulations. These areas are covered by a separate agreement, the Agreement on the Application of Sanitary and Phytosanitary Measures (SPS Agreement), where "sanitary" implies human and animal health, and "phytosanitary" implies plant health. This SPS Agreement is administered separately from the TBT Agreement in the Agriculture and Commodities Division of the WTO.

The main issue in the SPS Agreement is to ensure that food is safe and animal and plant health is protected, but at the same time that safety standards are not being used to prevent trade and protect domestic producers. The aims and procedures are similar to those for the TBT Agreement (WTO 2002c; Swinbank 1999). Countries are allowed to set their own regulations and standards on SPS issues, but these must be based on science and should not arbitrarily or unjustifiably discriminate against the exports of other countries. Member countries are encouraged to use international standards where available and, similarly, to follow international guidelines and recommendations. Members are allowed to set higher standards than internationally recognized, but these must be supported by science or be based on a proper assessment of risks (that is, not set arbitrarily).

Governments are required to notify other countries of any new or changed sanitary and phytosanitary requirements and, as with the TBT Agreement, to establish national enquiry points to provide information to exporters to that country. The agreement also established an SPS Committee, which reviews compliance with the agreement and examines the impact of SPS measures on international trade. This body is a forum for discussion (all WTO countries can have representation on it) that meets three or four times a year.

The SPS Agreement differs from the TBT Agreement in that it recognizes that a number of international bodies already exist in the area of food safety and animal and plant health. For food safety, it recognizes the authority of the Codex Alimentaurius Commission established in 1962 by the UN Food and Agricultural Organization (FAO) and the World Health Organization (WHO), which set standards and guidelines for food additives, veterinary drugs, and pesticide residues. In addition, it recognizes the International Office of Epizootics concerning animal health and the International Plant Protection Convention concerning plant health. While not encroaching on the activities of any of these bodies, the agreement seeks to ensure that, as far as possible, measures that are supported by the findings of these organizations do not restrict trade.

There is concern that SPS measures will have a significant effect in reducing world trade—that is, that as tariffs and other explicit barriers to agricultural trade come down, countries will use sanitary and phytosanitary measures to protect their home products. Such measures can be used ostensibly to raise food standards to protect domestic consumers, to pursue environmental goals, to avoid cross-contamination of domestic crops with pests brought in by foreign goods, and so on. By using these arguments, governments may be able to protect domestic producers while nominally allowing free trade.

Evidence on this is provided by Donna Roberts (1999), who discusses a survey by the U.S. Department of Agriculture (USDA) in 1996. This study examined technical barriers to U.S. exports in the agriculture, forestry, and fisheries sectors. It identified 339 measures across 62 countries that were seen as restricting or blockading U.S. agricultural goods and that could not be justified by science or international agreements. These mainly related to the protection of animal and plant health (210 cases), food safety (76 cases), or protection of domestic product quality (39 cases); the main measures used were restrictions by process standards (126 cases), product standards (72 cases), and import bans (72 cases). The cost of these restrictions was put at $4.9 billion in 1996 in terms of lost exports, or 7.1 percent of actual exports that year. These figures, when scaled up to represent the reduction in world trade as a whole, suggest that negative effects of SPS restrictions may be quite high.

Developing Countries

As already noted, developing countries face particular problems in dealing with technical regulations, standards, and conformity assessment procedures (WTO 1999). Such difficulties arise because these countries often lack human and financial resources, scientific infrastructure for laboratory testing and certification, awareness of international obligations, and technical expertise to frame and develop necessary standards and conformity assessment procedures.

These problems were noted in the TBT Agreement. Article 11 of the agreement requires members to advise other members (especially developing countries) on the preparation of technical regulations (that is, to give technical assistance to such countries). This assistance is to cover the establishment of national standardization bodies and participation in international standardization bodies. It also extends to testing products in the exporting country and providing technical assistance in setting up appropriate institutions and a corresponding legal framework. Article 12 of the agreement requires members to give different and more favorable treatment to developing countries in areas such as participation in international standardization bodies and technical assistance. The article also allows time-limited exceptions to the agreement for developing countries.

The First Triennial Review of the TBT Agreement raised a number of issues concerning developing countries and their participation in the agreement, and as a result a Workshop on Technical Assistance and Special and Differential Treatment in the Context of the TBT Agreement, organized by the WTO, was held on July 19–20, 2000 (WTO 2002d). The workshop identified four main areas of concern: implementation of the TBT Agreement, participation in international standard setting, conformity assessment procedures, and capacity building. Developing countries had problems in notifying the committee on the measures taken to implement the agreement because they lacked awareness of their TBT obligations, because they gave them relatively low priority, and because they lacked resources to implement the requirements. These problems also arose in dealing with notifications of other members of the agreement. Developing countries also had similar problems with establishing national enquiry points and in implementing the Code of Practice set out in the agreement.

Developing countries encountered problems with participating in international standardization bodies partly because of their lack of resources to attend meetings. They also argued that lack of technical expertise made it difficult for them to participate fully in such bodies and to have a significant impact on the proceedings. Developing countries often lack the physical and technical resources to engage in national conformity assessments, including accreditation. They have found it difficult to set up Mutual Recognition Agreements (MRAs) with other countries because their domestic testing procedures are often less developed than those used abroad, at least in developed countries. The implication here is that it is often necessary to engage in multiple tests of products (in the developing country and in the foreign country), that the testing increases costs, and that it delays the sale of goods. Finally, the workshop considered capacity building in developing countries, including provision of training, information dissemination, technology and infrastructure development, and efforts to raise awareness and participation.

Several important points emerged from the discussion. First, there is clearly an information problem, as well as a lack of resources and key skills, in developing countries, and these are areas in which technical assistance is currently being improved; but it may be that more assistance in this area is required. Second, in the case of international standard setting, it is probably desirable for developing countries to prioritize their activities, at least in the short term, by participating in areas of most relevance to them. Arguably, they could then take a larger role in other bodies when their technical expertise is further developed. Third, it is very important for developing countries to improve their products in line with the technical regulations of other (particularly, developed) countries so that they can more readily export to those countries. Again, technical assistance is likely to be important here.

Trade Blocs: NAFTA and the EU

Although the World Trade Organization is the principal world entity concerned with technical barriers to trade, some countries have formed regional bodies that are concerned with the same types of issues. Major world trade blocs have appeared, including the North American Free Trade Agreement (NAFTA), the European Union (EU), the Asia-Pacific Economic Cooperation (APEC) forum, and the Cairns Group. NAFTA, a free trade group formed on January 1, 1994, includes the United States, Canada, and Mexico. It is also considering allowing South American countries to join. The EU is a group of European nations that have formed a free trade area and consists of 25 full members, including France, Germany, the United Kingdom, and Spain, plus a number of transition economies from former East European countries. APEC, formed in 1989, is a loosely based free trade group of countries bordering the Pacific Ocean. It currently has twenty-one members, including China, Russia, the United States, Japan, and Australia. Finally, the Cairns Group, formed in 1986, is a group of seventeen agricultural exporting countries in North and South America, Africa, and the Asia-Pacific region pressing for free trade in agricultural products.

NAFTA was formed slightly earlier than the WTO, but many of the rules governing the two agreements are similar because the Uruguay Round had been under way for a number of years when NAFTA was negotiated. The influence of the Uruguay Round on NAFTA is reflected in the relevant clauses in the agreement covering technical barriers to trade and SPS arrangements. Chapter 9 of NAFTA deals with technical barriers to trade. Like the WTO agreement, it gives its members the right to take any standards-related measure, including measures relating to safety; to the protection of human, animal, or plant life or health; to the environment; or to consumers. However, members are not permitted to discriminate against the products or service providers of any country, must not create unnecessary obstacles to free trade, and must use international standards, where appropriate, in setting technical regulations and standards. The agreement also requires, where possible, that members make their standards-related measures compatible with those of other nations, with a view to encouraging trade between member countries. The chapter also establishes a Committee on Standards Related Measures and requires each country to set up an enquiry point to provide information about standards to member countries. The committee is, among other things, able to set up subcommittees or working groups on particular issues, and four subcommittees were established under the agreement to deal with land transportation standards, telecommunications, automotive standards, and labeling of textile and apparel goods.

It is difficult to see any major differences between NAFTA and the WTO agreement, and indeed, all three NAFTA countries are signatories to that agreement. One major difference, however, is that Chapter 9 covers land transport services (that is, services provided by motor carriers or by rail) and telecommunication services, whereas the WTO agreement relates only to goods.

Chapter 7 (Section B) of NAFTA relates to sanitary and phytosanitary measures and, again, is very similar to the WTO SPS Agreement. Member countries have the right to set their own SPS standards but must not apply technical regulations or standards that are discriminatory or create unnecessary obstacles to trade. SPS standards must also have a basis in scientific principles. The member countries are required to use international standards as appropriate and to work toward developing common standards. A Committee on Sanitary and Phytosanitary Measures was also created under NAFTA, as was a national enquiry point.

The EU also has its own policy on technical regulations, standards, and conformity assessment procedures. These are laid down in its Communication on Community External Trade Policy in the Field of Standards and Conformity Assessment (European Commission 2002; see also European Commission 2001). The EU has two trade objectives in this area: first, to reduce technical trade barriers in external markets and prevent the creation of new ones; and second, to encourage trading partners to adopt standards and regulatory approaches consistent with international and European practice. In its 1996 communication, its policy is based on two assumptions: that the impact of product standards and conformity assessment is increasing, creating possible technical barriers to trade, and that completion of the single market (in 1992) enables the Union to adopt a more outward-looking trade policy in this area. Its strategy has been: (1) to rely on the WTO TBT Agreement; (2) to conclude bilateral agreements with other countries on MRAs for conformity assessment and certification (in particular, with its leading trade partners); (3) to provide technical assistance to ensure that other countries' regimes are transparent, and to develop infrastructure in the areas of certification and testing; and (4) to support international cooperation in international standards setting and the harmonization of technical standards and regulations (European Commission 2001).

Considerable interest now exists in forming MRAs with the aim of eliminating multiple testing and speeding up trade. The EU has developed frameworks of agreement with four leading trading partners: with the United States, which came into force on December 1, 1998; Canada, which came into force on November 1, 1998; and with Australia and New Zealand, which came into force on January 1, 1999. These agreements cover a number of different product areas. The APEC group, through its Osaka Action Agenda, has also supported the formation of bilateral and multilateral MRAs among its members. Areas recognized for such actions are food and food products, automotive products, telecommunications equipment, and electrical and electronic equipment.

The Transatlantic Economic Partnership (TEP), which arose out of the EU-U.S. summit in London on May 18, 1998, also seeks to extend MRAs between the United States and the European Union. This agreement calls for further alignment of standards and regulatory requirements, where possible, between the two groups.

Future Action

It is clear that the Uruguay Round and the formation of the WTO constituted a major step forward in dealing with technical barriers to trade. By incorporating the TBT Agreement into the set of agreements on which the WTO was based, member countries made it an integral part of the move toward freer trade. The actual requirements of the agreement provide

a means of tackling obstacles to free trade that can arise as regulations and standards are extended to cover increasingly complex requirements for food safety, the protection of animal and plant life and health, protection of the environment, and protection of consumers. Policies adopted bilaterally (or multilaterally) such as MRAs also have a key role to play in preventing technical barriers to trade.

Standards and regulations tend to be developed mainly by developed countries, and this creates a continuing problem for developing countries attempting to meet the standards set. Developing countries lack the resources and the technical know-how to play a key role in the determination of international standards or in the formation of MRAs. There is a need to further develop technical assistance for developing countries so they can participate in and share the benefits of reducing TBTs.

Roger Clarke

See also Antidumping and Countervailing Duties; Nontariff Barriers; Tariffs; World Trade Organization (WTO)

References

Das, Lal B. 1999. *The World Trade Organization: A Guide to the Framework for International Trade.* London: Zed.

European Commission. 2001. "Implementing Policy for External Trade in the Fields of Standards and Conformity Assessment: A Tool Box of Instruments." Commission Staff Working Paper, SEC (2001), 1570.

———. "Community External Trade Policy in the Field of Standards and Conformity Assessment," http://europa.eu.int/comm/trade/pdf/mral.pdf (cited May 2, 2002).

Qureshi, Asif H. 1996. *The World Trade Organization: Implementing International Trade Norms.* Manchester: Manchester University Press.

Roberts, Donna. 1999. "Analyzing Technical Trade Barriers in Agricultural Markets: Challenges and Priorities." *Agribusiness* 15, no. 3: 335–354.

Swinbank, Alan. 1999. "The Role of the WTO and the International Agencies in SPS Standard Setting." *Agribusiness* 15, no. 3: 323–333.

World Trade Organization. 1999. "Technical Barriers to the Market Access of Developing Countries." WTO documents online, WT/CTE/W/101G/TBT/W/103,

http://docsonline.wto.ort/gen_home.asp?language=
1&_=1.

———. 2000. "Second Triennial Review of the Operation
and Implementation of the Agreement on Technical
Barriers to Trade." WTO documents online, G/TBT/9,
http://docsonline.wto.ort/gen_home.asp
?language=1&_=1.

———. 2002a. "Non-Tariff Barriers: Technicalities, Red
Tape, etc.," http://www.wto.org/english/thewto_e/
whatis_e/tif_e/agrm8_e.htm (cited May 2, 2002).

———. 2002b. "The WTO Agreement on Technical
Barriers to Trade," http://www.wto.org/english/
tratop_e/tbt_e/tbtagr_e.htm (cited March 22, 2002).

———. 2002c. "The WTO Agreement on the Application
of Sanitary and Phytosanitary Measures (SPS
Agreement)," http://www.wto.org/english/tratop_e/
sps_e/spsagr_e.htm (cited April 29, 2002).

———. 2002d. "Workshop on Technical Assistance and
Special and Differential Treatment in the Context of
the TBT Agreement—Session Reports," http://www.
wto.org/ english/news_e/news00_e/modrep_e.htm
(cited April 22, 2002).

Technology and Technical Change

In this period of adjustment to globalization, firms wanting to compete on world markets must aim at substantial improvement in their level of productivity. The influence of technological change on productivity, and consequently on the capacity of a country to keep pace with major industrialized countries, is now well recognized. The technological factor underpins the position of the national economies in the current international context.

Technology is not a commodity as any other. It is a body of knowledge that makes possible a certain rate of economic progress. That being the case, technology should not be confused with information; their respective characteristics are quite different. Information may be transmitted without prohibitive costs and may be assimilated relatively easily by the receiver; technology is altogether different. Technology is only partially a public good, which makes its transfer very difficult and costly, not to mention its assimilation. Investment in technology must take into account that technological development is both an ongoing and a cumulative process, which implies that what has been done in the past at the national and firm levels must serve as a basis for future investments.

Technology is increasingly recognized as being an important aspect of trade; competing internationally for market shares does not rely exclusively on price factors. Technology influences trade performance and therefore competitiveness and economic growth. However, the tacit nature of technology remains an important barrier to a global diffusion of technology. Therefore, to understand the dynamics of globalization, technological change provides an excellent viewpoint (Archibugi et al. 1999).

Some Notions Related to Technological Change

The first basic notion related to the nature of technology is that it is not an asset like others, that is, capable of being invested in, purchased, exchanged, or transferred in whole or in part in a straightforward manner, as is the case with a piece of equipment. An individual, a firm, or a country has distinctive technological capabilities enabling it to use certain technologies. At the same time, it can become locked into technologies presenting limited opportunities. To fully understand the nature of technology and to forecast technological opportunities requires looking backward to fully understand the present and assess the future possibilities. In this sense, an individual's, firm's, or country's technology "stock" is specific, idiosyncratic, and rarely reversible.

A second critical concept is that technology is integrally related to knowledge. Technology is more than blueprints; it is, above all, knowledge. Therefore, the process of the accumulation of technology is related to the embodiment of this knowledge in individuals and to the movement of individuals across occupations, industrial sectors, and countries. It takes place over time through learning-by-doing, by-using, and by interacting and can lead countries to be locked into some specialized activities. So, the accumulation of technology is not so much a matter of R&D investment, patenting activity, or having a certain type of machinery and equipment, but a rather more complicated process where knowledge and processes of learning lay at the core. Learning is therefore a core element of technological change. Linking technology to knowledge is a step toward better understanding the process underlying technological change. Recognizing this involves recognizing that skills, knowledge, and education are important and implies an increasing demand for high-skilled workers and a declining demand for less-skilled ones.

A third concept is that technological knowledge does not necessarily decrease when used. On the contrary, its use increases its value (Lundvall 1992). In economists' terms, there are "network effects" (Nye 2002) as a technology becomes more valuable once many people use it. This is the case with the Internet. However, not all technologies entirely share the characteristics of a public good and, therefore, not all can be appropriated unless a basis for understanding is present. To appropriate all the benefits of an investment in technological development, the investor must have exclusivity of knowledge. Against conventional wisdom among some economists, the nature of technology is not that of an international public good. Only firms and countries sharing some knowledge can eventually enjoy the returns and benefits of this investment. As will be seen later, it is hard to believe that all technology assets can flow freely across national borders.

Finally, the transfer of technology is an important notion, especially in the current global context. Such a transfer produces a knowledge spillover that the innovator firm or country developing technology cannot fully appropriate. The extent of the spillover is largely determined by the nature of the technology (tacit or codified) and the capacity of the initial investor, as well as competitors, to appropriate it. The most efficient transfer of technology occurs when the engineers involved in the development of a technology move from one firm to another or from one country to another.

A Variety of Technologies

Technologies are not all the same, nor do they rely on the same knowledge base. Some technologies are highly generic in the sense that they have major spillover effects on other industries. The information technologies are perhaps the best example, but there are many other technologies that can stimulate allied industries. Certain other technologies are complementary, in that combining them with other technologies helps improve production efficiency. For example, the combination of information and telecommunications technologies produced "telematics," and the merger of mechanics and electronics yielded "mechatronics."

The special nature of technology engenders great variety and diversity among firms, even those belonging to the same industry. The existence of such asymmetries among firms at the national level is not insignificant and has important consequences for the resource allocation process; special consideration must be given to the source of firms' technology, their transfer, and their means of appropriation in order to respond as effectively as possible to the true technological needs of the various industries.

Sources of Technology

As technologies differ tremendously, the sources of technological advance differ widely from one industry to another. For some industries, such as the chemical industry, science constitutes the main source feeding technological progress. Science, strictly speaking, arises out of activities occurring in different institutions such as universities, public institutes, and private laboratories.

The sources of innovation are numerous and cannot be limited strictly to expenditures on research (either basic or applied) and development (R&D). There appear to be more differences from one industry to another in the same country than within the same industry in different countries. Technology trends take shape in different forms resulting in diverse sources of technologies across industries. Keith Pavitt's taxonomy (Pavitt 1984) identified trends that, though not universal, can provide some indication of the diverse sources of technologies for various industries.. Technological knowledge can be acquired through various learning processes, such as through "learning-by-doing," through design, through production engineering, and so on.

Although R&D is not the only source of technological knowledge, it is nevertheless an essential investment (to varying degrees) leading to the recognition and integration of the technological development of both domestic and foreign competitors.

Conditions to Accumulate Technological Change

Influenced by the theories of Joseph Schumpeter, researchers have been preoccupied by the influence on technology of factors such as company size and industry concentration without ever reaching a consensus. As a result, experts have begun to take an interest in the influence of national technological conditions as incentives to increased investment in the innovation process.

Technological opportunities and the appropriation capacity of companies are two interrelated conditions associated with the innovation process in market economies (Dosi 1988). Far from being homogeneous, these opportunities vary across sectors and over time. Simply put, the variety in technological opportunities may be explained by the fact that investment in R&D and in other sources of technological change increases the supply of knowledge and makes it possible to use this knowledge in other sectors of the economy. The greater the

supply of knowledge and the more generic its applications, the greater will be the technological opportunities. Technological opportunities arise from a combination of factors, one being the nature of technology itself. Technology is constantly changing, and this impetus comes from new needs on the part of consumers (who then demand new products), from companies' efforts to remain competitive (that is, to produce efficiently), and from scientific and technological discoveries.

If these opportunities are to be converted into actual projects, companies must possess an appropriation capacity. This means that a number of mechanisms have to be put in place, either by government or in collaboration with government entities, in order to improve this appropriation capacity. Just as technological opportunities differ from one industry to another and from one industrial branch to another, conditions for appropriability vary considerably from industry to industry and from technology to technology. There are several sources of technological appropriation, including the tacit nature of technological capabilities in firms, the efficacy of the patent system, the degree of secrecy, lead times, and others.

Technological appropriation capacity is required because investment in technological change produces spillover effects. Spillovers refer to the idea that technological knowledge is created in one firm, sector, or country but inevitably spills over to another. This effect is sometimes unexpected and may also be an important source of technology for another firm, another sector of the economy, or other countries. However, the fact that a spillover effect occurs does not necessarily mean that firms in another industrial sector can automatically benefit from it. These companies must be in a position to appropriate the spinoffs of R&D, whether it was undertaken by the original firm or by another company with the necessary technological capacity. Two sets of conditions are required to develop technologies: technological opportunities and the development of a capacity to appropriate and take advantage of

Table 1: Internet Access by Region, 1999

	People Connected (millions)	Global Percentage of People Connected	Percentage of Global Population
Canada and the U.S.	97	56.6	5.1
Europe	40.1	23.4	13.7
Asia and the Pacific	27.0	15.8	6.2
Latin America	5.3	3.1	8.4
Africa	1.1	0.6	12.9
Middle East	0.9	0.5	3.6

Source: International Labour Office, *World Employment Report 2001: Life at Work in the Information Economy* (Geneva: ILO, 2001).

technological opportunities created abroad or in domestic industrial sectors.

Globalization and Technology

Globalization moves in tandem with the widespread use of new information and communications technologies (ICTs). By reducing the costs of communication, these technologies allow a rapid diffusion of information and codifiable knowledge. In this process, the Internet is the latest stage. If developed countries have, in general, easy access to the World Wide Web, many countries lag behind. As a result, there is a long way to go before ICTs can be globally diffused. Considerable distributional problems, in terms of the diffusion of ICTs' tangible equipment, such as personal computers or the number of Internet connections, arise among as well as within countries. A look at international indicators of connectivity shows that despite the profound transformation of people's private lives as well as of their work lives by ICTs, the diffusion of computers and Internet access is still quite concentrated in North America.

Technology has no national borders, and international scientific and technological influence represents a series of technological opportunities that governments tend to encourage rather than restrict. While encouraging technological opportunities, a national system of innovation must ensure that companies' adoption and appropriation capacity is

equal to the task of capitalizing on these technological opportunities.

It may seem contradictory to introduce the concept of a national system of innovation when globalization and internationalization are the dominant trends now and in the foreseeable future. However, as is the case for the diffusion of ICTs, technological situations and industrial structures are still highly national and vary from country to country. The existence of a national system implies a series of national institutions and firms linked in a coherent network of financial, production, commercial, and technological relationships. It involves, first and foremost, the creation of a climate of cooperation promoting a sense of partnerships and of trust in the national research system. Technological accumulation also requires a steady investment in skills at the national level in order to build a technological capability that possesses the momentum to continue its movement forward. Despite the porosity of national borders, the accumulation of technology is still national, meaning that national institutions influence the way technology accumulates within national borders.

Future Technological Paradigm

Although the ICT paradigm has an important potential for globalization, it is not the only technological paradigm, that is, there is not just one unique set of possibilities that exist at a given point in time with respect to technological development. The recent isolation of human embryonic stem cells will almost certainly lead to the next scientific/technological paradigm and will probably have the same magnitude as that offered by the ICTs (or still more). It is worth mentioning that technological paradigms are cumulative and complementary and not displacing or competitive. However, the emergence of an even spread of global innovative activities in both paradigms remains to be seen.

Marie Lavoie

See also Global Economic Growth; International Productivity; Computer Hardware and Electronics; Computer Software; Copyrights and Intellectual Property

References

Archibugi, Daniele, Jeremy Howells, and Jonathan Michie. 1999. *Innovation Policy in a Global Economy.* Cambridge: Cambridge University Press.

Dosi, Giovanni. 1988. "The Nature of the Innovative Process." Pp. 221–238 in G. Dosi, C. Freeman, R. Nelson, G. Silverberg, and L. Soete, eds., *Technical Change and Economic Theory.* London: Pinter.

International Labour Office. 2001. *World Employment Report 2001: Life at Work in the Information Economy.* Geneva: ILO.

Lundvall, Bengt-Ake, ed. 1992. *National Systems of Innovation: Towards a Theory of Innovation and Interactive Learning.* London: Pinter.

Nye, Joseph S. 2002. *The Paradox of American Power.* Oxford: Oxford University Press.

Pavitt, Keith. 1984. "Patterns of Technical Change: Towards a Taxonomy and a Theory." *Research Policy* 13, no. 6: 343–373.

Transportation and Communication

The essence of globalization is that it changes spatial interactions, entailing increased levels of trade, capital, and information flows and mobility of individuals across borders. Changes in transportation and communications technologies alter the manner in which space and time are perceived for such interactions. Advances in these technologies have led to a space/time collapse supporting greater economic integration of production and distribution systems and thus globalization. It is not surprising, therefore, that periods of increased globalization are associated with technological innovations that reduce transportation and communication costs.

Integration through Transportation and Communications

Global integration involves more interactions across national borders around the globe, and both the transportation and communications industries are basically geared toward making this possible. M. Mussa (2000) pointed to three fundamental factors that have affected the process of economic globalization. First, improvements in the technology of transportation and communications have reduced the cost of transporting goods, services, and factors of production and of communicating economically useful knowledge and technology. Second, the tastes of individuals and societies have generally favored taking advantage of the opportunities provided by declining costs of transportation and communication through

increasing economic integration. Third, public policies have significantly influenced the character and pace of economic integration, although not always in the direction of increasing it.

Clearly, these factors will continue to affect the process of globalization. Even though public policies (at each level of governance) are critical in determining the direction of global economic integration, advances in transportation and communication technologies act as major catalysts affecting the speed and magnitude of economic integration when public policy favors integration. Sometimes technological advances in communications can even counter restrictive public policies, as in the case of the Internet in China.

Decreasing Costs

Over the past two centuries there has been a dramatic decline in the cost of moving people, goods, and information across space. Broadly speaking, the changes can be divided into two periods. The first wave of globalization, which started roughly around 1820 and lasted until 1914, was largely associated with advances in transportation technologies. A second wave, which started from 1960 and has continued to the present, has been associated most significantly with advances in communications technologies (Baldwin and Martin 1999).

The world witnessed a rapid expansion of rail networks in the first half of the nineteenth century. Before the advent of railroads, land

Table 1: Real Costs of Ocean Shipping (1910 = 100)

Year	Costs	Year	Costs
1750	298	1910	100
1790	376	1930	107
1830	287	1960	47
1870	196	1990	51

Source: Nicholas Crafts and Anthony Venables, "Globalization in History: A Geographical Perspective." Paper prepared for NBER conference on Globalization in Historical Perspective.

transport was economically feasible only for goods with very high value-to-weight ratios. But with this new form of transport, vast tracts of land became potential markets for goods. The second half of the nineteenth century saw the widespread use of steam-driven ships for inland and oceanic routes (1840–1870). As a result, ocean-shipping costs saw substantial decreases between 1830 and 1910, revolutionizing ocean travel. In the 1830s, travel time from Liverpool to New York took about forty-eight days, but with the arrival of steamships the same journey could be completed in fourteen days. Costs also declined with the introduction of steel hulls in the 1870s that were lighter, stronger, and required less fuel (see Table 1).

The first transatlantic telegraph cable (1866) and the subsequent cabling of all the oceans revolutionized communications, lowering intercontinental communications times from weeks to minutes. Combined with low trade barriers, cheaper transport and faster communications spurred trade and investment, and the world witnessed a first wave of globalization between 1870 and 1914. However, protectionist barriers to trade, as well as the imposition of capital and migration controls, resurfaced with World War I, slowing down the integration process. The reductions in these technical and policy barriers to international transactions since 1960 led to a second wave of globalization that is still in progress. After World War II, new modes of transport by air became important, and by 1980 the real costs of airfreight had fallen to about a quarter of its level on the eve of World War II. The aviation sector's main contribution to the integration process has been the reduction in transit times and associated costs.

The costs of airfreight flattened out, however, in the 1980s, whereas the costs of communications continued to plunge. The second wave of globalization is therefore strongly associated with changes in the communications industry rather than in transportation. The cost of a three-minute call from New York to London has fallen from about $250 in 1930 to a few cents today (see Table 2). Furthermore, the capacity and speed of communications networks has increased enormously. In 1970, it would have cost $187 to transmit the *Encyclopaedia Britannica* as an electronic data file coast to coast in America because transmission speeds were slow and long-distance calls expensive. Nowadays the entire contents of the Library of Congress could be sent across America for just about $40. These advances have led to a revolutionary change in the way distance is perceived and have motivated proclamations of the "death of distance" (Cairncross 1997).

A distinct feature of the current globalization process is the ease with which ideas and information flow across the globe. The technological breakthroughs in the communications industry have taken services that used to be nontradable and made them internationally tradable. Economic integration today is the story of increased flows of goods, and more important, services and ideas, across the globe.

Table 2: Costs of Air Transportation and Telephone Calls (in 1990 U.S. dollars)

Year	Average Air Transportation Revenue per Passenger Mile	Cost of a 3-Minute Call, New York to London
1930	0.68	244.65
1940	0.46	188.51
1950	0.30	53.20
1960	0.24	45.86
1970	0.16	31.58
1980	0.10	4.80
1990	0.11	3.32

Source: International Monetary Fund, *World Economic Outlook: Globalization. Opportunities and Challenges* (Washington, DC: IMF, 1997).

Transportation in a Global Market

Over the past two decades, transportation costs and transit times have somewhat flattened out, unlike communications costs and speeds, which have dramatically declined. Yet the transport industry is being transformed by the global flow patterns and in turn affecting the globalization process. Globalization leads to reliance on outsourcing, customized production runs, flexibility of resource access (regardless of distance), just-in-time management of production and distribution, zero inventory, and information access and exchange. The transport industry has to facilitate reliable and synchronized movements across the globe, and it must cater to the demand for heavy volumes over longer distances for a global market. In general, transport demand is moving toward longer and more customized transport linkages with higher levels of sensitivity to the timing of connections, arrivals, and departures and heavier reliance on communications networks and information systems (Janelle and Beuthe 1997).

The changes in the transport industry are instigated by worldwide competitive forces to produce, transport, and distribute goods and services as efficiently as possible. Small variations in transport costs can have major impacts on the location of global production and export volumes if all other costs are similar.

Thus, even though transport costs may constitute a small proportion of the total product price, competitive pressures at the global level are such that these differences can be exploited. For example, sub-Saharan Africa has been unable to make significant inroads into world trade, despite low wages, partly because of adverse transport costs (Yeats 1998). Advances in transportation technologies thus stimulate globalization. The converse is also true, that is, the transportation industry itself adapts to meet the increased pressures of globalization.

The nature and volume of transport demand at each location stimulates a unique set of responses; however, a few common trends are noticeable. Three major trends in transportation, in particular, draw attention because of their interlinkage to the globalization process. First, there is intermodalism, that is, the integration of transport across modes and the attempt to standardize transport system designs. The second trend is the transformation of the industry structure through strategic alliances at the global level. The third is a shift in the focus from the standard line haul operations to operations at terminals because of the high levels of activity at these terminals. The interesting aspect is that all three processes, namely intermodalism, mergers and alliances, and improvement in transport terminals, are strongly interlinked.

Intermodalism

Intermodalism refers to the integration of two or more modes of transportation in moving passengers or freight through seamless connections from origin to destination. It facilitates globalization, and its further growth is dependent on continuing movement toward more globalization. Proponents of intermodal transport say that efficient trade flows across large distances entail movement through a complex chain of modes and therefore seek to reduce transit times and costs across modes. Also loading, unloading, transshipping, and setting up cargoes is costly in terms of both resources and time. To avoid repeated transactions between origin and destination points, freight movements are increasingly integrated seamlessly with a standard unit of transport, the container. The first container ship crossed the Atlantic in 1966, and today containers account for about 60 percent of the world trade in terms of value. Between 1982 and 1995, container use in developing-country ports grew 15.5 percent per annum (Hummels 1999). Containerization is an important source of shipping efficiency both in and out of port. But containerization is only the first level of standardization for intermodal transport, and seamless intermodal movement requires standardization at various other levels.

There are many constraints to such standardization because the transport industry in each region has developed under different policy regimes and with varied access to technological advances. For example, rail clearances differ across countries, creating problems for large containers, and overhead electrical equipment for traction often constrains double-stack movement of containers on railroads. The size of containers is an issue of debate as well: The United States favors large containers, whereas Europe and Asia have serious reservations on grounds of rail clearances, boat sizes, and terminal infrastructure facilities. Complete standardization may not even be viable because any solution would involve major, expensive changes. The intermodal solution therefore has to work within the constraints of nonstandardized designs and requires rationalized transport linkages and coordinated investments. Such linkages and investments would only be possible with partnerships, long-term contracts, and/or mergers among transport service providers in different modes. Coordination of investments in transport infrastructure would also require bilateral or multilateral trade agreements between governments to provide the environment of certainty necessary for such investments specific to the trading relationship (Bond 1997).

Strategic Alliances

Strategic alliances are taking place within the transportation industry to meet the requirements of a global supply chain that emphasizes network connectivity, reliability, and high levels of synchronization. Consortium and cooperative ventures between shipping lines have been common for more than thirty years now because containerization of freight movements have typically involved consortium and partnership arrangements. With globalization, these alliances are now spread over a global scale rather than confined to individual routes.

According to an estimate by the *Containerization International Yearbook* (1996), a few major alliances control nearly one-third of the world's shipboard TEU (container size of twenty "feet equivalent units") capacity. The concentration of assets is especially noticeable on the three major East/West container routes (Europe–Far East, Europe–North America, and Far East–North America), where it is estimated that companies involved in four alliances control as much as 50 percent of the capacity (McCalla 1999). Through cargo sharing on vessels and slot chartering, shipping lines are able to offer more services both in terms of frequency and routes serviced. As a result of these developments, the twenty largest carriers now control around 56 percent of the world container fleet, and the top five lines own or operate more than 25 percent (see Table 3). A similar trend is

Table 3: Summary of Services of Major Carrier Alliances and Megacarriers

Alliance Group	Participating Lines	Number of Sailings per Week			Slot Capacity (Number of Ships)
		Transpacific	Asia-Europe	Transatlantic	
Grand Alliance	P&O Nedlloyd NYK Hapag-Lloyd OOCL	West Coast 6 East Coast 2	7	2	645,748 TEU (278)
	Maersk Sea-Land	West Coast 5 East Coast 3	4	6	544,558 TEU (228)
New World Alliance	APL-NOL-MOL Hyundai	West Coast 9 East Coast 1	4	1	447,358 TEU (178)
United Alliance	Hanjin DSR-Senator Cho Yang UASC	West Coast 8 East Coast 2	5	2	342,566 TEU (152)
	Cosco/K Line/Yangming	West Coast 7 East Coast 1	4	3	380,689 TEU (207)
	Evergreen	West Coast 5 East Coast 2	3	1	311,951 TEU (132)

Source: United Nations Economic and Social Commission for Asia and the Pacific website, http://www.unescap.org.

evident with regard to airlines, especially passenger movements.

At the national level, governments are seeking to create competitive conditions in the railroad industry to improve efficiency and achieve reductions in costs. However, with increasing globalization, the main challenge for the railroad industry is to meet the overland transportation element of international trade. Since international trade is largely containerized, the interface between the railroads and the shipping industry at ports and at terminals near ports has become critical to the flow of goods. The trucking industry faces a similar challenge to meet overland transportation demand, sometimes competing with railroads and sometimes in a complementary role, catering to short lead traffic from rail terminals.

Terminals
Globalization and intermodal transportation have modified the economic and political environment in which transport terminals are evolving. Huge volumes of activity at terminals are highlighting space constraints, leading to changes in terminal operations technologies. Strategic alliances among service providers are also changing the relationship between terminals and users. The emphasis has therefore shifted from modes to terminals, since the real potential time savings are now at terminals and ports and, at the intra-urban scale, through synchronization of movements between transport terminals (Rodrigue 1999). Deregulation and privatization are creating conditions for integration between modes through terminals. The just-in-time inventory management environment reduces warehousing needs and increases the need for integration among elements of the production system. The transport industry's new role thus involves orchestrating inventory levels and adapting to constant fluctuations in demand from origin and destination clients. Achieving synchronization among transport terminals, regardless of the mode, necessitates an information exchange process supported by the information systems and by strategic alliances that include

information sharing. Strategic alliances, especially among maritime and air companies, have also enabled these companies to share their modes, terminals, and distribution networks and to improve the synchronization of their respective transport systems.

Communications

Communications technology plays a critical role in the linkages supported by the transport industry in the global supply chain. Advances in communication technologies have stimulated the dispersion of production, creating new demand for transport. Also, synchronization of traffic movements is achieved through information flows and networking. Transportation and communication industries are thus allies in the globalization process, feeding upon one another's technological advances and stimulating further integration.

Technological Advances

Over the past few decades, the communications industry has witnessed spectacular technological advances unparalleled in history. Analysts who attempt to understand the impact of these changes agree that the process has been rapid and exhibits many dimensions. The magnitude of the technological advances and their wide dissemination have led some to conclude that the globalization process is driven by communications technology. The digitization of information and the flow of ideas and information across national borders facilitated by the new technologies have even been viewed as weakening the authority of the sovereign state. This has raised concerns about imbalance in the communication flows between developed and developing nations. There is a large body of literature focusing on globalization and the effects of these flows. Basic features of these technological advances support a more integrated world and have affected the communications

industry in unprecedented ways. Indeed, advances in mobile cellular technology, cable, satellite, broadband, fiberoptics, the Internet, and other digital interactive telecommunications platforms have blurred the distinction between mass communications and interactive interpersonal communications systems.

Digitization and Networks

Digitization translates every kind of information into a universal binary code so that any kind of communication can be handled by the same medium and transmitted through its infrastructure. With the digital revolution, streams of voice, data, and video can flow ever faster around the globe, and the basic units of information are packets routed from one destination to the next. With compression technologies, one bandwidth can be used to transfer far larger amounts of information than was previously possible in an analog world. Digitization allows for information transfer through different media to occur seamlessly, somewhat similar to intermodalism in transport, only it is much more effective. Since different types of information can be sent over the same network, users can migrate from dedicated networks to universal networks. This technological development is leading to the *convergence* of communications technologies, which creates ideal conditions for mergers and alliances across corporations operating in different media. Combined with this development is the increase in the speeds with which information is processed and transmitted, features that clearly support greater global integration.

Information processing speeds have been increasing faster than predicted by Moore's law (named after Gordon Moore, writing as early as 1965), which stated that the information processing power of microprocessors would double every eighteen months. Indeed, the transmission speeds have more than kept pace, tripling every twelve months (meeting the requirements of Gilder's law, named after its originator George Gilder). The network systems of the predigital era required centralized organizational structures with networks controlled by the telephone or television company. However, the digital network, the Internet being a prime example, is built on a different paradigm (Mayer-Schonberger and Hurley 2000). The Internet, which evolved in a decentralized fashion, rests on standards such as TCP/IP—a convention that has been adopted globally. Thus four features of the new communication technology—digitization, processing power, network bandwidth, and globally standardized but decentralized communication architecture—are contributing to what is termed the "communication revolution." Global communication networks imply the decline of the importance of geographic proximity as a critical factor for transactions.

Digital networks caused global telecommunication network revenues to grow from US$600 billion in 1995 to $US1 trillion in 2002 (*World Telecommunication Indicators Database*). Within global communications, mobile telephony grew from about US$80 billion in 1995 to US$365 billion in 2002. Digital networks, with their capacity for permitting two-way communication, allow for a different model of production, namely, mass customization. In this system, concrete customer information is used to provide customized production meeting the buyer's specifications. Access to digital networks is becoming important in the new economy, and developing countries are moving faster into the information age than they have with other forms of technological advancement.

Convergence

On the one hand, the universal digital network permits decentralized communication architecture; on the other, the convergence of telecommunications, computing, and mass communications leads to consolidation efforts among media companies. For example, telecommunication services can be provided by TV cable networks, or TV signals can be carried by telecommunication operators. The technical convergence leads to institutional

convergence. There is evidence of increased convergence and consolidation in communications, media, and entertainment sectors. The bigger corporations have been buying up successful smaller enterprises to manage the competitive environment. In 1999, 921 deals worth almost US$568.3 billion were announced, up from 681 deals worth US$295.4 billion the year before (KPMG Web site). Industry alliances over the past two decades include alliances between CGE (France) and ITT (United States), Sony (Japan) and AT&T (United States), Philips (the Netherlands) and Matshushita (Japan), and so on (Hamelink 1995).

Another factor contributing to the communication revolution is satellite technology and its impact on telephony, television, and meteorological functions. Satellites placed in geostationary orbit can cover one-third of the earth's surface with their footprint. They have contributed to the globalization process through the rise of global news channels such as CNN and BBC World, global music channels such as MTV, and global sports channels.

Globalization, digitization, and consolidation go hand in hand with deregulated environments for world communications industries. Digitization reinforces technological integration and institutional consolidation and thus promotes globalization. Global operations create global markets necessitating deregulated national markets. Technological change has also facilitated the privatization of telecommunications structures, as the natural monopoly argument associated with network industries was no longer a strong argument for state monopolies.

Production Sharing and Capital Flows

Globalization alters patterns of production, distribution, and trade as well as the nature of the services provided and the manner in which they are delivered. The transportation and communication sectors, and especially the latter, are at the center of some of these changes.

Transportation and communications provide critical inputs to three key areas of the global economy: production sharing/outsourcing in the commodity markets, integration of capital markets, and transactions in all markets through the electronic medium.

Improved communication links have led to the emergence of international production networks by facilitating coordination of geographically dispersed production processes. International service networks have also led to dispersion of employment in the services sector, which now makes use of transcription and calling centers. Frances Cairncross (1997) supplied anecdotal evidence of this process, describing an accountancy firm in southern England (Dyer Partnership) that acts as the finance department for a Ukrainian manufacturer of wind turbines, using the Internet; Dyer handles all the financial reporting, including profit and loss statements. The retailing revolution, which began in the 1980s with the emergence of large-scale discount stores such as Wal-Mart and Target in the United States, is based on extensive outsourcing to low-wage countries combined with new inventory methods and rapid communications (Feenstra 1998). None of these methods of conducting business would have been possible without excellent communication networks and reliable transportation means.

In the nineteenth century, the high cost of transmitting knowledge favored long-term capital investments. The telecommunications revolution of the late twentieth century, however, favors the rapid, almost frenetic movement of highly liquid assets. The spread of information technology has strengthened real and financial linkages across countries. Although it is difficult to document, the increased ease, reliability, and lower cost of telecommunicatons have undoubtedly promoted the explosion of foreign direct investment (FDI). This is especially true of FDI in the service sector, where foreign affiliates are often selling information or expertise. Overall, world FDI flows more than tripled between 1988 and 1998, from US$192 billion to US$610 billion, and the share of FDI to gross domestic product (GDP) is generally rising in both developed and developing countries. Developing countries received about a quarter of world FDI inflows in 1988–1998, on average. This is now the largest form of private capital inflow to developing countries (World Bank).

Communication technologies have also been critical in changing the manner by which transactions are conducted. Numerous transactions now take place across the world through the electronic medium of the Internet. It is predicted that worldwide business-to-business (B2B) e-commerce revenues will surpass US$1.4 trillion by the end of 2003. By 2004, worldwide e-commerce revenues totaled US$2.7 trillion and are expected to continue this trend in 2005 (Emarketer 2005).

Conclusion

The transportation and communication sectors are the sinews and nerves, respectively, of globalization. The effects of globalization on standards of living in various regions of the world, the developed and the underdeveloped, is part of a heated debate. However, strong technological advances in the communication sector are leading to a world where borders are becoming less significant. Advances in the transportation and communication sectors may create a world where seamless movement of people, goods, services, and ideas across borders are possible. The question is whether public policies would continue to support such movement and reap the benefits of these technologies.

R. Badri Narayan and
Sunetra Sen Narayan

See also Transport Manufacturing: aircraft/automobiles/shipbuilding; Transport: Airlines/railroads/shipping

References

Baldwin, Richard E., and Phillipe Martin. 1999. "Two Waves of Globalization: Superficial Similarities, Fundamental Differences." NBER, Working Paper 6904.

Bond, Eric. 1997. "Transportation Infrastructure Investments and Regional Trade Liberalization", Policy Research Working Paper 1851, Pennsylvania State University.

Cairncross, Frances. 1997. *The Death of Distance.* London: Orion.

Containerization International Yearbook (1996), http://www.ci-online.co.uk.

Craft, Nicholas, and Anthony J. Venables. 2001. "Globalization in History: A Geographical Perspective" CEPR Discussion Paper No. 3079. http://ssrn.com/abstract=293626.

Emarketer, http://www.emarketer.com.

Feenstra, Robert. 1998. "Integration of Trade and Disintegration of Production in the Global Economy." *Journal of Economic Perspectives,* Fall, 31–50.

Hamelink, Cees. 1995. "Trends in World Communication." Pp. 69–119 in Cees Hamelink, *World Communication: Disempowerment and Self-Empowerment.* London: Zed.

Hummels, David. 1999. *Have International Transportation Costs Declined?* University of Chicago.

International Telecommunications Union, http://www.itu.int.

Janelle, Donald G., and Michel Beuthe. 1997. "Globalization and Research Issues in Transportation." *Journal of Transport Geography* 5, no. 3 (September): 199–206.

KPMG, http://www.kpmg.com.

Mayer-Schonberger, Victor, and Deborah Hurley. 2000. "Globalization of Communication." In Joseph S. Nye and John D. Donahue, eds., *Governance in a Globalizing World.* Washington, DC: Brookings Institution.

McCalla, Robert J. 1999. "Global Change, Local Pain: Intermodal Seaport Terminals and Their Service Areas." *Journal of Transport Geography* 7: 247–254.

Mussa, M. 2000. "Factors Driving Global Economic Integration." Paper presented at a symposium sponsored by the Federal Reserve Bank of Kansas City Jackson Hole, Wyoming. August 24–26, 2000.

Rodrigue, Jean-Paul. 1999. "Globalization and the Synchronization of Transport Terminals." *Journal of Transport Geography* 7: 255–261.

United Nations Economic and Social Commission for Asia and the Pacific (UNESCAP), http://www.unescap.org.

World Bank, http://www.worldbank.org.

World Telecommunication Indicators Database. 2002. ITU, International Telecommunication Union, http://www.itu.int/home.

Yeats, Alexander. 1998. "Just How Big Is Global Production Sharing?" World Bank Working Paper 1871.

PART TWO

Major Business and Economic Sectors

Agriculture

Primitive forms of agriculture existed thousands of years ago, involving the domestication of plants and animals. However, the application of scientific knowledge to agriculture dates back only about 200 years. The steel plow, the reaper, and the threshing machine were all patented in the early nineteenth century. In the developed part of the world, tractors did not replace horses until well into the twentieth century, and in many developing countries, animals are still used for power in agriculture today. About three-fourths of the world's population resides in developing countries where the most important source of employment is agriculture. So most of the world's poor are engaged in farming.

Global food production continues to outpace population growth (see Table 1), and food is now more available and more affordable to a larger share of the earth's population than ever before. Measured by calories per day, world per capita food supplies are about 25 percent higher than they were forty years ago, even though the global population has more than doubled over the same time period. As a result of the in-

creased supply, real agricultural commodity prices have shown a gradual downward trend. Over the past century, there have been recurring periods of rising and then falling raw commodity food prices, but the overall trend has been down (see Figure 1), with prices declining by about 0.4 percent per year, on average.

Approximately 10 to 15 percent of the world's population suffers from malnutrition today, and this figure has dropped spectacularly from over 50 percent in the early 1950s, according to the United Nations Food and Agriculture Organization. This success on the supply side of the food balance equation is due to large productivity gains associated with the intensification of agriculture and improvements in crop yields. Developing countries have been strong participants in this technological progress, as their per capita food supplies grew by about 40 percent over the past forty years, on average. However, the trend in increased supply has been uneven across continents. In Asia, the increase in per capita food supplies has exceeded the world average by a wide margin, whereas in sub-Saharan Africa

Table 1: Growth in Food Production and Production per Capita:
average annual % change

Annual % production	World	World per cap	Developing	Developing per cap	Developed	Developed per cap	Transition	Transition per cap
1971–80	2.39	0.59	2.93	0.75	1.91	1.10	1.34	0.48
1981–90	2.29	0.57	3.50	1.44	0.99	0.29	1.77	1.01
1991–00	2.35	0.95	3.72	2.04	0.30	–0.14	–3.44	–3.40

Source: Food and Agriculture Organization, FAOSTAT, www.fao.org.

Figure 1. Real Price of Foodstuffs, 1947 to 2002 (1947=100)

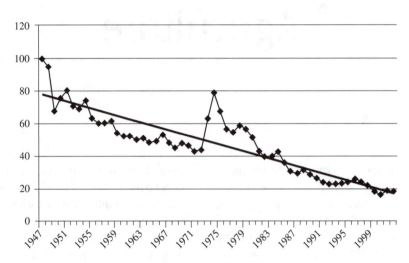

Source: Commodity Research Bureau. Index includes spot price of butter, cocoa, corn, hogs, lard, soybean oil, steers, sugar, soft wheat, and hard wheat. CRB index was deflated by the U.S. CPI.

food availability per capita has fallen since 1960.

The future of agriculture holds the promise of large benefits through bioengineered crop varieties that will serve to further boost yields through better control of pests, diseases, and resistance to frost and drought. These new crops will require fewer chemicals and therefore are expected to be more environmentally friendly. Once produced, bioengineered foods should offer nutritional and medical benefits to consumers. Per capita food production will therefore most likely continue to improve in terms of quantity and quality, especially as world population growth is showing signs of slowing down.

As economies grow, the general rule is that agriculture shrinks as a share of overall economic activity. Statistics from various nations illustrate the effects of economic development on agriculture's role in national economies. Agriculture's share of the economy in South Korea fell from 24 percent in 1970 to 4 percent in 2000. At the same time, the percent of the labor force in agriculture declined from 50 percent to 10 percent, and the national per capita income per annum rose from $250 to $9,700. In the United States in 1800, 75 percent of the labor force was directly engaged in agricultural production. By 1900, this share had dropped to less than 40 percent, and today the figure is around 2 percent. The decline in farm employment is largely due to rapid productivity growth in agriculture, about double that in manufacturing (Jorgenson and Gollop 1992). Figure 2 shows the global trends in agricultural employment in developed versus developing countries.

Agriculture is arguably one of the world's most important industries because everyone has to eat. Its importance in the global economy is shrinking to the point where it now accounts for less than 5 percent of the world's gross domestic product (GDP), yet it continues to employ over 40 percent of the global labor force. The gap between the small percent of GDP accounted for by agriculture and agriculture's relatively large share of the labor force underscores the fact that in most of the populous developing world, agriculture still accounts for a relatively large share of the economy. For instance, in China the figure is around 50 percent, and in India it is about 60 percent.

China and India have about 250 million to 300 million farmers each, and their average per

**Figure 2. Agricultural Employment as
Percentage of Total Employment**

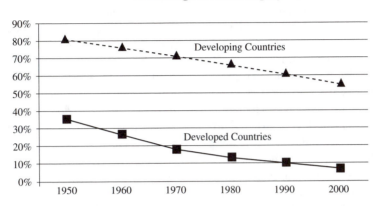

capita incomes are less than $2 per day (World Bank 2001). In sub-Saharan Africa, about 75 to 80 percent of the labor force is engaged in agriculture, with the average wage being less than $2 per day. Of course, these average figures obscure the wide variability in the role that agriculture plays in various economies around the world. For instance, in Afghanistan, agriculture accounts for 60 percent of the GDP and employs 80 percent of the labor force. In contrast, in Japan, agriculture accounts for only 2 percent of the GDP and employs 5 percent of the labor force.

Improvements in agricultural productivity have been impressive despite the fact that agriculture stands out as an industry that has not fully participated in the recent globalization trend. Agricultural input and output markets are not well integrated across nations because most governments continue to intervene in agricultural markets through subsidies, trade barriers, state-trading, and the like. In particular, farmers in developed countries, especially the European Union, Japan, and the United States, are politically organized in a way that allows them to tilt agricultural policy in their favor, collect large subsidies, and isolate themselves from the disciplines of the world marketplace. In developing countries, the state also plays a significant role in agriculture, but unlike the developed part of there world, where

farmers receive net subsidies, in the developing world the net effect is often to tax agriculture. Fortunately, there is political pressure for agricultural policy reform in both developed and developing countries, and if there is a breakthrough agriculture would become a more significant participant in globalization. Achieving this success could take a long time, however.

Agricultural Globalization: Historical Developments

Prior to the nineteenth century, nations were faced with recurring food shortages, and consequently, government food trade policies were highly protectionist. It wasn't until the 1840s, when the Industrial Revolution increased agricultural productivity (through mechanization), that the supply of food increased to the extent that international trade in food could be embraced. The repeal of the British Corn Laws in 1846 represents the beginning of modern agricultural trade. The complementary revolution in transportation at the time encouraged the growth of international agricultural commerce (McCalla 1969). The United Kingdom rapidly moved toward free trade during this period, whereas France and Germany chose to protect domestic landowners instead. These two influential continental nations continuously built up protective mechanisms for their domestic agriculture. Their trade barriers increased significantly in the 1870s when grain and livestock from North America started to flow into Europe and depress prices. Britain, meanwhile, adhered to the doctrines of free trade.

In the early part of the twentieth century, the two world wars and the Great Depression between the wars brought major changes in agricultural trade and trade policy. Food shortages in many European countries during World War I meant that supply security became a major issue following the war. The United States, Australia, and Canada expanded production rapidly to meet wartime demand. After the war, these abundant food supplies resulted in lower prices. Both Australia and Canada set up government agencies to market international wheat sales during the war period. Government control over grain also replaced the free market system in the United States in 1917 and 1918. The United States, Germany, and France all stepped up agricultural protection in the 1920s.

There were also major structural changes that took place in the world grain markets following World War I. For instance, prior to the war, Russia was the world's largest exporter of wheat, accounting for about 25 percent of the market. After the war, Canada, the United States, Australia, and Argentina came to dominate the market, and Russian exports were no longer of any significance. Interestingly, in the early part of the twenty-first century, Russia and the Ukraine once again emerged as large wheat exporters.

The New York stock market crash in 1929, which signaled the beginning of the Great Depression, also marked a period of rapid decline in agricultural commodity prices and the introduction of several new government policies to support farm incomes. The export price of Canadian wheat, which set the world standard at the time, fell from $1.75 per bushel in the summer of 1929 to below $1.00 the following June. By December 1930, the price declined to $0.55 and then hit rock bottom at $0.40 in December 1932.

The United States introduced a system of supporting farm incomes with the passage of the Agricultural Adjustment Act in 1933. Even the free trading nation of Britain introduced agricultural import restrictions in the 1930s. It was the depressed price levels in the world markets that led to increased protectionism. The percentage of traded agricultural commodities subject to domestic market regulation increased from 5 percent in 1929 to about 55 percent in 1935.

World War II resulted in a severe drop in agricultural production in Europe, the USSR, Southeast Asia, and North Africa. These regions became significant importers of food in the immediate postwar period. However, food production in Canada, the United States, Australia, and Argentina actually rose, just as it had during World War I. In North America alone, agricultural production during the war increased by about 30 percent.

The formation of the European Economic Community (EEC) in 1957 with the Treaty of Rome was a major event shaping the structure of world agriculture. One of the main reasons that the EEC was formed was to protect agricultural production in Europe from low-cost imports from North America and Oceania. Europe's Common Agricultural Policy (CAP) made no provisions for production limitations, and thus output increased dramatically while prices rose. Farmers in Europe responded by rapidly expanding the use of fertilizers and chemicals. As a result of CAP, Western Europe changed from a major net importer of agricultural commodities to a major exporter.

The 1950s witnessed the introduction of "cheap food policies" in many developing countries in Latin America, Africa, and Asia. At the time, the belief was that rapid economic growth could only be achieved through import-substitution industrialization. As a result, agriculture was discriminated against through high import tariffs on industrial goods, the formation of parastatal marketing boards, urban food subsidies, and overvalued exchange rates.

Perhaps the most extreme example of dis-

Figure 3. Use of Manufactured Fertilizer

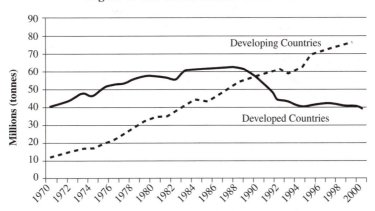

crimination against agriculture took place in China in the 1950s with the collectivization of agriculture and the establishment of communes based on the Soviet model. China's "Great Leap Forward" in the late 1950s diverted resources away from agriculture toward industrialization in an attempt to rapidly industrialize China's economy. China's grain output fell by about one-third in just two years, resulting in the worst famine of the nineteenth and twentieth centuries (Carter et al. 1996). An estimated 30 million people perished from the famine in China from 1959 to 1961. In comparison, the Irish famine of 1845–1851 resulted in 1.1 million deaths, the Bengal famine (in eastern India) in 1943 in 3 million to 4 million deaths, and the Ethiopian famine in 1984–1985 in about 1 million deaths.

The 1960s was a decade characterized by rapid technological change in agriculture, often called the "Green Revolution." Unlike previous periods of agricultural change, which were driven by advances in mechanical technology, the Green Revolution was characterized by breakthroughs in biological technology. In agriculture, mechanical technology has saved labor, whereas biological technology has generally served to save land.

Asia was the major benefactor of the Green Revolution because of major technological innovations that occurred in the production of hybrid rice and dwarf wheat. High-yielding

corn and wheat varieties were developed in Mexico in the 1950s, and high-yielding rice varieties were developed in China and the Philippines in the 1960s. These new varieties were very responsive to industrial inputs (such as chemical fertilizers, pesticides, and herbicides) and more effective soil and water management (including double cropping, that is, harvesting two crops per year on the same piece of land). These new techniques quickly replaced traditional farming practices throughout Asia and led to increased use of manufactured fertilizer in the developing world (see Figure 3).

The United Nations Conference on Trade and Development (UNCTAD) was established in the early 1960s with the goal of stabilizing and raising commodity prices in order to help developing countries, which were very dependent on primary commodity exports. Third World exporters faced falling commodity prices and price instability, slow growth in import demand, and trade restrictions in importing countries. UNCTAD worked to establish international commodity agreements (ICAs) that attempted to use buffer stocks and export controls to raise and stabilize world prices. ICAs in one form or another operated for wheat, sugar, rubber, and cocoa, and there were attempts to establish agreements for cotton, tea, jute, and sisal. The ICAs were unsuccessful owing to a lack of enthusiasm from member countries, "free riders" selling outside the agreements, and the general difficulties of attempting to manipulate world commodity markets that are subject to the disciplines of supply and demand (Gilbert 1987). For instance, the international coffee agreement was dominated by Brazil and Colombia for many years but could not control increased production in Africa and Asia that was sold outside the agreement to countries such as Russia.

An agricultural commodity price boom characterized the decade of the 1970s. Poor weather in parts of the world (partly due to El Niño) and policy failure elsewhere reduced food supplies and raised legitimate concerns over a potential world food crisis. The famous Russian "grain robbery" took place in 1972 when the Soviets purchased 30 million metric tons of grain from the United States over a short time period. The U.S. government even provided export subsidies on those sales, but immediately following the Russian purchases, the price of wheat, feed grains, and soybeans escalated sharply. The price of wheat and soybeans tripled in 1973. The volume of world agricultural trade expanded dramatically in the early part of the 1970s, and the U.S. government overreacted, imposing export controls on soybeans in 1973, a move which enraged Japanese importers and reignited food security fears in Japan. In 1974 and 1975, the United States also imposed volume restrictions on exports of corn and wheat to the USSR.

The 1980s saw a slowdown in the volume and value of agricultural trade and a collapse of commodity prices. In response to the USSR invasion of Afghanistan, the U.S. government (and other cooperating exporters) imposed an embargo on grain sales to the USSR in 1980. This embargo was not related to U.S. domestic supply concerns; rather, it was a foreign policy action aimed to punish the Soviet Union. The embargo was ultimately judged to be ineffective (USDA 1986), though Soviet import behavior did change after the embargo was lifted.

The most significant development in world agricultural policy during the 1980s was that China decollectivized its agriculture. To privatize farming, it established a "household responsibility system," supported rural industrial development (that is, township- and village-owned firms), and reformed mandatory procurement quotas and prices for agricultural commodities. Following reform, China's agricultural production growth was abnormally high for a few years owing to one-time productivity gains from improved incentives.

The Uruguay Round of trade negotiations was also launched in the 1980s, and the final 1994 agreement brought agriculture into the World Trade Organization (WTO). Agriculture thus became one of the last global industries to be subject to multilateral trade rules. The Uruguay Round Agreement on Agriculture (URAA) set new rules for trade in agricultural products and initiated a modest reduction in protection. The URAA also improved market access and disciplines on domestic support and export subsidies.

In the 1990s, the Asian financial crisis hit, and stock markets and currencies in the region fell between 30 and 50 percent. The Asian crisis was a reminder of the important linkage between macroeconomic variables (for example, interest rates, exchange rates, and income growth) and the agricultural sector. Macroeconomic shocks influence export competitiveness, import demand, and input prices. The agricultural producers in some Asian economies (such as Thailand) actually benefited from the crisis owing to currency depreciation, but consumers in those same countries suffered.

Agricultural Policy

Over thirty years ago, D. Gale Johnson wrote: "A significant fraction of world farm output is being produced in the wrong place. If significant benefits of a permanent nature were being derived from the distortions in location of output, there might be a reasonable basis for such interferences. However, the benefits that have been, and are being, derived are minimal; and the costs to consumers and taxpayers in many industrial countries, and to the possibilities of the developing countries to use their own resources to best advantage and to earn foreign exchange required for rapid economic growth, far outweigh any possible gains" (Johnson 1974, 23).

Johnson's description of how agricultural policies in rich countries have resulted in "world agriculture in disarray" is equally accurate today. He observed that the world's food supply is not produced in the regions with the lowest agricultural costs. Policies in developed nations tend to encourage agricultural output, while the opposite tends to be true in developing countries (Krueger et al. 1992). As a result, surplus agricultural production takes place in regions of the world where it isn't needed, and there is underproduction in regions of the world with a deficit in food supply. This implies that marketing and policy constraints are at least as important determinants of future food availability as biological or ecological constraints.

Despite considerable political rhetoric in the United States and the European Union about reforming and liberalizing agricultural policy, not much has changed; if anything, there is now more policy intervention than when Johnson made his observation many years ago. Agriculture remains one of the most distorted industries in the world economy.

The protection of agriculture has a long history. Prior to the nineteenth century, Britain employed import tariffs on grain (for example, through the Corn Laws) to raise food prices and benefit British landowners. The famous economist David Ricardo was concerned with this policy issue, and his theory of comparative advantage was directed at showing that free trade in grain was preferable to import duties.

Ricardo's principle of comparative advantage is recognized as one of the most important propositions in economics, but in today's global marketplace, much of what is observed in agriculture goes against the logic of Ricardo's theory. The standard free trade model

does not explain agricultural trade patterns. For example, the Japanese government pays its farmers $30 per bushel to produce wheat, when it could purchase all that it requires from other nations at $4 or $5 per bushel. Everywhere, agriculture remains heavily protected from imports—for instance, the U.S. import tariff on peanut butter is 130 percent, Canadian import tariffs on dairy products are 300 percent, and South Korean rice tariffs exceed 500 percent.

The staple nature of agricultural products makes the industry somewhat unique, and this is one reason that it receives special status with regard to government policy. Because human survival depends on food, agriculture and agricultural trade is highly political. This also means that the supply security issue is given undue attention in, for example, Europe and Japan. France is a classic example of a country where supply security is used as an argument in favor of high farm prices even though the country is a large food exporter. French politicians still use food shortages during World War II as justification for heavily subsidizing their farmers and others in the European Union.

Farmers in poor countries are adversely affected by subsidies in rich countries, which lead to overproduction and depressed world commodity prices. Annual agricultural support for developed countries now totals over $300 billion, double the value of total agricultural exports from developing countries (UNCTAD 1999). According to the Organisation for Economic Co-operation and Development (OECD), domestic policy support to agriculture in the United States, Japan, and the European Union accounts for 80 percent of the world's total subsidies. In 2001, total agricultural support in OECD countries was about $311 billion, accounting for about one-third of total farm receipts. Subsidies totaled about $100 billion in the EU, $55 billion in the United States, and $50 billion in Japan. For every metric ton of wheat produced in Australia in 1999, farmers received about $10 (in U.S. dollars) in subsidies from the government. In contrast, in the United States and in the EU, the subsidies per metric ton were $50 and $60, respectively, in the same year. The world wheat price in 1999 was only about $100 per metric ton.

U.S. farm policy is revamped every five years by measures commonly referred to as "Farm Bills." Prior to 1996, U.S. agricultural policy was based on a combination of features, including government-guaranteed farm prices, export subsidies, and government stockholding activities. The subsidies in the United States varied inversely with the global supply-demand balance. When world supplies were low and prices high, U.S. farmers received less in the way of government support. When global supplies were burdensome and prices low, farmers were paid not to produce but received very high prices for what they did produce.

The 1996 U.S. Farm Bill introduced the most fundamental changes in U.S. farm policy since the 1930s. Government payments were no longer linked to specific crops and crop prices, and farmers no longer had to take land out of production in order to receive subsidies. Furthermore, the U.S. government largely withdrew from holding reserve stocks and dramatically reduced the use of export subsidies. Under the 1996 bill, the government tied payments to individual producers based on historical plantings and yields. Individual growers could obtain government payments totaling up to $150,000 per year, and some growers receive multiples of this limit through partnerships and other business arrangements.

The EU has recently reformed its agricultural policy with the Agenda 2000 legislation, introduced in 1999. Agenda 2000 modified EU policy through a shift from price supports to direct payments. One impetus for the legislation was the EU enlargement to include several Central and Eastern European countries, including the Czech Republic, Hungary, and Poland. Another reason for the EU reform was that Europe needed to reduce its use of export subsidies in order to comply with its Uruguay Round commitments. A large share of the subsidies in the EU, Japan, and the United States becomes capitalized into land values. The WTO

offers the most hope for stopping this subsidization, as it helps governments in the EU, Japan, and the United States keep their own domestic special-interest groups in check. In order to comply with the spirit of the WTO rules, the United States is going to have to grant better access to its own markets—including sugar, dairy products, peanuts, and citrus—and to do so it must stand up to domestic lobby groups.

As traditional agricultural trade barriers are lowered, food safety and animal and plant quarantine measures are increasingly used as obstacles to international trade. The Uruguay Round Agreement on Sanitary and Phytosanitary Measures (SPS Agreement) established some basic rules for countries to set standards for food safety and the protection of domestic animal and plant species. It allows countries to set their own standards, but it also says regulations must be based on science.

Trade remedy laws are now being used in agriculture as a replacement for traditional trade barriers. There is an upward trend globally in the usage of trade remedy cases in both developed and developing countries—including antidumping (AD) and countervailing duty (CVD) laws and, to some extent, import relief (safeguard) laws. Developing countries have criticized the use of AD and CVD laws in developed countries. For instance, Brazil refused to fully engage itself in discussions on the Free Trade Area of the Americas because of the continued application of U.S. AD duties on products such as orange juice. In 2002, the filing of AD cases on exports of raspberries and spring table grapes to the United States troubled Chile. U.S. honey producers have also received AD protection from competition from Argentina and China as well as CVD protection from Argentina.

Food Supply and Demand

In 1972, the Club of Rome published "Limits to Growth," a very pessimistic study of population and food that predicted that by 2050 there would be a worldwide catastrophe due to food shortages (Meadows 1972). The Club of Rome predictions gave renewed attention to the writings of British economist Thomas Malthus, who in 1798 said the world would eventually face a large-scale famine because population growth would outstrip the food supply. Paul and Anne Ehrlich made a similar prediction in a 1990 book, *The Population Explosion,* in which they argued that humans are on a "collision course with massive famine." In 1995, Lester Brown, in *Who Will Feed China? Wake-Up Call for a Small Planet,* predicted that China will starve the rest of the world. These gloomy predictions have all been well off the mark; world per capita food supply (measured by available calories) has increased by 25 percent over the past forty years (FAO 2002).

Growth in agricultural production has been particularly impressive in Asia. In the 1980s and 1990s, agricultural production grew by 5.3 percent per year in China, 3.2 percent in India, and 3.3 percent in Indonesia. In contrast, agricultural production in the rich OECD countries only grew by 0.3 percent during the same period. China is the most successful story, as it boosted cereal grain production by more than 50 percent during this time period. Per capita food supply in China rose from 2,328 calories per day in 1980 to 3,029 calories in 2000, a 30 percent increase in just twenty years. In sharp contrast to Lester Brown's forecast, China's huge success with food production helps explain why developing countries as a group have done so well in terms of increasing supply.

The food situation has not performed as well in sub-Saharan Africa, where per capita food production fell by about 1.1 percent per year during the 1970s and 1980s. Food production grew at an annual rate of 1.7 percent between 1970 and 1989, but it could not keep pace with the rapid population growth in the region at the time, rising at 2.9 percent per year. Reasons for poor agricultural performance lie with a poor infrastructure (for example, less than 2 percent of the arable land is irrigated in sub-Saharan Africa), poor marketing

systems, unpredictable government policies, wars, and unstable macroeconomic conditions. However, there has been a movement away from centralized decisionmaking throughout Africa as marketing parastatals have been disbanded and market forces have been allowed to work. The results are encouraging, as sub-Saharan food production growth increased to an annual rate of 2.9 percent in the 1990s and growth in per capita food production was positive (0.2 percent per year).

Globally, per capita food production has grown at an average rate of approximately 0.6 percent a year over the past thirty years, and the growth rate has increased in the past decade. Developing countries, with increases in production due to the liberalization of regressive policies and the intensification of agriculture, have accounted for most of the growth in per capita world food production.

Of course, on the production side, agriculture is vulnerable to unplanned fluctuations in output resulting from weather phenomena. Moreover, supply fluctuations often give rise to price variations in the opposite direction. These factors combine to produce a large amount of revenue variability for agricultural exporters and fluctuating import costs for importers. Many developed nations have attempted to isolate themselves from fluctuating prices through the formation of trade barriers. However, this response tends to accentuate the amount of instability in the international marketplace (Zwart and Blandford 1989). For developing countries, variable agricultural prices are problematic, because their export base is often heavily concentrated on raw commodities.

"Engel's Law" (named after Ernst Engel, a nineteenth-century German statistician) states that with rising incomes, the share of expenditures for food products declines. Today, consumers residing in developing countries spend, on average, about 47 percent of their budget on food, whereas in rich countries consumers spend about 13 percent on average. It is also the case that increases in per capita food demand resulting from income growth slow as incomes rise. For example, as per capita incomes rose in Japan and South Korea, per capita rice consumption peaked and then started to decline.

Demographers, who once predicted the earth's population would peak at 12 billion over the next century, have revised their estimates; they now expect that the world's population will peak at 10 billion before 2200, when it may begin declining. The world's population, now 6.2 billion, quadrupled in the twentieth century. In 1900, 86 percent of the world's people lived in rural areas and about 14 percent in urban areas. By 2000, cities were home to 47 percent of the population, with 53 percent still in the countryside. Between now and 2030, when the global population is expected to reach about 8 billion, almost all the growth will be in cities. The largest percentage increase will take place in Africa, but the greatest absolute growth in population will occur in Asia, which has 56 percent of the world's population. The United Nations estimates that the world's population is growing at an annual rate of slightly more than 1.2 percent. Of this growth, 97 percent is taking place in less-developed countries.

Income growth and urbanization, and the resulting changes in dietary patterns, particularly in developing countries, have important implications for food consumption and agricultural trade. Urbanization leads to a decrease in calorie consumption per person (Clark et al. 1995) but greater demand for processed food products. At the same time, urbanization is correlated with income growth. Low-value staples, such as cereals, account for a larger share of the food budget of the poor, whereas high-value food items, such as dairy products and meat, make up a larger share of the food budget of the rich (Regmi 2001). Poor consumers are most responsive to income and price changes. Thus, rising incomes are usually associated with increased demand for meat, horticultural, and processed food products, and increased demand for meat, in turn, results in increased demand for feed grains and protein meals.

For instance, in 2000, per capita meat consumption (red meat, poultry, and fish) in China was 20 kilograms (kg) per year for rural households and 35 kg per year for urban households, and urban incomes were 2.5 times larger than rural incomes. On average, China's rural and urban meat consumption per person in 2000 was 24.5 kg per year. This figure compares to an annual consumption level of about 81 kg per person in the United States. The income gap between the United States and China is about 8:1. However, China's per capita incomes have more than tripled over the past twenty years, and as a result, some dramatic changes in food consumption have taken place. For instance, per capita meat consumption has also tripled over the past twenty years in China. Demand for improved quality and convenience, increased health awareness, and an aging population have all led to changes in food consumption patterns in developed countries (Regmi 2001). For example, in the United States, per capita consumption of red meat has fallen 12 percent over the past thirty years while per capita consumption of poultry increased by 92 percent. Per capita fruit and vegetable consumption in the United States increased by 21 percent over the same period.

International Trade

Global merchandise trade has grown seventeen-fold since 1950, but agricultural trade has grown only sixfold over the same time period. Agriculture now accounts for less than 10 percent of merchandise trade, down from 25 percent in the early 1960s. This lower growth rate in agricultural trade no doubt reflects the lower rate of world demand growth for food relative to the more price-elastic manufactures. However, average tariffs on manufactures have fallen from 40 percent to 4 percent during this period, whereas agricultural tariffs have remained in the 40 to 50 percent range, on average (USDA/ERS 1998). Thus, agriculture has not yet fully participated in the new globalization phenomenon. However, despite high protectionism, agricultural trade has expanded faster than agricultural production.

In 2001, the value of global agricultural trade was an estimated $412 billion, according to the FAO's categorization of agricultural products. Table 2 lists the annual value of global trade by major categories of agricultural products. The largest trade categories include fruits and vegetables ($69.8 billion), meat ($45.8 billion), cereal grains ($36 billion), milk and milk products ($27.6 billion), beverage crops ($25.1 billion), and soybeans and soybean products ($21.2 billion). The United States and the European Union are the largest food exporters in the world, each exporting around $50 billion per year. Tables 3 and 4 report the top agricultural trading nations. The two dominant exporters are followed by Canada, Australia, Brazil, China, and Argentina, in order of importance. On the import side (Table 4), the European Union, the United States, and Japan are by far the largest agricultural importers, followed by Canada, the former Soviet Union, Mexico, China, South Korea, and Hong Kong. China's official agricultural imports may be underreported because they do not take account of smuggling from Hong Kong, an activity that is prevalent for horticultural and animal products to avoid tariffs and other trade restrictions.

There have been some distinct changes in patterns of agricultural trade over the past few decades. The share of high-valued and processed food products has grown dramatically since the mid-1980s relative to trade in bulk agricultural commodities such as cereal grains, rising from about 39 percent in 1980 to more than 50 percent in 2000. The value of trade in fruits and vegetables has increased by over 30 percent over the past decade. Trade in meat has shown a similar upward trend, but at the same time, the value of trade in cereal grains has remained flat.

Cereal grain markets around the world remain a critical component of the world food

Table 2: Global Trade in Major Agricultural Products, 2001 (in billions of U.S. dollars)

Agricultural Product	2001
Fruits and vegetables	69.8
Meat	45.8
Cereal grains	36.0
Milk and milk products	27.6
Beverage crops (coffee, tea, & cocoa)	25.1
Soybeans and products	21.2
Wine	12.7
Distilled alcoholic beverages	10.6
Sugar	10.5
Cotton	6.2
Bananas	4.2
Orange juice	2.5
Other	161.3
Total	412.2

Source: Food and Agriculture Organization of the United Nations, FAOSTAT, www.fao.org.

equation because grain represents the single most important source of world food consumption, accounting for about 60 percent of the calories consumed. Total global production of wheat, coarse grains, and rice is approximately 1.8 billion metric tons per annum, with some 220 million metric tons (mmt) traded (about 12 percent). Oilseed production is around 215 mmt, and approximately 18 percent of this is traded. Because grain is one of the world's key staple products, it is a highly political commodity—it has been used in the past as an economic weapon (for example, in 1980 with the U.S. embargo on grain sales to the Soviet Union), and it receives special economic and political status in both developed and developing countries. Grain is a special commodity because the possibility of a grain shortage is real, although the probability of one is very low: World carryover stocks average about two to three months' supply, more or less the same as thirty years ago.

Wheat is the primary grain consumed by humans around the globe. About 75 percent of the world's wheat is consumed directly, and an-

Table 3: Top Ten Agricultural Exporters, 1998–2000 (in billions of U.S. dollars)

	1998	1999	2000
United States	53.1	50.3	52.9
European Union	49.5	47.4	48.1
Canada	14.7	14.8	15.8
Australia	13.4	14.2	15.1
Brazil	16.0	14.1	13.6
China	11.4	11.7	12.9
Argentina	12.9	11.5	11.2
Thailand	7.4	7.7	7.9
Mexico	6.5	6.5	6.8
New Zealand	6.4	6.3	6.6

Source: United States Department of Agriculture, Economic Research Service; Foreign Agricultural Trade of the United States.

other 15 percent indirectly in the form of animal products from animals that consume grain. This leaves 10 percent for seed and industrial use. The global consumption of wheat has doubled over the past thirty years to reach nearly 600 mmt per year in recent years. Consumption expanded by about 5.6 mmt per year in the 1990s, owing to rising population and incomes as well as increased urbanization, with its associated changing dietary patterns. Future growth in wheat consumption is expected to originate mainly from developing countries, the same source that accounted for recent growth in global wheat consumption.

Feed use accounts for a relatively small share of total world wheat consumption. During the 1990s, this share has dropped from approximately 20 percent of global use to just 15 percent. This shift in feed use was attributed mainly to a dramatic decline in the use of wheat for feed in the former Soviet Union (FSU). Between 1990/1991 and 1999/2000, the use of wheat for feed in the FSU fell by more than 46 mmt, a 74 percent decline. This was precipitated by the FSU's economic recession and the collapse of livestock production in that region.

The United States is the largest wheat exporter, followed by Canada, Australia, the EU, and Argentina. Recently, a number of smaller exporters have emerged that are of consequence in aggregate. These exporters include Kazakhstan, Hungary, India, Romania, Russia,

and the Ukraine. China and the former Soviet Union (FSU) together were large wheat importers during the early 1980s, at one point accounting for one-third of total world imports. However, their combined significance as importers declined sharply in the 1990s. At present, these two regions are immaterial importers. Looking forward, the FSU will most likely emerge as a major wheat exporter instead of an importer. At the same time, China will probably revert to importing wheat, with erratic swings in yearly import volumes.

Import demand for wheat in the developing nations of East Asia, Latin America, and North Africa has continued to grow—a trend that helps to explain why global trade in wheat has not fallen dramatically with the departure of China and the FSU from the import market. The strong possibility that developing countries will account for most of the import demand growth in the foreseeable future is extremely important for exporters, because developing countries tend to import lower quality wheat. The East Asian market (excluding China) is now the largest importing region, with its imports of wheat doubling over the 1990s.

Agricultural trade barriers were never seriously negotiated under the General Agreement on Tariffs and Trade (GATT) until the Uruguay Round in 1993. This meant that agricultural export subsidies were permitted under the GATT, as were quantitative domestic import re-

Table 4: Top Ten Agricultural Importers (in billions of U.S. dollars)

	1998	1999	2000
European Union	61.8	57.9	54.3
United States	41.1	41.4	40.5
Japan	31.4	31.1	31.4
Canada	10.8	11.5	12.1
Former Soviet Union	15.4	11.8	11.8
Mexico	8.7	9.0	10.3
China	7.6	6.8	9.5
South Korea	6.5	7.4	8.1
Hong Kong	9.0	7.7	7.8
Saudi Arabia	4.8	5.0	5.2

Source: United States Department of Agriculture, Economic Research Service; Foreign Agricultural Trade of the United States.

strictions. As a result, there was a rise in the use of quantitative trade barriers, tariffs, and nontariff import restrictions. Major agricultural products continue to enjoy a level of protection uncommon in merchandise trade. Certain developing countries now benefit from preferential trading arrangements with developed country importers. The EU has the most extensive set of preferential deals with nonmembers (Greenfield and Konandreas 1996). For instance, under the previous Lome Convention, the EU signed a series of preferential trade agreements with developing countries in Africa, the Caribbean, and the Pacific (the so-called "ACP countries"). Preferential trade concessions mean increased market access for those countries granted special access, but these types of trade preferences are inefficient relative to nondiscriminatory access. For this reason, special trade preferences contradict WTO rules. The EU's sugar import preferences are particularly controversial. The EU imports sugar from its former colonies and at the same time provides generous subsidies to its domestic sugar producers. As a result, the EU also is the world's largest exporter of sugar (accounting for 40 percent of world exports), and these subsidized exports are damaging the interests of many developing-country exporters.

In 2001, the United States and the EU settled a major trade dispute over bananas following a WTO ruling against the EU's banana import policies that gave import preferences to ACP growers. The quotas excluded U.S. companies with Latin American operations from exporting bananas from Latin America to the EU. After losing the WTO case, in 2001 the EU agreed to replace the preference system with a tariff-only system, which would give Latin America some access to the EU market.

Examples of regional trade agreements of importance to agriculture include the Andean Community (involving Bolivia, Colombia, Ecuador, and Venezuela); the Association of Southeast Asian Nations (ASEAN, including Cambodia, Indonesia, Singapore, the Philippines, Malaysia, Thailand, and Vietnam); the North American Free Trade Agreement (NAFTA, with Canada, Mexico, and the United States); Mercosur (Mercado Comùn del Sur, with Argentina, Brazil, Paraguay, and Uruguay); the Free Trade Area of the Americas; the Asia Pacific Economic Cooperation (APEC) forum; and, finally, the enlargement process of the European Union to include Central and Eastern European transition economies. Some economists believe that trade liberalization on a regional basis reduces the costs of liberalizing trade between blocs, hence making global liberalization easier to achieve. Others claim that regional integration reduces the motivation for liberalizing trade on a more global basis and results in excessive trade diversion (Krueger 1999).

Developing countries' share of world merchandise exports increased from 17.7 percent to 28.8 percent between 1980 and 1997. This greater involvement in global trade is largely due to a more outward-oriented trade policy and to trade liberalization that has been undertaken unilaterally by developing countries. However, developing countries have not been as successful in capturing a larger share of agricultural trade. During the period 1980–1997, developing countries' share of world agricultural exports was essentially unchanged, increasing only from 36.4 percent to 37.5 percent, and it remains surprisingly low. This inability to expand participation in world agricultural markets has held back economic growth and diversification in the developing world. Agriculture is the backbone of almost all developing countries, and for about fifty developing countries it accounts for one-third to one-half of export earnings.

Nontariff trade barriers of importance to agriculture include sanitary and phytosanitary measures—for example, Japan's testing requirements for imported apples, cherries, nectarines, and walnuts were found to be "without scientific merit" by the WTO. Scientific justification for trade measures is a complicated issue. A famous trade dispute in this area involves the European Union's long-running ban on growth hormones in beef production that has prevented the United States from selling beef into the EU. The WTO has found against the EU because the EU has failed to prove a public health risk, but the ban continues.

It can be argued that protectionism in agriculture and its success in expanding agricultural production have had adverse environmental consequences (Pinstrup-Andersen 2002). The expansion of acreage has led to deforestation and soil erosion. At the same time, the excessive use of fertilizer and chemicals in some countries has polluted the soil and water. For example, chemical fertilizer use in the EU ranges from 250 kg to 350 kg per hectare, compared to only 110 kg per hectare in the United States. Partly in response to policy reform and lower prices, the use of manufactured fertilizer in developed countries has actually declined in recent years, while it has continued to increase in the developing world (see Figure 3).

One of the most extreme examples of protectionism threatening the environment is the high cost of wheat production in Saudi Arabia's desert. Saudi Arabia has offered massive subsidies to encourage wheat production. Prices paid to farmers were five times the world level, and as a result, Saudi wheat production rose to exceed domestic consumption and the surplus grain was exported. In the early 1990s, Saudi Arabia was the world's sixth-largest wheat exporter. Through the use of modern irrigation, the desert wheat farms consume huge amounts of underground water, which is in short supply in that part of the world.

Recent arguments (for example, the multifunctionality approach) in the EU and the United States claim that agriculture provides "social benefits" not valued by the market, including environmental protectionism, food security, and the maintenance of rural communities. Those advancing this view claim that the agricultural industry must be subsidized because the value of social benefits is not included in the market prices.

Colin A. Carter

See Also Protectionism; Subsidies; Tariffs; Food and Beverages; World Trade Organization (WTO); Food Safety

References

Brown, Lester Russell. 1995. *Who Will Feed China? Wake-Up Call for a Small Planet.* New York: W. W. Norton.

Carter, Colin Andre, Fu-Ning Zhong, and Fang Cai. 1996. *China's Ongoing Agricultural Reform.* San Francisco: 1990 Institute.

Clark, Gregory, Michael Huberman, and Peter H. Lindert. 1995. "A British Food Puzzle, 1770–1850." *Economic History Review* 48, no. 2 (May): 215–237.

Ehrlich, Paul R., and Anne H. Ehrlich. 1990. *The Population Explosion.* New York: Simon and Schuster.

Food and Agriculture Organization. *The World Food Survey.* Various issues.

———. 2002. *Food Balance Sheets.* FAOSTAT, www.fao.org.

Gilbert, Christopher L. 1987. "International Commodity Agreements: Design and Performance." *World Development* 15, no. 5 (May): 591–616.

Greenfield Jim, and Panos Konandreas. 1996. "Implications of the Uruguay Round for Developing Countries. Introduction: An Overview of the Issues." *Food Policy* 21, no. 4–5 (Septerber-November): 345–350.

Johnson, D. Gale . 1974. US Agriculture in a World Context: Policies and Approaches for the Next Decade. New York: Praeger Press.

Jorgenson, Dale W., and Frank M. Gollop. 1992. "Productivity Growth in U.S. Agriculture: A Postwar Perspective." *American Journal of Agricultural Economics* 74, no. 3 (August): 745–750.

Josling, Timothy Edward, Stefan Tangermann, and T. K. Warley. 1996. *Agriculture in the GATT.* New York: St. Martin's.

Krueger, Anne O. 1999. "Are Preferential Trading Arrangements Trade-Liberalising or Protectionist?" *Journal of Economic Perspectives* 13, no. 4 (Fall): 105–124.

Krueger, Anne O., Maurice Schiff, and Alberto Valdés, eds. 1992. *The Political Economy of Agricultural Pricing Policy.* Baltimore: Published for the World Bank by Johns Hopkins University Press.

McCalla, Alex F. 1969. "Protectionism in International Agricultural Trade, 1850–1968." *Agricultural History* 43 (July): 329–343.

Meadows, Donella H. 1972. *The Limits to Growth: A Report for the Club of Rome's Project on the Predicament of Mankind.* New York: Universe Books.

Pinstrup-Andersen, Per. 2002. "Food and Agricultural Policy for a Globalizing World: Preparing for the Future." *American Journal of Agricultural Economics* 84, no. 5: 1201–1214.

Regmi, Anita, ed. 2001. "Changing Structure of Global Food Consumption and Trade." Market and Trade Economics Division, Economic Research Service, U.S. Department of Agriculture, Agriculture and Trade Report WRS-01-1.

United Nations Conference on Trade and Development. 1999. *Trade and Development Report.* Geneva: UNCTAD.

U.S. Department of Agriculture, Economic Research Service. 1986. *Embargoes, Surplus Disposal, and U.S. Agriculture.* Report No. 564.

———. 1998. *Agriculture in the WTO,* WRS-98-4, USDA/ERS, December.

World Bank. 2001. *Global Economic Prospects and the Developing Countries 2001.* Washington, DC: World Bank.

World Trade Organization. 2002. *International Trade Statistics 2002,* www.wto.org.

Zwart, Anthony C, and David Blandford. 1989. "Market Intervention and International Price Instability." *American Journal of Agricultural Economics* 71, no. 2 (May): 379–388.

Chemicals

Global Chemical Production

The overall value of world chemical production in 2002 was estimated at $1,738 billion. The chemical industry is spread somewhat unevenly across continents. About 29 percent of industry revenues, or $500 billion, were generated in North America, including about 26 percent in the United States alone. South America accounted for about 5 percent, or $95 billion; Western European countries for about 31 percent, or $530 billion; and the Middle East and Africa together generated about 4 percent, or some $70 billion. The Asia Pacific region ac-

counted for approximately 29 percent, or $504 billion, of which the Japanese chemical industry accounted for about 10 percent. The East Asian subregion, including China and the Republic of Korea (South Korea), accounted for about 13 percent.

The chemical industry has been slowing down in recent years in North America, particularly in the United States. The U.S. industry grew by only 2.5 percent in 1999 and had negative growth, of −0.1 percent, in 2002. In Western Europe, the chemical industry shows steady growth, with increases of 4.4 percent in 1999 and 5.2 percent in 2002. The East Asian

Table 1: Evolution of World Chemical Production, 1999–2004

	Actual Increase/Decrease				Chemical Production, 2002 (in billions of U.S. dollars)
	1999	2000	2001	2002	
North America	2.6	2.5	-0.5	0.1	498
USA	2.5	2.0	-0.6	-0.1	458
Canada	3.9	10.5	3.0	5.5	24
Mexico	3.4	3.9	3.2	-1.4	16
South America	0.3	5.0	2.9	1.1	95
Western Europe	4.4	5.1	2.3	5.2	534
Middle East and Africa	1.2	4.6	1.7	11.6	70
Asia and Pacific	5.6	6.3	3.2	6.3	504
Japan	2.5	0.7	2.1	3.1	181
East Asia	8.9	12.1	8.1	9.1	220
South Asia and other Asia and Pacific	5.7	6.0	3.1	5.7	103
World total	3.8	4.8	1.9	4.0	1,738

Source: Kagaku Keizai, special issue (March 2004): 7, and ILO.

328

Table 2: Chemical Production, United States, 1993–2003

	1993	1994	1995	1996	1997	1998	1999	2000	2001	2002	2003	Annual change: 1993–2003
Total index	80.8	85.2	89.3	93.1	100.0	105.9	110.6	115.4	111.5	110.9	111.2	3.2
Manufacturing, total	78.1	83.1	87.8	92.1	100.0	106.8	112.3	117.7	113.1	112.5	112.6	3.7
Nondurable manufacturing	91.4	94.6	96.2	96.5	100.0	101.5	102.2	102.8	99.8	99.2	97.0	0.6
Chemicals	89.0	91.3	92.7	94.6	100.0	101.8	103.8	105.5	103.9	105.3	105.6	1.7
Basic chemicals	92.4	93.2	93.1	93.1	100.0	97.6	101.8	98.9	91.4	95.3	93.9	0.2
Alkalies & chlorine	122.4	97.3	103.9	109.3	100.0	101.3	125.8	116.8	110.1	108.5	104.3	-1.6
Synthetic dyes & pigments	97.8	100.5	96.2	96.0	100.0	100.8	97.2	96.2	93.0	95.6	93.6	-0.4
Other basic inorganic chemicals	97.7	90.1	93.8	96.6	100.0	105.1	109.3	98.4	97.1	96.9	93.7	-0.4
Organic chemicals	86.4	91.2	90.4	90.2	100.0	92.2	99.1	99.9	88.2	94.9	94.6	0.9
Synthetic materials	88.4	95.5	96.1	94.1	100.0	104.1	105.6	103.2	92.1	96.2	94.9	0.7
Plastic material & resin	81.7	93.2	93.9	91.0	100.0	107.9	112.4	112.3	100.2	105.8	104.3	2.5
Artificial & synthetic fibers	105.7	104.4	105.5	105.9	100.0	100.8	92.1	83.0	72.6	72.5	71.0	-3.9
Chemical products	85.0	86.9	90.4	94.7	100.0	104.6	106.2	110.2	115.8	115.6	116.3	3.2
Pharmaceuticals & medicines	83.0	86.4	89.7	94.9	100.0	108.0	112.7	116.6	124.9	126.8	127.6	4.4
Soap, cleaning compounds & toiletries	87.7	87.1	91.8	94.4	100.0	98.5	94.2	99.0	101.3	96.3	96.6	1.0
Paint & coatings	95.6	102.6	99.5	99.3	100.0	100.4	98.9	98.6	96.1	106.2	111.6	1.6
Pesticide, fertilizer & other agricultural chemicals	95.0	94.9	94.5	96.4	100.0	102.4	91.8	84.9	80.6	81.7	80.9	-1.6

Note: Synthetic materials row includes synthetic rubber
Source: U.S. Federal Reserve Board, cited in *Chemical & Engineering News* (CEN), July 5, 2004, p. 50.

chemical industry shows almost two-digit growth. Tables 2 through 5 show the evolution of primary chemical production by the major chemical-producing countries, with 1997 as the base year, set at 100.

Global Chemical Trade

World trade in chemicals reached a record $660 billion in 2002 and accounted for 10.5 percent of overall world merchandise trade. The industry ranked fourth in world merchandise exports by product in 2002, after machinery and transport equipment ($2,539 billion, or 40.5 percent), office and telecommunications equipment ($838 billion, 13.4 percent), and mining products ($788 billion, 12.6 percent).

Table 6 shows leading exporters and importers of chemicals in 2002. The European Union is the largest exporter of chemicals. In 2002, the EU alone exported $363.34 billion of chemicals to the rest of world, accounting for 55 percent of the world chemical trade. It was followed by the United States, which exported $81.29 billion of chemicals in 2002. Japan ranks third, with $33.25 billion of exports in chemicals that year, followed by Switzerland with $29.70 billion and China with $15.32 billion. Canada ranks sixth. The world's seventh largest chemical-producing country is the Republic of Korea, which exported $12.65 billion, followed by Singapore, with $11.65 billion. From 1990 through 2002, the EU, the United States, Japan, and Switzerland reduced their shares in the world chemical trade, while China, Canada, the Republic of Korea, and Singapore increased their shares.

The EU is also the largest chemical importer. It imported $295.64 billion in chemicals in 2002, accounting for 43.5 percent of world chemical imports. The United States ranks second, importing $88.33 billion in chemicals in 2002. China ranks third, importing $39.04 billion, followed by Japan, Canada, Mexico, and the Republic of Korea. The United States, China, Canada, Switzerland, Mexico, Brazil,

Table 3: Chemical Production Index, Canada, 1993–2003

	1993	1994	1995	1996	1997	1998	1999	2000	2001	2002	2003	Annual Change, 1993–2003
All manufacturing	82.2	88.4	92.9	93.9	100.0	105.0	113.5	126.4	121.5	124.7	124.4	4.2
Chemicals	89.2	94.5	99.3	99.8	100.0	100.9	105.2	116.2	119.1	126.4	131.2	3.9
Basic chemicals	85.8	91.0	97.6	93.0	100.0	98.2	97.9	106.0	92.9	95.2	99.2	1.5
Pharmaceuticals & medicines	92.5	92.4	96.8	96.6	100.0	95.3	112.2	142.1	186.1	225.4	243.8	10.2

Source: Statistics Canada, cited in *Chemical & Engineering News* (CEN), July 5, 2004, p. 51.

Table 4: Chemical Production Index, Asia, 1993–2003

	1993	1994	1995	1996	1997	1998	1999	2000	2001	2002	2003	Annual Change, 1993–2003
Japan												
Mining & manufacturing	89.6	91.3	94.3	96.5	100.0	92.9	93.6	99.1	91.3	90.1	93.1	0.4
All chemicals	84.0	89.4	94.5	95.7	100.0	94.9	98.3	98.9	95.8	95.8	97.3	1.5
Petrochemicals	79.2	84.4	92.9	94.5	100.0	94.5	99.3	99.1	94.5	95.5	98.4	2.2
Aromatics	76.8	78.9	89.0	85.5	100.0	93.9	100.9	100.1	97.7	100.8	106.5	3.3
Industrial sodium chemicals	92.8	92.5	97.3	95.7	100.0	95.7	97.2	98.2	91.0	92.6	91.3	-0.2
Inorganic chemicals & dyes	95.9	94.5	98.5	96.8	100.0	97.7	103.3	106.8	101.8	103.8	106.3	1.0
Organic chemicals	79.6	82.0	90.4	93.2	100.0	96.6	101.9	100.6	94.3	94.6	100.0	2.3
Cyclic intermediates & dyes	80.7	89.3	96.9	96.8	100.0	95.1	98.2	97.7	93.9	95.6	96.6	1.8
Plastics	80.1	86.5	92.6	89.8	100.0	92.2	94.8	96.4	91.0	91.0	91.3	1.3
Synthetic rubber	82.3	84.9	94.1	95.8	100.0	95.5	99.1	99.9	92.0	96.1	99.6	1.9
Fertilizers	105.7	103.8	104.2	101.8	100.0	90.9	88.1	87.1	80.6	75.0	69.5	-4.1
Republic of Korea												
All manufacturing	71.0	78.9	88.3	95.9	100.0	93.4	116.8	136.8	137.1	148.3	156.0	8.2
Chemicals & chemical products	68.8	74.4	79.5	89.0	100.0	96.6	106.6	113.0	116.0	123.4	128.1	6.4
Rubber & plastic products	81.5	88.2	92.6	98.1	100.0	79.2	93.1	99.4	101.9	108.5	111.3	3.2
Taiwan, China												
All manufacturing	81.6	86.3	90.8	93.3	100.0	103.2	111.2	120.2	110.1	120.4	129.4	4.7
Chemicals	70.3	83.6	88.6	93.8	100.0	102.9	112.6	120.5	129.4	137.1	145.8	7.6
Basic chemicals	80.9	84.0	88.7	95.9	100.0	98.9	107.5	120.9	123.5	125.4	133.5	5.1
Petrochemicals	72.7	85.2	89.0	95.5	100.0	101.2	118.5	133.4	163.8	175.4	197.8	10.5
Fertilizers	84.6	88.1	94.7	96.5	100.0	92.3	85.0	83.0	77.5	74.2	73.8	-1.4
Synthetic fibers	74.5	82.8	85.6	91.1	100.0	105.5	107.6	111.8	107.7	112.2	111.8	4.1
Plastics & resins	64.6	84.8	91.5	95.1	100.0	103.3	113.2	117.8	118.0	125.3	129.0	7.2
Synthetic rubber	44.5	60.9	77.1	80.3	100.0	103.3	109.0	102.4	105.5	115.8	120.8	10.5

Note: "All chemicals" excludes pharmaceuticals.
Sources: Japan's Ministry of Economy, Trade and Industry; National Statistical Office, Republic of Korea; Taiwan's Ministry of Economic Affairs, Department of Statistics, cited in *Chemical & Engineering News* (CEN), July 5, 2004, p. 50.

Table 5: Chemical Production in Major Chemical-Producing Countries in Europe, 1993–2003

	1993	1994	1995	1996	1997	1998	1999	2000	2001	2002	2003	Annual Change, 1993–2003
Belgium	91.4	97.1	106.7	102.5	100.0	99.0	99.1	105.7	111.9	112.2	N/A	—
France	95.7	97.2	102.5	101.5	100.0	98.9	98.6	103.0	104.2	103.5	105.1	—
Germany	98.9	100.4	107.4	101.8	100.0	99.1	98.3	103.0	105.1	104.0	109.4	1.0
Italy	87.8	88.3	90.5	96.6	100.0	97.8	98.5	107.0	107.5	110.1	109.9	2.3
Netherlands	90.4	94.2	103.2	99.2	100.0	95.6	94.3	110.1	109.1	109.4	112.7	2.2
Spain	94.3	92.5	101.6	101.1	100.0	95.9	96.2	105.7	105.9	106.8	109.9	1.5
U.K.	83.1	85.7	85.9	86.5	100.0	98.9	100.0	108.3	111.6	111.8	115.6	3.4

N/A = Not available.
Sources: European Chemical Industry Council, national chemical associations, cited in *Chemical & Engineering News* (CEN), July 5, 2004, p. 51.

Poland, and Turkey imported more chemicals than they had twelve years earlier, whereas the EU, Japan, and Singapore imported less.

Characteristics of the Global Chemical Industry

Production of chemicals constitutes a key industry in many countries of the world. The chemical industry is science-based and uses high technology. It is one of history's grand enterprises. Its output includes more than 70,000 products, including paints and coatings; pharmaceuticals; soaps and detergents; perfumes and cosmetics; fertilizers, pesticides, herbicides, and other agricultural chemicals; solvents; packaging materials; composites, plastics, synthetic fibers, and rubbers; dyestuffs, inks, and photographic supplies; explosives; antifreeze; and many other materials. As it grew, the chemical industry revolutionized human life. Chemicals are building blocks at every level of production and consumption in agriculture, construction, manufacturing, and services industries. The chemical industry has contributed to improving standards of living. Figure 1 shows domestic consumption of chemicals in Western Europe.

The size of the chemical industry is impressive. In 2003, the chemical industry was Europe's third largest manufacturing industry, accounting for 2.4 percent of the EU's gross domestic product (GDP). On a value-added basis, chemicals represented 10.3 percent of all Japanese manufacturing sectors in 2000. The chemical industry was the fourth largest of the manufacturing sectors in Japan on this same basis, and the fifth largest Japanese exporter. The U.S. chemical industry is estimated to constitute about 10 percent of the country's manufacturing on a value-added basis.

The chemical industry has been responsible for the diffusion of new technologies and has spillover effects to other industries. It plays a central role in generating technological innovations for use by other industries. For exam-

Table 6: Leading Exporters and Importers of Chemicals, 2003 (in billions of U.S. dollars and annual percentage change)

	Value	Share in World Exports/Imports				Annual Percentage Change			
	2003	1980	1990	2000	2003	1995–2000	2001	2002	2003
Exporters									
European Union (15)	442.29	58.4	59.0	52.3	55.7	3	5	15	20
Extra-exports	174.58	23.3	21.1	20.4	22.0	4	7	15	19
United States	91.56	14.8	13.3	14.1	11.5	6	0	-1	13
Japan	38.96	4.7	5.3	6.0	4.9	3	-13	8	17
Switzerland	34.06	4.0	4.6	3.8	4.3	1	15	16	15
China	19.58	0.8	1.3	2.1	2.5	6	10	15	28
Canada	17.12	2.5	2.2	2.5	2.2	6	1	2	12
Singapore	16.88	0.5	1.1	1.6	2.1	6	3	18	45
Domestic exports	13.58	0.2	0.7	1.1	1.7	9	8	26	59
Re-exports	3.29	0.3	0.4	0.6	0.4	2	-7	-1	7
Korea, Republic of	16.82	0.5	0.8	2.4	2.1	9	-9	8	25
Taipei, China	12.19	0.4	0.9	1.6	1.5	4	-4	13	22
Hong Kong, China	10.85	-	-	-	-	-1	-11	4	12
Domestic exports	0.75	0.1	0.3	0.1	0.1	-7	-13	-4	10
Re-exports	10.10	-	-	-	-	0	-11	5	13
Russian Federation	9.08	-	-	1.2	1.1	...	2	0	25
Saudi Arabia	6.27	0.1	0.8	0.7	0.8	0	24	-2	23
Mexico	5.88	0.4	0.7	0.9	0.7	6	1	3	4
India	5.88	0.3	0.4	0.8	0.9	13	1	23	...
Malaysia	5.42	0.1	0.2	0.6	0.7	11	1	16	23
Above 15	719.47	87.0	91.0	89.5	90.8	-	-	-	-
Importers									
European Union (15)	358.77	46.4	50.6	41.7	44.0	2	4	14	20
Extra-imports	91.06	11.6	12.0	10.9	11.2	3	5	10	19
United States	103.81	6.2	7.7	12.5	12.7	12	7	9	18
China	48.98	2.0	2.2	5.0	6.0	12	6	22	25
Japan	29.43	4.1	5.0	4.3	3.6	2	-3	1	15
Canada	24.56	2.2	2.5	3.3	3.0	9	2	5	14
Switzerland	20.86	2.5	2.6	2.3	2.6	3	18	12	15
Mexico	18.29	1.5	1.2	2.5	2.2	16	2	7	11
Korea, Republic of	16.39	1.3	2.4	2.2	2.0	1	-4	8	18
Taipei, China	15.74	1.3	2.3	2.6	1.9	3	-22	11	17
Hong Kong, China	13.49	-	-	-	-	-1	-14	4	12
Retained imports	3.39	0.7	0.9	0.6	0.4	-5	-22	3	11
Brazil	10.50	2.4	1.1	1.7	1.3	5	2	-6	4
Turkey	10.20	0.8	0.9	1.2	1.3	7	-15	25	31
Poland	9.94	1.0	0.3	1.1	1.2	...	6	12	21
Australia	9.55	1.2	1.2	1.3	1.2	5	-8	7	21
Russian Federation	8.56	-	-	0.8	1.1	...	26	5	29
Above 15	688.95	73.6	81.0	83.2	84.6	-	-	-	-

Notes: Figures for China, Mexico, and Malaysia include significant shipments through processing zones. Figures for Korea and Russian Federation include Secretariat estimates. Figures for India are for 2002 instead of 2003. Import figures for Canada, Mexico, and Australia are valued f.o.b.

Source: World Trade Organization, International Trade Statistics 2004 (Geneva: WTO, 2004).

Figure 1. Chemicals in everyday use in Western Europe, 2003

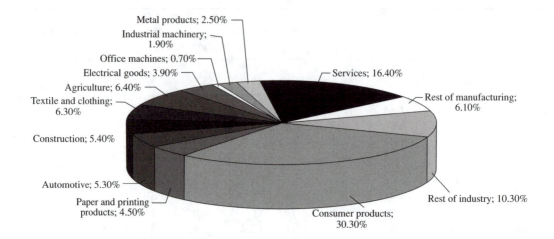

Source: European Chemical Industry Association (CEFIC)

ple, nanotechnology is the latest study of the unique properties of structures on the nanometer scale. Still a nascent field, nanotechnology promises to revolutionize manufacturing processes and products in almost all industry sectors, including medicine, plastics, energy, electronics, and aerospace.

In 2003, the total sales of the world's top 100 chemical companies reached $700 billion. Estimated net profits exceeded $15 billion, and total assets reached about $640 billion. These companies invested more than $17 billion, and their capital spending exceeded $40 billion. These companies altogether directly employ more than 1.5 million workers, accounting for about 20 percent of the global workforce in the chemical industry.

Keeping Competitive

The chemical industry is highly capital-intensive. In general, the more capital, the higher the profits. The integration of capital and cost-saving techniques are at the heart of the modern chemical industry. The industry is com-

posed of two main types of companies. There are "all-around companies," which are highly integrated across different value chains and operate in several of those chains on a large scale. Large chemical companies have a high degree of vertical integration compared with companies in other industries. Vertically integrated companies focus on direct control of strategic parts of the value chain in order to attain competitive advantage. There are also "focused" companies, which concentrate their business on one or only a few areas of chemicals. Focused companies tend to be smaller than all-around companies, but many of them are rather large in absolute terms.

Regardless of the scale on which they operate, chemical companies tend to pursue core focusing. They critically evaluate key elements of costs and value delivery and thereby focus on manufacturing and the process of developing specific products for high return against investment. One way to effectively increase core focusing is through mergers and acquisitions. Figures show that major transactions in the world chemical industry reached over $25 million in value, held steady at about $80 million

Table 7: Global Top 100 Chemical Companies, 2003

Company	Sales		Employees		Operating Profit or EBIT		Net Profit		Total Assets		R&D		Capital Spending	
	Millions of Dollars	Change from 2002 (%)		Change from 2002 (%)		Change from 2002(%)		Change from 2002(%)		Change from 2002(%)		Change from 2002(%)		Change from 2002%
1 BASF	42,025	3.6	87,159	-2.5	3,348	0.6	1,146	-39.5	42,328.4	-4.2	1,392.0	-2.6	2,888.5	-14.3
2 Bayer	35,986	-3.6	115,400	-5.9			-1,715	-228.4	47,169.5	-10.2	3,040.9	-6.3	2,190.6	-27.0
3 Dow Chemical	32,632	18.2	46,372	-7.2				312.3	41,891.0	5.9	981.0	-8.0	1,100.0	-32.2
4 DuPont	26,996	12.5	81,000	2.5			1,002	-45.6	37,039.0	7.0	1,349.0	6.7	1,713.0	33.8
5 Atofina	22,486	-9.3			320	-32.1							1,404.6	-9.9
6 Shell Chemicals	20,817	36.9			-277	-142.6	-209	-137.0	15,420.0	8.8			599.0	-40.0
7 ExxonMobil Chemical	20,190	23.1					1,432	72.5					692.0	-27.5
8 Mitsubishi Chemical	18,481	2.0	33,496	-11.0	942	6.7	332	61.5	19,219.9	-5.5	849.6	-2.8	665.5	-18.8
9 Akzo Nobel	16,440	-6.8	64,600	-4.9	1,340	-21.9	758	-26.4					731.9	-15.7
10 BP	15,483	23.8	15,950	-15.8	661	131.9		-100.0	10,591.0	5.1			775.0	-5.8
11 Degussa	14,395	-2.9	46,615	-2.2	829	0.5			17,640.8	-7.8			991.4	-21.4
12 Sabic	12,475	37.5			2,827	100.2	1,786	135.1	29,146.7	10.2			2,434.9	65.5
13 Asahi Kasei	12,032	5.0	25,011	-2.8	585	-1.0	266	-141.4	11,990.8	3.0	464.8	-1.8	829.2	-8.1
14 Sumitomo Chemical	11,119	4.3			640	-9.4	0		14,871.3	4.4				
15 Air Liquide	10,573	6.2	31,885	3.5	2,036	35.2	914	14.9	13,862.7	0.4			1,057.7	-27.5
16 ICI	10,436	-4.5	36,210	-4.8	767	-19.3	36	-88.8	9,292.1	-4.7	267.6	1.4	246.2	-25.0
17 Mitsui Chemical	10,109	10.6			542	33.2	195	165.6	11,760.4	-5.6	356.2	-5.1	659.9	-41.5
18 Sinopec	9,748	27.9			261	262.2							887.8	-0.9
19 Solvay	9,520	-4.6	30,139	-0.5			622		12,202.7	2.4	508.9	1.3	699.1	-14.0
20 Dainippon Inks & Chemicals (DIC)	9,357	1.3	26,522	-1.8	421	9.1	61	163.4	9,760.4	-2.4	143.8	16.1	439.0	6.0
21 Huntsman	9,252	15.5												
22 Merck KGaA	9,072	-2.7	34,206	-0.9	927	19.5	262	2.5	8,795.2	-7.0	762.1	-0.5	474.9	34.2
23 General Electric	8,371	9.4			803	-28.6								
24 Shin-Etsu	7,994	4.4	17,384	4.9	422	25.2	718	2.5	5,496.1	-9.7	252.7	-3.0	1,090.3	51.0
25 Norsk Hydro	7,839	-5.3	12,271	-32.1	222	64.6	144	61.5	7,187.5	-0.3				
26 Sekisui Chemical	7,822	1.9	11,783	-1.4	627	-0.3	391	-2.2	8,708.9	-0.2	227.5	1.3	231.3	-3.6
27 BOC	7,714	7.6							11,841.2					
28 DSM	7,621	7.3			370	-34.7	175	-88.3					2,511.8	302.0

(continues)

Table 7: Global Top 100 Chemical Companies, 2003 (continued)

Company	Sales — Millions of Dollars	Sales — Change from 2002(%)	Employees	Employees — Change from 2002(%)	Operating Profit or EBIT	Op — Change from 2002(%)	Net Profit	Net Profit — Change from 2002(%)	Total Assets	Total Assets — Change from 2002(%)	R&D	R&D — Change from 2002(%)	Capital Spending	Capital Spending — Change from 2002%
29 PKN Orlen	7,192	44.4					291	134.4	5,052.4	13.8				
30 Basell	7,180	-3.4					-87	-1,090.0						
31 Chevron Philips Chemical	6,907	28.2	5,451	-1.2			7	-123.3	6,242.0	2.2	55.0	17.0	223.0	-29.0
32 Clariant	6,879	-8.7	27,008	-3.0	494	-11.5	130	-124.8	6,464.5	-6.4	248.8	-12.5		
33 Rhodia	6,869	-10.0			-200	286.0	-1,702		8,224.6	-12.0	235.6	-7.0	293.5	-37.7
34 Showa Denko	6,617	2.3	20,500	-2.8	370	23.1	99	-20.8	9,021.7	-4.7	1,574.0	961.9	392.1	99.8
35 PPG Industries	6,606	10.2												
36 Syngenta	6,578	6.1			709	10.8	363	37.0	10,965.0	4.2	727.0	4.3		
37 Equistar	6,545	18.2	3,165	-6.9			-339	37.8	5,028.0	-0.5	38.0		106.0	-10.2
38 Rohm and Haas	6,421	12.1	17,245	-2.1			288	37.1	9,445.0	-1.5	238.0	-8.5	339.0	-16.7
39 Ineos	6,299		10,000											
40 Air Products	6,297	16.6	18,500	7.6	605	-21.9	397	-24.4	9,431.9	11.0			1,171.0	45.3
41 Reliance Industries	6,230	3.8			739	15.0	0		3,129.2	-4.8			96.3	-62.9
42 Eastman Chemical	5,800	9.0	15,000	-4.5			83	2.5	6,245.0	-1.1	173.0	8.8	230.0	-46.1
43 Eni Petrochemicals	5,652	-0.6	7,050	-6.4	-159				3,178.2	-10.6			177.6	-2.8
44 Praxair	5,613	9.5	25,438	1.7			585	6.8	8,305.0	12.2	75.0	8.7	644.0	29.3
45 Sasol	5,560	5.1	13,554	-0.4	260	-45.7	1,071	-19.8	5,403.7	-9.5			43.8	115.3
46 Sherwin-Williams	5,408	4.3	25,777	0.1			332	6.8	3,683.0	7.3				
47 Ciba Specialty Chemicals	5,368	-3.8	18,658	-1.8							227.0	-4.4		
48 Celanese	5,133	0.3	9,500	-9.5	134	3.5	278	-15.3	6,801.1	-11.9			233.1	-13.6
49 Linde	4,841	-1.0	17,420	-0.5	753	-47.5	165	-29.9					500.1	-1.0
50 LG Chem	4,758	4.4			402	-1.3	304	4.8	3,994.1	23.8			705.4	35.4
51 Borealis	4,627	4.5	5,037	-0.9	49	-7.2	13	166.7	3,944.1	-2.2	50.4	2.6	149.9	15.5
52 Tosoh	4,530	10.4	9,167	-2.5	269	-54.1	46	947.7	5,238.0	-4.6			116.4	-27.9
23 Johnson Matthey	4,493	3.9	1,524	0.3	4,493	79.4			1,370.7	3.1				
54 Grupo Alfa	4,163	17.6			416	3.9	100	8.7	7,172.4	5.7			177.3	4.2
55 Transammonia	4,000	48.1												
56 Nova Chemicals	3,949	27.8	4,700	9.3	-75	-0.2	-1	16.8	4,413.0	6.2	45.0	15.4	119.0	67.6
57 Kaneka	3,842	7.5			308	19.3	150	104.1	3,767.6	6.1			220.5	29.0
58 Lyondell Chemical	3,801	16.5	3,350				-302		7,633.0	2.5	37.0	23.3	268.0	1,118.2

(continues)

Table 7: Global Top 100 Chemical Companies, 2003 (continued)

Company	Sales (Millions of Dollars)	Sales Change from 2002 (%)	Employees	Employees Change from 2002 (%)	Operating Profit or EBIT	Op. Change from 2002(%)	Net Profit	Net Change from 2002(%)	Total Assets	T.A. Change from 2002(%)	R&D	R&D Change from 2002(%)	Capital Spending	Cap. Sp. Change from 2002%
59 UCB	3,736	18.0	11,559	11.9			428	2.4	3,893.7	17.9	340.1	3.1	823.8	298.8
60 Cognis	3,716	-5.6	8,660	-3.2	63	-64.8	-81	166.7	3,299.2	-11.2			153.7	24.5
61 Engelhard	3,715	-1.0	6,480	-2.6	282	-9.6	234	36.8	2,933.0	-2.9	93.0	5.7	114.0	0.9
62 Shangai Petrochemical	3,572	32.5					167	52.4	3,332.3	3.8				
63 Kuraray	3,188	3.0	6,760	-3.2	269	11.4	146	88.6	3,966.5	-3.2	131.4	9.3	308.7	68.5
64 Occidental Chemical	3,178	17.5	3,087	-8.4			210	89.2					0.0	-100.0
65 Honeywell	3,169	-1.1												
66 Wacker-Chemie	3,109	-7.8	15,622	-6.1	-74	-144.8	-120	-552.4	3,155.5	-9.3	191.5	-3.8	418.2	19.9
67 MG Technologies	2,933	-5.4	12,304	-2.0					3,031.0	5.2			249.4	10.6
68 Dow Corning	2,870		8,800											
69 Repsol	2,822	6.2			195	59.8	69	-52.8					102.0	-13.8
70 Orica	2,815	-2.5							2,415.0	5.6	20.4	7.1	79.5	6.4
71 Nalco	2,767	4.7	10,500						6,164.0	-5.0	0.0		101.0	-6.5
72 Kemira	2,738	4.8	10,536	1.5	144	260.0	74	797.6	2,495.1	0.2	0.0			
73 Agrium	2,499	20.0	4,667	-3.4			-21	-123.5	2,273.0	3.7			99.0	90.4
74 Ruters	2,491	2.7	11,290	3.6			64						132.0	-10.2
75 Tessenderlo Group	2,484	2.0	8,233	2.0	103	-28.7	54	-39.4			167.0	-22.0	149.9	8.2
76 Potash Corp of Saskatchewan	2,466	27.8	4,904	-5.7			77	42.6	4,567.0	-2.5				
77 Solutia	2,430	5.7	6,300	-13.7	-372	-1,078.9	-987	553.6	2,446.0	-26.8	53.0	12.8	151.0	-28.8
78 JSR	2,372	12.3			200	136.0	106	132.5	2,962.0	9.5	144.9	7.6	78.0	32.2
79 RPM	2,342	12.4	7,900	2.8			142	305.7	2,353.0	4.7			51.0	21.4
80 Danki Kagaku Kogyo (Denka)	2,340	1.3			173	7.7	46	-341.4			49.9	15.5		
81 Mitsubishi Gas Chemical	2,309	12.1			53	-583.1	57	-3,056.9	3,079.2	4.6				
82 NPC (Iran)	2,284	23.5	16,398	-5.2			302	-22.6	14,055.0	36.1	23.6	85.8	3,996.0	36.9
83 Thai Petrochemical	2,278	18.2					64	-160.4	3,556.7	6.5				
84 Israel Chemical	2,271	14.6			211	6.0					29.0	3.6		
85 Valspar	2,248	5.7	7,013	-0.6	228	41.6	113	-5.8	2,496.0	3.1	70.0	6.1	51.0	13.3
86 Givaudan	2,193	1.5	5,981	2.3	275	-16.1	175	-15.6	3,673.7	-0.3	140.6		50.9	28.6

(continues)

Table 7: Global Top 100 Chemical Companies, 2003 (continued)

Company	Sales		Employees		Operating Profit or EBIT		Net Profit		Total Assets		R&D		Capital Spending	
	Millions of Dollars	Change from 2002 (%)		Change from 2002(%)		Change from 2002(%)		Change from 2002(%)		Change from 2002(%)		Change from 2002(%)		Change from 2002%
87 IMC Global	2,191	6.5	5,017	-4.9			-38	171.4	3,671.0	0.9			120.0	-14.3
88 Crompton	2,185	4.5	5,521	-18.5			5	-91.1	2,529.0	-11.0	51.0	-5.6	88.0	-12.0
89 Asahi Glass	2,180													
90 Ube	2,066	3.6			87	-8.3			2,831.7	2.1			159.7	19.8
91 Lubrizol	2,052	3.4	5,032	-3.8			106	-15.9	1,942.0	4.4	167.0	-0.6	88.0	35.4
92 WR Grace	1,981	8.8	6,300	-1.6			-42	-290.9	2,875.0	6.8	52.0	0.0	86.0	-5.5
93 PolyOne	1,965	3.9	44,500	-41.4			-17	-522.0	1,901.0	-4.9			29.0	-55.4
94 Lonza	1,956	-4.5			244	-27.9	74	-58.8	3,621.2	9.4	65.4	17.4	87.0	3.6
95 FMC	1,921	3.7	5,300	-3.6	218	-5.6	27	-59.1	2,829.0	-1.4	87.0	6.1	65.0	-20.7
96 IFF	1,901	5.1	5,454	-4.8			173	-1.7	2,307.0	3.4	159.0	10.4		
97 Hercules	1,846	8.3	4,826	-5.3	255	15.9	45	-107.4	2,766.0	-1.5	39.0	-7.1	48.0	11.6
98 Cabot	1,795	15.3	4,400	-2.2			80	-24.5	2,308.0	11.1	64.0	33.3	129.0	-11.6
99 Millennium Chemicals	1,687	8.6			-51	-163.8	-184	-44.7	2,398.0	1.0				
100 British Vita	1,677	5.2			100	9.7	60	-60.5						

Note: Empty cell = data not available.

Source: European Chemical News (ECN), September 6–12, 2004, pp. 19–23.

Figure 2: M&A of Worldwide Chemical Companies in Total Number of Transactions

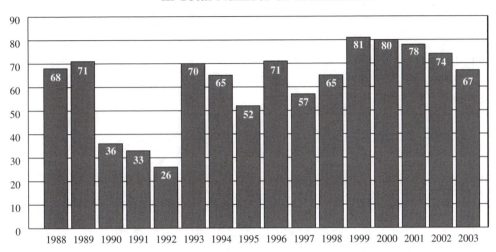

Source: Young & Partners

Figure 3: Mergers and Acquisitions, World Chemical Industry, 1988–2003 (in billions of U.S. dollars)

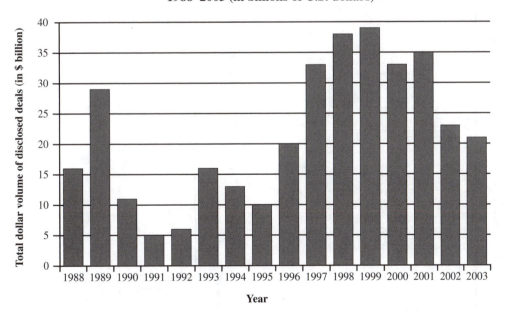

per year from 1999 to 2001, and dropped by 6 percent in 2002 and by 10 percent in 2003. In dollar value, major mergers and acquisitions in the world chemical industry amounted to around $35 billion during the period from 1997 to 2001.

U.S. chemical industry data help to explain why the industry needs to take cost-cutting measures. As Table 8 shows, the U.S. chemical industry improved by 32 percentage points between 1993 and 2003. Manufacturing sectors in general improved by 61.8 percentage points

Table 8: Productivity of the Chemical Industry in the United States, 1993–2003

	1993	1994	1995	1996	1997	1998	1999	2000	2001	2002	2003
Manufacturing	83.2	85.2	89.4	94.0	100.0	107.1	114.5	121.2	127.0	136.3	145.0
Chemicals	89.9	90.9	92.1	94.5	100.0	101.0	105.2	109.5	113.6	120.5	121.9
Basic chemicals	94.0	93.4	92.9	92.4	100.0	100.5	117.4	119.7	118.1	135.2	138.9
Resins, synthetic rubber & fibers	87.9	91.9	94.5	94.1	100.0	105.5	109.4	109.1	108.1	123.6	125.7
Agricultural chemicals	92.4	93.1	94.5	95.8	100.0	99.0	88.7	91.3	94.8	99.9	103.0
Pharmaceuticals	87.0	87.5	85.9	93.3	100.0	100.6	98.3	98.7	103.3	103.7	99.2
Paints, coatings, & adhesives	93.5	95.3	94.5	100.1	100.0	100.1	98.0	97.7	104.9	111.0	118.1
Soaps, cleaning compounds, & toilet preparations	87.0	87.8	94.0	96.4	100.0	95.2	90.1	100.9	104.8	104.9	105.4

Source: U.S. Federal Reserve Board and U.S. Department of Labor, cited in *Chemical & Engineering News* (CEN), July 5, 2004, p. 48.

Table 9: Establishment, Employment, Production, and Added Value in the Japanese Chemical Industry, 1990–2001 (in millions of Japanese yen)

	1990	1991	1992	1993	1994	1995	1996	1997	1998	1999	2000	2001
Establishment	5,352	5,391	5,340	5,340	5,160	5,230	5,224	5,184	5,426	5,280	5,263	5,152
Employment	401,076	405,572	415,073	412,879	398,114	392,1	388,586	383,089	382,814	370,694	365,953	364,06809
Production	23,606,820	24,395,096	24,243,305	23,221,656	22,502,206	23,42	23,509,017	24,683,252	23,267,239	23,025,095	23,792,798	23,308,2107,633
Added value	11,271,992	11,621,425	11,825,805	11,507,388	11,378,762	11,98	11,901,652	12,125,014	11,329,352	11,475,838	11,496,608	11,248,5043,632

Note: Establishments covered have more than four employees.
Source: Kagaku Keizai, January 2004, p. 96

over the same period. The pharmaceuticals sector, which requires a huge amount of investment and labor in order to grow, showed a decline in output per hour.

The chemical industry has maintained high added value while increasing productivity and integrating capital. Table 9 shows that this is true, for example, for the industry in Japan. Added value remained constant at 11 trillion Japanese yen (approximately $100,000 US) between 1990 and 2001. The Japanese chemical industry concentrated capital by eliminating 200 establishments during this period, with their numbers declining from 5,352 in 1990 to 5,152 in 2001. Over the same period, about 10 percent of the total workforce, or 37,000 people, lost their jobs; overall, employment fell from 401,076 in 1990 to 364,068 in 2001.

Employment loss has been an ongoing phenomenon in many chemical-producing countries over the past few years. In the United States, average chemical employment declined by about 1.2 percent, or by 125,000 workers, over a ten-year period, from 1,025,000 in 1993 to 900,000 in 2003. Among the chemical sectors, only pharmaceuticals scored an increase, adding 62,000 workers between 1993 and 2003, and reaching 294,000 workers in 2003. These figures compare with a 1.4 percent decline in employment for all manufacturing industries. Among the chemical sectors, basic chemicals saw the largest percentage drop, falling 3.9 percent from 1993 to 2003. Among the other chemical sectors, agricultural chemicals were down 2.5 percent, to 40,000 workers; resins, synthetic rubber, and fibers fell 2.6 percent, to 112,000 workers; paints, coating, and adhesives fell 1.6 percent, to 69,000 workers; soaps and toiletries declined 0.8 percent, to 118,000 workers; and all other chemicals fell 2.4 percent, to 111,000 workers. Table 10 shows the employment evolution of the chemical production workforce in the United States from 1993 to 2003.

In China, the workforce in the chemical industry declined from 3.82 million in 1996 to 3.7 million in 2003. This figure does not include the workforce in two large state-owned chemical companies. The reduction of workforce was accelerated by China's accession to the World Trade Organization (WTO) in 2001. Under the planned economy, the country followed a full-employment policy. However, globalization of the world economy put the Chinese chemical industry under severe competition, and this necessitated a restructuring of the chemical industry and further changes in management systems at the enterprise level in order to boost labor productivity.

Wages for chemical production workers are generally good. Workers in the industry in the United States receive some of the highest wages in manufacturing. For 2003, for example, wages for U.S. chemical manufacturing employees rose an average of 3.1 percent to reach $18.52 per hour. At the same time, the average hourly wage for all manufacturing increased only 2.9 percent, to $15.74. However, there have been some declines in hourly pay within specific chemical-industry sectors. For agricultural chemical workers, the average hourly wage fell by 3 percent, to $18.40 per hour, while the hourly wage for workers in the soaps and toiletries sector declined 0.8 percent, to $14.15, the lowest hourly wage in the chemical industry. By contrast, the largest increase was the 9.2 percent rise, to $19.78, for pharmaceutical workers.

Global Chemical Employment

Current global chemical employment is estimated at around 8 million workers. These employees account for almost 10 percent of the global manufacturing workforce, which has, of course, increased over time. In 1997, the global chemical workforce exceeded 5 million, and by 1999 it exceeded 7 million. This increase was due to rapid growth in East Asia and the Middle East. Employment in North America, Europe, and Japan experienced a downturn. Asian countries with increasing employment in the industrial chemical sector include India, where

Table 10: Evolution of Employment of Chemical Production Workers in the United States, 1993–2003

	1993	1994	1995	1996	1997	1998	1999	2000	2001	2002	2003	Change: 1993–2003
Manufacturing	12,070,000	12,361,000	12,566,000	12,532,000	12,673,000	12,729,000	12,524,000	12,428,000	11,677,000	10,768,000	10,200,000	- 1.7%
Chemicals	590,000	596,000	598,000	595,000	593,000	601,000	595,000	588,000	562,000	532,000	525,000	- 1.2%
Basic chemicals	139,000	139,000	139,000	139,000	137,000	136,000	126,000	122,000	115,000	104,000	101,000	- 3.2%
Resins, synthetic rubber & fibers	98,000	101,000	99,000	98,000	99,000	98,000	96,000	96,000	89,000	81,000	78,000	- 2.3%
Agricultural chemicals	34,000	33,000	33,000	33,000	33,000	34,000	34,000	32,000	30,000	30,000	28,000	- 1.9%
Pharmaceuticals	111,000	115,000	119,000	118,000	116,000	123,000	129,000	132,000	132,000	128,000	134,000	2.0%
Paints, coatings, & adhesives	41,000	41,000	41,000	40,000	40,000	40,000	41,000	42,000	39,000	38,000	37,000	- 1.1%
Soaps & toiletries	80,000	80,000	80,000	80,000	81,000	84,000	85,000	82,000	80,000	76,000	76,000	- 0.6%
Other chemicals	87,000	87,000	87,000	88,000	88,000	87,000	83,000	82,000	77,000	75,000	72,000	- 1.9%
Percent of chemicals against total manufacturing	4.9	4.8	4.8	4.7	4.7	4.7	4.8	4.7	4.8	4.9	5.1	

Source: U.S. Department of Labor, cited in *Chemical & Engineering News* (CEN), July 5, 2004, p. 48.

such employment doubled in a short time, going from about 190,000 in 1980 to about 380,000 in 1999. Chemical employment in the Republic of Korea peaked in 1996, reaching about 72,000. Malaysia's employment also increased, from about 10,000 in 1990 to 15,000 in 1999. In Singapore, chemical employment reached its peak of about 5,600 workers in 1994. There is some indication of rapid growth in recent years in the Middle East's chemical industry, although data are limited. Petrochemical facilities in the Middle East have been expanding, and the region is expected to almost double its share of world ethylene capacity, from 10 percent to about 20 percent, between 2003 and 2012.

The overall percentage of female workers in the world chemical industry is estimated to be as low as 20 percent. Figure 4 shows the percentage of female workers in the unionized workforce in selected chemical industries in 2000. In most of these countries, women accounted for less than 50 percent of the total workforce. Female workers are often found in peripheral jobs, and there are few women in top management.

Petrochemicals

The petrochemicals industry uses crude oil or natural gas to produce ethylene, propylene, butadiene, and benzene. It plays an essential role in supporting other industries in the development of new technologies and materials. Petrochemicals are first sold to customer industries, undergo several transformations, and then go into products that seem to bear no relation to the initial raw material. Because petrochemistry underpins a host of other essential industries, it is called an "enabling industry." It is, indeed, an enabling force behind innovation in numerous sectors, such as health care, telecommunications, construction, and transport. As such, the petrochemicals sector is central to the chemical industry as a whole.

Table 11: Wages of U.S. Chemical Production Workers, 2000–2003 (in U.S. dollars)

	Hourly Earnings				Weekly Earnings			
	2000	*2001*	*2002*	*2003*	*2000*	*2001*	*2002*	*2003*
Manufacturing	14.3	14.8	15.3	15.7	590.7	595.2	618.8	636.1
Chemicals	17.1	17.6	18.0	18.5	721.9	135.5	759.5	784.6
Basic chemicals	21.1	21.4	21.8	22.1	949.1	959.9	980.6	988.5
Resins, synthetic rubber & fibers	17.1	17.5	17.8	17.9	724.7	722.5	738.8	749.1
Agricultural chemicals	16.2	17.4	19.0	18.4	768.2	800.0	848.1	836.9
Pharmaceuticals	17.3	17.8	13.1	19.8	693.1	729.4	776.7	850.6
Paints, coatings, & adhesives	14.1	14.8	15.6	16.0	597.9	609.8	644.0	656.4
Soaps & toiletries	13.8	14.1	14.3	14.2	549.4	560.4	566.4	562.7
Other chemicals	15.5	16.0	16.4	17.0	642.4	647.8	665.8	694.3

Source: U.S. Department of Labor, cited in *Chemical & Engineering News* (CEN), July 5, 2004, p. 48.

Figure 4: Women in the Unionized Workforce in the Chemical Industry, 2000

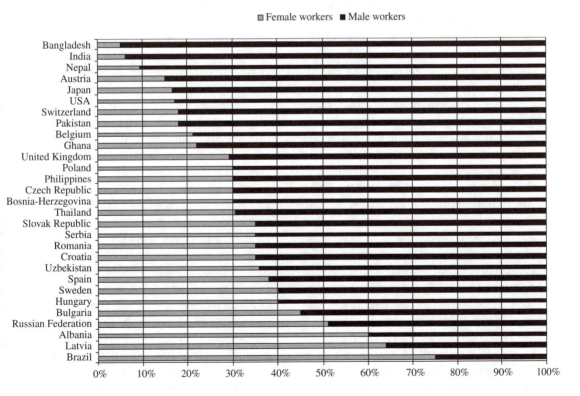

Source: International Federation of Chemical, Energy, Mine and General Workers' Unions (ICEM), "ICEM World Conference on the Chemical Industries," Background Paper, 26–28 November 2001, Bangkok, Thailand (Brussels: ICEM, 2001).

**Figure 5: Volatility of Ethylene and
Propylene Prices, 2003**

Contract price, cents per lb.

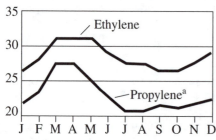

a Polymer grade.
Source: Chemical Market Associates Inc.

The U.S. petrochemical industry relies mostly on natural gas, whereas European, Latin American, and Asian production use petroleum-based feeds. The prices of crude oil and natural gas reflect the profit margins of the petrochemical industry. Figure 5 demonstrates the volatility of ethylene and propylene prices, and Figure 6 shows world ethylene production in 2003.

The North American petrochemical sector has been suffering from stagnant growth in recent years. The emergence of low-cost Middle Eastern players and a growing base of Asian producers coincided with the disappearance of the advantage that had benefited the North American petrochemical industry in the past. Relatively high prices for raw materials affect the Asian petrochemical industry, and it is becoming nearly impossible for countries in Asia, particularly China, to compete with the Middle East, which has the lowest feedstock prices in the world. China has an advantage in cost-savings because of downstream manufacturing.

China's chemical industry is also hugely important to the overall Chinese economy. In 2003, China's chemical industry produced chemicals worth about $106 billion, accounting for some 5 percent of total world output. The chemical industry is the third largest industry in China, followed by textiles and machinery, accounting for about 10 percent of China's GDP.

China accounts for about 40 percent of global demand growth for chemicals and represents about 45 percent of Asian demand for most chemical products. China's largest chemical companies, such as Sinopec and PetroChina, are still under state control. Table 12 shows the major Chinese chemical and petrochemical companies' sales in 2003.

China is described as the "powerhouse" of the market and will continue to drive demand growth in the petrochemical industry. According to Fortune Global 500, in 2002 CNPC/PetroChina and Sinopec ranked fifth and seventeenth, respectively, in profits among twenty-six global chemical companies. CNPC/PetroChina's profits in 2002 were equivalent to about half of those of ExxonMobil, and its profits as a percentage of total operating expenses reached 12 percent, or fourth in the world. Its operating return on chemical assets was 6 percent, or eleventh place. Because Chinese chemical/petrochemical companies are parts of integrated oil and gas companies, they can be more competitive than chemical companies elsewhere.

The Chinese petrochemical industry is forecast to grow an average of 11.3 percent per year through 2014. China's accession to the WTO appears to have increased its dependency on chemical imports, while also forcing improvements in infrastructure. China imports about 50 percent of its chemical consumption. Its heavy dependency on imported chemicals means that its chemical markets have become integrated with international markets. China committed to cutting chemical tariffs as part of its accession to the WTO. As a result, Chinese tariffs on polyethylene will fall from 18.1 percent in 2001 to 6.5 percent in 2008. Tariffs for polypropylene, PVC, and polystyrene will fall from 16 percent in 2001 to 6.5 percent in 2008. Lower tariffs will expose the inefficiency of much of China's outdated chemical capacity relative to more modern overseas plants. Some estimate that the loss of tariff protection could force closure of 15–20 percent of China's marginal operating capacity in polyethylene by

Figure 6: World Ethylene Production, by Country, 2003 (in millions of tons and percent of world production)

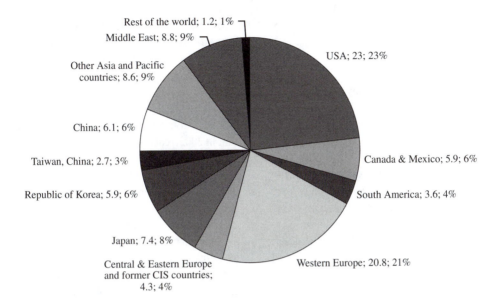

Source: Kagaku Keisai, March Special Edition, 2004, p.37

Table 12: Sales of Major Chinese Chemical Companies in 2003 (in billions of renminbi)

Sinopec	1	92.3
China National Chemical Corp.	2, 3	40.0
PetroChina	1	39.2
Shangai Petrochemical	4	29.6
Yangzi Petrochemical	4	22.0
Jilin Chemical Industrial	5	20.6
Shanghai Huayi Group	6	20.0
Beijing Yanhua Petrochemical	4	11.5
Yizheng Chemical Fibre	4	10.3

(1) chemical business; (2) proforma; (3) includes sales of nonchemical products; (4) Sinopec subsidiary; (5) PetroChina subsidiary; (6) Estimate

Source: Chemical Week, August 18/25, 2004, p. 25.

2008. In addition, the government's tightening of financial policy may harm private medium- and small-sized chemical companies, which account for about 55 percent of China's chemical production.

China also faces a huge energy crisis. It has a growing shortage of electricity and coal and a burgeoning demand for imported oil. However, some inadequate infrastructure is expected to be mitigated by an easing of restrictions on distribution by foreign companies operating in China. In connection with its accession to the WTO, China allowed foreign companies to distribute their products in Chinese markets without the need for local partners, for example.

Biotechnology

Biotechnology is taking its place at the center of the chemical industry, and statistics demonstrate its importance in the industry. In 2002, there were 1,466 biotechnology companies in the United States alone. These companies were marketing some 150 drugs and vaccines. Collectively, biotechnology firms amassed revenues of $33.6 billion in 2002. Success in developing drugs has led to enormous financial benefits for the chemical companies. In 2003, the U.S. chemical industry produced $460 billon in sales. More than one-quarter of the sales were within the pharmaceuticals sector, totaling $114.3 billion. The pharmaceuticals industry has been increasing in significance since the early 1990s. In 1993, pharmaceuticals represented 23 percent of the U.S. chemical industry. This share had increased by 4.5 percent by 2003. The industry's growth has been striking. It showed an increase of 8.4 percent in 2002–2003 alone. By contrast, chemicals excluding pharmaceuticals increased by only 2.8 percent between 1993 and 2003, from about $260 billion to about $344 billion. Similarly, pharmaceuticals in Japan increased from 24.2 percent of the chemical industry in 1993 to 29.2 percent in 2001. In the EU, the pharmaceuticals industry accounted for 24.1 percent of the chemical industry in 2003.

New medicines are now being developed with relatively small venture capital. There are some data indicating that small biotechnology "garage companies" have come of age. In San Francisco's East Bay region, biotechnology garnered 42 percent, or $101 million, of fourth-quarter 2003 funding. During the same year, life-science companies were awarded about $5 billion in funding, or about 30 percent of all venture funding, for the year in the United States.

By contrast, the growth of the biotechnology industry in Europe is still retained by publicly quoted companies. European biotechnology generated 12,861 million euros in 2002, of which publicly quoted companies generated about 60 percent, or 7,869 million euros, in the overall revenues in the sector. The number of publicly quoted companies increased by 2 percent in 2002, reaching 102 companies. The total workforce for the publicly quoted companies accounted for about 40 percent, or 33,304 workers, in the overall biotechnology industry, and saw an increase of 3 percent in 2002.

The pharmaceuticals industry is a global player in drug development. This is, in part, a result of global outsourcing. This sector continues to grow globally, particularly in the Asia and Pacific region. The global biotechnology industry increased its total revenues by 15 percent to more than $41 billion, while research and development (R&D) spending rose 34 percent to $22 billion, indicating a greater than 50 percent reinvestment of revenues in R&D. The number of biotechnology companies grew by about 2 percent in 2003, but the number of publicly quoted ones declined by 3 percent, suggesting that the downturn in global capital markets is taking its toll on new company formation. The one major hot spot is the Asia and Pacific region, where revenue was up 28 percent, the number of employees rose by 24 percent, and the number of public and private companies grew by 17 percent.

Growth of the biotechnology sector depends more on progress in developing its R&D segment than on drug manufacturing and export. During the past two decades, biotechnology companies have benefited from the intellectual strength of the workforce in science and technology in developed countries, focusing their efforts on biotechnology research. This emphasis has given the industry the potential to become a leading player in the drug discovery market.

India is the largest country stressing research and development in its biotechnology sector. It ranks high among developing countries in terms of technology, quality, and range of medicines manufactured. In October 2004, India opened the Wockhardt Biotech Park, the country's largest biotechnology complex, in Aurangabad. This complex has the capacity to serve 10–15 percent of global demand for biopharmaceuticals and symbolizes the rapid development of the country's pharmaceutical sector. In recent years, the international pharmaceutical industry has faced increasing pressures to reduce drug prices at a time when costs for R&D have risen sharply. These pressures have led international pharmaceutical companies to outsource their drug-related R&D operations to cost-saving countries. It is estimated that the Indian pharmaceutical industry is worth about $4.5 billion, and that it is growing at a rate of about 9 percent annually. The sector is highly fragmented, consisting of nearly 20,000 drug-production companies. The leading 250 companies control 70 percent of the market, and several are multinational firms.

Genetically Modified Crops

Chemical products are readily tradable items globally. Chemicals are sometimes also at the heart of international controversies. One example can be found in an international trade conflict over genetically modified (GM) crops. The United States, the largest exporter of GM crops, was particularly affected by the EU de facto moratorium on these products and claims to have lost $300 million annually in agricultural sales to Europe. The United States brought the case to the dispute settlement mechanism at the WTO in 2004, along with Canada and Brazil. These nations were later joined by Peru, Colombia, Mexico, New Zealand, Australia, India, Brazil, and Chile. The case was heard in June 2004 at the WTO.

At the center of the dispute is the EU's failure to process applications for genetically modified organisms (GMOs) to enter the European market. Since October 1998, the EU has operated a de facto moratorium, having previously approved eighteen GMOs for release into the environment and fifteen food products for marketing since 1990. The EU's ban was initially forced by five member states (Denmark, Greece, France, Italy, and Luxembourg), largely in response to rapidly growing public opposition to GM foods. U.S. concerns extend to the impact that the EU's precautionary stance will have on the future of the biotechnology market. Adoption of the European model of GM regulation by other countries would seriously curtail the international market for GM products and stunt the growth of the industry.

Despite the EU's moratorium, GM crops are now accepted by many countries. China has been a leading proponent of agricultural biotechnology among developing countries, and a decision to plant GM rice in China is expected soon. China was the first country to grow GM crops commercially in the mid-1990s. Cotton is the only GM crop currently grown on a commercial scale in China, accounting for about 60 percent of total national cotton production. However, a wide range of other GM crop varieties have been developed and tested. Rice may become the first GM food crop to be authorized for large-scale commercial planting in China.

Global Dialogue in the Chemical Industry

The International Labour Office (ILO), a United Nations specialized agency, provides unique opportunities to the chemical industries to discuss various social and labor issues. The ILO seeks to promote social justice and internationally recognized human and labor rights, to create employment opportunities, and to improve working conditions around the world. All activities at the ILO are carried out based on a consensus of labor, employers, and governments among the member states. The

Chemical Industries Committee was created in 1948 and meets on a regular basis. In 2003, chemical representatives from four continents met to discuss best practices in work-flexibility schemes and their impact on the quality of working life in the chemical industries. (Information about the ILO can be found at www. ilo.org.)

Major International Chemical Safety Initiatives

The chemical industry has a responsibility to help ensure that the chemicals it produces are safe for humans and for the environment. In 1984, in the middle of the night, a toxic cloud of gas from a Union Carbide pesticides plant crept over Bhopal, India. The toxic fumes cost 3,800 lives within days of the leak, and thousands more were injured. The chemical industry receives significant scrutiny from the public, partly as a result of this incident. Concerns about the potential ecological and human health impacts of chemicals have brought the safety of the industry as a whole into the global spotlight, resulting in an erosion of public trust and confidence.

The chemical industry responded to the erosion of public trust by establishing the Responsible Care (RC) program. The RC program was first developed in Canada. It has now become the international standard for stewardship in the chemical industry. It is practiced in more than forty countries, including the United States. All companies of exercising RC programs need to follow the RC standard in their day-to-day operations. RC uses a life-cycle approach to managing chemicals and consists of six management codes: (1) Community Awareness and Emergency Response (CARE); (2) research and development; (3) manufacturing; (4) transportation; (5) distribution; and (6) hazardous waste management.

In addition, the United Nations chemical safety initiatives emphasizing that hazardous substances need to be subject to standardized classification and labeling systems, with safety data sheets and easily understandable symbols. One of these initiatives was the Globally Harmonized System for the Classification and Labeling of Chemicals (GHS). GHS, drafted with the premise that existing systems in these areas should be harmonized into a single, global system , was designed to cover all chemicals, including both pure substances and mixtures, and to provide for the chemical hazard communication requirements of the workplace, transport of dangerous goods, safety of consumers, and protection of the environment. The International Chemical Safety Cards (ICSC) project, undertaken by the International Programme on Chemical Safety (IPCS), was another successful UN initiative addressing the issue of chemical safety. The ICSCs summarize essential health and safety information on chemical substances in a clear way and are intended for use at the shop floor level by workers and by those responsible for health and safety issues in factories, on farms, at construction worksites, and at any other place of work. They are also designed for use by employers when undertaking the duty of providing information and instruction to workers. (See www.ilo.org/safework.)

The United Nations Environment Programme (UNEP) was established in 1972 to coordinate and stimulate environmental action with the UN system and to provide technical and managerial assistance to countries requiring it. Under UNEP's auspices, governments have developed international treaties governing hazardous chemicals and substances, including the Stockholm Convention and the Rotterdam Convention.

The Stockholm Convention is a global treaty to protect humans and the environment from persistent organic pollutants (POPs). POPs are chemicals that remain intact in the environment for long periods, become widely distributed geographically, accumulate in the fatty tissue of living organisms, and are toxic to humans and wildlife. Their effects on humans and animals include birth defects, cancer, and damage to the immune system, to growth and development, and to the reproductive system. The convention calls for action on twelve initial POPs, nine of which are pesticides (aldrin, chlordane, DDT, dieldrin, endrin, heptachlor, hexachlorobenzen, mirex, and toxaphene). The other three are PCBs, dioxins, and furans.

The Rotterdam Convention aims to promote shared responsibility and cooperative efforts among parties in the international trade of certain hazardous chemicals in order to protect humans and the environment and to contribute to their environmentally sound use. Governments began to address the problem of toxic pesticides and other hazardous chemicals in the 1980s by establishing a voluntary Prior Informed Consent (PIC) procedure. PIC required exporters trading in any of a list of hazardous substances to obtain the consent of importers before proceeding with the trade. In 1988, governments decided to strengthen the procedure by adopting the Rotterdam Convention, which makes the PIC procedure legally binding. The convention establishes a first line of defense by giving importing countries the tools and information they need to identify potential hazards and to exclude chemicals they cannot manage safely. When a country agrees to import chemicals, the convention promotes their safe use through labeling standards, technical assistance, and other forms of support. It also ensures that exporters comply with the requirements. (For information about UNEP and its programs, consult www.unep.ch.)

The European Union is planning to introduce a regulatory regime for chemicals known as the REACH system (Registration, Evaluation and Authorisation of Chemicals). The REACH system is anticipated to go into effect in 2005. Although it is difficult to assess what effect REACH will have on the chemical industry, industry leaders are concerned because it is a massive regulatory undertaking and the costs may be substantial, both for the industry itself and for downstream users. Under REACH, the industry will bear the costs of registration, authorization, and testing. It is estimated that the cost to the chemical industry will be about $3 billion spread over an eleven-year period. However, the chemical industry is characterized by long, complex supply chains that touch nearly all sectors of the economy, so the actual costs may be much higher. It is estimated that the cost of REACH to European industry alone, including costs imposed on downstream users, could reach 5 billion euros over this period of time. The most ardent opponents of REACH have suggested that its costs may be 100 times higher than this and cause job losses for up to 2 million workers over its first decade in force.

The Future of the Chemical Industry

The chemical industry is an industry with innovation. Figures from the European Chemical Industry Association and the Organisation for Economic Co-operation and Development show that in Europe's chemical industry (excluding the pharmaceutical sector), the proportion of sales revenues devoted to R&D decreased in 2002, to just 1.9 percent, whereas in the United States it increased from 1.5 to 2.5 percent during the same period. To stay competitive, countries interested in advancing their chemical industry must ensure adequate R&D funding.

Innovation needs people to make it happen. The European Chemical Industry Association is concerned about a shortage of researchers, especially chemists. Since 1996, the numbers of chemistry graduates in many European countries have fallen, often by some 10 percent a year. Not only have the number of young people seeking a degree in chemistry dropped, but more of those completing chemistry degrees are seeking careers outside the sector. The chemical industry is working with academe and science organizations to increase the number of chemistry graduates. Government initiative in this area could make a significant difference. The EU aims to increase its research spending to 3 percent of GDP by 2010. But the future of the chemical industry worldwide re-

Table 13: Chemical Industry Research and Development (R&D) Spending (% of sales) in Japan, the United States, and the European Union, 1995–2002

	1995	1996	1997	1998	1999	2000	2001	2002
Japan	3.0	36.0	4.0	4.4	3.8	3.5	3.3	3.0
United States	2.5	3.0	2.2	2.9	2.6	2.6	2.6	2.5
European Union	2.4	2.4	2.3	2.4	2.2	2.1	2.0	1.9

Source: European Chemical Industry Association and Organisation of Economic Co-operation and Development, cited in European Chemical News (ECN), March 15–21, 2004, p. 17.

lies on young people to enter the industry and to keep it competitive and profitable.

Yasuhiko Kamakura

See Also Pharmaceuticals

References

Arora, A., et al. 1998. *Chemicals and Long-Term Economic Growth.* New York: John Wiley.

Baker, J. 2004. "Innovate for Growth." *European Chemical News,* March 15–21, 16–18.

"Conflicting Pressures Plague Biotech Policy." 2004. *Oxford Analytica,* September 10.

Davis, N. 2004. "A Year of Transition." *European Chemical News,* September 6–12, 18–23.

European Chemical Industry Council. 2004. "Facts and Figures: The European Chemical Industry in a Worldwide Perspective: July 2004," http://www.cefic.be.

"Facts and Figures for the Chemical Industry." 2004. *Chemical & Engineering News,* July 5, 24–63.

International Federation of Chemical, Energy, Mine and General Workers' Unions. 2001. "ICEM World Conference on the Chemical Industries, Background Paper, 26–28 November, Bangkok, Thailand." Brussels: ICEM.

Kamakura, Y. 2003. "Best Practices in Work-Flexibility Schemes and Their Impact on the Equality of Working Life in the Chemical Industries." Geneva: International Labour Office.

"Major New Chemicals Regime Ahead." 2004. *Oxford Analytica,* September 20.

McGarvy, R. 2004. "Biotech Comes of Age." *Biotech* (May).

"TRIP Regime Set to Bolster R&D Potential." 2004. *Oxford Analytica,* October 21.

United Nations Industrial Development Organization. 2003. Industrial Statistics DatabaseAU: New York: UNID. http://www.unido.org/

"World Chemical Industry White Paper (Sekai Kagaku Kogyo Hakusho)." 2004. Special Edition. Tokyo: *Kagaku Keizai,* March, pp. 7, 37.

World Trade Organization. 2003. *International Trade Statistics 2003.* Geneva: WTO.

"WTO Panel Hears GMO Trade Case." 2004. *Oxford Analytica,* June 9.

Computer Hardware and Electronics

The field of electronics is developing rapidly, with new products entering the market every day. The computer is arguably one of the most important tools of daily life. Computer hardware and electronics have played a major role in globalization, especially with the rise of the Internet, facilitating communication and the sharing of information worldwide and enabling firms to engage in greater trade and other international opportunities.

Definition of Electronics

Electronics is the field of engineering and applied physics dealing with the design and application of devices, usually electronic circuits, the operation of which depends on the flow of electrons for the generation, transmission, reception, and storage of information.

The history of electronics has its roots in the early twentieth century, with the invention of the first three-electrode vacuum tube—the "audion"—by Lee De Forest in 1906. Indeed, De Forest was building on previous inventions when he developed the device. Since then, vacuum tubes and other electronics components have been increasingly miniaturized and improved. The most important products in the field have either provided radically new ways to do important jobs, or made possible tasks that were previously unimagined. Their impact has been felt, if not right away, then eventually, by a large portion of humanity. Developments in the field have enabled significant new technological innovations and scientific discoveries to take place. And, finally, these products have had an enduring effect on the world.

The transistor, the television, and the computer are considered the main turning points of electronics history and development. It is noteworthy that each of these three inventions is developed further every day. They have affected every area of modern life, especially communications, the exchange of information, medicine, education, and business. In many fields, they increase efficiency and lower costs. They have become increasingly reliable, resulting in lower prices, and lower prices, in turn, have resulted in greater popularity and more widespread use of electronic devices.

The transistor, a device made of a crystalline semiconducting material, usually germanium, was one of the first important inventions in electronics because it helps to control the flow of electrons in electronic products. As such, it provided a key component of many other inventions. Radios have undergone countless improvements since the pioneering days of radio in the early 1900s. The telephone has seen dramatic improvement in recent years with the use of fiberoptic cables, which provide an alternative to bulky copper wire cables. This vital and important invention has been developed in size, capabilities, and functions, leading to huge leaps in the telecommunications industry. The development of wireless telephones, cellular telephones, and new features such as voice mail, conference calling, call forwarding, and other functions have given the telephone an essential role in global communications. The Internet, electronic mail (e-mail), and the ability to send and receive files and video streams further increased the ease of communicating over long distances.

Even video recorders, videocassette players, photocopiers, digital cameras, and the like have contributed in enormous ways to basic communication between people in many realms of their lives. Communication is a vital part of both personal life and business; it is also essential to education and, indeed, to any other situation that requires people to interact with each other. Communication, that is, the process of sharing ideas, information, and messages with others in a particular time and place, includes writing and speaking as well as nonverbal communication such as facial expressions, body language, or gestures; visual communication such as the use of images or pictures, photography, video, or film; and electronic communication such as telephone calls, e-mail, cable television, and satellite broadcasts.

One of the core developments in electronics is the communications satellite, which has become a linchpin of global communications. From modest beginnings, with a satellite that could handle only 240 voice circuits at a time, the technology has blossomed to the extent that satellites now carry about one-third of the voice traffic and essentially all the television signals between countries.

Definition of the Computer

Computers and information systems are tools that allow their users to transform data efficiently and effectively into digital format and distribute it wherever it is needed. If used properly, they can improve productivity in terms of both the time and the resources required to gain a desired result. In recent years, the growing use of microcomputers has brought the benefits of these tools to every continent and, in wealthy countries, to almost anyone who wants to take advantage of them. People use computers for many reasons, especially in economies based on information.

Computers process data by means of three basic functions: first, by performing arithmetic operations on numeric data; second, by testing relationships between data items by logically comparing values; and third, through the ability to store and retrieve data. These functions allow the computer to calculate numeric data, create documents, and manage data. Moreover, computers can work faster, more accurately, and more reliably than people. A computer is a machine that can be programmed to process data (input) into useful information (output). It can follow instructions to accept input, process that input, and produce information. The computer is a remarkable tool. Like humans, computers are complex; indeed, computers could be compared to humans in some ways. In a sense, they have hands (the keyboard or mouse); eyes (the monitor or scanners); ears (microphones); a mind (the central processing unit with its different parts); and even a memory (secondary storage).

Because computers can do certain types of jobs much faster than people and with far fewer errors, they have displaced people in many types of work at a great savings in labor costs. Moreover, they have enabled people in many professions to perform tasks that in the past were not possible. For instance, in the field of medicine, high-technology equipment is now used in virtually every area of specialization. It helps surgeons to perform operations (for example, laser technology), and it enables doctors to diagnose conditions more accurately (through the use of X-rays, ultrasounds, computerized tomography, magnetic resonance imaging, positron emission tomography, and the like). Medical electronics has progressed to systems that can image organs and other structures of the human body in great detail. Computers also facilitate research and compilation of documents and other projects, and they are now used in all aspects of business and education. Self-instructional computer programs help people learn new information and skills. Some programs present simulations of tasks, require the learner to perform in certain ways, and give the learner and/or instructor feedback about that performance. For example, airline pilots can sharpen their flying skills through the use of computer-generated flight simulators that duplicate the experience of flying in different types of aircraft.

Computers can be classified into four main types: (1) supercomputers, the most powerful type of computer, high-capacity machines used by very large organizations; (2) mainframes, large computers that occupy specially wired, air-conditioned rooms, which are capable of great processing speeds and data storage; (3) minicomputers, used by many businesses, colleges, and state and city agencies; and (4) microcomputers, common tools in all areas of life. The minicomputer market has diminished in recent years, squeezed at the high end by multifunction mainframes and at the low end by less expensive but increasingly powerful personal computers. Microcomputers are the most widely used and fastest-growing type of computer. This type includes desktop computers, laptop and notebook computers, and personal digital assistants. The memory and storage capacity of notebook computers today can compete with those of desktop computers. Personal digital assistants, also known as palmtop computers or handheld computers, combine pen input, writing recognition, personal organizational tools, and communications capabilities in a very small package. The pen-based computers weigh just over 5 ounces and fit in a shirt pocket. The newest kind of microcomputer, the net computer, is limited but useful for some purposes. It does have a central processing unit, but its memory is minimal. Microcomputers are the type of computer in most widespread use today.

It has become clear in most developed countries that access to computer technology is essential to success in education, business, government, and other realms. Thus, governments are faced with how to make computers more widely available to a broader range of citizens. The practical response to the digital divide was to establish national, state, and local programs to get more equipment and connections to a broader set of institutions. As a result, community technology is often available at libraries and schools, and ambitious grant-writing efforts to obtain computers for public access and to underwrite the costs of Internet connectivity continue.

Components and Developments of Hardware

Computer hardware, that is, the equipment associated with a computer system, comprises many different components. All computer hardware helps in some way to process "input," or the raw data accepted into the computer, to produce "output," that is, usable information, usually in the form of words, numbers, and graphics. The processor, or central processing unit (CPU), processes raw data into meaningful, useful information. The CPU interprets and executes program instructions and communicates with the input, output, and storage devices. Secondary storage provides additional storage space separate from memory. The most common secondary storage devices are magnetic disks or hard disks. Peripheral equipment includes all input, output, and secondary storage devices. In the case of personal computers, some of the input, output, and storage devices are built into the same physical unit; the CPU and disk drive are all contained in the same housing, whereas the keyboard, mouse, and screen are separate.

Hardware is only one of five components that make up a complete information system, however. The complete information system includes, first and foremost, people; the other four components are procedures, software, hardware, and data. People are the most important part of an information system because they program the computer to perform certain tasks or become users of the computer to achieve certain objectives related to business, private life, education, and so on. Procedures are the rules or guidelines that people follow when using software, hardware, and data. These procedures are documented in manuals written by computer specialists. Software and hardware manufacturers provide manuals with their products. Software is another name for a program or programs. It consists of the step-by-step instructions that tell the computer how to do its work. The purpose of the software is to convert data, or unprocessed facts, into information, or processed facts. Data consist of the raw, unprocessed facts, including text, numbers, images, and sounds. For example, for a payroll office worker, the raw facts might be the work hours and pay rate for a list of employees. After the data is processed by the computer, it is usually called information. Information in this case would be the total wages the company owes each employee for a week's work. Hardware is the equipment itself, the physically tangible pieces that make up the computer and that enable it to process input to produce output and to store data and information.

Because computers are made of electronic circuits, they can only recognize two distinct electrical states, "on" or "off." The on and off states are commonly represented by the numbers 1 and 0, respectively. The binary system is a base 2 number system using ones and zeros only. Various combinations of ones and zeros can be entered and stored in a computer to represent all of the numbers, letters, and symbols that people use in information processing, and data and instructions must be interpreted into binary code before they can be used by the computer. There are computer programs that take care of this conversion. Each individual 1 or 0 is called a "bit," short for binary digit. A bit is the smallest piece of data that a computer can process. Alphanumeric representation requires multiple bits. A group of eight bits is a "byte." The byte is the basic unit for measuring the size of memory. With today's memory sizes, a kilobyte (KB) is 1024 bytes, whereas a megabyte (MB) is 1024 kilobytes, and a gigabyte (GB) is 1024 megabytes. An "encoding system" permits alphanumeric characters to be coded in terms of bits using 1s and 0s. The two most widely used encoding systems are the American Standard Code for Information Interchange (ASCII) and the Extended Binary Coded Decimal Interchange Code (EBCDIC).

Besides hardware and software, there is also a category called "firmware." This term is often used to refer to microprocessors, which include aspects of both hardware and software. In some cases, they are still referred to as hardware.

A central processing unit has two principal parts, an arithmetic logic unit and a control unit. In addition, it contains several registers and a "bus." The arithmetic logic unit is the part of the CPU that performs arithmetic and logical operations. The control unit is the part of the CPU that directs the flow of electronic traffic. The bus connects the parts of the CPU that need to exchange data. The bus lines link the CPU to memory and peripheral cards. Registers are storage areas used by both the control unit and the arithmetic logic unit to speed up system processing. The CPU itself is a collection of electronic circuits. Electronic impulses enter the CPU from an input device. Within the CPU, these impulses move under program control through circuits to create a series of new impulses. Eventually, a set of impulses leaves the CPU, headed for an output device.

Input hardware consists of devices that provide information and instructions to the computer. There are two main types of input devices: keyboards and pointing devices. The keyboard is a composition of numerous keys arranged in a configuration similar to that of a typewriter that generates numbers and letters when pressed. Besides the numeric and alphabetical keys, there are function keys, a backspace key, a tab key, control keys, shift keys, the delete and insert keys, and arrow keys. Pointing devices are moving, on-screen pointers that control, for instance, an arrow, cursor, or insertion point. There are nine types of pointing devices that vary in function, specialization, and shape: mouse, light pen, touch screen, joystick, trackball, graphics tablet, stylus, puck, and head position and eye trackers. The mouse is the most common and the easiest pointing device.

Some input hardware records and generates images. Scanners and digital cameras, for example, enable users to prepare quality images for business or personal use. These images can be used on Internet Web sites or printed out and reproduced, thus enhancing advertising and other forms of media and communication. With the use of these tools, businesses and others can send images around the world instantaneously, and so this hardware, too, has contributed in important ways to the process of globalization. Digital imaging has made dazzling leaps in the half decade since the first digital cameras appeared. Digital cameras are ideal for four typical users: personal users, Web site designers, business users, and other professionals. Digital imaging is very useful for real estate agents, insurance adjusters, police officers, newspaper and magazine editors, and many other users who have a need for high-quality, high-resolution images to achieve various objectives.

Digital camcorders are vastly superior to the mid-level analog formats of a few years ago and provide better resolution and color quality. In addition, they enable users to get video from the camera to the computer via a simple file transfer that does not degrade the quality of the footage. Camcorders today have a number of advantages over the older analog ones. With the analog devices, video capture was a complicated operation involving a plethora of arcane settings that caused degradation in the quality of the video images. Over time, analog tape can suffer color shifts just sitting in a drawer. The new equipment uses flash memory, which has enough capacity and write speed to let the user capture reasonable amounts of fairly high-quality video. Thumbnail-size flash memory is used for smaller video cameras. Some small camcorders provide high-resolution stills along with video. In any case, these input devices all enable users to convey video streams worldwide.

Output hardware consists of external devices that transfer information from the computer's CPU to the computer user. There are two main types of output devices: display devices (monitors) and printers. A key characteristic of the monitor, or viewing screen, is its resolution, or sharpness. Resolution is measured by the density of the pixels. Monitors have improved greatly over the past two decades. Today, there are some that weigh less than 10 pounds; in size, most vary from 12 to 21 inches. Printers can be classified into three main types: personal printers, including most deskjet and laser printers; multifunction printers, which usually include a fax machine, a copier, and a scanner in addition to the printer; and photo printers, used mainly by professional photographers and graphic artists.

Storage hardware provides permanent storage of information and programs for retrieval by the computer. The two main types of storage devices are disk drives and memory. Memory refers to the computer chips that store information for quick retrieval by the CPU. Random access memory (RAM) is used to store the information and instructions that operate the computer's programs. Some devices serve more than one purpose. For example, floppy disks may also be used as input devices if they contain information to be used and processed by the computer user. Secondary storage provides additional storage separate from memory. The three most common secondary storage mediums are magnetic disks, magnetic tape, and optical disk systems, each with a number of subtypes.

Secondary storage devices have many properties: Besides the physical characteristics, which may differ, they may be volatile or nonvolatile, they may be removable or nonremovable, and they may access data via different methods. Any secondary storage system involves two physical parts: a peripheral device and an input/output medium. A disk drive and a tape drive are examples of peripheral devices, and diskettes and magnetic tape cartridges are types of media. The drives write data and programs onto the storage media and read them from the storage media. A medium must be situated on a peripheral device for the computer's CPU to process its contents. Peripheral storage devices can be internal or external. Nonvolatility means that when the computer is shutting down, the data stored on the medium remain there. This feature contrasts with many types of memory that are volatile. Data held in volatile storage disappear once the computer's power is shut off.

When the computer system receives an instruction pertaining to data or to a program in secondary storage, it must first find the materials. The process of retrieving data and programs in storage is called "access." There are two basic access methods: (1) sequential and direct access, by which a user can retrieve the records in a file only in the same order in which they are physically stored on the medium; and (2) direct access, sometimes called "random access," by which a user can retrieve records in any order.

There are two main types of magnetic disks: hard disks and diskettes. Hard disks consist of one or more rigid metal platters mounted onto a shaft and sealed along with an access mechanism inside a case. The size of hard disks vary. Diskettes, or floppy disks, store small amounts of data. They are round platters made of tough plastic. Most diskettes measure $3\frac{1}{2}$ inches in diameter, with the common capacity of 1.44 megabytes. Zip drives are magnetic-disk drives that accept removable $3\frac{1}{2}$ inch disk cartridges with capacities of 100 megabytes. Optical disks are metal disks varying in size from $3\frac{1}{2}$ to 14 inches and were originally developed as compact disks for video and audio applications. There are three formats of optical disks, namely, CD-ROM, WORM, and Erasable. Optical tape uses optical-laser techniques to store data. It is in cassette form, with a storage capacity of 8 gigabytes.

Storage technology will remain viable for a long time. Manufacturers are producing high-capacity super-floppy drives with large storage capacities using new materials such as metal

particles and barium ferrite. New disk-drive technology includes the wet disk, which separates the disk drive heads from the rotating disk with liquid instead of air, and the glass disk, which uses a glass platter instead of aluminum. Moreover, hardware advances are spawning growth in noncomputer devices. Televisions and computers are expected to merge into one device offering interactive television programming. Copiers are now equipped with storage devices for image capturing, and disk drives are found in printers, fax machines, and other document-imaging equipment.

Hardware connections are also very important, and their importance is increasing from day to day because of the Internet. E-mail messages may include not only the e-mail text itself but also a song, an attachment with a word-processed document, or a digital image, for example. There are many systems for connecting computers to the Internet, and all of them involve various types of hardware. Essentially, the computer should have a modem or make use of Ethernet technology. In other words, computer hardware requires physical connections that allow the components to communicate and interact.

The Computer Hardware and Electronics sector has been a major driving force in the process of globalization. Improvements in computer hardware, software, electronics, and telecommunications have created widespread access to information and economic potential. These advances have facilitated efficiency gains in all sectors of the economy. The use of computers and other electronic equipment provides the backbone that allows the expansion of products, ideas, and resources among nations and among people across borders. Thus, the computer and electronics industry has been a catalyst for global trade, innovation, and integration.

Nilly Kamal El-Amir

See Also Technology and Technical Change; Computer Software

References

Capron, H. L. 1998. *Computers: Tools for an Information Age,* Sixth ed. New York: Addison Wesley.

Curtin, Dennis P. 2003. *Information Technology: The Breaking Wave.* Chicago: Irwin McGraw-Hill.

Dvorak, John C. 2003. "The New Digital Camera." *PC Magazine* 22, no. 20 (November 11): 63.

Gibilisco, Stan. 1997. *The Illustrated Dictionary of Electronics.* Chicago: Irwin McGraw-Hill.

Ibrahim, Ahmed. 1996. *Introduction to Applied Fuzzy Electronics.* New York: Prentice Hall.

Howard, Bill. 2003. "On Technology, the New Digital Camcorder." *PC Magazine* 22, no. 19 (October 28): 65.

Hutchinson, Williams Sawyer. 1999. *Using Information Technology: A Practical Introduction to Computers and Communication.* Boston: Irwin McGraw-Hill.

O'Brien, James A. 1997. *Introduction to Information Systems.* Chicago: Irwin McGraw-Hill.

O'Leary, Timothy J., and Linda I. O'Leary. 2001. *Computing Essentials.* Chicago: Irwin McGraw-Hill.

Parsons, June Jamrich, and Dan Oja. 1998. *Computer Concepts.* Cambridge: Course Technology.

Pasahow, Edward. 1998. *Electronics Pocket Reference.* Chicago: Irwin McGraw-Hill.

Sandness, Donald H. 1988. *Computers Today.* Boston: Irwin McGraw Hill.

Scheurer, Thierry. 1994. *Foundations of Computing: System Development with Set Theory and Logic.* Boston: Addison Wesley.

Strover, Sharon. 2003. "Remapping the Digital Divide." *The Information Society* 1, no. 19: 275–277.

Szymanski, Robert A., Donald P. Szymanski, and Donna M. Pulschen. 1995. *Computers and Information Systems.* New Brunswick, NJ: Prentice Hall.

White, Ron, and Timothy Edward Downs. 2003. *How Computers Work.* New York: Que.

Computer Software

Software has been a key enabler of globalization in three ways. First, it has helped to integrate geographically dispersed activities by allowing electronic communication and transactions to take place and by providing a foundation for better use of central data repositories. Second, with computing becoming ubiquitous, the software industry, even though dominated by the United States, has fanned out to all continents to market its products, thereby standardizing the interface between humans and machines, and to recruit inexpensive talent, thereby innovating ways to synchronize work globally. Finally, software itself has globalized, which in industry jargon refers to a combination of internationalization (ensuring that software can handle multiple languages and cultural conventions) and localization (ensuring that software is appropriate for different local audiences). In all this, demand from government and businesses, not individuals, has been the central driver for the transformation of software from a niche market to a large, globalized sector.

Early Experiments in Defense

The roots of software-led globalization were in experiments in the 1950s by the U.S. military on communication and translation technology. The Advanced Research Projects Agency (ARPA) within the U.S. Department of Defense (DoD) explored decentralized, software-mediated means of communication that the Soviet Union would find difficult to penetrate or dis-able. The U.S. military also explored "machine translation" software intended to provide a quick, rough translation of intercepted Russian broadcasts.

In the 1960s, ARPA succeeded in establishing a network between a handful of "hosts," machines meant for managing electronic communications. Communications software was predicated on two key innovations that are still powering the Internet today: packets and protocols. Software broke data down into small packets and sent it to the recipient computer, where another software program would stitch the packets together into the full message. This activity eventually allowed the same physical line to be shared by multiple computers, thereby lowering the cost of data transmission. A set of protocols governed the transmission of packets. ARPANET, the precursor to the Internet, was founded in 1969 based on these innovations.

The Growth of Business Applications and Microcomputers

Only around 5,000 computers were in service in the United States in 1960. Software at that time was not standardized. Unlike today, most software was not bought "off the shelf" or even developed by software companies. It was developed by computer manufacturers, "bundled" and sold with computers, and meant to work only with the specific computer. Business customers hired in-house specialists and contract programmers to enhance software. Programming took place in "machine rooms" where large computers, called "mainframes," were housed. Different applications required different machines, making computing overall an expensive proposition limited to large businesses such as banks.

Within a few years, some companies began to identify opportunities to supply software in cases where manufacturers did not offer comparable products. To fill this niche, they developed the first packaged software and brought it to market. These products were made to complete specific tasks, usually for businesses or the military. The SAGE air defense project, developed at a cost of $8 billion, spawned the first private software developers in the United States. Demand from the Banque de Paris spurred the first European software company, the French SEMA. The first major project in which communications and business applications were developed together was Sabre, a system for travel agents in different locations to make airline reservations. Released in 1964 following seven years of development by IBM, Sabre was the harbinger of software's potential to transform global business by connecting computers through a communications link. Sabre is still used today, though in a much upgraded form.

Sabre's success showed the value of using communications-based software to facilitate transactions. Large companies began to establish proprietary networks to track sales, credit authorization, and research and development efforts across different branch offices. These systems began to store records in a central database for easier and faster access. As a result, managers had better insights into business generated by different branches. These transactional systems were custom-developed and "closed," that is, they were proprietary and could not communicate with other systems (in contrast, for example, to the telephone, which is an open system because you can plug the same telephone into the wall in different companies and it will still work and perform the same exact functions). A closed system can be ex-

panded internationally only in a limited manner. From the existence of multiple computing platforms with bundled software, which limited the use of computers to a select group, the industry had moved towards custom-designed programs. These programs, though still closed systems, enabled more companies to benefit from using computers. The widespread use of computers with a broad choice of standardized software was still another step in the evolution of the software industry.

Early corporate networks remained closed partly because of strict government regulation of the industry, especially in telecommunications. To circumvent regulation, the makers and buyers of network systems lobbied successfully to classify software-mediated exchange of data as a domain separate from telecom, even if they used telecom hardware. They persuaded the government to consider data networks and software as business tools, and like other business tools, as the private property of corporations. Although freed from regulation in this way, software was not protected by intellectual property rights. As opposed to hardware, the U.S. Patent and Trademark Office viewed software as mathematical formulas and algorithms, which were by definition "nonstatutory" (that is, they could not be patented). Inventions powered by software were also considered nonstatutory. The combination of treating software as proprietary but outside the realm of patents meant that companies were protective about their own software; as a result, the growth of commercial software remained limited to closed systems employed by large organizations.

For software to transform global business at an individual scale, more innovations needed to take place. The first, the floppy disk, arrived in the early 1970s, allowing software to be packaged, sold, and shipped at low cost. The software market expanded, and by the middle of the decade, fifty-two products had passed $5 million in revenue, though most were still used in specific business or scientific settings. The second innovation, e-mail software, was developed in 1971 and enabled people to send messages to addresses specific to individuals, not just to a computer. E-mail widened the potential use of computers beyond the programming community. By 1973, three-quarters of all traffic flowing through ARPANET consisted of e-mail.

The software industry was catapulted toward global growth through two innovative business decisions by IBM. In the early 1970s, IBM unbundled its software from its hardware, creating space for other companies worldwide to supply software for IBM's systems. Then, in 1981, IBM introduced the personal computer (PC), opening its architecture and allowing other companies to "clone" it. (Ironically, it was in the same year that the U.S. Supreme Court established that software-driven inventions were patentable.) These two decisions had several important ramifications: The number of players in the software market increased, prices declined, and eventually PCs were adopted in massive numbers in business environments. Companies could now run cheap word-processing programs, construct spreadsheets, develop databases, and increasingly, use e-mail programs.

These innovations made software useful for *individuals* within businesses. Its applicability was no longer restricted to mainframes and special circumstances. The growth of software was not uniform worldwide, however, and it became increasingly apparent that language could impose serious limitations on software. In Japan, for instance, IBM was not as dominant in the computer hardware market as it was in English-speaking countries. Fujitsu, Hitachi, and NEC were the leading manufacturers of computers in Japan. Business software there is still dominated by these three companies, and still bundled with hardware. Independent software players therefore did not flourish there the same way that they did in the United States after the PC revolution. Japan's entry into the world software market developed around recreational software such as video games,

where language was less of an issue. Video gaming software increased the computer's appeal for leisure use and spurred growth among home users in other non-English-speaking countries.

Centralization of Data and Standardization of Communications

Growth in the software industry, led by U.S. companies, skyrocketed from $2 billion in annual sales in 1979 to over $25 billion in 1985. Advances in centralized data analysis and communications bolstered this growth. Though corporate data software was still closed and expensive, ARPANET led innovations in free software, individual-level communications, and open systems (that is, usable across different computer platforms). The first international connection to ARPANET was made in 1973 when the University College of London (England) was linked to the network. In 1981, another research network, called BITNET, sprouted in the United States. Outside the United States, France led the way in consumerizing software-based communications by announcing Minitel in 1979. Minitel comprised terminals that French citizens could use free of charge to access a centralized electronic directory. It was a successful early example of integrating a single database with numerous terminals using communications technology—a hub-and-spoke architecture that still today drives much of software globalization.

The National Science Foundation established a wholly civilian network called the "NSFNET" in 1986. Based around five supercomputing centers, this network was critical to bringing more universities and international communities to the network. Several other networks were established around the world following the NSFNET model. These would eventually combine into a single network, giving rise to the Internet. A rapid international expansion in the number of hosts ensued, bringing the total to more than 100,000 by 1989. This growth was an indication of not just interest in networking but also the increasing maturity and stability of networks based on open (nonproprietary) protocols.

In the corporate world, the merger of data processing and networking happened in two stages, both of which sustained demand for software to connect distant computers and get them to "talk" or work together. The first was a growth in Electronic Data Interchange (EDI), a method of establishing a direct connection between computers. In the transportation sector, for instance, EDI began to replace or supplement manual documentation, ranging from invoices and purchase orders to bills of lading and acknowledgments, sent to and from different parties. The information could be stored in a central database. Different EDI software, however, used different proprietary methods, and a supplier that did business with multiple companies would require a custom software setup for each EDI connection. This led to high maintenance costs, and smaller companies were left out of EDI connections altogether.

The success of open networks led to the second stage: intranets, essentially networks based on protocols pioneered by the likes of ARPANET and NSFNET but closed off to those outside the company. Whereas EDI facilitated communication between a company and its external partners, intranets were used to enhance internal business within the company. By the late 1980s, for instance, Citicorp's network spanned ninety-four countries, transmitting calls, facilitating trades, and enabling employees to share information. Behind the scenes, large data-processing, reporting, and transactional software powered these networks, raising the pace of globalization.

ERP (Enterprise Resource Planning) software, developed by Oracle, Siebel, SAS, and PeopleSoft, added further integration capabilities across the entire international supply chain of large companies. In the late 1990s, online business-to-business (B2B) marketplaces be-

gan to connect buyers and suppliers from different countries within a particular industry. Unlike EDI, marketplace software is open and provided entirely on the Web. Transactions are open to all with a browser. B2B marketplaces have been successful especially in the aerospace, automotive, metals, energy, paper, and chemicals sectors. These virtual marketplaces facilitated regional integration. By 2001, B2B markets in Singapore, for instance, were conducting transactions exceeding U.S.$50 billion with companies in Malaysia, Indonesia, China, Taiwan, South Korea, and Japan.

While corporate software led globalization by connecting worldwide systems and companies virtually, a silent and more physical connection was occurring in the field of "embedded software." Almost everything with electronics—from digital wristwatches to thermostats, VCRs, cell phones, cars, and airplanes—has software embedded within it to perform certain tasks. The rapid growth of electronics since the 1980s has fueled growth in embedded software. In consumer goods markets, where innovation in hardware is increasingly sporadic, embedded software has become a key competitive differentiator. Some manufacturers of consumer electronics report that almost 70 percent of their product development costs go toward software development. Embedded software has been responsible for "convergence": that is, it has driven the standardization of the human-machine interface around the world, so that one can program a VCR using almost the same logic whether one is in Australia, Sri Lanka, or Canada.

Internationalization and Localization of Software

For most of software's history, U.S. firms have controlled the global market, and English has been the universal vernacular of software. Virtually all programming languages are based on English commands. The design of software's human interface (screens, features, and functionality) has been based on Western cultural norms. As U.S. businesses started to deploy software to integrate their foreign branches, and as software companies began to market their wares to other countries, the linguistic and cultural norms that had been taken for granted so far emerged as barriers. Although U.S. firms would likely dominate software production in the foreseeable future, they would no longer dominate its usage. By 2005, more than 70 percent of the world's software users were not native English speakers.

Software manufacturers and large businesses began to appreciate and tackle these issues systematically in the early 1980s. Initially they employed freelance translators and small in-house departments to translate "help" and other nonessential features into other languages. Packaging and instruction manuals were also translated, in some cases to comply with local law that required documentation to be in the local language. Core software functionality continued to be executed in English.

As software increased in size and complexity and as markets expanded beyond languages with Latin roots, manufacturers needed to rethink their approach to software development, especially in regard to internationalization and localization. First, software needed to accommodate different languages, including non-Latin ones. Akin to a telegraph using Morse Code, computers handle all letters and numbers by translating them to binary codes. To process English, computers employ a map called ASCII (American Standard Code for Information Interchange), set in 1963. ASCII defines binary code for 256 characters, more than enough for the English alphabet, including upper case, lower case, and special characters. But software based on ASCII cannot handle expansion into Japanese, which employs tens of thousands of characters. "Internationalization" refers to the process by which software is modified to accommodate such languages. Although it sounds very basic, internationalization is an extremely important task, without

which software would not be able to cross very many geographic boundaries.

Second, software needed to be "localized," that is, each local version or instance of software needed to appear in the local language and respect local cultural norms and legal requirements. A "locale definition" had to be added to software, where "locale" is defined as a combination of country and language. Canada-French and Belgium-French are different locales, and software deployed to a company with offices in Montreal or Brussels needs to be localized as such.

In the 1990s, the scope and complexity of internationalization and localization expanded significantly as the Internet became a basis for servicing a worldwide customer-base. By 1992, the number of hosts on the Internet exceeded 1 million worldwide. International organizations such as the World Bank and the United Nations, which were among the first to come online in the early 1990s, required internationalized and localized software. Key standards organizations adopted and clarified internationalization and localization guidelines for the Internet, and software manufacturers adopted many of those guidelines for their own development. Further innovations, such as "geolocation," which enables Web sites to automatically determine the geographic location of individual users and serve localized content or software accordingly, arose in the 1990s.

The number of Internet hosts worldwide now exceeds 180 million, and 171 countries have their own Internet identification. But localization by and large remains unidirectional. Almost 80 percent of software products are still developed in English and then localized. Due to the continued dominance of U.S. English in programming languages, standards, and conventions, most non-U.S. software manufacturers either develop their products in English or localize into English first, using that version as a basis for further localization. Regardless, thanks to software and the Internet, large firms, for the first time, can think globally and act locally almost instantaneously.

U.S. Capital, Foreign Labor, and Renegade Developers

A parallel exists in the software labor market. Just as U.S. English is the dominant language, even though the software user-base is global, U.S. capital is the engine that drives the software industry, even though labor is increasingly global. U.S. companies sell 77 percent of the packaged software in the world. Large software manufacturing and consulting firms in the United States have experimented with outsourcing labor-intensive tasks to Ireland and Wales, Southeast Asia, and India. Motorola, a leading U.S. manufacturer of cell phones and embedded chips, has software development centers in twenty-five countries. It developed software for its 3G phones by organizing teams in six countries. Between 1,300 and 9,900 miles apart from one another, the teams, who never got together physically, worked globally via advanced communication software, central databases, and management processes.

The goals of outsourcing have been to find specialized skills, to reduce labor-intensive programming costs, and to expedite production time by conducting "round-the-clock" product development. The biggest consumers of outsourced software labor, however, are not software manufacturers, but the IT (information technology) departments of large U.S. companies. Many have outsourced their routine IT maintenance and development jobs, focusing U.S. labor on higher value-added tasks, thereby generating 30 to 50 percent savings on wages.

The roots of outsourcing are in the diasporas of various nations, that is, their overseas immigrant populations. Employees of Indian or Chinese origin working for U.S. companies took advantage of their contacts within the United States (and later, Western Europe) to secure the initial contracts for data processing, the most labor-intensive of all IT-outsourced jobs. As the Internet boom took off in developing countries in the mid-1990s, and as higher bandwidth became available for communica-

tions, more outsourcing firms emerged. Success with data processing provided confidence to both overseas contractors and their U.S./European counterparts to allow the former to take on more complex programming projects.

Currently, almost 80 percent of the worldwide overseas outsourcing of software goes to India. India has aggressively marketed its highly skilled, English-speaking population and its wage differentials to Western clients while giving ample tax breaks, subsidies, incentives, and infrastructural investment for local entrepreneurs. Tata Consulting Services (TCS) was the first Indian software exporter, beginning operations in 1974. But tight government regulations and the lack of infrastructure kept growth checked, keeping it almost negligible until 1991. Since then, India's software production and services have boomed, exceeding $8.3 billion in sales in 2000 and making up 15 percent of India's total exports. The size of India's software industry is projected to exceed $50 billion by 2008, including exports and domestic use.

Outsourcing, though successful, has not been an entirely smooth experience for U.S. firms. The transition to managing teams in different countries has been difficult, as the productive work hours extended from eight or ten hours a day to almost twenty-four. Cultural norms and attitudes toward structure, decisionmaking, hierarchy, communication styles, and deadlines need to be bridged continually. Management of knowledge and information has also become problematic as intellectual capital and skills have become dispersed. Some studies indicate that because of these issues, multisite software development still takes longer than comparable projects colocated within a single firm, even with the virtually twenty-four-hour workday.

Populist politicians in the United States have attacked outsourcing as a labor-displacing and therefore reprehensible practice. Outsourcing is increasingly a threat to systems integration and programming jobs within IT departments in large firms, though it has been less menacing to software manufacturers. Sixty percent of India's software exports are sent to U.S. clients. U.S. software firms, in turn, have been vocal proponents of more lenient immigration and labor laws because they are in favor of allowing both employment of immigrants and outsourcing to the global labor market. India's provision of labor is centered on the least value-added and most labor-intensive activities in the software development chain. India is not a leading provider of either consumer-level or enterprise-level packaged software. To be sure, the leading Indian software companies do possess the management and programming skills required to complete large-scale software development. They have provided turnkey software projects to banking, manufacturing, retail, and other sectors in developing countries. However, they have not been able to shake the software leadership in most Western markets.

The main international challenge to large software companies has come from global communities of individual programmers. Although free software has existed since the mainframe days, the General Public License (GPL) and Linux movements catapulted it into a major player. These movements were a response to proprietary code, which renegades in the software community deemed wasteful and an example of capitalism being suboptimal for the common good. In 1983, the Free Software Foundation developed the concept of "copyleft," which, in contrast to "copyright," would allow anyone to use certain software and contribute to its development, provided that the source code remain nonproprietary and open. GPL is the license that codifies this concept and accompanies open-source products.

Linux, an operating system released in 1994 by Linus Torvalds of Finland, was based on this concept. It launched the first large-scale open-source threat to commercial U.S.-dominated software. Thanks to the Internet, a global community of contributors develops Linux and all other open-source software collaboratively. Because it is virtually free, nonprofit organizations were among the first adopters of open-source software. Parallel open-source software now exists for many commercial software titles. Because global volunteer talent nurtures it, many open-source software titles are proving to be more stable and flexible than their commercial counterparts, prompting an increasing number of large businesses to switch to open source. Some large manufacturers, such as IBM and Oracle, have already released Linux versions of some of their high-end business products. As of April 2003, more than 60,000 open-source projects involving over 600,000 collaborators worldwide were in progress at SourceForge, one of the leading online software collaboration hosts. Together, outsourcing and open-source software are poised to shape the foreseeable future of software globalization.

Jalal Alamgir

See Also Technology and Technical Change; Computer Hardware and Electronics

References

Campbell-Kelly, Martin. 2003. *From Airline Reservations to Sonic the Hedgehog: A History of the Software Industry.* Cambridge: MIT Press.

D'Costa, Anthony. 2003. "Uneven and Combined Development: Understanding India's Software Exports." *World Development* 31, no. 1 (January): 211–226.

Herbsleb, James D., and Deependra Moitra. 2001. "Global Software Development." *IEEE Software* (March/April): 16–20.

O'Hara-Devereaux, M., and R. Johansen. 1994. *Globalwork: Bridging Distance, Culture, and Time.* San Francisco: Jossey-Bass.

Schiller, Dan. 1999. *Digital Capitalism: Networking the Global Market System.* Cambridge: MIT Press.

Energy and Utilities

Energy and utilities industries are essential to all societies. They include such activities as telephony and telegraphy, water and sanitation, electricity and power supplies, and public transportation. Since shortcomings in public utility systems can lead to problems in health care and exacerbate economic inequality, governments generally make it a top priority to ensure these services are provided to all who are within their jurisdiction. The investment in infrastructure necessary to provide services is extremely high, however, and the possibilities of extracting profits from rural and remote areas very low. Consequently, service provision often follows the model of the natural monopoly. This pattern is being increasingly challenged as states look for ways to introduce market mechanisms to the provision of energy and utilities.

Utilities generally operate under the terms of a license or contract with a central government. Typically, they are obliged to provide certain services to the public, and in return they may receive government funding or other forms of support. The exact nature of such arrangements differs considerably around the world, just as legislative and constitutional arrangements vary. However, with the spread of privatization and deregulation, more complex but also more internationally standardized arrangements are being introduced. These often make an important distinction between bodies that maintain a distribution network of some sort (for example, water pipelines or train tracks) and those that provide services to the public (for example, generating electricity or driving trains). As technology and society change, the types of industries generally considered public utilities also change, with new technologies becoming important and older services less so. On the one hand, for example, different forms of broadcasting and radio-frequency wavelength usage have been considered public utilities in some cases in recent years. On the other hand, historical monopolies in commodities such as salt and spices would now no longer be considered a public service anywhere.

As industrial development deepens and spreads around the world, the demand for energy and utilities continually increases. Since resources are finite, inevitably states will increasingly compete with each other for access to those resources. Climate change will also have an impact upon further demand for energy and utilities, and there will be enhanced need for the development and delivery of alternative sources of energy, including nuclear power. In many cases, greater levels of efficiency may be obtained through cross-border public utility provision, although in these cases many political and logistical problems remain.

Public utilities may be classified into several categories: energy (fossil fuels, nuclear power, and alternative sources of energy), water, public transportation, telecommunications and broadcasting, and other services that take a public-utility role, such as provision of health care. Management of each type of utility involves specific issues, especially with respect to privatization and deregulation. Finally, globalization and cross-border issues affect the provision of public utilities.

Varieties of Public Utilities

Energy

The production of energy is necessary to keep modern society running. Without it, wealth production would be almost impossible, public health would rapidly deteriorate, and disorder would soon become rampant. Most energy is produced from fossil fuels, although alternative sources are likely to become increasingly important as fossil fuel supplies become depleted. Many governments, especially in developing countries, subsidize energy production and consumption; in many cases, their policies render populations vulnerable to external shocks and especially to the impact of climate change (Heller and Mani 2002).

Fossil Fuels. Fossil fuels—primarily oil, coal, and natural gas—remain the most important sources of energy in the world. These fuels are unevenly distributed, however, often relatively inaccessible, and contribute to pollution and global warming when burned. Existing supplies are, of course, finite, though how long they will last under current levels of demand is a contested issue. In part, it depends on the feasibility of employing new techniques to extract already known sources of supply that would not be economical to extract at the present time. Although oil production may have already peaked, it is unknown how long supplies will last: There may be as much as 120 years' worth of supply still remaining, or there may be significantly less. In any case, attention will have to be focused on continued improved efficiency in machinery and operations. International diplomacy will also be required to limit military threats and armed confrontation over the distribution and use of fossil fuels for particular states.

Alternative Energy. Research is under way to explore various forms of energy that are renewable and that do not depend on fossil fuels. These include wind, wave, and solar power, together with different types of fuels that may

cause less environmental degradation than fossil fuels. It is hoped that these alternatives will soon begin to replace fossil fuels as researchers find ways to make them feasible. Although some progress has been made with providing alternative energy, such sources make up a very small proportion of energy provision globally. The alternatives are not without environmental concerns. Hydroelectricity, in particular, has attracted negative scrutiny with regard to the impact of dams on indigenous peoples and their lifestyles, and wind power sites have also been criticized by some for unsightliness and noise pollution.

Many projects related to alternative energy are organized by the private sector, although public-sector initiatives do exist. Universities in a number of developed countries are leading the way with some technologies and have formed partnerships with other public- and private-sector institutions. To date, most forms of alternative energy generate power to only small-scale local areas or else contribute to the conventional distribution network.

Nuclear Power. Nuclear power depends upon the decomposition of certain heavy metals that release energy in the form of radioactive particles, or fission energy. The energy is typically used to heat water, which then drives generating equipment. Fission energy produces nuclear waste, which can remain harmful for many years. Management of this waste remains of crucial importance to the production of nuclear power. Proponents point to ongoing successful management of waste from existing nuclear power plants, whereas detractors highlight the fact that accidents could still occur, that successful management would have to continue for many years into the future, and that it would take just one serious incident to cause widespread suffering and possible loss of life. In any case, the issues surrounding the disposal of nuclear waste remain unresolved, and any possible international trade in waste would need to be thoroughly regulated and monitored. These factors make nuclear power a very expensive prospect and reduce its attractiveness to potential recipient states. A new phase of development of nuclear power would be the use of fusion energy, which, if it were feasible, would reduce the amount of dangerous byproducts released into the environment.

Despite the unsolved potential problems, nuclear power is seen as inescapable in countries such as South Korea and China where demand for energy far outstrips resources to generate it. Countries such as Iran and North Korea, which are also apparently investigating the use of nuclear power, have come under suspicion of wishing to use the nuclear power generation program to hide potential weapons development programs. As the United Nations–led efforts to identify nuclear and other programs in Iraq demonstrated, finding evidence of such activities is a complex and time-consuming undertaking.

Water

A safe and secure supply of water is necessary for individuals as consumers and also for industry. Additional, related services include sewage removal, sewage treatment, and desalination. Parts of the same network are generally required for conducting each of these services, and the cost of maintaining the network, not to mention extending it, means that only states will have the ability to manage the process. However, a number of countries have found that allowing independent providers of some services may be a feasible alternative. Nevertheless, the increasing global demand for water, deriving from increasing population and increasing industrial development, together with changes in demand patterns resulting from climate change, mean that competition for water resources is likely to become more intense. As water resources are rarely located wholly within the boundaries of a single state, it is possible that political or armed confrontation could develop around water issues in the future. This seems particularly true in the case of the Middle East; the supply of water from Malaysia to Singapore and the use of the upper Mekong River by China are other areas where controversy is possible.

Public Transportation

Some states have deemed the provision of public transportation to be a public utility because of the importance of moving people conveniently to and from workplaces, public institutions, and the like. Forms of transportation that fall under the public utility umbrella often include rail and underground rail (subway), bus, and air transportation. Geography and society affect the type of transport considered to be a utility, however. For example, in Australia, remote distances promoted the idea of the Royal Flying Doctor Service, and ferries are common forms of transportation when island communities are involved. Transportation facilities can also provide additional services. In South Korea, for example, underground railway systems in the capital, Seoul, were built in part to provide shelter in the event of bombardment or chemical attack from North Korea or other enemies, and the highway system was created not only to boost economic development and national unity but also to assist in military deployment.

Transportation consists of a network along which services may be provided, together with vehicles and attendant services such as cleaning, catering, and maintenance. Public safety services may also be required, especially with respect to air services. Deregulation and privatization of transportation services generally work to the disadvantage of people in remote, rural locations, whereas those in profitable urban locations may find themselves facing intense competition under such a system.

Telecommunications and Broadcasting

Telecommunications can be used to provide important information and services to people and industry and hence may be considered a public utility. The development of mobile telecommunications and its integration with personal computing suggest that it may not be necessary to expand existing communication networks to cover the remaining unconnected regions of states. In Brunei, for example, mobile telephones have rendered the need for conventional landlines redundant. However, this option requires individual members of the population to own handsets, which remain expensive in many countries for the average person. The inability to develop inclusive networks in some regions may intensify the problem of the digital divide—that is, the differences in economic opportunities available to those who have access to Internet services and those who do not.

Although some states have sought to regulate the types of services used within their borders, economies of scale and scope dictate that the more successful mobile telephone providers will be large multinational enterprises. Insofar as companies act together to create industry standards, their collaboration can increase efficiency and hence reduce costs for consumers. Generally, private-sector institutions dominate these industries, although they may be subject to regulation by a state body.

State broadcasting services have been favored in many countries on the basis that they can be used to convey important security information and other forms of public announcements to people in a wide area. Further, some believe that an unbiased approach would result from the absence of commercial interests. Unfortunately, state broadcasting services have in many cases been subject to powerful influences over content that compromise the impartiality of the news and information sent over the airwaves. Further, the complexity and sophistication required of modern broadcasting services require resources beyond the ability of states to provide without commercial sponsorship. Nevertheless, in states where broadcasting and telecommunications technology may play an important role in nation-building, integrating people into society and widening economic opportunities, the provision of such services may be helpful. Examples include Thailand, where open-distance learning, sponsored by the king, helps to overcome the problem of meager educational resources in remote areas. Planned satellite and telecommunication services can also reduce inequalities stimulated by the digital divide.

Public Health

Because infectious diseases and other health hazards can represent significant social problems, many governments provide public health services in the same way that they provide public utilities. These services vary considerably from country to country. Services may be created and delivered on very short notice in the event of a medical emergency. Examples of this phenomenon in recent years have included crises arising from Severe Acute Respiratory Syndrome (SARS) in East Asia and North America, Avian Influenza ("bird flu") in Southeast Asia, and Bovine Spongiform Encephalopathy (BSE, or "mad cow disease") in the United Kingdom and elsewhere. The nature of public health services range from provision of information to health inspection, vaccination, and other preventive measures. Voluntary groups may also become involved in public health services, especially internationally.

Other Utilities

Almost any industry may be classified as a public utility in one context or another. Industries that play a significant role in economic development, such as mining or banking in some economies with few other resources, are good examples.

Privatization and Competition

Particularly since the collapse of the Soviet system at the end of the 1980s, a single model of economic development has assumed supremacy worldwide. This model has been adopted by the International Monetary Fund (IMF) and aggressively promoted around the world, notably in countries requiring structural adjustment funding. The model strongly promotes privatization of state-owned enterprises and increases in market competition. Numerous countries have voluntarily privatized energy and utility services, but with mixed results. In Russia, for example, the rapid privatization of resource industries resulted in a concentration of power in a small number of corporate hands before an effective taxation system could be established (Stiglitz 2002, 157–160). Other privatizations in the country were conducted without an appropriate legal or market infrastructure and have been ruinous for the Russian economy.

Privatization is considered a necessary precursor to competition, and deregulation is required to ensure that privatization enables market actors to perform to their highest ability. However, evidence from privatization of power-generating companies illustrates a number of difficulties attendant upon the process. In California, for example, privatization and partial deregulation led to competition in wholesale markets for electricity, while retail prices were capped. The motivation for the deregulation was to allow for companies to recover their losses from failed investments in nuclear power (Palast 2001). California normally relies upon hydroelectricity and natural gas for significant portions of its energy supply, and deregulation initially made little difference, as excess generating capacity ensured that wholesale prices remained lower than retail prices. However, in 2000, drought and a large increase in natural gas prices caused major increases in demand for conventional electricity, and the wholesale price increased beyond the capped retail limit. Independent producers were then able to manipulate the price through transmission restraints and other manipulations of the supply. Distributors were forced to buy power at a loss from the independent producers and could not pass on price increases to consumers. They were soon in financial difficulties and appealed for state support. Governor Gray Davis was required to implement emergency legislation to allow for the purchase of power at levels acceptable to consumers, although the deregulation had

been instituted by his predecessor. Newly elected president George W. Bush refused to lend assistance to California, and Davis, beset by corporate scandals and obliged to close down state programs through lack of money, was subsequently recalled following a politically motivated right-wing campaign (McCrum 2003).

The privatization of water services has also grown in importance internationally. Thanks in large part to the support of the World Bank and the IMF, the number of people in the world dependent on water supplies from private corporations rose from 51 million in 1990 to around 460 million in 2004 (Hacher 2004). Many of these privatization projects have had negative consequences, such as increased pollution, increased costs to consumers, and corporate difficulties in meeting expected targets. From South America to South Africa and Southeast Asia, many thousands have faced increased costs and decreased service as a result of water privatization. There are few significant reports of positive outcomes outside of Western countries, which already possessed sophisticated institutions able to deal effectively with powerful corporations. Furthermore, regulatory bodies have proved themselves incapable of administering corporations in any country, as scandals over companies such as Enron have demonstrated. However, there are occasions in which privatization of some public utilities may be managed successfully.

Globalization and Cross-Border Issues

Many complex issues cross political borders by nature. These include issues related to environmental degradation, migration, and climate change. In some cases, these issues may be ameliorated through provision of public services and cross-border cooperation is required. This may be bilateral or multilateral in nature, depending on the particular issue concerned, although multilateral fora are more likely to be effective in dealing with widespread problems.

Acid rain, for example, affects countries quite removed from those where it is created. Similarly, water resources are rarely concentrated wholly within the boundaries of a single state. Such actions as the refusal of the United States to ratify the Kyoto Protocol dealing with global warming, the collapse of World Trade Organization (WTO) negotiations, and the like have reduced global collaboration on such matters.

Corporate power in many cases far outstrips the ability of states to regulate the provision of public services. The creation of international regulatory bodies with genuine power to control private-sector institutions involved in energy and utility provision will therefore become essential. Public policy must begin to ensure that gains from energy consumption are matched by efforts to mitigate the costs, especially to the environment. Global economic development and the attendant demand for energy cannot be constrained, but governments will need to provide for reduced emissions from oil consumption and increased use of alternative energy sources, together with appropriate institutional arrangements to administer them.

John Walsh

See Also Environmental Impacts of Globalization; Global Climate Change

References

Hacher, Sebastian. 2004. "Argentina Water Privatization Scheme Runs Dry." *Corp Watch,* February 26, http://corpwatch.radicaldesigns.org/article.php?id=10088.

Heller, Peter S., and Muthukumara Mani. 2002. "Adapting to Climate Change." *Finance and Development* 39, no.1 (March), http://www.imf.org/external/pubs/ft/fandd/2002/03/heller.htm.

McCrum, Robert. 2003. "Judgement Day." *The Observer,* September 28, http://observer.guardian.co.uk/magazine/story/0,11913,1050825,00.html.

Nuclear Energy Agency and Organisation for Economic Co-operation and Development. 2003. *Nuclear Energy Today,* http://www1.oecd.org/publications/e-book/6603111E.PDF.

Palast, Gregory. 2001. "A High Price to Pay for the Power and the Glory." *The Observer,* February 4, http://observer.guardian.co.uk/business/story/0,433094,00.html.

Stiglitz, Joseph. 2002. *Globalization and Its Discontents.* London: Penguin.

Financial Services

The term "financial services" generally covers all services offered by banks, credit institutions, insurance companies, financial intermediaries, and other institutions that deal with investments or financial instruments. In order to avoid disputes on the definition of financial services, the World Trade Organization (WTO) devised a listing of financial services under the General Agreement on Trade in Services (GATS), where financial services are divided into four main categories: (1) insurance services—direct insurance (life and property insurance), reinsurance, insurance provision, and auxiliary services such as insurance statistics; (2) banking services—acceptance of deposits, issuance of loans; (3) securities services—asset management, trade with and participation in the issue of securities, invoicing and clearing services; and (4) other services, such as provision of financial information and consultation services. Virtually all national and international financial operations fall into one of these categories.

Revolutionary Changes in the Financial Services Industry

The financial services industry has undergone revolutionary changes, particularly in the past decade, and continues to evolve today. The revolution has mainly concerned the organization and structure of markets, the role of financial intermediaries, and the pathways taken by monetary flows around the globe (Gentle 1993). These changes have left no corner of the industry untouched. Consequently, the direct investments of the industrial countries in the financial service sector increased from $63 billion to $356 billion between 1980 and 1990, representing an approximate average annual increase of 18 percent (UNCTAD 2003).

The institutions involved in providing financial services are being rocked by new competition both domestically and internationally. For instance, the Hong Kong and Shanghai Banking Corporation (Hong Kong Bank, or HSBC) has been transformed from an Asian giant to a global financial services provider—with its headquarters now in London and with a huge U.S. network of affiliates—based on its acquisitions of Republic Bank of New York, Marine Midland Bank, and other smaller institutions. Even insurance companies are finding it necessary to enter the domain of other financial services in a major way—the acquisition of Dresdner Bank, Germany's second largest, by Allianz, and the rapid global expansion of the latter through acquisitions of insurance companies in the United States and Europe, is a case in point. Moreover, these changes are redefining the financial services industry through the use of electronic methods replacing people and physical documentary activities.

Traditionally, households in many countries have used commercial banks for checking accounts and credit cards. People have generally had their savings accounts and home mortgages at savings institutions, purchased life insurance policies from insurance companies, and bought securities from a securities broker. Similarly, companies have generally borrowed from commercial banks and used security firms to issue debt or equity securities. Moreover, there has been a desire to delineate boundaries for each financial institution. For example, in the United States, a variety of constraints have prohibited bank branching across state lines. There were also restrictions that limited the range of products banks could offer and that kept other companies out of the banking business. In several countries, banking and securities have been relatively separate businesses, in some cases by law and regulation (United States and Japan) and in others by practice (United Kingdom).

The historical separation of financial service functions has come under increasing strains in recent times. Under the competitive pressures unleashed by decreasing legal and regulatory barriers, returns in traditional financial services have drastically decreased. On the one hand, these forces have worked as a catalyst to financial service providers, forcing them to expand beyond the traditional boundaries with new combinations of activities. On the other hand, other factors have encouraged highly focused firms to specialize in particular activities. A number of factors have contributed to the changing economics of the financial services industry. A complete list of these factors would have to include more volatile interest rates and exchange rates, liberalization and deregulation, the formation of international pools of funds, new product development, and asset securitization. These are not independent factors. The collapse of the Bretton Woods system and the subsequent shift to floating exchange rates in the early 1970s made it easier for central banks to pursue easy monetary policies, encouraging inflation, higher domestic rates, and wider swings in interest rates and exchange rates (Meerschwam 1991). These effects, in turn, put pressure on domestic regulatory structures and institutional relationships, setting the stage, for example, for low interest rates on savings deposits.

The rise of euro markets—international money outside of domestic regulation—has been the key underlying force that propelled a decisive change. Previously, corporate figures who wanted to borrow a particular currency had to rely on the local institutions in the home country of the currency desired. Now corporations can obtain funds from several locations. This internationalization of the capital markets has greatly increased the competitive pressure on domestic financial institutions and the pressure for more uniform financial regulation. Moreover, the development of the swap market, a new financial instrument, has encouraged the process of integration. Swaps and other products, such as interest rate options and forward contracts, have greatly facilitated the management of financial risk in the corporate world and have strengthened links in international markets. For instance, a borrower can take advantage of an attractive financing opportunity in one financial market and then swap the repayment obligation into the form and currency desired through the swap market.

Securitization, a process of homogenizing and packaging financial instruments into a new fungible one with functions such as acquisition, classification, collateralization, composition, pooling, and distribution, has also been a vital force for change. Loans normally made by banks to large borrowers increasingly have taken the form of securities sold to an array of institutional buyers. Instead of loaning the money, commercial banks now act as agents in the transaction, sometimes providing credit guarantees to borrowers. This has led to the development of the euro-commercial paper market, note issuance facilities, and other security products in the international marketplace. Securities backed by a pool of managers have been particularly important for securitization in the United States. These changes have allowed various institutions to invest in mortgages, converting the U.S. mortgage market from a highly segmented and localized market into a broad-based market in which mortgage rates are driven by other long-term rates available in the financial marketplace.

With increasing international and domestic competition, declining margins in traditional businesses, and greater regulatory freedom, financial service firms have sought new opportunities outside their traditional businesses. The changes under way, however, are more fundamental than institutions simply managing by broadening their horizons. The basic cost structure of most financial service firms developed in a different world than that of the early 1990s. These institutions were protected from potential competitors; their cost of funds was relatively low and stable; and the rates they charged on assets were determined by local market conditions. In this environment, institutions often competed by building up expensive delivery systems in the form of branch offices, loan officers, securities brokers, life insurance agents, and the like. Because delivery systems were highly labor intensive and often involved handling a large paper flow of checks and securities, economies of scale were difficult to achieve (Humphrey 1990). But, with high and stable margins, firms could afford to compete through "service" by adding staff and opening new offices.

The changed state of savings banks demonstrates what has really happened in the new environment. In the United States, the earnings rate on new mortgages is determined by the national marketplace because of the large mortgage-backed securities market. The savings rate paid to customers is also heavily determined by national money market rates because savers have ready access to money market mutual funds. Thus, the net interest spread is effectively out of the hands of the savings bank. Even worse, mortgage brokers in competition with savings banks can originate mortgages without an expensive branch network, and the operating cost of a money market mutual fund is way below that of a savings bank. The mutual fund can provide a money market rate with checking account privileges for an all-in cost of 0.50 to 0.75 percent of assets, approximately one-third of the operating cost of a savings bank. Faced with this situation, many financial service firms are seeking economies of scope, trying to distribute more products through their expensive delivery systems (Crane et al. 1983). Regulators are generally helping in this process in an effort to improve the profitability of weakened institutions. For instance, in Australia, commercial banks are allowed to distribute virtually all consumer financial products.

Technology changes and expanding customer needs are also affecting the configuration of financial service firms. Taking corporate customers as an example, short-term borrowing and long-term debt were formerly treated as separate products. These products were purchased by different people within the company and provided by different suppliers. Now, debt is a highly integrated set of products purchased in a centralized manner. Financial service firms are reorganizing their functions to face the evolving realities of the marketplace. Whereas some products are being bundled together in new ways, others are becoming unbundled. Credit cards in the United States are more and more spun off into separate businesses. Nonbank competitors have discovered that credit card services can be delivered successfully nationally or internationally without the need for conventional bank branches. Furthermore, there are substantial economies of scale in the card business. With advances in technology and customer solicitation, the business has become much less paper- and labor-intensive. These changes have led to substantial increases in the concentration of business among the leading credit card issuers.

New Trends in the Financial Services

The financial services sector has experienced far-reaching structural and directional changes over the past two decades. An extremely dynamic period of growth in this sector began in 1973, the year that ushered in a new floating exchange rate regime. It was the end of the postwar order of the international financial system and its fixed dollar-tied exchange rate mechanism. With the floating exchange rate regime, a powerful wave of liberalization and deregulation swept across the financial sector, leading to the rise of global financial markets. Under the new set of conditions, the financial services industry experienced an enormous upswing and became itself a driving force behind the dynamics of the financial markets. This process was characterized by some new trends, including, on the one hand, a high degree of concentration, and on the other numerous new products and institutions.

Expansions, Mergers, and Concentrations
The internationalization of banks and other financial service providers has been observable since the 1960s. Euro markets created the need to circumvent national regulation. For example, during the 1950s German banks were largely devoted to reconstruction, but during the 1960s they began to follow their customers, the multinational companies abroad. At that time, corporations involved in cross-border activities were already initiating international mergers. In the 1970s, rapid development of international financial business created new fields of activity for internationally oriented companies. With the addition of the foreign exchange trade, "new" financial centers in London, New York, Tokyo, Hong Kong, and Frankfurt started to emerge. The international credit trade became an important and rapidly growing area of business. Commercial banks, too, were no longer involved in their original areas of operation, but through diversification of their service and financial product range, and through mergers and takeovers, increasingly tried to expand into other money-spinning areas. Thus, a major new trend has been toward one-stop banking. As a result, up to 75 percent of the sales volume of the big banks has been achieved through the trading activities of the investment banking sector.

Financial services have become more important in the context of a substantial increase in the indebtedness of consumer households as

well as the privatization initiatives that have taken place in waves for more than two decades. The financial services industry is therefore among the big winners of globalization. Nevertheless, financial markets outside the United States are still regarded as highly regulated. Numerous financial service providers are still in public ownership, despite the fact that privatization programs have been moving ahead in many developed and developing economies. Therefore, it is no coincidence that a concentration wave, based on mergers and takeovers as well as a further increase in the supply of financial products, has swept across the industry. The growing derivative trade is a product of unregulated financial markets.

Since international financial markets are given considerable control and steering functions, with regard to all other macroeconomic areas their weaknesses and systemic risks are viewed as dangerous to stability. Highlighting this point, the Bank for International Settlements (BIS) has noted that with an increasing degree of concentration of the banks, the systemic risks grew, as did the distortion of market rates, which ultimately led to the misallocation of capital. The concentration processes are exemplified as well by the worldwide unofficial trade in derivatives and foreign exchange, almost 50 percent of which is concluded at only two financial centers, London and New York. Only three U.S. banks hold almost 90 percent of the nominal circulation of foreign currency derivatives. The concentration in the market for interest and credit derivatives, 86 percent and 94 percent, respectively, is similar. Globally, about three-quarters of exchange transactions are concluded by only thirty dealers (BIS 2002).

A glance at the share of overall worldwide capital holdings in the hands of a few banks and pension funds makes the oligopolization trend even clearer. And yet, this type of concentration could be used to make directive power of supervisory and regulative authorities more efficient, since the number of players is very limited. Another trend is the strong development of wealth and asset management in the banks, an indicator of the considerable increase in large fortunes (World Bank 2002), which is an expression of the increasing social polarization that has taken place worldwide over the past two decades. These circumstances, in any case, have further strengthened the influential role of banks and insurance service providers. The financial service providers and banks—and primarily the investment banks, such as Citigroup, Deutsche Bank, Credit Suisse, First Boston, Goldman Sachs, Morgan Stanley, JP Morgan, and Merrill Lynch—have thus at the same time secured a leading role in the process of economic globalization.

Institutional Investors

Institutional investors, such as insurance companies, pension funds, investment funds, and investment companies, are a new, strategically important group of players in the financial markets. They clearly demonstrate the problem of the concentration of large amounts of capital in a few hands. Their decisions on inflows and outflows of capital can have far-reaching economic effects. They therefore are increasingly courted by state and private capital recipients, and increasingly included in the political-economic decisionmaking process. Certainly, like banks, institutional investors collect savings deposits; rather than passing them on to companies and governments in the form of loans, however, they invest in bond issues and stocks, putting together a mixture of portfolio investments. The significance of institutional investors for national economies gets even clearer if one places the assets managed by them in relationship to gross domestic product (GDP). For instance, in the United States, institutionally invested assets to some extent amount to more than one and a half times the value of the GDP.

Private Pension Funds

Owing to demographic developments in industrial countries, a wide-ranging discussion about the future of the public pension systems, which are based on the intergenerational-contract concept and financed by payments, has taken place. The providers of private retirement plans have a major stake in this discussion. For them, it is extremely attractive to open up, at least partially, the gigantic sums of money that move through the public pension funds. The optimistic idea that commercial pension funds would bring about a solution to the demographic problem, however, has subsided considerably. The burst of the speculative bubble in 2001, after almost a decade of apparently irreversibly high-flying stock-exchange quotations, has brought the supporters of private retirement provisions back to earth. In the United States, thousands have lost their pensions, and millions of privately insured people the world over have seen their payments drop considerably. The pension insurance companies, which once seemed so solid, have obviously miscalculated and are now facing massive losses. Besides the high-capital market risk, there is a problem inherent in the system for the mass of wage-earning policyholders. On the one hand, high salaries are necessary in order to be able to afford sufficient private insurance protection in the first place; on the other, if those salaries rise too high, the returns on the private funds will drop.

Moreover, regardless of crisis-type developments, the gigantic financial assets that are moved around by the pension funds in "normal" times also contribute to increasing the volatility of the financial markets. Developing countries are placed at a particular disadvantage, since they are frequently forced to use their foreign currency reserves to stabilize their foreign trade earnings and their debt service, creating a permanent redistribution effect from the weak currencies to the strong currencies. The privatization of the retirement-pension system not only further strengthens the economic power of the financial services industry but also increases its influence on basic sociopolitical conditions. The experience with the private pension systems in the United States and Great Britain demonstrates that the pensions are getting unstable, that the polarization between wealthy seniors and poor pensioners is increasing, and that old-age poverty is rising.

Financial Conglomerates

The financial services industry is increasingly dominated by financial conglomerates—commonly defined as a group of companies under common control whose predominant activities consist of providing significant services in at least two of the three major financial sectors. The three sectors are commercial banking, investment banking, and insurance. In countries where the boundaries between the different subsectors have broken down, the majority of the banks and insurance companies have engaged in cross-selling each other's products. Even in countries where deregulation could not move that fast, distribution alliances between banks and insurance companies are very common. Researchers have referred to this phenomenon by the term "bancassurance," but other terms, such as "assurfinance," "assurbanque," "allfinanz," "all finance" and "financial conglomerates," have been used to identify the phenomenon of financial convergence. Sometimes, the term "allfinanz" has been used to indicate both bancassurance and assurfinance strategies. For example, Lafferty Business Research (1991) used the term "allfinanz," which some people have translated into "all finance," because it better conveys the blurring of barriers that has been taking place, not just between banks and insurance companies, but among all types of financial service providers.

The largest financial services provider worldwide is the U.S. financial holding company Citigroup—formerly Citicorp—since its merger with the Traveler's Group, which was a financial services provider for travel insurance companies. Citigroup encompasses Citibank as well as various other banks and insurance companies, including one of the largest investment banks, Salomon Smith Barney (SSB), and also Visa. These major mergers and takeovers took place in the 1990s, during a period that saw the overall consolidation of financial service providers. The companies and subsidiaries belonging to Citigroup can be found worldwide—in more than 100 countries. According to the criterion of market capitalization, Citigroup now occupies fifth place in the overall worldwide corporate ranking, behind only Microsoft, General Electric, Exxon Mobil, and Wal-Mart.

In the European ranking, the Allianz Group is in the top seven, surpassed, for instance, by the oil majors Totalfina and BP and the automobile manufacturers DaimlerChrysler and Volkswagen. Allianz is not only in the insurance service sector, the group's traditional line of business, but also in asset management and other financial services. The Allianz Group includes more than 700 companies, subsidiaries, or partial ownerships on all continents. Allianz, with more than 1 trillion euros in assets under management, is one of the largest investors worldwide. The second largest European insurer, Axa, also a one-stop banking company, intends to expand its banking transactions and thus to double the number of its bank customers, create new distribution channels for traditional products, and extend its product range by expanding into home-building, consumer credit, and savings accounts.

The Lobby of the Financial Services Industry

Financial service providers have a strong lobby by which they influence the political decision-making process and public opinion. They include representatives of the most influential financial service industries (with the highest sales volumes) in the most economically and financially dominant economies. One of the most important lobby associations is the Financial Leaders Group (FLG), whose members are leading financial services representatives from the United States, Canada, the European Union, Hong Kong, Japan, and Switzerland. The lobby was founded principally to promote the position of its members in the negotiations for financial services agreements in the WTO.

Without the pressure from this powerful lobby, there probably would have been no agreement on the deregulation of financial services.

The most influential national group in the Financial Leaders Working Group (FLWG) is the U.S. Coalition of Service Industries (USCSI), which was founded in 1982. At its initiative, the issue of trade in services was for the first time placed on the international agenda in 1986, at the beginning of the Uruguay Round. Between 1982 and 1985, the coalition cooperated closely with U.S. trade representatives and tried, through intensive lobbying, to win Congress members over to a stronger stand on trade liberalization (Wesselius 2002).

The result of this lobbying was a real symbiosis between the Trade Desk of the government and the representatives of the service industry. The USCSI was given privileged access to all decisionmaking processes relevant to trade policy via the Industry Sectoral Advisory Committee on Services (ISAC). During the negotiations of the Uruguay Round, the USCSI became the most important support of the official negotiators. The conclusion of the Uruguay Round could therefore also be regarded as a victory for the service industry. At that time, financial services were not yet a component of the liberalization negotiations. The first progress was made in 1997. During the preparations for the next round of negotiations, GATS 2000, the cooperation of the two parties was intensified. There was a business-government dialogue between the government and the service industry regarding future expansion aims. At a joint conference, the USCSI and the Department of Commerce discussed increased market access and the implementation of additional regulatory and supervisory standards. In 1997, the negotiations on the financial services agreement as an additional protocol to the GATS were concluded. A so-called interim agreement had been reached in 1995. A temporary result of the untiring lobbying effort was the implementation of the final agreement in 1999, which even liberalization proponents regard as far-reaching. The agreement covers 95 percent of all international financial services in the banking, security, and insurance sectors. The lobbying of the Financial Leaders Group and of several large financial services providers, including AIG, Citigroup, Merrill Lynch, and Goldman Sachs, had paid off. Founded in 1999, the European Service Forum (ESF) is the counterpart to the USCSI, but less effective in its influence.

Activities of Financial Service Providers

Together with the telecommunications and information sectors, the financial services form the core of a modern economy. Information technology, telecommunications, and financial services are mutually determinant and supporting. Without the innovations in information and communications technology, noncash commercial traffic, remote-sales transactions, interbank commercial traffic, electronic floor trading, and the like would not have been possible. Telecommunications technology facilitates all these operations, allowing them to take place in real time and at very low transaction costs. Because of their intangible nature, financial services are particularly well suited for transactions in remote sales. With the global IT revolution, the international volume of trade in financial services has also increased, as has product diversification. A few central fields of activity among providers of financial services demonstrate the economic function of the sector.

Financial Intermediaries

Financial intermediaries include all market participants who offer services to providers and recipients of money or capital in the broadest sense. They may be individuals or such financial service institutions as banks or stock exchanges, insurance or investment companies, or leasing or factoring companies. Basically, the term covers all the players in the capital markets who can act as agents in any form whatsoever. One area of responsibility is oriented toward the mediation of financial need and potential financial investment, that is, the funds of investors are accepted against the promise of later repayment (investment service) and then provided to recipients, again against a promise of later repayment.

The services provided fall into three main categories. First, there are agency services, which include two primary areas of activity: (1) those that bring together provider and recipient to facilitate business transactions between them, usually through agents such as financial brokers, credit agents, insurance institutions, or agents/brokers, including reinsurance institutions (an example would be the issuance and placement of short-term credit instruments—for example, euro-notes); and (2) those involving the transfer of already-existing claims or obligations from a previous provider to a new provider, usually through agents such as securities firms or securities dealers, including reinsurance brokers and companies (an example would be the revolving trade in promissory note loans). Since the original providers or recipients have a multilevel agency system available to them owing to the passing on of claims and obligations, the network of relationships between and among the contracting parties is often very difficult to elucidate. The second main category is information services, such as stock exchange services, rating agencies, securities issuers, evidence centers, and institutions that collect information about money and borrowers and pass it on to donors on request. Third are risk-assumption or risk-transfer services, and hence also liability services, including all kinds of credit insurance, such as credit sureties, leasing sureties, and factoring.

The services of financial intermediaries are viewed by investors as opportunity enhancing. The existence of market intermediaries is also seen as an indicator of the stage of development of the market itself: The more the intermediaries, the more highly developed the markets. Financial intermediaries are legally independent and receive not salaries but so-called acquisition commissions.

Other Financial Services

Reinsurance. Reinsurance exchanges (prevalent in the United Kingdom) or reinsurance brokers (widespread in Germany) are among the financial intermediaries that are at work in today's global economy. Their role stems from the fact that insurance companies can reinsure themselves through other insurance companies. These reinsurance companies then assume the obligations that the insurance companies have taken on through their actual insurance policies (primary or direct insurance)—the future-based protection promise toward the policyholder. They therefore cover both the risk from the direct insurance and that from the reinsurance. Almost all primary insurance companies pass on a part of their risk in this way. Furthermore, reinsurance companies cover risks of further reinsurance by other insurance companies. In this way, a variety of insurance companies are involved in the risks. The reinsurance stock exchange is the place where insurance companies are traded. Reinsurance companies are regarded as particularly dependent on the assessment of the rating agencies, which are responsible for the credit standing classification of countries, financial institutes, and monetary and capital market securities in certain classification systems. Leading rating agencies are Standard and Poor's (New York), Moody's Investors Service (New York), and International Banking Credit Analysis (London), since the primary insurance companies judge the credit standing of the reinsurance companies on the basis of these classifications.

Factoring. Factoring means nothing more than the continuous purchase of short-term receivables. In other words, it provides funding, or cash flow, that is locked up in a company's sales ledger. With the assumption of the receivable, the factor also assumes the risks of failure and liability. Before assumption of risk, a credit standing and respectability investigation of the receivable seller (client) is carried out; the level of the receivable must be beyond reproach, and the receivable itself must be free of any claims by third parties. Collection companies are an example. They insure that due receivables, usually following multiple reminders and nonpayment of invoices and charges, are returned as fast as possible to their customers. Thus, they do not assume the failure or liability risk. This form of receivables assumption is therefore also described as "recourse factoring." As a fee, one receives a proportional share of the amount collected, which is in turn charged to the debtor.

Brokerage Services. The main activity of the broker is to manage the trade in securities, funds, and foreign exchange. When acting as a business agent, the broker either acts on the part of a third party or as a commission agent in his own name, but with the money of others. Current developments are, however, increasingly moving brokers away from the classic broker's position—one in which they do not execute any trading activity of their own—and toward that of so-called broker-dealers, who do hold risk positions of their own. The broker gets a "brokerage fee," or commission, for his services.

Portfolio Management. A securities portfolio is a mixture of different types of investments, such as stocks, securities, federal bonds, bills of exchange, and the like. The mixture serves the purpose of spreading the risk. Portfolio management means the optimum planning and choice of securities for the purpose of an ongoing optimization among companies, investment trusts, and banks. The attempt is also made, with the aid of mathematical statistics, to take into account the risks of single investment, in addition to yields. The main function of portfolio management is to spread or diversify the risk in the interest of securing long-term profits.

Portfolio investments, unlike direct investments, are short-term capital investments that mainly serve speculative interests. Profits are made through the continual use of exchange

and interest-rate differences. They involve all cross-border purchases of tradable monetary and pension-fund-market securities as well as those stock purchases by which the foreign investor does not gain a controlling influence on the business policy of the issuing company (that is, less than 10 percent of corporate capital). Portfolio investments have fallen into disrepute since the Asian financial crisis of 1997, as so-called "hot money" (the money invested in currency markets by speculators) was one of the main causes of the crisis. After 1998, their share has declined dramatically, from 22 percent in 1994 to around 2 percent in 1998.

Investment Banking. Unlike commercial banks, which traditionally have handled deposit and credit transactions, investment banks operate mainly on the security markets, that is, they issue no loans, concentrating instead on consulting services concerning the issue of securities and capital investments as well as trade in securities, either in their own name or on the part of others. Thus, investment banks could also be described as financial intermediaries. The customers of the investment banks are large corporations, governments, and high-net-worth individuals. They support governments and corporations in procuring financing on the capital market or through the new issue of shares and loans. This support service extends from consultation on setting the issue price of new shares through the composition of bank consortiums, the placement of securities on the markets, and the assumption of placement risk through obligations to purchase securities not sold. All in all, they are responsible for investing and utilizing public and private funds as profitably as possible. Their area of operations thus extends into asset management. Market research, consulting, and risk management are also among the services of the investment banks.

Furthermore, investment banks also handle currency-hedging transactions for transnational companies, including the trade in derivatives. This description shows that the areas of operation of the dominant players—financial intermediaries, brokers, investment bankers, and fund and portfolio managers—increasingly overlap. Because the boundaries of their fields of activity are becoming blurred or hard to differentiate, it has become much more difficult for outsiders to get a picture of the structures and power relations, and hence to assign responsibilities within them. Regulatory authorities, and supervisory bodies, too, have had to contend with this problem.

General Agreement on Trade in Services (GATS)

The WTO is the most important international institution, next to the International Monetary Fund (IMF) and the World Bank, involved in the economic—or rather, financial—globalization that has been occurring over the past decade. The goal of the WTO is to open all markets by means of multilateral liberalization agreements. The doctrine of free trade is the ideological basis of WTO policy initiatives. Until the establishment of the WTO in 1995, trade in goods was the only focus of the multilateral trade regime, under the General Agreement on Tariffs and Trade (GATT). Now, agricultural trade, intellectual property, trade-related investments, and services have also been integrated, through such devices as the Agreement on Trade-Related Aspects of Intellectual Property Rights (TRIPS Agreement), the Agreement on Trade-Related Investment Measures (TRIMS agreement), and of course the GATS.

From its main principles—reciprocity, most-favored-nation clause, and nondiscrimination—the WTO has developed a strong liberalization dynamic. The only multilateral economic organization with a dispute settlement procedure that can authorize economic sanctions, the WTO has a strong capability to intervene in the economy and social policy of its member countries. The WTO Agreement on Financial Services is a component of GATS, which regulates the services trade in general.

In 1986, financial services became the object of multilateral negotiations for the first time with the beginning of the Uruguay Round (1986–1993). At that time, however, there still was resistance on the part of developing countries to the liberalization of financial services, so that at the end of the Uruguay Round, there was no agreement on the integration of a financial services component into the WTO treaty framework.

When the WTO took up its work in 1995, and the GATS went into effect, there was merely an interim agreement on financial services. The liberalization requirements in the banking, insurance, and securities sectors lagged far behind the expectations of the industrial countries. During two follow-up rounds of negotiations, developed economies were able, thanks to far-reaching concessions by the developing countries, to achieve a considerably better result. Thus, on December 12, 1997, an agreement on financial services was successfully concluded. It went into effect upon ratification in 1999. The agreement brings trade in the financial services sector under the WTO's multilateral rules on a permanent and full most-favored-nation basis. The agreement covers more than 95 percent of trade in banking, insurance, securities, and financial information.

Jitendra Uttam

See Also International Financial Markets; World Trade Organization (WTO)

References

Bank for International Settlement. 2002. *72nd Annual Report.* Basel: BIS.

Benston, G. J. 1994. "Universal Banking." *Journal of Economic Perspectives* 3 (Summer): 121–143.

Crane, D. B., R. C. Kimball, and W. C. Gregor. 1983. *The Effects of Banking Deregulation.* Chicago: Association of Reserve City Bankers.

Gardener, E. P. M., ed. 1990. *The Future of Financial Systems and Services.* London: Macmillan.

Gentle, Christopher J. S. 1993. *The Financial Service Industry: The Impact of Corporate Reorganization on Regional Economic Development.* Avebury: Aldershot.

Humphrey, D. B. 1990. "Why Do Estimates of Bank Scale
Economies Differ?" *Economic Review of the Federal
Reserve Bank of Richmond,* September-October,
38–50.

Lafferty Business Research. 1991. *The Allfinanz
Revolution: Winning Strategies for the 1990s.* Dublin:
Lafferty.

Maycok, J. 1986. *Financial Conglomerates: The New
Phenomenon.* Gower: Aldershot.

Meerschwam, D. M. 1991. *Breaking Financial Boundaries:
Global Capital, National Deregulation, and Financial
Service Firms.* Boston: Harvard Business School
Press.

Moran, Michael. 1991. *The Politics of Financial Services
Revolution: The USA, UK and Japan.* Basingstoke:
Macmillan.

Tamirisa, Natalia. 1999. "Trade in Financial Services and
Capital Movements." WP/99/89, International
Monetary Fund.

United Nations Conference on Trade and Development.
2003. *Trade in Services, Statistics.* New York: UNCTAD.

Van den Berghe, L. A. A., and K. Verweire. 1998. *Creating
the Future with All Finance and Financial
Conglomerates.* Boston: Kluwer Academic.

Wesselius, Erik. 2002. "Behind GATS 2000: Corporate
Energy at Work." TNI Briefing Series, no. 2002/6.
Amsterdam: Transnational Institutes.

———. 2004. "Driving the GATS Juggernaut,"
www.globalpolicy.org (cited June 26, 2004).

World Bank. 2002. *World Development Report 2000–2001:
Attacking Poverty.* Washington, DC: World Bank.

Food and Beverages

The United Nations Food and Agriculture Organization (FAO) defined globalization as "the ongoing process of rapid global economic integration facilitated by lower transaction costs and lower barriers to movements in capital and goods" (FAO 2003). Like other industrial sectors, the food and beverage sector is influenced by the globalization process. Economic growth and the universalization of the modes of food consumption—that is, the diffusion of the Western model—offer multinational enterprises (MNEs) new and important markets, mainly in high-density demographic areas such as Asia and South and Central America.

Three main lines of research have emerged in globalization studies (Traill 1997). First, researchers study the increasing weight of international trade and its role in promoting economic growth. Second, they look at the importance of MNEs in both trade and foreign direct investment (FDI), and especially in promoting an integrated economy (that is, one in which firms make production and distribution decisions without regard to national boundaries). The expressions "international" and "global" are not used synonymously: "Internationalization" refers simply to the expansion of operations across national boundaries; "globalization" involves more than this, implying a degree of purposive functional integration among geographically scattered operations. According to this analysis, trade is a form of internationalization, whereas the operations of MNEs can represent true globalization. A third perspective comes from the marketing profession. In this line of research, globalization is seen in terms of consumer markets (demographics as well as food preferences and attitudes, for example). Researchers in this area thus deal with questions related to the convergence of consumer markets and the extent to which this convergence enables firms to use global marketing strategies to target consumers.

Food processing is the largest industrial sector in the United States, Canada, and the European Union, with the U.S. processed-food industry dominating the developed world's food industries overall. The sector has undergone significant structural changes. The size and market of the world food majors have had profound implications for basic agricultural commodity producers globally, particularly for products such as coffee, cocoa, and bananas, and also for the value-added capabilities of those industries. The orchestrated corporate strategies executed by MNEs imply a certain maneuverability in the ways in which commodity input producers relate to the value-added capabilities of the processed-food industry. Current consolidation trends in the industry, through mergers and acquisitions, strategic alliances, and the construction of bigger plants, have resulted in fewer and larger enterprises.

Characteristics of the Food and Beverages Sector

Food and agribusiness constitute one of the major sectors of the world economy. Therefore, much necessary development has been directed toward raw inputs and technology that will convert food products and market them to consumers. The sector faces a constantly changing industrial environment. The global market can be described as the result of vacillating influences from the realms of science and sociology. Advances in biological and information technologies are in turn affected by globalization as well as by increasing social concerns about the environment, health, and nutrition. From a broad view, the distinctive characteristics of the sector include:

- the unique cultural, institutional, and political aspects of food, both domestically and internationally;
- the uncertainty that arises from the underlying biological processes of crop and livestock production;
- the alternative goals and forms of political intervention across subsectors and between nations in an increasingly global industry;
- the institutional arrangements that place significant portions of the technology development process in the public sector; and
- the differing competitive structures within and among the subsectors of the food and agribusiness industries.

This is a sector that has traditionally been characterized by interference from governments, either through regulations intended to protect consumers or through measures directed toward the organization of the sector. The economic and sociopolitical weight of this sector for centuries, as well as its importance for the well-being of the general population, have led to an intricate and complex set of rules embedded in layers of devices. The endless international controversies regarding public subsidies and protection rules testify to this complexity.

Two cofactors in the distribution of inven-

tory are (1) the dependency on the nature of perishable goods, and (2) the rate of consumption as determined by consumer behavior (within a socioprofessional and cultural context). Perishable agricultural products from U.S. growers were not feasible in the international market prior to ten years ago. Today, with 20 percent of U.S. foreign agricultural trade, the U.S. farmer is competitive in sales to a global market. Moreover, the cost of transporting perishable products is, in many cases, substantially more than for bulk commodities, amounting to over 30 percent of the free on board (FOB) value of important agricultural products such as citrus and frozen potatoes, compared to only 5 to 10 percent for grain. Perishable products are becoming available to new and more distant regions partly because of declining transportation costs and partly because of new technologies to increase shelf life. Moreover, consumer demand is fueling research and development into even more high-tech preservation of perishable goods, making them a rising component of international food and agricultural trade.

Food and beverage products have been an important part of most countries' economies for hundreds of years. In the past, sustenance was primarily locally produced. Consumer demand and other factors have combined today to make domestic produce only one of the choices. Cheeses, wines, citrus fruits, and other special foods might have been imported from other regions previously, but most foods were grown locally. Two modern developments, in particular, have enabled producers to bring a spectrum of choices to market: (1) the advent of refrigeration, and (2) rapid transportation systems. In former years, fruits such as bananas, pineapples, and papayas were exotic foods to regions outside the region of origin. Transporting these items long distances took time, and the food would be ruined by the time it arrived at its destination. When, and if, limited amounts of tropical fruits made it into foreign markets, their shelf life was considerably shorter than it is today.

Table 1: Top Fifteen Agricultural Exporters and Importers, 2001

Exporters	Amount Exported (in billions of U.S. (dollars)	Share in the World (%)	Importers	Amount Imported (in billions of U.S. (dollars)	Share in the World (%)
EU members	215.53	39.0	EU members	235.51	39.7
EU to rest of the world	57.81	10.6	EU from rest of world	79.87	13.5
U.S.	70.02	12.8	United States	68.40	11.5
Canada	33.57	6.1	Japan	56.94	9.6
Brazil	18.43	3.4	China	20.12	3.4
China	16.63	3.0	Canada	15.55	2.6
Australia	16.56	3.0	Mexico	12.79	2.2
Argentina	12.20	2.2	Korea, Rep. of	12.50	2.1
Thailand	12.06	2.2	Russian Fed.	11.40	1.9
Mexico	9.07	1.7	Hong Kong, China	11.06	—
Russian Federation	8.17	1.5	Retained imports	6.99	1.1
New Zealand	7.97	1.5	Switzerland	5.65	1.0
Malaysia	7.19	1.3	Indonesia	5.35	0.9
Indonesia	7.02	1.3	Saudi Arabia	5.01	0.8
Chile	6.97	1.3	Malaysia	4.83	0.8
India	6.41	1.2	Thailand	4.83	0.8
Above 15	445.80	81.4	Above 15	472.32	79.6

Source: World Trade Organization, International Trade Statistics 2002.

Food and Agricultural Trade

Trade is of continuing importance for both developed and developing countries. The benefits of international agricultural trade to the domestic economic climate cannot be underestimated. Further, it can be argued that international trade augments the domestic supplies to meet consumer consumption needs; reduces supply variability while possibly causing stability of prices; fosters income growth; makes efficient use of world resources; and permits global production to take place in those regions most suited for it. According to the FAO, the value of U.S. agricultural goods traded worldwide, including fishery and forestry products, reached close to $650 billion in 1995—more than doubling since 1980.

The relative weight of trade in agricultural products in relation to world exports of goods in general has been diminishing for decades, however. From 46 percent, the share of agricultural trade declined to 10–12 percent in 1998 (Rastoin and Ghersi 2001; FAO 2003). The share of exports represented by processed foods and beverages increased considerably during the same period. According to FAO data, developing countries accounted for about 26 percent of total food trade in 1996–1997. This trend follows a historical pattern in which the volume of processed products tends to increase in the global food system.

Only a few commodities account for a large share of total agricultural trade (wheat, coffee, cotton, and so on). The food system is steadily becoming more internationally oriented. However, this trend is sensitive to changes in demography. Developed countries have played a dominant role in the changing structure of world agricultural trade. The fact that food products are essential makes their consumption dependent on the consumers' purchasing power capacity. Economic growth in countries with high population densities will create new and important food markets.

The world trade in agricultural products is characterized by three main features. First, the internationalization of the food system is relatively low, that is, specific foods are still intensively produced by certain countries. The ratio of agricultural exports to agricultural gross domestic product (AGDP) is about 40 percent, on average (Rastoin and Ghersi 2001). However, only 15 high-revenue countries exceed this ratio. The evidence reveals a competitive relationship between domestic and international markets, with economic wealth being a determining factor in the outcome. Other determining factors are the demand location (for example, temperate zones for tropical products) and the degree of perishability of products. Second, agricultural trade by the main triad of producers (the United States, the European Union, and Japan) is far ahead of trade by other countries, causing substantial polarization: It accounted for about 62 percent of the world agricultural exports and 70 percent of the world agricultural imports in 1996. However, after the opening of Eastern European economies in 1989, world trade expanded considerably for those countries. Third, the formation of new free trade areas and regional agreements, such as the North American Free Trade Agreement (NAFTA), Mercosur, ASEAN, and the like, should promote international trade. The expanding consumer base resulting from open markets in Eastern Europe, along with other factors causing increases in worldwide food-product commerce, should lower costs for consumers and erase nonfiscal barriers for businesses.

Many countries produce only a few major crops, especially bananas, coffee, or rice. Plantation countries are economically vulnerable because of their complete dependence on fluctuating market prices, and market collapses could be extremely detrimental. Additionally, the ecosystems of plantation countries are entirely at risk because they are subject to hazardous environmental damage from large-scale agricultural production (for example, from pesticide use).

Evolving interconnected economics and political dynamics have an effect on trade and food consumption patterns across regions. In turn, changes in food consumption in one region have implications for production and trade in other countries (Gehlhar and Coyle 2001). Trade acts to balance the differences between production and consumption. Therefore, trade links countries, helping to form an interlaced global economy. The common market trend creates a demand for a wider range of products, especially in developed countries, and increases the distribution of products from both developed and developing countries. Further, other factors, such as the role of urbanization in developing countries, a country's stage of development, its unique cultural features, and geography, also help to determine growth in trade.

Trends in Consumption Patterns and Behavior

Over the past fifty years, the food consumption model was characterized by five phases (see Table 2). Patterns of food consumption changed considerably, especially in developed countries, during the period. The "satiety society," which emerged after 1980, had four main features:

- income was not the primary factor explaining consumption;
- there was a strong and generalized preference for agro-industrial foods;
- nutritional patterns of food consumption improved; and
- food consumption expenditures increased in absolute terms.

In Organisation for Economic Co-operation and Development (OECD) countries, caloric consumption increased by 5 percent between 1969 and 1988. The minimum range by the end

Table 2: Evolution of Food Representations in Western Countries

	Before 1955	1955–1980	1980–1987	1987–1992	After 1992
Dominant Model	The quantity of eating	Reduction of quantity	Distance/food consumption	Reconstitution	Choice among products
Products	Basic products	Reduction of "bad" products	New products, new practices	Similarities among products (without or more)	Variety and diversity of products
	Bread,meat, feculent	Hunting Kcal, sugar, fattening	Frozen, "4th range," unstructured meals	Traditional plates	Exploration, rehabilitation
Symbols	Health	Slim	Good shape, social winner	Balancing the way of life	Rhythm, bio-individual
	Additional quantities	Less quantity	Minimalism	Substitutes	Quality, taste
	Eating more	Eating less	Eating rapidly	Eating without	Eating balanced

Source: Adapted from A. Defrance, "To Eat or Not to Eat, 25 ans du discours alimentaire dans la presse," *Les Cahiers de l'OCHA,* no. 4 (1994).

of the period went from 2,647 calories per capita per day in Japan to 3,698 calories per capita per day in ex-Yugoslavia. This increase, however, was not continuous over time; rather, it peaked in 1983 at 3,279 calories per capita per day and declined thereafter. The average protein intake for OECD countries showed similar trends over the same period.

Though still important, expenditures for food have become less important for households as a share of expenditures overall (see Figure 1). Food consumption at home decreased sharply, while expenditures for food outside the home progressively increased over the 1980s and 1990s. Changes in society, in other words, have led to new consumption habits and patterns.

Changes in society have brought other issues to prominence as well. Food security is one of the main issues faced by policymakers because of the threat of terrorism. The pursuit of value capture through "quality" is assuming primacy in the corporate strategies of the world MNEs. Quality is increasingly associated with lifestyle considerations, health awareness, convenience,

consumer social aspirations, and, especially for advanced industrial economies, increased female workforce participation. Research and development (R&D) activities of MNEs increasingly take these factors into account.

Since the 1970s, free-market economies have seen an increase in the consumption of "high-value" products among families and individuals (see Figure 2). Urbanization and changing lifestyles have reduced the consumption of products with high nutritional value and increased the consumption of highly processed foods that are convenient. Consumer marketing and supply are dependent in part on consumer purchase analyses. People in developed countries have less time for meal planning and preparation. Because of changes in women's roles and in the economic needs of families, the two-income family has become common in many nations. The food industry recognizes this and has responded to the fact that traditional, labor-intensive meal preparation has become impractical. Working women, with more purchasing power, lead an active life outside the home, have to commute long dis-

Figure 1. U.S. Food Expenditures by Families and
Individuals as a Share of Disposable Personal Income (1929–2001)

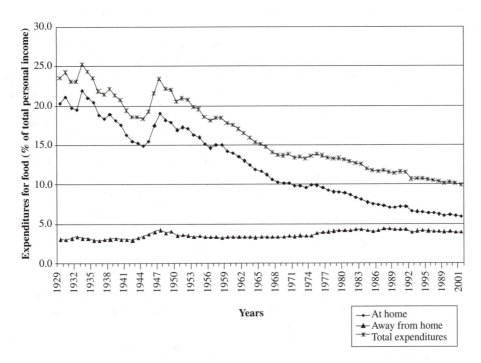

Years

- At home
- Away from home
- Total expenditures

Figure 2. U.S. Food Supply: Food Servings Available per Capita
and per Day (1970–1997)

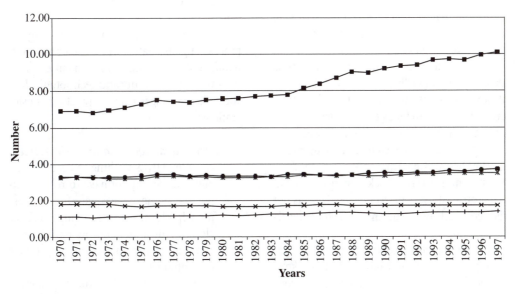

Years

■ Bread, cereal, rice, and pasta ✕ Milk, yogurt, and cheese ✳ Meat, poultry, fish, dry beans, eggs, and nuts ● Vegetables ＋ Fruits

tances for work, and desire to have more leisure time.

This shift in the social and economic role of women within the family creates a demand for new products that cater to a new market. Industry-wide changes implemented by the food trade in response to shopper demands include extended store hours, greater availability of convenience foods, and the like. Industrial analysis of current trends projects an increasing demand for healthy choices in meal planning. The consumer is "king" with business; therefore, keeping a pulse on current changes in habits and preferences is vital to industry growth.

Consumers have busy schedules and are expected to progressively organize commitments. The average consumer in industrial nations divides his or her time between work, family, and leisure pursuits. Thus, the average shopper in this hyper-demand culture devalues traditional, time-consuming methods of preparing meals and prefers to take "shortcuts" in menu planning. Major food companies are responding by developing partially or totally prepared meals. A growing share of food companies' output is due to the popularity of prepared meal items among these consumers. Trade in single-ingredient items has been declining in market practice. Market trends, in other words, follow consumer demands as revealed through purchasing habits.

Another factor in the current food market is that the concept of "healthy" food is changing. It now means, above all, safe food, but it increasingly refers to foods that are rich in nutrients and wholesome. Nutritional awareness among consumers is encouraging a closer integration between pharmaceutical and food interests. This pattern is quickly being adopted in the industrial Asian markets, though it has not gained much momentum in Western developed nations.

Moreover, behavioral trends are clearly favoring some foods over others in all markets. Generally, snack foods are favored for their convenience, and low-fat dairy products and fruits for their health attributes. At the same time, individual buyers are lowering their consumption of meat, refined sugar, and eggs. Vegetarianism is another emerging trend. Meat substitutes and alternatives are a fast-growing market.

"Functional foods," or foods chosen primarily for their nutrient quality and for their perceived ability to counter disease and maintain health, are also becoming important. Particularly in the aging population, the belief that nutritious foods may be used as medicinal agents is becoming more widespread. Consumers have even more fundamental requirements covering food safety, and issues concerning environmental sustainability and greater fairness throughout the food chain are growing in importance.

Food-Processing Multinationals and Investment Flows

Traditionally, the food industry was almost wholly focused on developments within the domestic market. However, this is no longer the case. Food processing is becoming an increasingly global industry. MNEs are moving their investments and operations around the globe to site facilities where costs are low and quality is high.

Some of the current changes driving the process of globalization in the sector are international liberalization of investment controls, liberalization of trade, and technological issues. These changes relate to practical considerations:

> *International liberalization of investment controls.* MNEs wishing to access a foreign market do not have to rely on exporting to those markets—they can establish a local manufacturing presence close to consumers in the market or license a local manufacturer to produce their product.
> *Liberalization of trade.* Exports generally provide an option for penetrating foreign

markets that carries less risk than the option of expanding operations to another country, keeping costs low. Reduced trade barriers, through the World Trade Organization (WTO), and bilateral or regional agreements, through, for example, NAFTA, the European Union, Mercosur, and the like, facilitate this route.

Technological issues. Advances in food and food storage technologies have facilitated increases in shelf life. New production technologies, rapid transportation of goods, improved logistics, and advanced food safety techniques are examples. Further upstream in the chain, the use of equipment and chemicals has expanded considerably in the middle-income countries over the past decade.

Along with these innovations, the expanding tastes of consumers (related to the diffusion of information and cultural influences in international markets) have driven globalization.

Even with massive global changes in technology and the opening of new markets, there are still formidable barriers to increased agricultural trade. Guarded nations can effectively hamper and discourage the free transfer of products, capital, and goods, leaving the buyer's demand for variety and choices from international sources unsatisfied. Potential investments can be curtailed or circumscribed by restrictive conditions that are subject to government enforcement. Most at fault are developing countries, which often legislate protectionist trade policies in an effort to shelter and enhance the position of their domestic food industries. "Tariff escalation," or the practice of raising tariffs on processed goods, is an example of the methods used.

Even in developed nations, tastes do not change quickly. The vast majority of food consumed is in accordance with a nation's traditional staple diet. However, even traditional fare is being highly processed for the sake of convenience, longer shelf life, more attractive packaging, and so on. In this way, previously unconventional means of packaging are now inculcated into the traditional staple-food system.

The intense emphasis on quality in the food industries of advanced industrial countries, and in the corporate strategies of MNEs, has had a profound impact on the agribusiness chain and on corporations themselves. Sluggish growth in real expenditures has triggered an ever-increasing pursuit for new high-value, quality food products in the advanced developed countries, yielding record-breaking profits. As the premium consumer needs of lifestyle, health, and convenience are exploited, the food suppliers are generating large profit margins. Profitability of MNEs has been high, and consequently, various food entities are segmenting (concentrating) within the food industry at a startling pace.

Indeed, concentration has been the main issue in the industry since the end of the 1980s. For example, meat-packing and grain-milling enterprises see themselves as separate industries rather than as subcategories within the food industry. "Horizontal integration" takes place through consolidation; "vertical integration" connects the retail sector back to the production and processing stages of the food system (see Table 3). However, the trend toward a world oligopoly headed by MNEs will not mean the disappearance of small and medium-sized enterprises (SMEs).

Those corporate strategies pursue profitability in advanced developed markets through extensive international reach. The multi-nation selling strategy assumes that members of the target population are dynamic, informed buyers. Sellers make substantial investments annually toward establishing brand recognition, launching new products, and repositioning high value-added products. Food industrialists conduct research into current consumer lifestyles and demands for quality. Only 10 of the top 190 world food companies receive more than half their revenues from standardized staple products (Rama 1992, 23).

MNEs increasingly make investment decisions by comparing opportunities in emerging

Table 3: Concentration in Protein

Beef Packers	Pork Packers	Broilers
CR4 = 81%	CR4 = 59%	CR4 = 50%
1. Tyson (IBP Inc.)	1. Smithfield	1. Tyson Foods
2. Cargill (Excel)	2. Tyson (IBP Inc.)	2. Gold Kist
3. Swift & Co. (ConAgra)	3. ConAgra (Swift)	3. Pilgrim's Pride
4. Farmland National Beef	4. Cargill (Excel)	4. ConAgra

Note: CR4 is the concentration ratio (relative to 100 percent) of the top four firms in a specific food industry.
Source: Adapted from Mary Hendrickson, "An Overview of Concentration in the Food System," University of Missouri, available at http://www.foodcircles.missouri.edu.

Table 4: The World's 100 Largest Food Firms

Home Country	1978	1985	2002
United States	50	38	38
United Kingdom	21	25	7
Japan	9	11	19
France	4	8	5
Canada	7	7	4
Netherlands	2	2	7
Switzerland	2	2	2
Other countries	5	6	18
Total	100	100	100

Sources: Ruth Rama, *Investing in Food* (Paris: Organisation for Economic Co-operation and Development, 1992), 41; *Food Engineering,* October 2002.

economies such as China with alternatives in other countries. Investors weigh the potential of emerging markets against the combination of market opportunities available. Profit-driven decisionmakers consider the logistical practicality and risk control that competing locations offer. U.S. food and beverage businesses look to minimize the uncertainties in maintaining the value of their product, including their brand names, trademarks, and patents.

In 2002, the world's top 100 companies in the food and beverage sector accounted for US$679.4 billion. Each year, new names enter the rankings. For example, in 2002, Constellation Brands, Wrigley, Pilgrim's Pride, and Barilla appeared, replacing some companies that no longer exist, including IBP, which merged with Tyson in September 2001; Quaker Oats, now part of PepsiCo; Ralston Purina, which was sold to Nestlé in December 2001; and Earthgrains, now the centerpiece of Sara Lee's bakery division. Also disappearing were Suiza Foods, which acquired Dean Foods and adopted the Dean name; and Eridania Beghin-Say, a French company that separated into four companies.

Major companies are streamlining business operations. Products with poor profit margins are divested of the brand and business without hesitation. Entire operations may be restructured as management acts to shed "extra baggage" in order to be competitive and strive to be flexible enough to quickly respond to market trends with new product and idea development. After reorganization, MNEs often emerge leaner, more goal oriented, and more profitable.

Table 5: Number of Subsidiaries of the 100 Largest Food and Beverage MNEs by Region, 1996

HEADQUARTERS			HOST REGION				
	Africa	Latin America and the Caribbean	North America	Asia	Eastern and Central Europe	Western Europe	Total
Africa	58	0	0	1	3	2	64
Latin America	8	45	14	5	0	49	121
North America	52	390	1295	234	114	818	2903
Asia	9	37	103	587	1	90	827
Western Europe	84	233	312	268	104	1948	2949
Australasia	1	8	5	25	0	46	85
Total	212	713	1729	1120	222	2953	6949

Source: Jean-Louis Rastoin, Gérard Ghersi, Roland Perez, and Selma Tozanli. "Structures, performances et stratégies des groupes agroindustriels multinationaux," *Agrodata 1998* (Montpellier: CIHEAM-IAMM, 1998).

Table 5 shows the number of subsidiaries of the top 100 food and beverage MNEs by region, indicating the extent to which MNEs have spread their activities and the regions most affected. Most of the MNEs host subsidiaries based in both North America and Western Europe. Together they account for approximately 84 percent of all MNEs that have invested in markets abroad. MNEs from North America and from the European Union have, to some extent, also established foreign affiliates in developing countries. Together, Asia and Latin America host almost the same number of subsidiaries as North America. Limited North American and European Union subsidiaries are present on the African continent.

Food companies in such countries as South Africa, Brazil, and Mexico are also beginning to offer serious competition to the large U.S. and European food companies as their products continue to be exported worldwide (for example, Ambev, Grupo Modelo, Bimbo, Femsa SABMiller). Like many primary nations with established and trusted food businesses, the secondary nations are making it their objective to bring goods to the global market.

MNEs have a global vision of the food system and act in a synchronized network, accountable to the customer's well-being. Infor-
mation technologies are indispensable to the future of MNEs worldwide because they will help them to function in the web of multiple transactions (intranet, data warehouse, electronic data interchange, and the like) required by a global economy. Also, the restructuring of large commodity chains leads to the implementation of international standards (HACCP [Hazard Analysis and Critical Control Point], ISO [International Organization for Standardization] 9000) in order to ensure quality and safety. Traceability has become increasingly important in most of the global food chains (dairy products, fresh fruits and vegetables, meat, and so on) because of the rare but essential need to determine the origin of food safety problems.

Networks of Food Retailers

In retailing, supermarkets are changing as chains construct larger stores in a variety of formats (Wal-Mart, Ahold, Carrefour, and so on), which further affects the structuring of suppliers on through distributors. Mergers among supermarket chains have led to increased concentration of the industry within countries and cities. At the same time, nontraditional food retailers such as Wal-Mart and

Sam's Club have expanded their presence, and e-commerce providers have begun to offer services in some major metropolitan areas. According to some industry rankings, Wal-Mart is now the world's largest grocery retailer, followed by Carrefour of France and Ahold of the Netherlands. The top five grocery retailers in the United States now control about half of the U.S. market, and their share is increasing. Heavy concentration at the retail level is forcing processors, manufacturers, and seed suppliers to cluster even further to supply mass-produced, uniform supplies at margins acceptable to these mega-firms. Farms, in turn, will need to grow larger to produce the raw materials in mass quantities at lower prices.

Increasing control from large chains in retailing improves the efficiency of the food and beverage sector and changes the dynamics of conducting business. Although efficiency is advantageous, the negotiating ability of the industry diminishes under these conditions. The concentration of retailers and the movement toward increasing domination by a few large retail chains will clarify several functions in the food sector. Logistical obstacles for big retail chains will be gradually overcome through strategic planning throughout larger territories. As a counterweight, the negotiating power of retailers will increase, and hence the retail sector will display growing similarities across countries. Retailers will emphasize private label products, and it will be possible to conduct competition bidding and purchasing in, for example, the whole European Union. In another example, in the Baltic market, competitive emerging Finnish firms would need to provide accessible products to an assortment of retailers for survival in the food industry.

In many countries today, the large retailers have increased their use of upgraded information systems, computerized technology known in the field as electronic data interchange (EDI). The EDI system provides an electronic link between manufacturers and retailers in such areas as order placement and inventory control. When retail formats use EDI methods success-

fully in one country, they are rapidly adapted, tested, and modified for use in receiving nations. In addition, hard-discount chain retailers (holding a relative short range of products at low prices), such as Lidl, Aldi, Netto, Ed, and Leader Price, are diffused. The largest grocery retailers compete in an almost saturated market. Competition for the same customer base within Western countries in the food retail market is good for consumers, but it is a challenge for established organizations. Already familiar giant food retailers must compete fiercely with emerging retail food chains for revenue.

Food Service

The diverse food service industry is a fast-developing sector that may be quantified by its growing share of revenue and by the surge in the number of facilities that cater to consumer appetites. In response to consumer demands, fast-food franchises and other restaurants continue to multiply. The "food service industry" includes all companies involved in the catering of prepared meals and snacks intended for on-premise or immediate consumption. Catering in the food industry may be either commercial (drinking and eating places, lodging, recreation/entertainment, and retail hosts) or non-commercial (establishments where meals and snacks are prepared as an adjunct, supportive service to the primary purpose of the establishment, such as schools, colleges, hospitals, or the military).

Enterprising business acumen has been well rewarded in the U.S. food service market, which has seen sales soar, reaching some US$358 billion in 2000. Separate eating places deriving revenue mainly from the sale of meals and snacks accounted for about 70 percent of total food service sales. These establishments included full-service restaurants, fast-food or quick-service outlets, lunchrooms, commercial cafeterias, and social caterers.

The four largest restaurant chains in 2002 sales were McDonald's Corporation, Burger

**Table 6: Top 10 Restaurant Chains in the
United States by Market Share, 2002**

Restaurant Chain	Market Share
McDonald's	7.3%
Burger King	3.0%
Wendy's	2.4%
Subway	1.9%
Taco Bell (Yum Brands)	1.9%
Pizza Hut (Yum Brands)	1.8%
KFC (Yum Brands)	1.7%
Applebee's	1.1%
Starbucks	1.1%
Domino's Pizza	1.0%

Source: Http://www.adbrands.net.

King, Wendy's, and Subway (see Table 6). McDonald's and Yum! operate about 30,000 stores each worldwide. These franchises are opening new units outside the United States at a faster rate than they are domestically. McDonald's, the leading franchise, has opened 1,000 units per year in other countries in recent years.

McDonald's is the most popular fast-food entity worldwide. Yum! Brands owns three of the world's best-known fast-food franchises: Pizza Hut, KFC, and Taco Bell. None of the three individually matches the global strength of the McDonald's brand. However, sales of the three brands combined make it the number one restaurant worldwide by number of outlets, although McDonald's outperforms it by sales.

The food industry is largely unaffected by recessions. Although the industry was affected by waves of job cuts and major restructurings in the early 2000s, it nevertheless remains a strong business segment nourished by the resourcefulness of its highly professionalized management ranks.

The European market strategy of the food franchises has been savvy. In Europe, where these establishments are well represented, they invest in high-growth business segments (sandwiches, pizzerias, and coffee shops) favoring the emergence of new concepts, which has raised the level of competition among existing food service firms.

In the United States, consumer tastes have become sophisticated with exposure to exotic foods. Confident market strategists have taken advantage of this element to market vegetarian meals as ethnic fare to nonvegetarians.

Emerging Regional and Niche Products and the Social Construction of Quality

Regional products are specialty goods that are unique products of specific geographical locales. To qualify as an official regional product, a food should meet three criteria (the first two are mandatory to attain the specific-origin label):

1. It must have *geographic specificity.* The product must have intrinsic characteristics that differentiate it from similar products. These characteristics must depend upon a specificity in the production process and/or in the raw agricultural input that can be found only in a well-defined geographical area.
2. It must arise out of *historical tradition.* There must be historical evidence of the existence of the product in the past, and it must have characteristics similar to the traditional item.
3. It should have *cultural and social specificity.* In the region of origin, there should be a consensus, depending on the local, social, and cultural environment, about the identification and appraisal of specific attributes that differentiate the product from others. The cultural value of the product might be associated with particular celebrations or with local gastronomic customs or social norms, for example.

In the case of regional products, it can be assumed that quality is a social construction. In other words, in consuming their regional products, people are guided by social and cultural norms. These norms operate on three levels:

1. They help to construct a reference standard (accounting for the horizontal dimension of quality).
2. They play a role in enforcing the standard. Whereas formal standards are enforced by law (through the quality standards of a governing body), informal standards must be informally enforced. The enforcement mechanisms may rely on competitive as well as on cooperative behaviors.
3. They have the effect of raising the value of the product. Since regional products give consumers socially and psychosocially rooted benefits different from those given by the closest substitute products, they are perceived as high-quality goods.

Regional food products may have three important functions: (1) enhancing the degree of competitiveness within the food and beverages sector through the strong influence of market strategy; (2) preserving agriculture in regions with cost disadvantages but where rural communities perform considerable positive environmental and social functions; (3) keeping alive local traditions by avoiding the loss of social and cultural diversity stemming from globalization.

Regional products are vulnerable to many modern practices. In the international food market, they suffer from the progressive standardization of food consumption patterns, from the use of biotechnology in the industry, and from the consolidation of retail sectors. Perpetuating the demand for regional products will require both public and private interventions to be carried out. Public interventions concern the preservation of local cultural environments that sustain the "social construction of quality" of regional products. Private interventions will likely involve producers' associations in marketing efforts that promote regional products in order to stimulate demand in food-market niches.

The Road to Sustainability: Future Challenges

Within the competitive food and beverage industry, organizations must confront and challenge interests of special stakeholders in order to preserve the quality of trustworthiness—an open, customer-centered relationship—that is needed to satisfy the expectations of the general public. Greater competitiveness can be achieved through increased economic efficiency of inputs, such as precision farming and biotechnology. However, greater regulation, which limits competition, and a lack of standards could encourage market segmentation.

The tendencies of countries exposed to globalization have changed the position of sectors within given societies, and government statutes reflect this latest transformation. In nations open to internationalization, the role of the public sector in many areas of food security and nutrition appears to be shrinking, whereas the involvement of civil society and the private sector is increasing. There is a precautionary principle in all of this that applies to the resolution of certain disputes: Do governments have the right to create trade barriers to protect human health and/or the environment, and if so, are there also corporate rights to conduct export commerce? Related questions are also emerging:

- What are the consequences of restructuring for rural communities?
- What are the implications for large, nonlocal firms, whether they hire labor as wage earners or as piece rate workers, which often view laborers as a "commodity" to be purchased at the lowest rate?
- How do these changes affect U.S. food imports, in light of a stronger U.S. dollar and increases in low-dollar-value imports as a share of U.S. trade activity?
- How can food quality and especially food safety be assured?
- How do food-industry events affect the

genetic diversity of various domestic animals?

These are complex questions. The global food system is becoming more like other economic sectors, however, except that food is a human necessity, thus always in demand. The primary participants in global food commerce thus have enormous economic power.

Gaining more acceptance and popularity on the local level of food trade are "niche markets." In a niche, farmers and other participants try to satisfy a specific consumer demand. Such opportunities do exist: There has been a major resurgence of farmers' markets, local food routes (for example, in the wine sector), subscription, and other forms of direct marketing between farmers and consumers. Of course, minor processing agents are involved in small-scale "niche market" transactions, when necessary.

Although a more centralized food system continues to emerge, the industry lacks organized, public-sanctioned direction. The ruling minority of large retail food entities makes choices for the masses. But many observers believe that consumers have a right to more choices. Rather than allowing themselves to be supplied with food from dictatorial conglomerates because of networks supported by information systems and many other collaborators, informed buyers should question the fairness of the control imposed by retail food vendors within the food system. And, more important, the public, both now and for future generations, has interests in the food supply chain that should be given the attention they deserve.

Conclusion

Although the effects of globalization on the food and beverage sector have been systemic, they are difficult to accurately assess. A few things are clear. The open market has been beneficial to the food industry. Changes in the global marketplace have resulted in increased global food consumption, changing patterns of food consumption, and trade liberalization. In addition, due to increasing popular demand, developing environmentally sustainable agricultural products has become a high priority internationally. The prevailing government forces affecting the industry stem from state interventionism through agricultural, sectoral, and food and nutrition policies. Furthermore, in many nations, economic and social policies inadvertently affect the globalized distribution of the food and beverage sectors.

Food consumption is not globally monitored in any systematic way; therefore, the impact of nation-to-nation policies on consumption of perishable goods alone cannot be adequately quantified. There are clearly some forces at work that amplify the convergence of consumption patterns (see Connor 1994). International trade, when complicated by cultural differences, is beginning to produce segments of consumers with common preferences. As the decades advance, supermarkets and manufacturers can be expected to add yet more distinctive brands to their already existing lines of products. Vendors indisputably will research ways to market to a global consumer base and increase consumer confidence in the sector as a fair and responsible industry.

The food industry, like a cartel, has a monopolistic reach and is formed by independent organizations. The large retail food chains perceive that the benefits of globalization in food and agriculture could outweigh the risks and costs of commerce. Globalization has generally helped to reduce poverty in Asia, for example. But, as the FAO has pointed out, it has "also led to the rise of multinational food companies with the potential to disempower farmers in many countries" (FAO 2003).

The expansion of MNEs into developing countries may have some positive effects. The MNEs bring in important financial resources but do not maximize reinvestments into the community. The developing countries gain an influx of skilled management staff to areas with few skilled laborers. Local employment is also generated, though predominantly for low-level positions.

A critical task for international communities is to have the foresight to form progressive agendas while staying mindful of the importance of including developing nations in the decisionmaking process. Ethical business practices support the integration of all nations into a world economy. When such integration occurs, then and only then will developing nations have a voice to protect and advocate their own interests. Underrepresented nations can gain multiple benefits, along with the food and beverage sectors, upon integration into the "cartel" of food industrialists.

Moreover, economically challenged nations, by lobbying other nations, can present the case for decreasing high-trade distortion barriers. Developing nations would have greater economic viability, with representation within the circle of food magnates, once trade barriers were diminished. The immediate result would be to favor economic growth and viability. In addition, healthy diets and proper nutrition should be a global focus, especially since such goals are achievable through an equally represented international alliance of food suppliers, handlers, and vendors.

Alfredo Coelho

See Also Agriculture; Food Safety

References

Bolling, Christine, and Samwaru Agapi. 2001. "U.S. Food Companies Access to Foreign Markets through Direct Investment." *Food Review* 24, no. 3: 23–28.

Connor, John. 1994. "North America as a Precursor of Changes in Western European Food-Purchasing Patterns. *European Review of Agricultural Economics* 21: 155–173.

———. 1997. "Comments on the Structural Convergence Hypothesis." In Julie A. Caswell and Ronald W. Cotterill, eds., *Strategy and Policy in the Food System: Emerging Issues.* Proceedings of the NE-165

Conference, June 20–21, 1996, Washington, DC, Food Marketing Policy Center, University of Connecticut, and Department of Resource Economics, University of Massachusetts, Amherst.

Coyle, W., Mark Gehlar, Thomas W. Hertel, Zhi Wang, and Wusheng Yu. 1998. "Understanding the Determinants of Structural Change in the World Food Markets." *American Journal of Agricultural Economics* 80, no. 5: 1051–1061.

Cranfield, John A. L., Thomas H. Hertel, James S. Eales, and Paul V. Preckel. 1998. "Changes in the Structure of Global Food Demand." *American Journal of Agricultural Economics* 80: 1042–1050.

Defrance, A. 1994. "To Eat or Not to Eat, 25 ans du discours alimentaire dans la presse." *Les Cahiers de l'OCHA,* no. 4.

Food and Agriculture Organization. "World Agriculture 2003," http://www.fao.org (cited June 26, 2003).

———. "World Agriculture towards 2015/2030," http://www.fao.org (cited June 26, 2003).

Gehlhar, Mark, and William Coyle. 2001. "Global Food Consumption and Impacts on Trade Patterns." In Anita Regmi, ed., *Changing Structure of Global Food Consumption and Trade,* WRS-01-1. Washington, DC: U.S. Department of Agriculture.

Hendrickson, Mary. "An Overview of Concentration in the Food System," http://www.foodcircles.missouri.edu (cited June 10, 2003).

Herrmann, Roland, and Claudia Röder. 1995. "Does Food Consumption Converge Internationally? Measurement, Empirical Tests and Determinants." *European Agricultural Economics* 22: 400–414.

Higgins, Kevin T. 2003. "The World's Top 100 Food and Beverage Companies," http://www. foodengineeringmag.com (cited April 10, 2003).

Kinkes, Jean D. 2001. "The New Food Economy: Consumers, Farms, Pharms, and Science." *American Journal of Agricultural Economics* 83, no. 5: 113–1130.

Murdock, Jonathan, and Mara Miele. 1999. "'Back to Nature': Changing 'Worlds of Production' in the Food Sector." *Sociologia Ruralis* 39, no. 9: 465–483.

Price, Charlene. 2002. "Food Service." *U.S. Food Marketing System,* AER-811, 34–46.

Raiikes, Philip, Michael Friis Jensen, and Stefano Ponte. 2000. "Global Commodity Chain Analysis and the French *Filière* Approach: Comparison and Critique." *Economy and Society* 29, no. 3 (August): 390–417.

Rama, Ruth. 1992. *Investing in Food.* Paris: Organisation for Economic Co-operation and Development.

Rastoin, Jean-Louis, and Gérard Ghersi. 2001. "Agroalimentaire: La mondialisation." *Problèmes Economiques,* no. 2719 (June 27): 29–32.

Rastoin, Jean-Louis, Gérard Ghersi, Roland Perez, and Selma Tozanli. 1998. "Structures, performances et stratégies des groupes agroindustriels multinationaux." *Agrodata 1998*. Montpellier: CIHEAM-IAMM.

"Restaurants and Bars," http://www.adbrands.net (cited June 26, 2003).

Traill, Bruce. 1997. "Globalisation in the food industries?" *European Review of Agricultural Economics* 24: 390–410.

World Trade Organization. "International Statistics," http://www.wto.org.

Media and Entertainment

In an increasingly global environment, the media are facing new challenges, including audience fragmentation and erosion, ownership regulations, and the need for more sales in more markets. The boundaries of media and entertainment continue to expand, including movies, television, radio, sound recordings, newspapers, magazines, books, and advertising. The addition of new media technologies, such as video games and the Internet, have further blurred the line between entertainment and information.

The biggest problem that media companies around the world are tackling is rapidly changing audiences. Audiences now have more competitive media products to choose from, and less time in which to consume them. For example, the average American receives more than 100 television channels at home and is exposed to dozens of media outlets every day, including Web sites, advertising, television, and print publications. This media fragmentation leads to smaller audiences for all media and to a decrease in the percentage of the population using specific media or outlets. In order to keep audiences, entertainment companies have to expand their holdings and saturate the marketplace with well-promoted products beyond the domestic sphere. These global media companies are often multinational conglomerates trying to sell diverse products in an increasingly competitive environment but are criticized for enabling "cultural imperialism"—the belief that American entertainment is colonizing the rest of the world through technological devices such as cable and satellite broadcasting as well as remote printing presses, movies, and music. Some critics are also concerned that the diffusion of "American taste" will be detrimental to nationalism and cultural identity around the globe.

Historical Overview

The first step in creating a global entertainment environment was Hollywood's perfection of mass production and distribution in the first half of the twentieth century. Between 1919 and 1939, Hollywood engaged in international motion picture trade, especially with England, France, and Germany. The increasing tension in Europe, however, encouraged American companies to focus more on the domestic market. At the height of the Studio System from the mid-1930s to late 1940s, eight companies produced and released more than 500 films in a year, owing much of their success to a codified structure of market domination, a dizzying schedule of mass production and distribution, and the star system, which created movie icons out of actors under contract. At its height in 1946, the annual American box office took in $1,692,000, even with a third fewer releases than in the previous seven years (Finler 1988, 288). But in 1938 the Justice Department launched an antitrust suit against the major studios with the aim of dismantling the vertical integration of the motion picture industry. The suit took one step forward and two steps backward over the next ten years, while Hollywood basked in the glow of sky-high revenues and popularity. In 1949, the district court demanded that the studios divest themselves of theater chains—the most contentious issue in the suit.

The "Paramount Decree" forced the competition of quality, not quantity. Studios now had to compete in the market based on the intrinsic value of their products. This market was becoming increasingly crowded as television lured families away from theaters. As television grew more popular, particularly with young postwar families, box-office revenues plummeted by the early 1960s. It became very clear that in order to build up the audience again, entertainment companies would have to expand their interests, particularly overseas. The import, but mostly export, of cultural products was stepped up, particularly by the United States, Europe, and Asia. By the 1970s, all the major Hollywood studios were also engaged in television production and were starting to branch out into other media outlets. The biggest battle for market saturation, however, was being played out between the three television networks—NBC, ABC, and CBS. As cable networks began to expand and audience share decreased, networks were caught up in the merger mania sweeping the nation. NBC was purchased by military-industry giant General Electric, CBS by Westinghouse, and in the 1990s, ABC became part of Disney's holdings.

Ownership and Conglomeration

Currently, globalization in entertainment is best exemplified by the trend toward conglomeration, where fewer and larger corporations own more and more media properties. This trend continued throughout the 1980s and 1990s, until a massive system of horizontally integrated companies was built. Previously, media had been primarily vertically integrated, where each organization had control over a product through the production, distribution, and exhibition process. Now, conglomerates that are horizontally integrated own production facilities, distribution networks, and exhibition outlets in a number of different media industries. They all join together to create an efficient and synergistic media environment in which the whole of the company is greater than the sum of its parts, both ideologically and financially. Companies such as Disney can not only produce and distribute a movie in theaters and on video/DVD, but can create tie-in books, soundtracks, toys, and computer games and market their products in Disney-owned newspapers, magazines, and radio and television networks around the globe.

Most companies do not set out to become a transnational conglomerate, but become invested in foreign markets through a process of evolution. Globalization in media is influenced by the trend toward deregulation and privatization and significant changes in technology and markets. These conglomerates can only flourish in a free market economy, where players are willing to compete internationally for foreign direct investment. The push for media companies to expand across domestic borders is usually influenced by three things:

1. interest in penetrating a foreign market, which may or may not already be developed;
2. access to production and distribution resources, such as lower labor costs, tax incentives, or technical talent; and
3. desire to circumvent import quotas and tariffs through strategic foreign partnerships.

Although the expansion of these conglomerates is usually successful, they often run into roadblocks in the form of governments wanting to protect domestic markets and activist groups wanting to protect local culture. Transnational media ownership is aided, however, by the realization by most players that conglomeration is an inevitability in the new global economy. These conglomerates make financial sense because they fit into "economies of scope" and "economies of scale." In a media economy of scope, it costs less for one company to produce vastly different cultural products than it would for different companies to specialize. An economy of scale occurs if the average cost of creating one particular product is lower for firms capable of higher levels of output. Media conglomeration allows for both of these economies to flourish.

Over the past twenty years, international distribution has been crucial in the success of global media but has met with criticism over allegations of discriminatory pricing strategies, product "dumping," and the fears that many countries have over losing control of their own domestic markets. As the market for American cultural artifacts opened up, including newly vital trade in Asia and Central America, many governments and trade organizations had to contend with the reality that exports from the United States were becoming more popular than local products. Exacerbating this situation was the low level of U.S. export prices, especially on television programming. Of particular concern were accusations of "dumping," which occurs when the price charged in the foreign market is below cost and less than domestic producers would charge for the same product. In other words, in many foreign markets it is cheaper to buy an American television program than it would be to produce the program themselves. Some countries, such as Canada, Australia, England, France, Germany, Brazil, and Japan, have relatively thriving film and television industries but still retain protectionist measures, such as tariffs and taxes, on entertainment imports. Many of these same countries, however, have benefited from participating in coproductions, wherein creative talent and financing is assembled from different nations. International coproductions are sometimes hampered by difficulty in communication, but the advantage of gaining access to international markets, as well as quotas,

subsidies, and tax incentives, often outweighs any concerns over culturally muddled projects.

Global Media and National Identity

Some countries are concerned that the prevalence of American media is undermining their own cultural identity, not just their domestic market. Although satellite television and electronic media have virtually erased national borders, cultural boundaries still exist around the world, and many cultures are struggling to maintain themselves in the face of Western media colonization. In the twentieth century, this struggle against the domination of American culture has been located around the globe. In the 1940s, the French government lobbied unsuccessfully to ban Coca-Cola. For most of the twentieth century, South Korea banned Japanese cultural products, and other countries, such as Singapore and South Africa, have struggled to extend their geographical borders to include media and entertainment importation.

Many countries have decided to assimilate American culture in their own way. McDonald's has different menus around the globe, ranging from kosher in Israel to teriyaki burgers in Japan. American media conglomerates often pride themselves on hiring local talent to run their global operations. In another example, MTV is available in more than 140 countries on every continent except Africa and Antarctica and relies on regional talent to produce 60 percent of its content for broadcast on nearly fifty localized channels and Web sites (Turow 2003, 186). Some local media, recognizing that imported television and music may always be more popular than domestic content, privileges American programming in coveted time-slots. Another popular strategy is simply to borrow successful American genres and remold them with local talent. The television soap opera, which has a long tradition in both the United States and the United Kingdom, is increasing in prominence all over the globe. One notable example was *Dallas,* which had a worldwide audience of more than 300 million people tuning in to displays of American excess on a weekly basis during the 1980s. Even popular British soap *Coronation Street* was appropriated by Dutch producers, who planned to resituate the show in the Netherlands. In the early twenty-first century, reality shows have become the most exportable genre of television programming—they are cheap to produce, easy to translate and adapt to different cultural markets, and very popular with audiences. Even the brackets around television shows—television commercials—are now a global media commodity, enjoying collective success at film festivals such as Cannes.

One explanation for the success of commercials, soap operas, and now reality shows around the world is that they often have a low cultural discount. A cultural discount exists if a television program, film, or other media product is easily marketed in different cultures. A product rooted in specific cultural values, myths, style, language, and history will be less appealing to viewers outside of that culture and therefore will garner fewer viewers. This reduced value will affect the domestic and international trade in the media product. The cultural discount for an imported program or movie can be calculated as the value of the domestic equivalent minus the value of the import divided by the value of the domestic equivalent. A product with a low cultural discount will be more successful outside the domestic market, which is an important consideration for entertainment companies with global interests.

The Global Village and Cultural Imperialism

In the 1960s, communications theorist Marshall McLuhan envisioned a "global village" whose citizens would be inextricably linked by media and a common popular culture. McLuhan's prediction is now a reality thanks to the speed and immediacy of electronic communication and satellite technology, but it still does not mean that media products will be received the same way by geographically and culturally diverse audiences. It has been argued that the overseas success of American movies and television is a form of cultural imperialism. This theory has gained prominence since the 1970s, as mergers between media companies continue to create huge international conglomerates such as AOL Time Warner, Viacom, and Newscorp. Researchers believed that the flow of international cultural products, particularly in film and television, was one-way—from the United States to the rest of the world. This "hegemony" uses cultural ideology to exert force over other nations, in the form of entertainment, and is often exacerbated by lackluster domestic production in poorer countries. One example of this is the "CNN effect." The global reach of Cable News Network's operations has arguably influenced American (and international) foreign policy and diplomacy through the "parachute journalism" encouraged by instantaneous satellite news delivery (Kamalipour 2002, 232).

The tension between consent and coercion is especially present in global media, but the "cultural imperialism" thesis has also been criticized for not taking the "active" viewer into account. The theory presupposes that audiences are passive vessels, who use media products as the producers intended. Cultural studies theory argues that media texts are polysemous, meaning that they are interpreted and used differently by different groups. For example, American audiences may make meaning out of a television show like *The West Wing* and relate to its discussions of domestic politics and democracy, but viewers in China are unlikely to interpret the program the same way.

Not all popular culture is American. Although products with a low cultural discount, such as action movies and reality television, continue to dominate the international market, in some arenas media producers have realized that American tastes are not universal. Popular music, for example, is hugely different from country to country, as are the newspaper, magazine, and book industries. But often the cost of creating these products is incremental, so it makes financial sense to continue to pursue segmented audiences. Media conglomerates are particularly adept at expanding the breadth and depth of their international divisions, while still channeling the profits back to the head office. Some companies believe that their global brand is crucial to continued success. For example, Disney has consistently focused on international venues, opening Disneyland Tokyo (1983), Disneyland Paris (1992), and Disneyland Hong Kong (set for 2006). Romance publisher Harlequin Books has also thrived in the global marketplace, selling approximately 200 million paperbacks a year in 23 languages and more than 100 countries.

Globalization in the Digital World

At the turn of the twenty-first century, the Internet and digital technology has an enormous influence over media and entertainment around the world. It is now not only possible for media producers to reach global audiences simultaneously and immediately, but also for consumers to connect with each other. Digital technology means that media products such as motion pictures and newspapers can be reproduced electronically and sent anywhere at a fraction of the cost, time, and space required previously to distribute material. The Internet and e-mail make it possible for consumers to provide feedback to producers and to keep in touch with people around the globe with similar interests. The combination of these technologies also makes piracy easier than ever before.

Pirated movies and television shows on videotape have been problematic for Hollywood producers for twenty years, particularly in regions where American culture is not politically popular, such as the Middle East and Africa. Popular music also continues to be a hot property in the international black market, particularly since the refinement of compact disc burners. But new communications technologies, such as the Internet, have made the production and consumption of copyrighted materials accessible, fast, and even acceptable in some circles. Peer-to-peer file-sharing services, which allow Internet users to freely trade digital copies of movies, television shows, and especially music, are increasingly popular among amateur and professional bootleggers. Unlike traditional distribution of media goods, Internet file sharing rarely delivers income of any kind to the producer. Creative personnel and corporate accounting offices alike are not being paid for the usage of these pirated products.

This is troubling to movie studios, recording companies, and professional associations. The Recording Industry Association of America estimates that it loses more than $1 billion a year from illegal Internet downloads. Some companies and professional associations have attempted to combat this problem with lawsuits against users, but they are battling a shift in popular ideology that suggests that current copyright laws are outdated. Producers who have tried to convince users to pay for downloading materials are largely disappointed, and while the Internet expands and flourishes, so will piracy of entertainment products. In the global marketplace, digital convergence and the Internet have been a double-edged sword. On one hand, they have facilitated international trade in media goods and services, reaching previously untapped audiences with ease and speed. On the other hand, they have also smoothed the path for illegal distribution and protests against perceived cultural invasion.

Nicola Simpson

See Also Copyrights and Intellectual Property; Culture and Globalization; Gender

References

Albarran, A. B. 1998. *Global Media Economics: Commercialization, Concentration, and Integration of World Media Markets.* Ames: Iowa State University Press.

Finler, Joel. 1988. *The Hollywood Story.* New York: Crown.

Herman, Edward S., and Robert W. McChesney. 1997. *The Global Media: The New Missionaries of Corporate Capitalism.* London: Cassell.

Hoskins, Colin, Stuart McFadyen, and Adam Finn. 1997. *Global Television and Film: An Introduction to the Economics of the Business.* Oxford: Oxford University Press.

Kamalipour, Yahya R., ed. 2002. *Global Communication.* Belmont, CA: Wadsworth Thomson Learning.

Liebes, Tamar, and Elihu Katz. 1990. *The Export of Meaning: Cross-Cultural Readings of* Dallas. New York: Oxford University Press.

Mosco, Vincent, and Janet Wasko. 1988. *The Political Economy of Information.* Madison: University of Wisconsin Press.

Price, Monroe E. 2002. *Media and Sovereignty: The Global Information Revolution and Its Challenge to State Power.* Cambridge: MIT Press.

Sreberny-Mohammadi, Annabelle, Dwayne Winseck, Jim McKenna, and Oliver Boyd-Barrett, eds. 1997. *Media in Global Context: A Reader.* London: Hodder Headline Group.

Thussu, D. K. 1998. *Electronic Empires: Global Media and Local Resistance.* New York: Oxford University Press.

Turow, Joseph. 2003. *Media Today: An Introduction to Mass Communication.* 2d ed. Boston: Houghton Mifflin.

Wilkin, Peter. 2001. *The Political Economy of Global Communication: An Introduction.* London: Pluto.

Pharmaceuticals

The pharmaceutical industry consists of thousands of firms engaged in one or several of the functions of discovering, developing, manufacturing, and marketing medicines for human use. More narrowly, the industry can be taken to include firms supplying prescription drugs. This market segment is dominated by around twenty-five research-based companies headquartered in the United States, Europe, and Japan. Known as the "big pharma" group, these firms participate as "insiders" within national policy processes and markets across the world yet operate globally integrated innovation, production, and marketing networks. Firms specializing in the production of out-of-patent generic drugs constitute another increasingly significant segment of the pharmaceutical industry.

The recent period of globalization has brought about a wave of mergers and acquisitions and the reengineering of corporate structures to achieve greater flexibility and increased capacity to engage in external collaborations. Changes in the structure of the industry are closely associated with a technological paradigm shift from chemistry-based drugs toward biopharmaceutical drugs requiring more complex and diverse capabilities.

History of the Pharmaceutical Industry

Early medicines were derived from natural sources such as plants and animals and had limited or nonexistent therapeutic effects. The nineteenth-century development of chemistry into a major science made possible the production of a new type of synthetic drugs. Morphine was extracted from crude opium in 1805, and other discoveries, such as digitalis and strychnine, followed. In the 1880s, the medicinal effects of dyestuffs and other organic chemicals were discovered, and in 1897 aspirin was introduced by the German company Bayer. German and Swiss companies such as Bayer, Hoechst, Ciba, Geigy, and Hoffman–La Roche were trailblazers in the emergence of the modern pharmaceutical industry. Germany alone represented around 80 percent of the world production of pharmaceuticals in the years leading up to 1914. The outbreak of World War I provided a strong stimulus for England, France, and the United States to develop their own chemical and pharmaceutical industries, and these gradually acquired capacities comparable to those of their German and Swiss competitors (Gassmann et al. 2004; Silverman and Lee, 1974).

Merck and several other U.S. drug companies were first established by German chemical firms, while SmithKline Beckman (which merged with Beecham in 1989 and in 2000 with GlaxoWellcome) and Upjohn (now absorbed by Pfizer) originated as wholesale pharmacists and moved into drug discovery only after 1945. The pharmaceutical industry became research intensive in the middle of the twentieth century. Sulfanilamide, effective in the treatment of infections, is considered the first of the modern drugs. It was introduced by Bayer in 1935 under the name of Prontosil and represented a breakthrough in synthetic organic chemistry, opening the way for the discovery, patenting, and marketing of other sulfanilamide derivatives. During World War II, pharmaceutical firms in the United States worked closely with the government in support of the war effort. Particular achievements in this period included the production of dried plasma and penicillin. Penicillin, discovered by Alexander Fleming in 1928 and first manufactured by Merck and Pfizer during the war, provided a major boost to the growth of the industry. By 1945, penicillin was produced by twenty-one companies (Pratt 1985).

The decades after 1945 were the golden age of the pharmaceutical industry. The large companies multiplied their research and development (R&D) spending, and several hundred new chemical entities (NCEs) were discovered. Many effective new products were launched, and this had a major impact on life expectancy throughout the world. It is likely, however, that environmental public health and political, economic, and social measures were at least equally important in changing mortality patterns. The economics of scale of research and marketing prevented new firms from challenging the dominance of incumbents such as Bristol-Myers, Warner Lambert, Plough, Merck, Pfizer, Lilly, Hoechst, Hoffmann–La Roche, and Ciba.

From the 1970s, commercial drug developments became increasingly intertwined with expanding systems of public health research such as the U.S. National Institutes of Health. Advances in the biological sciences have since had a major impact on the drug development process and the structure of the industry. The first of the new biotechnology companies— Genentech—was established in 1976, signaling that the revolution in molecular biology would have significant commercial implications. Big pharma companies, adapting successfully to new scientific and technological paradigms, have become less self-sufficient than in the past and now engage extensively in collaborations with external organizations. Firms seek efficiencies and innovative capaci-

ties from outsourcing (including outsourcing of manufacturing and clinical trials), licensing and marketing alliances, strategic partnerships, joint ventures, and other forms of collaborative arrangements with both competitors and science-intensive "spin-offs" from universities and the public research sector. Even the largest of the pharmaceutical firms now draw extensively on external resources, typically spending around 30 percent of R&D budgets on outside collaborations (Goozner 2004; Henderson et al. 1999).

Regulation of the Pharmaceutical Sector

The pharmaceutical sector is characterized by market failures that, in the absence of state intervention, would produce unacceptable outcomes. The principal failure is the inability of consumers to make informed decisions about the quality, efficacy, and appropriate use of medicines with potentially harmful or even fatal consequences. Individual medical practitioners are also unable to assess the therapeutic value of thousands of pharmaceuticals and must rely to a large extent on the claims made by the suppliers.

The current system of government controls to ensure drug quality, safety, and efficacy evolved in parallel with the growth of the modern pharmaceutical industry. The U.S. Food and Drug Act of 1906 established the agency that became the Food and Drug Administration (FDA), though initially its primary focus was on problems in the food industry. Recurrent disasters resulting from unsafe drugs impelled the U.S. and other governments progressively to extend their regulation of the industry. The Food, Drug, and Cosmetic Act, passed by the U.S. Congress in 1938 after the death of 107 people poisoned by a toxic medicine, introduced the requirement that manufacturers provide scientific proof of the safety of new products. In the late 1950s and early 1960s, the birth of more than 8,000 infants with severe deformities of the limbs in forty-six countries, as a result of their pregnant mothers' consumption of the drug thalidomide, paved the way for more rigorous safety regulation achieved through the Kefauver-Harris 1962 Amendments to the 1938 act. The FDA's role in preventing market clearance for thalidomide strengthened a public perception in the United States of the indispensability of strict government drug controls (Burkholz 1994).

Similar steps to make the process of market approval more stringent were soon taken in other developed countries. Complex government controls now affect all stages of the pharmaceutical production and distribution chain: basic research, product development, manufacturing, exports and imports, market access, pricing and profits, marketing, wholesaling, and retail distribution, most countries also have direct or indirect regulation of drug prices and profits. Since the early 1990s, the drug safety control system has been largely harmonized at the transnational level through a process known as the International Conference on Harmonization of Technical Requirements for Registration of Pharmaceuticals for Human Use (ICH). The key participants in this process are the pharmaceutical industry associations and the government drug regulatory agencies of the European Union, Japan, and the United States (Abraham and Smith 2003).

The very nature of medicinal drugs introduces a powerful ethical element to the activity of firms and to public policy in this domain. Universal access to essential drugs irrespective of ability to pay is an accepted policy objective in most countries. Doctors and pharmacists operate as intermediaries between drug suppliers and consumers. The effect of public and private insurance schemes is to insulate consumers and doctors to a significant extent from normal market signals. Consumers generally do not have to bear the full cost of the medicines, while doctors can prescribe drugs with scant regard to their cost. In the countries of the European Union and in Canada, Australia, and elsewhere, governments subsidize a significant proportion of the cost of prescription

pharmaceuticals through public insurance schemes. In the United States, some of the drug costs of the elderly and disabled are subsidized through Medicaid, a joint federal-state program, but most consumers rely on health maintenance organizations (HMOs) and other forms of private insurance for some protection against high drug costs. Approximately 20 percent of the population, however, does not have prescription drug coverage.

Both public and private third-party payers around the world are concerned about the growing cost of medicinal drugs associated with the aging of the population and the availability of new expensive medicines, including "lifestyle" drugs for conditions such as obesity and hair loss. Concerns about prices and political pressures on the industry are also fueled by the very high profitability of big pharma. The annual Fortune 500 list regularly records profits in the pharma industry that, as a percentage of revenue, far outstrip most or all other American industries. A standard cost-containment tool is to undertake a cost-effectiveness assessment before accepting a new drug on a "formulary" of products approved for use or reimbursement. Expert committees managing formularies now expect prices paid for a new drug to reflect its relative benefits compared to alternative treatments, as it is simply not rational to pay a substantially higher price for a new drug that delivers only marginal additional benefits compared to an older, cheaper product. Companies must therefore pay increasingly close attention to the economics of new drugs. The complexity of economic analyses of drug development and drug use gave rise in the 1990s to the applied discipline of pharmacoeconomics (Schweizer 1997).

The extent of government regulation makes political and legal action critical to the prosperity of the pharma industry. National and international industry associations—including the Pharmaceutical Research and Manufacturers of America (PhRMA) and the International Federation of Pharmaceutical Manufacturers Associations (IFPMA)—lobby effectively on its behalf. The relationship between regulators and the drug industry has fluctuated over time and across countries. Regulatory agencies have at times been unduly influenced by the industry, and there are recurrent examples of corruption. The industry at other times has criticized regulators for being unresponsive and hostile. In particular, the time taken by regulatory agencies to approve new products for marketing was a source of persistent industry apprehension throughout the 1980s and 1990s. Interaction between regulators, companies, and other interests is, however, normally characterized by routine exchange.

The trend in the recent period of globalization has been toward a blurring of public-private boundaries and more trust-based interaction among a wider range of actors, including pharma companies, doctors, pharmacists, consumer and patient advocacy groups, and government agencies. Both the pharma industry and regulators now aim for partnerships rather than conflict. Yet, scientific and technological developments, including the emergence of biotechnology, and the globalization of innovation, production, and markets have spurred ever more complex regulation at national and transnational levels. The capacity of government agencies to impose regulatory controls unilaterally, however, has diminished.

Product and Market Characteristics

More than 20,000 different medicinal drugs, derived from around 5,000 active substances, are available in major pharmaceutical markets (Ballance et al. 1992). The value of the global prescription drug market in 2004 approached $500 billion. The United States accounts for approximately 50 percent of worldwide sales, and the European Union for a further 25 percent. In the early 1990s, the value of U.S. pharmaceutical sales was of the same magnitude as in Europe. The rapid expansion of the U.S. market in the past fifteen years is due largely to the fact that prices are higher in the United States than

in other industrially developed countries as a consequence of the absence of government price controls. Countries outside of North America, Europe, and Japan represent only about 10 percent of the global market.

Medicinal products are divided into patented prescription drugs; out-of-patent, or multisource (generic), prescription drugs; and over-the-counter (OTC) medicines (which may or may not be patented). A strict categorization is made difficult by the fact that the same drug may have a different status in different markets, and products also move between these categories. Prescription medicines are also known as "ethical" drugs. Generics are copies of an original product whose patent has expired. OTC products are medicines for self-medication sold directly to the public through pharmacies and other retail outlets. Research-based firms seek to recoup R&D costs and generate a profit from sales of prescription drugs during the period of effective patent protection, whereas OTC products can have a long product life, sometimes more than fifty years (for example, aspirin).

Big pharma companies derive a high proportion of revenue from so-called "blockbuster" drugs generating more than $1 billion in annual sales. There were sixty-six blockbuster drugs in 2003; forty-seven of these were sold by the top ten companies. The best-selling product was Pfizer's Lipitor, which generated $9.23 billion in revenue, followed by Merck's Zocor, which was worth $5 billion (Sellers 2004). Prices normally fall substantially following patent expiration when generic competitors enter the market.

The 1984 U.S. Drug Price Competition and Patent Restoration (Hatch-Waxman) Act was a decisive moment in the development of the generics industry. The Hatch-Waxman Act introduced facilitated market entry for generic versions of all post-1962 approved products. Generic competition in the 1990s transformed the dynamics of the U.S. pharmaceutical market (Congressional Budget Office 1998). A key driver of that market came in the form of health maintenance organizations and pharmaceutical benefit management companies spearheading cost-containment measures such as generic prescribing, brand substitution by pharmacists, and reimbursement on the basis of cheapest brand (called "reference pricing"). Generics in the United States now account for more than 50 percent of all prescriptions dispensed and in 2003 sold at an average price of $31 per prescription, compared to brand prescriptions averaging $84 (according to data provided by the National Association of Chain Drug Stores). In other countries, public-sector insurance programs similarly encourage or mandate prescribers and consumers to substitute cheaper generics for more expensive brand products. The value of the global generics market is around $40 billion, and growth fueled by recent and future patent expirations of many blockbuster drugs is expected to continue at around 10 to 15 percent per annum.

Litigation between brand and generic companies about intellectual property rights is a conspicuous feature of the contemporary pharma industry. Patents and exclusive marketing rights enable research-based companies to charge monopoly prices, and the extension of patent protection often translates into many millions of dollars. Yet, the boundary between the research-based and the generics segments of the pharma industry is increasingly blurred. Most big pharma companies also supply generics, including so-called "pseudo-generics," that are identical (not copies but produced on the same production lines) to their branded equivalents. Conversely, some generics companies also supply patented products.

Industry Consolidation and the R&D Productivity Crisis

The ten largest companies ranked as follows in 2003 (by global prescription drug sales): Pfizer, GlaxoSmithKline, Merck, Johnson & Johnson, Aventis, AstraZeneca, Novartis, Bristol-Myers Squibb, Wyeth, and Eli Lilly (Sellers 2004). Six

were headquartered in the United States, two in the United Kingdom (GlaxoSmithKline and AstraZeneca), one in France (Aventis), and one in Switzerland (Novartis). Other countries with a significant research-based industry include Germany and Japan. Over several decades, the composition of the group of twenty-five or so leading companies has changed, mainly through mergers and acquisitions. Firm rankings are also affected by the launch and patent expiry of blockbuster drugs, which can result in significant shifts in market share. At least thirty-eight major drug companies have merged since 1994, and the process of consolidation is continuing. Recent examples include the merger in 2000 between Glaxo Wellcome and SmithKline Beecham to form GlaxoSmithKline, and Pfizer's 2002 acquisition of Pharmacia (formed through earlier mergers between Pharmacia, Upjohn, and Monsanto). Pfizer had previously absorbed Warner-Lambert, Parke-Davis, and Searle.

The generics industry is also undergoing consolidation at a global level as companies seek to expand their geographical and technological reach. The market leaders in 2004 were Teva Pharmaceutical Industries of Israel and Sandoz (owned by Novartis of Switzerland). Indian companies, including Ranbaxy and Dr Reddy's Laboratories, drawing on low-cost, quality-manufacturing facilities and a strong engineering tradition, are also important global suppliers of generics. In 2003, around 20 percent of all generic drugs sold in the United States were manufactured in India.

To sustain growth, big pharma must be able to substitute new products for their old ones as patents expire and prices fall with the onset of generic competition. This requires large investments in R&D. The top ten companies reported total R&D spending in 2003 of close to $36 billion, which for most firms represented around 15 percent of sales revenue. Occasionally, a "new product" means a truly innovative drug that treats a disease for which an effective medicine was not previously available. Most new drugs, however, are "me-too" products that provide a marginal improvement on existing medicines. It is estimated that about 18 percent of R&D spending is directed at research to discover new breakthrough medicines, while 82 percent is expended on incremental improvements on existing drugs and clinical trials (National Science Foundation 2003). Governments also contribute to drug discovery research with commercial spin-offs through deductions and tax credits and through the basic research undertaken within organizations such as the National Institutes of Health and the U.S. Department of Defense (Goozner 2004).

Explanations for industry consolidation most commonly emphasize pressures to improve R&D productivity. The discovery of innovative new drugs has become increasingly difficult and expensive. The R&D cost per new drug more than doubled between the late 1980s and the late 1990s. For most of the 1990s, the top twenty firms each launched an average of 1.5 new products per year, but in 2000 to 2003 they launched less than one new product per year. In 2003, the FDA approved twenty-one new molecular entities (NMEs), which can be compared to the peak in 1996, when fifty-six new NMEs were approved. Scientific and technological developments, including the advent of genomics, have opened up promising new avenues of drug discovery. But the R&D process has also become more complex, and the prospect of a wave of new, effective drugs has not yet been realized (Cockburn 2004).

Industry consolidation is pursued as a means of mobilizing and rationalizing the massive resources required for R&D and can also facilitate the management of the regulatory approval process throughout the world. Mergers enable companies to widen their product portfolio through the acquisition of existing products and drugs in the R&D pipeline, and also enable them to eliminate duplicate overhead costs, partly through the shedding of employees. Moreover, a larger size extends the global reach of companies and provides for scale advantages in manufactur-

ing and marketing. Yet, bigger size does not automatically solve the productivity problem. Since the 1980s, a high proportion of drug innovations have emerged from biotechnology and other small science-intensive companies. Some of the new biotechnology companies, including Amgen and Genentech, have become fully integrated competitors with big pharma. Others have been acquired by the big pharmaceutical companies, but most operate as specialist suppliers to big pharma.

Global Disparities

The big pharma companies are central actors within a global system for discovering, developing, regulating, and marketing prescription drugs. Firms in some developing countries (including India, China, Brazil, and South Africa) participate within this network, but the global pharma sector remains primarily a "triad" system of companies, regulatory agencies, and research organizations in North America, Europe, and Japan. Drugs are developed first and foremost to meet the needs of patients and doctors in industrially developed countries, accounting for almost 90 percent of global pharmaceutical sales. The majority of the population in developing countries lacks purchasing power to access patented drugs, and cheaper generic medicines are also out of reach for billions of people (Médecins Sans Frontières 2001). A minuscule proportion of R&D expenditure focuses on diseases affecting mainly poor countries, such as sleeping sickness, river blindness, Chagas disease, and leishmaniasis. Of 1,393 new drugs launched between 1975 and 1999, only 16 were for tropical diseases and tuberculosis (Trouillier et al. 2002).

In the industrially developed world, drugs account for around 15 percent of total (public and private) health expenditure, and in most of these countries between 50 and 80 percent of pharmaceuticals expenditure is publicly funded. In poor countries, by contrast, drugs account for between 25 percent and more than

60 percent of total health expenditure, and most consumers must pay the full cost of drugs out-of-pocket. Also, safety regulation is often unreliable or nonexistent, and many drugs are of poor quality. Since 1977, the World Health Organization (WHO) has operated an "essential drugs program" to assist developing countries in spending their limited resources in a way that maximizes health outcomes. Through the careful selection of a limited range of essential medicines, most medical needs can be met cost-effectively. The 12th Model List of Essential Drugs, prepared in 2002, includes 325 individual drugs, most of which are out-of-patent and can therefore be supplied relatively cheaply as generics (WHO 2004).

The calamity of AIDS in Africa and elsewhere has brought issues of access and affordable pricing to the fore in global drug policy debates. The 1995 Trade Related Aspects of Intellectual Property Rights (TRIPS) Agreement has been a central focus of such discussions. The TRIPS Agreement progressively extends a standard twenty-year patent period for drugs to all member countries of the World Trade Organization, including developing countries. Big pharma, and governments in countries where these firms are based, consider intellectual property rights to provide essential incentives for investments in the discovery of new effective medicines. From the perspective of the population of many poor countries, however, an extended patent period means delayed access to cheaper generics, including access to generic AIDS medications.

Following international lobbying and media controversy, the November 2001 ministerial meeting of the WTO at Doha agreed on a consensus statement called the "Doha Declaration on TRIPS and Public Health." This agreement allows developing countries to produce generic versions of patented drugs through "compulsory licensing" to protect public health and meet national emergencies. The least developed countries, however, lack the capacity to produce generic drugs, and the issue of importation and effective distribution of affordable

generics in these countries continues to be the subject of international dispute.

The Pharmaceutical Industry in the Era of Globalization

Pharmaceuticals have become a quintessentially global high-tech industry. The huge companies emerging from mergers and acquisitions operate discovery, development, and marketing processes stretching across many countries, linking into the best science anywhere in the world and the most cost-effective locations for production. Yet, the United States is by far the primary location for pharmaceutical and biotechnology R&D. In the past, the manufacturing of active ingredients, and other core activities, were concentrated in companies' home countries, with secondary plants located elsewhere for conversion into final products and local distribution. Today, regional or global markets are supplied with ready-made products from a small number of strategic sites, and the manufacturing of active ingredients is often outsourced to low-income countries such as China and India. Clinical trials, which can encompass up to 40 percent of total development costs, are shaping up as the next major activity for global outsourcing. India offers the advantages of large pools of patients, many qualified doctors and clinicians, and low costs. Thus, the corporate strategies successfully applied for most of the postwar period are being redesigned to meet the new opportunities posed by globalization.

At the same time, corporate strategies must also meet the challenges of globalization. These include:

- Growing pressures on prices resulting from the application of market power by public and private insurance providers. Companies must increasingly be able to demonstrate the cost-effectiveness of drugs to cost-conscious group buyers.
- Price competition as drugs go out of

patent. The market share for generics is increasing steadily.

- A lack of new breakthrough drugs. The long-expected major commercial breakthrough for biotechnology-based drugs has not yet become reality.
- A more complex political environment, and the growing expectation that companies demonstrate "corporate social responsibility."

The hallmark of the global big pharma corporation is the replacement of traditional command-and-control systems with less hierarchical forms of management and control. In particular, the science- and technology-intensive nature of innovation requires openness toward external organizations such as universities and smaller biotechnology companies.

Pharmaceutical firms remain very sensitive to decisions taken by government regulators. The failure to bring a research project to fruition, or a delay of market approval for a major drug product, can have devastating commercial consequences. All actors within the sector retain an awareness of the risk and unacceptable consequences of unsafe products. Global company webs and global markets are, however, inducing a reconfiguration of regulatory arrangements, and some functions previously wielded by nation-states are being shifted upward to the transnational level. Companies and their associations are engaged forcefully in the process of international harmonization and in broader discussions on health policy. The international regime now emerging is characterized by a complex intermeshing of private and public players in a process shaped and influenced, to a significant extent, by the power of big pharma. National regulatory agencies have not been superseded, but the trend is for such agencies to operate as components of a global system.

Pharmaceutical companies have been much criticized in debates about affordable access and have in response initiated a range of humanitarian and charitable activities, including partnership programs with WHO and with the governments of many developing countries. The role of international organizations such as WHO, UNICEF, and nongovernment organizations (NGOs) such as Médecins Sans Frontières (MSF), Health Action International (HAI), and Oxfam International impose some constraints on the global power of big pharma. As globalization proceeds, however, there will be growing pressures for transparency and democratic accountability in respect to the worldwide system for discovering, developing, and providing access to medical drugs.

Hans Lofgren

See Also World Health Organization (WHO); World Trade Organization (WTO); Copyrights and Intellectual Property; Public Health

References

Abraham, John, and Helen Lawton Smith, eds. 2003. *Regulation of the Pharmaceutical Industry.* Houndsmills, Basingstoke: Palgrave Macmillan.

Angell, Marcia. 2004. *Drug Money: How Pharmaceutical Companies Deceive Us and What We Can Do about It.* New York: Random House.

Ballance, Robert H., Janos Pogany, and Helmut Forstner. 1992. *The World's Pharmaceutical Industries: An International Perspective on Innovation, Competition and Policy.* Aldershot: Edward Elgar.

Burkholz, Herbert. 1994. *The FDA Follies.* New York: Basic.

Cockburn, Iain. 2004. "The Changing Structure of the Pharmaceutical Industry." *Health Affairs* 23, no. 1: 10–22.

Congressional Budget Office. 1998. *How Increased Competition from Generic Drugs Has Affected Prices and Returns in the Pharmaceutical Industry.* Washington, DC: Congress of the United States.

Croghan, Thomas W., and Patricia M. Croghan. 2004. "The Medicine Cabinet: What's in It, Why, and Can We Change the Contents?" *Health Affairs* 23, no. 1: 23–33.

Gassmann, Oliver, Gerrit Reepmeyer, and Maximilian von Zedtwitz. 2004. *Leading Pharmaceutical Innovation: Trends and Drives for Growth in the Pharmaceutical Industry.* Berlin: Springer.

Goozner, Merrill. 2004. *The $800 Million Pill: The Truth behind the Cost of New Drugs.* Berkeley: University of California Press.

Harrison, Christopher Scott. 2004. *The Politics of the International Pricing of Prescription Drugs.* Westport, CT: Praeger.

Henderson, Rebecca, Luigi Oresenigo, and Gary P. Pisano. 1999. "The Pharmaceutical Industry and the Revolution in Molecular Biology: Interactions among Scientific, Institutional, and Organizational Change." Pp. 267–311 in David C. Mowery and Richard R. Nelson, eds., *Sources of Industrial Leadership: Studies of Seven Industries.* Cambridge: Cambridge University Press.

Kassirer, Jerome P. 2004. *On the Take: How Medicine's Complicity with Big Business Can Endanger Your Health.* New York, Oxford University Press.

Médecins Sans Frontières. 2001. *Fatal Imbalance: The Crisis in Research and Development for Drugs for Neglected Diseases.* Geneva: MSF.

National Science Foundation. 2003. *Research and Developments in Industry: 2000.* NSF 03–318. Arlington, VA: NSF.

Pratt, Edmund T., Jr. 1985. *Pfizer: Bringing Science to Life.* New York: Newcomen Society of the United States.

Schweizer, Stuart O. 1997. *Pharmaceutical Economics and Policy.* New York: Oxford University Press.

Sellers, L. J. "Special Report: Pharm Exec 50," http://www. pharmexec.com/pharmexec/article/articleDetail.jsp? id=95192 (cited July 2004).

Silverman, Milton, and Philip R. Lee. 1974. *Pills, Profits, and Politics.* Berkeley: University of California Press.

Trouillier, P., et al. 2002. "Drug Development for Neglected Diseases: A Deficient Market and a Public-Health Policy Failure." *The Lancet* 359, no. 9324 (October 5): 2188–2194.

World Health Organization. "Essential Drugs and Medicines Policy," http://www.who.int/medicines/ rationale.shtml (cited August 2004).

Textiles and Apparel

Textiles and apparel have been referred to as the most globalized industries in the world. They are also the industries most associated with the first stages of industrialization, having fulfilled this role in both the industrialized nations during the nineteenth and early twentieth centuries and in the developing world in the late twentieth and early twenty-first centuries. Currently, both textiles and apparel are technology-intensive industries with complex supply-chain management systems, computerized production, highly competitive time-sensitive sales, research and development, and truly global manufacturing. The labor-intensive apparel industry is frequently at the center of international labor standards debates, especially child labor issues. The more capital-intensive textile industry is often at the center of environmental issues, particularly in regard to dyes and colorings.

The international textile and apparel trade has been regulated on a multilateral basis since the 1960s and remained outside the jurisdiction of the General Agreement on Tariffs and Trade (GATT) until 1994, when it was agreed that the quota system would be phased out. On January 1, 2005, textiles and apparel became fully integrated into the World Trade Organization (WTO) system. Textile and apparel trade still plays a sizable role in the economy of industrialized countries, but it is most important for some developing and least-developed countries, accounting for a dominant portion of industrial capacity, industrial employment, total exports, and gross domestic product (GDP) for many. Because of this role, the quota system phase-out became the most controversial trade issue of the first years of the twenty-first century.

Global Economic Impact

The textile and apparel industries constitute a significant sector in the world economy. World exports of textiles and apparel in 2002 exceeded $400 billion. This accounts for over 6 percent of world trade, and over 8 percent of world trade in manufactured goods. Apparel represents 60 percent of this combined total. There are 30 million apparel production jobs worldwide. The international garment industry works in far more countries than almost any other industry today, dealing with more products and with more suppliers. Virtually all countries produce and export garments. This means that some 192 countries export garments from more than 250,000 garment factories. For many developing countries, garment manufacturing represents the overwhelming majority of total exports. For example, in terms of total exports, apparel accounts for 85.9 percent for Bangladesh, 84.4 percent for Macau, 72.5 percent for Cambodia, 72.1 percent for Pakistan, 60.2 percent for El Salvador, 56.6 percent for Mauritius, 54.3 percent for Sri Lanka, 50.9 percent for the Dominican Republic, 48.7 percent for Nepal, and 42.4 percent for Tunisia.

413

Table 1: Global Textile and Apparel Trade, 1995–2003 (aggregate figures)

	European Union				USA				Japan			
	1995	2001	2002	2003	1995	2001	2002	2003	1995	2001	2002	2003
IMPORTS (in billions of euros)												
WORLD	45.25	72.49	71.41	70.24	37.45	85.52	83.23		19.38	26.21	22.96	
European Union	1.87	1.91	1.59	1.28	3.31	5.51	5.23		2.76	2.29	2.1	
USA	0.12	0.15	0.13	0.11					1.48	0.87	0.7	
Canada	0.7	0.78	0.69	0.57	1.46	3.9	3.74		0.03	0.03	0.03	
Japan	4.28	6.43	6.26	5.92	0.52	0.75	0.72					
Acceding countries	1.36	4.56	4.85	5.03	0.21	0.28	0.26		0.02	0.04	0.05	
Bulgaria & Romania	1.25	1.42	1.33	1.21	0.09	0.32	0.3		0	0.02	0.03	
CIS	6.82	12.14	12.97	13.24	0.17	0.73	0.71		0.01	0.02	0.01	
Mediterranean countries	0.85	0.77	0.77	0.73	1.31	3.46	3.72		0.05	0.08	0.08	
Latin America	4.81	10.44	11.37	12.32	7.42	22.88	21.59		0.11	0.12	0.11	
China	2.6	2.64	2.34	2.08	4.68	9.69	10.71		9.45	18.34	16.35	
Hong Kong	0.83	1.75	1.56	1.39	3.58	5.14	4.5		0.25	0.08	0.07	
South Korea	3.6	6.17	5.61	4.94	1.94	3.69	3.52		1.78	0.99	0.68	
ASEAN	5.84	9.85	9.69	9.99	4.38	10.97	11.01		1.6	1.99	1.69	
South Asia	1.08	1.05	0.87	0.76	4.02	10.33	9.98		0.67	0.53	0.43	
Australia and New Zealand	1.11	1.84	1.53	1.36	0.22	0.38	0.36		0.43	0.29	0.19	
ACP	0.21	0.38	0.33	0.33	2.27	3.84	3.43		0.04	0.02	0.02	
Gulf countries					0.41	1.06	0.87		0	0.01	0.01	
OPEC	2.18	3.01	2.53	2.25	1.34	3.65	3.18		0.52	0.61	0.49	
EXPORTS (in billions of euros)												
WORLD	29.23	43.59	43.51	41.71	13.96	21.41	19.45		6.65	8.16	7.53	
European Union	3.24	5.72	5.2	4.64	1.63	1.66	1.48		0.62	0.68	0.62	
USA	0.43	0.61	0.58	0.55					0.48	0.59	0.54	
Canada	2.54	2.39	2.16	2.01	2.07	3.5	3.14		0.04	0.04	0.04	
Japan	3.82	6.43	6.51	6.38	1.22	0.71	0.6					
Acceding Countries	1.06	3.28	3.53	3.68	0.04	0.05	0.04		0.01	0.01	0.01	
Bulgaria & Romania	0.98	2.22	2.43	2.49	0.02	0.01	0.01		0	0	0	
CIS	2.68	4.32	4.58	4.33	0.03	0.04	0.03		0.01	0.01	0.01	
Mediterranean countries	0.74	1.32	1.22	1.02	0.33	0.38	0.37		0.04	0.04	0.05	
Latin America	0.29	0.59	0.65	0.74	4.76	11.94	10.79		0.07	0.07	0.05	
China	1.28	1.55	1.47	1.37	0.83	0.32	0.49		1.8	3.17	2.94	
Hong Kong	0.67	0.73	0.77	0.72	0.41	0.41	0.39		0.92	0.97	0.91	
South Korea	0.7	0.77	0.74	0.69	0.44	0.34	0.29		0.58	0.54	0.49	
ASEAN	0.25	0.39	0.42	0.43	0.76	0.66	0.66		0.87	1.02	0.96	
South Asia	0.38	0.41	0.46	0.45	0.27	0.46	0.35		0.14	0.15	0.14	
Australia and New Zealand	0.64	1.15	1.11	1.02	0.16	0.14	0.13		0.09	0.05	0.05	
ACP	0.82	1.16	1.21	1.05	1.28	1.94	1.79		0.05	0.06	0.06	
Gulf countries					0.21	0.12	0.11		0.32	0.28	0.25	
OPEC	1.24	1.72	1.72	1.54	0.69	0.55	0.47		0.54	0.54	0.46	

(continues)

Table 1: Global Textile and Apparel Trade, 1995–2003 (aggregate figures) Continued

	European Union				USA				Japan			
	1995	2001	2002	2003	1995	2001	2002	2003	1995	2001	2002	2003
					BALANCE (in billions of euros)							
WORLD	-16.02	-28.9	-27.9	-28.53	-23.49	-64.11	-63.79		-12.73	-18.05	-15.43	
European Union					-1.67	-3.85	-3.75		-2.14	-1.61	-1.48	
USA	1.37	3.81	3.61	3.36					-1	-0.28	-0.17	
Canada	0.31	0.46	0.45	0.44	0.61	-0.4	-0.59		0.01	0.01	0.01	
Japan	1.84	1.61	1.47	1.44	0.7	-0.03	-0.12					
Acceding countries	-0.46	0	0.25	0.46	-0.17	-0.23	-0.22		-0.01	-0.03	-0.03	
Bulgaria & Romania	-0.3	-1.28	-1.32	-1.35	-0.08	-0.31	-0.29		0	-0.01	-0.03	
CIS	-0.27	0.8	1.1	1.28	-0.14	-0.69	-0.68		-0.01	0	0	
Mediterranean countries	-4.14	-7.82	-8.39	-8.91	-0.98	-3.08	-3.35		-0.01	-0.03	-0.02	
Latin America	-0.11	0.55	0.45	0.29	-2.66	-10.94	-10.79		-0.04	-0.05	-0.06	
China	-4.52	-9.85	-10.72	-11.58	-3.85	-9.37	-10.22		-7.65	-15.18	-13.41	
Hong Kong	-1.32	-1.09	-0.87	-0.71	-3.17	-4.72	-4.11		0.67	0.89	0.84	
South Korea	-0.16	-1.02	-0.79	-0.67	-1.5	-3.35	-3.23		-1.2	-0.45	-0.19	
ASEAN	-2.9	-5.4	-4.87	-4.25	-3.62	-10.31	-10.35		-0.73	-0.97	-0.72	
South Asia	-5.59	-9.46	-9.27	-9.56	-3.75	-9.86	-9.63		-0.53	-0.38	-0.29	
Australia and New Zealand	-0.7	-0.64	-0.41	-0.31	-0.06	-0.24	-0.23		-0.34	-0.23	-0.14	
ACP	-0.47	-0.69	-0.42	-0.34	-0.98	-1.9	-1.63		0.01	0.04	0.04	
Gulf countries	0.61	0.78	0.88	0.72	-0.2	-0.94	-0.76		0.31	0.27	0.25	
OPEC	-0.94	-1.29	-0.81	-0.71	-0.65	-3.1	-2.71		0.02	-0.07	-0.03	

Note: Figures for world totals exclude intra-EU trade
Sources: EUROSTAT/COMEXT, March 23, 2004; COMTRADE, March 23, 2004.

The Quota System

Global trade of textiles and apparel among WTO members is governed by the Agreement on Textiles and Clothing (ATC), which came into force at the founding of the WTO on January 1, 1995. According to this agreement there was a progressive application of GATT rules and a progressive phasing out of quotas in the European Union, the United States, and Canada over a ten-year period. The ATC further established that following the ten-year phase-out period ending on January 1, 2005, the ATC would expire and all quotas would be abolished, allowing all WTO members unrestricted access to the European, U.S., and Canadian textile and apparel markets.

The quota system began in the postwar period. Industrialized countries such as the United States and the United Kingdom negotiated a series of bilateral arrangements restricting their textile and apparel markets as early as the 1950s. Multilateral arrangements began with the Long-Term Arrangement Regarding International Trade in Cotton Textiles (LTA) in 1962. The LTA gave way to the Multi-Fiber Agreement (MFA) (also called the Multi-Fiber Arrangement) in 1974. The aim of the MFA was to stem a steady fall in employment in the textile and apparel industries in the West. Under the MFA framework, the United States, for example, negotiated access to its market with each country, and then each other government allocated quotas among its own domestic textile and apparel firms as it saw fit. When an apparel-exporting country reached a limit in a given category of product, the category was said to be "embargoed," that is, that country could not ship more goods of that kind until the following year. Companies that ran into unexpected embargoes were allowed to work around them through a program known as "carry forward," which allowed them to borrow against the next year's quota allocation. The response of the apparel industry in the industrialized countries to the import quotas was to globalize production by creating a "quota-

hopping" system, which encouraged development of the industry in places where none existed previously. The demise of the quota system came about during the Uruguay trade rounds, spearheaded by the developing countries. In practice, the MFA carved up the world market, thereby shielding some of the weaker producers from competition.

The Impact of Quota Phase-Out

MFA quotas were quantitative restrictions that had a number of characteristics. They were applied on a discriminatory basis to some exporting countries but not to others; were negotiated on a bilateral basis rather than imposed globally and, therefore, differed from country to country in terms of product coverage and degree of restrictiveness; and involved limits on exports, transferring rents from the importing country to the exporting country. Xinshen Diao and Agapi Somwaru (2001) estimated that over the twenty-five-year period following ATC implementation, the annual growth of world textile and apparel trade would be at least 5 percent faster than it would have been in the absence of the ATC. This acceleration translates into as much as $200 billion over the period. They also predicted that world apparel trade would increase twice as fast as textile trade in the post-quota world, but that the impact would differ across countries and regions. For all countries, quota elimination represents both an opportunity and a threat: an opportunity because markets will no longer be restricted, and a threat because suppliers will no longer be restrained and major markets will be open to intense competition.

China is expected to be the biggest winner from the phase-out of the quota system, followed by India. At the time the phase-out was negotiated, China's production was comparatively minimal, and China was not a member of the WTO. Developing countries thought the phase-out agreement would help them expand exports to the industrialized world. Reinstatement of the MFA or some form of quota system appears unlikely because of a lack of interest from the United States and the European Union as well as because of the potential WTO challenges if the quotas are not removed.

Some have argued that the phase-out could lead to a reallocation of production to the detriment of developing-country exporters that in the past were "effectively protected" from more competitive suppliers by the quota system. Others have predicted that the apparel production of the restrained exporters as a whole, generally Asian countries, would increase by almost 20 percent, and that their textile production would increase by almost 6 percent once the MFA has been phased out. It has been estimated that the market shares of non-quota-constrained suppliers (such as Mexico and African, Caribbean, and Central American countries) would shrink. It is thought that Mercosur and Chile will reduce their exports of clothing significantly and their exports of textiles moderately.

Richard Avisse and Michel Fouquin (2001) estimated that Asian apparel exports would rise by 54 percent over the phase out period and that their share of the world market would increase to 60 percent from 40 percent in 1995. China's apparel exports are expected to rise by 87 percent, and their share of world apparel exports should rise by more than 10 percentage points during the same period. Meanwhile both South Asia's and Southeast Asia's apparel exports also should experience substantial gains, increasing by 36 percent combined. Latin American apparel exports, in contrast, are predicted to decrease by 39 percent during this period.

Asian countries should also experience some increases in textile exports. It is estimated that China's exports will increase by 9 percent, and South Asia's by 22 percent. Avisse and Fouquin estimated that Chinese production would rise by 70 percent, and that of other Asian countries by 26 percent. Some industry observers expect much higher rates and believe that China will dominate world apparel

production within a few years of quota elimination. Joseph Francois and Dean Spinanger (2001) have argued that the "protective shield" will disappear gradually as quotas are phased out and that preferred supplying groups will probably see dramatic increases in competition from Chinese and other Asian exporters. They asserted that preferential access to North America (by Mexico) and Europe (by Turkey and Eastern European countries) will be reduced considerably when quotas are eliminated for competing exporters and that there will be a shift in demand away from these countries to other suppliers (especially Asian countries). Mexico, in their view, stands to be the largest loser among exporting countries.

The growth in domestic demand in Asian countries, particularly China, might lessen the dramatic changes in trade patterns after 2005. Mike Flanagan (2003) argued that wealth in rich countries (and therefore the people's ability to buy clothes) is not growing as quickly as wages in the world's middle-income countries—especially in the world's two most populous countries, China and India. He further argued that faster economic growth would be accompanied by even faster growth in apparel purchases and apparel importing. For example, in 2001 China's retail sales of apparel grew twice as fast as its economy.

Lower prices in manufactures may be offset by higher prices in some raw materials, especially cotton. Total world cotton production in 2004 was over 22 million tons. The top ten countries accounted for nearly 86 percent of world output. These are: China (5.42 million tons), the United States (4.39 million tons), India (3.12 million tons), Pakistan (1.73 million tons), Brazil (1.38 million tons), Uzbekistan (1.01 million tons), Turkey (0.99 million tons), Greece (0.35 million tons), Australia (0.34 million tons), and Mali (0.29 million tons). The United States is the leading cotton exporter, with more than 40 percent of global market share. The WTO ruled in June 2004 that U.S. cotton subsidies violated international trade rules. The landmark decision is expected to eventually drive up world prices and give cotton growers from Brazil to West Africa an incentive to increase production. In its WTO complaint, Brazil charged that the more than $3 billion in annual subsidies paid out to U.S. cotton growers led to increased output in the United States and artificially depressed global prices, robbing Brazil of potential export markets and undercutting the livelihood of its farmers. Brazil argued that U.S. cotton exports would fall by 41 percent, that U.S. production would drop by 29 percent, and that world cotton prices would rise by 12.6 percent if the United States ended its cotton subsidies. If Brazil's WTO challenge survives U.S. appeals, the United States may eventually be forced to reduce all agricultural subsidies.

The Global Fight for Quotas

The changes slated to occur in the global textile and apparel quota system sparked a trade debate within individual countries and within the international community. The Fair Trade Textile Alliance, a coalition of 123 textile and apparel trade associations representing 56 countries, called for an extension of quotas beyond 2005. In this alliance, industry leaders in industrial countries joined forces with their counterparts in developing countries, thus grouping, for example, some U.S. industry leaders and Bangladesh on the same side of the battle. Throughout 2003–2004, representatives of the U.S. textile industry actively campaigned both domestically and abroad for continued protection. Textile firms, led by Milliken & Co., lobbied heavily to change policy and elect congressional candidates who would back policies favorable to U.S. mills.

The textile industry has never been a large campaign contributor in the United States, and since the latest revenue and job declines, its political action committees have been largely dormant, according to the Federal Election Commission. U.S. domestic textile groups, including the National Coalition of Textile Organizations

and the American Manufacturing Trade Action Coalition (AMTAC), issued a call for textile producers around the world to lobby their governments to continue providing protection through 2007. In conjunction with Turkey's textile and apparel industry association, they issued the Istanbul Declaration for Fair Trade in Textiles and Clothing—a letter to the director general of the WTO urging him to convene an emergency meeting to discuss the quota phase-out. The press release announcing the declaration states that China's accession to the WTO "represents a severe and disruptive change in circumstances not present during consideration in the early 1990s of a timetable for the phase-out of quotas." The U.S. groups toured the world to enlist the support of textile and apparel industry associations.

The movement, however, miscalculated its strategy because: (1) it did not focus on governments, which make up the membership in the WTO, but on industry associations; (2) the WTO operates by consensus, which means that any quota resolution could be blocked by expected winners of the phase-out such as Pakistan, India, and China; (3) the Istanbul Declaration assumes that China's accession was not contemplated in the Uruguay agreement, when in fact it was a consideration; and (4) the elimination of the quota system was put into the Uruguay agreement as a condition by the developing world in return for accepting some of the other standards put into place by the request of the developed world (such as intellectual property rights).

Moreover, although textile and apparel manufacturers in the United States and many other countries were united in maintaining the quota system, apparel importers around the world, especially in the giant U.S. market, were active and vocal in their support for the quota system phase-out. The diverging interests produced clashes within the United States between the two sides of the industry (importers vs. manufacturers). Domestic manufacturers successfully pushed the George W. Bush administration to accept threat-based safeguard peti-

Global Textile and Apparel Trade—A Snapshot of Major Events

1950s The United States and the United Kingdom negotiate with Japan, Hong Kong, China, India, and Pakistan to restrict textile and apparel exports out of fear of undermining domestic producers.

1961 The United States initiates the Short-Term Arrangement Regarding International Trade in Cotton Textiles (STA)—a multilateral agreement to formalize one year restrictions on trade in cotton products in sixty-four categories in order to avoid market disruption until a more permanent agreement can be put in place.

1962 Nineteen major trading nations agree to the Long-Term Arrangement Regarding International Trade in Cotton Textiles (LTA)—a multilateral agreement to regulate international trade in cotton textiles and apparel.

1974 The Multi-Fiber Arrangement comes into effect covering all textiles and clothing goods except silk, with seventy-three countries as signatories. This arrangement would be renegotiated four times (1977, 1981, 1986, 1991).

1995 The Agreement on Textiles and Clothing, negotiated in the Uruguay Round, comes into force, committing WTO members to progressively eliminating all quotas by January 1, 2005.

2003 In May, EU Commissioner Pascal Lamy chairs the Global Conference on the Future of Textiles and Clothing After 2005. Also, the Istanbul Declaration for Fair Trade in Textiles and Clothing is issued, whereby trade associations and labor unions from twenty-six countries appeal to the WTO for an emergency meeting and delay in the phase-out of quotas, emphasizing the threat from China. By August 2004, a total of 123 organizations from 56 countries at all stages of development had signed the declaration.

2004 The debate on the WTO's impending phase-out system intensifies, and the following events occur:

June The Brussels Summit on Fair Trade in Textiles and Apparel is held, with thirty-six industry associations in attendance warning that ending quotas will result in 30 million job losses around the world and one or two countries monopolizing the market.

September The Euro-Mediterranean trade ministers conference on the future of textiles and clothing, chaired by Tunisia, is held.

December The United States Association of Importers of Textiles and Apparel challenges the ability of the Committee for the Implementation of Textile Agreements to consider threat-based safeguard petitions and wins a temporary injunction barring the U.S. government from considering further proposals. In addition, Turkey becomes the first country to announce the imposition of new quotas on Chinese apparel imports to protect its domestic industry, and China announces voluntary export taxes on exports of textiles and apparel.

tions in August 2004 and went on to submit twelve such petitions by December. Apparel importers, who saw their interests hurt by any safeguards, took legal action against the U.S. government. In December, the United States Association of Importers of Textiles and Apparel (USA-ITA) successfully sued the Committee for the Implementation of Textile Agreements, chaired by the U.S. Department of Commerce, securing a court injunction preventing the U.S. government from considering further threat-based petitions (see section on United States under the heading "Current Trends: Technology and Consolidation"). In the same month, Turkey became the first country to announce new restrictions on Chinese imports of textiles and apparel, and China announced voluntary imposition of export taxes on certain textile and apparel categories.

Supply Chain Management

The end of the quota system makes the global apparel industry essentially a buyers' market. However, labor costs, normally assumed to be the deciding factor in production, are not the only factor. Competition is exacerbated by complex supply chains. Apparel may have the most difficult supply chain of any business because of the seasonality of clothing and fast-changing consumer preferences and trends. In such an environment, competitiveness depends on service, quality, speed, logistical support, and infrastructure as well as price.

For this reason, lowest-cost producers in terms of labor are not always preferable, and thus they are unlikely to be major beneficiaries of a post-quota world. Niki Tait (2002) has asserted that purchasers are likely to concentrate on four or five politically and financially stable countries. According to Tait, factors that are considered important include respect for basic human ethics such as minimum wages, absence of child or forced labor, good working conditions, and reliable delivery and lead times. David Birnbaum (2002b) argued that current and future sourcing decisions depend in great part on which countries offer the best facilities and greatest logistical advantages. Tait also stressed the importance of infrastructure to support the buying process (such as good telecommunications, ease of import and export documentation and procedures, international logistics, quality controllers, and test centers). Proximity to the export market, or the ability to quickly respond to changes in market conditions, is also considered to be an important determinant of the pattern of trade. Birnbaum (2001) noted that since U.S. buyers are increasingly demanding "quick response" services, distant factories will find it harder to satisfy customer requirements.

Regional sourcing will remain important for flexibility and for technical innovation, and having regionally available producers that offer a six-week versus a 120-day lead time will also be important. For example, shipping time from Sri Lanka, Bangladesh, and India to the United States averages twenty-eight days, compared to two days from Mexico or Canada. Similarly, Turkey, Romania, the Czech Republic, and Hungary are all within one or two days by road freight to the EU. Moreover, the availability of local or regional raw material greatly improves a country's ability to respond to orders with shorter lead times. Also, technological innovation is more easily accomplished when the factory is near the design firm. Significant speculation over whether safeguard measures will be employed against Chinese imports may prevent China from dominating market share as has been predicted. As purchasers consolidate and rationalize their sources, the degree of vertical integration in countries or firms becomes an important competitiveness factor.

According to Birnbaum (2002b), today's sourcing decisions are increasingly based on which factories can best meet customers' ever-increasing requirements. He noted that buyers go to China because Chinese factories give the customers what they want, from pattern-making to final stock garment shipment. Tait (2002) argued that the level of service required by buyers is evolving and that a "full package from design to delivery of the finished product, inclusive of fabric and trim sourcing, right down to the delivery of store-ready items to individual shops," is now in demand. Not all apparel products have the same requirements. Some firms (such as those producing higher priced or specialty products) don't expect big changes for their supply chain as a result of quota elimination because of their focus on maintaining a high standard of quality, and they expect to maintain more vendor continuity than the majority of fashion firms because of the steep learning curve required for producers of certain products. Others expect larger, more integrated manufacturers to develop that coordinate and deliver more services and product development while supplying directly to the retailer. For trendy fashion items, speed to market is critical, and so proximity plays a greater role; thus, firms in that sector also may be slow in making big changes if closer suppliers are available. More apparel firms are interested in vertical integration (full-package manufacturers). This can be accomplished within a particular firm or even within a particular region/country. The general industry agreement, however, is that only the strongest, most efficient supply chains will remain. With quota elimination comes sourcing consolidation. U.S. companies are cutting the number of offshore suppliers and countries with which they do business, and they are asking those that remain for more involvement in design and logistics. In general, the U.S. industry plans to do more business with fewer suppliers that are bigger.

Employment, Labor Standards, and Social Responsibility

Social responsibility also plays an increasingly important role in textile and apparel imports. For example, in 2003, the Gap chain dropped 136 of its factory suppliers because they had committed violations of its code of vendor conduct. It also began to deliver a social responsibility practices report to shareholders at its annual meeting. The Gap has a supply chain of 3,000 factories in more than 50 countries and 4,000 stores around the world, along with 93 compliance officers. Its code of conduct includes both broad human rights standards, such as forbidding the use of child or forced labor, as well as safety and hours rules, such as ensuring corridors remain clear and not allowing workers to toil more than sixty hours a week. One of its reports said that "few factories, if any, are in full compliance all of the time." The firm's compliance officers strive to correct problems in noncompliant factories rather than just dropping vendors at the first sign of a

violation, with the goal of improving the conditions of factories and the well-being of workers.

However, there is concern that the post-MFA competition could threaten labor standards. The International Labour Organization (ILO) monitors garment factories around the world. According to a 2004 ILO report, "ensuring that working conditions and labor relations throughout the sector are generally acceptable is now, more than ever, of the utmost importance," referring to the elimination of quotas in 2005. The impact on jobs will be tremendous. Vertical manufacturing facilities could grow so large that they would employ 40,000 workers. More than 150,000 people in Latin America today earn a living making pants for the U.S. market. It is expected that the majority of those jobs will disappear as manufacturing shifts to Asia. In 2004, Honduran exports to the United States declined by 20.5 percent, and Turkey's declined 16.2 percent, while exports to the United States from South Korea rose by 20.3 percent, from Pakistan by 8.3 percent, and from Indonesia by 16.7 percent; China's shipments rose 20.26 percent a month. About half of the 500,000 jobs in the Central American region's 1,000 garment companies could vanish in the next five years.

Current Trends: Technology and Consolidation

Technology increasingly plays an important role in the apparel industry, and especially in the textile manufacturing process. In addition to supply-chain management technology, computerized design and production and radio-frequency identification (RFID) tags are now industry standards. Computer-aided design and computer-integrated design manufacturing (CAD/CAM) are used to digitize, record, and automate pattern production and sizing. The development and integration of 3D pattern-making tools allow designers to visualize the interaction between body form, garment shape, and fabric. Increasing global competition is forcing manufacturers around the world to look seriously at their methods of production in the quest for ways to rapidly turn out good quality merchandise. They seek flexible methods that will enable them to react to consumer demands and maintain low work-in-process (WIP) levels.

Within a few years, industry experts expect to see widespread use of RFID tags on high-value items where size and color choices add complexity to stock management, on items where counterfeiting is an issue, and for items that are a security risk. RFID was already in use in 2004 by retailers in the United States, Germany, and the United Kingdom such as Wal-Mart, Asda, Metro Group, Marks & Spencer, and Woolworths. Other uses for RFID include customer service. Prada, for example, tested RFID tags in its New York City boutique in 2003 for customer benefits, installing tag readers in fitting rooms so shoppers could check on related merchandise or alternate size availability from a self-serve kiosk rather than having to call an assistant. In the textile industry, innovations include infrared fabrics that improve circulation; stain-fighting, odor-fighting, and antimicrobial bacteria–resistant fabrics; fabrics that protect against ultraviolet light; automatic cutting machines, single-process seamless-garment knitting machines, and digital textile printing and computerized fabric printers; body scanning virtual measurement; and 3-D visualization technology.

In the United States, a number of large apparel firms were established as mergers, acquisitions, and consolidations rippled through the industry to produce multibrand marketing giants such as the VF Corporation, Kellwood, Warnaco, Liz Claiborne, Jones New York, and PVH. In Europe, similar trends produced LVMH and PPR, the luxury giants controlling many of the most well-known brands in luxury fashion and accessories. Expectations are for even more consolidation after 2005. This may result in greater industry unity, which has been lacking for more than a decade. Financing within the textile and apparel industries tends to be in-house or through traditional channels of commercial banking, with only a tiny fraction of firms becoming publicly listed. Even commercial bank financing is tricky. Banks have traditionally viewed the apparel sector as too risky, thereby imposing punitively high interest rates on companies that want to expand. The industry frequently finances internally with suppliers offering credit to buyers at all levels. Factoring (or selling at a discount to a third-party financial entity) of receivables is also common.

United States

The United States is the largest textile and apparel importer in the world, importing more than $77 billion worth of textiles and apparel in 2003, representing more than 90 percent of all clothing sold at retail in the country. Of that total, more than $61 billion was under quota. By 2004, U.S.-made apparel represented less than 10 percent of the clothing sold in the country. The U.S. textile and apparel industries have been hurt severely by increased competition, losing more than 740,000 jobs in the past ten years, with factories closing continuously. A number of textile firms filed for bankruptcy over this period, while hours worked fluctuated for those workers still employed. Meanwhile, retail employment grew as retailing dramatically expanded into what some have called "the over-storing of America." For example, department store employment in the United States, as of June 2004, totaled 1.6 million. After the remaining quotas are removed, the expectation is that there will be a wave of textile plant closures in the United States and that an estimated $42 billion in export orders from non-U.S. countries will shift to China. Currently, China supplies 16 percent of the U.S. market, but after quotas are eliminated, it is expected to supply 50 percent or more. India is expected to move from 4 percent to 15 percent, while the rest of the Americas drop from 16 percent to 5 percent. In cotton pants, for example, which represents 10 percent of the U.S. market, U.S. importers purchased from more than seventy countries in 2003. This number is expected to drop to ten countries within five years.

U.S. officials have said they are committed to quota elimination. However, import restrictions under alternate mechanisms are likely. Under the terms of China's WTO entry agreement, China remains subject to temporary "safeguard quotas" that could cap its shipments up to 2008. Importing nations are allowed to place safeguard quotas on Chinese exports in specific categories where Chinese products cause market disruption. The one-year quotas can limit shipments in affected categories to no more than 7.5 percent above the previous year's level, and they can be renewed for as many as three years. In accordance with these guidelines, safeguard measures that were negotiated bilaterally between China and the United States in 1993 allow the United States to preserve its trade laws and to unilaterally impose temporary quota-like safeguard limitations lasting one year (renewable) on Chinese exports if requested to do so by U.S. industry. These safeguards can be used until the end of 2008, and under these provisions, China can only export goods at a level 7.5 percent higher than in the previous year. These safeguard limits could be imposed prior to the removal of the quotas. The relaxation of restrictions on some textile and apparel categories has already resulted in surges of 24,000 percent in imports from China to the United States. In 2003, as quotas for some products expired, U.S. safeguard measures were imposed for bras, dressing gowns, robes, and knit fabrics. Because only a low threshold of evidence was needed for the measures to prevail in these earlier cases, some analysts predict that safeguards will be used extensively after quotas are removed.

In August 2004, the Bush administration determined that the industry had the right to file petitions based on the threat of market disruption, rather than waiting for actual disruption to occur. A coalition of U.S. textile associations filed twelve "threat-based" safeguard petitions between October and December 2004

alone, covering U.S. imports from China of such items as cotton pants and trousers, cotton knit shirts and blouses, men's and boy's cotton and synthetic fiber shirts (not knit), synthetic fiber knit shirts and blouses, and synthetic fiber pants and trousers. Under the safeguard procedures, once petitions were filed the Committee for the Implementation of Textile Agreements (CITA), established in 1974, had fifteen days to decide whether it would accept them for review. Following that was a thirty-day public comment period. CITA then had sixty days to review the petitions and render a decision.

CITA manages bilateral and multilateral textile trade issues for the United States. It is a five-member interagency governmental body established in 1972, chaired by the Department of Commerce, and includes the Department of Treasury, the Department of Labor, the Department of State, and the chief textile negotiator of the Office of the U.S. Special Trade Representative. On December 1, 2004, a lawsuit was filed against CITA by the United States Association of Importers of Textiles and Apparel to try to block the U.S. government from taking safeguard action based on the threat of market disruption. The U.S. Court of International Trade issued a temporary injunction prohibiting the U.S. government from reviewing any new threat-based petitions. Importers, represented by USA-ITA, alleged that by considering the preemptive safeguard quotas CITA was endangering their livelihood and argued that there is no legal basis for safeguard petitions based on threat rather than actual damage.

Another important association, the American Apparel and Footwear Association (AAFA), has ardently supported free trade in textiles and apparel, arguing against safeguards, but has not taken legal action. Antidumping action is distinct from safeguard action and remains an option for the U.S. government regardless of the ultimate outcome of the CITA lawsuit. AAFA supports U.S. efforts to expand free trade agreements and has been a proponent of U.S. preferential trade legislation such as the Caribbean Basin Trade Partnership Act, the

African Growth Opportunity Act (AGOA), and the Andean Trade and Drug Eradication Act, all of which allow duty-free and quota-free entry into the United States of regionally made apparel produced using American fabrics, or third-country fabric under special circumstances.

The European Union

Although the U.S. market is larger in terms of sales, textiles and apparel are much more important in the European Union than in the United States in terms of share of industrial production and employment. The textile and apparel industries account for 4 percent of all EU manufacturing production and 7 percent of all manufacturing employment, at 2.5 million jobs. The EU was the world's largest exporter of textiles (not including clothing) in 2002, with a 15 percent share, and the world's second largest exporter of textile and apparel (combined), accounting for an 11 percent share, just behind China. In the same year, the EU imported textile and clothing goods worth some 71 billion euros, or around 20 percent of total world imports, second after the United States, which accounted for 24 percent of world imports. In 2003, more than 107,000 textile and apparel companies, mostly small and medium-sized enterprises averaging twenty-three employees (only 2,500 firms have 1,000 employees or more), comprised an annual turnover of approximately 190 billion euros. The EU has progressively liberalized textile and clothing imports (one-third are duty free), it has not imposed many quotas on less developed countries, and its imports under quota in the sector represent only 25 percent of total imports.

To prepare for the challenges faced by the textile and apparel industries, on October 29, 2003, the European Commission adopted a communication on "The Future of the Textiles and Clothing Sector in the Enlarged European Union." In order to follow up on the ideas and suggestions contained in this document, early in 2004 the commission set up a High Level Group on textiles and clothing. This commis-

sion comprises all stakeholders of the textiles and clothing industry and is composed of commissioners, representatives from governments of four EU member states, a member of the European Parliament, industrialists, retailers and distributors, European trade associations, trade unions, and local textile and clothing association representatives. Its mandate is to formulate recommendations on initiatives to improve conditions for the competitiveness of the European textile and clothing industry.

The group produced a report, "The Challenge of 2005—European Textiles and Clothing in a Quota Free Environment," on June 30, 2004. The report made several major recommendations, urging EU officials to complete the EU-Mediterranean free trade area and asserting that the EU should promote research and development in clothing technology, establish an action plan in respect to China, secure genuine market access to third-world countries, improve skills of workers, facilitate and protect intellectual property rights, simplify the internal regulatory framework, establish a monitoring system for imports from China, and look at the possible use of safeguards as a last resort. In addition, the commission proposed that the EU provide special structural funds (1 percent of the structural fund annual contribution for the "Convergence" objective and 3 percent of the "Regional Competitiveness and Employment" objective) in order "to cover unforeseen crises" and help the textiles industry restructure, modernize, and adjust to trade opening and to mitigate the socioeconomic impact on regions with a high concentration of textiles employment. In late 2004, Euratex, a lobby group of European textile manufacturers, applied to the European Commission for safeguard measures in five categories.

Canada

The Canadian apparel industry is the tenth largest manufacturing sector in Canada, with more than 79,000 employees working in 2,700 establishments. It accounts for 2 percent of Canada's total manufacturing GDP, 0.4 percent of manufacturing investment, and 4.4 percent of total manufacturing employment. In 2003, the industry shipped some $4 billion of apparel in total, of which $2.7 billion (38.3 percent) was exported. Apparel aggregate shipments in 2003 recorded a decline of 6.3 percent from the previous year, with exports declining 11.9 percent, from $3.1 billion to $2.7 billion, and domestic shipments falling 2.5 percent, from $4.5 billion to $4.4 billion. Notwithstanding the year-to-year decline, in the seven-year period of 1996–2003, apparel aggregate shipments were 5.9 percent higher, having risen from $6.7 billion in 1996 to $7.1 billion in 2003.

As in other industrial countries, apparel manufacturers in Canada continue to lose market share to offshore suppliers. In 1996, domestic supply accounted for over 70 percent of the Canadian apparel market. By 2003, domestic producers accounted for only 41.7 percent. The continuing loss of market share by domestic manufacturers is being offset by apparel manufacturers' export-market development activity. Between 1996 and 2003, apparel exports increased 62.9 percent, rising from $1.7 billion to $2.7 billion. In this seven-year period, men's and boy's apparel exports rose 46.8 percent, from $514.2 million to $755 million; women's and girl's apparel exports rose 85.2 percent, from $540 million to $1 billion; and children's apparel exports rose 25.4 percent, from $9.6 million to $12.1 million. The United States, accounting for some 94.3 percent of Canadian apparel exports in 2003, continues to be Canada's main market. Canada nevertheless continues to carry an apparel trade deficit determined primarily by imports from low-wage countries, led by China, India, Mexico, and Bangladesh. In 2003, the aggregate textiles trade deficit rose to $3.4 billion, an increase of 12.3 percent from the previous year and 98.1 percent from seven years earlier.

China

China is the world's largest producer of textiles and apparel, which accounted for 10 percent of its manufacturing output in 2000 and 20 percent of its total exports in 2001. Reflecting the dominance of textiles and apparel for the Chinese economy, China is continually upgrading its production capacity in the sector. It was the world's largest investor in new spinning and weaving equipment during 1997–2001. China is highly price competitive, largely because of its large supply of low-cost labor, but is also considered to have effective middle management and the technical know-how to produce a wide range of sector goods.

According to the China National Textile Industry Council (CNTIC), the national federation of all textile-related industries in China, the sector comprises textiles, including knit apparel (62 percent of sector sales in 2002), woven apparel (31.5 percent), and synthetic fibers (6.5 percent). Official Chinese statistics for 2001 show that the sector comprised about 21,000 enterprises with total output of $116 billion and employment of 7.9 million workers, or 14.5 percent of Chinese industrial employment. However, sector production and employment levels are believed to be much higher, because the official statistics include data only for "statistically sizable enterprises" (SSEs), or firms having an annual output of more than 5 million *renminbi* (RMB, approximately $600,000). As such, the official statistics do not include data for the many small firms (mainly family-based production units) involved in production of sector goods in China. In 2002, CNTIC estimated that there were about 15 million workers in the Chinese textile and apparel sector, including both SSEs and smaller firms.

China is the world's largest exporter of textiles and apparel (combined), accounting for 16 percent of the total in 2001, and is expected to become the "supplier of choice" for many U.S. importers following quota elimination in 2005 because of its ability to produce almost any type of textile and apparel article at any quality level at a competitive price. Chinese apparel is sold at all price levels and in all types of stores, ranging from low end discount stores to specialty and department stores. However, many U.S. importers have said that the uncertainty over whether safeguards (quotas) will be placed on U.S. textile and apparel imports from China likely will temper growth in sourcing from China, at least in the early years following quota elimination (see section on the "United States" above for information on the China textile safeguards). China is able to compete based not only on price, but also based on its industry-wide ability to respond rapidly and reliably, its business-like attitude and excellent understanding of customer demand. China offers internal and external economies of scale—not the cheapest wages, but the highest productivity.

The obstacles to Chinese success stem from the fact that, according to the terms of China's WTO accession agreement, other countries could reimpose quotas on Chinese exports until 2008. Moreover, antidumping measures could be applied as well. Furthermore, protectionist lobbies could use eco-labeling schemes and other regulatory devices to keep out Chinese imports. An additional problem for China is its lack of raw materials, particularly cotton. There is some speculation that reduced prices could be offset by a rise in the cost of raw materials, which China will increasingly have to import.

By September 2004, China's share of the U.S. market was 23.2 percent and far ahead of the second largest supplier, Mexico, with 9 percent. China continues to gain every month (outpacing other sources) in products no longer under the quota. Industry analysts predict that megafactories in China will dwarf anything found in Latin America. China's efficiencies of size, lower cost, and cheap credit are expected to push prices down further, and by 2010 China could supply more than 80 percent of all U.S. clothing and 50 percent of the world market. China has made major investments in infrastructure and has been building apparel-manufacturing capacity at a very rapid rate.

According to Wilbur Ross, chairman of the International Textile Group (ITG) based in Greensboro, North Carolina, "There is a tremendous amount of unused capacity in the Chinese mills. Many of them seem to have op-

erating rates at only about 50 percent of capacity." This observation suggests that China is reacting to potential safeguards that could limit growth to 7.5 percent each year through 2009, according to Ross. "It's likely that their real strategy is to have this huge capacity built up and throw in as much as they can right at the bell starting 1/1/05—so when the President finally puts in the safeguards, the base to which they are applied will be bigger and they [the safeguards] won't be particularly meaningful" (Kusterbeck 2004, 5). Some related sectors and subsectors are likely to benefit from China's rise as a textile and apparel powerhouse. For example, China is the number one importer of U.S. cotton, and increasingly, affluent Chinese consumers have demonstrated a strong preference for garments made outside of China. For this group of consumers, luxury items from the United States and the European Union that reflect status, craftsmanship, and quality are becoming more popular.

In late December 2004, China announced plans to impose export taxes on 148 categories of textiles and apparel beginning January 1, 2005, in an effort to control its exports of those products as the world liberalized trade in textiles and apparel. The export duties ranged from 2.4 cents to 3.6 cents per piece or per set of clothing and 6 cents per kilogram for parts or accessories. Observers speculated that the surprising move had a dual purpose of assuaging global fears of China dominating apparel production and allowing the Chinese government to recoup a portion of the revenue it would lose from quota allocation fees as the quota system ended. Others believed the move was intended to stem U.S. and EU safeguard actions.

ASEAN

The countries of the Association of Southeast Asian Nations (ASEAN) expanded their exports of textiles and apparel by 17 percent during 1997–2001 to $26 billion. Three-fourths of the exports in 2001 came from Indonesia, Thailand, Malaysia, and the Philippines. Most

ASEAN countries benefit from low labor costs, established textile manufacturing infrastructures and export markets, and access to many raw materials. The elimination of quotas in 2005 likely will intensify competition for ASEAN countries in their home and export markets, particularly from China. Two of the world's fastest-growing exporters of textiles and apparel, Vietnam and Cambodia, are ASEAN countries. Neither is a member of the World Trade Organization, and as such, the countries are ineligible for quota liberalization under the WTO Agreement on Textiles and Clothing. Vietnam and Cambodia have greatly expanded their exports of apparel to the United States in recent years, leading to the establishment of U.S. quotas on their apparel shipments. This, however, has not stopped dramatic growth. Approximately 70 percent of all growth in apparel imports to the United States in 2002 came from China and Vietnam. Vietnam had almost no apparel or textile trade with the United States until 2001. In 2002, Vietnam was the second largest supplier, behind Mexico, despite Mexico's tariff-free status under the North American Free Trade Agreement (NAFTA).

India and South Asia
The textile and apparel sector remains the primary engine for economic growth in South Asia, an area that includes Bangladesh, India, Pakistan, and Sri Lanka. For each of these countries, the textile and apparel sector accounts for a significant portion of traded goods, contributing between 25 percent (India) and 86 percent (Bangladesh) of the total value of exports in 2001. South Asian countries are highly dependent on the sector for both jobs and export earnings.

The textile and apparel sectors in Bangladesh, India, Pakistan, and Sri Lanka exhibit different degrees of specialization. Firms in Pakistan specialize in cotton textile intermediate goods (yarn and grey fabric), as well as towels and bed linens, whereas firms in Bangladesh and Sri Lanka remain export-oriented apparel producers and are dependent on imported inputs such as yarn and fabric to augment local textile production. India has developed a highly complex sector covering the entire value and production chain from fiber production to garment manufacture and packaging. Firms in South Asia generally are not vertically integrated and, for the most part, are independent, privately owned small and medium-sized firms. Textile and apparel exports from South Asian countries rose during 1997–2001. Total Bangladeshi exports increased from $3.9 billion in 1997 to $5.5 billion in 2001; almost all of the increase was in exports of apparel products to U.S. and EU markets.

India is positioned to become a superpower of apparel manufacturing in 2005. Its clothing and textile industry is preparing for quota removal by investing to expand capacity. Potential problems, however, are that current Indian labor laws make it easier to manage smaller separate factories than one large factory. India has good design, availability of raw materials, low-cost labor, and the English language, and its legal system provides protection for workers rights. Worldwide, India exports about $6 billion worth of apparel each year, slightly more than half of which has gone to the United States. Problems include poor infrastructure (especially access to port facilities and electricity), poor roads, high-cost power, low productivity, random strikes, and corruption.

Bangladesh is leading the movement among developing countries seeking to halt the quota phase-out. It sent a letter to the WTO in July 2004 asking to extend the quotas beyond the end of the year and calling on developed countries to extend special duty-free treatment toward developing countries' exports. This proposal lacked support among key WTO members. It is expected that when the quotas are removed, Bangladesh will lose 40 percent of its exports. The fear is that the result will be high unemployment and social disruption as women who were formerly in the apparel industry will turn to prostitution. The main problem is that Bangladesh produces few textiles and as a result has to import most textiles used in its apparel exports. Additionally, the infrastructure is poor and results in slow deliveries, which is not good in a fast-paced apparel industry. As of July 2004, Bangladesh's government had no plan in place to stem the potentially devastating effect of quota elimination.

Central America and the Caribbean Basin

Though comparatively few textiles are produced in the region, Central America and the Caribbean are major apparel producers and highly dependent on apparel production. Major apparel producers in the area include Costa Rica, the Dominican Republic, El Salvador, Guatemala, Haiti, Honduras, Jamaica, and Nicaragua. The region maintains a special relationship with the United States based on historical ties, geographic proximity, and special preferences granted by U.S. trade legislation. U.S. imports of textiles and apparel from beneficiary countries under the 1983 Caribbean Basin Economic Recovery Act (CBERA) and the subsequent Caribbean Basin Trade Partnership Act (CBTPA), which covered the island nations of the Caribbean and the nations of Central America, have grown sixfold since 1986, when the United States liberalized apparel quotas for the region, reaching 3.7 billion square meters equivalent (SMEs), valued at $9.5 billion, in 2002. The growth in such imports, which consisted almost entirely of apparel, largely reflected the expanded use of production-sharing operations in the region by U.S. apparel producers. In addition, firms based in Korea and Taiwan have made significant investments in Caribbean and Central American apparel production. Apparel is still the largest import from the region, representing 45 percent of total regional shipments in 2002. In October 2002, the United States announced its intent to enter into negotiations on a proposed free-trade agreement with Central America and the Dominican Republic. On August 2, 2005, President Bush signed the CAFTA-DR agreement.

It is estimated that Central America will lose $6.2 billion in export orders to China,

which represents a 90 percent net loss in market share over the phase out. To compete with China, nations such as Honduras have worked to consolidate their supply chain, investing heavily in capital, such as cutting, spreading, embroidery, and screen-printing operations. These firms are attempting to offer full-package programs to form a vertical supply chain. Additionally, the industry is working cooperatively to form external economies of scale through the sharing of mutual experience, technology, and expertise. There are also efforts under way to designate some locations in the region as official U.S. Customs ports so that exports destined for the United States can clear customs before actual shipment.

In Honduras, the expectation is that companies already vertically integrated will continue to stay in business, especially those with links to foreign producers, but the prospects for small and medium-sized enterprises are not hopeful. The result could be devastating for national employment. In Honduras, the apparel sector employs 114,000 people, or 30 percent of the country's total formal industrial employment, with an average wage of about $3,500 per year—or more than four times the national average. Some hope that a mix of flexibility and speed (two days to Miami as opposed to two weeks from China) will enable the region's apparel industry to withstand the expected flood of cheaper apparel from China and other parts of Asia. Central America's position is based on its reputation as a fast turnaround producer and quick-response exporter. The largest Latin American apparel producers are investing heavily to overhaul their operations in a bid to survive. Apparel makers in Central America are heavily dependent on fabric imported from the United States, Asia, or elsewhere, with local textile makers supplying only an estimated 10 percent of the fabric used in the region.

Mexico

In 2004, the Mexican textile and apparel sector accounted for about 1.2 percent of Mexico's GDP, 7 percent of manufacturing GDP, and 18 percent of all manufacturing employment, making it Mexico's largest industrial employer, with 11,000 apparel firms and 2,000 textile firms. Many in Mexico have done little to adapt to the MFA phase-out. Mexico became the largest foreign supplier of textiles and apparel to the United States in the late 1980s and early 1990s. In 2002, however, it was surpassed by China as the largest foreign supplier, largely reflecting the effects of the appreciation of the peso and the acceleration of imports from China in quota-free product categories. The sector accounted for only 2.4 percent of foreign direct investment (FDI) in the manufacturing sector. The U.S. market accounted for 95 percent ($9.6 billion) of Mexico's textile and apparel exports in 2001.

Mexico is facing growing competition in the U.S. textile and apparel market from lower-cost countries in Asia and the Caribbean Basin, and the recent appreciation of its currency is effectively reducing the price competitiveness of its textile and apparel products. A large part of the increased competition for Mexico in the U.S. market reflects the entrance of China into the WTO, which resulted in the elimination of certain quotas on Chinese exports to North American markets, and implementation of U.S. trade preferences for certain textile and apparel products from Caribbean Basin and sub-Saharan African countries. According to Mexican industry consultants, to remain a major supplier of textiles and apparel to the United States, Mexican firms will have to continue their efforts to shift production from low-value-added basic garments to more "full-package" and technology-intensive products.

According to one U.S. apparel retailer, Mexican apparel producers, faced with increasing competitive pressure from countries such as China, will need to focus more on higher fashion, brand-name products that require smaller and more flexible runs. The Mexican textile and apparel sector comprised 14,000 firms and employed 909,000 workers in 2001. The sector can be divided into three distinct segments: apparel firms, *maquila* (maquilas or maquila-

doras are manufacturing or export assembly plants in northern Mexico, producing parts and products for the United States establishments), and textile producers. Apparel firms constitute the largest share of the sector (79 percent, or 11,076 firms). Maquilas produce mostly garments for export. In 2001, there were 860 maquilas (6 percent) and 2,100 textile producers (15 percent). Nearly 98 percent of Mexican firms are considered small to medium sized (averaging forty-four employees per plant), and 2 percent of the firms are large apparel firms. Most apparel firms are family owned and managed, and they are largely subcontractors that do cut-and-sew operations. The Mexican apparel industry produces primarily basic garments, particularly five-pocket denim jeans and knit tops (such as T-shirts), mainly for export to the United States. NAFTA preferences apply to products made in North America from the yarn stage forward (the "yarn forward" rule). Mexican textile producers have not always provided consistent quality in fabric production, particularly in the finishing processes.

Turkey

Turkey ranks among the world's largest exporters of textiles and apparel, and the textile and apparel industry is the country's largest industrial sector, with 10 percent of its GDP and 21 percent of industrial output and total employment. The textile and apparel sector is also its largest source of export earnings, accounting for 33 percent of the total in 2001. Since implementation of the EU-Turkey customs union agreement in 1996, Turkey has benefited from duty-free and quota-free access to the EU textile and apparel market. It has a modern and diverse textile and apparel infrastructure, with production capacity in all sectors of the supply chain, and a relatively flexible, low-cost, and highly skilled workforce. Turkey's strategic geographical location between Europe and Asia enables Turkish producers to ship goods to both markets quickly, and at reduced shipping costs. Flexible manufacturing also results in shorter lead times and the ability to increase production runs quickly.

In December 2004, Turkey decided to impose textile quotas limiting imports from China to an annual increase of only 7.5 percent for one year in forty-two categories to protect its large domestic industry from Chinese imports expected to surge in 2005. The first country to unilaterally impose quotas in the wake of apparel and textile trade liberalization, Turkey announced that booming imports from China threatened fair trade, would drive down prices, and would squeeze out local manufacturers. The move followed China's voluntary imposition of an export tax. The Istanbul Ready-Made Garment Exporters Association called on the EU to impose similar quotas.

Africa

Sub-Saharan Africa (SSA) is a relatively small supplier of textiles and apparel to the global market, accounting for less than 1 percent of world exports in 2001. However, SSA textile and apparel exports have been growing in recent years, particularly to the United States, largely reflecting duty-free and quota-free access to the U.S. market under the provisions of the African Growth and Opportunity Act (AGOA). SSA production and exports tend to be concentrated in a few countries, particularly Mauritius, Madagascar, South Africa, Lesotho, and Kenya. Swaziland has recently increased production and exports, and other countries, such as Namibia, are in the process of making investments in new production to take advantage of AGOA eligibility. The majority of SSA-sector production and exports consists of apparel (not textiles). In 2002, U.S. textile and apparel imports from SSA consisted almost entirely of apparel. South Africa and Mauritius are the only SSA countries with an established textile sector. South Africa is the largest SSA exporter of textiles. Its principal markets include the European Union, the United States, and other African countries. Other countries with textile capacity include Madagascar, which has a fully integrated supply chain for producing trousers

from heavyweight fabrics, and Zambia, which exports cotton yarn to other SSA countries.

The textile and apparel sector in South Africa has been undergoing restructuring since international anti-apartheid trade sanctions were lifted in the early 1990s. In 2001, the sector accounted for 1.2 percent of the country's GDP (down from 1.5 percent in 1997). It constituted the second-largest source of government revenue (after the mining sector) and ranked as the sixth largest source of manufacturing employment, with 15 percent of the total. Textiles and apparel accounted for 2 percent, or $471 million, of South Africa's total exports in 2001. The South African government has encouraged foreign direct investment by allowing 100 percent foreign ownership, eliminating foreign exchange controls, and extending tax allowances to foreign firms, among other investment-sector promotion activities. Although some foreign investors have found the lower wages in other SSA countries more attractive, others have found that South Africa's more developed export infrastructure and the availability of more highly skilled labor offset some of the country's additional production costs.

South Africa benefits from AGOA preferences, but it is ineligible for AGOA preferential treatment for apparel made from "third-country" fabrics or yarns (other than of U.S. or SSA origin). The textile and apparel sector in South Africa is vertically integrated from the production of natural fibers (such as cotton and wool) and synthetic fibers (such as polyester) through the manufacture of intermediate inputs (mainly yarns and fabrics) to the production of finished goods, including apparel, home textiles, and industrial textiles. The sector benefits from South Africa having the most advanced transportation, telecommunications, and utilities infrastructure in SSA. South Africa's geographic location provides ready access for imports of raw materials from neighboring countries and ocean access to foreign markets. During 1997–2001, employment declined by 30 percent in the textile industry (excluding knitting mills), to 53,372 workers, and by 42 percent in the knitting mill segment, to 10,701 workers. Employment in the apparel industry fluctuated within a narrow range during 1997–2001, totaling about 122,500 workers in 2001.

Conclusion

The elimination of quotas will have a massive global impact, including the emergence of new manufacturers and low-cost production areas, the slashing of margins among existing producers, tumbling prices, and importers driving decisions. The results should be lower clothing prices for consumers, further consolidation within the apparel industry, stronger competition among suppliers, and expansion of vertical manufacturing. The dramatic global restructuring of apparel manufacturing will also impact employment, exports, and income for many countries and may threaten social disruption for some.

Anastasia Xenias

See Also Nontariff Barriers; Protectionism

References

Avisse, Richard, and Michel Fouquin. 2001. "Textiles and Clothing: The End of Discriminatory Protection." *La Lettre du CEPII,* no 198 (February).

Birnbaum, David. 2001. "The Coming Garment Massacre," http://www.just-style.com, October 15.

———. 2002a. "Life after Quota," http://www.just-style.com, April 22.

———. 2002b. "Marginal Countries and Marginal Factories," http://www.just-style.com, November 18.

Diao, Xinshen, and Agapi Somwaru. 2001. "Impact of the MFA Phase-Out on the World Economy: An Intertemporal Global General Equilibrium Analysis." TMD Discussion Paper, no. 79, Trade and Macroeconomics Division, International Food Policy Research Institute, October.

Dowlah, C. A. F. 1999. "The Future of the Readymade Clothing Industry of Bangladesh in the Post–Uruguay Round World." *World Economy* 22, no. 7.

European Commission. 2004. "Textiles and Clothing after 2005: Recommendations of the High Level Group for Textiles and Clothing." COM(2004) 668 final (October), http://europa.eu.int/comm/enterprise/textile/com2004.htm.

Flanagan, Mike. 2003. "Apparel Sourcing in the 21st Century, the 10 Lessons So Far," http://www.just-style.com, January.

Francois, Joseph, and Dean Spinanger. 2001. "With Rags to Riches but Then What? Hong Kong's T&C Industry vs. the ATC and China's WTO Accession." Paper prepared for the Fourth Annual Conference on Global Economic Analysis, Purdue University, West Lafayette, Indiana, June 27–29.

Gereffi, Gary. 2002. "The International Competitiveness of Asian Economies in the Apparel Commodity Chain." Asian Development Bank, ERD Working Paper Series, no. 5, February.

Hummels, David. 2001. 2001. "Time as a Trade Barrier." Mimeo, Purdue University, July.

Hyvarinen, Antero. 2001. "Implications of the Introduction of the Agreement of Textiles and Clothing (ATC) on the African Textiles and Clothing Sector." Papers on the Introduction of the Agreement of Textiles and Clothing (ATC), International Trade Center, United Nations Conference on Trade and Development/World Trade Organization, January.

International Monetary Fund/World Bank. 2002. "Market Access for Developing Country Exports—Selected Issues." Report prepared by the staffs of the IMF and the World Bank, September 26.

Kathuria, Sanjay, and Anjali Bhardwaj. 1998. "Export Quotas and Policy Constraints in the Indian Textile and Garment Industries." Mimeo, World Bank.

Kathuria, Sanjay, Will Martin, and Anjali Bhardwaj. 2001. "Implications for South Asian Countries of Abolishing the Multifibre Arrangement." World Bank Policy Research Working Paper 2721, November.

Kusterbeck, Staci. 2004. "US Trade Delegates Discuss China's Open Textile Capacity." *Apparel* (June).

Tait, N (2002). "Prospects for the textile and clothing industries of Madagascar." *Textile Outlook International* 98.

U.S. Department of Commerce, Office of Textiles and Apparel. 2004. "Textiles and Apparel: Assessment of the Competitiveness of Certain Foreign Suppliers to the U.S. Market." Investigation no. 332–448, Publication 3671. January, http://otexa.ita.doc.gov.

Transport: Airlines, Railroads, and Shipping

Industry Characteristics

Transportation is an ever-expanding global industry with the main goals of moving people and goods, locally and abroad, through the supply chain by using a system of interconnected public and private roads, airports, railroads, terminals, seaports, and waterways. Transport modes, including airplanes, ships, rail, and trucks, transfer raw materials, commercial goods, and consumer products to wholesalers, retailers, and end users over long distances, between nations and continents, or for shorter hauls through intermodal facilities. Aviation and maritime segments mainly focus on international freight transport, whereas trucking and rail segments are highly capable in shorter shipments connecting long-haul movements with local points of origin or destination.

Most international deliveries involve the transfer of goods and passengers from origin to destination using more than one mode of transport, known as intermodal transport. Efficient intermodal facilities have the ability to switch transport modes securely and reliably while modifying accordingly as transport demand grows or retracts. Transportation also enhances the process of globalization, expands trade growth, and advances world economies by employing workers, amassing revenues, and consuming resources and services generated across multiple sectors within the economy.

Globalization and Transport

Globalization transforms the international and domestic transportation industries by redefining the standard for cargo and passenger movements and creating a rapid evolution within the industry to meet progressive demand for goods in the world market. Transport companies are altering their operation methods, implementing new organization techniques, utilizing recent technology, improving customer service, and expanding geographic reach to meet this additional demand.

For example, air cargo carriers are ensuring speedy delivery times so that customers can maintain slim just-in-time (JIT) inventory systems; trucking and rail companies are installing navigation and positioning systems that will track and report more complete and accurate information on shipments and equipment; and ocean transport firms are focusing on containerization to increase delivery times on intermodal transport. Other factors that impact the transportation revolution include economic factors; government involvement; competitive pressures; transport costs; vehicle, equipment, and infrastructure availability; labor skill and productivity; technology; and environmental and safety issues.

Economic Factors

Economic trends and events directly affect the performance of and govern the demand for freight transportation services, causing international transport companies to be subject to fluctuations in the world economy. Economic expansion results in volume increases in demand for goods and services, whereas economic contractions yield demand reductions. Currency variations and exchange rates produce substantial gains or losses that impact shipping costs and affect management decisions. Changes in global industry production and operations techniques, such as the use of the JIT inventory system, alter the frequency of deliveries and shipment size. Also, the overall economic condition designates the buying and purchasing power of populations, determining the types and values of commodities produced and consumed and the volume of goods that shippers will carry.

Unforeseeable economic events and other global concerns impact the health and welfare of the transport industry. Such events include the 1997 Asian financial crisis and various recessions; the September 11, 2001, terrorist attacks; outbreaks of disease, such as Sudden Acute Respiratory Syndrome (SARS); the West Coast Port Shutdown in the United States in October 2002; and the continued instability of the Middle East. The Asian financial crisis placed a heavy toll on the transportation industry, especially marine shipping, because of the imbalance of trade between Asia, Europe, and the United States that occurred as a result of a depreciation in Asian currency. Marine shipping revenue was mainly affected by the decrease in demand for Asian trade, forcing marine shipping companies to reposition containers, modify schedules, and incur operating

costs. The Asian crisis also created capacity issues for many carriers because companies lacked the capital to invest in fleet expansion.

The 9/11 terrorist attacks led to implementation of new security laws and techniques but also caused delayed shipments, increased costs, and decreased shipping volumes within the transport industry. The U.S. West Coast Port Shutdown froze the global supply chain and ocean carriers' ability to deliver services as U.S. dockworkers went on strike. During 2003, SARS created a wave of panic among shippers impacting operational aspects, supply and demand for goods, and trade between countries. Transport carriers faced new regulations at seaports and airports, health checks, and increased waiting times, along with large fines for noncompliance. Finally, the ongoing friction in the Middle East causes significant impact on fuel supply and great fluctuations in the cost of fuel, decreasing carrier operating profits and shipping performance. These problems may cause either an increase in the freight rate to customers, leading to the decline of demand for shipping transport, or a decrease in profit, when the rate remains constant.

Government and Industry Involvement

Multiple political and governmental factors, such as transportation operating agreements, carrier-shipper alliances, and taxes, influence the transport trade environment by influencing global production and distribution. International trade agreements such as the European Union, the Association of Southeast Asian Nations (ASEAN) Free Trade Area (AFTA), and the North American Free Trade Agreement (NAFTA), create regional trading blocs that drive the global marketplace. These blocs were established to lower total distribution and logistics costs for exporting companies through reduced and eliminated tariffs. The regional trading blocs and international trade agreements shape carrier decisions on volume, trade routes, and frequency of shipping. Nations within these regional trading blocs, seeking to create opportunities and economic growth, negotiate bilateral and multilateral international transportation agreements. International ocean shipping is usually free from route restrictions, but carrier conferences and cargo preferences influence rates and services in major markets. Other types of transportation agreements within the transport environment include intermodal operating agreements and carrier-shipper alliances. With transportation carriers becoming increasingly multimodal, there is a need to build cooperative relationships between carrier modes. Intermodal operating agreements combine the services of rail, truck, and water; allow carriers to offer a broader range of services; and tailor service packages for individual shippers, thus lowering costs and increasing levels of service for freight transportation. Shippers and carriers are also entering into partnerships to ensure better, faster, and more reliable transportation services. These carrier-shipper alliances focus on arranging, managing, and monitoring shipments. Transport companies understand the benefits these alliances can have, such as lower logistics costs per unit of commodity, higher reliability of on-time delivery, and lower probability of loss or damage claim.

Competitive Pressures

Transport firms must adjust shipping practices to meet customer needs for varied and timely shipment deliveries, or be subject to competition from other modes of transport more capable of accommodating service needs. Each transportation mode specializes in certain market areas segmented by product type, length of haul, and speed of delivery, but in some instances overlapping competition can occur between modes. Railroads and trucking companies compete for short movements of bulk commodities and for medium- to long-distance movements for general merchandise.

Competition is escalating between less-than-truckload (LTL) motor carriers and air cargo companies. LTL firms now aggressively pursue time-sensitive freight mainly transported by air carriers, and air carriers assume ground shipment responsibilities usually tackled by motor carriers. United Parcel Service (UPS), a major competitor in the trucking industry, recently acquired Fritz Companies and Menlo Worldwide Forwarding, both of which specialize in freight forwarding, customs brokerage, and logistics. UPS can now offer customers a combination of transport services ranging from road transport and airfreight forwarding to ocean shipping and international trade management services.

Transport Cost

Shippers want to minimize costs associated with transport and logistics, including the major components of fuel, weather, labor, and equipment. Cargo carriers operating their own vehicles have a high sensitivity to fuel cost. In many cases, carriers include rate hikes or fluctuating surcharges in customer contracts to reduce the impact of fuel costs. Severe weather patterns impact all modes of commercial transportation by delaying shipments, lengthening travel time, and contributing to greater labor, maintenance, and fuel costs. Rain and fog create additional costs and diminish productivity by delaying air-carrier schedules or by forcing truckers to decrease driving speeds. Railroads also use financial resources to have snow removed from tracks, delaying service, but railroad companies are most exposed to high costs by floods, which damage infrastructure, necessitating repairs that must take place before service can be resumed.

Vehicle, Equipment, and Infrastructure Availability

Many transportation firms allocate a majority of their revenue to support, maintain, and update vehicle fleets, equipment, infrastructure, and facilities. These financial investments are necessary to enhance the quality and condition of current international transport systems, keep systems running efficiently, and reduce problems such as infrastructure overcapacity, pollution, safety concerns, and labor conflicts. For example, the marine shipping industry is strongly dependent on efficient intermodal transport facilities for retrieval and distribution of goods, thus demanding a fixed infrastructure of road, rail, and terminal access. Ports, which provide the infrastructure for marine carriers, invest in berth and cargo space, storage, stevedoring, fueling, and loading facilities to combat capacity constraints and maintain system fluidity.

Railroads outlay large dollar amounts to purchase, build, repair, and maintain track, signals, and terminals. New entrants to the rail industry have to privately purchase track and undeveloped land in which to place the track; indeed, these high infrastructure costs may present a barrier to entry. Trucking companies and integrated air carriers face substantial asset-related costs involving fleet numbers, terminal facilities, and equipment repair shops as well as costly equipment expenditures related to fleets of ground delivery equipment, which, again, may discourage some investment in these industries.

Labor Productivity and Skill

It is essential that the transport employment environment have a highly skilled and capable workforce that understands the business and can meet fast-changing transportation needs. Today's transport employees need a diversified set of skills ranging from technological and computer skills to management and fiscal knowledge. The transport arena has become more specialized, and knowledge of policy writing, environmental impacts, energy needs, and transportation, in regards to urban structure and economic development, are increasingly important. With the emergence of new

technologies applicable to the industry, especially related to safety and security, workers need to update their skills to maintain system efficiency.

Challenges within the transport employment environment are tighter labor markets, rising labor costs, and occasional labor disturbances. Demographics and geographic regions challenge labor markets to maintain a qualified workforce at all levels within the industry. For example, rural economies with lower populations are deficient in specialized workers, such as planners and engineers, and for more populated urban areas with high-tech economies, those who can construct, operate, and maintain transport infrastructure are desired. Once an appropriate level of employment is achieved, that staff must be accurately managed. The less-than-truckload carriers, constituting a highly labor-intensive segment of freight transport, manually collect packages and consolidate these packages onto larger vehicles for distribution.

Solid management skills and large outlays of financial resources are required to integrate and maintain such a large sales staff and to handle crew and equipment and facilities maintenance personnel. Maintenance of labor pools is important, and labor disturbances may occur if a steady integration and communication is not upheld. In 2003, then again in 2004, the ports of Los Angeles and Long Beach were failing to accommodate an influx of container imports owing to a lack of dockworkers, resulting in prolonged and financially draining port lockouts as ocean carriers and port administrators battled with longshoremen over labor issues.

Impact of Technology

Technology continues to evolve and improve transportation with advances in equipment and information systems. Examples include containerization, double-stack technology, automation, robotics, handling systems, electronic data interchange (EDI), automated equipment identification (AEI), applications of Intelligent Transportation Systems (ITS) to commercial vehicle operations, global positioning systems, and cargo routing and tracking systems. These new advances affect carriers by altering transportation type and size, the weight of commodities, methods of production and distribution, and associated costs. Many of the technologies enable significant increases in productivity to occur but require a significant financial investment.

Environmental and Safety Issues

Transportation is often connected with environmental difficulties related to air, water, and noise pollution as well as energy and natural resource consumption. Environmentalists and governments are concerned that unfavorable environmental consequences, such as pollution and congestion, create individual health problems and ecological damage; therefore, new restrictions are placed on transport carriers to reduce negative outcomes. Transport firms are concerned that these restrictions, which affect the choice of routes, vehicle usage, and delivery times, will significantly increase freight transport cost. For example, the trucking industry has been accused of straining the world energy supply through large engine fuel consumption, of contributing to congestion, of slowing down travel times for everyone, and of causing air pollution due to high levels of emissions released into the environment by idling vehicles. Governments now require emission-control devices in transport vehicles, restrict vehicle size and weight, and control fuel components, thereby improving efficiency, safety, and quality of life.

As major priorities in the transport system, safety and security issues have led to the introduction of new regulations, technologies, and security practices across all modes. Traffic safety laws are of greater importance today than in the past because large trucks now share the road with more cars, resulting in collisions.

Overcrowding at transport facilities has made vehicle operation more dangerous, especially at airports and railroads with increased volumes of business.

Major Trends in Transport

Globalization has revolutionized the transportation industry's continuous goal of improving speed, service, and flexibility by bringing opportunities to all transport modes through increased demand, enhanced competition from a greater number of entrants, improved international networks, and updated innovations.

Air Transport

The global air transportation industry focuses on the movement of passengers and freight worldwide using many types of aircraft, ranging from single-engine planes to multi-engine airliners. This industry, composed of multiple players, including air carriers, express companies, forwarders, and passenger airlines with freight-carrying ability, concentrates on shipping high-value and time-sensitive goods across great distances while extending an arm into the acquisition and operation of ground transport equipment and facilities.

Demand for air transport is on the rise, recovering from market tremors of the past decade, which had a negative impact on growth and passenger volume, placing several major airlines in financial trouble. According to the International Air Transport Association (IATA), an industry trade group, demand for international air cargo services from Asia, Europe, and the Middle East will increase revenues within the industry. The fastest growing airfreight trade region with the United States is Asia, supported by exports from China. Major industry players, such as FedEx, UPS, and Emery Worldwide, have taken advantage of this growing market, increasing competition along with their presence in the region. Smaller shippers may have difficulty entering this market owing to anticompetitive practices regarding

Table 1: Air Carriers and Air Express Carriers, 2004

Air Carriers	
Company	*2004 Revenue (in U.S. dollars)*
Lufthansa	$24.31 billion
KLM	$7,154.10 million
Singapore Airlines	$5,795.6 million
Korean Air	$5,170.30 million

Air Express Carriers	
Company	*2004 Revenue (in U.S. dollars)*
FedEx Express	$2.869 billion
UPS Airlines	N/A
Menlo WorldWide	$2.89 billion
EGL Inc.	$2.53 billion
ABX Air Inc.	$1.20 billion

international traffic rights that favor certain carriers, introducing a competitive advantage.

Currently, Lufthansa Cargo is the world's largest airfreight carrier, followed by Korean Air and Singapore Airlines. In the United States, FedEx and UPS are the major carriers of air express packages, and Emery Worldwide and BAX global handle heavy cargo.

Industry regulations try to reduce anticompetitive practices by overseeing traffic rights and Air Service Agreements (ASAs), airport and landing slots, and environmental and security standards. These regulations, imposed by national and international organizations such as the U.S. Federal Aviation Administration and the United Nations International Civil Aviation Organization, often act as barriers to entry or hinder daily operations. As a trend toward deregulation spreads through air travel and freight markets, new entrants become aware of the benefits within the consumer, business, and tourism industries, thus increasing competition among airlines. Deregulation and increased competition have introduced global air transport networks and lenient ASAs, known as Open Skies agreements, resulting in lower rates, new service routes, and job creation. Open Skies agreements are multilateral agreements between countries that allow passenger demand and market conditions to set landing and departure schedules, rather

than government regulations. Airlines have also formed international networks through the creation of alliances, resulting in improved efficiency by way of better customer connection to the global marketplace and a wider range of low-cost transport-service choices.

Technological innovations are being created to meet the needs of this rapidly integrating segment of the transport industry. Developments in telecommunications, e-commerce, customs, and delivery services have changed traditional airline services by providing travel information, ticket sales, Internet check-in, automatic paging, and onboard Internet access as well as by establishing an infrastructure to order, ship, track, and deliver goods to customers. Advances in safety, security, and environmental protection systems have also become a high priority within the industry. With innovations constantly changing, the air employment environment must also change to keep up with new systems. Job opportunities will increase as passenger and cargo traffic expand in response to increases in population, income, and business activity. Positions as pilots, flight attendants, baggage handlers, aircraft and avionics equipment mechanics, and computer and service technicians are seen as growth opportunities, and applicants with a college degree, technician training, and flying experience will be in demand.

Marine Transport

The marine freight shipping industry transports large amounts of deferrable, lower value goods across oceans using commodity-specific vessels. Ocean carriers are segregated into classes of bulk, specialized, and general cargo carriers. Bulk carrier vessels are designed to deliver large shipments of a single commodity. The commodities fall into three categories: dry bulk, liquid bulk, and specialist bulk. Dry bulk products include iron ore, coal, grain, phosphates, and bauxite as well as steel products, cement, gypsum, sugar, salt, and forest products. Major liquid bulk products are oil and liquid chemicals. Specialized bulk commodities include motor vehicles, refrigerated cargo, and cargo with specific handling instructions. General cargo and containership lines concentrate on the smaller shipments of manufactured or intermediate goods, such as electronics and textiles, but have the ability to carry small amounts of grain and liquid chemicals.

Since 1956, containerization within the international transport industry has led to considerable improvements in economic efficiency. The use of standardized containers, with common unit measures of usually twenty and forty feet, eases cargo movement between modes. Steamship lines and railways have encountered the benefits of standardized containers and, in turn, have designed large-scale container ships and double-stack container train cars to profit from these benefits. These innovations have heightened competition, reduced costs, and lowered international freight rates.

Along with constructing larger vessels, ocean carrier companies are gaining bargaining power, reliability, and profitability through mergers, alliances, and partnerships. Recent acquisitions in the industry have been by foreign companies purchasing U.S. carriers, which has led to the reorganization of major players in the industry. For example, Neptune Orient Lines purchased American President Lines; Maersk took over Sealand Service; and certain Crowly operations were bought by Hamburg-Sud.

Ocean transport demand was traditionally characterized by seasonal demand cycles, with volumes continually surging upward in the months from September through November and declining to previous levels as demand slowed during the beginning months of the year. But with a heavy influx of exports from China, ports are seeing major increases in container volumes throughout all months of the year. This increased volume has created problems of congestion and capacity strain at current port facilities, leading to delays in shipments, escalating rates, and soaring storage fees. As importers, such as major industry players Maersk Sealand and P&O Nedlloyd, became frustrated with delivery delays, they sought different options, including alternative routes and vessel deployments, to reduce capacity constraints and congestion. The idea of port diversion bloomed during the port lockouts in 2003, and shippers jumped at the chance to alter routes through the Panama Canal to the Gulf Coast. Even with the labor dispute solved, many shipping companies continued to divert cargo and are now better able to handle congestion. Panama Canal operators have seen the jump in demand and are developing infrastructure and management techniques to cope with the change.

Maersk Sealand, Hanjin Shipping, and Evergreen Line are the world's largest container shipping lines, according to Port Import Export Reporting Services. In the container shipping business, the top twenty carriers account for 82.3 percent of the worldwide TEU capacity.

Rail Transport

Railroads move large quantities of goods and passengers long distances over land, specializing in the movement of low-value bulk goods such as coal, ores, chemicals, and forest products. Railroads are also seen as a complement transport type linking water, land, and air-based modes. Rail transportation has embraced globalization and has since seen ascending productivity through technological advances, larger capacity equipment, and al-

Table 2: U.S. Waterborne Foreign Trade, Containerized Cargo, Top Twenty Shipping Lines, 2003 (in thousands of twenty-foot equivalent units [TEUs])

Shipping Lines	Export	Import	Total
Maersk Sealand	940	1,802	2,742
Hanjin Shipping Col. Ltd	442	953	1,395
Evergreen Line	405	966	1,371
American President Lines	408	934	1,342
Mediterranean Shipping Company	402	609	1.011
P&O Nedlloyd	328	616	943
Orient Overseas Container Line	301	595	869
China Ocean Shipping	251	594	845
NYK Line	249	594	836
Hapag Lloyd	325	494	819
Hyundai	274	536	810
K Line	249	532	781
Yang Ming Line	267	459	726
MOL	191	377	568
Zim Container	183	339	522
China Shipping Container Line	110	383	493
CMA-CGM The French Line	106	307	413
Lykes	184	191	375
Lloyd Triestino	87	254	341
Dole Fresh Fruit Co	50	239	289
Top 20 Shipping Lines	5,752	11,774	17,525
Grand Total	7,389	13,899	21,289
Top 20 Shipping Lines as a % of Grand Total	77.9%	84.7%	82.3%

Source: Port Import/Export Reporting Services (PIERS)

liances between rail, maritime, and road transportation.

Strong freight demand and a tight trucking capacity benefit rail volumes and prices. Coal shipments are the main driver of railroads, but intermodal container traffic is the fastest-growing segment of the railroad freight industry, fueled by growth of imports and exports. The intermodal transport of goods is growing, mainly in response to the increasing expense and restricted capacity of long-haul trucking. Rail transport has a competitive advantage through its cost structure; rail enterprises can charge lower rates for long-haul bulk movements than motor carriers, and rail has the capability to carry triple the amount of bulk product of truckload carriers. Economies of scale are prevalent in rail transport for its ability to stack containers two high per flatcar, for up to 200 containers per trip, using a minimal amount of labor, whereas truck carriers can transport only one or two containers per trip.

Railroad companies are focusing on increasing margins and operating efficiency by improving and maintaining customer relations and commercial alliances through on-time performance, value, equipment and operations, and information technology. Concerns for rail company profitability arise because of high fuel and employment costs as well as because of the need to maintain system fluidity with increased volumes. An increased demand for rail services has revealed decreasing railroad performance. The problems need to be addressed, especially the slower travel times and increased wait times, which are due mostly to the lack of skilled workers available to run the system. These issues weaken the rail indus-

Table 3: Rail Industry Leaders, 2003

Rail Line	Location	2003 Revenue (in billions of U.S. dollars)
East Japan Railway Company	Japan	N/A
Deutsche Bahn AG	Germany	N/A
Societe Nationale des Chemins Fer Francais	France	N/A
Central Japan Railway Company	Japan	N/A
West Japan Railway Company	Japan	N/A
Union Pacific Railroad	United States	$12.22
Burlington Northern Railroad Co.	United States	$10.95
CSX Corporation	United States	$8.02
Norfolk Southern Corp.	United States	$7.31
Canadian Pacific Ltd.	Canada	$5.42

try, causing overdue shipments, increasing expenditures, and discouraging customers.

Demand for railroad service has increased, however, in regions where rail technology has focused on speed, reliability, capacity, and efficiency. New computer innovations command train movements, braking systems, and grade crossings and monitor inconsistencies within rail rights-of-way, decreasing chances of collision and making the railroad system safer and more efficient. Productivity and revenue advancement is also alive in the rail passenger sector, mainly in Europe and Japan, with the introduction of high-speed rail. Railroads are providing more availability of high-speed rail service, which is seen as a possible substitute for short-haul air movements. This type of service takes the pressure off of airport capacity and reduces road congestion.

Trucking

The trucking industry, inspired by fierce competition, low margins, and minimal barriers to entry, transports goods and information to destinations of varying distances through integrated road and highway systems. The three categories of shipment capacity are truckload (TL), or shipments greater than 10,000 pounds; less-than-truckload (LTL), shipments less than or equal to 10,000 pounds; and pack-age express. Recent industry trends have added a fourth element, logistics, to the industry. Logistics uses precise information to deliver goods in a cost-effective and timely manner. New technological advances in tracking and communication, combined with mergers and alliances, support growth of logistics by allowing motor carriers to track fleets, organize customers and loads, and provide a variety of transportation services that create optimal freight movement strategies for the customer. The trucking industry has undergone changes recently as numerous mergers and bankruptcies have taken place. First, in September 2002, the number three LTL in the United States, Consolidated Freightways, filed for bankruptcy, leaving the remaining LTLs to gain market share and post revenue growth in 2003. Then, in December 2003, the number two LTL carrier in the United States, Yellow Freight, purchased the number one carrier, Roadway.

Motor carriers have been enjoying higher prices and improved yields owing to recent industry consolidation and increased demand. Along with the increased demand, carriers are starting to struggle with capacity constraints, fuel costs, driver retention issues, and regulations regarding hours of service and environmental standards. The economic upturn has increased demand for TL freight transporta-

Table 4: Trucking Industry Players, 2003

Industry Participants	2003 Revenues (in billions of U.S. dollars)
Private Carriers	
Sysco Corp.	N/A
Wal-Mart	N/A
Truckload Carriers	
Publicly Owned:	
J.B. Hunt Transport Services Inc.	$2.43
Swift Transportation Co. Inc.	$2.40
Land Star System Inc.	$1.60
Privately Owned:	
Schneider National	$2.90
Less than Truckload Carriers	
Yellow Freight System	$2.81
ABF Freight System Inc.	$1.37
USF Corp.	$2.31
Con-Way Transportation	$2.20

tion, but concerns over driver shortages and high turnover rates continue to plague the TL industry, raising recruitment and training expenditures. As stated by *Traffic World,* a transportation trade weekly, hiring a new driver costs between $3,000 and $9,000, and replacing a driver can cost up to $15,000 (http://www.trafficworld.com). The need for drivers is so great that trucking companies are hiring inexperienced drivers and finding they have to make outlays for insurance costs and claims paid out for damaged cargo.

Key reasons for the driver shortage include inadequate pay, extended time away from home, and pay based on miles rather than hours, which does not account for time spent loading or waiting in congested traffic. Companies are changing operation methods in an attempt to retain drivers. In addition, the new hours-of-service regulations are expected to decrease productivity and increase labor cost per mile, causing carriers to pass additional costs to customers through rate increases, loading charges, and wait time at terminals. In

2004, after sixty-four years under the same system, truckers were introduced to new hours-of-service rules. These rules set an industry standard limiting the amount of consecutive hours drivers are allowed to work. The Federal Motor Carrier Safety Administration (FMCSA), a division of the U.S. Department of Transportation, put these rules in place as a way to reduce driver fatigue and highway accidents. Some carriers responded in a positive way, saying the new rules had little or no effect on operations, and saw improved coordination with shippers and higher driver retention.

To combat these externalities, however, carriers have to create strategies to compensate for the extra expenditures. They may raise rates, put surcharges into contracts, update their use of technology, or eliminate routes to maintain profitability. Innovations in electronic commerce and navigation extend the operations of freight movement to encompass information management, customer satisfaction, and improved business processes. These innovations revised motor-carrier roles by varying the size, distance, and frequency of shipments and by increasing shipment timeliness and speed.

Future of Transport

The future of transport depends on the industry's ability to meet the challenges of growing trade and travel and to adjust to changing market conditions. Addressing the problems of increasing demand, congestion, and pollution that hinder transport access to intermodal terminals at airports and seaports and through all transport infrastructures will be a major public policy challenge for all nations wishing to conquer the global marketplace. Cooperation among nations and international organizations is needed to formulate guidelines addressing worldwide transport concerns for acceptable infrastructure, safety, security, labor practice, and environmental issues across all modes. Presently, carriers strive to make greater progress and seek further growth in the new millennium. These carriers will continue to face internal and external challenges, but with the improvement in the supply-and-demand balance and the increase in efficiency throughout the whole transportation chain, a positive outcome is nevertheless expected.

With the incredible economic events that occurred during the past decade, transport carrier management personnel have learned that they must take account of uncontrollable risks and uncertainties that could cause the decline of their profits. External events such as the Asian financial crisis, the 9/11 terrorist attacks, SARS, and the like have shown transport carriers the importance of a strong macroeconomic policy framework. They will have to use this knowledge to develop ways to strengthen their organizations and reduce the severity of similar future events. For example, they will have to learn to manage economic change by becoming well versed in various tools against currency fluctuation risks and by implementing contingency plans to ensure that their services will not be interrupted.

They will also have to focus on technological development and investments in new technologies to control costs, regulate environmental standards, and improve reliability, service levels, and safety. E-commerce has quickly become a permanent component of the transportation infrastructure, from the delivery of goods and services to the sales and marketing of those services, and will be used more extensively in the future as transportation continues to play a major role in trade facilitation and economic growth.

Tracey Zuliani

See Also Global Economic Growth; Transportation and Communication; Transport: Equipment Manufacturing

References

Coyle, John J., E. J. Bardi, and R. A. Novack. 1999. *Transportation.* South-Western College Publishers.

De Old, Alan, E. Sheets, and W. Alexander. 1986. *Transportation: The Technology of Moving People and Products.* Davis Publications.

Doganis, Rigas. 2001. *The Airline Business in the 21st Century.* Routledge.

Gardiner, Robert, ed. 1994. *The Golden Age of Shipping: The Classic Merchant Ship, 1900–1960.* Annapolis, MD: Naval Institute Press.

Green, William, G. Swanborough, and J. Mowinski. 1987. *Modern Commercial Aircraft.* New York: Portland House.

Kahn, Alfred. 2004. *Lessons from Deregulation: Telecommunications and Airlines after the Crunch.* Washington, DC: Brookings Institution Press.

Kendall, Lane, and James J. Buckley. 2001. *The Business of Shipping.* 7th ed. Cornell Maritime Press.

Tames, Richard L. 1970. *The Transport Revolution in the 19th Century: A Documentary Approach.* London: Oxford University Press.

Taylor, John, and Susan Young. 1975. *Passenger Aircraft and Airlines.* New York: Marshall Cavendish.

Transport: Equipment Manufacturing

Industry Profile

The transport equipment manufacturing (TEM) sector—whose members might be more properly termed "providers of transportation systems"—is a highly concentrated industry. Although many of the major motor vehicle companies are becoming less vertically integrated, they nevertheless remain horizontally consolidated. The majority of the companies are in many, if not most, of the subsectors of the industry, ranging from the manufacture of motorcycles, passenger cars, light commercial vehicles, heavy trucks, coaches, and buses to the production of locomotives, subway cars, airplanes, and marine engines. Only the manufacturers of bicycles, shipbuilders, and the makers of some heavy trucks seem to stand on their own.

The manufacturers of transportation systems hold a significant position in many developed economies, measured in terms of their share in employment, production, value added, exports, imports, and sales. The sector as a whole accounted for 13 percent of manufacturing employment in Canada and Germany, 12 percent in France and Sweden; 11 percent in the Republic of Korea; 10 percent in Spain, the United Kingdom, Mexico, and Belgium; 9.5 percent in the United States; and 8.3 percent in Japan. Most of these workers were in the "triad" consisting of Japan, the United States, and the European Union (EU), with the EU accounting for half, followed by the United States with one-third and Japan with 16 percent. The automotive industry alone (components sup-

pliers plus final assemblers) employed some 10 million workers.

The TEM sector accounted for between 30 and 40 percent of Canada's manufactured exports during the past ten years, 31 percent of Spain's, 24 percent of Japan's, and 21 percent of Germany's. However, the absolute value of exports from the TEM sector was the highest for Germany, followed by Japan and the United States. Italy, Belgium, and the United Kingdom also have high TEM export ratios, accounting for as much as one-fifth of their exports in the manufacturing sector (followed by Austria, France, and Sweden).

Although motor vehicles, and automobiles in particular, have the largest share of exports within the TEM sector, the export of aircraft and their parts represents a significant share of the export sector for the United States, the United Kingdom, and France, and their value can be almost as significant as that of automobiles.

Workers in the TEM sector tend to be the best paid in the manufacturing industry (which is shrinking) and more highly unionized, with multiyear collective agreements characterized by pattern bargaining, and with many benefits other workers do not enjoy. The remuneration of TEM workers is typically above the manufacturing average; within the sector, auto workers are the highest compensated.

Three automotive companies (General Motors, Ford, and DaimlerChrysler) are the top research and development (R&D) spenders in the world, followed by an electronics giant

(Siemens) that also supplies auto parts and builds locomotives. Together with aerospace, these transport equipment manufacturers account for at least 20 percent of world spending on research and development.

Decisions of regulatory bodies such as the World Trade Organization (WTO) and the EU are having an increasing influence on the world's economy, including manufacturers of transport equipment. The progressive reduction and elimination of tariffs and customs duties will affect the international sourcing of parts and sales of vehicles. Trade disputes are being increasingly referred to the WTO for adjudication, which will ultimately have an impact on the location of jobs. The EU Commission also has a watchdog function concerning subsidies, pricing policies, and mergers that would have repercussions on the industry (where it could lead to a dominant position). The introduction of the euro has had an effect on pricing policies and on how cars are bought and sold in Europe.

The Motor Vehicle Sector

The industry is highly concentrated, with six major companies producing automobiles and half a dozen makers of trucks and buses. Mergers and acquisitions are taking place at an unprecedented pace and increasingly involve cross-border alliances. The Mercedes-Benz merger with Chrysler catapulted them from seventeenth and twenty-fifth place, respectively, on the Fortune 500 list of the largest companies in the world into second place, just behind General Motors. And with the sale of its parts supplier Delphi Automotive, General Motors may in fact find its position vis-à-vis DaimlerChrysler reversed in next year's listing. A similar leapfrog effect would put the Renault/Nissan alliance, currently thirty-third and forty-ninth in the world (ranked by assets), into about tenth place, if their activities were considered together. Companies that do not merge are likely to conduct joint research to

economize (especially on green technologies) or to secure their independence.

Although the automobile industry already directly employs up to 10 percent of the manufacturing workforce in many countries, if indirect backward and forward linkages were added, the overall employment- and income-generating effects could easily be increased by a factor of two or three. These linkages include upstream activities such as rubber, tires, plastics, glass, paint, electronics, and textile manufacturing as well as downstream operations such as sales, service, repair, motor fuel, and finance and insurance personnel.

In fact, the automobile industry is so paramount in many countries that it is often considered by governments to be a barometer of their economies. For this reason, too, governments go to great lengths to attract new investment or keep ailing companies alive with subsidies. Many developing countries have also attempted to build up automobile industries, with varying degrees of success. Two-thirds of world automobile production is concentrated in just six countries: Japan, the United States, Germany, France, Spain, and the Republic of Korea. Another five—the United Kingdom, Canada, Italy, Belgium, and Brazil—account for over 20 percent. Of the developing countries only the Republic of Korea and Brazil have made it into the major producers. Mexico has potential in the North American Free Trade Agreement (NAFTA), and Asian countries such as Thailand, Malaysia, the Philippines, and Indonesia are pinning their hopes on future projections. With the exception of South Africa, few countries on that continent have been able to mount large-scale assembly (or manufacturing) activities, although many are trying, such as Botswana, which hopes for export opportunities with the disappearance of customs duties.

However, the industry is characterized by overcapacity, it is sensitive to economic downturns and currency fluctuations, and it is subject to the dictates of the market, since consumer response to new models cannot be anticipated. It is because of these ups and downs that employers want to introduce flexible labor-market arrangements with respect to working time and work organization.

Some projections predict that the world car parc will more than double in the next fifteen years, with as many vehicles being produced in the next twenty years as were produced in the first 100 years of the industry. Much of the increase will be due to cars produced and sold in Asia, especially in India and China. This would bring enormous employment opportunities to the region but may pose severe infrastructure and pollution problems as well as pressures on world petroleum markets.

The strikes and lockouts of the past have been avoided in recent times and would be extremely costly and difficult for the industry if they were to occur again in the future. In North America, four-year collective agreements are common. Volkswagen has just signed an agreement guaranteeing jobs up to 2011, and GM has offered generous severance benefits to workers being made redundant at Opel. With just-in-time (JIT) production methods, and in the absence of huge inventories, companies would not be able to continue production while some or all of their workers were on strike. They also would be more vulnerable than in the past if a single supplier were to strike and disrupt deliveries. However, with global sourcing, companies can theoretically order parts from anywhere in the world.

Since the margins on various operations remain small, especially for the mass-volume producers, most companies have established financial divisions or separate companies to fund leasing agreements or to provide loans or other services (such as insurance) to their customers, and quite often they earn more on these operations than on the sale of the car itself. Some are also involved in the repair and rental markets. For example, the consolidation of Daimler and Chrysler's financial-service activities into a single business (Debis AG) makes it the world's fourth largest nonbank provider of such services, and it is DaimlerChrysler's

biggest earner after its core automotive activities. General Motors improved its position by simply buying a local bank, and Boeing is considering leasing out its planes.

Suppliers: A Sunrise Industry

Throughout the world, the makers of automotive components, most of which are original equipment manufacturers (OEM), are on the rise. All the major employment increases in the sector have been in components manufacturers, a trend that is likely to continue, especially given the fact that workers in the car parts industry in Canada and the United States already outnumber those in final automobile assembly by a factor of 2:1, and that the second largest employer in the auto industry in Canada is a components' manufacturer (Magna International), soon to be number one, perhaps. The data available show wages in the supplier industries to be lower than in the factories where final assembly is done.

Although some of the growth in the independent parts industry can be attributed to increased orders, much of it, too, has come from the latest trend to spin off in-house or captive suppliers previously owned by automobile companies, or to outsource work formerly done in the automobile factories to outside companies. Since many of the parts manufacturers—unlike the automotive companies—tend to be in small, low-wage, unorganized establishments, unions are concerned that previously well-paid jobs are being replaced by lower-paid ones.

In the future, there may be only three types of Tier-1 suppliers, each specializing in either the interior or the exterior (or chassis) platform. The major automotive companies will allow these first-tier suppliers (or "systems integrators," as they are coming to be known) to design and install these systems (the components for which they, in turn, will subcontract out to second- and third-tier suppliers). The automotive companies themselves may simply become marketing devices grouping a transportation system around a recognized logo and providing the customer with credit, insurance, financing, and replacement parts.

Suppliers of seats, dashboards, and instrument panels can furnish all subsegments of the TEM industry with parts that are flexible enough to be used in cars, trucks, buses, airplanes, or trains. The current wave of mergers and acquisitions (M&As) in the components sector of the automotive industry also reflects the global trend toward consolidation, both at the national and international levels (with foreign companies entering Japan for the first time).

With zero inventory and just-in-sequence production, the pressure to deliver on time is now transferred to the suppliers, whose workforces become human buffers. Internet advances will help to facilitate the process. The Internet is also changing the way people order cars, how companies sell them, how parts (suppliers) are coordinated, and how production is organized. Honda is now offering a five-day customized car order service. Auto.com has become a virtual reality, and companies such as Opel now have WYSIWYG home pages that allow customers to configure and order their own cars. Ford, meanwhile, has entered into a deal with Oracle. As these innovations grow in popularity, car dealerships may become a thing of the past.

Suppliers today play an increasingly important role in the automotive industry as a whole. Already, for cars they contribute up to two-thirds of the value added by manufacturing, an amount forecast to rise in the next few years to as much as 75 percent. The worldwide employment breakdown in the automotive sector currently is estimated to be at an average 54:46 of assemblers-to-suppliers, reaching 33:66 in some cases. The trend appears likely to move toward the latter ratio.

Emerging markets will increase their share of global components production. This will happen chiefly through the increase in automotive assembly in Central and Eastern Europe, China, and India. Although component production in developing countries is increasing rapidly, and despite a potential for outsourcing from companies in advanced countries due to lower labor costs, developing countries accounted for only 12 percent of world exports of components in 1999. However, domestic suppliers in emerging automotive economies may not always be able to fully capitalize on increased demand for components, as foreign Tier-1 suppliers colocate in emerging markets, with their major customers as inward investors.

Nevertheless, vehicle assemblers who market the final product dictate requirements to suppliers, inter alia, in terms of cost, quality, and the location of production. It is inevitable that many suppliers will remain vulnerable (despite their technological strength), since—with few exceptions—the automobile assemblers are their only customers. Those, however, that are able to innovate, exploit intellectual property, and support a balanced product base will be in the driver's seat.

To match the consolidation taking place in the assembly sector, more and more Tier-1 suppliers are expected to merge and to reinforce the coordination role they already play vis-à-vis the activities of other, Tier-2 and Tier-3, suppliers. However, should the financial weakness of many of the vehicle assemblers continue—an unhealthy situation for suppliers, in particular—and should there continue to be an assumption of greater responsibilities and risks by suppliers, the balance of decision-making power *may* tilt in favor of the Tier-1 suppliers. This would be still more likely once the supplier sector has undergone further merger and acquisition activity.

The pressure to continuously reduce costs, diversify, and deliver to increasingly just-in-time schedules will invariably have an impact on working conditions among suppliers, requiring even greater flexibility on the part of the workforce. Assemblers are passing more responsibility and risk on to supplier firms in areas as diverse as product liability, research and development, and stock keeping. This shift, in turn, affects the position of workers within those firms. Perhaps one positive result of this process is the continued migration of competencies from assemblers to components manufacturers. One supplier, for example, registered more patents in 2003 than any automobile manufacturer. Meanwhile, in one major automobile-producing country, a supplier is poised to become the largest employer in the sector.

With the share per vehicle of electronic components and synthetic material increasing, other firms now outside the automotive industry may enter the market as suppliers, thereby transforming the shape of the industry. However, the trend toward an ever greater electronics content per vehicle may not continue as systems become too complex and subject to failure.

Other Transport Equipment Manufacturing Industries

As a result of global competition, shipbuilding is one of the industries to have suffered the largest declines in Europe and North America in recent years. The major winner has been Asia (Japan, the Republic of Korea, and China). Most new orders are in Japan and China. Although Vietnam and India are developing capabilities, their output is limited to only a few vessels. As a result of reunification, Germany still maintains a prominent position in Europe. Poland and Romania have potential but are still relatively small, and they may have more of a role in supplying parts of vessels for assembly elsewhere.

Most civilian shipbuilding is now carried out in the Republic of Korea (with 38 percent of the current order book and 43 percent of new orders), followed by Japan. China is third, with 19 percent of new orders and an official target of capturing 25 percent of the world market in the near future. Other countries with a still significant industry presence, or significant niche

products, include Vietnam, Singapore (repair, conversion), India, Germany, Croatia (third largest builder of tankers in Europe), Romania (hulls), Ukraine (eighth in Europe), Russia, the United States, and Brazil. In a reverse trend, Korean workers are now worried that outsourcing by Korean companies could transfer jobs to Romania and other countries. Many nations continue to build their own naval vessels.

One of the major problems facing the industry is that order books are full and vessels ordered today will take four years to deliver, and for most ships, the rising cost of steel means a loss for the shipbuilders over the original contract price. Recent decisions by the European Union and the International Maritime Organization (IMO) to speed up the phase-out of single-hull vessels will increase the demand for new vessels and the amount of steel required for double hulls. The down side of globalization in the shipping industry is the hazardous work of scrapping obsolete vessels by hand on beaches in Bangladesh, China, India, and Pakistan, where over 90 percent of shipbreaking takes place.

With regard to negotiations on a new shipbuilding agreement for subsidies, an earlier agreement on subsidies, brokered by the Organisation for Economic Co-operation and Development (OECD), failed because of the stringent requirement that it would only enter into force after all countries had ratified it. (The U.S. Senate did not ratify it.) A new initiative may suffer a similar fate, but with the EU complaint against Korea in the WTO, Korea's countercharge against the EU—and the fact that China's continued growth is not possible without subsidies—some kind of agreement is desirable to regularize the situation. Hidden subsidies also exist for yards that build dual-purpose vessels, which benefit from military contracts to produce civilian versions of naval vessels.

With only two manufacturers of large civilian aircraft, the competition between them will increase. Although there are fewer and fewer makers of military aircraft, they also follow the global trend of large-scale cross-border mergers and strategic alliances, as in the case of the recently formed European Aeronautic, Defence and Space Company (EADS). Three companies are competing for the market for passenger planes with fewer than 100 seats, but these rivals also rely heavily on government subsidies and backing for R&D. This subsector of the industry shows similar trends to those occurring in the automobile sector in terms of outsourcing and lean production, with offset-manufacturing often being used as a carrot to secure large orders.

There are only three manufacturers of aircraft engines, all of which suffered job losses in recent years, and none of which manufacture a single part. Virtually all components are supplied through subcontracting. Under the pressures of global competition, these companies, too, will have to invent strategies to secure orders.

Social and Labor Issues

Many of the production techniques introduced in the automotive industry have been named after their founders and emulated elsewhere. For example, "Fordism" was named after Henry Ford's assembly line, "Toyotism" after that company's lean-production methods, and the "Kalmar model" of group work after Volvo's experiments in Sweden. There is some speculation today that the industry is already in the post-lean era, and questions still surround teamwork (one of the essential ingredients of new production methods) and how it can best be implemented.

Major new forms of work organization, such as teamwork, flexible working arrangements, time accounts, the four-day week, and so on, have been pioneered in the automobile industry. Often these developments can be imitated in other sectors of the economy. For example, lean production seems to have been copied by the aircraft manufacturing industry. However, many of these flexible arrangements are also introduced under the menace of global competition and the threat that work and jobs will have to go elsewhere unless established work patterns become less rigid.

Throughout the world, people tend to live longer than in the past, and as a consequence they may also need to work longer. Nevertheless, there is an observed tendency in the automotive industry, in almost every country, to offer early retirement (or even preretirement schemes, beginning at fifty-five) to bring the current average age down from around forty-five to something in the mid- to lower thirties. From the employer's side, it is argued that this is necessary to remain competitive, since older workers have difficulty in adapting to new production techniques, whereas the trade unions argue that lean-production methods have increased the pace to the point that workers can no longer cope. One thing is clear: Golden handshakes are rarely turned down, given their high-income replacement value, and they are usually subsidized in one form or another by governments, which may use them as a device to combat youth unemployment. Nevertheless, there is a trend to increase both working hours and the retirement age in most European countries.

Despite the fact that Germany's dual system was the model that others were once called upon to emulate, German TEM manufacturers often find, after three or four years of training, at a cost of up to DM100,000, that the worker they have turned out is not the one they need. In addition, there appears to be a shortage of engineering graduates. Most countries could probably benefit from a revamping of their apprenticeship training programs and a move toward lifelong learning. With only four schools in the world teaching vehicle design, graduates are highly sought after as companies seek to differentiate their products.

Occupational safety and health (OSH) problems, such as repetitive strain injury (RSI), have emerged and warrant further study. In addition to promoting more environmentally friendly and fuel-efficient cars, the EU has recently introduced the concept of end-of-life vehicles (ELV), whereby the manufacturer is required to take the vehicle back when the owner is finished with it, much like returnable bottles and cans. Making the most of this approach will require more research into recyclable materials. Eventually, such a model could be applied to the shipbreaking industry.

Opportunities for Social Dialogue

Whether they are Japanese transplants or German companies with long-standing union traditions at home, it is quite apparent that when companies embark on greenfield investments they tend to do so in environments that are not conducive to unionization. Some examples are Mercedes in Tuscaloosa (Alabama), BMW in Spartanburg (Tennessee), or the Smart car in Alsace. To combat these tendencies, which are a matter of concern to unions, one tactic has been to negotiate "neutrality letters" (or agreements) with employers in which the employers agree not to hinder union-organizing campaigns. The concept has recently been extended in Canada, where the Big Three (DaimlerChrysler, Ford, and General Motors) have issued neutrality letters to their suppliers urging them not to stand in the way of union-organizing campaigns.

There are many ways of giving workers a voice in enterprise affairs—through, for example, their shop-floor representation, works councils (whether at the plant, company, or group level), supervisory boards (the German *Mitbestimmung,* or codetermination model), European Works Councils (EWCs), and World Company Councils. Although the automotive companies and components suppliers seem to have been quick in setting up EWCs, not enough time has passed for analysts to fairly assess their effectiveness.

Major automobile manufacturers (Daimler-Chrysler, VW, and Renault) and Tier-1 suppliers (Robert Bosch, Leoni, and so on) have been in the forefront of signing International Framework Agreements (IFAs) with the International Metalworkers' Federation and local union representatives. These IFAs recognize the core labor standards of the International Labour Organization (ILO). The companies involved state that they expect their suppliers to adhere to the same standards as part of their continuing business relationship. The Global Reporting Initiative (GRI) also contains reference to ILO core standards. Companies are expected to report on their own compliance, as well as that of their suppliers throughout the value-added chain.

"Work ownership" is a new concept pioneered by the National Automobile, Aerospace, Transportation and General Workers' Union of Canada (CAW), whereby companies recognize that the worker owns the contribution to the product he or she makes. Thus, a company cannot be sold off during a collective agreement or work outsourced without the master contract also applying to the new supplier. One example of an employee ownership scheme is provided by Dasa, which instead of closing down or laying off workers sold its Speyer facilities to its employees for a symbolic DM1, (Deutsch Mark, Germany's currency before the Euro) and even provided material and training on how to run the new company, now called Pfalz-Flugzeugwerke GmbH.

An increasing number of "employment pacts" are being concluded in the form of the Alliance for Jobs, *Standortsicherungsvereinbarungen* (production site guarantees), and multiyear collective agreements. In Germany, in particular, but also in other European countries, unions have been able to secure guarantees from major companies about employment and the continuation of production at local sites over a certain period of time. The four-year agreements signed in the United States between the United Auto Workers (UAW) and the auto producers, and between the International Association of Machinists (IAM) and Boeing, can likewise be seen as attempts to obtain more security.

Paul Bailey

See Also Transportation and Communication; Transport: Airlines, Railroads, and Shipping

References

Conybeare, J. 2004. *Merging Traffic: The Consolidation of the International Automobile Industry.* Rowman and Littlefield.

European Industrial Relations Observatory. "Industrial Relations in the Automotive Sector," www.eiro.eurofund.eu.int/2003/12/study/tn0312101s.htm (cited June 7, 2004).

Humphrey, John, and Olga Memedovic. 2003. *The Global Automotive Industry Value Chain: What Prospects for Upgrading by Developing Countries?* Vienna: United Nations Industrial Development Organization, http://www.unido.org/en/doc/12769.

International Labour Office. 2000. *The social and labour impact of globalization in the manufacture of transport equipment.* Report for discussion at the Tripartite Meeting on the Social and Labour Impact of Globalization in the Manufacture of Transport Equipment. Geneva, 8–12 May 2000. International Labour Office, Geneva.

———. 2005. *Automotive Industry Trends Affecting Components Suppliers.* Tripartite Meeting on Employment, Social Dialogue, Rights at Work and Industrial Relations in Transport Equipment Manufacturing. Geneva: ILO

———. World Commission on the Social Dimensions of Globalization. 2004. *A Fair Globalization: Creating Opportunities for All.* Geneva: ILO.

Posthuma, Anne. 2004. *Industrial Renewal and Inter-Firm Relations in the Supply Chain of the Brazilian Automotive Industry.* Working Paper 46. Geneva: ILO.